PREFACE

The Manual for Courts-Martial (MCM), United States (2016 Edition) updates the MCM (2012 Edition). It is a complete reprinting and incorporates the MCM (2012 Edition), including all amendments to the Preamble, Rules for Courts-Martial (R.C.M.), Military Rules of Evidence (Mil. R. Evid.), Punitive Articles, and Nonjudicial Punishment Procedures made by the President in Executive Orders (EO) from 1984 to present, and specifically including EO 13643 (15 May 2013); EO 13669 (13 June 2014); EO 13696 (17 June 2015); EO 13730 (20 May 2016); and EO 13740 (16 September 2016). *See* Appendix 25. This edition also contains amendments to the Uniform Code of Military Justice (UCMJ) made by the National Defense Authorization Acts (NDAA) for Fiscal Years 2014 through 2016. Finally, this edition incorporates amendments to the Supplementary Materials accompanying the MCM as published in the Federal Register on 8 July 2015, 16 July 2015, 22 March 2016, 15 June 2016, 8 November 2016, and 8 December 2016. The aforementioned NDAAs, EOs, and Supplementary Materials are available at the Joint Service Committee on Military Justice website at http://jsc.defense.gov. Because this manual includes numerous changes, practitioners should consider the MCM completely revised.

JOINT SERVICE COMMITTEE ON MILITARY JUSTICE

CONTENTS

CHAPTER III. INITIATION OF CHARGES; APPREHENSION; PRETRIAL RESTRAINT; RELATED MATTERS

CHAPTER IX.   TRIAL PROCEDURES THROUGH FINDINGS

PART I
PREAMBLE

1. Sources of military jurisdiction

The sources of military jurisdiction include the Constitution and international law. International law includes the law of war.

2. Exercise of military jurisdiction

(a) *Kinds.* Military jurisdiction is exercised by:

(1) A government in the exercise of that branch of the municipal law which regulates its military establishment. (Military law).

(2) A government temporarily governing the civil population within its territory or a portion of its territory through its military forces as necessity may require. (Martial law).

(3) A belligerent occupying enemy territory. (Military government).

(4) A government with respect to offenses against the law of war.

(b) *Agencies.* The agencies through which military jurisdiction is exercised include:

(1) Courts-martial for the trial of offenses against military law and, in the case of general courts-martial, of persons who by the law of war are subject to trial by military tribunals. *See* Parts II, III, and IV of this Manual for rules governing courts-martial.

(2) Military commissions and provost courts for the trial of cases within their respective jurisdictions. Subject to any applicable rule of international law or to any regulations prescribed by the President or by other competent authority, military commissions and provost courts shall be guided by the appropriate principles of law and rules of procedures and evidence prescribed for courts-martial.

(3) Courts of inquiry for the investigation of any matter referred to such court by competent authority. *See* Article 135. The Secretary concerned may prescribe regulations governing courts of inquiry.

(4) Nonjudicial punishment proceedings of a commander under Article 15. *See* Part V of this Manual.

3. Nature and purpose of military law

Military law consists of the statutes governing the military establishment and regulations issued thereunder, the constitutional powers of the President and regulations issued thereunder, and the inherent authority of military commanders. Military law includes jurisdiction exercised by courts-martial and the jurisdiction exercised by commanders with respect to nonjudicial punishment. The purpose of military law is to promote justice, to assist in maintaining good order and discipline in the armed forces, to promote efficiency and effectiveness in the military establishment, and thereby to strengthen the national security of the United States.

4. Structure and application of the Manual for Courts-Martial

The Manual for Courts-Martial shall consist of this Preamble, the Rules for Courts-Martial, the Military Rules of Evidence, the Punitive Articles, and Nonjudicial Punishment Procedures (Part I-V). This Manual shall be applied consistent with the purpose of military law.

The Department of Defense, in conjunction with the Department of Homeland Security, publishes supplementary materials to accompany the Manual for Courts-Martial. These materials consist of a Preface, a Table of Contents, Discussions, Appendices, and an Index. These supplementary materials do not have the force of law.

The Manual shall be identified by the year in which it was printed; for example, "Manual for Courts-Martial, United States (20xx edition)." Any amendments to the Manual made by Executive Order shall be identified as "20xx" Amendments to the Manual for Courts-Martial, United States, "20xx" being the year the Executive Order was signed.

The Department of Defense Joint Service Committee (JSC) on Military Justice reviews the Manual for Courts-Martial and proposes amendments to the Department of Defense (DoD) for consideration by the President on an annual basis. In conducting its annual review, the JSC is guided by DoD Directive 5500.17, "Role and Responsibilities of the Joint Service Committee (JSC) on Military Justice." DoD Directive 5500.17 includes provisions allowing public participation in the annual review process.

Discussion

The Department of Defense, in conjunction with the Department of Homeland Security, has published supplementary materials to accompany the Manual for Courts-Martial. These materials consist of a Discussion (accompanying the Preamble, the Rules for Courts-Martial, the Military Rules of Evidence, and the Punitive Articles), an Analysis, and various appendices. These supplementary materials do not constitute the official views of the Department of Defense, the Department of Homeland Security, the Department of Justice, the military departments, the United States Court of Appeals for the Armed Forces, or any other authority of the Government of the United States, and they do not constitute rules. *Cf., e.g.,* 5 U.S.C. § 551(4). The supplementary materials do not create rights or responsibilities that are binding on any person, party, or other entity (including any authority of the Government of the United States whether or not included in the definition of "agency" in 5 U.S.C. § 551(1)). Failure to comply with matter set forth in the supplementary materials does not, of itself, constitute error, although these materials may refer to requirements in the rules set forth in the Executive Order or established by other legal authorities (for example, binding judicial precedents applicable to courts-martial) that are based on sources of authority independent of the supplementary materials. *See* Appendix 21 in this Manual.

The 1995 amendment to paragraph 4 of the Preamble eliminated the practice of identifying the Manual for Courts-Martial, United States, by a particular year. Historically the Manual had been published in its entirety sporadically (*e.g.,* 1917, 1921, 1928, 1949, 1951, 1969, and 1984) with amendments to it published piecemeal. It was therefore logical to identify the Manual by the calendar year of publication, with periodic amendments identified as "Changes" to the Manual. Beginning in 1995, however, a new edition of the Manual was published in its entirety and a new naming convention was adopted. *See* Exec. Order No. 12960 of May 12, 1995. Beginning in 1995, the Manual was to be referred to as "Manual for Courts-Martial, United States (19xx edition)." In 2013, the Preamble was amended to identify new Manuals based on their publication date.

Amendments made to the Manual can be researched in the relevant Executive Order as referenced in Appendix 25. Although the Executive Orders were removed from Appendix 25 of the Manual in 2012 to reduce printing requirements, they can be accessed online. *See* Appendix 25.

PART II
RULES FOR COURTS–MARTIAL

CHAPTER I. GENERAL PROVISIONS

Rule 101. Scope, title

(a) *In general.* These rules govern the procedures and punishments in all courts-martial and, whenever expressly provided, preliminary, supplementary, and appellate procedures and activities.

(b) *Title.* These rules may be known and cited as the Rules for Courts-Martial (R.C.M.).

Rule 102. Purpose and construction

(a) *Purpose.* These rules are intended to provide for the just determination of every proceeding relating to trial by court-martial.

(b) *Construction.* These rules shall be construed to secure simplicity in procedure, fairness in administration, and the elimination of unjustifiable expense and delay.

Rule 103. Definitions and rules of construction

The following definitions and rules of construction apply throughout this Manual, unless otherwise expressly provided.

(1) "Article" refers to articles of the Uniform Code of Military Justice unless the context indicates otherwise.

(2) "Capital case" means a general court-martial to which a capital offense has been referred with an instruction that the case be treated as capital, and, in the case of a rehearing or new or other trial, for which offense death remains an authorized punishment under R.C.M. 810(d).

(3) "Capital offense" means an offense for which death is an authorized punishment under the code and Part IV of this Manual or under the law of war.

(4) "Code" refers to the Uniform Code of Military Justice, unless the context indicates otherwise.

Discussion

The Uniform Code of Military Justice is set forth at Appendix 2.

---

(5) "Commander" means a commissioned officer in command or an officer in charge except in Part V or unless the context indicates otherwise.

(6) "Convening authority" includes a commissioned officer in command for the time being and successors in command.

Discussion

See R.C.M. 504 concerning who may convene courts-martial.

---

(7) "Copy" means an accurate reproduction, however made. Whenever necessary and feasible, a copy may be made by handwriting.

(8) "Court-martial" includes, depending on the context:

  (A) The military judge and members of a general or special court-martial;

  (B) The military judge when a session of a general or special court-martial is conducted without members under Article 39(a);

  (C) The military judge when a request for trial by military judge alone has been approved under R.C.M. 903;

  (D) The members of a special court-martial when a military judge has not been detailed; or

  (E) The summary court-martial officer.

(9) "Days." When a period of time is expressed in a number of days, the period shall be in calendar days, unless otherwise specified. Unless otherwise specified, the date on which the period begins shall not count, but the date on which the period ends shall count as one day.

(10) "Detail" means to order a person to perform a specific temporary duty, unless the context indicates otherwise.

(11) "Explosive" means gunpowders, powders used for blasting, all forms of high explosives, blasting materials, fuzes (other than electrical circuit breakers), detonators, and other detonating agents, smokeless powders, any explosive bomb, grenade, missile, or similar device, and any incendiary bomb or grenade, fire bomb, or similar device, and any other compound, mixture, or device which is an explosive within the meaning of 18 U.S.C. § 232(5) or 844(j).

(12) "Firearm" means any weapon which is de-

signed to or may be readily converted to expel any projectile by the action of an explosive.

(13) "Joint" in connection with military organization connotes activities, operations, organizations, and the like in which elements of more than one military service of the same nation participate.

(14) "Members." The members of a court-martial are the voting members detailed by the convening authority.

(15) "Military judge" means the presiding officer of a general or special court-martial detailed in accordance with Article 26. Except as otherwise expressly provided, in the context of a summary court-martial "military judge" includes the summary court-martial officer or in the context of a special court-martial without a military judge, the president. Unless otherwise indicated in the context, "the military judge" means the military judge detailed to the court-martial to which charges in a case have been referred for trial.

(16) "Party." Party, in the context of parties to a court-martial, means:

(A) The accused and any defense or associate or assistant defense counsel and agents of the defense counsel when acting on behalf of the accused with respect to the court-martial in question; and

(B) Any trial or assistant trial counsel representing the United States, and agents of the trial counsel when acting on behalf of the trial counsel with respect to the court-martial in question.

(17) "Staff judge advocate" means a judge advocate so designated in Army, Air Force, or Marine Corps, and means the principal legal advisor of a command in the Navy and Coast Guard who is a judge advocate.

(18) "*sua sponte*" means that the person involved acts on that person's initiative, without the need for a request, motion, or application.

(19) "War, time of." For purpose of R.C.M. 1004(c)(6) and of implementing the applicable paragraphs of Parts IV and V of this Manual only, "time of war" means a period of war declared by Congress or the factual determination by the President that the existence of hostilities warrants a finding that a "time of war" exists for purposes of R.C.M. 1004(c)(6) and Parts IV and V of this Manual.

(20) "Writing" includes printing and typewriting and reproductions of visual symbols by handwriting, typewriting, printing, photostating, photographing, magnetic impulse, mechanical or electronic recording, or other form of data compilation.

Discussion

The definition of "writing" includes letters, words, or numbers set down by handwriting, typewriting, printing, photostating, photographing, magnetic impulse, mechanical or electronic recording, or any other form of data compilation. This section makes it clear that computers and other modern reproduction systems are included in this definition, and consistent with the definition of "writing" in Military Rule of Evidence 1001. The definition is comprehensive, covering all forms of writing or recording of words or word-substitutes.

---

(21) The definitions and rules of construction in 1 U.S.C. §§ 1 through 5 and in 10 U.S.C. §§ 101 and 801.

Discussion

1 U.S.C. §§ 1 through 5, 10 U.S.C. § 101, and 10 U.S.C. § 801 (Article 1) are set forth below.

1 U.S.C. § 1. Words denoting number, gender, and so forth.

In determining the meaning of any Act of Congress, unless the context indicates otherwise—

words importing the singular include and apply to several persons, parties, or things; words importing the plural include the singular;

words importing the masculine gender include the feminine as well;

words used in the present tense include the future as well as the present;

the words "insane" and "insane person" and "lunatic" shall include every idiot, lunatic, insane person, and person non compos mentis; the words "person" and "whoever" include corporations, companies, associations, firms, partnerships, societies, and joint stock companies, as well as individuals;

"officer" includes any person authorized by law to perform the duties of the office;

"signature" or "subscription" includes a mark when the person making the same intended it as such;

"oath" includes affirmation, and "sworn" includes affirmed;

§ 2. "County" as including "parish," and so forth.

The word "county" includes a parish, or any other equivalent subdivision of a State or Territory of the United States.

§ 3. "Vessel" as including all means of water transportation.

The word "vessel" includes every description of watercraft or other artificial contrivance used or capable of being used, as a means of transportation on water.

§ 4. "Vehicle" as including all means of land transportation.

The word "vehicle" includes every description of carriage or other artificial contrivance used or capable of being used, as a means of transportation on land.

§ 5. "Company" or "association" as including successors and assigns.

The word "company" or "association", when used in reference to a corporation, shall be deemed to embrace the words "successors and assigns of such company or association", in like manner as if these last-named words, or words of similar import, were expressed.

10 U.S.C. § 101. *Definitions*

In addition to the definitions in sections 1-5 of title 1, the following definitions apply in this title:

(1) "United States", in a geographic sense, means the States and the District of Columbia.

(2) Except as provided in section 101(1) of title 32 for laws relating to the militia, the National Guard, the Army National Guard of the United States, and the Air National Guard of the United States, "Territory" means any Territory organized after this title is enacted, so long as it remains a Territory.

(3) "Possessions" includes the Virgin Islands, the Canal Zone, Guam, American Samoa, and the Guano islands, so long as they remain possessions, but does not include any Territory or Commonwealth.

(4) "Armed forces" means the Army, Navy, Air Force, Marine Corps, and Coast Guard.

(5) "Department", when used with respect to a military department, means the executive part of the department and all field headquarters, forces, reserve components, installations, activities, and functions under the control or supervision of the Secretary of the department. When used with respect to the Department of Defense, it means the executive part of the department, including the executive parts of the military departments, and all field headquarters, forces, reserve components, installations, activities, and functions under the control or supervision of the Secretary of Defense, including those of the military departments.

(6) "Executive part of the department" means the executive part of the Department of the Army, Department of the Navy, or Department of the Air Force, as the case may be, at the seat of government.

(7) "Military departments" means the Department of the Army, the Department of the Navy, and the Department of the Air Force.

(8) "Secretary concerned" means—

(A) the Secretary of the Army, with respect to matters concerning the Army;

(B) the Secretary of the Navy, with respect to matters concerning the Navy, the Marine Corps, and the Coast Guard when it is operating as a service in the Navy;

(C) the Secretary of the Air Force, with respect to matters concerning the Air Force; and

(D) the Secretary of Homeland Security, with respect to matters concerning the Coast Guard when it is not operating as a service in the Navy.

(9) "National Guard" means the Army National Guard and the Air National Guard.

(10) "Army National Guard" means that part of the organized militia of the several States and Territories, Puerto Rico, and the Canal Zone, and the District of Columbia, active and inactive, that—

(A) is a land force;

(B) is trained, and has its officers appointed, under the sixteenth clause of section 8, article 1, of the Constitution;

(C) is organized, armed, and equipped wholly or partly at Federal expense; and

(D) is federally recognized.

(11) "Army National Guard of the United States" means the reserve component of the Army all of whose members are members of the Army National Guard.

(12) "Air National Guard" means that part of the organized militia of the several States and Territories, Puerto Rico, the Canal Zone, and the District of Columbia, active and inactive, that—

(A) is an air force;

(B) is trained, and has its officers appointed, under the sixteenth clause of section 8, article 1, of the Constitution;

(C) is organized, armed, and equipped wholly or partly at Federal expense; and

(D) is federally recognized.

(13) "Air National Guard of the United States" means the reserve component of the Air Force all of whose members are members of the Air National Guard.

(14) "Officer" means commissioned or warrant officer.

(15) "Commissioned officer" includes a commissioned warrant officer.

(16) "Warrant officer" means a person who holds a commission or warrant in a warrant officer grade.

(17) "Enlisted member" means a person in an enlisted grade.

(18) "Grade" means a step or degree, in a graduated scale of office or military rank that is established and designated as a grade by law or regulation.

(19) "Rank" means the order of precedence among members of the armed forces.

[Definitions established in clauses (18) and (19) post-date the enactment of the code and, as a result, differ from usage of the same terms in the code and current and prior Manual provisions. *See* Articles 1(5) and 25(d)(1); R.C.M. 1003(c)(2); paragraphs 13c(1), 83c(2), and 84c, Part IV, MCM, 1984. MCM 1951 referred to officer personnel by 'rank' and enlisted personnel by "grade." *See* paragraphs 4c, 16b, 126d, 126i, and 168, MCM, 1951. "Rank" as defined in 10 U.S.C. § 101, clause (19) above, refers to the MCM, 1951 provision regarding "lineal precedence, numbers, and seniority." Paragraph 126i, MCM, 1951; *see also* paragraph 126i, MCM, 1969 (Rev). Except where lineal position or seniority is clearly intended, rank, as commonly and traditionally used, and grade refer to the current definition of "grade."]

(20) "Rating" means the name (such as "boatswain's mate") prescribed for members of an armed force in an occupational field. "Rate" means the name (such as "chief boatswain's mate") prescribed for members in the same rating or other category who are in the same grade (such as chief petty officer or seaman apprentice).

[Note: The definitions in clauses (3), (15), (18)-(21), (23)-(30), and (31)-(33) reflect the adoption of terminology which, though undefined in the source statutes restated in this title, represents the closest practicable approximation of the ways in which the terms defined have been most commonly used. A choice has been made where established uses conflict.]

(21) "Authorized strength" means the largest number of members authorized to be in an armed force, a component, a branch, a grade, or any other category of the armed forces.

(22) "Active duty" means full-time duty in the active military service of the United States. It includes full-time training duty, annual training duty, and attendance, while in the active military service, at a school designated as a service school by law or by the Secretary of the military department concerned.

(23) "Active duty for a period of more than 30 days"

means active duty under a call or order that does not specify a period of 30 days or less.

(24) "Active service" means service on active duty.

(25) "Active status" means the status of a reserve commissioned officer, other than a commissioned warrant officer, who is not in the inactive Army National Guard or inactive Air National Guard, on an inactive status list, or in the Retired Reserve.

(26) "Supplies" includes material, equipment, and stores of all kinds.

(27) "Pay" includes basic pay, special pay, retainer pay, incentive pay, retired pay, and equivalent pay, but does not include allowances.

(28) "Shall" is used in an imperative sense.

(29) "May" is used in a permissive sense. The words "no person may . . ." mean that no person is required, authorized, or permitted to do the act prescribed.

(30) "Includes" means "includes but is not limited to."

(31) "Inactive-duty training" means—

(A) duty prescribed for Reserves by the Secretary concerned under section 206 of title 37 or any other provision of law; and

(B) special additional duties authorized for Reserves by an authority designated by the Secretary concerned and performed by them on a voluntary basis in connection with the prescribed training or maintenance activities of the units to which they are assigned.

It includes those duties when performed by Reserves in their status as members of the National Guard.

(32) "Spouse" means husband or wife, as the case may be.

(33) "Regular", with respect to an enlistment, appointment, grade, or office, means enlistment, appointment, grade, or office in a regular component of an armed force.

(34) "Reserve", with respect to an enlistment, appointment, grade, or office, means enlistment, appointment, grade, or office held as a Reserve of an armed force.

(35) "Original", with respect to the appointment of a member of the armed forces in a regular or reserve component, refers to his most recent appointment in the component that is neither a promotion nor a demotion.

(36) Repealed.

(37) "Active-duty list" means a single list for the Army, Navy, Air Force or Marine Corps (required to be maintained under section 620 of this title) which contains the names of all officers of that armed force, other than officers described in section 641 of this title, who are serving on active duty.

(38) "Medical officer" means an officer of the Medical Corps of the Army, an officer of the Medical Corps of the Navy, or an officer in the Air Force designated as a medical officer.

(39) "Dental officer" means an officer of the Dental Corps of the Army, an officer of the Dental Corps of the Navy, or an officer of the Air Force designated as a dental officer.

(40) "General officer" means an officer of the Army, Air Force, or Marine Corps serving in or having the grade of general, lieutenant general, major general, or brigadier general.

(41) "Flag officer" means an officer of the Navy or Coast Guard serving in or having the grade of admiral, vice admiral, rear admiral, or commodore.

10 U.S.C. § 801. *Article 1. Definitions*   In this chapter:

(1) "Judge Advocate General" means, severally, the Judge Advocates General of the Army, Navy, and Air Force and, except when the Coast Guard is operating as a service in the Navy, an official designated to serve as Judge Advocate General of the Coast Guard by the Secretary of Homeland Security. [NOTE: The Secretary of Homeland Security has designated the Chief Counsel, U.S. Coast Guard, to serve as the Judge Advocate General of the Coast Guard.].

(2) The Navy, the Marine Corps, and the Coast Guard when it is operating as a service in the Navy, shall be considered as one armed force.

(3) "Commanding officer" includes only commissioned officers.

(4) "Officer in charge" means a member of the Navy, the Marine Corps, or the Coast Guard designated as such by appropriate authority.

(5) "Superior commissioned officer" means a commissioned officer superior in rank or command.

(6) "Cadet" means a cadet of the United States Military Academy, the United States Air Force Academy, or the United States Coast Guard Academy.

(7) "Midshipman" means a midshipman of the United States Naval Academy and any other midshipman on active duty in the naval service.

(8) "Military" refers to any or all of the armed forces.

(9) "Accuser" means a person who signs and swears to charges, any person who directs that charges nominally be signed and sworn to by another, and any other person who has an interest other than an official interest in the prosecution of the accused.

(10) "Military judge" means an official of a general or special court-martial detailed in accordance with section 826 of this title (article 26). [*See also* R.C.M. 103(15).]

(11) REPEALED

[Note: The definition for "law specialist" was repealed by Public Law 109-241, title II, § 218(a)(1), July 11, 2006, 120 Stat. 256. The text was stricken but subsequent paragraphs were not renumbered.]

(12) "Legal officer" means any commissioned officer of the Navy, Marine Corps, or Coast Guard designated to perform legal duties for a command.

(13) "Judge Advocate" means—

(A) an officer of the Judge Advocate General's Corps of the Army or Navy;

(B) an officer of the Air Force or the Marine Corps who is designated as a judge advocate; or

(C) a commissioned officer of the Coast Guard designated for special duty (law).

(14) "Classified information" (A) means any information or material that has been determined by an official of the United States pursuant to law, an Executive Order, or regulation to require protection against unauthorized disclosure for reasons of national security, and (B) any restricted data, as defined in section 2014(y) of title 42, United States Code.

(15) "National security" means the national defense and foreign relations of the United States.

Rule 104. Unlawful command influence

(a) *General prohibitions.*

(1) *Convening authorities and commanders.* No convening authority or commander may censure, reprimand, or admonish a court-martial or other military tribunal or any member, military judge, or counsel thereof, with respect to the findings or sentence adjudged by the court-martial or tribunal, or with respect to any other exercise of the functions of the court-martial or tribunal or such persons in the conduct of the proceedings.

(2) *All persons subject to the code.* No person subject to the code may attempt to coerce or, by any unauthorized means, influence the action of a court-martial or any other military tribunal or any member thereof, in reaching the findings or sentence in any case or the action of any convening, approving, or reviewing authority with respect to such authority's judicial acts.

(3) *Exceptions.*

(A) *Instructions.* Subsections (a)(1) and (2) of the rule do not prohibit general instructional or informational courses in military justice if such courses are designed solely for the purpose of instructing personnel of a command in the substantive and procedural aspects of courts-martial.

(B) *Court-martial statements.* Subsections (a)(1) and (2) of this rule do not prohibit statements and instructions given in open session by the military judge or counsel.

(C) *Professional supervision.* Subsections (a)(1) and (2) of this rule do not prohibit action by the Judge Advocate General concerned under R.C.M. 109.

(D) *Offense.* Subsection (a)(1) and (2) of this rule do not prohibit appropriate action against a person for an offense committed while detailed as a military judge, counsel, or member of a court-martial, or while serving as individual counsel.

(b) *Prohibitions concerning evaluations.*

(1) *Evaluation of member, defense counsel, or special victims' counsel.* In the preparation of an effectiveness, fitness, or efficiency report or any other report or document used in whole or in part for the purpose of determining whether a member of the armed forces is qualified to be advanced in grade, or in determining the assignment or transfer of a member of the armed forces, or in determining whether a member of the armed forces should be retained on active duty, no person subject to the code may:

(A) Consider or evaluate the performance of duty of any such person as a member of a court-martial; or

(B) Give a less favorable rating or evaluation of any defense counsel or special victims' counsel because of the zeal with which such counsel represented any client. As used in this rule, "special victims' counsel" are judge advocates who, in accordance with 10 U.S.C. 1044e, are designated as Special Victims' Counsel.

(2) *Evaluation of military judge.*

(A) *General courts-martial.* Unless the general court-martial was convened by the President or the Secretary concerned, neither the convening authority nor any member of the convening authority's staff may prepare or review any report concerning the effectiveness, fitness, or efficiency of the military judge detailed to a general court-martial, which relates to the performance of duty as a military judge.

(B) *Special courts-martial.* The convening authority may not prepare or review any report concerning the effectiveness, fitness, or efficiency of a military judge detailed to a special court-martial which relates to the performance of duty as a military judge. When the military judge is normally rated or the military judge's report is reviewed by the convening authority, the manner in which such military judge will be rated or evaluated upon the performance of duty as a military judge may be as prescribed in regulations of the Secretary concerned which shall ensure the absence of any command influence in the rating or evaluation of the military judge's judicial performance.

Discussion

See paragraph 22 of Part IV concerning prosecuting violations of Article 37 under Article 98.

Rule 105. Direct communications: convening authorities and staff judge advocates; among staff judge advocates

(a) *Convening authorities and staff judge advocates.* Convening authorities shall at all times communicate directly with their staff judge advocates in matters relating to the administration of military justice.

(b) *Among staff judge advocates and with the Judge Advocate General.* The staff judge advocate of any command is entitled to communicate directly with the staff judge advocate of a superior or subordinate command, or with the Judge Advocate General.

Discussion

See R.C.M. 103(17) for a definition of staff judge advocate.

Rule 106. Delivery of military offenders to civilian authorities

Under such regulations as the Secretary concerned may prescribe, a member of the armed forces accused of an offense against civilian authority may be delivered, upon request, to the civilian authority for trial. A member may be placed in restraint by military authorities for this purpose only upon receipt of a duly issued warrant for the apprehension of the member or upon receipt of information establishing probable cause that the member committed an offense, and upon reasonable belief that such restraint is necessary. Such restraint may continue only for such time as is reasonably necessary to effect the delivery.

Discussion

See R.C.M. 1113(e)(2)(A)(ii) for the effect of such delivery on the execution of a court-martial sentence.

Rule 107. Dismissed officer's right to request trial by court-martial

If a commissioned officer of any armed force is dismissed by order of the President under 10 U.S.C. § 1161(a)(3), that officer may apply for trial by general court-martial within a reasonable time.

Discussion

See Article 4 for the procedures to be followed. *See also* Article 75(c).

Rule 108. Rules of court

The Judge Advocate General concerned and persons designated by the Judge Advocate General may make rules of court not inconsistent with these rules for the conduct of court-martial proceedings. Such rules shall be disseminated in accordance with procedures prescribed by the Judge Advocate General concerned or a person to whom this authority has been delegated. Noncompliance with such procedures shall not affect the validity of any rule of court with respect to a party who has received actual and timely notice of the rule or who has not been prejudiced under Article 59 by the absence of such notice. Copies of all rules of court issued under this rule shall be forwarded to the Judge Advocate General concerned.

Rule 109. Professional supervision of military judges and counsel

(a) *In general.* Each Judge Advocate General is responsible for the professional supervision and discipline of military trial and appellate military judges, judge advocates, and other lawyers who practice in proceedings governed by the code and this Manual. To discharge this responsibility each Judge Advocate General may prescribe rules of professional conduct not inconsistent with this rule or this Manual. Rules of professional conduct promulgated pursuant to this rule may include sanctions for violations of such rules. Sanctions may include but are not limited to indefinite suspension from practice in courts-martial and in the Courts of Criminal Appeals. Such suspensions may only be imposed by the Judge Advocate General of the armed service of such courts. Prior to imposing any discipline under this rule, the subject of the proposed action must be provided notice and an opportunity to be heard. The Judge Advocate General concerned may upon good cause shown modify or revoke suspension. Procedures to investigate complaints against military trial judges and appellate military judges are contained in subsection (c) of this rule.

(b) *Action after suspension or disbarment.* When a Judge Advocate General suspends a person from practice or the Court of Appeals for the Armed Forces disbars a person, any Judge Advocate General may suspend that person from practice upon written notice and opportunity to be heard in writing.

(c) *Investigation of judges.*

(1) *In general.* These rules and procedures promulgated pursuant to Article 6a are established to investigate and dispose of charges, allegations, or information pertaining to the fitness of a military

trial judge or appellate military judge to perform the duties of the judge's office.

(2) *Policy.* Allegations of judicial misconduct or unfitness shall be investigated pursuant to the procedures of this rule and appropriate action shall be taken. Judicial misconduct includes any act or omission that may serve to demonstrate unfitness for further duty as a judge, including, but not limited to violations of applicable ethical standards.

Discussion

The term "unfitness" should be construed broadly, including, for example, matters relating to the incompetence, impartiality, and misconduct of the judge. Erroneous decisions of a judge are not subject to investigation under this rule. Challenges to these decisions are more appropriately left to the appellate process.

(3) *Complaints.* Complaints concerning a military trial judge or appellate military judge will be forwarded to the Judge Advocate General of the service concerned or to a person designated by the Judge Advocate General concerned to receive such complaints.

Discussion

Complaints need not be made in any specific form, but if possible complaints should be made under oath. Complaints may be made by judges, lawyers, a party, court personnel, members of the general public or members of the military community. Reports in the news media relating to the conduct of a judge may also form the basis of a complaint.

An individual designated to receive complaints under this subsection should have judicial experience. The chief trial judge of a service may be designated to receive complaints against military trial judges.

(4) *Initial action upon receipt of a complaint.* Upon receipt, a complaint will be screened by the Judge Advocate General concerned or by the individual designated in subsection (c)(3) of this rule to receive complaints. An initial inquiry is necessary if the complaint, taken as true, would constitute judicial misconduct or unfitness for further service as a judge. Prior to the commencement of an initial inquiry, the Judge Advocate General concerned shall be notified that a complaint has been filed and that an initial inquiry will be conducted. The Judge Advocate General concerned may temporarily suspend the subject of a complaint from performing judicial duties pending the outcome of any inquiry or investigation conducted pursuant to this rule. Such inquiries or investigations shall be conducted with reasonable promptness.

Discussion

Complaints under this subsection will be treated with confidentiality. Confidentiality protects the subject judge and the judiciary when a complaint is not substantiated. Confidentiality also encourages the reporting of allegations of judicial misconduct or unfitness and permits complaints to be screened with the full cooperation of others.

Complaints containing allegations of criminality should be referred to the appropriate criminal investigative agency in accordance with Appendix 3 of this Manual.

(5) *Initial inquiry.*

(A) *In general.* An initial inquiry is necessary to determine if the complaint is substantiated. A complaint is substantiated upon finding that it is more likely than not that the subject judge has engaged in judicial misconduct or is otherwise unfit for further service as a judge.

(B) *Responsibility to conduct initial inquiry.* The Judge Advocate General concerned, or the person designated to receive complaints under subsection (c)(3) of this rule will conduct or order an initial inquiry. The individual designated to conduct the inquiry should, if practicable, be senior to the subject of the complaint. If the subject of the complaint is a military trial judge, the individual designated to conduct the initial inquiry should, if practicable, be a military trial judge or an individual with experience as a military trial judge. If the subject of the complaint is an appellate military judge, the individual designated to conduct the inquiry should, if practicable, have experience as an appellate military judge.

Discussion

To avoid the type of conflict prohibited in Article 66(g), the Judge Advocate General's designee should not ordinarily be a member of the same Court of Criminal Appeals as the subject of the complaint. If practicable, a former appellate military judge should be designated.

(C) *Due process.* During the initial inquiry, the subject of the complaint will, at a minimum, be given notice and an opportunity to be heard.

(D) *Action following the initial inquiry.* If the complaint is not substantiated pursuant to subsection (c)(5)(A) of this rule, the complaint shall be dismissed as unfounded. If the complaint is substantiated, minor professional disciplinary action may be taken or the complaint may be forwarded, with findings and recommendations, to the Judge Advocate General concerned. Minor professional disciplinary action is defined as counseling or the issuance of an oral or written admonition or reprimand. The Judge Advocate General concerned will be notified prior to taking minor professional disciplinary action or dismissing a complaint as unfounded.

(6) *Action by the Judge Advocate General.*

(A) *In general.* The Judge Advocates General are responsible for the professional supervision and discipline of military trial and appellate military judges under their jurisdiction. Upon receipt of findings and recommendations required by subsection (c)(5) of this rule the Judge Advocate General concerned will take appropriate action.

(B) *Appropriate actions.* The Judge Advocate General concerned may dismiss the complaint, order an additional inquiry, appoint an ethics commission to consider the complaint, refer the matter to another appropriate investigative agency or take appropriate professional disciplinary action pursuant to the rules of professional conduct prescribed by the Judge Advocate General under subsection (a) of this rule. Any decision of the Judge Advocate General, under this rule, is final and is not subject to appeal.

Discussion

The discretionary reassignment of military trial judges or appellate military judges to meet the needs of the service is not professional disciplinary action.

(C) *Standard of proof.* Prior to taking professional disciplinary action, other than minor disciplinary action as defined in subsection (c)(5) of this rule, the Judge Advocate General concerned shall find, in writing, that the subject of the complaint engaged in judicial misconduct or is otherwise unfit for continued service as a military judge, and that

such misconduct or unfitness is established by clear and convincing evidence.

(D) *Due process.* Prior to taking final action on the complaint, the Judge Advocate General concerned will ensure that the subject of the complaint is, at a minimum, given notice and an opportunity to be heard.

(7) *The Ethics Commission.*

(A) *Membership.* If appointed pursuant to subsection (c)(6)(B) of this rule, an ethics commission shall consist of at least three members. If the subject of the complaint is a military trial judge, the commission should include one or more military trial judges or individuals with experience as a military trial judge. If the subject of the complaint is an appellate military judge, the commission should include one or more individuals with experience as an appellate military judge. Members of the commission should, if practicable, be senior to the subject of the complaint.

(B) *Duties.* The commission will perform those duties assigned by the Judge Advocate General concerned. Normally, the commission will provide an opinion as to whether the subject's acts or omissions constitute judicial misconduct or unfitness. If the commission determines that the affected judge engaged in judicial misconduct or is unfit for continued judicial service, the commission may be required to recommend an appropriate disposition to The Judge Advocate General concerned.

Discussion

The Judge Advocate General concerned may appoint an ad hoc or a standing commission.

---

(8) *Rules of procedure.* The Secretary of Defense or the Secretary of the service concerned may establish additional procedures consistent with this rule and Article 6a.

CHAPTER II. JURISDICTION

Rule 201. Jurisdiction in general

(a) *Nature of courts-martial jurisdiction.*

(1) The jurisdiction of courts-martial is entirely penal or disciplinary.

Discussion

"Jurisdiction" means the power to hear a case and to render a legally competent decision. A court-martial has no power to adjudge civil remedies. For example, a court-martial may not adjudge the payment of damages, collect private debts, order the return of property, or order a criminal forfeiture of seized property. A summary court-martial appointed under 10 U.S.C. §§ 4712 or 9712 to dispose of the effects of a deceased person is not affected by these Rules or this Manual.

(2) The code applies in all places.

Discussion

Except insofar as required by the Constitution, the Code, or the Manual, such as jurisdiction over persons listed under Article 2(a)(10), jurisdiction of courts-martial does not depend on where the offense was committed.

(3) The jurisdiction of a court-martial with respect to offenses under the code is not affected by the place where the court-martial sits. The jurisdiction of a court-martial with respect to military government or the law of war is not affected by the place where the court-martial sits except as otherwise expressly required by this Manual or applicable rule of international law.

Discussion

In addition to the power to try persons for offenses under the code, general courts-martial have power to try certain persons for violations of the law of war and for crimes or offenses against the law of the territory occupied as an incident of war or belligerency whenever the local civil authority is superseded in whole or part by the military authority of the occupying power. *See* R.C.M. 201(f)(1)(B). In cases where a person is tried by general court-martial for offenses against the law of an occupied territory, the court-martial normally sits in the country where the offense is committed, and must do so under certain circumstances. *See* Articles 4, 64, and 66, Geneva Convention Relative to the Protection of Civilian Persons in Time of War, August 12, 1949, arts. 4, 64, and 66, 6 U.S.T. 3516, 3559-60 T.I.A.S. No. 3365.

(b) *Requisites of court-martial jurisdiction.* A court-martial always has jurisdiction to determine whether it has jurisdiction. Otherwise for a court-martial to have jurisdiction:

(1) The court-martial must be convened by an official empowered to convene it;

Discussion

See R.C.M. 504; 1302.

(2) The court-martial must be composed in accordance with these rules with respect to number and qualifications of its personnel. As used here "personnel" includes only the military judge, the members, and the summary court-martial;

Discussion

See R.C.M. 501-504; 1301.

(3) Each charge before the court-martial must be referred to it by competent authority;

Discussion

See R.C.M. 601.

(4) The accused must be a person subject to court-martial jurisdiction; and

Discussion

See R.C.M. 202.

(5) The offense must be subject to court-martial jurisdiction.

Discussion

See R.C.M. 203.

The judgment of a court-martial without jurisdiction is void and is entitled to no legal effect. *See* R.C.M. 907(b)(2)(C)(iv). *But see* R.C.M. 810(d) concerning the effect of certain decisions by courts-martial without jurisdiction.

(c) *Contempt.* A judge detailed to a court-martial may punish for contempt any person who uses any menacing word, sign, or gesture in the presence of the judge during the proceedings of the court-martial; disturbs the proceedings of the court-martial by any riot or disorder; or willfully disobeys the lawful writ, process, order, rule, decree, or command of the court-martial. The punishment may not exceed confinement for 30 days or a fine of $1,000, or both.

Discussion

See R.C.M. 809 for procedures and standards for contempt proceedings.

(d) *Exclusive and nonexclusive jurisdiction.*

(1) Courts-martial have exclusive jurisdiction of purely military offenses.

(2) An act or omission which violates both the code and local criminal law, foreign or domestic, may be tried by a court-martial, or by a proper civilian tribunal, foreign or domestic, or, subject to R.C.M. 907(b)(2)(C) and regulations of the Secretary concerned, by both.

(3) Where an act or omission is subject to trial by court-martial and by one or more civil tribunals, foreign or domestic, the determination which nation, state, or agency will exercise jurisdiction is a matter for the nations, states, and agencies concerned, and is not a right of the suspect or accused.

Discussion

In the case of an act or omission which violates the code and a criminal law of a State, the United States, or both, the determination which agency shall exercise jurisdiction should normally be made through consultation or prior agreement between appropriate military officials (ordinarily the staff judge advocate) and appropriate civilian authorities (United States Attorney, or equivalent). *See also* Memorandum of Understanding Between Departments of Justice and Defense Relating to the Investigation and Prosecution of Crimes Over Which the Two Departments Have Concurrent Jurisdiction at Appendix 3.

Under the Constitution, a person may not be tried for the same misconduct by both a court-martial and another federal court. *See* R.C.M. 907(b)(2)(C). Although it is constitutionally permissible to try a person by court-martial and by a State court for the same act, as a matter of policy a person who is pending trial or has been tried by a State court should not ordinarily be tried by court-martial for the same act. Overseas, international agreements might preclude trial by one state of a person acquitted or finally convicted of a given act by the other state.

Under international law, a friendly foreign nation has jurisdiction to punish offenses committed within its borders by members of a visiting force, unless expressly or impliedly consents to relinquish its jurisdiction to the visiting sovereign. The procedures and standards for determining which nation will exercise jurisdiction are normally established by treaty. *See*, for example, NATO Status of Forces Agreement, June 19, 1951, 4 U.S.T. 1792, T.I.A.S. No. 2846. As a matter of policy, efforts should be made to maximize the exercise of court-martial jurisdiction over per-

sons subject to the code to the extent possible under applicable agreements.

See R.C.M. 106 concerning delivery of offenders to civilian authorities.

See also R.C.M. 201(g) concerning the jurisdiction of other military tribunals.

(e) *Reciprocal jurisdiction.*

(1) Each armed force has court-martial jurisdiction over all persons subject to the code.

(2)(A) A commander of a unified or specified combatant command may convene courts-martial over members of any of the armed forces.

(B) So much of the authority vested in the President under Article 22(a)(9) to empower any commanding officer of a joint command or joint task force to convene courts-martial is delegated to the Secretary of Defense, and such a commanding officer may convene general courts-martial for the trial of members of any of the armed forces assigned or attached to a combatant command or joint command.

(C) A commander who is empowered to convene a court-martial under subsections (e)(2)(A) or (e)(2)(B) of this rule may expressly authorize a commanding officer of a subordinate joint command or subordinate joint task force who is authorized to convene special and summary courts-martial to convene such courts-martial for the trial of members of other armed forces assigned or attached to a joint command or joint task force, under regulations which the superior command may prescribe.

(3) A member of one armed force may be tried by a court-martial convened by a member of another armed force, using the implementing regulations and procedures prescribed by the Secretary concerned of the military service of the accused, when:

(A) The court-martial is convened by a commander authorized to convene courts-martial under subsection (e)(2) of this rule; or

(B) The accused cannot be delivered to the armed force of which the accused is a member without manifest injury to the armed forces.

An accused should not ordinarily be tried by a court-martial convened by a member of a different armed force except when the circumstances described in (A) or (B) exist. However, failure to comply with this policy does not affect an otherwise valid referral.

(4) Nothing in this rule prohibits detailing to a

court-martial a military judge, member, or counsel who is a member of an armed force different from that of the accused or the convening authority, or both.

(5) In all cases, departmental review after that by the officer with authority to convene a general court-martial for the command which held the trial, where that review is required by the code, shall be carried out by the department that includes the armed force of which the accused is a member.

(6) When there is a disagreement between the Secretaries of two military departments or between the Secretary of a military department and the commander of a unified or specified combatant command or other joint command or joint task force as to which organization should exercise jurisdiction over a particular case or class of cases, the Secretary of Defense or an official acting under the authority of the Secretary of Defense shall designate which organization will exercise jurisdiction.

(7) Except as provided in subsections (5) and (6) or as otherwise directed by the President or Secretary of Defense, whenever action under this Manual is required or authorized to be taken by a person superior to—

(A) a commander of a unified or specified combatant command or;

(B) a commander of any other joint command or joint task force that is not part of a unified or specified combatant command, the matter shall be referred to the Secretary of the armed force of which the accused is a member. The Secretary may convene a court-martial, take other appropriate action, or, subject to R.C.M. 504(c), refer the matter to any person authorized to convene a court-martial of the accused.

Discussion

As to the authority to convene courts-martial, see R.C.M. 504. "Manifest injury" does not mean minor inconvenience or expense. Examples of manifest injury include direct and substantial effect on morale, discipline, or military operations, substantial expense or delay, or loss of essential witnesses.

As to the composition of a court-martial for the trial of an accused who is a member of another armed force, *see* R.C.M. 503(a)(3) Discussion. Cases involving two or more accused who are members of different armed forces should not be referred to a court-martial for a common trial.

(f) *Types of courts-martial.*
[Note: R.C.M. 201(f)(1)(D) and (f)(2)(D) apply to offenses committed on or after 24 June 2014.]

(1) *General courts-martial.*

(A) *Cases under the code.*

(i) Except as otherwise expressly provided, general courts-martial may try any person subject to the code for any offense made punishable under the code. General courts-martial also may try any person for a violation of Article 83, 104, or 106.

(ii) Upon a finding of guilty of an offense made punishable by the code, general courts-martial may, within limits prescribed by this Manual, adjudge any punishment authorized under R.C.M. 1003.

(iii) Notwithstanding any other rule, the death penalty may not be adjudged if:

(a) Not specifically authorized for the offense by the code and Part IV of this Manual; or

(b) The case has not been referred with a special instruction that the case is to be tried as capital.

(B) *Cases under the law of war.*

(i) General courts-martial may try any person who by the law of war is subject to trial by military tribunal for any crime or offense against:

(a) The law of war; or

(b) The law of the territory occupied as an incident of war or belligerency whenever the local civil authority is superseded in whole or part by the military authority of the occupying power. The law of the occupied territory includes the local criminal law as adopted or modified by competent authority, and the proclamations, ordinances, regulations, or orders promulgated by competent authority of the occupying power.

Discussion

Subsection (f)(1)(B)(i)(b) is an exercise of the power of military government.

(ii) When a general court-martial exercises jurisdiction under the law of war, it may adjudge any punishment permitted by the law of war.

Discussion

Certain limitations on the discretion of military tribunals to adjudge punishment under the law of war are prescribed in international conventions. *See*, for example, Geneva Convention Relative to the Protection of Civilian Persons in Time of War, Aug. 12, 1949, art. 68, 6 U.S.T. 3516, T.I.A.S. No. 3365.

(C) *Limitations in judge alone cases.* A general court-martial composed only of a military judge does not have jurisdiction to try any person for any offense for which the death penalty may be adjudged unless the case has been referred to trial as noncapital.

(D) *Jurisdiction for certain sexual offenses.* Only a general court-martial has jurisdiction to try offenses under Articles 120(a), 120(b), 120b(a), and 120b(b), forcible sodomy under Article 125, and attempts thereof under Article 80.

(2) *Special courts-martial.*

(A) *In general.* Except as otherwise expressly provided, special courts-martial may try any person subject to the code for any noncapital offense made punishable by the code and, as provided in this rule, for capital offenses.

(B) *Punishments.*

(i) Upon a finding of guilty, special courts-martial may adjudge, under limitations prescribed by this Manual, any punishment authorized under R.C.M. 1003 except death, dishonorable discharge, dismissal, confinement for more than 1 year, hard labor without confinement for more than 3 months, forfeiture of pay exceeding two-thirds pay per month, or any forfeiture of pay for more than 1 year.

(ii) A bad-conduct discharge, confinement for more than six months, or forfeiture of pay for more than six months, may not be adjudged by a special court-martial unless:

(a) Counsel qualified under Article 27(b) is detailed to represent the accused; and

(b) A military judge is detailed to the trial, except in a case in which a military judge could not be detailed because of physical conditions or military exigencies. Physical conditions or military exigencies, as the terms are here used, may exist under rare circumstances, such as on an isolated ship on the high seas or in a unit in an inaccessible area, provided compelling reasons exist why trial must be held at that time and at that place. Mere inconvenience does not constitute a physical condition or military exigency and does not excuse a failure to detail a military judge. If a military judge cannot be detailed because of physical conditions or military exigencies, a bad-conduct discharge, confinement for more than six months, or forfeiture of pay for more than six months, may be adjudged provided the other conditions have been met. In that event, however, the convening authority shall, prior to trial, make a written statement explaining why a military judge could not be obtained. This statement shall be appended to the record of trial and shall set forth in detail the reasons why a military judge could not be detailed, and why the trial had to be held at that time and place.

Discussion

See R.C.M. 503 concerning detailing the military judge and counsel.

The requirement for counsel is satisfied when counsel qualified under Article 27(b), and not otherwise disqualified, has been detailed and made available, even though the accused may not choose to cooperate with, or use the services of, such detailed counsel.

The physical condition or military exigency exception to the requirement for a military judge does not apply to the requirement for detailing counsel qualified under Article 27(b).

See also R.C.M. 1103(c) concerning the requirements for a record of trial in special courts-martial.

(C) *Capital offenses*

(i) A capital offense for which there is prescribed a mandatory punishment beyond the punitive power of a special court-martial shall not be referred to such a court-martial.

(ii) An officer exercising general court-martial jurisdiction over the command which includes the accused may permit any capital offense other than one described in subsection (f)(2)(C)(i) of this rule to be referred to a special court-martial for trial.

(iii) The Secretary concerned may authorize, by regulation, officers exercising special court-martial jurisdiction to refer capital offenses, other than those described in subsection (f)(2)(C)(i) of this rule, to trial by special court-martial without first obtaining the consent of the officer exercising general court-martial jurisdiction over the command.

Discussion

See R.C.M. 103(3) for a definition of capital offenses.

(D) *Certain offenses under Articles 120, 120b, and 125.* Notwithstanding subsection (f)(2)(A), special courts-martial do not have jurisdiction over offenses under Articles 120(a), 120(b), 120b(a), and 120b(b), forcible sodomy under Article 125, and attempts thereof under Article 80. Such offenses shall not be referred to a special court-martial.

Discussion

Pursuant to the National Defense Authorization Act for Fiscal Year 2014, only a general court-martial has jurisdiction over penetrative sex offenses under subsections (a) and (b) of Article 120, subsections (a) and (b) of Article 120b, Article 125, and attempts to commit such penetrative sex offenses under Article 80.

---

(3) *Summary courts-martial. See* R.C.M. 1301(c) and (d)(1).

(g) *Concurrent jurisdiction of other military tribunals.* The provisions of the code and this Manual conferring jurisdiction upon courts-martial do not deprive military commissions, provost courts, or other military tribunals of concurrent jurisdiction with respect to offenders or offenses that by statute or by the law of war may be tried by military commissions, provost courts, or other military tribunals.

Discussion

See Articles 104 and 106 for some instances of concurrent jurisdiction.

Rule 202. Persons subject to the jurisdiction of courts-martial

(a) *In general.* Courts-martial may try any person when authorized to do so under the code.

Discussion

(1) *Authority under the code.* Article 2 lists classes of persons who are subject to the code. These include active duty personnel (Article 2(a)(1)); cadets, aviation cadets, and midshipmen (Article 2(a)(2)); certain retired personnel (Article 2(a)(4) and (5)); members of Reserve components not on active duty under some circumstances (Article 2(a)(3) and (6)); persons in the custody of the armed forces serving a sentence imposed by court-martial (Article 2(a)(7)); and, under some circumstances, specified categories of civilians (Article 2(a)(8), (9), (10), (11), and (12); *see* subsection (3) and (4) of this discussion). In addition, certain persons whose status as members of the armed forces or as persons otherwise subject to the code apparently has ended may, nevertheless, be amendable to trial by court-martial. *See*

Article 3, 4, and 73. A person need not be subject to the code to be subject to trial by court-martial under Articles 83, 104, or 106. *See also* Article 48 and R.C.M. 809 concerning who may be subject to the contempt powers of a court-martial.

(2) *Active duty personnel.* Court-martial jurisdiction is most commonly exercised over active duty personnel. In general, a person becomes subject to court-martial jurisdiction upon enlistment in or induction into the armed forces, acceptance of a commission, or entry onto active duty pursuant to orders. Court-martial jurisdiction over active duty personnel ordinarily ends on delivery of a discharge certificate or its equivalent to the person concerned issued pursuant to competent orders. Orders transferring a person to the inactive reserve are the equivalent of a discharge certificate for purposes of jurisdiction.

These are several important qualifications and exceptions to these general guidelines.

(A) *Inception of court-martial jurisdiction over active duty personnel.*

(i) *Enlistment.* "The voluntary enlistment of any person who has the capacity to understand the significance of enlisting in the armed forces shall be valid for purposes of jurisdiction under [Article 2(a)] and a change of status from civilian to member of the armed forces shall be effective upon taking the oath of enlistment." Article 2(b). A person who is, at the time of enlistment, insane, intoxicated, or under the age of 17 does not have the capacity to enlist by law. No court-martial jurisdiction over such a person may exist as long as the incapacity continues. If the incapacity ceases to exist, a "constructive enlistment" may result under Article 2(c). *See* discussion of "constructive enlistment" below. Similarly, if the enlistment was involuntary, court-martial jurisdiction will exist only when the coercion is removed and a "constructive enlistment" under Article 2(c) is established.

Persons age 17 (but not yet 18) may not enlist without parental consent. A parent or guardian may, within 90 days of its inception, terminate the enlistment of a 17-year-old who enlisted without parental consent, if the person has not yet reached the age of 18. 10 U.S.C. § 1170. *See also* DOD Directive 1332.14 and service regulations for specific rules on separation of persons 17 years of age on the basis of a parental request. Absent effective action by a parent or guardian to terminate such an enlistment, court-martial jurisdiction exists over the person. An application by a parent for release does not deprive a court-martial of jurisdiction to try a person for offenses committed before action is completed on such an application.

Even if a person lacked capacity to understand the effect of enlistment or did not enlist voluntarily, a "constructive enlistment" may be established under Article 2(c), which provides:

Notwithstanding any other provision of law, a person serving with an armed force who—

(1) submitted voluntary to military authority;

(2) met the mental competency and minimum age qualifications of sections 504 and 505 of this title at the time of voluntary submission to military authority [that is, not insane, intoxicated, or under the age of 17]

(3) received military pay or allowances; and

(4) performed military duties;

is subject to [the code] until such person's active service has been terminated in accordance with law or regulations promulgated by the Secretary concerned.

Even if a person never underwent an enlistment or induction

proceeding of any kind, court-martial jurisdiction could be established under this provision.

(ii) *Induction.* Court-martial jurisdiction does not extend to a draftee until: the draftee has completed an induction ceremony which was in substantial compliance with the requirements prescribed by statute and regulations; the draftee by conduct after an apparent induction, has waived objection to substantive defects in it; or a "constructive enlistment" under Article 2(c) exists.

The fact that a person was improperly inducted (for example, because of incorrect classification or erroneous denial of exemption) does not of itself negate court-martial jurisdiction. When a person has made timely and persistent efforts to correct such an error, court-martial jurisdiction may be defeated if improper induction is found, depending on all the circumstances of the case.

(iii) *Call to active duty.* A member of a reserve component may be called or ordered to active duty for a variety of reasons, including training, service in time of war or national emergency, discipline, or as a result of failure to participate satisfactorily in unit activities.

When a person is ordered to active duty for failure to satisfactorily participate in unit activities, the order must substantially comply with procedures prescribed by regulations, to the extent due process requires, for court-martial jurisdiction to exist. Generally, the person must be given notice of the activation and the reasons therefor, and an opportunity to object to the activation. A person waives the right to contest involuntary activation by failure to exercise this right within a reasonable time after notice of the right to do so.

(B) *Termination of jurisdiction over active duty personnel.* As indicated above, the delivery of a valid discharge certificate or its equivalent ordinarily serves to terminate court-martial jurisdiction.

(i) *Effect of completion of term of service.* Completion of an enlistment or term of service does not by itself terminate court-martial jurisdiction. An original term of enlistment may be adjusted for a variety of reasons, such as making up time lost for unauthorized absence. Even after such adjustments are considered, court-martial jurisdiction normally continues past the time of scheduled separation until a discharge certificate or its equivalent is delivered or until the Government fails to act within a reasonable time after the person objects to continued retention.

As indicated in subsection (c) of this rule, servicemembers may be retained past their scheduled time of separation, over protest, by action with a view to trial while they are still subject to the code. Thus, if action with a view to trial is initiated before discharge or the effective terminal date of self-executing orders, a person may be retained beyond the date that the period of service would otherwise have expired or the terminal date of such orders.

(ii) *Effect of discharge and reenlistment.* For offenses occurring on or after 23 October 1992, under the 1992 Amendment to Article 3(a), a person who reenlists following a discharge may be tried for offenses committed during the earlier term of service. For offenses occurring prior to 23 October 1992, a person who reenlists following a discharge may be tried for offenses committed during the earlier term of service only if the offense was punishable by confinement for five (5) years or more and could not be tried in the courts of the United States or of a State, a Territory, or the District of Columbia. However, *see* (iii)(a) below.

(iii) *Exceptions.* There are several exceptions to the general principle that court-martial jurisdiction terminates on discharge or its equivalent.

(a) A person who was subject to the code at the time an offense was committed may be tried by court-martial for that offense despite a later discharge or other termination of that status if:

(1) For offenses occurring on or after 23 October 1992, the person is, at the time of the court-martial, subject to the code, by reentry into the armed forces or otherwise. *See* Article 3(a) as amended by the National Defense Authorization Act for Fiscal Year 1993, Pub. L. No. 102-484, 106 Stat. 2315, 2505 (1992);

(2) For offenses occurring before 23 October 1992,

(A) The offense is one for which a court-martial may adjudge confinement for five (5) or more years;

(B) The person cannot be tried in the courts of the United States or of a State, Territory, or the District of Columbia; and

(C) The person is, at the time of the court-martial, subject to the code, by reentry into the armed forces or otherwise. *See* Article 3(a) prior to the 1992 amendment.

(b) A person who was subject to the code at the time the offense was committed is subject to trial by court-martial despite a later discharge if—

(1) The discharge was issued before the end of the accused's term of enlistment for the purpose of reenlisting;

(2) The person remains, at the time of the court-martial, subject to the code; and

(3) The reenlistment occurred after 26 July 1982.

(c) Persons in the custody of the armed forces serving a sentence imposed by a court-martial remain subject to the code and court-martial jurisdiction. A prisoner who has received a discharge and who remains in the custody of an armed force may be tried for an offense committed while a member of the armed forces and before the execution of the discharge as well as for offenses committed after it.

(d) A person discharged from the armed forces who is later charged with having fraudulently obtained that discharge is, subject to the statute of limitations, subject to trial by court-martial on that charge, and is after apprehension subject to the code while in the custody of the armed forces for trial. Upon conviction of that charge such a person is subject to trial by court-martial for any offenses under the code committed before the fraudulent discharge.

(e) No person who has deserted from the armed forces is relieved from court-martial jurisdiction by a separation from any later period of service.

(f) When a person's discharge or other separation does not interrupt the status as a person belonging to the general category of persons subject to the code, court-martial jurisdiction over that person does not end. For example, when an officer holding a commission in a Reserve component of an armed force is discharged from that commission while on active duty because of acceptance of a commission in a Regular component of that armed force, without an interval between the periods of service under the two commissions, that officer's military status does not end. There is merely a change in personnel status from temporary to permanent officer, and court-martial jurisdiction over an offense committed before the discharge is not affected.

(3) *Public Health Service and National Oceanic and Atmospheric Administration.* Members of the Public Health Service and the National Oceanic and Atmospheric Administration become subject to the code when assigned to and serving with the armed forces.

(4) *Limitations on jurisdiction over civilians.* Court-martial jurisdiction over civilians under the code is limited by the Constitution and other applicable laws, including as construed in judicial decisions. The exercise of jurisdiction under Article 2(a)(11) in peace time has been held unconstitutional by the Supreme Court of the United States. Before initiating court-martial proceedings against a civilian, relevant statutes, decisions, service regulations, and policy memoranda should be carefully examined.

(5) *Members of a Reserve Component.* Members of a reserve component in federal service on active duty, as well as those in federal service on inactive-duty training, are subject to the code. Moreover, members of a reserve component are amenable to the jurisdiction of courts-martial notwithstanding the termination of a period of such duty. *See* R.C.M. 204.

───────────

(b) *Offenses under the law of war.* Nothing in this rule limits the power of general courts-martial to try persons under the law of war. *See* R.C.M. 201(f)(1)(B).

(c) *Attachment of jurisdiction over the person.*

(1) *In general.* Court-martial jurisdiction attaches over a person when action with a view to trial of that person is taken. Once court-martial jurisdiction over a person attaches, such jurisdiction shall continue for all purposes of trial, sentence, and punishment, notwithstanding the expiration of that person's term of service or other period in which that person was subject to the code or trial by court-martial. When jurisdiction attaches over a servicemember on active duty, the servicemember may be held on active duty over objection pending disposition of any offense for which held and shall remain subject to the code during the entire period.

Discussion

Court-martial jurisdiction exists to try a person as long as that person occupies a status as a person subject to the code. *See also* Article 104 and 106. Thus, a servicemember is subject to court-martial jurisdiction until lawfully discharged or, when the servicemember's term of service has expired, the government fails to act within a reasonable time on objection by the servicemember to continued retention.

Court-martial jurisdiction attaches over a person upon action with a view to trial. Once court-martial jurisdiction attaches, it continues throughout the trial and appellate process, and for purposes of punishment.

If jurisdiction has attached before the effective terminal date of self-executing orders, the person may be held for trial by court-martial beyond the effective terminal date.

───────────

(2) *Procedure.* Actions by which court-martial jurisdiction attaches include: apprehension; imposition of restraint, such as restriction, arrest, or confinement; and preferral of charges.

Rule 203. Jurisdiction over the offense

To the extent permitted by the Constitution, courts-martial may try any offense under the code and, in the case of general courts-martial, the law of war.

Discussion

(a) *In general.* Courts-martial have power to try any offense under the code except when prohibited from so doing by the Constitution. The rule enunciated in *Solorio v. United States*, 483 U.S. 435 (1987) is that jurisdiction of courts-martial depends solely on the accused's status as a person subject to the Uniform Code of Military Justice, and not on the "service-connection" of the offense charged.

(b) *Pleading and proof.* Normally, the inclusion of the accused's rank or grade will be sufficient to plead the service status of the accused. Ordinarily, no allegation of the accused's armed force or unit is necessary for military members on active duty. *See* R.C.M. 307 regarding required specificity of pleadings.

───────────

Rule 204. Jurisdiction over certain reserve component personnel

(a) *Service regulations.* The Secretary concerned shall prescribe regulations setting forth rules and procedures for the exercise of court-martial jurisdiction and nonjudicial punishment authority over reserve component personnel under Article 2(a)(3) and 2(d), subject to the limitations of this Manual and the UCMJ.

Discussion

Such regulations should describe procedures for ordering a reservist to active duty for disciplinary action, preferral of charges, preliminary hearings, forwarding of charges, referral of charges, designation of convening authorities and commanders authorized to conduct nonjudicial punishment proceedings, and for other appropriate purposes.

See definitions in R.C.M. 103 (Discussion). *See* paragraph 5e and f, Part V, concerning limitations on nonjudicial punishments imposed on reservists while on inactive-duty training.

Members of the Army National Guard and the Air National

Guard are subject to Federal court-martial jurisdiction only when the offense concerned is committed while the member is in Federal service.

(b) *Courts-Martial*

(1) *General and special court-martial proceedings.* A member of a reserve component must be on active duty prior to arraignment at a general or special court-martial. A member ordered to active duty pursuant to Article 2(d) may be retained on active duty to serve any adjudged confinement or other restriction on liberty if the order to active duty was approved in accordance with Article 2(d)(5), but such member may not be retained on active duty pursuant to Article 2(d) after service of the confinement or other restriction on liberty. All punishments remaining unserved at the time the member is released from active duty may be carried over to subsequent periods of inactive-duty training or active duty.

Discussion

An accused ordered to active duty pursuant to Article 2(d) may be retained on active duty after service of the punishment if permitted by other authority. For example, an accused who commits another offense while on active duty ordered pursuant to Article 2(d) may be retained on active duty pursuant to R.C.M. 202(c)(1).

---

(2) *Summary courts-martial.* A member of a reserve component may be tried by summary court-martial either while on active duty or inactive-duty training. A summary court-martial conducted during inactive-duty training may be in session only during normal periods of such training. The accused may not be held beyond such periods of training for trial or service or any punishment. All punishments remaining unserved at the end of a period of active duty or the end of any normal period of inactive duty training may be carried over to subsequent periods of inactive-duty training or active duty.

Discussion

A "normal period" of inactive-duty training does not include periods which are scheduled solely for the purpose of conducting court-martial proceedings.

(c) *Applicability.* This subsection is not applicable when a member is held on active duty pursuant to R.C.M. 202(c).

(d) *Changes in type of service.* A member of a reserve component at the time disciplinary action is initiated, who is alleged to have committed an offense while on active duty or inactive-duty training, is subject to court-martial jurisdiction without regard to any change between active and reserve service or within different categories of reserve service subsequent to commission of the offense. This subsection does not apply to a person whose military status was completely terminated after commission of an offense.

Discussion

A member of a regular or reserve component remains subject to court-martial jurisdiction after leaving active duty for offenses committed prior to such termination of active duty if the member retains military status in a reserve component without having been discharged from all obligations of military service.

See R.C.M. 202(a), Discussion, paragraph (2)(B)(ii) and (iii) regarding the jurisdictional effect of a discharge from military service. A "complete termination" of military status refers to a discharge relieving the servicemember of any further military service. It does not include a discharge conditioned upon acceptance of further military service.

CHAPTER III. INITIATION OF CHARGES; APPREHENSION; PRETRIAL RESTRAINT; RELATED MATTERS

Rule 301. Report of offense

(a) *Who may report.* Any person may report an offense subject to trial by court-martial.

(b) *To whom reports conveyed for disposition.* Ordinarily, any military authority who receives a report of an offense shall forward as soon as practicable the report and any accompanying information to the immediate commander of the suspect. Competent authority superior to that commander may direct otherwise.

Discussion

Any military authority may receive a report of an offense. Typically such reports are made to law enforcement or investigative personnel, or to appropriate persons in the chain of command. A report may be made by any means, and no particular format is required. When a person who is not a law enforcement official receives a report of an offense, that person should forward the report to the immediate commander of the suspect unless that person believes it would be more appropriate to notify law enforcement or investigative authorities.

If the suspect is unidentified, the military authority who receives the report should refer it to a law enforcement or investigative agency.

Upon receipt of a report, the immediate commander of a suspect should refer to R.C.M. 306 (Initial disposition). *See also* R.C.M. 302 (Apprehension); R.C.M. 303 (Preliminary inquiry); R.C.M. 304, 305 (Pretrial restraint, confinement).

Rule 302. Apprehension

(a) *Definition and scope.*

(1) *Definition.* Apprehension is the taking of a person into custody.

Discussion

Apprehension is the equivalent of "arrest" in civilian terminology. (In military terminology, "arrest" is a form of restraint. *See* Article 9; R.C.M. 304.) *See* subsection (c) of this rule concerning the bases for apprehension. An apprehension is not required in every case; the fact that an accused was never apprehended does not affect the jurisdiction of a court-martial to try the accused. However, *see* R.C.M. 202(c) concerning attachment of jurisdiction.

An apprehension is different from detention of a person for investigative purposes, although each involves the exercise of government control over the freedom of movement of a person. An apprehension must be based on probable cause, and the custody initiated in an apprehension may continue until proper authority is notified and acts under R.C.M. 304 or 305. An investigative detention may be made on less than probable cause (*see* Mil. R. Evid. 314(f)), and normally involves a relatively short period of custody. Furthermore, an extensive search of the person is not authorized incident to an investigative detention, as it is with an apprehension. *See* Mil. R. Evid. 314(f) and (g). This rule does not affect any seizure of the person less severe than apprehension.

Evidence obtained as the result of an apprehension which is in violation of this rule may be challenged under Mil. R. Evid. 311(c)(1). Evidence obtained as the result of an unlawful civilian arrest may be challenged under Mil. R. Evid. 311(c)(1), (2).

(2) *Scope.* This rule applies only to apprehensions made by persons authorized to do so under subsection (b) of this rule with respect to offenses subject to trial by court-martial. Nothing in this rule limits the authority of federal law enforcement officials to apprehend persons, whether or not subject to trial by court-martial, to the extent permitted by applicable enabling statutes and other law.

Discussion

R.C.M. 302 does not affect the authority of any official to detain, arrest, or apprehend persons not subject to trial under the code. The rule does not apply to actions taken by any person in a private capacity.

Several federal agencies have broad powers to apprehend persons for violations of federal laws, including the Uniform Code of Military Justice. For example, agents of the Federal Bureau of Investigation, United States Marshals, and agents of the Secret Service may apprehend persons for any offenses committed in their presence and for felonies. 18 U.S.C. §§ 3052, 3053, 3056. Other agencies have apprehension powers include the General Services Administration, 40 U.S.C. § 318 and the Veterans Administration, 38 U.S.C. § 218. The extent to which such agencies become involved in the apprehension of persons subject to trial by courts-martial may depend on the statutory authority of the agency and the agency's formal or informal relationships with the Department of Defense.

(b) *Who may apprehend.* The following officials may apprehend any person subject to trial by court-martial:

(1) *Military law enforcement officials.* Security police, military police, master at arms personnel, members of the shore patrol, and persons designated by proper authorities to perform military criminal investigative, guard, or police duties, whether subject to the code or not, when in each of the foregoing instances, the official making the apprehension is in the execution of law enforcement duties;

Discussion

Whenever enlisted persons, including police and guards, and civilian police and guards apprehend any commissioned or warrant officer, such persons should make an immediate report to the commissioned officer to whom the apprehending person is responsible.

The phrase "persons designated by proper authority to perform military criminal investigative, guard or police duties" includes special agents of the Defense Criminal Investigative Service.

---

(2) *Commissioned, warrant, petty, and noncommissioned officers.* All commissioned, warrant, petty, and noncommissioned officers on active duty or inactive duty training;

Discussion

Noncommissioned and petty officers not otherwise performing law enforcement duties should not apprehend a commissioned officer unless directed to do so by a commissioned officer or in order to prevent disgrace to the service or the escape of one who has committed a serious offense.

---

(3) *Civilians authorized to apprehend deserters.* Under Article 8, any civilian officer having authority to apprehend offenders under laws of the United States or of a State, Territory, Commonwealth, or possession, or the District of Columbia, when the apprehension is of a deserter from the armed forces.

Discussion

The code specifically provides that any civil officer, whether of a State, Territory, district, or of the United States may apprehend any deserter. However, this authority does not permit state and local law enforcement officers to apprehend persons for other violations of the code. *See* Article 8.

(c) *Grounds for apprehension.* A person subject to the code or trial thereunder may be apprehended for an offense triable by court-martial upon probable cause to apprehend. Probable cause to apprehend exists when there are reasonable grounds to believe that an offense has been or is being committed and the person to be apprehended committed or is committing it. Persons authorized to apprehend under subsection (b)(2) of this rule may also apprehend persons subject to the code who take part in quarrels, frays, or disorders, wherever they occur.

Discussion

"Reasonable grounds" means that there must be the kind of reliable information that a reasonable, prudent person would rely on which makes it more likely than not that something is true. A mere suspicion is not enough but proof which would support a conviction is not necessary. A person who determines probable cause may rely on the reports of others.

(d) *How an apprehension may be made.*

(1) *In general.* An apprehension is made by clearly notifying the person to be apprehended that person is in custody. This notice should be given orally or in writing, but it may be implied by the circumstances.

(2) *Warrants.* Neither warrants nor any other authorization shall be required for an apprehension under these rules except as required in subsection (e)(2) of this rule.

(3) *Use of force.* Any person authorized under these rules to make an apprehension may use such force and means as reasonably necessary under the circumstances to effect the apprehension.

Discussion

In addition to any other action required by law or regulation or proper military officials, any person making an apprehension under these rules should maintain custody of the person apprehended and inform as promptly as possible the immediate commander of the person apprehended, or any official higher in the chain of command of the person apprehended if it is impractical to inform the immediate commander.

(e) *Where an apprehension may be made.*

(1) *In general.* An apprehension may be made at any place, except as provided in subsection (e)(2) of this rule.

(2) *Private dwellings.* A private dwelling includes dwellings, on or off a military installation, such as single family houses, duplexes, and apartments. The quarters may be owned, leased, or rented by the residents, or assigned, and may be occupied on a temporary or permanent basis. "Private dwelling" does not include the following, whether or not subdivided into individual units: living areas in military barracks, vessels, aircraft, vehicles, tents, bunkers, field encampments, and similar places. No person may enter a private dwelling for the purpose of making an apprehension under these rules unless:

(A) Pursuant to consent under Mil. R. Evid. 314(e) or 316(d)(2);

(B) Under exigent circumstances described in Mil. R. Evid. 315(g) or 316(d)(4)(B);

(C) In the case of a private dwelling which is military property or under military control, or non-military property in a foreign country

(i) if the person to be apprehended is a resident of the private dwelling, there exists, at the time of the entry, reason to believe that the person to be apprehended is present in the dwelling, and the apprehension has been authorized by an official listed in Mil. R. Evid. 315(d) upon a determination that probable cause to apprehend the person exists; or

(ii) if the person to be apprehended is not a resident of the private dwelling, the entry has been authorized by an official listed in Mil. R. Evid. 315(d) upon a determination that probable cause exists to apprehend the person and to believe that the person to be apprehended is or will be present at the time of the entry;

(D) In the case of a private dwelling not included in subsection (e)(2)(C) of this rule,

(i) if the person to be apprehended is a resident of the private dwelling, there exists at the time of the entry, reason to believe that the person to be apprehended is present and the apprehension is authorized by an arrest warrant issued by competent civilian authority; or

(ii) if the person to be apprehended is not a resident of the private dwelling, the apprehension is authorized by an arrest warrant and the entry is authorized by a search warrant, each issued by competent civilian authority. A person who is not a resident of the private dwelling entered may not challenge the legality of an apprehension of that person on the basis of failure to secure a warrant or authorization to enter that dwelling, or on the basis of the sufficiency of such a warrant or authorization. Nothing in this subsection ((e)(2)) affects the legality of an apprehension which is incident to otherwise lawful presence in a private dwelling.

Discussion

For example, if law enforcement officials enter a private dwelling pursuant to a valid search warrant or search authorization, they may apprehend persons therein if grounds for an apprehension exist. This subsection is not intended to be an independent grant of authority to execute civilian arrest or search warrants. The authority must derive from an appropriate Federal or state procedure. *See e.g.* Fed. R. Crim. P. 41 and 28 C.F.R. 60.1.

Rule 303. Preliminary inquiry into reported offenses

Upon receipt of information that a member of the command is accused or suspected of committing an offense or offenses triable by court-martial, the immediate commander shall make or cause to be made a preliminary inquiry into the charges or suspected offenses.

Discussion

The preliminary inquiry is usually informal. It may be an examination of the charges and an investigative report or other summary of expected evidence. In other cases a more extensive investigation may be necessary. Although the commander may conduct the investigation personally or with members of the command, in serious or complex cases the commander should consider whether to seek the assistance of law enforcement personnel in conducting any inquiry or further investigation. The inquiry should gather all reasonably available evidence bearing on guilt or innocence and any evidence relating to aggravation, extenuation, or mitigation.

The Military Rules of Evidence should be consulted when conducting interrogations (*see* Mil. R. Evid. 301-306), searches (*see* Mil. R. Evid. 311-317), and eyewitness identifications (*see* Mil. R. Evid. 321).

If the offense is one for which the Department of Justice has investigative responsibilities, appropriate coordination should be made under the Memorandum of Understanding, *see* Appendix 3, and any implementing regulations.

If it appears that any witness may not be available for later proceedings in the case, this should be brought to the attention of appropriate authorities. *See also* R.C.M. 702 (depositions).

A person who is an accuser (*see* Article 1(9)) is disqualified from convening a general or special court-martial in that case. R.C.M. 504(c)(1). Therefore, when the immediate commander is a general or special court-martial convening authority, the preliminary inquiry should be conducted by another officer of the command. That officer may be informed that charges may be preferred if the officer determines that preferral is warranted.

Rule 304. Pretrial restraint

(a) *Types of pretrial restraint.* Pretrial restraint is moral or physical restraint on a person's liberty which is imposed before and during disposition of offenses. Pretrial restraint may consist of conditions on liberty, restriction in lieu of arrest, arrest, or confinement.

(1) *Conditions on liberty.* Conditions on liberty are imposed by orders directing a person to do or

refrain from doing specified acts. Such conditions may be imposed in conjunction with other forms of restraint or separately.

(2) *Restriction in lieu of arrest.* Restriction in lieu of arrest is the restraint of a person by oral or written orders directing the person to remain within specified limits; a restricted person shall, unless otherwise directed, perform full military duties while restricted.

(3) *Arrest.* Arrest is the restraint of a person by oral or written order not imposed as punishment, directing the person to remain within specified limits; a person in the status of arrest may not be required to perform full military duties such as commanding or supervising personnel, serving as guard, or bearing arms. The status of arrest automatically ends when the person is placed, by the authority who ordered the arrest or a superior authority, on duty inconsistent with the status of arrest, but this shall not prevent requiring the person arrested to do ordinary cleaning or policing, or to take part in routine training and duties.

(4) *Confinement.* Pretrial confinement is physical restraint, imposed by order of competent authority, depriving a person of freedom pending disposition of offenses. *See* R.C.M. 305.

Discussion

Conditions on liberty include orders to report periodically to a specified official, orders not to go to a certain place (such as the scene of the alleged offense), and orders not to associate with specified persons (such as the alleged victim or potential witnesses). Conditions on liberty must not hinder pretrial preparation, however. Thus, when such conditions are imposed, they must by sufficiently flexible to permit pretrial preparation.

Restriction in lieu of arrest is a less severe restraint on liberty than is arrest. Arrest includes suspension from performing full military duties and the limits of arrest are normally narrower than those of restriction in lieu of arrest. The actual nature of the restraint imposed, and not the characterization of it by the officer imposing it, will determine whether it is technically an arrest or restriction in lieu of arrest.

Breach of arrest or restriction in lieu of arrest or violation of conditions on liberty are offenses under the code. *See* paragraphs 16, 19, and 102, Part IV. When such an offense occurs, it may warrant appropriate action such as nonjudicial punishment or court-martial. *See* R.C.M. 306. In addition, such a breach or violation may provide a basis for the imposition of a more severe form of restraint.

R.C.M. 707(a) requires that the accused be brought to trial within 120 days of preferral of charges or imposition of restraint under R.C.M. 304(a)(2)-(4).

(b) *Who may order pretrial restraint.*

(1) *Of civilians and officers.* Only a commanding officer to whose authority the civilian or officer is subject may order pretrial restraint of that civilian or officer.

Discussion

Civilians may be restrained under these rules only when they are subject to trial by court-martial. *See* R.C.M. 202.

(2) *Of enlisted persons.* Any commissioned officer may order pretrial restraint of any enlisted person.

(3) *Delegation of authority.* The authority to order pretrial restraint of civilians and commissioned and warrant officers may not be delegated. A commanding officer may delegate to warrant, petty, and noncommissioned officers authority to order pretrial restraint of enlisted persons of the commanding officer's command or subject to the authority of that commanding officer.

(4) *Authority to withhold.* A superior competent authority may withhold from a subordinate the authority to order pretrial restraint.

(c) *When a person may be restrained.* No person may be ordered into restraint before trial except for probable cause. Probable cause to order pretrial restraint exists when there is a reasonable belief that:

(1) An offense triable by court-martial has been committed;

(2) The person to be restrained committed it; and

(3) The restraint ordered is required by the circumstances.

Discussion

The decision whether to impose pretrial restraint, and, if so, what type or types, should be made on a case-by-case basis. The factors listed in the Discussion of R.C.M. 305(h)(2)(B) should be considered. The restraint should not be more rigorous than the circumstances require to ensure the presence of the person restrained or to prevent foreseeable serious criminal misconduct.

Restraint is not required in every case. The absence of pretrial restraint does not affect the jurisdiction of a court-martial. However, *see* R.C.M. 202(c) concerning attachment of jurisdiction. *See* R.C.M. 305 concerning the standards and procedures governing pretrial confinement.

(d) *Procedures for ordering pretrial restraint.* Pretrial restraint other than confinement is imposed by notifying the person orally or in writing of the restraint, including its terms or limits. The order to an enlisted person shall be delivered personally by the authority who issues it or through other persons subject to the code. The order to an officer or a civilian shall be delivered personally by the authority who issues it or by another commissioned officer. Pretrial confinement is imposed pursuant to orders by a competent authority by the delivery of a person to a place of confinement.

(e) *Notice of basis for restraint.* When a person is placed under restraint, the person shall be informed of the nature of the offense which is the basis for such restraint.

Discussion

See R.C.M. 305(e) concerning additional information which must be given to a person who is confined. If the person ordering the restrain is not the commander of the person restrained, that officer should be notified.

(f) *Punishment prohibited.* Pretrial restraint is not punishment and shall not be used as such. No person who is restrained pending trial may be subjected to punishment or penalty for the offense which is the basis for that restraint. Prisoners being held for trial shall not be required to undergo punitive duty hours or training, perform punitive labor, or wear special uniforms prescribed only for post-trial prisoners. This rule does not prohibit minor punishment during pretrial confinement for infractions of the rules of the place of confinement. Prisoners shall be afforded facilities and treatment under regulations of the Secretary concerned.

Discussion

Offenses under the code by a person under restraint may be disposed of in the same manner as any other offenses.

(g) *Release.* Except as otherwise provided in R.C.M. 305, a person may be released from pretrial restraint by a person authorized to impose it. Pretrial restraint shall terminate when a sentence is adjudged, the accused is acquitted of all charges, or all charges are dismissed.

Discussion

Pretrial restraint may be imposed (or reimposed) if charges are to be reinstated or a rehearing or "other" trial is to be ordered.

(h) *Administrative restraint.* Nothing in this rule prohibits limitations on a servicemember imposed for operational or other military purposes independent of military justice, including administrative hold or medical reasons.

Discussion

See also R.C.M. 306.

Rule 305. Pretrial confinement

(a) *In general.* Pretrial confinement is physical restraint, imposed by order of competent authority, depriving a person of freedom pending disposition of charges.

Discussion

No member of the armed forces may be placed in confinement in immediate association with enemy prisoners or other foreign nationals not members of the armed forces of the United States. Article 12. However, if members of the armed forces of the United States are separated from prisoners of the other categories mentioned, they may be confined in the same confinement facilities.

(b) *Who may be confined.* Any person who is subject to trial by court-martial may be confined if the requirements of this rule are met.

Discussion

See R.C.M. 201 and 202 and the discussions therein concerning persons who are subject to trial by courts-martial.

(c) *Who may order confinement.* See R.C.M. 304(b).

Discussion

"No provost marshal, commander of a guard, or master at arms may refuse to receive or keep any prisoner committed to his charge by a commissioned officer of the armed forces, when the committing officer furnishes a statement, signed by him, of the offense charged against the prisoner." Article 11(a).

(d) *When a person may be confined.* No person may be ordered into pretrial confinement except for probable cause. Probable cause to order pretrial confinement exists when there is a reasonable belief that:

(1) An offense triable by court-martial has been committed;

(2) The person confined committed it; and

(3) Confinement is required by the circumstances.

Discussion

The person who directs confinement should consider the matters discussed under subsection (h)(2)(B) of this rule before ordering confinement. However, the person who initially orders confinement is not required to make a detailed analysis of the necessity for confinement. It is often not possible to review a person's background and character or even the details of an offense before physically detaining the person. For example, until additional information can be secured, it may be necessary to confine a person apprehended in the course of a violent crime.

"[W]hen charged only with an offense normally tried by summary court-martial, [an accused] shall not ordinarily be paced in confinement." Article 10.

Confinement should be distinguished from custody. Custody is restraint which is imposed by apprehension and which may be, but is not necessarily, physical. Custody may be imposed by anyone authorized to apprehend (*see* R.C.M. 302(b)), and may continue until a proper authority under R.C.M. 304(B) is notified and takes action. Thus, a person who has been apprehended could be physically restrained, but this would not be pretrial confinement in the sense of this rule until a person authorized to do so under R.C.M. 304(b) directed confinement.

(e) *Advice to the accused upon confinement.* Each person confined shall be promptly informed of:

(1) The nature of the offenses for which held;

(2) The right to remain silent and that any statement made by the person may be used against the person;

(3) The right to retain civilian counsel at no expense to the United States, and the right to request assignment of military counsel; and

(4) The procedures by which pretrial confinement will be reviewed.

(f) *Military counsel.* If requested by the prisoner and such request is made known to military authorities, military counsel shall be provided to the prisoner before the initial review under subsection (i) of this rule or within 72 hours of such a request being first communicated to military authorities, whichever occurs first. Counsel may be assigned for the limited purpose of representing the accused only during the pretrial confinement proceedings before charges are referred. If assignment is made for this limited pur-

pose, the prisoner shall be so informed. Unless otherwise provided by regulations of the Secretary concerned, a prisoner does not have a right under this rule to have military counsel of the prisoner's own selection.

(g) *Who may direct release from confinement.* Any commander of a prisoner, an officer appointed under regulations of the Secretary concerned to conduct the review under subsection (i) and/or (j) of this rule, or, once charges have been referred, a military judge detailed to the court-martial to which the charges against the accused have been referred, may direct release from pretrial confinement. For purposes of this subsection, "any commander" includes the immediate or higher commander of the prisoner and the commander of the installation on which the confinement facility is located.

(h) *Notification and action by commander.*

(1) *Report.* Unless the commander of the prisoner ordered the pretrial confinement, the commissioned, warrant, noncommissioned, or petty officer into whose charge the prisoner was committed shall, within 24 hours after that commitment, cause a report to be made to the commander that shall contain the name of the prisoner, the offenses charged against the prisoner, and the name of the person who ordered or authorized confinement.

Discussion

This report may be made by any means. Ordinarily, the immediate commander of the prisoner should be notified. In unusual cases any commander to whose authority the prisoner is subject, such as the commander of the confinement facility, may be notified. In the latter case, the commander so notified must ensure compliance with subsection (h)(2) of this rule.

---

(2) *Action by commander.*

(A) *Decision.* Not later than 72 hours after the commander's ordering of a prisoner into pretrial confinement or, after receipt of a report that a member of the commander's unit or organization has been confined, whichever situation is applicable, the commander shall decide whether pretrial confinement will continue. A commander's compliance with this subsection may also satisfy the 48-hour probable cause determination of subsection R.C.M. 305(i)(1) below, provided the commander is a neutral and detached officer and acts within 48 hours of the imposition of confinement under military control. Nothing in subsections R.C.M. 305(d), R.C.M.

305(i)(1), or this subsection prevents a neutral and detached commander from completing the 48-hour probable cause determination and the 72-hour commander's decision immediately after an accused is ordered into pretrial confinement.

(B) *Requirements for confinement.* The commander shall direct the prisoner's release from pretrial confinement unless the commander believes upon probable cause, that is, upon reasonable grounds, that:

(i) An offense triable by a court-martial has been committed;

(ii) The prisoner committed it; and

(iii) Confinement is necessary because it is foreseeable that:

(a) The prisoner will not appear at trial, pretrial hearing, preliminary hearing, or investigation, or

(b) The prisoner will engage in serious criminal misconduct; and

(iv) Less severe forms of restraint are inadequate.

Serious criminal misconduct includes intimidation of witnesses or other obstruction of justice, serious injury of others, or other offenses which pose a serious threat to the safety of the community or to the effectiveness, morale, discipline, readiness, or safety of the command, or to the national security of the United States. As used in this rule, "national security" means the national defense and foreign relations of the United States and specifically includes: a military or defense advantage over any foreign nation or group of nations; a favorable foreign relations position; or a defense posture capable of successfully resisting hostile or destructive action from within or without, overt or covert.

Discussion

A person should not be confined as a mere matter of convenience or expedience.

Some of the factors which should be considered under this subsection are:

(1) The nature and circumstances of the offenses charged or suspected, including extenuating circumstances;

(2) The weight of the evidence against the accused;

(3) The accused's ties to the locale, including family, off-duty employment, financial resources, and length of residence;

(4) The accused's character and mental condition;

(5) The accused's service record, including any record of previous misconduct;

(6) The accused's record of appearance at or flight from other preliminary hearings, trials, and similar proceedings; and

(7) The likelihood that the accused can and will commit further serious criminal misconduct if allowed to remain at liberty.

Although the Military Rules of Evidence are not applicable, the commander should judge the reliability of the information available. Before relying on the reports of others, the commander must have a reasonable belief that the information is believable and has a factual basis. The information may be received orally or in writing. Information need not be received under oath, but an oath may add to its reliability. A commander may examine the prisoner's personnel records, police records, and may consider the recommendations of others.

Less serious forms of restraint must always be considered before pretrial confinement may be approved. Thus the commander should consider whether the prisoner could be safely returned to the prisoner's unit, at liberty or under restriction, arrest, or conditions on liberty. See R.C.M. 304.

(C) *72-hour memorandum.* If continued pretrial confinement is approved, the commander shall prepare a written memorandum that states the reasons for the conclusion that the requirements for confinement in subsection (h)(2)(B) of this rule have been met. This memorandum may include hearsay and may incorporate by reference other documents, such as witness statements, investigative reports, or official records. This memorandum shall be forwarded to the 7-day reviewing officer under subsection (i)(2) of this rule. If such a memorandum was prepared by the commander before ordering confinement, a second memorandum need not be prepared; however, additional information may be added to the memorandum at any time.

(i) *Procedures for review of pretrial confinement.*

(1) *48-hour probable cause determination.* Review of the adequacy of probable cause to continue pretrial confinement shall be made by a neutral and detached officer within 48 hours of imposition of confinement under military control. If the prisoner is apprehended by civilian authorities and remains in civilian custody at the request of military authorities, reasonable efforts will be made to bring the prisoner under military control in a timely fashion.

(2) *7-day review of pretrial confinement.* Within 7 days of the imposition of confinement, a neutral and detached officer appointed in accordance with regulations prescribed by the Secretary concerned shall review the probable cause determination and necessity for continued pretrial confinement. In calculating the number of days of confinement for pur-

poses of this rule, the initial date of confinement under military control shall count as one day and the date of the review shall also count as one day.

(A) *Nature of the 7-day review.*

(i) *Matters considered.* The review under this subsection shall include a review of the memorandum submitted by the prisoner's commander under subsection (h)(2)(C) of this rule. Additional written matters may be considered, including any submitted by the prisoner. The prisoner and the prisoner's counsel, if any, shall be allowed to appear before the 7-day reviewing officer and make a statement, if practicable. A representative of the command may also appear before the reviewing officer to make a statement.

(ii) *Rules of evidence.* Except for Mil. R. Evid., Section V (Privileges) and Mil. R. Evid. 302 and 305, the Military Rules of Evidence shall not apply to the matters considered.

(iii) *Standard of proof.* The requirements for confinement under subsection (h)(2)(B) of this rule must be proved by a preponderance of the evidence.

(iv) *Victim's right to be reasonably heard.* A victim of an alleged offense committed by the prisoner has the right to reasonable, accurate, and timely notice of the 7-day review; the right to confer with the representative of the command and counsel for the government, if any; and the right to be reasonably heard during the review. However, the hearing may not be unduly delayed for this purpose. The right to be heard under this rule includes the right to be heard through counsel and the right to be reasonably protected from the prisoner during the 7-day review. The victim of an alleged offense shall be notified of these rights in accordance with regulations of the Secretary concerned.

Discussion

Personal appearance by the victim is not required. A victim's right to be reasonably heard at a 7-day review may also be accomplished telephonically, by video teleconference, or by written statement. The right to be heard under this rule includes the right to be heard through counsel.

(B) *Extension of time limit.* The 7-day reviewing officer may, for good cause, extend the time limit for completion of the review to 10 days after the imposition of pretrial confinement.

(C) *Action by 7-day reviewing officer.* Upon completion of review, the reviewing officer shall approve continued confinement or order immediate release. If the reviewing officer orders immediate release, a victim of an alleged offense committed by the prisoner has the right to reasonable, accurate, and timely notice of the release, unless such notice may endanger the safety of any person.

(D) *Memorandum.* The 7-day reviewing officer's conclusions, including the factual findings on which they are based, shall be set forth in a written memorandum. The memorandum shall also state whether the victim was notified of the review, was given the opportunity to confer with the representative of the command or counsel for the government, and was given a reasonable opportunity to be heard. A copy of the memorandum and all documents considered by the 7-day reviewing officer shall be maintained in accordance with regulations prescribed by the Secretary concerned and provided to the accused or the Government on request.

(E) *Reconsideration of approval of continued confinement.* The 7-day reviewing officer shall upon request, and after notice to the parties, reconsider the decision to confine the prisoner based upon any significant information not previously considered.

(j) *Review by military judge.* Once the charges for which the accused has been confined are referred to trial, the military judge shall review the propriety of pretrial confinement upon motion for appropriate relief.

(1) *Release.* The military judge shall order release from pretrial confinement only if:

(A) The 7-day reviewing officer's decision was an abuse of discretion, and there is not sufficient information presented to the military judge justifying continuation of pretrial confinement under subsection (h)(2)(B) of this rule;

(B) Information not presented to the 7-day reviewing officer establishes that the prisoner should be released under subsection (h)(2)(B) of this rule; or

(C) The provisions of subsection (i)(1) or (2) of this rule have not been complied with and information presented to the military judge does not establish sufficient grounds for continued confinement under subsection (h)(2)(B) of this rule.

Discussion

Upon a motion for release from pretrial confinement, a victim of an alleged offense committed by the prisoner has the right to reasonable, accurate, and timely notice of the motion and any hearing, the right to confer with counsel representing the government, and the right to be reasonably heard. Inability to reasonably afford a victim these rights shall not delay the proceedings. The right to be heard under this rule includes the right to be heard through counsel. *See* R.C.M. 906(b)(8).

---

(2) *Credit.* The military judge shall order administrative credit under subsection (k) of this rule for any pretrial confinement served as a result of an abuse of discretion or failure to comply with the provisions of subsections (f), (h), or (i) of this rule.

(k) *Remedy.* The remedy for noncompliance with subsections (f), (h), (i), or (j) of this rule shall be an administrative credit against the sentence adjudged for any confinement served as the result of such noncompliance. Such credit shall be computed at the rate of 1 day credit for each day of confinement served as a result of such noncompliance. The military judge may order additional credit for each day of pretrial confinement that involves an abuse of discretion or unusually harsh circumstances. This credit is to be applied in addition to any other credit the accused may be entitled as a result of pretrial confinement served. This credit shall be applied first against any confinement adjudged. If no confinement is adjudged, or if the confinement adjudged is insufficient to offset all the credit to which the accused is entitled, the credit shall be applied against hard labor without confinement, restriction, fine, and forfeiture of pay, in that order, using the conversion formula under R.C.M. 1003(b)(6) and (7). For purposes of this subsection, 1 day of confinement shall be equal to 1 day of total forfeiture or a like amount of fine. The credit shall not be applied against any other form of punishment.

(l) *Confinement after release.* No person whose release from pretrial confinement has been directed by a person authorized in subsection (g) of this rule may be confined again before completion of trial except upon the discovery, after the order of release, of evidence or of misconduct which, either alone or in conjunction with all other available evidence, justifies confinement.

Discussion

See R.C.M. 304(b) concerning who may order confinement.

(m) *Exceptions.*

(1) *Operational necessity.* The Secretary of Defense may suspend application of subsections (e)(2) and (3), (f), (h)(2)(A) and (C), and (i) of this rule to specific units or in specified areas when operational requirements of such units or in such areas would make application of such provisions impracticable.

(2) *At sea.* Subsections (e)(2) and (3), (f), (h)(2)(C), and (i) of this rule shall not apply in the case of a person on board a vessel at sea. In such situations, confinement on board the vessel at sea may continue only until the person can be transferred to a confinement facility ashore. Such transfer shall be accomplished at the earliest opportunity permitted by the operational requirements and mission of the vessel. Upon such transfer the memorandum required by subsection (h)(2)(C) of this rule shall be transmitted to the reviewing officer under subsection (i) of this rule and shall include an explanation of any delay in the transfer.

Discussion

Under this subsection the standards for confinement remain the same (although the circumstances giving rise to the exception could bear on the application of those standards). Also, pretrial confinement remains subject to judicial review. The prisoner's commander still must determine whether confinement will continue under subsection (h)(2)(B) of this rule. The suspension of subsection (h)(2)(A) of this rule removes the 72-hour requirement since in a combat environment, the commander may not be available to comply with it. The commander must make the pretrial confinement decision as soon as reasonably possible, however. (This provision is not suspended under subsection (2) since the commander of a vessel is always available.)

(n) *Notice to victim of escaped prisoner.* A victim of an alleged offense committed by the prisoner for which the prisoner has been placed in pretrial confinement has the right to reasonable, accurate, and timely notice of the escape of the prisoner, unless such notice may endanger the safety of any person.

Discussion

For purposes of this rule, the term "victim of an alleged offense" means a person who has suffered direct physical, emotional, or pecuniary harm as a result of the commission of an offense under the UCMJ.

Rule 306. Initial disposition

(a) *Who may dispose of offenses.* Each commander has discretion to dispose of offenses by members of that command. Ordinarily the immediate commander of a person accused or suspected of committing an offense triable by court-martial initially determines how to dispose of that offense. A superior commander may withhold the authority to dispose of offenses in individual cases, types of cases, or generally. A superior commander may not limit the discretion of a subordinate commander to act on cases over which authority has not been withheld.

Discussion

Each commander in the chain of command has independent, yet overlapping discretion to dispose of offenses within the limits of that officer's authority. Normally, in keeping with the policy in subsection (b) of this rule, the initial disposition decision is made by the official at the lowest echelon with the power to make it. A decision by a commander ordinarily does not bar a different disposition by a superior authority. *See* R.C.M. 401(c); 601(f). Once charges are referred to a court-martial by a convening authority competent to do so, they may be withdrawn from that court-martial only in accordance with R.C.M. 604.

See Appendix 3 with respect to offenses for which coordination with the Department of Justice is required.

(b) *Policy.* Allegations of offenses should be disposed of in a timely manner at the lowest appropriate level of disposition listed in subsection (c) of this rule.

Discussion

The disposition decision is one of the most important and difficult decisions facing a commander. Many factors must be taken into consideration and balanced, including, to the extent practicable, the nature of the offenses, any mitigating or extenuating circumstances, the views of the victim as to disposition, any recommendations made by subordinate commanders, the interest of justice, military exigencies, and the effect of the decision on the accused and the command. The goal should be a disposition that is warranted, appropriate, and fair.

In deciding how an offense should be disposed of, factors the commander should consider, to the extent they are known, include:

(A) the nature of and circumstances surrounding the offense and the extent of the harm caused by the offense, including the offense's effect on morale, health, safety, welfare, and discipline;

(B) when applicable, the views of the victim as to disposition;

(C) existence of jurisdiction over the accused and the offense;

(D) availability and admissibility of evidence;

(E) the willingness of the victim or others to testify;

(F) cooperation of the accused in the apprehension or prosecution of another accused;

(G) possible improper motives or biases of the person(s) making the allegation(s);

(H) availability and likelihood of prosecution of the same or similar and related charges against the accused by another jurisdiction;

(I) appropriateness of the authorized punishment to the particular accused or offense.

(c) *How offenses may be disposed of.* Within the limits of the commander's authority, a commander may take the actions set forth in this subsection to initially dispose of a charge or suspected offense.

Discussion

Prompt disposition of charges is essential. *See* R.C.M. 707 (speedy trial requirements).

Before determining an appropriate disposition, a commander should ensure that a preliminary inquiry under R.C.M. 303 has been conducted. If charges have not already been preferred, the commander may, if appropriate, prefer them and dispose of them under this rule. *But see* R.C.M. 601 (c) regarding disqualification of an accuser.

If charges have been preferred, the commander should ensure that the accused has been notified in accordance with R.C.M. 308, and that charges are in proper form. *See* R.C.M. 307. Each commander who forwards or disposes of charges may make minor changes therein. *See* R.C.M. 603(a) and (b). If major changes are necessary, the affected charge should be preferred anew. *See* R.C.M. 603(d).

When charges are brought against two or more accused with a view to a joint or common trial, *see* R.C.M. 307(c)(5); 601(e)(3). If it appears that the accused may lack mental capacity to stand trial or may not have been mentally responsible at the times of the offenses, *see* R.C.M. 706; 909; 916(k).

(1) *No action.* A commander may decide to take no action on an offense. If charges have been preferred, they may be dismissed.

Discussion

A decision to take no action or dismissal of charges at this stage does not bar later disposition of the offenses under subsection (c)(2) through (5) of this rule.

See R.C.M. 401(a) concerning who may dismiss charges, and R.C.M. 401(c)(1) concerning dismissal of charges.

When a decision is made to take no action, the accused should be informed.

(2) *Administrative action.* A commander may take or initiate administrative action, in addition to or instead of other action taken under this rule, subject to regulations of the Secretary concerned. Administrative actions include corrective measures such as counseling, admonition, reprimand, exhortation, disapproval, criticism, censure, reproach, rebuke, extra

military instruction, or the administrative withholding of privileges, or any combination of the above.

Discussion

Other administrative measures, which are subject to regulations of the Secretary concerned, include matters related to efficiency reports, academic reports, and other ratings; rehabilitation and reassignment; career field reclassification; administrative reduction for inefficiency; bar to reenlistment; personnel reliability program reclassification; security classification changes; pecuniary liability for negligence or misconduct; and administrative separation.

---

(3) *Nonjudicial punishment.* A commander may consider the matter pursuant to Article 15, nonjudicial punishment. *See* Part V.

(4) *Disposition of charges.* Charges may be disposed of in accordance with R.C.M. 401.

Discussion

If charges have not been preferred, they may be preferred. *See* R.C.M. 307 concerning preferral of charges. However, *see* R.C.M. 601(c) concerning disqualification of an accuser.

Charges may be disposed of by dismissing them, forwarding them to another commander for disposition, or referring them to a summary, special, or general court-martial. Before charges may be referred to a general court-martial, compliance with R.C.M. 405 and 406 is necessary. Therefore, if appropriate, an investigation under R.C.M. 405 may be directed. Additional guidance on these matters is found in R.C.M. 401-407.

---

(5) *Forwarding for disposition.* A commander may forward a matter concerning an offense, or charges, to a superior or subordinate authority for disposition.

Discussion

The immediate commander may lack authority to take action which that commander believes is an appropriate disposition. In such cases, the matter should be forwarded to a superior officer with a recommendation as to disposition. *See also* R.C.M. 401(c)(2) concerning forwarding charges. If allegations are forwarded to a higher authority for disposition, because of lack of authority or otherwise, the disposition decision becomes a matter within the discretion of the higher authority.

A matter may be forwarded for other reasons, such as for investigation of allegations and preferral of charges, if warranted (*see* R.C.M. 303, 307), or so that a subordinate can dispose of the matter.

(d) *National security matters.* If a commander not authorized to convene general courts-martial finds that an offense warrants trial by court-martial, but believes that trial would be detrimental to the prosecution of a war or harmful to national security, the matter shall be forwarded to the general court-martial convening authority for action under R.C.M. 407(b).

(e) *Sex-related offenses.*

(1) For purposes of this subsection, a "sex-related offense" means any allegation of a violation of Article 120, 120a, 120b, 120c, or 125, or any attempt thereof under Article 80, UCMJ.

(2) Under such regulations as the Secretary concerned may prescribe, for alleged sex-related offenses committed in the United States, the victim of the sex-related offense shall be provided an opportunity to express views as to whether the offense should be prosecuted by court-martial or in a civilian court with jurisdiction over the offense. The commander, and if charges are preferred, the convening authority, shall consider such views as to the victim's preference for jurisdiction, if available, prior to making an initial disposition decision. For purposes of this rule, "victim" is defined as an individual who has suffered direct physical, emotional, or pecuniary harm as a result of the commission of an alleged sex-related offense as defined in subparagraph (1) of this rule.

Discussion

Any preferences as to disposition expressed by the victim regarding jurisdiction, while not binding, should be considered by the cognizant commander prior to making initial disposition.

The cognizant commander should continue to consider the views of the victim as to jurisdiction until final disposition of the case.

---

(3) Under such regulations as the Secretary concerned may prescribe, if the victim of an alleged sex-related offense expresses a preference for prosecution of the offense in a civilian court, the commander, and if charges are preferred, the convening authority, shall ensure that the civilian authority with jurisdiction over the offense is notified of the victim's preference for civilian prosecution. If the commander, and if charges are preferred, the convening authority learns of any decision by the civilian authority to prosecute or not prosecute the offense in civilian court, the convening authority shall ensure the victim is notified.

Rule 307. Preferral of charges

(a) *Who may prefer charges.* Any person subject to the code may prefer charges.

Discussion

No person may be ordered to prefer charges to which that person is unable to make truthfully the required oath. *See* Article 30(a) and subsection (b) of this rule. A person who has been the accuser or nominal accuser (*see* Article 1(9)) may not also serve as the convening authority of a general or special court-martial to which the charges are later referred. *See* Articles 22(b) and 23(b); R.C.M. 601; however, *see* R.C.M. 1302(b) (summary court-martial convening authority is not disqualified by being the accuser). A person authorized to dispose of offenses (*see* R.C.M. 306(a); 401–404 and 407) should not be ordered to prefer charges when this would disqualify that person from exercising that person's authority or would improperly restrict that person's discretion to act on the case. *See* R.C.M. 104 and 504(c).

Charges may be preferred against a person subject to trial by court-martial at any time but should be preferred without unnecessary delay. *See* the statute of limitations prescribed by Article 43. Preferral of charges should not be unnecessarily delayed. When a good reason exists—as when a person is permitted to continue a course of conduct so that a ringleader or other conspirators may also be discovered or when a suspected counterfeiter goes uncharged until guilty knowledge becomes apparent—a reasonable delay is permissible. However, *see* R.C.M. 707 concerning speedy trial requirements.

(b) *How charges are preferred; oath.* A person who prefers charges must:

(1) Sign the charges and specifications under oath before a commissioned officer of the armed forces authorized to administer oaths; and

(2) State that the signer has personal knowledge of or has investigated the matters set forth in the charges and specifications and that they are true in fact to the best of that person's knowledge and belief.

Discussion

See Article 136 for authority to administer oaths. The following form may be used to administer the oath:

"You (swear) (affirm) that you are a person subject to the Uniform Code of Military Justice, that you have personal knowledge of or have investigated the matters set forth in the foregoing charge(s) and specification(s), and that the same are true in fact to the best of your knowledge and belief. (So help you God.)"

The accuser's belief may be based upon reports of others in whole or in part.

(c) *How to allege offenses.*

(1) *In general.* The format of charge and specification is used to allege violations of the code.

Discussion

See Appendix 4 for a sample of a Charge Sheet (DD Form 458).

(2) *Charge.* A charge states the article of the code, law of war, or local penal law of an occupied territory which the accused is alleged to have violated.

Discussion

The particular subdivision of an article of the code (for example, Article 118(1)) should not be included in the charge. When there are numerous infractions of the same article, there will be only one charge, but several specifications thereunder. There may also be several charges, but each must allege a violation of a different article of the code. For violations of the law of war, *see* (D) below.

(A) *Numbering charges.* If there is only one charge, it is not numbered. When there is more than one charge, each charge is numbered by a Roman numeral.

(B) *Additional charges.* Charges preferred after others have been preferred are labeled "additional charges" and are also numbered with Roman numerals, beginning with "I" if there is more than one additional charge. These ordinarily relate to offenses not known at the time or committed after the original charges were preferred. Additional charges do not require a separate trial if incorporated in the trial of the original charges before arraignment. *See* R.C.M. 601(e)(2).

(C) *Preemption.* An offense specifically defined by Articles 81 through 132 may not be alleged as a violation of Article 134. *See* paragraph 60c(5)(a) of Part IV. *But see* subsection (d) of this rule.

(D) *Charges under the law of war.* In the case of a person subject to trial by general court-martial for violations of the law of war (*see* Article 18), the charge should be: "Violation of the Law of War"; or "Violation of _____, _____" referring to the local penal law of the occupied territory. *See* R.C.M. 201(f)(1)(B). *But see* subsection (d) of this rule. Ordinarily persons subject to the code should be charged with a specific violation of the code rather than a violation of the law of war.

(3) *Specification.* A specification is a plain, concise, and definite statement of the essential facts constituting the offense charged. A specification is sufficient if it alleges every element of the charged offense expressly or by necessary implication; however, specifications under Article 134 must expressly allege the terminal element. Except for aggravating factors under R.C.M 1003(d) and R.C.M. 1004, facts that increase the maximum authorized punishment must be alleged in order to permit the possible in-

creased punishment. No particular format is required.

Discussion

How to draft specifications. For Article 134 offenses, also refer to paragraph 60c(6) in Part IV.

(A) *Sample specifications.* Before drafting a specification, the drafter should read the pertinent provisions of Part IV, where the elements of proof of various offenses and forms for specifications appear.

[Note: Be advised that the sample specifications in this Manual have not been amended to comport with *United States v. Jones*, 68 M.J. 465 (C.A.A.F. 2010) and *United States v. Fosler*, 70 M.J. 225 (C.A.A.F. 2011). Practitioners should read the notes above and draft specifications in conformity with the cases cited therein.]

(B) *Numbering specifications.* If there is only one specification under a charge it is not numbered. When there is more than one specification under any charge, the specifications are numbered in Arabic numerals. The term "additional" is not used in connection with the specifications under an additional charge.

(C) *Name and description of the accused.*

(i) *Name.* The specification should state the accused's full name: first name, middle name or initial, last name. If the accused is known by more than one name, the name acknowledged by the accused should be used. If there is no such acknowledgment, the name believed to be the true name should be listed first, followed by all known aliases. For example: Seaman John P. Smith, U.S. Navy, alias Lt. Robert R. Brown, U.S. Navy.

(ii) *Military association.* The specification should state the accused's rank or grade. If the rank or grade of the accused has changed since the date of an alleged offense, and the change is pertinent to the offense charged, the accused should be identified by the present rank or grade followed by rank or grade on the date of the alleged offense. For example: In that Seaman _____, then Seaman Apprentice _____, etc.

(iii) *Social security number or service number.* The social security number or service number of an accused should not be stated in the specification.

(iv) *Basis of personal jurisdiction.*

(a) *Military members on active duty.* Ordinarily, no allegation of the accused's armed force or unit or organization is necessary for military members on active duty.

(b) *Persons subject to the code under Article 2(a), subsections (3) through (12), or subject to trial by court-martial under Articles 3 or 4.* The specification should describe the accused's armed force, unit or organization, position, or status which will indicate the basis of jurisdiction. For example: John Jones, (a person employed by and serving with the U.S. Army in the field in time of war) (a person convicted of having obtained a fraudulent discharge), etc.

(D) *Date and time of offense*

(i) *In general.* The date of the commission of the offense charged should be stated in the specification with sufficient precision to identify the offense and enable the accused to understand what particular act or omission to defend against.

(ii) *Use of "on or about."* In alleging the date of the offense it is proper to allege it as "on or about" a specified day.

(iii) *Hour.* The exact hour of the offense is ordinarily not alleged except in certain absence offenses. When the exact time is alleged, the 24-hour clock should be used. The use of "at or about" is proper.

(iv) *Extended periods.* When the acts specified extend(s) over a considerable period of time it is proper to allege it (or them) as having occurred, for example, "from about 15 June 1983 to about 4 November 1983," or "did on divers occasions between 15 June 1983 and 4 November 1983."

(E) *Place of offense.* The place of the commission of the offense charged should be stated in the specification with sufficient precision to identify the offense and enable the accused to understand the particular act or omission to defend against. In alleging the place of the offense, it is proper to allege it as "at or near" a certain place if the exact place is uncertain.

(F) *Subject-matter jurisdiction allegations.* Pleading the accused's rank or grade along with the proper elements of the offense normally will be sufficient to establish subject-matter jurisdiction.

(G) *Description of offense.*

(i) *Elements.* The elements of the offense must be alleged, either expressly or by necessary implication, except that Article 134 specifications must expressly allege the terminal element. *See* paragraph 60.c.(6) in Part IV. If a specific intent, knowledge, or state of mind is an element of the offense, it must be alleged.

(ii) *Words indicating criminality.* If the alleged act is not itself an offense but is made an offense either by applicable statute (including Articles 133 and 134), or regulation or custom having the effect of law, then words indicating criminality such as "wrongfully," "unlawfully," or "without authority" (depending upon the nature of the offense) should be used to describe the accused's acts.

(iii) *Specificity.* The specification should be sufficiently specific to inform the accused of the conduct charged, to enable the accused to prepare a defense, and to protect the accused against double jeopardy. Only those facts that make the accused's conduct criminal ordinarily should be alleged. Specific evidence supporting the allegations ordinarily should not be included in the specifications.

(iv) *Duplicitousness.* One specification should not allege more than one offense, either conjunctively (the accused "lost and destroyed") or alternatively (the accused "lost or destroyed"). However, if two acts or a series of acts constitute one offense, they may be alleged conjunctively. *See* R.C.M. 906(b)(5).

(v) *Lesser Included Offenses.* The elements of the contemplated lesser included offense should be compared with the elements of the greater offense to determine if the elements of the lesser offense are derivative of the greater offense and vice versa. *See* discussion following paragraph 3.b.(1)(c) in Part IV and the related analysis in Appendix 23.

(H) *Other considerations in drafting specifications.*

(i) *Principals.* All principals are charged as if each was the perpetrator. *See* paragraph 1 of Part IV for a discussion of principals.

(ii) *Victim.* In the case of an offense against the person or property of a person, the first name, middle initial, and last name or first, middle, and last initials of such person should be alleged, if known. If the name of the victim is unknown, a general physical description may be used. If this cannot be done, the victim may be described as "a person whose name is unknown." Military rank or grade should be alleged, and must be alleged if an element of the offense, as in an allegation of disobedience of the command of a superior officer. If the person has no military position, it may otherwise be necessary to allege the status as in an allegation of using provoking words toward a person subject to the code. *See* paragraph 42 of Part IV. Counsel for the government should be aware that if initials of victims are used, additional notice of the identity of victims will be required.

(iii) *Property.* In describing property generic terms should be used, such as "a watch" or "a knife," and descriptive details such as make, model, color, and serial number should ordinarily be omitted. In some instances, however, details may be essential to the offense, so they must be alleged. For example: the length of a knife blade may be important when alleging a violation of general regulation prohibiting carrying a knife with a blade that exceeds a certain length.

(iv) *Value.* When the value of property or other amount determines the maximum punishment which may be adjudged for an offense, the value or amount should be alleged, for in such a case increased punishments that are contingent upon value may not be adjudged unless there is an allegation, as well as proof, of a value which will support the punishment. If several articles of different kinds are the subject of the offense, the value of each article should be stated followed by a statement of the aggregate value. Exact value should be stated, if known. For ease of proof an allegation may be "of a value not less than _____." If only an approximate value is known, it may be alleged as "of a value of about _____." If the value of an item is unknown but obviously minimal, the term "of some value" may be used. These principles apply to allegations of amounts.

(v) *Documents.* When documents other than regulations or orders must be alleged (for example, bad checks in violation of Article 123a), the document may be set forth verbatim (including photocopies and similar reproductions) or may be described, in which case the description must be sufficient to inform the accused of the offense charged.

(vi) *Orders.*

(a) *General orders.* A specification alleging a violation of a general order or regulation (Article 92(1)) must clearly identify the specific order or regulation allegedly violated. The general order or regulation should be cited by its identifying title or number, section or paragraph, and date. It is not necessary to recite the text of the general order or regulation verbatim.

(b) *Other orders.* If the order allegedly violated is an "other lawful order" (Article 92(2)), it should be set forth verbatim or described in the specification. When the order is oral, *see* (vii) below.

(c) *Negating exceptions.* If the order contains exceptions, it is not necessary that the specification contain a specific allegation negating the exceptions. However, words of criminality may be required if the alleged act is not necessarily criminal. *See* subsection (G)(ii) of this discussion.

(vii) *Oral statements.* When alleging oral statements the phrase "or words to that effect" should be added.

(viii) *Joint offense.* In the case of a joint offense each accused may be charged separately as if each accused acted alone or all may be charged together in a single specification. For example:

(a) If Doe and Roe are joint perpetrators of an offense and it is intended to charge and try both at the same trial, they should be charged in a single specification as follows:

"In that Doe and Roe, acting jointly and pursuant to a common intent, did. . . ."

(b) If it is intended that Roe will be tried alone or that Roe will be tried with Doe at a common trial, Roe may be charged in the same manner as if Roe alone had committed the offense. However, to show in the specification that Doe was a joint actor with Roe, even though Doe is not to be tried with Roe, Roe may be charged as follows:

"In that Roe did, in conjunction with Doe, ..."

(ix) *Matters in aggravation.* Matters in aggravation that do not increase the maximum authorized punishment ordinarily should not be alleged in the specification. Prior convictions need not be alleged in the specification to permit increased punishment. Aggravating factors in capital cases should not be alleged in the specification. Notice of such factors is normally provided in accordance with R.C.M. 1004(b)(1).

(x) *Abbreviations.* Commonly used and understood abbreviations may be used, particularly abbreviations for ranks, grades, units and organizations, components, and geographic or political entities, such as the names of states or countries.

---

(4) *Multiple offenses.* Charges and specifications alleging all known offenses by an accused may be preferred at the same time. Each specification shall state only one offense. What is substantially one transaction should not be made the basis for an unreasonable multiplication of charges against one person. Unreasonable multiplication of charges is addressed in R.C.M. 906(b)(12); multiplicity is addressed in R.C.M. 907(b)(3)(B); and punishment limitations are addressed in R.C.M. 1003(c)(1)(C).

Discussion

The prohibition against unreasonable multiplication of charges addresses those features of military law that increase the potential for overreaching in the exercise of prosecutorial discretion. It is based on reasonableness, and has no foundation in Constitutional rights. To determine if charges are unreasonably multiplied, see R.C.M. 906(b)(12). Because prosecutors are free to charge in the alternative, it may be reasonable to charge two or more offenses that arise from one transaction if sufficient doubt exists as to the facts or the law. In no case should both an offense and a lesser included offense thereof be separately charged. See also Part IV, paragraph 3, and R.C.M. 601(e)(2) concerning referral of several offenses.

See R.C.M. 906(b)(12) and 1003(c)(1)(C). For example, a person should not be charged with both failure to report for a routine scheduled duty, such as reveille, and with absence without leave if the failure to report occurred during the period for which the accused is charged with absence without leave. There are times, however, when sufficient doubt as to the facts or the law exists to warrant making one transaction the basis for charging two or more offenses. In no case should both an offense and a lesser included offense thereof be separately charged.

See also R.C.M. 601(e)(2) concerning referral of several

offenses.

(5) *Multiple offenders.* A specification may name more than one person as an accused if each person so named is believed by the accuser to be a principal in the offense which is the subject of the specification.

Discussion

See also R.C.M. 601(e)(3) concerning joinder of accused.

A joint offense is one committed by two or more persons acting together with a common intent. Principals may be charged jointly with the commission of the same offense, but an accessory after the fact cannot be charged jointly with the principal whom the accused is alleged to have received, comforted, or assisted. Offenders are properly joined only if there is a common unlawful design or purpose; the mere fact that several persons happen to have committed the same kinds of offenses at the time, although material as tending to show concert of purpose, does not necessarily establish this. The fact that several persons happen to have absented themselves without leave at about the same time will not, in the absence of evidence indicating a joint design, purpose, or plan justify joining them in one specification, for they may merely have been availing themselves of the same opportunity. In joint offenses the participants may be separately or jointly charged. However, if the participants are members of different armed forces, they must be charged separately because their trials must be separately reviewed. The preparation of joint charges is discussed in subsection (c)(3) Discussion (H) (viii)*(a)* of this rule. The advantage of a joint charge is that all accused will be tried at one trial, thereby saving time, labor, and expense. This must be weighed against the possible unfairness to the accused which may result if their defenses are inconsistent or antagonistic. An accused cannot be called as a witness except upon that accused's own request. If the testimony of an accomplice is necessary, the accomplice should not be tried jointly with those against whom the accomplice is expected to testify. *See also* Mil. R. Evid. 306.

See R.C.M. 603 concerning amending specifications.

See R.C.M. 906(b)(5) and (6) concerning motions to amend

specifications and bills of particulars.

(d) *Harmless error in citation.* Error in or omission of the designation of the article of the code or other statute, law of war, or regulation violated shall not be ground for dismissal of a charge or reversal of a conviction if the error or omission did not prejudicially mislead the accused.

Rule 308. Notification to accused of charges

(a) *Immediate commander.* The immediate commander of the accused shall cause the accused to be informed of the charges preferred against the accused, and the name of the person who preferred the charges and of any person who ordered the charges to be preferred, if known, as soon as practicable.

Discussion

When notice is given, a certificate to that effect on the Charge Sheet should be completed. *See* Appendix 4.

(b) *Commanders at higher echelons.* When the accused has not been informed of the charges, commanders at higher echelons to whom the preferred charges are forwarded shall cause the accused to be informed of the matters required under subsection (a) of this rule as soon as practicable.

(c) *Remedy.* The sole remedy for violation of this rule is a continuance or recess of sufficient length to permit the accused to adequately prepare a defense, and no relief shall be granted upon a failure to comply with this rule unless the accused demonstrates that the accused has been hindered in the preparation of a defense.

CHAPTER IV. FORWARDING AND DISPOSITION OF CHARGES

Rule 401. Forwarding and disposition of charges in general

(a) *Who may dispose of charges.* Only persons authorized to convene courts-martial or to administer nonjudicial punishment under Article 15 may dispose of charges. A superior competent authority may withhold the authority of a subordinate to dispose of charges in individual cases, types of cases, or generally.

Discussion

See R.C.M. 504 as to who may convene courts-martial and paragraph 2 of Part V as to who may administer nonjudicial punishment. If the power to convene courts-martial and to administer nonjudicial punishment has been withheld, a commander may not dispose of charges under this rule.

Ordinarily charges should be forwarded to the accused's immediate commander for initial consideration as to disposition. Each commander has independent discretion to determine how charges will be disposed of, except to the extent that the commander's authority has been withheld by superior competent authority. *See also* R.C.M. 104.

Each commander who forwards or disposes of charges may make minor changes therein. *See* R.C.M. 603(a) and (b). If major changes are necessary, the affected charge should be preferred anew. *See* R.C.M. 603(d). If a commander is an accuser (*see* Article 1(9); 307(a)) that commander is ineligible to refer such charges to a general or special court-martial. *See* R.C.M. 601(c). However, see R.C.M. 1302(b) (accuser may refer charges to a summary court-martial).

(b) *Prompt determination.* When a commander with authority to dispose of charges receives charges, that commander shall promptly determine what disposition will be made in the interest of justice and discipline.

Discussion

In determining what level of disposition is appropriate, *see* R.C.M. 306(b) and (c). When charges are brought against two or more accused with a view to a joint or common trial, *see* R.C.M. 307(c)(5); 601(e)(3). If it appears that the accused may lack mental capacity to stand trial or may not have been mentally responsible at the times of the offenses, *see* R.C.M. 706; 909; 916(k).

As to the rules concerning speedy trial, *see* R.C.M. 707. *See also* Articles 10; 30; 33; 98.

Before determining an appropriate disposition, a commander who receives charges should ensure that: (1) a preliminary inquiry under R.C.M. 303 has been conducted; (2) the accused has been notified in accordance with R.C.M. 308; and (3) the charges are in proper form.

(c) *How charges may be disposed of.* Unless the authority to do so has been limited or withheld by superior competent authority, a commander may dispose of charges by dismissing any or all of them, forwarding any or all of them to another commander for disposition, or referring any or all of them to a court-martial which the commander is empowered to convene. Charges should be disposed of in accordance with the policy in R.C.M. 306(b).

Discussion

When an alleged offense involves a victim, the victim should, whenever practicable, be provided an opportunity to express views regarding the disposition of the charges. The commander with authority to dispose of charges should consider such views of the victim prior to deciding how to dispose of the charges and should continue to consider the views of the victim until final disposition of the case. A "victim" is an individual who is alleged to have suffered direct physical, emotional, or pecuniary harm as a result of the matters set forth in a charge or specification under consideration and is named in one of the specifications under consideration.

A commander may dispose of charges individually or collectively. If charges are referred to a court-martial, ordinarily all known charges should be referred to a single court-martial.

See Appendix 3 when the charges may involve matters in which the Department of Justice has an interest.

---

(1) *Dismissal.* When a commander dismisses charges further disposition under R.C.M. 306(c) of the offenses is not barred.

Discussion

Charges are ordinarily dismissed by lining out and initialing the deleted specifications or otherwise recording that a specification is dismissed. When all charges and specifications are dismissed, the accuser and the accused ordinarily should be informed.

A charge should be dismissed when it fails to state an offense, when it is unsupported by available evidence, or when there are other sound reasons why trial by court-martial is not appropriate. Before dismissing charges because trial would be detrimental to the prosecution of a war or harmful to national security, *see* R.C.M. 401(d); 407(b).

If the accused has already refused nonjudicial punishment, charges should not be dismissed with a view to offering nonjudicial punishment unless the accused has indicated willingness to accept nonjudicial punishment if again offered. The decision whether to dismiss charges in such circumstances is within the sole discretion of the commander concerned.

Charges may be amended in accordance with R.C.M. 603.

It is appropriate to dismiss a charge and prefer another charge anew when, for example, the original charge failed to state an offense, or was so defective that a major amendment was required (*see* R.C.M. 603(d)), or did not adequately reflect the nature or seriousness of the offense.

See R.C.M. 907(b)(2)(C) concerning the effect of dismissing charges after the court-martial has begun.

---

(2) *Forwarding charges.*

(A) *Forwarding to a superior commander.* When charges are forwarded to a superior commander for disposition, the forwarding commander shall make a personal recommendation as to disposition. If the forwarding commander is disqualified from acting as convening authority in the case, the basis for the disqualification shall be noted.

Discussion

A commander's recommendation is within that commander's sole discretion. No authority may direct a commander to make a specific recommendation as to disposition.

When charges are forwarded to a superior commander with a view to trial by general or special court-martial, they should be forwarded by a letter of transmittal or indorsement. To the extent practicable without unduly delaying forwarding the charges, the letter should include or carry as enclosures: a summary of the available evidence relating to each offense; evidence of previous convictions and nonjudicial punishments of the accused; an indication that the accused has been offered and refused nonjudicial punishment, if applicable; and any other matters required by superior authority or deemed appropriate by the forwarding commander. Other matters which may be appropriate include information concerning the accused's background and character of military service, and a description of any unusual circumstances in the case. The summary of evidence should include available witness statements, documentary evidence, and exhibits. When practicable, copies of signed statements of the witnesses should be forwarded, as should copies of any investigative or laboratory reports. Forwarding charges should not be delayed, however, solely to obtain such statements or reports when it otherwise appears that sufficient evidence to warrant trial is or will be available in time for trial. If because of the bulk of documents or exhibits, it is impracticable to forward them with the letter of transmittal, they should be properly preserved and should be referred to in the letter of transmittal.

When it appears that any witness may not be available for later proceedings in the case or that a deposition may be appropriate, that matter should be brought to the attention of the convening authority promptly and should be noted in the letter of transmittal.

When charges are forwarded with a view to disposition other than trial by general or special court-martial, they should be accompanied by sufficient information to enable the authority receiving them to dispose of them without further investigation.

(B) *Other cases.* When charges are forwarded to a commander who is not a superior of the forwarding commander, no recommendation as to disposition may be made.

Discussion

Except when directed to forward charges, a subordinate commander may not be required to take any specific action to dispose of charges. *See* R.C.M. 104. *See also* paragraph 1d(2) of Part V. When appropriate, charges may be sent or returned to a subordinate commander for compliance with procedural requirements. *See*, for example, R.C.M. 303 (preliminary inquiry); R.C.M. 308 (notification to accused of charges).

---

(3) *Referral of charges. See* R.C.M. 403, 404, 407, 601.

(d) *National security matters.* If a commander who is not a general court-martial convening authority finds that the charges warrant trial by court-martial but believes that trial would probably be detrimental to the prosecution of a war or harmful to national security, the charges shall be forwarded to the officer exercising general court-martial convening authority.

Discussion

See R.C.M. 407(b).

Rule 402. Action by commander not authorized to convene courts-martial

When in receipt of charges, a commander authorized to administer nonjudicial punishment but not authorized to convene courts-martial may:

(1) Dismiss any charges; or

Discussion

See R.C.M. 401(c)(1) concerning dismissal of charges, the effect of dismissal, and options for further action.

---

(2) Forward them to a superior commander for disposition.

Discussion

See R.C.M. 401(c)(2) for additional guidance concerning forwarding charges. *See generally* R.C.M. 303 (preliminary inquiry); 308

(notification to accused of charges) concerning other duties of the immediate commander when in receipt of charges.

When the immediate commander is authorized to convene courts-martial, *see* R.C.M. 403, 404, or 407, as appropriate.

Rule 403. Action by commander exercising summary court-martial jurisdiction

(a) *Recording receipt.* Immediately upon receipt of sworn charges, an officer exercising summary court-martial jurisdiction over the command shall cause the hour and date of receipt to be entered on the charge sheet.

Discussion

See Article 24 and R.C.M. 1302(a) concerning who may exercise summary court-martial jurisdiction.

The entry indicating receipt is important because it stops the running of the statute of limitations. *See* Article 43; R.C.M. 907(b)(2)(B). Charges may be preferred and forwarded to an officer exercising summary court-martial jurisdiction over the command to stop the running of the statute of limitations even though the accused is absent without authority.

(b) *Disposition.* When in receipt of charges a commander exercising summary court-martial jurisdiction may:

(1) Dismiss any charges;

Discussion

See R.C.M. 401(c)(1) concerning dismissal of charges, the effect of dismissing charges, and options for further action.

(2) Forward charges (or, after dismissing charges, the matter) to a subordinate commander for disposition;

Discussion

See R.C.M. 401(c)(2)(B) concerning forwarding charges to a subordinate. When appropriate, charges may be forwarded to a subordinate even if the subordinate previously considered them.

(3) Forward any charges to a superior commander for disposition;

Discussion

See R.C.M. 401(c)(2)(A) for guidance concerning forwarding charges to a superior.

(4) Subject to R.C.M. 601(d), refer charges to a summary court-martial for trial; or

Discussion

See R.C.M. 1302(c) concerning referral of charges to a summary court-martial.

(5) Unless otherwise prescribed by the Secretary concerned, direct a preliminary hearing under R.C.M. 405, and, if appropriate, forward the report of preliminary hearing with the charges to a superior commander for disposition.

Discussion

A preliminary hearing should be directed when it appears the charges are of such a serious nature that trial by general court-martial may be warranted. *See* R.C.M. 405. If a preliminary hearing of the subject has already been conducted, see R.C.M. 405(b).

Rule 404. Action by commander exercising special court-martial jurisdiction

When in receipt of charges, a commander exercising special court-martial jurisdiction may:

(a) Dismiss any charges;

Discussion

See R.C.M. 401(c)(1) concerning dismissal of charges, the effect of dismissing charges, and options for further action.

(b) Forward charges (or, after dismissing charges, the matter) to a subordinate commander for disposition;

Discussion

See R.C.M. 401(c)(2)(B) concerning forwarding charges to a subordinate. When appropriate, charges may be forwarded to a subordinate even if that subordinate previously considered them.

(c) Forward any charges to a superior commander for disposition;

Discussion

See R.C.M. 401(c)(2)(A) for guidance concerning forwarding charges to a superior.

(d) Subject to R.C.M. 601(d), refer charges to a

summary court-martial or to a special court-martial for trial; or

Discussion

See Article 23 and R.C.M. 504(b)(2) concerning who may convene special courts-martial.

See R.C.M. 601 concerning referral of charges to a special court-martial. *See* R.C.M. 1302(c) concerning referral of charges to a summary court-martial.

(e) Unless otherwise prescribed by the Secretary concerned, direct a preliminary hearing under R.C.M. 405, and, if appropriate, forward the report of preliminary hearing with the charges to a superior commander for disposition.

Discussion

A preliminary hearing should be directed when it appears that the charges are of such a serious nature that trial by general court-martial may be warranted. *See* R.C.M. 405. If a preliminary hearing of the subject matter already has been conducted, see R.C.M. 405(b) and 405(e)(2).

Rule 404A. Disclosure of matters following direction of preliminary hearing

(a) When a convening authority directs a preliminary hearing under R.C.M. 405, counsel for the government shall, subject to subsections (b) through (d) of this rule, within 5 days of issuance of the Article 32 appointing order, provide to the defense the following information or matters:

(1) charge sheet;

(2) Article 32 appointing order;

(3) documents accompanying the charge sheet on which the preferral decision was based;

(4) documents provided to the convening authority when deciding to direct the preliminary hearing;

(5) documents the counsel for the government intends to present at the preliminary hearing; and

(6) access to tangible objects counsel for the government intends to present at the preliminary hearing.

(b) *Contraband.* If items covered by subsection (a) of this rule are contraband, the disclosure required under this rule is a reasonable opportunity to inspect said contraband prior to the hearing.

(c) *Privilege.* If items covered by subsection (a) of this rule are privileged, classified or otherwise pro-

tected under Section V of Part III, no disclosure of those items is required under this rule. However, counsel for the government may disclose privileged, classified, or otherwise protected information covered by subsection (a) of this rule if authorized by the holder of the privilege, or in the case of Mil. R. Evid. 505 or 506, if authorized by a competent authority.

(d) *Protective order if privileged information is disclosed.* If the government agrees to disclose to the accused information to which the protections afforded by Section V of Part III may apply, the convening authority, or other person designated by regulation of the Secretary concerned, may enter an appropriate protective order, in writing, to guard against the compromise of information disclosed to the accused. The terms of any such protective order may include prohibiting the disclosure of the information except as authorized by the authority issuing the protective order, as well as those terms specified by Mil. R. Evid. 505(g)(2)–(6) or 506(g)(2)–(5).

Discussion

The purposes of this rule are to provide the accused with the documents used to make the determination to prefer charges and direct a preliminary hearing, and to allow the accused to prepare for the preliminary hearing. This rule is not intended to be a tool for discovery and does not impose the same discovery obligations found in R.C.M. 405 prior to amendments required by the National Defense Authorization Act for Fiscal Year 2014 or R.C.M. 701. Additional rules for disclosure of witnesses and other evidence in the preliminary hearing are provided in R.C.M. 405(g).

Rule 405. Preliminary hearing

(a) *In general.* Except as provided in subsection (k) of this rule, no charge or specification may be referred to a general court-martial for trial until completion of a preliminary hearing in substantial compliance with this rule. A preliminary hearing conducted under this rule is not intended to serve as a means of discovery and will be limited to an examination of those issues necessary to determine whether there is probable cause to conclude that an offense or offenses have been committed and whether the accused committed it; to determine whether a court-martial would have jurisdiction over the offense(s) and the accused; to consider the form of the charge(s); and to recommend the disposition that should be made of the charge(s). Failure to comply with this rule shall have no effect on the disposition of the charge(s) if the charge(s) is not referred to a general court-martial.

Discussion

The function of the preliminary hearing is to ascertain and impartially weigh the facts needed for the limited scope and purpose of the preliminary hearing. The preliminary hearing is not intended to perfect a case against the accused and is not intended to serve as a means of discovery or to provide a right of confrontation required at trial. Determinations and recommendations of the preliminary hearing officer are advisory.

Failure to substantially comply with the requirements of Article 32, which failure prejudices the accused, may result in delay in disposition of the case or disapproval of the proceedings. *See* R.C.M. 905(b)(1) and 906(b)(3) concerning motions for appropriate relief relating to the preliminary hearing.

The accused may waive the preliminary hearing. *See* subsection (k) of this rule. In such case, no preliminary hearing need be held. However, the convening authority authorized to direct the preliminary hearing may direct that it be conducted notwithstanding the waiver.

(b) *Earlier preliminary hearing.* If a preliminary hearing of the subject matter of an offense has been conducted before the accused is charged with an offense, and the accused was present at the preliminary hearing and afforded the rights to counsel, cross-examination, and presentation of evidence required by this rule, no further preliminary hearing is required.

(c) *Who may direct a preliminary hearing.* Unless prohibited by regulations of the Secretary concerned, a preliminary hearing may be directed under this rule by any court-martial convening authority. That authority may also give procedural instructions not inconsistent with these rules.

(d) *Personnel.*

(1) *Preliminary hearing officer.* Whenever practicable, the convening authority directing a preliminary hearing under this rule shall detail an impartial judge advocate certified under Article 27(b), not the accuser, as a preliminary hearing officer, who shall conduct the preliminary hearing and make a report that addresses whether there is probable cause to believe that an offense or offenses have been committed and that the accused committed the offense(s); whether a court-martial would have jurisdiction over the offense(s) and the accused; the form of the charge(s); and a recommendation as to the disposition of the charge(s).

When the appointment of a judge advocate as the preliminary hearing officer is not practicable, or in exceptional circumstances in which the interest of justice warrants, the convening authority directing the preliminary hearing may detail an impartial commissioned officer, who is not the accuser, as the preliminary hearing officer. If the preliminary hearing officer is not a judge advocate, an impartial judge advocate certified under Article 27(b) shall be available to provide legal advice to the preliminary hearing officer.

When practicable, the preliminary hearing officer shall be equal or senior in grade to the military counsel detailed to represent the accused and the government at the preliminary hearing. The Secretary concerned may prescribe additional limitations on the appointment of preliminary hearing officers.

The preliminary hearing officer shall not depart from an impartial role and become an advocate for either side. The preliminary hearing officer is disqualified to act later in the same case in any other capacity.

Discussion

The preliminary hearing officer, if not a judge advocate, should be an officer in the grade of O-4 or higher. The preliminary hearing officer may seek legal advice concerning the preliminary hearing officer's responsibilities from an impartial source, but may not obtain such advice from counsel for any party or counsel for a victim.

---

(2) *Counsel to represent the United States.* A judge advocate, not the accuser, shall serve as counsel to represent the United States, and shall present evidence on behalf of the government relevant to the limited scope and purpose of the preliminary hearing as set forth in subsection (a) of this rule.

(3) *Defense counsel.*

(A) *Detailed counsel.* Except as provided in subsection (d)(3)(B) of this rule, military counsel certified in accordance with Article 27(b) shall be detailed to represent the accused.

(B) *Individual military counsel.* The accused may request to be represented by individual military counsel. Such requests shall be acted on in accordance with R.C.M. 506(b).

(C) *Civilian counsel.* The accused may be represented by civilian counsel at no expense to the United States. Upon request, the accused is entitled to a reasonable time to obtain civilian counsel and to have such counsel present for the preliminary hearing. However, the preliminary hearing shall not be unduly delayed for this purpose. Representation by civilian counsel shall not limit the rights to military counsel under subsections (d)(3)(A) and (B) of this rule.

(4) *Others.* The convening authority who directed the preliminary hearing may also, as a matter of discretion, detail or request an appropriate authority to detail:

(A) A reporter; and

(B) An interpreter.

(e) *Scope of preliminary hearing.*

(1) The preliminary hearing officer shall limit the inquiry to the examination of evidence, including witnesses, necessary to:

(A) Determine whether there is probable cause to believe an offense or offenses have been committed and whether the accused committed it;

(B) Determine whether a court-martial would have jurisdiction over the offense(s) and the accused;

(C) Consider whether the form of the charge(s) is proper; and

(D) Make a recommendation as to the disposition of the charge(s).

(2) If evidence adduced during the preliminary hearing indicates that the accused committed any uncharged offense(s), the preliminary hearing officer may examine evidence and hear witnesses relating to the subject matter of such offense(s) and make the findings and recommendations enumerated in subsection (e)(1) of this rule regarding such offense(s) without the accused first having been charged with the offense. The accused's rights under subsection (f)(2) of this rule, and, where it would not cause undue delay to the proceedings, subsection (g) of this rule, are the same with regard to both charged and uncharged offenses. When considering uncharged offenses identified during the preliminary hearing, the preliminary hearing officer shall inform the accused of the general nature of each uncharged offense considered, and otherwise afford the accused the same opportunity for representation, cross-examination, and presentation afforded during the preliminary hearing of any charged offense.

Discussion

Except as set forth in subsection (h) of this rule, the Mil. R. Evid. do not apply at a preliminary hearing. Except as prohibited elsewhere in this rule, a preliminary hearing officer may consider evidence, including hearsay, which would not be admissible at trial.

(f) *Rights of the accused.*

(1) Prior to any preliminary hearing under this rule the accused shall have the right to:

(A) Notice of any witnesses that the government intends to call at the preliminary hearing and copies of or access to any written or recorded statements made by those witnesses that relate to the subject matter of any charged offense;

(i) For purposes of this rule, a "written statement" is one that is signed or otherwise adopted or approved by the witness that is within the possession or control of counsel for the government; and

(ii) For purposes of this rule, a "recorded statement" is an oral statement made by the witness that is recorded contemporaneously with the making of the oral statement and contained in a digital or other recording or a transcription thereof that is within the possession or control of counsel for the government.

(B) Notice of, and reasonable access to, any other evidence that the government intends to offer at the preliminary hearing; and

(C) Notice of, and reasonable access to, evidence that is within the possession or control of counsel for the government that negates or reduces the degree of guilt of the accused for an offense charged.

(2) At any preliminary hearing under this rule the accused shall have the right to:

(A) Be advised of the charges under consideration;

(B) Be represented by counsel;

(C) Be informed of the purpose of the preliminary hearing;

(D) Be informed of the right against self-incrimination under Article 31;

(E) Except in the circumstances described in R.C.M. 804(c)(2), be present throughout the taking of evidence;

(F) Cross-examine witnesses on matters relevant to the limited scope and purpose of the preliminary hearing;

(G) Present matters in defense and mitigation

relevant to the limited scope and purpose of the preliminary hearing; and

Discussion

Unsworn statements by the accused, unlike those made under R.C.M. 1001(c)(2), shall be limited to matters in defense and mitigation.

(H) Make a statement relevant to the limited scope and purpose of the preliminary hearing.

(g) *Production of Witnesses and Other Evidence.*

(1) *Military Witnesses.*

(A) Prior to the preliminary hearing, defense counsel shall provide to counsel for the government the names of proposed military witnesses whom the accused requests that the government produce to testify at the preliminary hearing, and the requested form of the testimony, in accordance with the timeline established by the preliminary hearing officer. Counsel for the government shall respond that either: (1) the government agrees that the witness's testimony is relevant, not cumulative, and necessary for the limited scope and purpose of the preliminary hearing and will seek to secure the witness's testimony for the hearing; or (2) the government objects to the proposed defense witness on the grounds that the testimony would be irrelevant, cumulative, or unnecessary based on the limited scope and purpose of the preliminary hearing.

(B) If the government objects to the proposed defense witness, defense counsel may request that the preliminary hearing officer determine whether the witness is relevant, not cumulative, and necessary based on the limited scope and purpose of the preliminary hearing.

(C) If the government does not object to the proposed defense military witness or the preliminary hearing officer determines that the military witness is relevant, not cumulative, and necessary, counsel for the government shall request that the commanding officer of the proposed military witness make that person available to provide testimony. The commanding officer shall determine whether the individual is available based on operational necessity or mission requirements, except that a victim, as defined in this rule, who declines to testify shall be deemed to be not available. If the commanding officer determines that the military witness is available, counsel for the government shall make arrangements

for that individual's testimony. The commanding officer's determination of unavailability due to operational necessity or mission requirements is final. If there is a dispute among the parties, the military witness's commanding officer shall determine whether the witness testifies in person, by video teleconference, by telephone, or by similar means of remote testimony.

Discussion

A commanding officer's determination of whether an individual is available, as well as the means by which the individual is available, is a balancing test. The more important the testimony of the witness, the greater the difficulty, expense, delay, or effect on military operations must be to deny production of the witness. Based on operational necessity and mission requirements, the witness's commanding officer may authorize the witness to testify by video teleconference, telephone, or similar means of remote testimony. Factors to be considered in making this determination include the costs of producing the witness; the timing of the request for production of the witness; the potential delay in the proceeding that may be caused by the production of the witness; and the likelihood of significant interference with operational deployment, mission accomplishment, or essential training.

---

(2) *Civilian Witnesses.*

(A) Defense counsel shall provide to counsel for the government the names of proposed civilian witnesses whom the accused requests that the government produce to testify at the preliminary hearing, and the requested form of the testimony, in accordance with the timeline established by the preliminary hearing officer. Counsel for the government shall respond that either: (1) the government agrees that the witness's testimony is relevant, not cumulative, and necessary for the limited scope and purpose of the preliminary hearing and will seek to secure the witness's testimony for the hearing; or (2) the government objects to the proposed defense witness on the grounds that the testimony would be irrelevant, cumulative, or unnecessary based on the limited scope and purpose of the preliminary hearing.

(B) If the government objects to the proposed defense witness, defense counsel may request that the preliminary hearing officer determine whether the witness is relevant, not cumulative, and necessary based on the limited scope and purpose of the preliminary hearing.

(C) If the government does not object to the proposed civilian witness or the preliminary hearing officer determines that the civilian witness's testimony is relevant, not cumulative, and necessary, counsel for the government shall invite the civilian witness to provide testimony and, if the individual agrees, shall make arrangements for that witness's testimony. If expense to the government is to be incurred, the convening authority who directed the preliminary hearing, or the convening authority's delegate, shall determine whether the witness testifies in person, by video teleconference, by telephone, or by similar means of remote testimony.

Discussion

Factors to be considered in making this determination include the costs of producing the witness; the timing of the request for production of the witness; the potential delay in the proceeding that may be caused by the production of the witness; the willingness of the witness to testify in person; and, for child witnesses, the traumatic effect of providing in-person testimony. Civilian witnesses may not be compelled to provide testimony at a preliminary hearing. Civilian witnesses may be paid for travel and associated expenses to testify at a preliminary hearing. *See* Department of Defense Joint Travel Regulations.

---

(3) *Other evidence.*

(A) *Evidence under the control of the government.*

(i) Prior to the preliminary hearing, defense counsel shall provide to counsel for the government a list of evidence under the control of the government the accused requests the government produce to the defense for introduction at the preliminary hearing. The preliminary hearing officer may set a deadline by which defense requests must be received. Counsel for the government shall respond that either: (1) the government agrees that the evidence is relevant, not cumulative, and necessary for the limited scope and purpose of the preliminary hearing and shall make reasonable efforts to obtain the evidence; or (2) the government objects to production of the evidence on the grounds that the evidence would be irrelevant, cumulative, or unnecessary based on the limited scope and purpose of the preliminary hearing.

(ii) If the government objects to production of the evidence, defense counsel may request that the preliminary hearing officer determine whether the evidence should be produced. The preliminary hearing officer shall determine whether the evidence is relevant, not cumulative, and necessary based on the limited scope and purpose of the hearing. If the preliminary hearing officer determines that the evidence shall be produced, counsel for the government shall make reasonable efforts to obtain the evidence.

(B) *Evidence not under the control of the government.*

(i) Evidence not under the control of the government may be obtained through noncompulsory means or by *subpoenas duces tecum* issued by counsel for the government in accordance with the process established by R.C.M. 703.

(ii) Prior to the preliminary hearing, defense counsel shall provide to counsel for the government a list of evidence not under the control of the government that the accused requests the government obtain. The preliminary hearing officer may set a deadline by which defense requests must be received. Counsel for the government shall respond that either: (1) the government agrees that the evidence is relevant, not cumulative, and necessary for the limited scope and purpose of the preliminary hearing and shall issue *subpoenas duces tecum* for the evidence; or (2) the government objects to production of the evidence on the grounds that the evidence would be irrelevant, cumulative, or unnecessary based on the limited scope and purpose of the preliminary hearing.

(iii) If the government objects to production of the evidence, defense counsel may request that the preliminary hearing officer determine whether the evidence should be produced. If the preliminary hearing officer determines that the evidence is relevant, not cumulative, and necessary based on the limited scope and purpose of the preliminary hearing and that the issuance of *subpoenas duces tecum* would not cause undue delay to the preliminary hearing, the preliminary hearing officer shall direct counsel for the government to issue *subpoenas duces tecum* for the defense-requested evidence. The preliminary hearing officer shall note in the report of preliminary hearing any failure on the part of counsel for the government to issue *subpoenas duces tecum* directed by the preliminary hearing officer.

Discussion

A *subpoena duces tecum* to produce books, papers, documents, data, electronically stored information, or other objects for a preliminary hearing pursuant to Article 32 may be issued by counsel for the government. The preliminary hearing officer has no authority to issue a *subpoena duces tecum*. However, the preliminary hearing officer may direct counsel for the government to issue a *subpoena duces tecum* for defense-requested evidence.

(h) *Military Rules of Evidence.* The Military Rules of Evidence do not apply in preliminary hearings under this rule except as follows:

(1) Mil. R. Evid. 301-303 and 305 shall apply in their entirety.

(2) Mil. R. Evid. 412 shall apply in any case that includes a charge defined as a sexual offense in Mil. R. Evid. 412(d), except that Mil. R. Evid. 412(b)(1)(C) shall not apply.

(3) Mil. R. Evid., Section V, Privileges, shall apply, except that Mil. R. Evid. 505(f)-(h) and (j); 506(f)-(h), (j), (k), and (m); and 514(d)(6) shall not apply.

(4) In applying these rules to a preliminary hearing, the term "military judge," as used in these rules, shall mean the preliminary hearing officer, who shall assume the military judge's authority to exclude evidence from the preliminary hearing, and who shall, in discharging this duty, follow the procedures set forth in the rules cited in subsections (h)(1)-(3) of this rule. However, the preliminary hearing officer is not authorized to order production of communications covered by Mil. R. Evid. 513 and 514.

Discussion

The prohibition against ordering production of evidence does not preclude a preliminary hearing officer from considering evidence offered by the parties under Mil. R. Evid. 513 or 514.

---

(5) Failure to meet the procedural requirements of the applicable rules of evidence shall result in exclusion of that evidence from the preliminary hearing, unless good cause is shown.

Discussion

Before considering evidence offered under subsection (h)(2), the preliminary hearing officer must determine that the evidence offered is relevant for the limited scope and purpose of the hearing, that the evidence is proper under subsection (h)(2), and that the probative value of such evidence outweighs the danger of unfair prejudice to the alleged victim's privacy. The preliminary hearing officer shall set forth any limitations on the scope of such evidence.

Evidence offered under subsection (h)(2) must be protected pursuant to the Privacy Act of 1974, 5 U.S.C. 552a. Although Mil. R. Evid. 412(b)(1)(C) allows admission of evidence of the victim's sexual behavior or predisposition at trial when it is constitutionally required, there is no constitutional requirement at an

Article 32 hearing. There is likewise no constitutional requirement for a preliminary hearing officer to consider evidence under Mil. R. Evid. 514(d)(6) at an Article 32 hearing. Evidence deemed admissible by the preliminary hearing officer should be made a part of the report of preliminary hearing. *See* subsection (j)(2)(C), of this rule. Evidence not considered, and the testimony taken during a closed hearing, should not be included in the report of preliminary hearing but should be appropriately safeguarded or sealed. The preliminary hearing officer and counsel representing the government are responsible for careful handling of any such evidence to prevent unauthorized viewing or disclosure.

(i) *Procedure.*

(1) *Generally.* The preliminary hearing shall begin with the preliminary hearing officer informing the accused of the accused's rights under subsection (f) of this rule. Counsel for the government will then present evidence. Upon the conclusion of counsel for the government's presentation of evidence, defense counsel may present matters in defense and mitigation consistent with subsection (f) of this rule. For the purposes of this rule, "matters in mitigation" are defined as matters that may serve to explain the circumstances surrounding a charged offense. Both counsel for the government and defense shall be afforded an opportunity to cross-examine adverse witnesses. The preliminary hearing officer may also question witnesses called by the parties. If the preliminary hearing officer determines that additional evidence is necessary to satisfy the requirements of subsection (e) of this rule, the preliminary hearing officer may provide the parties an opportunity to present additional testimony or evidence relevant to the limited scope and purpose of the preliminary hearing. The preliminary hearing officer shall not consider evidence not presented at the preliminary hearing. The preliminary hearing officer shall not call witnesses *sua sponte.*

Discussion

A preliminary hearing officer may only consider evidence within the limited purpose of the preliminary hearing and shall ensure that the scope of the hearing is limited to that purpose. When the preliminary hearing officer finds that evidence offered by either party is not within the scope of the hearing, he shall inform the parties and halt the presentation of that information.

---

(2) *Notice to and presence of the victim(s).*

(A) The victim(s) of an offense under the UCMJ has the right to reasonable, accurate, and timely notice of a preliminary hearing relating to the alleged offense, the right to be reasonably protected from the accused, and the reasonable right to confer with counsel for the government during the preliminary hearing. For the purposes of this rule, a "victim" is a person who is alleged to have suffered a direct physical, emotional, or pecuniary harm as a result of the matters set forth in a charge or specification under consideration and is named in one of the specifications under consideration.

(B) A victim of an offense under consideration at the preliminary hearing is not required to testify at the preliminary hearing.

(C) A victim has the right not to be excluded from any portion of a preliminary hearing related to the alleged offense, unless the preliminary hearing officer, after receiving clear and convincing evidence, determines the testimony by the victim would be materially altered if the victim heard other testimony at the proceeding.

(D) A victim shall be excluded if a privilege set forth in Mil. R. Evid. 505 or 506 is invoked or if evidence is offered under Mil. R. Evid. 412, 513, or 514, for charges other than those in which the victim is named.

(3) *Presentation of evidence.*

(A) *Testimony.* Witness testimony may be provided in person, by video teleconference, by telephone, or by similar means of remote testimony. All testimony shall be taken under oath, except that the accused may make an unsworn statement. The preliminary hearing officer shall only consider testimony that is relevant to the limited scope and purpose of the preliminary hearing.

Discussion

The following oath may be given to witnesses:
"Do you (swear) (affirm) that the evidence you give shall be the truth, the whole truth, and nothing but the truth (so help you God)?"

The preliminary hearing officer is required to include in the report of the preliminary hearing, at a minimum, a summary of the substance of all testimony. *See* subsection (j)(2)(B) of this rule.

All preliminary hearing officer notes of testimony and recordings of testimony should be preserved until the end of trial.

If during the preliminary hearing any witness subject to the Code is suspected of an offense under the Code, the preliminary hearing officer should comply with the warning requirements of Mil. R. Evid. 305(c), (d), and, if necessary, (e).

Bearing in mind that counsel are responsible for preparing and presenting their cases, the preliminary hearing officer may ask a witness questions relevant to the limited scope and purpose of the

hearing. When questioning a witness, the preliminary hearing officer may not depart from an impartial role and become an advocate for either side.

(B) *Other evidence.* If relevant to the limited scope and purpose of the preliminary hearing, and not cumulative, a preliminary hearing officer may consider other evidence, in addition to or in lieu of witness testimony, including statements, tangible evidence, or reproductions thereof, offered by either side, that the preliminary hearing officer determines is reliable. This other evidence need not be sworn.

(4) *Access by spectators.* Preliminary hearings are public proceedings and should remain open to the public whenever possible. The convening authority who directed the preliminary hearing or the preliminary hearing officer may restrict or foreclose access by spectators to all or part of the proceedings if an overriding interest exists that outweighs the value of an open preliminary hearing. Examples of overriding interests may include: preventing psychological harm or trauma to a child witness or an alleged victim of a sexual crime, protecting the safety or privacy of a witness or alleged victim, protecting classified material, and receiving evidence where a witness is incapable of testifying in an open setting. Any closure must be narrowly tailored to achieve the overriding interest that justified the closure. Convening authorities or preliminary hearing officers must conclude that no lesser methods short of closing the preliminary hearing can be used to protect the overriding interest in the case. Convening authorities or preliminary hearing officers must conduct a case-by-case, witness-by-witness, circumstance-by-circumstance analysis of whether closure is necessary. If a convening authority or preliminary hearing officer believes closing the preliminary hearing is necessary, the convening authority or preliminary hearing officer must make specific findings of fact in writing that support the closure. The written findings of fact must be included in the report of preliminary hearing.

(5) *Presence of accused.* The further progress of the taking of evidence shall not be prevented and the accused shall be considered to have waived the right to be present whenever the accused:

(A) After being notified of the time and place of the proceeding is voluntarily absent; or

(B) After being warned by the preliminary hearing officer that disruptive conduct will cause removal from the proceeding, persists in conduct that is such as to justify exclusion from the proceeding.

(6) *Recording of the preliminary hearing.* Counsel for the government shall ensure that the preliminary hearing is recorded by a suitable recording device. A victim, as defined by subsection (i)(2)(A) of this rule, may request access to, or a copy of, the recording of the proceedings. Upon request, counsel for the government shall provide the requested access to, or a copy of, the recording to the victim not later than a reasonable time following dismissal of the charges, unless charges are dismissed for the purpose of re-referral, or court-martial adjournment. A victim is not entitled to classified information or access to or a copy of a recording of closed sessions that the victim did not have the right to attend under subsections (i)(2)(C) or (i)(2)(D) of this rule.

Discussion

Counsel for the government shall provide victims with access to, or a copy of, the recording of the proceedings in accordance with such regulations as the Secretary concerned may prescribe.

---

(7) *Objections.* Any objection alleging failure to comply with this rule shall be made to the convening authority via the preliminary hearing officer.

(8) *Sealed exhibits and proceedings.* The preliminary hearing officer has the authority to order exhibits, proceedings, or other matters sealed as described in R.C.M. 1103A.

(j) *Report of preliminary hearing.*

(1) *In general.* The preliminary hearing officer shall make a timely written report of the preliminary hearing to the convening authority who directed the preliminary hearing.

Discussion

If practicable, the charges and the report of preliminary hearing should be forwarded to the general court-martial convening authority within 8 days after an accused is ordered into arrest or confinement. *See* Article 33.

---

(2) *Contents.* The report of preliminary hearing shall include:

(A) A statement of names and organizations or addresses of defense counsel and whether defense counsel was present throughout the taking of evidence, or, if not present, the reason why;

(B) The substance of the testimony taken on both sides;

(C) Any other statements, documents, or matters considered by the preliminary hearing officer, or recitals of the substance or nature of such evidence;

(D) A statement that an essential witness may not be available for trial;

(E) An explanation of any delays in the preliminary hearing;

(F) A notation if counsel for the government failed to issue a *subpoena duces tecum* that was directed by the preliminary hearing officer;

(G) The preliminary hearing officer's determination as to whether there is probable cause to believe the offense(s) listed on the charge sheet or otherwise considered at the preliminary hearing occurred;

(H) The preliminary hearing officer's determination as to whether there is probable cause to believe the accused committed the offense(s) listed on the charge sheet or otherwise considered at the preliminary hearing;

(I) The preliminary hearing officer's determination as to whether a court-martial has jurisdiction over the offense(s) and the accused;

(J) The preliminary hearing officer's determination as to whether the charge(s) and specification(s) are in proper form; and

(K) The preliminary hearing officer's recommendations regarding disposition of the charge(s).

Discussion

The preliminary hearing officer may include any additional matters useful to the convening authority in determining disposition. The preliminary hearing officer may recommend that the charges and specifications be amended or that additional charges be preferred. *See* R.C.M. 306 and 401 concerning other possible dispositions.

---

(3) *Sealed exhibits and proceedings.* If the report of preliminary hearing contains exhibits, proceedings, or other matters ordered sealed by the preliminary hearing officer in accordance with R.C.M. 1103A, counsel for the government shall cause such materials to be sealed so as to prevent unauthorized viewing or disclosure.

(4) *Distribution of the report.* The preliminary

hearing officer shall cause the report to be delivered to the convening authority who directed the preliminary hearing. That convening authority shall promptly cause a copy of the report to be delivered to each accused.

(5) *Objections.* Any objection to the report shall be made to the convening authority who directed the preliminary hearing, via the preliminary hearing officer. Upon receipt of the report, the accused has 5 days to submit objections to the preliminary hearing officer. The preliminary hearing officer will forward the objections to the convening authority as soon as practicable. This subsection does not prohibit a convening authority from referring the charge(s) or taking other action within the 5-day period.

(k) *Waiver.* The accused may waive a preliminary hearing under this rule. However, the convening authority authorized to direct the preliminary hearing may direct that it be conducted notwithstanding the waiver. Failure to make a timely objection under this rule, including an objection to the report, shall constitute waiver of the objection. Relief from the waiver may be granted by the convening authority who directed the preliminary hearing, a superior convening authority, or the military judge, as appropriate, for good cause shown.

Discussion

See also R.C.M. 905(b)(1); 906(b)(3).

The convening authority who receives an objection may direct that the preliminary hearing be reopened or take other action, as appropriate.

Rule 406. Pretrial advice

(a) *In general.* Before any charge may be referred for trial by a general court-martial, it shall be referred to the staff judge advocate of the convening authority for consideration and advice.

Discussion

A pretrial advice need not be prepared in cases referred to special or summary courts-martial. A convening authority may, however, seek the advice of a lawyer before referring charges to such a court-martial. When charges have been withdrawn from a general court-martial (*see* R.C.M. 604) or when a mistrial has been declared in a general court-martial (*see* R.C.M. 915), supplementary advice is necessary before the charges may be referred to another general court-martial.

The staff judge advocate may make changes in the charges

and specifications in accordance with R.C.M. 603.

(b) *Contents.* The advice of the staff judge advocate shall include a written and signed statement which sets forth that person's:

(1) Conclusion with respect to whether each specification alleges an offense under the code;

(2) Conclusion with respect to whether the allegation of each offense is warranted by the evidence indicated in the report of preliminary hearing (if there is such a report);

(3) Conclusion with respect to whether a court-martial would have jurisdiction over the accused and the offense; and

(4) Recommendation of the action to be taken by the convening authority.

Discussion

The staff judge advocate is personally responsible for the pretrial advice and must make an independent and informed appraisal of the charges and evidence in order to render the advice. Another person may prepare the advice, but the staff judge advocate is, unless disqualified, responsible for it and must sign it personally. Grounds for disqualification in a case include previous action in that case as preliminary hearing officer, military judge, trial counsel, defense counsel, or member.

The advice need not set forth the underlying analysis or rationale for its conclusions. Ordinarily, the charge sheet, forwarding letter, endorsements, and report of investigation are forwarded with the pretrial advice. In addition, the pretrial advice should include when appropriate: a brief summary of the evidence; discussion of significant aggravating, extenuating, or mitigating factors; any recommendations for disposition of the case by commanders or others who have forwarded the charges; and the recommendation of the Article 32 preliminary hearing officer. However, there is no legal requirement to include such information, and failure to do so is not error.

Whatever matters are included in the advice, whether or not they are required, should be accurate. Information which is incorrect or so incomplete as to be misleading may result in a determination that the advice is defective, necessitating appropriate relief. *See* R.C.M. 905(b)(1); 906(b)(3).

The standard of proof to be applied in R.C.M. 406(b)(2) is probable cause. *See* R.C.M. 601(d)(1). Defects in the pretrial advice are not jurisdictional and are raised by pretrial motion. *See* R.C.M.905(b)(1) and its Discussion.

(c) *Distribution.* A copy of the advice of the staff judge advocate shall be provided to the defense if charges are referred to trial by general court-martial.

Rule 407. Action by commander exercising general court-martial jurisdiction

(a) *Disposition.* When in receipt of charges, a commander exercising general court-martial jurisdiction may:

(1) Dismiss any charges;

Discussion

See R.C.M. 401(c)(1) concerning dismissal of charges and the effect of dismissing charges.

(2) Forward charges (or, after dismissing charges, the matter) to a subordinate commander for disposition;

Discussion

See R.C.M. 401(c)(2)(B) concerning forwarding charges to a subordinate.

A subordinate commander may not be required to take any specific action or to dispose of charges. *See* R.C.M. 104. *See also* paragraph 1d(2) of Part V. When appropriate, charges may be sent or returned to a subordinate commander for compliance with procedural requirements. *See*, for example, R.C.M. 303 (preliminary inquiry); R.C.M. 308 (notification to accused of charges).

(3) Forward any charges to a superior commander for disposition;

Discussion

See R.C.M. 401 (c)(2)(A) for guidance concerning forwarding charges to a superior.

(4) Refer charges to a summary court-martial or a special court-martial for trial;

Discussion

See R.C.M. 601; 1302(c).

(5) Unless otherwise prescribed by the Secretary concerned, direct a preliminary hearing under R.C.M. 405, after which additional action under this rule may be taken;

Discussion

A preliminary hearing should be directed when it appears the charges are of such a serious nature that trial by general court-martial may be warranted. *See* R.C.M. 405. If a preliminary hearing of the subject has already been conducted, see R.C.M. 405(b).

(6) Subject to R.C.M. 601(d), refer charges to a general court-martial.

Discussion

See Article 22 and R.C.M. 504(b)(1) concerning who may exercise general court-martial jurisdiction.

See R.C.M. 601 concerning referral of charges. *See* R.C.M. 306 and 401 concerning other dispositions.

(b) *National security matters.* When in receipt of charges the trial of which the commander exercising general court-martial jurisdiction finds would probably be inimical to the prosecution of a war or harmful to national security, that commander, unless otherwise prescribed by regulations of the Secretary concerned, shall determine whether trial is warranted and, if so, whether the security considerations involved are paramount to trial. As the commander finds appropriate, the commander may dismiss the charges, authorize trial of them, or forward them to a superior authority.

Discussion

In time of war, charges may be forwarded to the Secretary concerned for disposition under Article 43(e). Under Article 43(e), the Secretary may take action suspending the statute of limitations in time of war.

CHAPTER V. COURT-MARTIAL COMPOSITION AND PERSONNEL; CONVENING COURTS-MARTIAL

Rule 501. Composition and personnel of courts-martial

(a) *Composition of courts-martial.*

(1) *General courts-martial.*

(A) Except in capital cases, general courts-martial shall consist of a military judge and not less than five members, or of the military judge alone if requested and approved under R.C.M. 903.

(B) In all capital cases, general courts-martial shall consist of a military judge and no fewer than 12 members, unless 12 members are not reasonably available because of physical conditions or military exigencies. If 12 members are not reasonably available, the convening authority shall detail the next lesser number of reasonably available members under 12, but in no event fewer than five. In such a case, the convening authority shall state in the convening order the reasons why 12 members are not reasonably available.

(2) *Special courts-martial.* Special courts-martial shall consist of:

(A) Not less than three members;

(B) A military judge and not less than three members; or

(C) A military judge alone if a military judge is detailed and if requested and approved under R.C.M. 903.

Discussion

See R.C.M. 1301(a) concerning composition of summary courts-martial.

(b) *Counsel in general and special courts-martial.* Military trial and defense counsel shall be detailed to general and special courts-martial. Assistant trial and associate or assistant defense counsel may be detailed.

(c) *Other personnel.* Other personnel, such as reporters, interpreters, bailiffs, clerks, escorts, and orderlies, may be detailed or employed as appropriate but need not be detailed by the convening authority personally.

Discussion

The convening authority may direct that a reporter not be used in special courts-martial. Regulations of the Secretary concerned may also require or restrict the use of reporters in special courts-martial.

Rule 502. Qualifications and duties of personnel of courts-martial

(a) *Members.*

(1) *Qualifications.* The members detailed to a court-martial shall be those persons who in the opinion of the convening authority are best qualified for the duty by reason of their age, education, training, experience, length of service, and judicial temperament. Each member shall be on active duty with the armed forces and shall be:

(A) A commissioned officer;

(B) A warrant officer, except when the accused is a commissioned officer; or

(C) An enlisted person if the accused is an enlisted person and has made a timely request under R.C.M. 503(a)(2).

Discussion

Retired members of any Regular component and members of Reserve components of the armed forces are eligible to serve as members if they are on active duty.

Members of the National Oceanic and Atmospheric Administration and of the Public Health Service are eligible to serve as members when assigned to and serving with an armed force. The Public Health Service includes both commissioned and warrant officers. The National Oceanic and Atmospheric Administration includes only commissioned officers.

---

(2) *Duties.* The members of a court-martial shall determine whether the accused is proved guilty and, if necessary, adjudge a proper sentence, based on the evidence and in accordance with the instructions of the military judge. Each member has an equal voice and vote with other members in deliberating upon and deciding all matters submitted to them, except as otherwise specifically provided in these rules. No member may use rank or position to influence another member. No member of a court-martial may have access to or use in any open or closed session this Manual, reports of decided cases, or any other reference material, except the president of a special

court-martial without a military judge may use such materials in open session.

Discussion

Members should avoid any conduct or communication with the military judge, witnesses, or other trial personnel during the trial which might present an appearance of partiality. Except as provided in these rules, members should not discuss any part of a case with anyone until the matter is submitted to them for determination. Members should not on their own visit or conduct a view of the scene of the crime and should not investigate or gather evidence of the offense. Members should not form an opinion on any matter in connection with a case until that matter has been submitted to them for determination.

(b) *President.*

(1) *Qualifications.* The president of a court-martial shall be the detailed member senior in rank then serving.

(2) *Duties.* The president shall have the same duties as the other members and shall also:

(A) Preside over closed sessions of the members of the court-martial during their deliberations;

(B) Speak for the members of the court-martial when announcing the decision of the members or requesting instructions from the military judge; and

(C) In a special court-martial without a military judge, perform the duties assigned by this Manual to the military judge except as otherwise expressly provided.

(c) *Qualifications of military judge.* A military judge shall be a commissioned officer of the armed forces who is a member of the bar of a Federal court or a member of the bar of the highest court of a State and who is certified to be qualified for duty as a military judge by the Judge Advocate General of the armed force of which such military judge is a member. In addition, the military judge of a general court-martial shall be designated for such duties by the Judge Advocate General or the Judge Advocate General's designee, certified to be qualified for duty as a military judge of a general court-martial, and assigned and directly responsible to the Judge Advocate General or the Judge Advocate General's designee. The Secretary concerned may prescribe additional qualifications for military judges in special courts-martial. As used in this subsection "military judge" does not include the president of a special court-martial without a military judge.

Discussion

See R.C.M. 801 for description of some of the general duties of the military judge.

Military judges assigned as general court-martial judges may perform duties in addition to the primary duty of judge of a general court-martial only when such duties are assigned or approved by the Judge Advocate General, or a designee, of the service of which the military judge is a member. Similar restrictions on other duties which a military judge in special courts-martial may perform may be prescribed in regulations of the Secretary concerned.

(d) *Counsel.*

(1) *Certified counsel required.* Only persons certified under Article 27(b) as competent to perform duties as counsel in courts-martial by the Judge Advocate General of the armed force of which the counsel is a member may be detailed as defense counsel or associate defense counsel in general or special courts-martial or as trial counsel in general courts-martial.

Discussion

To be certified by the Judge Advocate General concerned under Article 27(b), a person must be a member of the bar of a Federal court or the highest court of a State. The Judge Advocate General concerned may establish additional requirements for certification.

When the accused has individual military or civilian defense counsel, the detailed counsel is "associate counsel" unless excused from the case. *See* R.C.M. 506(b)(3).

---

(2) *Other military counsel.* Any commissioned officer may be detailed as trial counsel in special courts-martial, or as assistant trial counsel or assistant defense counsel in general or special courts-martial. The Secretary concerned may establish additional qualifications for such counsel.

(3) *Qualifications of individual military and civilian defense counsel.* Individual military or civilian defense counsel who represents an accused in a court-martial shall be:

(A) A member of the bar of a Federal court or of the bar of the highest court of a State; or

(B) If not a member of such a bar, a lawyer who is authorized by a recognized licensing authority to practice law and is found by the military judge to be qualified to represent the accused upon a showing to the satisfaction of the military judge that the counsel has appropriate training and familiarity with the general principles of criminal law which apply in a court-martial.

Discussion

In making such a determination—particularly in the case of civilian defense counsel who are members only of a foreign bar—the military judge also should inquire into:

(i) the availability of the counsel at times at which sessions of the court-martial have been scheduled;

(ii) whether the accused wants the counsel to appear with military defense counsel;

(iii) the familiarity of the counsel with spoken English;

(iv) practical alternatives for discipline of the counsel in the event of misconduct;

(v) whether foreign witnesses are expected to testify with whom the counsel may more readily communicate than might military counsel; and

(vi) whether ethnic or other similarity between the accused and the counsel may facilitate communication and confidence between the accused and civilian defense counsel.

---

(4) *Disqualifications.* No person shall act as trial counsel or assistant trial counsel or, except when expressly requested by the accused, as defense counsel or associate or assistant defense counsel in any case in which that person is or has been:

(A) The accuser;

(B) An investigating or preliminary hearing officer;

(C) A military judge; or

(D) A member.

No person who has acted as counsel for a party may serve as counsel for an opposing party in the same case.

Discussion

In the absence of evidence to the contrary, it is presumed that a person who, between referral and trial of a case, has been detailed as counsel for any party to the court-martial to which the case has been referred, has acted in that capacity.

---

(5) *Duties of trial and assistant trial counsel.* The trial counsel shall prosecute cases on behalf of the United States and shall cause the record of trial of such cases to be prepared. Under the supervision of trial counsel an assistant trial counsel may perform any act or duty which trial counsel may perform under law, regulation, or custom of the service.

Discussion

(A) *General duties before trial.* Immediately upon receipt of referred charges, trial counsel should cause a copy of the charges to be served upon accused. *See* R.C.M. 602.

Trial counsel should: examine the charge sheet and allied papers for completeness and correctness; correct (and initial) minor errors or obvious mistakes in the charges but may not without authority make any substantial changes (*see* R.C.M. 603); and assure that the information about the accused on the charge sheet and any evidence of previous convictions are accurate.

(B) *Relationship with convening authority.* Trial counsel should: report to the convening authority any substantial irregularity in the convening orders, charges, or allied papers; report an actual or anticipated reduction of the number of members below quorum to the convening authority; bring to the attention of the convening authority any case in which trial counsel finds trial inadvisable for lack of evidence or other reasons.

(C) *Relations with the accused and defense counsel.* Trial counsel must communicate with a represented accused only through the accused's defense counsel. However, *see* R.C.M. 602. Trial counsel may not attempt to induce an accused to plead guilty or surrender other important rights.

(D) *Preparation for trial.* Trial counsel should: ensure that a suitable room, a reporter (if authorized), and necessary equipment and supplies are provided for the court-martial; obtain copies of the charges and specifications and convening orders for each member and all personnel of the court-martial; give timely notice to the members, other parties, other personnel of the court-martial, and witnesses for the prosecution and (if known) defense of the date, time, place, and uniform of the meetings of the court-martial; ensure that any person having custody of the accused is also informed; comply with applicable discovery rules (*see* R.C.M. 701); prepare to make a prompt, full, and orderly presentation of the evidence at trial; consider the elements of proof of each offense charged, the burden of proof of guilt and the burdens of proof on motions which may be anticipated, and the Military Rules of Evidence; secure for use at trial such legal texts as may be available and necessary to sustain the prosecution's contentions; arrange for the presence of witnesses and evidence in accordance with R.C.M. 703; prepare to make an opening statement of the prosecution's case (*see* R.C.M. 913); prepare to conduct the examination and cross-examination of witnesses; and prepare to make final argument on the findings and, if necessary, on sentencing (*see* R.C.M. 919; 1001(g)).

(E) *Trial.* Trial counsel should bring to the attention of the military judge any substantial irregularity in the proceedings. Trial counsel should not allude to or disclose to the members any evidence not yet admitted or reasonably expected to be admitted in evidence or intimate, transmit, or purport to transmit to the military judge or members the views of the convening authority or others as to the guilt or innocence of the accused, an appropriate sentence, or any other matter within the discretion of the court-martial.

(F) *Post-trial duties.* Trial counsel must promptly provide written notice of the findings and sentence adjudged to the convening authority or a designee, the accused's immediate commander, and (if applicable) the officer in charge of the confinement facility (*see* R.C.M. 1101(a)), and supervise the preparation, authentication, and distribution of copies of the record as required by these rules and regulations of the Secretary concerned (*see* R.C.M. 1103; 1104).

(G) *Assistant trial counsel.* An assistant trial counsel may act in that capacity only under the supervision of the detailed trial counsel. Responsibility for trial of a case may not devolve to an assistant not qualified to serve as trial counsel. Unless the contrary appears, all acts of an assistant trial counsel are presumed to have been done by the direction of the trial counsel. An assistant trial counsel may not act in the absence of trial counsel at trial in a general court-martial unless the assistant has the qualifications required of a trial counsel. *See* R.C.M. 805(c).

---

(6) *Duties of defense and associate or assistant defense counsel.* Defense counsel shall represent the accused in matters under the code and these rules arising from the offenses of which the accused is then suspected or charged. Under the supervision of the defense counsel an associate or assistant defense counsel may perform any act or duty which a defense counsel may perform under law, regulation, or custom of the service.

Discussion

(A) *Initial advice by military defense counsel.* Defense counsel should promptly explain to the accused the general duties of the defense counsel and inform the accused of the rights to request individual military counsel of the accused's own selection, and of the effect of such a request, and to retain civilian counsel. If the accused wants to request individual military counsel, the defense counsel should immediately inform the convening authority through trial counsel and, if the request is approved, serve as associate counsel if the accused requests and the convening authority permits. Unless the accused directs otherwise, military counsel will begin preparation of the defense immediately after being detailed without waiting for approval of a request for individual military counsel or retention of civilian counsel. *See* R.C.M. 506.

(B) *General duties of defense counsel.* Defense counsel must: guard the interests of the accused zealously within the bounds of the law without regard to personal opinion as to the guilt of the accused; disclose to the accused any interest defense counsel may have in connection with the case, any disqualification, and any other matter which might influence the accused in the selection of counsel; represent the accused with undivided fidelity and may not disclose the accused's secrets or confidences except as the accused may authorize (*see also* Mil. R. Evid. 502). A defense counsel designated to represent two or more co-accused in a joint or common trial or in allied cases must be particularly alert to conflicting interests of those accused. Defense counsel should bring such matters to the attention of the military judge so that the accused's understanding and choice may be made a matter of record. *See* R.C.M. 901(d)(4)(D).

Defense counsel must explain to the accused: the elections available as to composition of the court-martial and assist the accused to make any request necessary to effect the election (*see* R.C.M. 903); the right to plead guilty or not guilty and the meaning and effect of a plea of guilty; the rights to introduce evidence, to testify or remain silent, and to assert any available defense; and the rights to present evidence during sentencing and the rights of the accused to testify under oath, make an unsworn statement, and have counsel make a statement on behalf of the accused. These explanations must be made regardless of the intentions of the accused as to testifying and pleading.

Defense counsel should try to obtain complete knowledge of the facts of the case before advising the accused, and should give the accused a candid opinion of the merits of the case.

(C) *Preparation for trial.* Defense counsel may have the assistance of trial counsel in obtaining the presence of witnesses and evidence for the defense. *See* R.C.M. 703.

Defense counsel should consider the elements of proof of the offenses alleged and the pertinent rules of evidence to ensure that evidence that the defense plans to introduce is admissible and to be prepared to object to inadmissible evidence offered by the prosecution.

Defense counsel should: prepare to make an opening statement of the defense case (*see* R.C.M. 913(b)); and prepare to examine and cross-examine witnesses, and to make final argument on the findings and, if necessary, on sentencing (*see* R.C.M. 919; 1001(g)).

(D) *Trial.* Defense counsel should represent and protect the interests of the accused at trial.

When a trial proceeds in the absence of the accused, defense counsel must continue to represent the accused.

(E) *Post-trial duties.*

(i) *Deferment of confinement.* If the accused is sentenced to confinement, the defense counsel must explain to the accused the right to request the convening authority to defer service of the sentence to confinement and assist the accused in making such a request if the accused chooses to make one. *See* R.C.M. 1101(c).

(ii) *Examination of the record; appellate brief.* The defense counsel should in any case examine the record for accuracy and note any errors in it. This notice may be forwarded for attachment to the record. *See* R.C.M. 1103(b)(3)(C). *See* also R.C.M. 1103(i)(1)(B).

(iii) *Submission of matters.* If the accused is convicted, the defense counsel may submit to the convening authority matters for the latter's consideration in deciding whether to approve the sentence or to disapprove any findings. *See* R.C.M. 1105. Defense counsel should discuss with the accused the right to submit matters to the convening authority and the powers of the convening authority in taking action on the case. Defense counsel may also submit a brief of any matters counsel believes should be considered on further review.

(iv) *Appellate rights.* Defense counsel must explain to the accused the rights to appellate review that apply in the case, and advise the accused concerning the exercise of those rights. If the case is subject to review by the Court of Criminal Appeals, defense counsel should explain the powers of that court and advise the accused of the right to be represented by counsel before it. *See* R.C.M. 1202 and 1203. Defense counsel should also explain the possibility of further review by the Court of Appeals for the Armed Forces and the Supreme Court. *See* R.C.M. 1204 and 1205. If the case may be examined in the office of the Judge Advocate General under Article 69(a), defense counsel should explain the nature of such review to the accused. *See* R.C.M. 1201(b)(1). Defense counsel must explain the consequences of waiver of appellate review, when applicable, and, if the accused elects to waive appellate review, defense counsel will assist in preparing the waiver. *See* R.C.M. 1110. If the accused waives appellate review, or if it is not available, defense counsel should explain that the case will be reviewed by a judge advocate and should submit any appropriate matters for consideration by the judge advocate. *See* R.C.M. 1112. The accused should be advised of the right to apply to the Judge Advocate General for relief under Article 69(b) when such review is available. *See* R.C.M. 1201(b)(3).

(v) *Examination of post-trial recommendation.* When the post-trial recommendation is served on defense counsel, defense counsel should examine it and reply promptly in writing, noting any errors or omissions. Failure to note defects in the recommendation waives them. *See* R.C.M. 1106(f).

(F) *Associate or assistant defense counsel.* Associate or assistant counsel may act in that capacity only under the supervision and by the general direction of the defense counsel. A detailed defense counsel becomes associate defense counsel when the accused has individual military or civilian counsel and detailed counsel is not excused. Although associate counsel acts under the general supervision of the defense counsel, associate defense counsel may act without such supervision when circumstances require. *See,* for example, R.C.M. 805(c). An assistant defense counsel may do this only if such counsel has the qualifications to act as defense counsel. Responsibility for trial of a case may not devolve upon an assistant who is not qualified to serve as defense counsel. An assistant defense counsel may not act in the absence of the defense counsel at trial unless the assistant has the qualifications required of a defense counsel. *See also* R.C.M. 805. Unless the contrary appears, all acts of an assistant or associate defense counsel are presumed to have been done under the supervision of the defense counsel.

(e) *Interpreters, reporters, escorts, bailiffs, clerks, and guards.*

(1) *Qualifications.* The qualifications of interpreters and reporters may be prescribed by the Secretary concerned. Any person who is not disqualified under subsection (e)(2) of this rule may serve as escort, bailiff, clerk, or orderly, subject to removal by the military judge.

(2) *Disqualifications.* In addition to any disqualifications which may be prescribed by the Secretary concerned, no person shall act as interpreter, reporter, escort, bailiff, clerk, or orderly in any case in which that person is or has been in the same case:

(A) The accuser;

(B) A witness;

(C) An investigating or preliminary hearing officer;

(D) Counsel for any party; or

(E) A member of the court-martial or of any earlier court-martial of which the trial is a rehearing or new or other trial.

(3) *Duties.* In addition to such other duties as the Secretary concerned may prescribe, the following persons may perform the following duties.

(A) *Interpreters.* Interpreters shall interpret for the court-martial or for an accused who does not speak or understand English.

Discussion

The accused also may retain an unofficial interpreter without expense to the United States.

(B) *Reporters.* Reporters shall record the proceedings and testimony and shall transcribe them so as to comply with the requirements for the record of trial as prescribed in these rules.

(C) *Others.* Other personnel detailed for the assistance of the court-martial shall have such duties as may be imposed by the military judge.

(4) *Payment of reporters, interpreters.* The Secretary concerned may prescribe regulations for the payment of allowances, expenses, per diem, and compensation of reporters and interpreters.

Discussion

See R.C.M. 807 regarding oaths for reporters, interpreters, and escorts.

(f) *Action upon discovery of disqualification or lack of qualifications.* Any person who discovers that a person detailed to a court-martial is disqualified or lacks the qualifications specified by this rule shall cause a report of the matter to be made before the court-martial is first in session to the convening authority or, if discovered later, to the military judge.

Rule 503. Detailing members, military judge, and counsel

(a) *Members.*

(1) *In general.* The convening authority shall detail qualified persons as members for courts-martial.

Discussion

The following persons are subject to challenge under R.C.M. 912(f) and should not be detailed as members: any person who is, in the same case, an accuser, witness, preliminary hearing officer, or counsel for any party; any person who, in the case of a new trial, other trial, or rehearing, was a member of any court-martial which previously heard the case; any person who is junior to the accused, unless this is unavoidable; an enlisted member from the same unit as the accused; or any person who is in arrest or confinement.

(2) *Enlisted members.* An enlisted accused may, before assembly, request orally on the record or in writing that enlisted persons serve as members of the general or special court-martial to which that accused's case has been or will be referred. If such a request is made, an enlisted accused may not be tried by a court-martial the membership of which does not include enlisted members in a number comprising at least one-third of the total number of members unless eligible enlisted members cannot be obtained because of physical conditions or military exigencies. If the appropriate number of enlisted members cannot be obtained, the court-martial may be assembled, and the trial may proceed without them, but the convening authority shall make a detailed written explanation why enlisted members could not be obtained which must be appended to the record of trial.

Discussion

When such a request is made, the convening authority should:

(1) Detail an appropriate number of enlisted members to the court-martial and, if appropriate, relieve an appropriate number of commissioned or warrant officers previously detailed;

(2) Withdraw the charges from the court-martial to which they were originally referred and refer them to a court-martial which includes the proper proportion of enlisted members; or

(3) Advise the court-martial before which the charges are then pending to proceed in the absence of enlisted members if eligible enlisted members cannot be detailed because of physical conditions or military exigencies.

See also R.C.M. 1103(b)(2)(D)(iii).

(3) *Members from another command or armed force.* A convening authority may detail as members of general and special courts-martial persons under that convening authority's command or made available by their commander, even if those persons are members of an armed force different from that of the convening authority or accused.

Discussion

Concurrence of the proper commander may be oral and need not be shown by the record of trial.

Members should ordinarily be of the same armed force as the accused. When a court-martial composed of members of different armed forces is selected, at least a majority of the members should be of the same armed force as the accused unless exigent circumstances make it impractical to do so without manifest injury to the service.

(b) *Military judge.*

(1) *By whom detailed.* The military judge shall be detailed, in accordance with regulations of the Secretary concerned, by a person assigned as a military judge and directly responsible to the Judge Advocate General or the Judge Advocate General's designee. The authority to detail military judges may be delegated to persons assigned as military judges. If authority to detail military judges has been delegated to a military judge, that military judge may detail himself or herself as military judge for a court-martial.

(2) *Record of detail.* The order detailing a military judge shall be reduced to writing and included in the record of trial or announced orally on the record at the court-martial. The writing or announcement shall indicate by whom the military judge was detailed. The Secretary concerned may require that the order be reduced to writing.

(3) *Military judge from a different armed force.* A military judge from one armed force may be detailed to a court-martial convened in a different armed force, a combatant command or joint command when permitted by the Judge Advocate General of the armed force of which the military judge is a member. The Judge Advocate General may delegate authority to make military judges available for this purpose.

(c) *Counsel.*

(1) *By whom detailed.* Trial and defense counsel, assistant trial and defense counsel, and associate defense counsel shall be detailed in accordance with regulations of the Secretary concerned. If authority to detail counsel has been delegated to a person, that person may detail himself or herself as counsel for a court-martial.

(2) *Record of detail.* The order detailing a counsel shall be reduced to writing and included in the record of trial or announced orally on the record at the court-martial. The writing or announcement shall indicate by whom the counsel was detailed. The Secretary concerned may require that the order be reduced to writing.

(3) *Counsel from a different armed force.* A person from one armed force may be detailed to serve as counsel in a court-martial in a different armed

force, a combatant command or joint command when permitted by the Judge Advocate General of the armed force of which the counsel is a member. The Judge Advocate General may delegate authority to make persons available for this purpose.

Rule 504. Convening courts-martial

(a) *In general.* A court-martial is created by a convening order of the convening authority.

(b) *Who may convene courts-martial.*

(1) *General courts-martial.* Unless otherwise limited by superior competent authority, general courts-martial may be convened by persons occupying positions designated in Article 22(a) and by any commander designated by the Secretary concerned or empowered by the President.

Discussion

The authority to convene courts-martial is independent of rank and is retained as long as the convening authority remains a commander in one of the designated positions. The rule by which command devolves are found in regulations of the Secretary concerned.

(2) *Special courts-martial.* Unless otherwise limited by superior competent authority, special courts-martial may be convened by persons occupying positions designated in Article 23(a) and by commanders designated by the Secretary concerned.

Discussion

See the discussion of subsection (b)(1) of this rule. Persons authorized to convene general courts-martial may also convene special courts-martial.

(A) *Definition.* For purposes of Articles 23 and 24, a command or unit is "separate or detached" when isolated or removed from the immediate disciplinary control of a superior in such manner as to make its commander the person held by superior commanders primarily responsible for discipline. "Separate or detached" is used in a disciplinary sense and not necessarily in a tactical or physical sense. A subordinate joint command or joint task force is ordinarily considered to be "separate or detached."

Discussion

The power of a commander of a separate or detached unit to

convene courts-martial, like that of any other commander, may be limited by superior competent authority.

(B) *Determination.* If a commander is in doubt whether the command is separate or detached, the matter shall be determined:

(i) In the Army or the Air Force, by the officer exercising general court-martial jurisdiction over the command; or

(ii) In the Naval Service or Coast Guard, by the flag or general officer in command or the senior officer present who designated the detachment; or

(iii) In a combatant command or joint command, by the officer exercising general court-martial jurisdiction over the command.

(3) *Summary courts-martial. See* R.C.M. 1302(a).

Discussion

See the discussion under subsection (b)(1) of this rule.

(4) *Delegation prohibited.* The power to convene courts-martial may not be delegated.

(c) *Disqualification.*

(1) *Accuser.* An accuser may not convene a general or special court-martial for the trial of the person accused.

Discussion

See also Article 1(9); 307(a); 601(c). However, *see* R.C.M. 1302(b) (accuser may convene a summary court-martial).

(2) *Other.* A convening authority junior in rank to an accuser may not convene a general or special court-martial for the trial of the accused unless that convening authority is superior in command to the accuser. A convening authority junior in command to an accuser may not convene a general or special court-martial for the trial of the accused.

(3) *Action when disqualified.* When a commander who would otherwise convene a general or special court-martial is disqualified in a case, the charges shall be forwarded to a superior competent authority for disposition. That authority may personally dispose of the charges or forward the charges to another convening authority who is superior in rank to the accuser, or, if in the same chain of command, who is superior in command to the accuser.

Discussion

See also R.C.M. 401(c).

(d) *Convening orders.*

(1) *General and special courts-martial.* A convening order for a general or special court-martial shall designate the type of court-martial and detail the members and may designate where the court-martial will meet. If the convening authority has been designated by the Secretary concerned, the convening order shall so state.

Discussion

See Appendix 6 for a suggested format for a convening order.

---

(2) *Summary courts-martial.* A convening order for a summary court-martial shall designate that it is a summary court-martial and detail the summary court-martial, and may designate where the court-martial will meet. If the convening authority has been designated by the Secretary concerned, the convening order shall so state.

Discussion

See also R.C.M. 1302(c).

---

(3) *Additional matters.* Additional matters to be included in convening orders may be prescribed by the Secretary concerned.

(e) *Place.* The convening authority shall ensure that an appropriate location and facilities for courts-martial are provided.

Rule 505. Changes of members, military judge, and counsel

(a) *In general.* Subject to this rule, the members, military judge, and counsel may be changed by an authority competent to detail such persons. Members also may be excused as provided in subsections (c)(1)(B)(ii) and (c)(2)(A) of this rule.

Discussion

Changes of the members of the court-martial should be kept to a minimum. If extensive changes are necessary and no session of the court-martial has begun, it may be appropriate to withdraw

the charges from one court-martial and refer them to another. *See* R.C.M. 604.

(b) *Procedure.* When new persons are added as members or counsel or when substitutions are made as to any members or counsel or the military judge, such persons shall be detailed in accordance with R.C.M. 503. An order changing the members of the court-martial, except one which excuses members without replacement, shall be reduced to writing before authentication of the record of trial.

Discussion

When members or counsel have been excused and the excusal is not reduced to writing, the excusal should be announced on the record. A member who has been temporarily excused need not be formally reappointed to the court-martial.

(c) *Changes of members.*

(1) *Before assembly.*

(A) *By convening authority.* Before the court-martial is assembled, the convening authority may change the members of the court-martial without showing cause.

(B) *By convening authority's delegate.*

(i) *Delegation.* The convening authority may delegate, under regulations of the Secretary concerned, authority to excuse individual members to the staff judge advocate or legal officer or other principal assistant to the convening authority.

(ii) *Limitations.* Before the court-martial is assembled, the convening authority's delegate may excuse members without cause shown; however, no more than one-third of the total number of members detailed by the convening authority may be excused by the convening authority's delegate in any one court-martial. After assembly the convening authority's delegate may not excuse members.

(2) *After assembly.*

(A) *Excusal.* After assembly no member may be excused, except:

(i) By the convening authority for good cause shown on the record;

(ii) By the military judge for good cause shown on the record; or

(iii) As a result of challenge under R.C.M. 912.

(B) *New members.* New members may be detailed after assembly only when, as a result of excusals under subsection (c)(2)(A) of this rule, the number of members of the court-martial is reduced below a quorum, or the number of enlisted members, when the accused has made a timely written request for enlisted members, is reduced below one-third of the total membership.

(d) *Changes of detailed counsel.*

(1) *Trial counsel.* An authority competent to detail trial counsel may change the trial counsel and any assistant trial counsel at any time without showing cause.

(2) *Defense counsel.*

(A) *Before formation of attorney-client relationship.* Before an attorney-client relationship has been formed between the accused and detailed defense counsel or associate or assistant defense counsel, an authority competent to detail defense counsel may excuse or change such counsel without showing cause.

(B) *After formation of attorney-client relationship.* After an attorney-client relationship has been formed between the accused and detailed defense counsel or associate or assistant defense counsel, an authority competent to detail such counsel may excuse or change such counsel only:

(i) Under R.C.M. 506(b)(3);

(ii) Upon request of the accused or application for withdrawal by such counsel under R.C.M. 506(c); or

(iii) For other good cause shown on the record.

(e) *Change of military judge.*

(1) *Before assembly.* Before the court-martial is assembled, the military judge may be changed by an authority competent to detail the military judge, without cause shown on the record.

(2) *After assembly.* After the court-martial is assembled, the military judge may be changed by an authority competent to detail the military judge only when, as a result of disqualification under R.C.M. 902 or for good cause shown, the previously detailed military judge is unable to proceed.

(f) *Good cause.* For purposes of this rule, "good cause" includes physical disability, military exigency, and other extraordinary circumstances which render the member, counsel, or military judge unable to proceed with the court-martial within a reasonable

time. "Good cause" does not include temporary inconveniences which are incident to normal conditions of military life.

Rule 506. Accused's rights to counsel

(a) *In general.* The accused has the right to be represented before a general or special court-martial by civilian counsel if provided at no expense to the Government, and either by the military counsel detailed under Article 27 or military counsel of the accused's own selection, if reasonably available. The accused is not entitled to be represented by more than one military counsel.

Discussion

See R.C.M. 502(d)(3) as to qualifications of civilian counsel or individual military counsel.

(b) *Individual military counsel.*

(1) *Reasonably available.* Subject to this subsection, the Secretary concerned shall define "reasonably available." While so assigned, the following persons are not reasonably available to serve as individual military counsel because of the nature of their duties or positions:

(A) A general or flag officer;

(B) A trial or appellate military judge;

(C) A trial counsel;

(D) An appellate defense or government counsel;

(E) A principal legal advisor to a command, organization, or agency and, when such command, organization, or agency has general court-martial jurisdiction, the principal assistant of such an advisor;

(F) An instructor or student at a service school or academy:

(G) A student at a college or university;

(H) A member of the staff of the Judge Advocate General of the Army, Navy, or Air Force, the Chief Counsel of the Coast Guard, or the Director, Judge Advocate Division, Headquarters, Marine Corps.

The Secretary concerned may determine other persons to be not reasonably available because of the nature or responsibilities of their assignments, geographic considerations, exigent circumstances, or military necessity. A person who is a member of an armed force different from that of which the accused is a member shall be reasonably available to serve as individual military counsel for such accused to the same extent as that person is available to serve as individual military counsel for an accused in the same armed force as the person requested. The Secretary concerned may prescribe circumstances under which exceptions may be made to the prohibitions in this subsection when merited by the existence of an attorney-client relationship regarding matters relating to a charge in question. However, if the attorney-client relationship arose solely because the counsel represented the accused on review under Article 70, this exception shall not apply.

(2) *Procedure.* Subject to this subsection, the Secretary concerned shall prescribe procedures for determining whether a requested person is "reasonably available" to act as individual military counsel. Requests for an individual military counsel shall be made by the accused or the detailed defense counsel through the trial counsel to the convening authority. If the requested person is among those not reasonably available under subsection (b)(1) of this rule or under regulations of the Secretary concerned, the convening authority shall deny the request and notify the accused, unless the accused asserts that there is an existing attorney-client relationship regarding a charge in question or that the person requested will not, at the time of the trial or preliminary hearing for which requested, be among those so listed as not reasonably available. If the accused's request makes such a claim, or if the person is not among those so listed as not reasonably available, the convening authority shall forward the request to the commander or head of the organization, activity, or agency to which the requested person is assigned. That authority shall make an administrative determination whether the requested person is reasonably available in accordance with the procedure prescribed by the Secretary concerned. This determination is a matter within the sole discretion of that authority. An adverse determination may be reviewed upon request of the accused through that authority to the next higher commander or level of supervision, but no administrative review may be made which requires action at the departmental or higher level.

(3) *Excusal of detailed counsel.* If the accused is represented by individual military counsel, detailed defense counsel shall normally be excused. The au-

thority who detailed the defense counsel, as a matter of discretion, may approve a request from the accused that detailed defense counsel shall act as associate counsel. The action of the authority who detailed the counsel is subject to review only for abuse of discretion.

Discussion

A request under subsection (b)(3) should be considered in light of the general statutory policy that the accused is not entitled to be represented by more than one military counsel. Among the factors that may be considered in the exercise of discretion are the seriousness of the case, retention of civilian defense counsel, complexity of legal or factual issues, and the detail of additional trial counsel.

See R.C.M. 905(b)(6) and 906(b)(2) as to motions concerning denial of a request for individual military counsel or retention of detailed counsel as associate counsel.

(c) *Excusal or withdrawal.* Except as otherwise provided in R.C.M. 505(d)(2) and subsection (b)(3) of this rule, defense counsel may be excused only with the express consent of the accused, or by the military judge upon application for withdrawal by the defense counsel for good cause shown.

(d) *Waiver.* The accused may expressly waive the right to be represented by counsel and may thereafter conduct the defense personally. Such waiver shall be accepted by the military judge only if the military judge finds that the accused is competent to understand the disadvantages of self-representation and that the waiver is voluntary and understanding. The military judge may require that a defense counsel remain present even if the accused waives counsel and conducts the defense personally. The right of the accused to conduct the defense personally may be revoked if the accused is disruptive or fails to follow basic rules of decorum and procedure.

(e) *Nonlawyer present.* Subject to the discretion of the military judge, the accused may have present and seated at the counsel table for purpose of consultation persons not qualified to serve as counsel under R.C.M. 502.

Discussion

See also Mil. R. Evid. 615 if the person is a potential witness in the case.

CHAPTER VI. REFERRAL, SERVICE, AMENDMENT, AND WITHDRAWAL OF CHARGES

Rule 601. Referral

(a) *In general.* Referral is the order of a convening authority that charges against an accused will be tried by a specified court-martial.

Discussion

Referral of charges requires three elements: a convening authority who is authorized to convene the court-martial and is not disqualified (*see* R.C.M. 601(b) and (c)); preferred charges which have been received by the convening authority for disposition (*see* R.C.M. 307 as to preferral of charges and Chapter IV as to disposition); and a court-martial convened by that convening authority or a predecessor (*see* R.C.M. 504).

If trial would be warranted but would be detrimental to the prosecution of a war or inimical to national security, *see* R.C.M. 401(d) and 407(b).

(b) *Who may refer.* Any convening authority may refer charges to a court-martial convened by that convening authority or a predecessor, unless the power to do so has been withheld by superior competent authority.

Discussion

See R.C.M. 306(a), 403, 404, 407, and 504.

The convening authority may be of any command, including a command different from that of the accused, but as a practical matter the accused must be subject to the orders of the convening authority or otherwise under the convening authority's control to assure the appearance of the accused at trial. The convening authority's power over the accused may be based upon agreements between the commanders concerned.

(c) *Disqualification.* An accuser may not refer charges to a general or special court-martial.

Discussion

Convening authorities are not disqualified from referring charges by prior participation in the same case except when they have acted as accuser. For a definition of "accuser," *see* Article 1(9). A convening authority who is disqualified may forward the charges and allied papers for disposition by competent authority superior in rank or command. *See* R.C.M. 401(c) concerning actions which the superior may take.

See R.C.M. 1302 for rules relating to convening summary courts-martial.

(d) *When charges may be referred.*

(1) *Basis for referral.* If the convening authority finds or is advised by a judge advocate that there are reasonable grounds to believe that an offense triable by a court-martial has been committed and that the accused committed it, and that the specification alleges an offense, the convening authority may refer it. The finding may be based on hearsay in whole or in part. The convening authority or judge advocate may consider information from any source and shall not be limited to the information reviewed by any previous authority, but a case may not be referred to a general court-martial except in compliance with subsection (d)(2) of this rule. The convening authority or judge advocate shall not be required before charges are referred to resolve legal issues, including objections to evidence, which may arise at trial.

Discussion

For a discussion of selection among alternative dispositions, *see* R.C.M. 306. The convening authority is not obliged to refer all charges which the evidence might support. The convening authority should consider the options and considerations under R.C.M. 306 in exercising the discretion to refer.

---

(2) *General courts-martial.* The convening authority may not refer a specification under a charge to a general court-martial unless—

(A) There has been substantial compliance with the preliminary hearing requirements of R.C.M. 405; and

(B) The convening authority has received the advice of the staff judge advocate required under R.C.M. 406. These requirements may be waived by the accused.

Discussion

See R.C.M. 201(f)(2)(C) concerning limitations on referral of capital offenses to special courts-martial. *See* R.C.M. 103(3) for the definition of a capital offense.

See R.C.M. 1301(c) concerning limitations on the referral of certain cases to summary courts-martial.

(e) *How charges shall be referred.*

(1) *Order, instructions.* Referral shall be by the personal order of the convening authority. The con-

vening authority may include proper instructions in the order.

Discussion

Referral is ordinarily evidenced by an indorsement on the charge sheet. Although the indorsement should be completed on all copies of the charge sheet, only the original must be signed. The signature may be that of a person acting by the order or direction of the convening authority. In such a case the signature element must reflect the signer's authority.

If, for any reason, charges are referred to a court-martial different from that to which they were originally referred, the new referral is ordinarily made by a new indorsement attached to the original charge sheet. The previous indorsement should be lined out and initialed by the person signing the new referral. The original indorsement should not be obliterated. *See also* R.C.M. 604.

If the only officer present in a command refers the charges to a summary court-martial and serves as the summary court-martial under R.C.M. 1302, the indorsement should be completed with the additional comments, "only officer present in the command."

The convening authority may instruct that the charges against the accused be tried with certain other charges against the accused. *See* subsection (2) below.

The convening authority may instruct that charges against one accused be referred for joint or common trial with another accused. *See* subsection (3) below.

The convening authority shall indicate that the case is to be tried as a capital case by including a special instruction in the referral block of the charge sheet. Failure to include this special instruction at the time of the referral shall not bar the convening authority from later adding the required special instruction, provided that the convening authority has otherwise complied with the applicable notice requirements. If the accused demonstrates specific prejudice from such failure to include the special instruction, a continuance or a recess is an adequate remedy.

The convening authority should acknowledge by an instruction that a bad-conduct discharge, confinement for more than six months, or forfeiture of pay for more than six months, may not be adjudged when the prerequisites under Article 19 will not be met. *See* R.C.M. 201(f)(2)(B)(ii). For example, this instruction may be given when a court reporter is not detailed.

Any special instructions must be stated in the referral indorsement.

When the charges have been referred to a court-martial, the indorsed charge sheet and allied papers should be promptly transmitted to the trial counsel.

---

(2) *Joinder of offenses.* In the discretion of the convening authority, two or more offenses charged against an accused may be referred to the same court-martial for trial, whether serious or minor offenses or both, regardless whether related. Additional charges may be joined with other charges for a single trial at any time before arraignment if all necessary procedural requirements concerning the additional charges have been complied with. After arraignment of the accused upon charges, no additional charges may be referred to the same trial without consent of the accused.

Discussion

Ordinarily all known charges should be referred to a single court-martial.

---

(3) *Joinder of accused.* Allegations against two or more accused may be referred for joint trial if the accused are alleged to have participated in the same act or transaction or in the same series of acts or transactions constituting an offense or offenses. Such accused may be charged in one or more specifications together or separately, and every accused need not be charged in each specification. Related allegations against two or more accused which may be proved by substantially the same evidence may be referred to a common trial.

Discussion

A joint offense is one committed by two or more persons acting together with a common intent. Joint offenses may be referred for joint trial, along with all related offenses against each of the accused. A common trial may be used when the evidence of several offenses committed by several accused separately is essentially the same, even though the offenses were not jointly committed. *See* R.C.M. 307(c)(5) Discussion. Convening authorities should consider that joint and common trials may be complicated by procedural and evidentiary rules.

(f) *Superior convening authorities.* Except as otherwise provided in these rules, a superior competent authority may cause charges, whether or not referred, to be transmitted to the authority for further consideration, including, if appropriate, referral.

(g) *Parallel convening authorities.* If it is impracticable for the original convening authority to continue exercising authority over the charges, the convening authority may cause the charges, even if referred, to be transmitted to a parallel convening authority. This transmittal must be in writing and in accordance with such regulations as the Secretary concerned may prescribe. Subsequent actions taken by the parallel convening authority are within the sole discretion of that convening authority.

Discussion

Parallel convening authorities are those convening authorities that possess the same court-martial jurisdiction authority. Examples of permissible transmittal of charges under this rule include the transmittal from a general court-martial convening authority to another general court-martial convening authority, or from one special court-martial convening authority to another special court-martial convening authority. It would be impracticable for an original convening authority to continue exercising authority over the charges, for example, when a command is being decommissioned or inactivated, or when deploying or redeploying and the accused is remaining behind. If charges have been referred, there is no requirement that the charges be withdrawn or dismissed prior to transfer. *See* R.C.M. 604. In the event that the case has been referred, the receiving convening authority may adopt the original court-martial convening order, including the court-martial panel selected to hear the case as indicated in that convening order. When charges are transmitted under this rule, no recommendation as to disposition may be made.

Rule 602. Service of charges

The trial counsel detailed to the court-martial to which charges have been referred for trial shall cause to be served upon each accused a copy of the charge sheet. In time of peace, no person may, over objection, be brought to trial—including an Article 39(a) session—before a general court-martial within a period of five days after service of charges, or before a special court-martial within a period of three days after service of charges. In computing these periods, the date of service of charges and the date of trial are excluded; holidays and Sundays are included.

Discussion

Trial counsel should comply with this rule immediately upon receipt of the charges. Whenever after service the charges are amended or changed the trial counsel must give notice of the changes to the defense counsel. Whenever such amendments or changes add a new party, a new offense, or substantially new allegations, the charge sheet so amended or changed must be served anew. *See also* R.C.M. 603.

Service may be made only upon the accused; substitute service upon defense counsel is insufficient. The trial counsel should promptly inform the defense counsel when charges have been served.

If the accused has questions when served with charges, the accused should be told to discuss the matter with defense counsel.

Rule 603. Changes to charges and specifications

(a) *Minor changes defined.* Minor changes in charges and specifications are any except those which add a party, offenses, or substantial matter not fairly included in those previously preferred, or which are likely to mislead the accused as to the offenses charged.

Discussion

Minor changes include those necessary to correct inartfully drafted or redundant specifications; to correct a misnaming of the accused; to allege the proper article; or to correct other slight errors. Minor charges also include those which reduce the seriousness of an offense, as when the value of an allegedly stolen item in a larceny specification is reduced, or when a desertion specification is amended to allege only unauthorized absence.

(b) *Minor changes before arraignment.* Any person forwarding, acting upon, or prosecuting charges on behalf of the United States except a preliminary hearing officer appointed under R.C.M. 405 may make minor changes to charges or specifications before arraignment.

Discussion

Charges forwarded or referred for trial should be free from defects of form and substance. Minor errors may be corrected and the charge may be redrafted without being sworn anew by the accuser. Other changes should be signed and sworn to by an accuser. All changes in the charges should be initialed by the person who makes them. A trial counsel acting under this provision ordinarily should consult with the convening authority before making any changes which, even though minor, change the nature or seriousness of the offense.

(c) *Minor changes after arraignment.* After arraignment the military judge may, upon motion, permit minor changes in the charges and specifications at any time before findings are announced if no substantial right of the accused is prejudiced.

(d) *Major changes.* Changes or amendments to charges or specifications other than minor changes may not be made over the objection of the accused unless the charge or specification affected is preferred anew.

Discussion

If there has been a major change or amendment over the accused's objection to a charge already referred, a new referral is necessary. Similarly, in the case of a general court-martial, a new preliminary hearing under R.C.M. 405 will be necessary if the charge as amended or changed was not covered in the prior preliminary hearing. If the substance of the charge or specification as amended or changed has not been referred or, in the case of a general court-martial, has not been subject to a preliminary hearing, a new referral and, if appropriate, preliminary hearing are necessary. When charges are re-referred, they must be served anew under R.C.M. 602.

Rule 604. Withdrawal of charges

(a) *Withdrawal.* The convening authority or a superior competent authority may for any reason cause any charges or specifications to be withdrawn from a court-martial at any time before findings are announced.

Discussion

Charges which are withdrawn from a court-martial should be dismissed (*see* R.C.M. 401(c)(1)) unless it is intended to refer them anew promptly or to forward them to another authority for disposition.

Charges should not be withdrawn from a court-martial arbitrarily or unfairly to an accused. *See also* subsection (b) of this rule.

Some or all charges and specifications may be withdrawn. In a joint or common trial the withdrawal may be limited to charges against one or some of the accused.

When an alleged offense involves a victim, the victim should, whenever practicable, be provided an opportunity to express views regarding the withdrawal of any charges or specifications in which the victim is named. The convening authority or other individual authorized to act on the charges should consider such views of the victim prior to withdrawing said charges or specifications and should continue to consider the views of the victim until final disposition of the case. A "victim" is an individual who is alleged to have suffered direct physical, emotional, or pecuniary harm as a result of the matters set forth in a charge or specification under consideration and is named in one of the specifications under consideration.

Charges which have been properly referred to a court-martial may be withdrawn only by the direction of the convening authority or a superior competent authority in the exercise of that officer's independent judgment. When directed to do so by the convening authority or a superior competent authority, trial counsel may withdraw charges or specifications by lining out the affected charges or specifications, renumbering remaining charges or specifications as necessary, and initialing the changes. Charges and specifications withdrawn before commencement of trial will not be brought to the attention of the members. When charges or specifications are withdrawn after they have come to the attention of the members, the military judge must instruct them that the withdrawn charges or specifications may not be considered for any reason.

(b) *Referral of withdrawn charges.* Charges which have been withdrawn from a court-martial may be referred to another court-martial unless the withdrawal was for an improper reason. Charges withdrawn after the introduction of evidence on the general issue of guilt may be referred to another court-martial only if the withdrawal was necessitated by urgent and unforeseen military necessity.

Discussion

See also R.C.M. 915 (Mistrial).

When charges which have been withdrawn from a court-martial are referred to another court-martial, the reasons for the withdrawal and later referral should be included in the record of the later court-martial, if the later referral is more onerous to the accused. Therefore, if further prosecution is contemplated at the time of the withdrawal, the reasons for the withdrawal should be included in or attached to the record of the earlier proceeding.

Improper reasons for withdrawal include an intent to interfere with the free exercise by the accused of constitutional rights or rights provided under the code, or with the impartiality of a court-martial. A withdrawal is improper if it was not directed personally and independently by the convening authority or by a superior competent authority.

Whether the reason for a withdrawal is proper, for purposes of the propriety of a later referral, depends in part on the stage in the proceedings at which the withdrawal takes place. Before arraignment, there are many reasons for a withdrawal which will not preclude another referral. These include receipt of additional charges, absence of the accused, reconsideration by the convening authority or by a superior competent authority of the seriousness of the offenses, questions concerning the mental capacity of the accused, and routine duty rotation of the personnel constituting the court-martial. Charges withdrawn after arraignment may be referred to another court-martial under some circumstances. For example, it is permissible to refer charges which were withdrawn pursuant to a pretrial agreement if the accused fails to fulfill the terms of the agreement. *See* R.C.M. 705. Charges withdrawn after some evidence on the general issue of guilty is introduced may be re-referred only under the narrow circumstances described in the rule.

CHAPTER VII. PRETRIAL MATTERS

Rule 701. Discovery

(a) *Disclosure by the trial counsel.* Except as otherwise provided in subsections (f) and (g)(2) of this rule, the trial counsel shall provide the following information or matters to the defense—

(1) *Papers accompanying charges; convening orders; statements.* As soon as practicable after service of charges under R.C.M. 602, the trial counsel shall provide the defense with copies of, or, if extraordinary circumstances make it impracticable to provide copies, permit the defense to inspect:

(A) Any paper which accompanied the charges when they were referred to the court-martial, including papers sent with charges upon a rehearing or new trial;

(B) The convening order and any amending orders; and

(C) Any sworn or signed statement relating to an offense charged in the case which is in the possession of the trial counsel.

(2) *Documents, tangible objects, reports.* After service of charges, upon request of the defense, the Government shall permit the defense to inspect:

(A) Any books, papers, documents, photographs, tangible objects, buildings, or places, or copies of portions thereof, which are within the possession, custody, or control of military authorities, and which are material to the preparation of the defense or are intended for use by the trial counsel as evidence in the prosecution case-in-chief at trial, or were obtained from or belong to the accused; and

(B) Any results or reports of physical or mental examinations, and of scientific tests or experiments, or copies thereof, which are within the possession, custody, or control of military authorities, the existence of which is known or by the exercise of due diligence may become known to the trial counsel, and which are material to the preparation of the defense or are intended for use by the trial counsel as evidence in the prosecution case-in-chief at trial.

Discussion

For specific rules concerning certain mental examinations of the accused or third party patients, *see* R.C.M. 701(f), R.C.M. 706, Mil. R. Evid. 302 and Mil. R. Evid. 513.

---

(3) *Witnesses.* Before the beginning of trial on the merits the trial counsel shall notify the defense of the names and addresses of the witnesses the trial counsel intends to call:

(A) In the prosecution case-in-chief; and

(B) To rebut a defense of alibi, innocent ingestion, or lack of mental responsibility, when trial counsel has received timely notice under subsection (b)(1) or (2) of this rule.

Discussion

Such notice should be in writing except when impracticable.

---

(4) *Prior convictions of accused offered on the merits.* Before arraignment the trial counsel shall notify the defense of any records of prior civilian or court-martial convictions of the accused of which the trial counsel is aware and which the trial counsel may offer on the merits for any purpose, including impeachment, and shall permit the defense to inspect such records when they are in the trial counsel's possession.

(5) *Information to be offered at sentencing.* Upon request of the defense the trial counsel shall:

(A) Permit the defense to inspect such written material as will be presented by the prosecution at the presentencing proceedings; and

(B) Notify the defense of the names and addresses of the witnesses the trial counsel intends to call at the presentencing proceedings under R.C.M. 1001(b).

(6) *Evidence favorable to the defense.* The trial counsel shall, as soon as practicable, disclose to the defense the existence of evidence known to the trial counsel which reasonably tends to:

(A) Negate the guilt of the accused of an offense charged;

(B) Reduce the degree of guilt of the accused of an offense charged; or

(C) Reduce the punishment.

Discussion

In addition to the matters required to be disclosed under subsection (a) of this rule, the Government is required to notify the defense of or provide to the defense certain information under other rules. Mil. R. Evid. 506 covers the disclosure of unclassified information which is under the control of the Government. Mil. R. Evid. 505 covers disclosure of classified information.

Other R.C.M. and Mil. R. Evid. concern disclosure of other specific matters. *See* R.C.M. 308 (identification of accuser), 405 (report of Article 32 preliminary hearing), 706(c)(3)(B) (mental examination of accused), 914 (production of certain statements), and 1004(b)(1) (aggravating circumstances in capital cases); Mil. R. Evid. 301(c)(2) (notice of immunity or leniency to witnesses), 302 (mental examination of accused), 304(d)(1) (statements by accused), 311(d)(1) (evidence seized from accused), 321(c)(1) (evidence based on lineups), 507 (identity of informants), 612 (memoranda used to refresh recollection), and 613(a) (prior inconsistent statements).

Requirements for notice of intent to use certain evidence are found in: Mil. R. Evid. 201A(b) (judicial notice of foreign law), 301(c)(2) (immunized witnesses), 304(d)(2) (notice of intent to use undisclosed confessions), 304(f) (testimony of accused for limited purpose on confession), 311(d)(2)(B) (notice of intent to use undisclosed evidence seized), 311(f) (testimony of accused for limited purpose on seizures), 321(c)(2)(B) (notice of intent to use undisclosed line-up evidence), 321(e) (testimony of accused for limited purpose of line-ups), 412(c)(1) and (2) (intent of defense to use evidence of sexual misconduct by a victim); 505(h) (intent to disclose classified information), 506(h) (intent to disclose privilege government information), and 609(b) (intent to impeach with conviction over 10 years old).

(b) *Disclosure by the defense.* Except as otherwise provided in subsections (f) and (g)(2) of this rule, the defense shall provide the following information to the trial counsel—

(1) *Names of witnesses and statements.*

(A) Before the beginning of trial on the merits, the defense shall notify the trial counsel of the names and addresses of all witnesses, other than the accused, whom the defense intends to call during the defense case in chief, and provide all sworn or signed statements known by the defense to have been made by such witnesses in connection with the case.

(B) Upon request of the trial counsel, the defense shall also

(i) Provide the trial counsel with the names and addresses of any witnesses whom the defense intends to call at the presentencing proceedings under R.C.M. 1001(c); and

(ii) Permit the trial counsel to inspect any written material that will be presented by the defense at the presentencing proceeding.

Discussion

Such notice shall be in writing except when impracticable. *See*

R.C.M. 701(f) for statements that would not be subject to disclosure.

---

(2) *Notice of certain defenses.* The defense shall notify the trial counsel before the beginning of trial on the merits of its intent to offer the defense of alibi, innocent ingestion, or lack of mental responsibility, or its intent to introduce expert testimony as to the accused's mental condition. Such notice by the defense shall disclose, in the case of an alibi defense, the place or places at which the defense claims the accused to have been at the time of the alleged offense, and, in the case of an innocent ingestion defense, the place or places where, and the circumstances under which the defense claims the accused innocently ingested the substance in question, and the names and addresses of the witnesses upon whom the accused intends to rely to establish any such defenses.

Discussion

Such notice should be in writing except when impracticable. *See* R.C.M. 916(k) concerning the defense of lack of mental responsibility. *See* R.C.M. 706 concerning inquiries into the mental responsibility of the accused. *See* Mil. R. Evid. 302 concerning statements by the accused during such inquiries. If the defense needs more detail as to the time, date, or place of the offense to comply with this rule, it should request a bill of particulars. *See* R.C.M. 906(b)(6).

---

(3) *Documents and tangible objects.* If the defense requests disclosure under subsection (a)(2)(A) of this rule, upon compliance with such request by the Government, the defense, on request of the trial counsel, shall permit the trial counsel to inspect books, papers, documents, photographs, tangible objects, or copies or portions thereof, which are within the possession, custody, or control of the defense and which the defense intends to introduce as evidence in the defense case-in-chief at trial.

(4) *Reports of examination and tests.* If the defense requests disclosure under subsection (a)(2)(B) of this rule, upon compliance with such request by the Government, the defense, on request of trial counsel, shall (except as provided in R.C.M. 706, Mil. R. Evid. 302, and Mil. R. Evid. 513) permit the trial counsel to inspect any results or reports of physical or mental examinations and of scientific tests or experiments made in connection with the particular case, or copies thereof, that are within the

possession, custody, or control of the defense that the defense intends to introduce as evidence in the defense case-in-chief at trial or that were prepared by a witness whom the defense intends to call at trial when the results or reports relate to that witness' testimony.

(5) *Inadmissibility of withdrawn defense.* If an intention to rely upon a defense under subsection (b)(2) of this rule is withdrawn, evidence of such intention and disclosures by the accused or defense counsel made in connection with such intention is not, in any court-martial, admissible against the accused who gave notice of the intention.

Discussion

In addition to the matters covered in subsection (b) of this rule, defense counsel is required to give notice or disclose evidence under certain Military Rules of Evidence: Mil. R. Evid. 201A(b) (judicial notice of foreign law), 304(f) (testimony by the accused for a limited purpose in relation to a confession), 311(b) (same, search), 321(e) (same, lineup), 412(c)(1) and (2) (intent to offer evidence of sexual misconduct by a victim), 505(h) (intent to disclose classified information), 506(h) (intent to disclose privileged government information), 609(b) (intent to impeach a witness with a conviction older than 10 years), 612(2) (writing used to refresh recollection), and 613(a) (prior inconsistent statements).

(c) *Failure to call witness.* The fact that a witness' name is on a list of expected or intended witnesses provided to an opposing party, whether required by this rule or not, shall not be ground for comment upon a failure to call the witness.

(d) *Continuing duty to disclose.* If, before or during the court-martial, a party discovers additional evidence or material previously requested or required to be produced, which is subject to discovery or inspection under this rule, that party shall promptly notify the other party or the military judge of the existence of the additional evidence or material.

(e) *Access to witnesses and evidence.* Each party shall have adequate opportunity to prepare its case and equal opportunity to interview witnesses and inspect evidence, subject to the limitations in subsection (e)(1) of this rule. No party may unreasonably impede the access of another party to a witness or evidence.

(1) *Counsel for the Accused Interview of Victim of Alleged Sex-Related Offense.*

(A) Upon notice by counsel for the government to counsel for the accused of the name of an alleged victim of a sex-related offense whom counsel for the government intends to call to testify at a court-martial, counsel for the accused, or that lawyer's representative, as defined in Mil. R. Evid. 502(b)(3), shall make any request to interview that victim through special victims' counsel or other counsel for the victim, if applicable.

(B) If requested by an alleged victim of a sex-related offense who is subject to a request for interview under subsection (e)(1)(A) of this rule, any interview of the victim by counsel for the accused, or that lawyer's representative, as defined in Mil. R. Evid. 502(b)(3), shall take place only in the presence of counsel for the government, counsel for the victim, or a sexual assault victim advocate.

(C) In this subsection, the term "sex-related offense" means–

(i) a violation of Article 120, 120a, 120b, 120c, or 125; or

(ii) an attempt to commit an offense specified in subsection (e)(1)(C)(i) of this rule under Article 80.

Discussion

Convening authorities, commanders and members of their immediate staffs should make no statement, oral or written, and take no action which could reasonably be understood to discourage or prevent witnesses from testifying truthfully before a court-martial, or as a threat of retribution for such testimony.

Counsel must remain cognizant of professional responsibility rules regarding communicating with represented persons.

(f) *Information not subject to disclosure.* Nothing in this rule shall be construed to require the disclosure of information protected from disclosure by the Military Rules of Evidence. Nothing in this rule shall require the disclosure or production of notes, memoranda, or similar working papers prepared by counsel and counsel's assistants and representatives.

(g) *Regulation of discovery.*

(1) *Time, place, and manner.* The military judge may, consistent with this rule, specify the time, place, and manner of making discovery and may prescribe such terms and conditions as are just.

(2) *Protective and modifying orders.* Upon a sufficient showing the military judge may at any time order that the discovery or inspection be denied, restricted, or deferred, or make such other order as is appropriate. Upon motion by a party, the military judge may permit the party to make such showing,

in whole or in part, in writing to be inspected only by the military judge. If the military judge grants relief after such an ex parte showing, the entire text of the party's statement shall be sealed and attached to the record of trial as an appellate exhibit. Such material may be examined by reviewing authorities in closed proceedings for the purpose of reviewing the determination of the military judge.

(3) *Failure to comply.* If at any time during the court-martial it is brought to the attention of the military judge that a party has failed to comply with this rule, the military judge may take one or more of the following actions:

(A) Order the party to permit discovery;

(B) Grant a continuance;

(C) Prohibit the party from introducing evidence, calling a witness, or raising a defense not disclosed; and

(D) Enter such other order as is just under the circumstances. This rule shall not limit the right of the accused to testify in the accused's behalf.

Discussion

Factors to be considered in determining whether to grant an exception to exclusion under subsection (3)(C) include: the extent of disadvantage that resulted from a failure to disclose; the reason for the failure to disclose; the extent to which later events mitigated the disadvantage caused by the failure to disclose; and any other relevant factors.

The sanction of excluding the testimony of a defense witness should be used only upon finding that the defense counsel's failure to comply with this rule was willful and motivated by a desire to obtain a tactical advantage or to conceal a plan to present fabricated testimony. Moreover, the sanction of excluding the testimony of a defense witness should only be used if alternative sanctions could not have minimized the prejudice to the Government. Before imposing this sanction, the military judge must weigh the defendant's right to compulsory process against the countervailing public interests, including (1) the integrity of the adversary process; (2) the interest in the fair and efficient administration of military justice; and (3) the potential prejudice to the truth-determining function of the trial process.

Procedures governing refusal to disclose classified information are in Mil. R. Evid. 505. Procedures governing refusal to disclose other government information are in Mil. R. Evid. 506. Procedures governing refusal to disclose an informant's identity are in Mil. R. Evid. 507.

(h) *Inspect.* As used in this rule "inspect" includes the right to photograph and copy.

Rule 702. Depositions

(a) *In general.* A deposition may be ordered whenever, after preferral of charges, due to exceptional circumstances of the case it is in the interest of justice that the testimony of a prospective witness be taken and preserved for use at a preliminary hearing under Article 32 or a court-martial. A victim's declination to testify at a preliminary hearing or a victim's declination to submit to pretrial interviews shall not, by themselves, be considered exceptional circumstances. In accordance with subsection (b) of this rule, the convening authority or military judge may order a deposition of a victim only if it is determined, by a preponderance of the evidence, that the victim will not be available to testify at court-martial.

Discussion

A deposition is the out-of-court testimony of a witness under oath in response to questions by the parties, which is reduced to writing or recorded on videotape or audiotape or similar material. A deposition taken on oral examination is an oral deposition, and a deposition taken on written interrogatories is a written deposition. Written interrogatories are questions, prepared by the prosecution, defense, or both, which are reduced to writing before submission to a witness whose testimony is to be taken by deposition. The answers, reduced to writing and properly sworn to, constitute the deposition testimony of the witness.

Note that under subsection (i) of this rule a deposition may be taken by agreement of the parties without necessity of an order.

Part or all of a deposition, so far as otherwise admissible under the Military Rules of Evidence, may be used on the merits or on an interlocutory question as substantive evidence if the witness is unavailable under Mil. R. Evid. 804(a) except that a deposition may be admitted in a capital case only upon offer by the defense. *See* Mil. R. Evid. 804(b)(1). In any case, a deposition may be used by any party for the purpose of contradicting or impeaching the testimony of the deponent as a witness. *See* Mil. R. Evid. 613. If only a part of a deposition is offered in evidence by a party, an adverse party may require the proponent to offer all which is relevant to the part offered, and any party may offer other parts. *See* Mil. R. Evid. 106.

A deposition which is transcribed is ordinarily read to the court-martial by the party offering it. *See also* subsection (g)(3) of this rule. The transcript of a deposition may not be inspected by the members. Objections may be made to testimony in a written deposition in the same way that they would be if the testimony were offered through the personal appearance of a witness.

Part or all of a deposition so far as otherwise admissible under the Military Rules of Evidence may be used in presentencing proceedings as substantive evidence as provided in R.C.M. 1001.

DD Form 456 (Interrogatories and Deposition) may be used in conjunction with this rule.

(b) *Who may order.* A convening authority who has the charges for disposition or, after referral, the convening authority or the military judge may order that a deposition be taken on request of a party.

(c) *Request to take deposition.*

(1) *Submission of request.* At any time after charges have been preferred, any party may request in writing that a deposition be taken.

Discussion

A copy of the request and any accompanying papers ordinarily should be served on the other parties when the request is submitted.

(2) *Contents of request.* A request for a deposition shall include:

(A) the name and address of the person whose deposition is requested, or, if the name of the person is unknown, a description of the office or position of the person;

(B) a statement of the matters on which the person is to be examined; and

(C) whether an oral or written deposition is requested.

(3) *Action on request.*

(A) Upon receipt of a request for a deposition, the convening authority or military judge shall determine whether the requesting party has shown, by a preponderance of the evidence, that due to exceptional circumstances and in the interest of justice, the testimony of the prospective witness must be taken and preserved for use at a preliminary hearing under Article 32 or court-martial.

(B) *Written deposition.* A request for a written deposition may not be approved without the consent of the opposing party except when the deposition is ordered solely in lieu of producing a witness for sentencing under R.C.M. 1001 and the authority ordering the deposition determines that the interests of the parties and the court-martial can be adequately served by a written deposition.

Discussion

A request for an oral deposition may be approved without the consent of the opposing party.

(C) *Notification of decision.* The authority who acts on the request shall promptly inform the requesting party of the action on the request and, if the request is denied, the reasons for denial.

(D) *Waiver.* Failure to review before the military judge a request for a deposition denied by a convening authority waives further consideration of the request.

(d) *Action when request is approved.*

(1) *Detail of deposition officer.* When a request for a deposition is approved, the convening authority shall detail a judge advocate certified under Article 27(b) to serve as deposition officer. When the appointment of a judge advocate as deposition officer is not practicable, the convening authority may detail an impartial commissioned officer or appropriate civil officer authorized to administer oaths, not the accuser, to serve as deposition officer. If the deposition officer is not a judge advocate, an impartial judge advocate certified under Article 27(b) shall be made available to provide legal advice to the deposition officer.

Discussion

See Article 49(c).

When a deposition will be at a point distant from the command, an appropriate authority may be requested to make available an officer to serve as deposition officer.

(2) *Assignment of counsel.* If charges have not yet been referred to a court-martial when a request to take a deposition is approved, the convening authority who directed the taking of the deposition shall ensure that counsel qualified as required under R.C.M. 502(d) are assigned to represent each party.

Discussion

The counsel who represents the accused at a deposition ordinarily will form an attorney-client relationship with the accused which will continue through a later court-martial. *See* R.C.M. 506.

If the accused has formed an attorney-client relationship with military counsel concerning the charges in question, ordinarily that counsel should be appointed to represent the accused.

(3) *Instructions.* The convening authority may give instructions not inconsistent with this rule to the deposition officer.

Discussion

Such instruction may include the time and place for taking the deposition.

(e) *Notice.* The party at whose request a deposition is to be taken shall give to every other party reasonable written notice of the time and place for taking the deposition and the name and address of each person to be examined. On motion of a party upon whom the notice is served the deposition officer may for cause shown extend or shorten the time or change the place for taking the deposition, consistent with any instructions from the convening authority.

(f) *Duties of the deposition officer.* In accordance with this rule, and subject to any instructions under subsection (d)(3) of this rule, the deposition officer shall:

(1) Arrange a time and place for taking the deposition and, in the case of an oral deposition, notify the party who requested the deposition accordingly;

(2) Arrange for the presence of any witness whose deposition is to be taken in accordance with the procedures for production of witnesses and evidence under R.C.M. 703(e);

(3) Maintain order during the deposition and protect the parties and witnesses from annoyance, embarrassment, or oppression;

(4) Administer the oath to each witness, the reporter, and interpreter, if any;

(5) In the case of a written deposition, ask the questions submitted by counsel to the witness;

(6) Cause the proceedings to be recorded so that a verbatim record is made or may be prepared;

(7) Record, but not rule upon, objections or motions and the testimony to which they relate;

(8) Authenticate the record of the deposition and forward it to the authority who ordered the deposition; and

(9) Report to the convening authority any substantial irregularity in the proceeding.

Discussion

When any unusual problem, such as improper conduct by counsel or a witness, prevents an orderly and fair proceeding, the deposition officer should adjourn the proceedings and inform the convening authority.

The authority who ordered the deposition should forward copies to the parties.

(g) *Procedure.*

(1) *Oral depositions.*

(A) *Rights of accused.* At an oral deposition, the accused shall have the rights to:

(i) Be present except when: *(a)* the accused, absent good cause shown, fails to appear after notice of time and place of the deposition; *(b)* the accused is disruptive within the meaning of R.C.M. 804(b)(2); or *(c)* the deposition is ordered in lieu of production of a witness on sentencing under R.C.M. 1001 and the authority ordering the deposition determines that the interests of the parties and the court-martial can be served adequately by an oral deposition without the presence of the accused; and

(ii) Be represented by counsel as provided in R.C.M. 506.

(B) *Examination of witnesses.* Each witness giving an oral deposition shall be examined under oath. The scope and manner of examination and cross-examination shall be such as would be allowed in the trial itself. The Government shall make available to each accused for examination and use at the taking of the deposition any statement of the witness which is in the possession of the United States and to which the accused would be entitled at the trial.

Discussion

As to objections, *see* subsections (f)(7) and (h) of this rule. As to production of prior statements of witnesses, *see* R.C.M. 914; Mil. R. Evid. 612, 613.

A sample oath for a deposition follows.

"You (swear) (affirm) that the evidence you give shall be the truth, the whole truth, and nothing but the truth (so help you God)?"

---

(2) *Written depositions.*

(A) *Rights of accused.* The accused shall have the right to be represented by counsel as provided in R.C.M. 506 for the purpose of taking a written deposition, except when the deposition is taken for use at a summary court-martial.

(B) *Presence of parties.* No party has a right to be present at a written deposition.

(C) *Submission of interrogatories to opponent.* The party requesting a written deposition shall submit to opposing counsel a list of written questions to be asked of the witness. Opposing counsel may examine the questions and shall be allowed a reasonable time to prepare cross-interrogatories and objections, if any.

Discussion

The interrogatories and cross-interrogatories should be sent to the deposition officer by the party who requested the deposition. *See* subsection (h)(3) of this rule concerning objections.

(D) *Examination of witnesses.* The deposition officer shall swear the witness, read each question presented by the parties to the witness, and record each response. The testimony of the witness shall be recorded on videotape, audiotape, or similar material or shall be transcribed. When the testimony is transcribed, the deposition shall, except when impracticable, be submitted to the witness for examination. The deposition officer may enter additional matters then stated by the witness under oath. The deposition shall be signed by the witness if the witness is available. If the deposition is not signed by the witness, the deposition officer shall record the reason. The certificate of authentication shall then be executed.

(3) *How recorded.* In the discretion of the authority who ordered the deposition, a deposition may be recorded by a reporter or by other means including videotape, audiotape, or sound film. In the discretion of the military judge, depositions recorded by videotape, audiotape, or sound film may be played for the court-martial or may be transcribed and read to the court-martial.

Discussion

A deposition read in evidence or one that is played during a court-martial, is recorded and transcribed by the reporter in the same way as any other testimony. The deposition need not be included in the record of trial.

(h) *Objections.*

(1) *In general.* A failure to object prior to the deposition to the taking of the deposition on grounds which may be corrected if the objection is made prior to the deposition waives such objection.

(2) *Oral depositions.* Objections to questions, testimony, or evidence at an oral deposition and the grounds for such objection shall be stated at the time of taking such deposition. If an objection relates to a matter which could have been corrected if the objec-

tion had been made during the deposition, the objection is waived if not made at the deposition.

Discussion

A party may show that an objection was made during the deposition but not recorded, but, in the absence of such evidence, the transcript of the deposition governs.

---

(3) *Written depositions.* Objections to any question in written interrogatories shall be served on the party who proposed the question before the interrogatories are sent to the deposition officer or the objection is waived. Objections to answers in a written deposition may be made at trial.

(i) *Deposition by agreement not precluded.*

(1) *Taking deposition.* Nothing in this rule shall preclude the taking of a deposition without cost to the United States, orally or upon written questions, by agreement of the parties.

(2) *Use of deposition.* Subject to Article 49, nothing in this rule shall preclude the use of a deposition at the court-martial by agreement of the parties unless the military judge forbids its use for good cause.

Rule 703. Production of witnesses and evidence

(a) *In general.* The prosecution and defense and the court-martial shall have equal opportunity to obtain witnesses and evidence, subject to the limitations set forth in R.C.M. 701(e)(1), including the benefit of compulsory process.

Discussion

See also R.C.M. 801(c) concerning the opportunity of the court-martial to obtain witnesses and evidence.

(b) *Right to witnesses.*

(1) *On the merits or on interlocutory questions.* Each party is entitled to the production of any witness whose testimony on a matter in issue on the merits or on an interlocutory question would be relevant and necessary. With the consent of both the accused and Government, the military judge may authorize any witness to testify via remote means. Over a party's objection, the military judge may authorize any witness to testify on interlocutory questions via remote means or similar technology if the practical difficulties of producing the witness

outweigh the significance of the witness' personal appearance (although such testimony will not be admissible over the accused's objection as evidence on the ultimate issue of guilt). Factors to be considered include, but are not limited to: the costs of producing the witness; the timing of the request for production of the witness; the potential delay in the interlocutory proceeding that may be caused by the production of the witness; the willingness of the witness to testify in person; the likelihood of significant interference with military operational deployment, mission accomplishment, or essential training; and, for child witnesses, the traumatic effect of providing in-court testimony.

Discussion

See Mil. R. Evid. 401 concerning relevance.

Relevant testimony is necessary when it is not cumulative and when it would contribute to a party's presentation of the case in some positive way on a matter in issue. A matter is not in issue when it is stipulated as a fact.

The procedures for receiving testimony via remote means and the definition thereof are contained in R.C.M. 914B. An issue may arise as both an interlocutory question and a question that bears on the ultimate issue of guilt. See R.C.M. 801(e)(5). In such circumstances, this rule authorizes the admission of testimony by remote means or similar technology over the accused's objection only as evidence on the interlocutory question. In most instances, testimony taken over a party's objection will not be admissible as evidence on the question that bears on the ultimate issue of guilt; however, there may be certain limited circumstances where the testimony is admissible on the ultimate issue of guilt. Such determinations must be made based upon the relevant rules of evidence.

---

(2) *On sentencing.* Each party is entitled to the production of a witness whose testimony on sentencing is required under R.C.M. 1001(e).

(3) *Unavailable witness.* Notwithstanding subsections (b)(1) and (2) of this rule, a party is not entitled to the presence of a witness who is unavailable within the meaning of Mil. R. Evid. 804(a). However, if the testimony of a witness who is unavailable is of such central importance to an issue that it is essential to a fair trial, and if there is no adequate substitute for such testimony, the military judge shall grant a continuance or other relief in order to attempt to secure the witness' presence or shall abate the proceedings, unless the unavailability of the witness is the fault of or could have been prevented by the requesting party.

(c) *Determining which witness will be produced.*

(1) *Witnesses for the prosecution.* The trial counsel shall obtain the presence of witnesses whose testimony the trial counsel considers relevant and necessary for the prosecution.

(2) *Witnesses for the defense.*

(A) *Request.* The defense shall submit to the trial counsel a written list of witnesses whose production by the Government the defense requests.

(B) *Contents of request.*

(i) *Witnesses on merits or interlocutory questions.* A list of witnesses whose testimony the defense considers relevant and necessary on the merits or on an interlocutory question shall include the name, telephone number, if known, and address or location of the witness such that the witness can be found upon the exercise of due diligence and a synopsis of the expected testimony sufficient to show its relevance and necessity.

(ii) *Witnesses on sentencing.* A list of witnesses wanted for presentencing proceedings shall include the name, telephone number, if known, and address or location of the witness such that the witness can be found upon the exercise of due diligence, a synopsis of the testimony that it is expected the witness will give, and the reasons why the witness' personal appearance will be necessary under the standards set forth in R.C.M. 1001(e).

(C) *Time of request.* A list of witnesses under this subsection shall be submitted in time reasonably to allow production of each witness on the date when the witness' presence will be necessary. The military judge may set a specific date by which such lists must be submitted. Failure to submit the name of a witness in a timely manner shall permit denial of a motion for production of the witness, but relief from such denial may be granted for good cause shown.

(D) *Determination.* The trial counsel shall arrange for the presence of any witness listed by the defense unless the trial counsel contends that the witness' production is not required under this rule. If the trial counsel contends that the witness' production is not required by this rule, the matter may be submitted to the military judge. If the military judge grants a motion for a witness, the trial counsel shall produce the witness or the proceedings shall be abated.

Discussion

When significant or unusual costs would be involved in producing witnesses, the trial counsel should inform the convening authority, as the convening authority may elect to dispose of the matter by means other than a court-martial. *See* R.C.M. 906(b)(7). *See also* R.C.M. 905(j).

(d) *Employment of expert witnesses.* When the employment at Government expense of an expert is considered necessary by a party, the party shall, in advance of employment of the expert, and with notice to the opposing party, submit a request to the convening authority to authorize the employment and to fix the compensation for the expert. The request shall include a complete statement of reasons why employment of the expert is necessary and the estimated cost of employment. A request denied by the convening authority may be renewed before the military judge who shall determine whether the testimony of the expert is relevant and necessary, and, if so, whether the Government has provided or will provide an adequate substitute. If the military judge grants a motion for employment of an expert or finds that the Government is required to provide a substitute, the proceedings shall be abated if the Government fails to comply with the ruling. In the absence of advance authorization, an expert witness may not be paid fees other than those to which entitled under subsection (e)(2)(D) of this rule.

Discussion

See Mil. R. Evid. 702, 706.

(e) *Procedures for production of witnesses.*

(1) *Military witnesses.* The attendance of a military witness may be obtained by notifying the commander of the witness of the time, place, and date the witness' presence is required and requesting the commander to issue any necessary orders to the witness.

Discussion

When military witnesses are located near the court-martial, their presence can usually be obtained through informal coordination with them and their commander. If the witness is not near the court-martial and attendance would involve travel at government expense, or if informal coordination is inadequate, the appropriate superior should be requested to issue the necessary order.

If practicable, a request for the attendance of a military witness should be made so that the witness will have at least 48 hours notice before starting to travel to attend the court-martial.

The attendance of persons not on active duty should be obtained in the manner prescribed in subsection (e)(2) of this rule.

---

(2) *Civilian witnesses—subpoena.*

(A) *In general.* The presence of witnesses not on active duty may be obtained by subpoena.

Discussion

A subpoena is not necessary if the witness appears voluntarily at no expense to the United States.

Civilian employees of the Department of Defense may be directed by appropriate authorities to appear as witnesses in courts-martial as an incident of their employment. Appropriate travel orders may be issued for this purpose.

A subpoena may not be used to compel a civilian to travel outside the United States and its territories.

A witness must be subject to United States jurisdiction to be subject to a subpoena. Foreign nationals in a foreign country are not subject to subpoena. Their presence may be obtained through cooperation of the host nation.

(B) *Contents.* A subpoena shall state the command by which the proceeding is directed, and the title, if any, of the proceeding. A subpoena shall command each person to whom it is directed to attend and give testimony at the time and place specified therein. A subpoena may also command the person to whom it is directed to produce books, papers, documents, data, or other objects or electronically stored information designated therein at the proceeding or at an earlier time for inspection by the parties. A subpoena issued for a preliminary hearing pursuant to Article 32 shall not command any person to attend or give testimony at an Article 32 preliminary hearing.

Discussion

A subpoena may not be used to compel a witness to appear at an examination or interview before trial, but a subpoena may be used to obtain witnesses for a deposition or a court of inquiry. In accordance with subsection (f)(4)(B) of this rule, a *subpoena duces tecum* to produce books, papers, documents, data, or other objects or electronically stored information for preliminary hearings pursuant to Article 32 may be issued, following the convening authority's order directing such preliminary hearing, by the counsel representing the United States.

A subpoena normally is prepared, signed, and issued in duplicate on the official forms. *See* Appendix 7 for an example of a subpoena with certificate of service (DD Form 453) and a Travel Order (DD Form 453-1).

(C) *Who may issue.*

(1) A subpoena to secure evidence may be issued by:

(a) the summary court-martial;

(b) at an Article 32 preliminary hearing, detailed counsel for the government;

(c) after referral to a court-martial, detailed trial counsel;

(d) the president of a court of inquiry; or

(e) an officer detailed to take a deposition.

(2) A subpoena to secure witnesses may be issued by:

(a) the summary court-martial;

(b) after referral to a court-martial, detailed trial counsel;

(c) the president of a court of inquiry; or

(d) an officer detailed to take a deposition.

(D) *Service.* A subpoena may be served by the person authorized by this rule to issue it, a United States Marshal, or any other person who is not less than 18 years of age. Service shall be made by delivering a copy of the subpoena to the person named and by providing to the person named travel orders and a means for reimbursement for fees and mileage as may be prescribed by the Secretary concerned, or in the case of hardship resulting in the subpoenaed witness's inability to comply with the subpoena absent initial government payment, by providing to the person named travel orders, fees, and mileage sufficient to comply with the subpoena in rules prescribed by the Secretary concerned.

Discussion

If practicable, a subpoena should be issued in time to permit service at least 24 hours before the time the witness will have to travel to comply with the subpoena.

Informal service. Unless formal service is advisable, the person who issued the subpoena may mail it to the witness in duplicate, enclosing a postage-paid envelope bearing a return address, with the request that the witness sign the acceptance of service on the copy and return it in the envelope provided. The return envelope should be addressed to the person who issued the subpoena. The person who issued the subpoena should include with it a statement to the effect that the rights of the witness to fees and mileage will not be impaired by voluntary compliance with the request and that a voucher for fees and mileage will be delivered to the witness promptly on being discharged from attendance.

Formal service. Formal service is advisable whenever it is anticipated that the witness will not comply voluntarily with the subpoena. Appropriate fees and mileage must be paid or tendered.

See Article 47. If formal service is advisable, the person who issued the subpoena must assure timely and economical service. That person may do so by serving the subpoena personally when the witness is in the vicinity. When the witness is not in the vicinity, the subpoena may be sent in duplicate to the commander of a military installation near the witness. Such commanders should give prompt and effective assistance, issuing travel orders for their personnel to serve the subpoena when necessary.

Service should ordinarily be made by a person subject to the code. The duplicate copy of the subpoena must have entered upon it proof of service as indicated on the form and must be promptly returned to the person who issued the subpoena. If service cannot be made, the person who issued the subpoena must be informed promptly. A stamped, addressed envelope should be provided for these purposes.

For purposes of this Rule, "hardship" is defined as any situation which would substantially preclude reasonable efforts to appear that could be solved by providing transportation or fees and mileage to which the witness is entitled for appearing at the hearing in question.

(E) *Place of service.*

(i) *In general.* A subpoena requiring the attendance of a witness at a deposition, court-martial, or court of inquiry may be served at any place within the United States, it Territories, Commonwealths, or possessions.

(ii) *Foreign territory.* In foreign territory, the attendance of civilian witnesses may be obtained in accordance with existing agreements or, in the absence of agreements, with principles of international law.

(iii) *Occupied territory.* In occupied enemy territory, the appropriate commander may compel the attendance of civilian witnesses located within the occupied territory.

(F) *Relief.* If a person subpoenaed requests relief on grounds that compliance is unreasonable or oppressive, the convening authority or, after referral, the military judge may direct that the subpoena be modified or withdrawn if appropriate.

(G) *Neglect or refusal to appear.*

(i) *Issuance of warrant of attachment.* The military judge or, if there is no military judge, the convening authority may, in accordance with this rule, issue a warrant of attachment to compel the attendance of a witness or production of documents.

Discussion

A warrant of attachment (DD Form 454) may be used when necessary to compel a witness to appear or produce evidence under this rule. A warrant of attachment is a legal order addressed to an official directing that official to have the person named in the order brought before a court.

Subpoenas issued under R.C.M. 703 are federal process and a person not subject to the code may be prosecuted in a federal civilian court under Article 47 for failure to comply with a subpoena issued in compliance with this rule and formally served.

Failing to comply with such a subpoena is a felony offense, and may result in a fine or imprisonment, or both, at the discretion of the district court. The different purposes of the warrant of attachment and criminal complaint under Article 47 should be borne in mind. The warrant of attachment, available without the intervention of civilian judicial proceedings, has as its purpose the obtaining of the witness's presence, testimony, or documents. The criminal complaint, prosecuted through the civilian federal courts, has as its purpose punishment for failing to comply with process issued by military authority. It serves to vindicate the military interest in obtaining compliance with its lawful process.

For subpoenas issued for a preliminary hearing pursuant to Article 32 under subsection (f)(4)(B), the general court-martial convening authority with jurisdiction over the case may issue a warrant of attachment to compel production of documents.

_____

(ii) *Requirements.* A warrant of attachment may be issued only upon probable cause to believe that the witness was duly served with a subpoena, that the subpoena was issued in accordance with these rules, that a means of reimbursement of fees and mileage was provided to the witness or advanced to the witness in cases of hardship, that the witness is material, that the witness refused or willfully neglected to appear at the time and place specified on the subpoena, and that no valid excuse is reasonably apparent for the witness's failure to appear.

(iii) *Form.* A warrant of attachment shall be written. All documents in support of the warrant of attachment shall be attached to the warrant, together with the charge sheet and convening orders.

(iv) *Execution.* A warrant of attachment may be executed by a United States marshal or such other person who is not less than 18 years of age as the authority issuing the warrant may direct. Only such nondeadly force as may be necessary to bring the witness before the court-martial or other proceeding may be used to execute the warrant. A witness attached under this rule shall be brought before the court-martial or proceeding without delay and shall testify as soon as practicable and be released.

Discussion

In executing a warrant of attachment, no more force than necessary to bring the witness to the court-martial, deposition, or court of inquiry may be used.

_____

(v) *Definition.* For purposes of subsection (e)(2)(G) of this rule "military judge" does not include a summary court-martial or the president of a special court-martial without a military judge.

(f) *Right to evidence.*

(1) *In general.* Each party is entitled to the production of evidence which is relevant and necessary.

Discussion

Relevance is defined by Mil. R. Evid. 401. Relevant evidence is necessary when it is not cumulative and when it would contribute to a party's presentation of the case in some positive way on a matter in issue. A matter is not in issue when it is stipulated as a fact. The discovery and introduction of classified or other government information is controlled by Mil. R. Evid. 505 and 506.

_____

(2) *Unavailable evidence.* Notwithstanding subsection (f)(1) of this rule, a party is not entitled to the production of evidence which is destroyed, lost, or otherwise not subject to compulsory process. However, if such evidence is of such central importance to an issue that it is essential to a fair trial, and if there is no adequate substitute for such evidence, the military judge shall grant a continuance or other relief in order to attempt to produce the evidence or shall abate the proceedings, unless the unavailability of the evidence is the fault of or could have been prevented by the requesting party.

(3) *Determining what evidence will be produced.* The procedures in subsection (c) of this rule shall apply to a determination of what evidence will be produced, except that any defense request for the production of evidence shall list the items of evidence to be produced and shall include a description of each item sufficient to show its relevance and necessity, a statement where it can be obtained, and, if known, the name, address, and telephone number of the custodian of the evidence.

(4) *Procedures for production of evidence.*

(A) *Evidence under the control of the Government.* Evidence under the control of the Government may be obtained by notifying the custodian of the evidence of the time, place, and date the evidence is required and requesting the custodian to send or deliver the evidence.

(B) *Evidence not under the control of the gov-*

ernment. Evidence not under the control of the government may be obtained by a subpoena issued in accordance with subsection (e)(2) of this rule. A *subpoena duces tecum* to produce books, papers, documents, data, or other objects or electronically stored information for a preliminary hearing pursuant to Article 32 may be issued, following the convening authority's order directing such preliminary hearing, by counsel for the government. A person in receipt of a *subpoena duces tecum* for an Article 32 hearing need not personally appear in order to comply with the subpoena.

Discussion

The National Defense Authorization Act for Fiscal Year 2012, P.L. 112-81, § 542, amended Article 47 to allow the issuance of *subpoenas duces tecum* for Article 32 hearings. Although the amended language cites Article 32(b), this new subpoena power extends to documents subpoenaed by counsel representing the United States, whether or not requested by the defense.

(C) *Relief.* If the person having custody of evidence requests relief on grounds that compliance with the subpoena or order of production is unreasonable or oppressive, the convening authority or, after referral, the military judge may direct that the subpoena or order of production be withdrawn or modified. Subject to Mil. R. Evid. 505 and 506, the military judge may direct that the evidence be submitted to the military judge for an in camera inspection in order to determine whether such relief should be granted.

Rule 704. Immunity

(a) *Types of immunity.* Two types of immunity may be granted under this rule.

(1) *Transactional immunity.* A person may be granted transactional immunity from trial by court-martial for one or more offenses under the code.

(2) *Testimonial immunity.* A person may be granted immunity from the use of testimony, statements, and any information directly or indirectly derived from such testimony or statements by that person in a later court-martial.

Discussion

"Testimonial" immunity is also called "use" immunity.

Immunity ordinarily should be granted only when testimony or other information from the person is necessary to the public interest, including the needs of good order and discipline, and

when the person has refused or is likely to refuse to testify or provide other information on the basis of the privilege against self-incrimination.

Testimonial immunity is preferred because it does not bar prosecution of the person for the offenses about which testimony or information is given under the grant of immunity.

In any trial of a person granted testimonial immunity after the testimony or information is given, the Government must meet a heavy burden to show that it has not used in any way for the prosecution of that person the person's statements, testimony, or information derived from them. In many cases this burden makes difficult a later prosecution of such a person for any offense that was the subject of that person's testimony or statements. Therefore, if it is intended to prosecute a person to whom testimonial immunity has been or will be granted for offenses about which that person may testify or make statements, it may be necessary to try that person before the testimony or statements are given.

(b) *Scope.* Nothing in this rule bars:

(1) A later court-martial for perjury, false swearing, making a false official statement, or failure to comply with an order to testify; or

(2) Use in a court-martial under subsection (b)(1) of this rule of testimony or statements derived from such testimony or statements.

(c) *Authority to grant immunity.* Only a general court-martial convening authority may grant immunity, and may do so only in accordance with this rule.

Discussion

Only general court-martial convening authorities are authorized to grant immunity. However, in some circumstances, when a person testifies or makes statements pursuant to a promise of immunity, or a similar promise, by a person with apparent authority to make it, such testimony or statements and evidence derived from them may be inadmissible in a later trial. Under some circumstances a promise of immunity by someone other than a general court-martial convening authority may bar prosecution altogether. Persons not authorized to grant immunity should exercise care when dealing with accused or suspects to avoid inadvertently causing statements to be inadmissible or prosecution to be barred.

A convening authority who grants immunity to a prosecution witness in a court-martial may be disqualified from taking post-trial action in the case under some circumstances.

----

(1) *Persons subject to the code.* A general court-martial convening authority may grant immunity to any person subject to the code. However, a general court-martial convening authority may grant immunity to a person subject to the code extending to a prosecution in a United States District Court only when specifically authorized to do so by the Attor-

ney General of the United States or other authority designated under 18 U.S.C. § 6004.

Discussion

When testimony or a statement for which a person subject to the code may be granted immunity may relate to an offense for which that person could be prosecuted in a United States District Court, immunity should not be granted without prior coordination with the Department of Justice. Ordinarily coordination with the local United States Attorney is appropriate. Unless the Department of Justice indicates it has no interest in the case, authorization for the grant of immunity should be sought from the Attorney General. A request for such authorization should be forwarded through the office of the Judge Advocate General concerned. Service regulations may provide additional guidance. Even if the Department of Justice expresses no interest in the case, authorization by the Attorney General for the grant of immunity may be necessary to compel the person to testify or make a statement if such testimony or statement would make the person liable for a Federal civilian offense.

(2) *Persons not subject to the code.* A general court-martial convening authority may grant immunity to persons not subject to the code only when specifically authorized to do so by the Attorney General of the United States or other authority designated under 18 U.S.C. § 6004.

Discussion

See the discussion under subsection (c)(1) of this rule concerning forwarding a request for authorization to grant immunity to the Attorney General.

(3) *Other limitations.* The authority to grant immunity under this rule may not be delegated. The authority to grant immunity may be limited by superior authority.

Discussion

Department of Defense Directive 1355.1 (21 July 1981) provides: "A proposed grant of immunity in a case involving espionage, subversion, aiding the enemy, sabotage, spying, or violation of rules or statutes concerning classified information or the foreign relations of the United States, shall be forwarded to the General Counsel of the Department of Defense for the purpose of consultation with the Department of Justice. The General Counsel shall obtain the view of other appropriate elements of the Department of defense in furtherance of such consultation."

(d) *Procedure.* A grant of immunity shall be written and signed by the convening authority who issues it. The grant shall include a statement of the authority

under which it is made and shall identify the matters to which it extends.

Discussion

A person who has received a valid grant of immunity from a proper authority may be ordered to testify. In addition, a servicemember who has received a valid grant of immunity may be ordered to answer questions by investigators or counsel pursuant to that grant. *See* Mil. R. Evid. 301(c). A person who refuses to testify despite a valid grant of immunity may be prosecuted for such refusal. Persons subject to the code may be charged under Article 134. *See* paragraph 108, Part IV. A grant of immunity removes the right to refuse to testify or make a statement on self-incrimination grounds. It does not, however, remove other privileges against disclosure of information. *See* Mil. R. Evid., Section V.

An immunity order or grant must not specify the contents of the testimony it is expected the witness will give.

When immunity is granted to a prosecution witness, the accused must be notified in accordance with Mil. R. Evid. 301(c)(2).

(e) *Decision to grant immunity.* Unless limited by superior competent authority, the decision to grant immunity is a matter within the sole discretion of the appropriate general court-martial convening authority. However, if a defense request to immunize a witness has been denied, the military judge may, upon motion by the defense, grant appropriate relief directing that either an appropriate convening authority grant testimonial immunity to a defense witness or, as to the affected charges and specifications, the proceedings against the accused be abated, upon findings that:

(1) The witness intends to invoke the right against self-incrimination to the extent permitted by law if called to testify; and

(2) The Government has engaged in discriminatory use of immunity to obtain a tactical advantage, or the Government, through its own overreaching, has forced the witness to invoke the privilege against self-incrimination; and

(3) The witness' testimony is material, clearly exculpatory, not cumulative, not obtainable from any other source and does more than merely affect the credibility of other witnesses.

Rule 705. Pretrial agreements

(a) *In general.* Subject to such limitations as the Secretary concerned may prescribe, an accused and the convening authority may enter into a pretrial agreement in accordance with this rule.

Discussion

The authority of convening authorities to refer cases to trial and approve pretrial agreements extends only to trials by courts-martial. To ensure that such actions do not preclude appropriate action by Federal civilian authorities in cases likely to be prosecuted in the United States District Courts, convening authorities shall ensure that appropriate consultation under the "Memorandum of Understanding Between the Departments of Justice and Defense Relating to the Investigation and Prosecution of Crimes Over Which the Two Departments Have Concurrent Jurisdiction " has taken place prior to trial by court-martial or approval of a pretrial agreement in cases where such consultation is required. *See* Appendix 3.

(b) *Nature of agreement.* A pretrial agreement may include:

(1) A promise by the accused to plead guilty to, or to enter a confessional stipulation as to one or more charges and specifications, and to fulfill such additional terms or conditions which may be included in the agreement and which are not prohibited under this rule; and

(2) A promise by the convening authority to do one or more of the following:

(A) Refer the charges to a certain type of court-martial;

(B) Refer a capital offense as noncapital;

(C) Withdraw one or more charges or specifications from the court-martial;

Discussion

A convening authority may withdraw certain specifications and/or charges from a court-martial and dismiss them if the accused fulfills the accused's promises in the agreement. Except when jeopardy has attached (*see* R.C.M. 907(b)(2)(C)), such withdrawal and dismissal does not bar later reinstitution of the charges by the same or a different convening authority. A judicial determination that the accused breached the pretrial agreement is not required prior to reinstitution of withdrawn or dismissed specifications and/or charges. If the defense moves to dismiss the reinstituted specifications and/or charges on the grounds that the government remains bound by the terms of the pretrial agreement, the government will be required to prove, by a preponderance of the evidence, that the accused has breached the terms of the pretrial agreement. If the agreement is intended to grant immunity to an accused, *see* R.C.M. 704.

(D) Have the trial counsel present no evidence

as to one or more specifications or portions thereof; and

(E) Take specified action on the sentence adjudged by the court-martial.

Discussion

For example, the convening authority may agree to approve no sentence in excess of a specified maximum, to suspend all or part of a sentence, to defer confinement, or to mitigate certain forms of punishment into less severe forms.

(c) *Terms and conditions.*

(1) *Prohibited terms or conditions.*

(A) *Not voluntary.* A term or condition in a pretrial agreement shall not be enforced if the accused did not freely and voluntarily agree to it.

(B) *Deprivation of certain rights.* A term or condition in a pretrial agreement shall not be enforced if it deprives the accused of: the right to counsel; the right to due process; the right to challenge the jurisdiction of the court-martial; the right to a speedy trial; the right to complete sentencing proceedings; the complete and effective exercise of post-trial and appellate rights.

Discussion

A pretrial agreement provision which prohibits the accused from making certain pretrial motions (*see* R.C.M. 905–907) may be improper.

---

(2) *Permissible terms or conditions.* Subject to subsection (c)(1)(A) of this rule, subsection (c)(1)(B) of this rule does not prohibit either party from proposing the following additional conditions:

(A) A promise to enter into a stipulation of fact concerning offenses to which a plea of guilty or a confessional stipulation will be entered;

(B) A promise to testify as a witness in the trial of another person;

Discussion

See R.C.M. 704(a)(2) concerning testimonial immunity. Only a general court-martial convening authority may grant immunity.

(C) A promise to provide restitution;

Discussion

A promise to provide restitution includes restitution to a victim of an alleged offense committed by the accused in accordance with Article 6b(a)(6).

(D) A promise to conform the accused's conduct to certain conditions of probation before action by the convening authority as well as during any period of suspension of the sentence, provided that the requirements of R.C.M. 1109 must be complied with before an alleged violation of such terms may relieve the convening authority of the obligation to fulfill the agreement; and

(E) A promise to waive procedural requirements such as the Article 32 preliminary hearing, the right to trial by court-martial composed of members or the right to request trial by military judge alone, or the opportunity to obtain the personal appearance of witnesses at sentencing proceedings.

(d) *Procedure.*

(1) *Negotiation.* Pretrial agreement negotiations may be initiated by the accused, defense counsel, trial counsel, the staff judge advocate, convening authority, or their duly authorized representatives. Either the defense or the government may propose any term or condition not prohibited by law or public policy. Government representatives shall negotiate with defense counsel unless the accused has waived the right to counsel.

(2) *Formal submission.* After negotiation, if any, under subsection (d)(1) of this rule, if the accused elects to propose a pretrial agreement, the defense shall submit a written offer. All terms, conditions, and promises between the parties shall be written. The proposed agreement shall be signed by the accused and defense counsel, if any. If the agreement contains any specified action on the adjudged sentence, such action shall be set forth on a page separate from the other portions of the agreement.

Discussion

The first part of the agreement ordinarily contains an offer to plead guilty and a description of the offenses to which the offer extends. It must also contain a complete and accurate statement of any other agreed terms or conditions. For example, if the convening authority agrees to withdraw certain specifications, or if the accused agrees to waive the right to an Article 32 preliminary hearing, this should be stated. The written agreement should contain a statement by the accused that the accused enters it freely and voluntarily and may contain a statement that the accused has been advised of certain rights in connection with the agreement.

(3) *Acceptance.*

(A) *In general.* The convening authority may either accept or reject an offer of the accused to enter into a pretrial agreement or may propose by counteroffer any terms or conditions not prohibited by law or public policy. The decision whether to accept or reject an offer is within the sole discretion of the convening authority. When the convening authority has accepted a pretrial agreement, the agreement shall be signed by the convening authority or by a person, such as the staff judge advocate or trial counsel, who has been authorized by the convening authority to sign.

(B) *Victim consultation.* Whenever practicable, prior to the convening authority accepting a pretrial agreement the victim shall be provided an opportunity to express views concerning the pretrial agreement terms and conditions in accordance with regulations prescribed by the Secretary concerned. The convening authority shall consider any such views provided prior to accepting a pretrial agreement. For purposes of this rule, a "victim" is an individual who is alleged to have suffered direct physical, emotional, or pecuniary harm as a result of the matters set forth in a charge or specification under consideration and is named in one of the specifications under consideration

Discussion

The convening authority should consult with the staff judge advocate or trial counsel before acting on an offer to enter into a pretrial agreement.

(4) *Withdrawal.*

(A) *By accused.* The accused may withdraw from a pretrial agreement at any time; however, the accused may withdraw a plea of guilty or a confessional stipulation entered pursuant to a pretrial agreement only as provided in R.C.M. 910(h) or 811(d), respectively.

(B) *By convening authority.* The convening authority may withdraw from a pretrial agreement at any time before the accused begins performance of promises contained in the agreement, upon the failure by the accused to fulfill any material promise or condition in the agreement, when inquiry by the military judge discloses a disagreement as to a material term in the agreement, or if findings are set aside because a plea of guilty entered pursuant to the agreement is held improvident on appellate review.

(e) *Nondisclosure of existence of agreement.* Except in a special court-martial without a military judge, no member of a court-martial shall be informed of the existence of a pretrial agreement. In addition, except as provided in Mil. R. Evid. 410, the fact that an accused offered to enter into a pretrial agreement, and any statements made by an accused in connection therewith, whether during negotiations or during a providence inquiry, shall not be otherwise disclosed to the members.

Discussion

See also R.C.M. 910(f) (plea agreement inquiry).

Rule 706. Inquiry into the mental capacity or mental responsibility of the accused

(a) *Initial action.* If it appears to any commander who considers the disposition of charges, or to any preliminary hearing officer, trial counsel, defense counsel, military judge, or member that there is reason to believe that the accused lacked mental responsibility for any offense charged or lacks capacity to stand trial, that fact and the basis of the belief or observation shall be transmitted through appropriate channels to the officer authorized to order an inquiry into the mental condition of the accused. The submission may be accompanied by an application for a mental examination under this rule.

Discussion

See R.C.M. 909 concerning the capacity of the accused to stand trial and R.C.M. 916(k) concerning mental responsibility of the accused.

(b) *Ordering an inquiry.*

(1) *Before referral.* Before referral of charges, an inquiry into the mental capacity or mental responsibility of the accused may be ordered by the convening authority before whom the charges are pending for disposition.

(2) *After referral.* After referral of charges, an inquiry into the mental capacity or mental responsibility of the accused may be ordered by the military judge. The convening authority may order such an inquiry after referral of charges but before beginning

of the first session of the court-martial (including any Article 39(a) session) when the military judge is not reasonably available. The military judge may order a mental examination of the accused regardless of any earlier determination by the convening authority.

(c) *Inquiry.*

(1) *By whom conducted.* When a mental examination is ordered under subsection (b) of this rule, the matter shall be referred to a board consisting of one or more persons. Each member of the board shall be either a physician or a clinical psychologist. Normally, at least one member of the board shall be either a psychiatrist or a clinical psychologist. The board shall report as to the mental capacity or mental responsibility or both of the accused.

(2) *Matters in inquiry.* When a mental examination is ordered under this rule, the order shall contain the reasons for doubting the mental capacity or mental responsibility, or both, of the accused, or other reasons for requesting the examination. In addition to other requirements, the order shall require the board to make separate and distinct findings as to each of the following questions:

(A) At the time of the alleged criminal conduct, did the accused have a severe mental disease or defect? (The term "severe mental disease or defect" does not include an abnormality manifested only by repeated criminal or otherwise antisocial conduct, or minor disorders such as nonpsychotic behavior disorders and personality defects.)

(B) What is the clinical psychiatric diagnosis?

(C) Was the accused, at the time of the alleged criminal conduct and as a result of such severe mental disease or defect, unable to appreciate the nature and quality or wrongfulness of his or her conduct?

(D) Is the accused presently suffering from a mental disease or defect rendering the accused unable to understand the nature of the proceedings against the accused or to conduct or cooperate intelligently in the defense?

Other appropriate questions may also be included.

(3) *Directions to board.* In addition to the requirements specified in subsection (c)(2) of this rule, the order to the board shall specify:

(A) That upon completion of the board's investigation, a statement consisting only of the board's ultimate conclusions as to all questions specified in the order shall be submitted to the officer ordering the examination, the accused's commanding officer, the preliminary hearing officer, if any, appointed pursuant to Article 32 and to all counsel in the case, the convening authority, and, after referral, to the military judge;

(B) That the full report of the board may be released by the board or other medical personnel only to other medical personnel for medical purposes, unless otherwise authorized by the convening authority or, after referral of charges, by the military judge, except that a copy of the full report shall be furnished to the defense and, upon request, to the commanding officer of the accused; and

(C) That neither the contents of the full report nor any matter considered by the board during its investigation shall be released by the board or other medical personnel to any person not authorized to receive the full report, except pursuant to an order by the military judge.

Discussion

Based on the report, further action in the case may be suspended, the charges may be dismissed by the convening authority, administrative action may be taken to discharge the accused from the service or, subject to Mil. R. Evid. 302, the charges may be tried by court-martial.

(4) *Additional examinations.* Additional examinations may be directed under this rule at any stage of the proceedings as circumstances may require.

(5) *Disclosure to trial counsel.* No person, other than the defense counsel, accused, or, after referral of charges, the military judge may disclose to the trial counsel any statement made by the accused to the board or any evidence derived from such statement.

Discussion

See Mil. R. Evid. 302.

Rule 707. Speedy trial

(a) *In general.* The accused shall be brought to trial within 120 days after the earlier of:

(1) Preferral of charges;

Discussion

Delay from the time of an offense to preferral of charges or the imposition of pretrial restraint is not considered for speedy trial purposes. *See also* Article 43 (statute of limitations). In some circumstances such delay may prejudice the accused and may result in dismissal of the charges or other relief. Offenses ordinarily should be disposed of promptly to serve the interests of good order and discipline. Priority shall be given to persons in arrest or confinement.

(2) The imposition of restraint under R.C.M. 304(a)(2)–(4); or

(3) Entry on active duty under R.C.M. 204.

(b) *Accountability.*

(1) *In general.* The date of preferral of charges, the date on which pretrial restraint under R.C.M. 304 (a)(2)-(4) is imposed, or the date of entry on active duty under R.C.M. 204 shall not count for purpose of computing time under subsection (a) of this rule. The date on which the accused is brought to trial shall count. The accused is brought to trial within the meaning of this rule at the time of arraignment under R.C.M. 904.

(2) *Multiple Charges.* When charges are preferred at different times, accountability for each charge shall be determined from the appropriate date under subsection (a) of this rule for that charge.

(3) *Events which affect time periods.*

(A) *Dismissal or mistrial.* If charges are dismissed, or if a mistrial is granted, a new 120-day time period under this rule shall begin on the date of dismissal or mistrial for cases in which there is no repreferral and cases in which the accused is in pretrial restraint. In all other cases, a new 120-day time period under the rule shall begin on the earlier of

(i) the date of repreferral; or

(ii) the date of imposition of restraint under R.C.M. 304(a)(2)–(4).

(B) *Release from restraint.* If the accused is released from pretrial restraint for a significant period, the 120-day time period under this rule shall begin on the earlier of

(i) the date of preferral of charges;

(ii) the date on which restraint under R.C.M. 304(a) (2)-(4) is reimposed; or

(iii) the date of entry on active duty under R.C.M. 204.

(C) *Government appeals.* If notice of appeal under R.C.M. 908 is filed, a new 120-day time period under this rule shall begin, for all charges neither proceeded on nor severed under R.C.M. 908(b)(4), on the date of notice to the parties under R.C.M. 908(b)(8) or 908(c)(3), unless it is determined that the appeal was filed solely for the purpose of delay with the knowledge that it was totally frivolous and without merit. After the decision of the Court of Criminal Appeals under R.C.M. 908, if there is a further appeal to the Court of Appeals for the Armed Forces or, subsequently, to the Supreme Court, a new 120-day time period under this rule shall begin on the date the parties are notified of the final decision of the Court of Appeals for the Armed Forces, or, if appropriate, the Supreme Court.

(D) *Rehearings.* If a rehearing is ordered or authorized by an appellate court, a new 120-day time period under this rule shall begin on the date that the responsible convening authority receives the record of trial and the opinion authorizing or directing a rehearing. An accused is brought to trial within the meaning of this rule at the time of arraignment under R.C.M. 904 or, if arraignment is not required (such as in the case of a sentence-only rehearing), at the time of the first session under R.C.M. 803.

(E) *Commitment of the incompetent accused.* If the accused is committed to the custody of the Attorney General for hospitalization as provided in R.C.M. 909(f), all periods of such commitment shall be excluded when determining whether the period in subsection (a) of this rule has run. If, at the end of the period of commitment, the accused is returned to the custody of the general court-martial convening authority, a new 120-day time period under this rule shall begin on the date of such return to custody.

(c) *Excludable delay.* All periods of time during which appellate courts have issued stays in the proceedings, or the accused is absent without authority, or the accused is hospitalized due to incompetence, or is otherwise in the custody of the Attorney General, shall be excluded when determining whether the period in subsection (a) of this rule has run. All other pretrial delays approved by a military judge or the convening authority shall be similarly excluded.

(1) *Procedure.* Prior to referral, all requests for pretrial delay, together with supporting reasons, will be submitted to the convening authority or, if authorized under regulations prescribed by the Secretary concerned, to a military judge for resolution.

After referral, such requests for pretrial delay will be submitted to the military judge for resolution.

Discussion

The decision to grant or deny a reasonable delay is a matter within the sole discretion of the convening authority or a military judge. This decision should be based on the facts and circumstances then and there existing. Reasons to grant a delay might, for example, include the need for: time to enable counsel to prepare for trial in complex cases; time to allow examination into the mental capacity of the accused; time to process a member of the reserve component to active duty for disciplinary action; time to complete other proceedings related to the case; time requested by the defense; time to secure the availability of the accused, substantial witnesses, or other evidence; time to obtain appropriate security clearances for access to classified information or time to declassify evidence; or additional time for other good cause.

Pretrial delays should not be granted ex parte, and when practicable, the decision granting the delay, together with supporting reasons and the dates covering the delay, should be reduced to writing.

Prior to referral, the convening authority may delegate the authority to grant continuances to an Article 32 preliminary hearing officer.

---

(2) *Motions.* Upon accused's timely motion to a military judge under R.C.M. 905 for speedy trial relief, counsel should provide the court a chronology detailing the processing of the case. This chronology should be made a part of the appellate record.

(d) *Remedy.* A failure to comply with this rule will result in dismissal of the affected charges, or, in a sentence-only rehearing, sentence relief as appropriate.

(1) *Dismissal.* Dismissal will be with or without prejudice to the government's right to reinstitute court-martial proceedings against the accused for the same offense at a later date. The charges must be dismissed with prejudice where the accused has been deprived of his or her constitutional right to a speedy trial. In determining whether to dismiss charges with or without prejudice, the court shall consider, among others, each of the following factors: the seriousness of the offense; the facts and circumstances of the case that lead to dismissal; the impact of a re-prosecution on the administration of justice; and any prejudice to the accused resulting from the denial of a speedy trial.

(2) *Sentence relief.* In determining whether or how much sentence relief is appropriate, the military judge shall consider, among others, each of the following factors: the length of the delay, the reasons

for the delay, the accused's demand for speedy trial, and any prejudice to the accused from the delay. Any sentence relief granted will be applied against the sentence approved by the convening authority.

Discussion

See subsection (c)(1) and the accompanying Discussion concerning reasons for delay and procedures for parties to request delay.

———————

(e) *Waiver.* Except as provided in R.C.M. 910(a)(2), a plea of guilty which results in a finding of guilty waives any speedy trial issue as to that offense.

Discussion

Speedy trial issues may also be waived by a failure to raise the issue at trial. *See* R.C.M. 905(e) and 907(b)(2).

———————

CHAPTER VIII. TRIAL PROCEDURE GENERALLY

Rule 801. Military judge's responsibilities; other matters

(a) *Responsibilities of military judge.* The military judge is the presiding officer in a court-martial.

Discussion

The military judge is responsible for ensuring that court-martial proceedings are conducted in a fair and orderly manner, without unnecessary delay or waste of time or resources. Unless otherwise specified, the president of a special court-martial without a military judge has the same authority and responsibility as a military judge. *See* R.C.M. 502(b)(2).

The military judge shall:

(1) Determine the time and uniform for each session of a court-martial;

Discussion

The military judge should consult with counsel concerning the scheduling of sessions and the uniform to be worn. The military judge recesses or adjourns the court-martial as appropriate. Subject to R.C.M. 504(d)(1), the military judge may also determine the place of trial. *See also* R.C.M. 906(b)(11).

---

(2) Ensure that the dignity and decorum of the proceedings are maintained;

Discussion

See also R.C.M. 804 and 806. Courts-martial should be conducted in an atmosphere which is conducive to calm and detached deliberation and determination of the issues presented and which reflects the seriousness of the proceedings.

---

(3) Subject to the code and this Manual, exercise reasonable control over the proceedings to promote the purposes of these rules and this Manual;

Discussion

See R.C.M. 102. The military judge may, within the framework established by the code and this Manual, prescribe the manner and order in which the proceedings may take place. Thus, the military judge may determine: when, and in what order, motions will be litigated (*see* R.C.M. 905); the manner in which voir dire will be conducted and challenges made (*see* R.C.M. 902(d) and 912); the order in which witnesses may testify (*see* R.C.M. 913; Mil. R. Evid. 611); the order in which the parties may argue on a motion or objection; and the time limits for argument (*see* R.C.M. 905; 919; 1001(g)).

The military judge should prevent unnecessary waste of time

and promote the ascertainment of truth, but must avoid undue interference with the parties' presentations or the appearance of partiality. The parties are entitled to a reasonable opportunity to properly present and support their contentions on any relevant matter.

---

(4) Subject to subsection (e) of this rule, rule on all interlocutory questions and all questions of law raised during the court-martial; and

(5) Instruct the members on questions of law and procedure which may arise.

Discussion

The military judge instructs the members concerning findings (*see* R.C.M. 920) and sentence (*see* R.C.M. 1005), and when otherwise appropriate. For example, preliminary instructions to the members concerning their duties and the duties of other trial participants and other matters are normally appropriate. *See* R.C.M. 913. Other instructions (for example, instructions on the limited purpose for which evidence has been introduced, *see* Mil. R. Evid. 105) may be given whenever the need arises.

---

(6) In the case of a victim of an offense under the UCMJ who is under 18 years of age and not a member of the armed forces, or who is incompetent, incapacitated, or deceased, designate in writing a family member, a representative of the estate of the victim, or another suitable individual to assume the victim's rights under the UCMJ.

(A) For the purposes of this rule, the individual is designated for the sole purpose of assuming the legal rights of the victim as they pertain to the victim's status as a victim of any offense(s) properly before the court.

Discussion

The rights that a designee may exercise on behalf of a victim include the right to receive notice of public hearings in the case; the right to be reasonably heard at such hearings, if permitted by law; and the right to confer with counsel representing the government at such hearings. The designee may also be the custodial guardian of the child.

When determining whom to appoint under this rule, the military judge may consider the following: the age and maturity, relationship to the victim, and physical proximity of any proposed designee; the costs incurred in effecting the appointment; the willingness of the proposed designee to serve in such a role; the previous appointment of a guardian by another court of competent jurisdiction; the preference of the victim; any potential delay in any proceeding that may be caused by a specific appointment; and any other relevant information.

(B) *Procedure to determine appointment of designee.*

(i) As soon as practicable, trial counsel shall notify the military judge, counsel for the accused, and the victim(s) of any offense(s) properly before the court when there is an apparent requirement to appoint a designee under this rule.

Discussion

In the event a case involves multiple victims who are entitled to notice under this rule, each victim is only entitled to notice relating to his or her own designated representative.

(ii) The military judge will determine if the appointment of a designee is required under this rule.

(iii) At the discretion of the military judge, victim(s), trial counsel, and the accused may be given the opportunity to recommend to the military judge individual(s) for appointment.

(iv) The military judge is not required to hold a hearing before determining whether a designation is required or making such an appointment under this rule.

(v) If the military judge determines a hearing pursuant to Article 39(a), UCMJ, is necessary, the following shall be notified of the hearing and afforded the right to be present at the hearing: trial counsel, accused, and the victim(s).

(vi) The individual designated shall not be the accused.

(C) At any time after appointment, a designee shall be excused upon request by the designee or a finding of good cause by the military judge.

(D) If the individual appointed to assume the victim's rights is excused, the military judge shall appoint a successor consistent with this rule.

Discussion

The term "victim of an offense under the UCMJ" means a person who has suffered direct physical, emotional, or pecuniary harm as a result of the commission of an offense under the UCMJ. "Good cause" means adequate or reasonable grounds to believe that the individual appointed to assume the victim's rights

is not acting or does not intend to act in the best interest of the victim.

(b) *Rules of court; contempt.* The military judge may:

(1) Subject to R.C.M. 108, promulgate and enforce rules of court.

(2) Subject to R.C.M. 809, exercise contempt power.

(c) *Obtaining evidence.* The court-martial may act to obtain evidence in addition to that presented by the parties. The right of the members to have additional evidence obtained is subject to an interlocutory ruling by the military judge.

Discussion

The members may request and the military judge may require that a witness be recalled, or that a new witness be summoned, or other evidence produced. The members or military judge may direct trial counsel to make an inquiry along certain lines to discover and produce additional evidence. *See also* Mil. R. Evid. 614. In taking such action, the court-martial must not depart from an impartial role.

(d) *Uncharged offenses.* If during the trial there is evidence that the accused may be guilty of an untried offense not alleged in any specification before the court-martial, the court-martial shall proceed with the trial of the offense charged.

Discussion

A report of the matter may be made to the convening authority after trial. If charges are preferred for an offense indicated by the evidence referred to in this subsection, no member of the court-martial who participated in the first trial should sit in any later trial. Such a member would ordinarily be subject to a challenge for cause. *See* R.C.M. 912. *See also* Mil. R. Evid. 105 concerning instructing the members on evidence of uncharged misconduct.

(e) *Interlocutory questions and questions of law.* For purposes of this subsection "military judge" does not include the president of a special court-martial without a military judge.

(1) *Rulings by the military judge.*

(A) *Finality of rulings.* Any ruling by the military judge upon a question of law, including a motion for a finding of not guilty, or upon any interlocutory question is final.

(B) *Changing a ruling.* The military judge may change a ruling made by that or another military judge in the case except a previously granted motion for a finding of not guilty, at any time during the trial.

(C) *Article 39(a) sessions.* When required by this Manual or otherwise deemed appropriate by the military judge, interlocutory questions or questions of law shall be presented and decided at sessions held without members under R.C.M. 803.

Discussion

Sessions without members are appropriate for interlocutory questions, questions of law, and instructions. *See also* Mil. R. Evid. 103; 304; 311; 321. Such sessions should be used to the extent possible consistent with the orderly, expeditious progress of the proceedings.

---

(2) *Ruling by the president of a special court-martial without a military judge.*

(A) *Questions of law.* Any ruling by the president of a special court-martial without a military judge on any question of law other than a motion for a finding of not guilty is final.

(B) *Questions of fact.* Any ruling by the president of a special court-martial without a military judge on any interlocutory question of fact, including a factual issue of mental capacity of the accused, or on a motion for a finding of not guilty, is final unless objected to by a member.

(C) *Changing a ruling.* The president of a special court-martial without a military judge may change a ruling made by that or another president in the case except a previously granted motion for a finding of not guilty, at any time during the trial.

(D) *Presence of members.* Except as provided in R.C.M. 505 and 912, all members will be present at all sessions of a special court-martial without a military judge, including sessions at which questions of law or interlocutory questions are litigated. However, the president of a special court-martial without a military judge may examine an offered item of real or documentary evidence before ruling on its admissibility without exposing it to other members.

(3) *Procedures for rulings by the president of a special court-martial without a military judge which are subject to objection by a member.*

(A) *Determination.* The president of a special court-martial without a military judge shall determine whether a ruling is subject to objection.

(B) *Instructions.* When a ruling by the president of a special court-martial without a military judge is subject to objection, the president shall so advise the members and shall give such instructions on the issue as may be necessary to enable the members to understand the issue and the legal standards by which they will determine it if objection is made.

(C) *Voting.* When a member objects to a ruling by the president of a special court-martial without a military judge which is subject to objection, the court-martial shall be closed, and the members shall vote orally, beginning with the junior in rank, and the question shall be decided by a majority vote. A tie vote on a motion for a finding of not guilty is a determination against the accused. A tie vote on any other question is a determination in favor of the accused.

(D) *Consultation.* The president of a special court-martial without a military judge may close the court-martial and consult with other members before ruling on a matter, when such ruling is subject to the objection of any member.

(4) *Standard of proof.* Questions of fact in an interlocutory question shall be determined by a preponderance of the evidence, unless otherwise stated in this Manual. In the absence of a rule in this Manual assigning the burden of persuasion, the party making the motion or raising the objection shall bear the burden of persuasion.

Discussion

A ruling on an interlocutory question should be preceded by any necessary inquiry into the pertinent facts and law. For example, the party making the objection, motion, or request may be required to furnish evidence or legal authority in support of the contention. An interlocutory issue may have a different standard of proof. *See,* for example, Mil. R. Evid. 314(e)(5), which requires consent for a search to be proved by clear and convincing evidence.

Most of the common motions are discussed in specific rules in this Manual, and the burden of persuasion is assigned therein. The prosecution usually bears the burden of persuasion (*see* Mil. R. Evid. 304(e); 311(e); *see also* R.C.M. 905 through 907) once an issue has been raised. What "raises" an issue may vary with the issue. Some issues may be raised by a timely motion or objection. *See,* for example, Mil. R. Evid. 304(e). Others may not be raised until the defense has made an offer of proof or presented evidence in support of its position. *See,* for example, Mil. R. Evid. 311(g)(2). The rules in this Manual and relevant decisions should be consulted when a question arises as to whether an issue is raised, as well as which side has the burden of persuasion. The military judge or president of a special court-martial may require a party to clarify a motion or objection or to make an offer of proof, regardless of the burden of persuasion, when it appears that the motion or objection is vague, inapposite, irrelevant, or spurious.

---

(5) *Scope.* Subsection (e) of this rule applies to the disposition of questions of law and interlocutory questions arising during trial except the question whether a challenge should be sustained.

Discussion

Questions of law and interlocutory questions include all issues which arise during trial other than the findings (that is, guilty or not guilty), sentence, and administrative matters such as declaring recesses and adjournments. A question may be both interlocutory and a question of law. Challenges are specifically covered in R.C.M. 902 and 912.

Questions of the applicability of a rule of law to an undisputed set of facts are normally questions of law. Similarly, the legality of an act is normally a question of law. For example, the legality of an order when disobedience of an order is charged, the legality of restraint when there is a prosecution for breach of arrest, or the sufficiency of warnings before interrogation are normally questions of law. It is possible, however, for such questions to be decided solely upon some factual issue, in which case they would be questions of fact. For example, the question of what warnings, if any, were given by an interrogator to a suspect would be a factual question.

A question is interlocutory unless the ruling on it would finally decide whether the accused is guilty. Questions which may determine the ultimate issue of guilt are not interlocutory. An issue may arise as both an interlocutory question and a question which may determine the ultimate issue of guilt. An issued is not purely interlocutory if an accused raises a defense or objection and the disputed facts involved determine the ultimate question of guilt. For example, if during a trial for desertion the accused moves to dismiss for lack of jurisdiction and presents some evidence that the accused is not a member of an armed force, the accused's status as a military person may determine the ultimate question of guilt because status is an element of the offense. If the motion is denied, the disputed facts must be resolved by each member in deliberation upon the findings. (The accused's status as a servicemember would have to be proved by a preponderance of the evidence to uphold jurisdiction, *see* R.C.M. 907, but beyond a reasonable doubt to permit a finding of guilty.) If, on the other hand, the accused was charged with larceny and presented the same evidence as to military status, the evidence would bear only upon amenability to trial and the issue would be disposed of solely as an interlocutory question.

Interlocutory questions may be questions of fact or questions of law. This distinction is important because the president of a special court-martial without a military judge rules finally on interlocutory questions of law, but not on interlocutory questions of fact. On interlocutory questions of fact the president of a special court-martial without a military judge rules subject to the objection of any other member. On mixed questions of fact and law, rulings by the president are subject to objection by any

member to the extent that the issue of fact can be isolated and considered separately.

(f) *Rulings on record.* All sessions involving rulings or instructions made or given by the military judge or the president of a special court-martial without a military judge shall be made a part of the record. All rulings and instructions shall be made or given in open session in the presence of the parties and the members, except as otherwise may be determined in the discretion of the military judge. For purposes of this subsection [R.C.M. 801(f)] "military judge" does not include the president of a special court-martial without a military judge.

Discussion

See R.C.M. 808 and 1103 concerning preparation of the record of trial.

(g) *Effect of failure to raise defenses or objections.* Failure by a party to raise defenses or objections or to make requests or motions which must be made at the time set by this Manual or by the military judge under authority of this Manual, or prior to any extension thereof made by the military judge, shall constitute waiver thereof, but the military judge for good cause shown may grant relief from the waiver.

Rule 802. Conferences

(a) *In general.* After referral, the military judge may, upon request of any party or *sua sponte*, order one or more conferences with the parties to consider such matters as will promote a fair and expeditious trial.

Discussion

Conferences between the military judge and counsel may be held when necessary before or during trial. The purpose of such conference is to inform the military judge of anticipated issues and to expeditiously resolve matters on which the parties can agree, not to litigate or decide contested issues. *See* subsection (c) below. No party may be compelled to resolve any matter at a conference.

A conference may be appropriate in order to resolve scheduling difficulties, so that witnesses and members are not unnecessarily inconvenienced. Matters which will ultimately be in the military judge's discretion, such as conduct of voir dire, seating arrangements in the courtroom, or procedures when there are multiple accused may be resolved at a conference. Conferences may be used to advise the military judge of issues or problems, such as unusual motions or objections, which are likely to arise during trial.

Occasionally it may be appropriate to resolve certain issues, in addition to routine or administrative matters, if this can be done with the consent of the parties. For example, a request for a witness which, if litigated and approved at trial, would delay the proceedings and cause expense or inconvenience, might be resolved at a conference. Note, however, that this could only be done by an agreement of the parties and not by a binding ruling of the military judge. Such a resolution must be included in the record. *See* subsection (b) below.

A military judge may not participate in negotiations relating to pleas. *See* R.C.M. 705 and Mil. R. Evid. 410.

No place or method is prescribed for conducting a conference. A conference may be conducted by remote means or similar technology consistent with the definition in R.C.M. 914B.

(b) *Matters on record.* Conferences need not be made part of the record, but matters agreed upon at a conference shall be included in the record orally or in writing. Failure of a party to object at trial to failure to comply with this subsection shall waive this requirement.

(c) *Rights of parties.* No party may be prevented under this rule from presenting evidence or from making any argument, objection, or motion at trial.

(d) *Accused's presence.* The presence of the accused is neither required nor prohibited at a conference.

Discussion

Normally the defense counsel may be presumed to speak for the accused.

(e) *Admission.* No admissions made by the accused or defense counsel at a conference shall be used against the accused unless the admissions are reduced to writing and signed by the accused and defense counsel.

(f) *Limitations.* This rule shall not be invoked in the case of an accused who is not represented by counsel, or in special court-martial without a military judge.

Rule 803. Court-martial sessions without members under Article 39(a)

A military judge who has been detailed to the court-martial may, under Article 39(a), after service of charges, call the court-martial into session without the presence of members. Such sessions may be held before and after assembly of the court-martial, and when authorized in these rules, after adjournment and before action by the convening authority. All such sessions are a part of the trial and shall be

conducted in the presence of the accused, defense counsel, and trial counsel, in accordance with R.C.M. 804 and 805, and shall be made a part of the record. For purposes of this rule "military judge" does not include the president of a special court-martial without a military judge.

Discussion

The purpose of Article 39(a) is "to give statutory sanction to pretrial and other hearings without the presence of the members concerning those matters which are amenable to disposition on either a tentative or final basis by the military judge." The military judge and members may, and ordinarily should, call the court-martial into session without members to ascertain the accused's understanding of the right to counsel, the right to request trial by military judge alone, or when applicable, enlisted members, and the accused's choices with respect to these matters; dispose of interlocutory matters; hear objections and motions; rule upon other matters that may legally be ruled upon by the military judge, such as admitting evidence; and perform other procedural functions which do not require the presence of members. *See*, for example, R.C.M. 901–910. The military judge may, if permitted by regulations of the Secretary concerned, hold the arraignment, receive pleas, and enter findings of guilty upon an accepted plea of guilty.

Evidence may be admitted and process, including a subpoena, may be issued to compel attendance of witnesses and production of evidence at such sessions. *See* R.C.M. 703.

Article 39(a) authorizes sessions only after charges have been referred to trial and served on the accused, but the accused has an absolute right to object, in time of peace, to any session until the period prescribed by Article 35 has run.

See R.C.M. 804 concerning waiver by the accused of the right to be present. *See also* R.C.M. 802 concerning conferences.

Rule 804. Presence of the accused at trial proceedings

(a) *Presence required.* The accused shall be present at the arraignment, the time of the plea, every stage of the trial including sessions conducted under Article 39(a), voir dire and challenges of members, the return of the findings, sentencing proceedings, and post-trial sessions, if any, except as otherwise provided by this rule.

(b) *Presence by remote means.* If authorized by the regulations of the Secretary concerned, the military judge may order the use of audiovisual technology, such as videoteleconferencing technology, between the parties and the military judge for purposes of Article 39(a) sessions. Use of such audiovisual technology will satisfy the "presence" requirement of the accused only when the accused has a defense counsel physically present at his location. Such technology may include two or more remote sites as long as all parties can see and hear each other.

(c) *Continued presence not required.* The further progress of the trial to and including the return of the findings and, if necessary, determination of a sentence shall not be prevented and the accused shall be considered to have waived the right to be present whenever an accused, initially present:

(1) Is voluntarily absent after arraignment (whether or not informed by the military judge of the obligation to remain during the trial); or

(2) After being warned by the military judge that disruptive conduct will cause the accused to be removed from the courtroom, persists in conduct which is such as to justify exclusion from the courtroom.

Discussion

Express waiver. The accused may expressly waive the right to be present at trial proceedings. There is no right to be absent, however, and the accused may be required to be present over objection. Thus, an accused cannot frustrate efforts to identify the accused at trial by waiving the right to be present. The right to be present is so fundamental, and the Government's interest in the attendance of the accused so substantial, that the accused should be permitted to waive the right to be present only for good cause, and only after the military judge explains to the accused the right, and the consequences of foregoing it, and secures the accused's personal consent to proceeding without the accused.

Voluntary absence. In any case the accused may forfeit the right to be present by being voluntarily absent after arraignment.

"Voluntary absence" means voluntary absence from trial. For an absence from court-martial proceedings to be voluntary, the accused must have known of the scheduled proceedings and intentionally missed them. For example, although an accused servicemember might voluntarily be absent without authority, this would not justify proceeding with a court-martial in the accused's absence unless the accused was aware that the court-martial would be held during the period of the absence.

An accused who is in military custody or otherwise subject to military control at the time of trial or other proceeding may not properly be absent from the trial or proceeding without securing the permission of the military judge on the record.

The prosecution has the burden to establish by a preponderance of the evidence that the accused's absence from trial is voluntary. Voluntariness may not be presumed, but it may be inferred, depending on the circumstances. For example, it may be inferred, in the absence of evidence to the contrary, that an accused who was present when the trial recessed and who knew when the proceedings were scheduled to resume, but who nonetheless is not present when court reconvenes at the designated time, is absent voluntarily.

Where there is some evidence that an accused who is absent for a hearing or trial may lack mental capacity to stand trial,

capacity to voluntarily waive the right to be present for trial must be shown. *See* R.C.M. 909.

Subsection (1) authorizes but does not require trial to proceed in the absence of the accused upon the accused's voluntary absence. When an accused is absent from trial after arraignment, a continuance or a recess may be appropriate, depending on all the circumstances.

Presence of the accused by remote means does not require the consent of the accused.

Removal for disruption. Trial may proceed without the presence of an accused who has disrupted the proceedings, but only after at least one warning by the military judge that such behavior may result in removal from the courtroom. In order to justify removal from the proceedings, the accused's behavior should be of such a nature as to materially interfere with the conduct of the proceedings.

The military judge should consider alternatives to removal of a disruptive accused. Such alternatives include physical restraint (such as binding, shackling, and gagging) of the accused, or physically segregating the accused in the courtroom. Such alternatives need not be tried before removing a disruptive accused under subsection (2). Removal may be preferable to such an alternative as binding and gagging, which can be an affront to the dignity and decorum of the proceedings.

Disruptive behavior of the accused may also constitute contempt. *See* R.C.M. 809. When the accused is removed from the courtroom for disruptive behavior, the military judge should—

(A) Afford the accused and defense counsel ample opportunity to consult throughout the proceedings. To this end, the accused should be held or otherwise required to remain in the vicinity of the trial, and frequent recesses permitted to allow counsel to confer with the accused.

(B) Take such additional steps as may be reasonably practicable to enable the accused to be informed about the proceedings. Although not required, technological aids, such as closed-circuit television or audio transmissions, may be used for this purpose.

(C) Afford the accused a continuing opportunity to return to the courtroom upon assurance of good behavior. To this end, the accused should be brought to the courtroom at appropriate intervals, and offered the opportunity to remain upon good behavior.

(D) Ensure that the reasons for removal appear in the record.

(d) *Voluntary absence for limited purpose of child testimony.*

(1) *Election by accused.* Following a determination by the military judge that remote live testimony of a child is appropriate pursuant to Mil. R. Evid. 611(d)(3), the accused may elect to voluntarily absent himself from the courtroom in order to preclude the use of procedures described in R.C.M. 914A.

(2) *Procedure.* The accused's absence will be conditional upon his being able to view the witness' testimony from a remote location. Normally, transmission of the testimony will include a system that will transmit the accused's image and voice into the courtroom from a remote location as well as trans-

mission of the child's testimony from the courtroom to the accused's location. A one-way transmission may be used if deemed necessary by the military judge. The accused will also be provided private, contemporaneous communication with his counsel. The procedures described herein shall be employed unless the accused has made a knowing and affirmative waiver of these procedures.

(3) *Effect on accused's rights generally.* An election by the accused to be absent pursuant to subsection (c)(1) shall not otherwise affect the accused's right to be present at the remainder of the trial in accordance with this rule.

(e) *Appearance and security of accused.*

(1) *Appearance.* The accused shall be properly attired in the uniform or dress prescribed by the military judge. An accused servicemember shall wear the insignia of grade and may wear any decorations, emblems, or ribbons to which entitled. The accused and defense counsel are responsible for ensuring that the accused is properly attired; however, upon request, the accused's commander shall render such assistance as may be reasonably necessary to ensure that the accused is properly attired.

Discussion

This subsection recognizes the right, as well as the obligation, of an accused servicemember to present a good military appearance at trial. An accused servicemember who refuses to present a proper military appearance before a court-martial may be compelled to do so.

---

(2) *Custody.* Responsibility for maintaining custody or control of an accused before and during trial may be assigned, subject to R.C.M. 304 and 305, and subsection (c)(3) of this rule, under such regulations as the Secretary concerned may prescribe.

(3) *Restraint.* Physical restraint shall not be imposed on the accused during open sessions of the court-martial unless prescribed by the military judge.

Rule 805. Presence of military judge, members, and counsel

(a) *Military judge.* No court-martial proceeding, except the deliberations of the members, may take place in the absence of the military judge, if detailed. If authorized by regulations of the Secretary concerned, for purposes of Article 39(a) sessions solely, the presence of the military judge at Article

39(a) sessions may be satisfied by the use of audio-visual technology, such as videoteleconferencing technology.

(b) *Members.* Unless trial is by military judge alone pursuant to a request by the accused, no court-martial proceeding may take place in the absence of any detailed member except: Article 39(a) sessions under R.C.M. 803; examination of members under R.C.M. 912(d); when the member has been excused under R.C.M. 505 or 912(f); or as otherwise provided in R.C.M. 1102. No general court-martial proceeding requiring the presence of members may be conducted unless at least five members are present, or in capital cases, at least 12 members are present except as provided in R.C.M. 501(a)(1)(B), where 12 members are not reasonably available because of physical conditions or military exigencies. No special court-martial proceeding requiring the presence of members may be conducted unless at least three members are present except as provided in R.C.M. 912(h). Except as provided in R.C.M. 503(a)(2), when an enlisted accused has requested enlisted members, no proceeding requiring the presence of members may be conducted unless at least one-third of the members actually sitting on the court-martial are enlisted persons.

(c) *Counsel.* As long as at least one qualified counsel for each party is present, other counsel for each party may be absent from a court-martial session. An assistant counsel who lacks the qualifications necessary to serve as counsel for a party may not act at a session in the absence of such qualified counsel. If authorized by regulations of the Secretary concerned, for purposes of Article 39(a) sessions solely, the presence of counsel at Article 39(a) sessions may be satisfied by the use of audiovisual technology, such as videoteleconferencing technology. At least one qualified defense counsel shall be physically present with the accused.

Discussion

See R.C.M. 504(d) concerning qualifications of counsel.

Ordinarily, no court-martial proceeding should take place if any defense or assistant defense counsel is absent unless the accused expressly consents to the absence. The military judge may, however proceed in the absence of one or more defense counsel, without the consent of the accused, if the military judge finds that, under the circumstances, a continuance is not warranted and that the accused's right to be adequately represented would not be impaired.

See R.C.M. 502(d)(6) and 505(d)(2) concerning withdrawal or substitution of counsel. *See* R.C.M. 506(d) concerning the right of the accused to proceed without counsel.

(d) *Effect of replacement of member or military judge.*

(1) *Members.* When after presentation of evidence on the merits has begun, a new member is detailed under R.C.M. 505(c)(2)(B), trial may not proceed unless the testimony and evidence previously admitted on the merits, if recorded verbatim, is read to the new member, or, if not recorded verbatim, and in the absence of a stipulation as to such testimony and evidence, the trial proceeds as if no evidence has been presented.

Discussion

When a new member is detailed, the military judge should give such instructions as may be appropriate. *See also* R.C.M. 912 concerning voir dire and challenges.

When the court-martial has been reduced below a quorum, a mistrial may be appropriate. See *R.C.M.* 915.

---

(2) *Military judge.* When, after the presentation of evidence on the merits has begun in trial before military judge alone, a new military judge is detailed under R.C.M. 505(e)(2) trial may not proceed unless the accused requests, and the military judge approves, trial by military judge alone, and a verbatim record of the testimony and evidence or a stipulation thereof is read to the military judge, or the trial proceeds as if no evidence had been presented.

Rule 806. Public trial

(a) *In general.* Except as otherwise provided in this rule, courts-martial shall be open to the public. For purposes of this rule, "public" includes members of both the military and civilian communities.

Discussion

Because of the requirement for public trials, courts-martial must be conducted in facilities which can accommodate a reasonable number of spectators. Military exigencies may occasionally make attendance at courts-martial difficult or impracticable, as, for example, when a court-martial is conducted on a ship at sea or in a unit in a combat zone. This does not violate this rule. However, such exigencies should not be manipulated to prevent attendance at a court-martial. The requirements of this rule may be met even though only servicemembers are able to attend a court-martial. Although not required, servicemembers should be encouraged to attend courts-martial.

When public access to a court-martial is limited for some reason, including lack of space, special care must be taken to avoid arbitrary exclusion of specific groups or persons. This may include allocating a reasonable number of seats to members of the press and to relatives of the accused, and establishing procedures for entering and exiting from the courtroom. *See also* subsection (b) below. There is no requirement that there actually be spectators at a court-martial.

The fact that a trial is conducted with members does not make it a public trial.

(b) *Control of spectators and closure.*

(1) *Control of spectators.* In order to maintain the dignity and decorum of the proceedings or for other good cause, the military judge may reasonably limit the number of spectators in, and the means of access to, the courtroom, and exclude specific persons from the courtroom. When excluding specific persons, the military judge must make findings on the record establishing the reason for the exclusion, the basis for the military judge's belief that exclusion is necessary, and that the exclusion is as narrowly tailored as possible.

(2) *Right of victim to notice.* A victim of an alleged offense committed by the accused has the right to reasonable, accurate, and timely notice of court-martial proceedings relating to the offense.

Discussion

The military judge must ensure that the dignity and decorum of the proceedings are maintained and that the other rights and interests of the parties and society are protected. Public access to a session may be limited, specific persons may be excluded from the courtroom, and, under unusual circumstances, a session may be closed.

Exclusion of specific persons, if unreasonable under the circumstances, may violate the accused's right to a public trial, even though other spectators remain. Whenever specific persons or some members of the public are excluded, exclusion must be limited in time and scope to the minimum extent necessary to achieve the purpose for which it is ordered. Prevention of over¡ crowding or noise may justify limiting access to the courtroom. Disruptive or distracting appearance or conduct may justify excluding specific persons. Specific persons may be excluded when necessary to protect witness's from harm or intimidation. Access may be reduced when no other means is available to relieve a witness's inability to testify due to embarrassment or extreme nervousness. Witnesses will ordinarily be excluded from the courtroom so that they cannot hear the testimony of other witnesses. *See* Mil. R. Evid. 615.

For purposes of this rule, the term "victim of an alleged offense" means a person who has suffered direct physical, emotional, or pecuniary harm as a result of the commission of an offense under the UCMJ.

---

(3) *Right of victim to attend.* A victim of an al-

leged offense committed by the accused may not be excluded from a court-martial relating to the offense unless the military judge, after receiving clear and convincing evidence, determines that testimony by the victim would be materially altered if the victim heard other testimony at that hearing or proceeding. The right to attend requires reasonable, accurate, and timely notice of a court-martial relating to the offense.

(4) *Right of victim to confer.* A victim of an alleged offense committed by the accused has the reasonable right to confer with the trial counsel.

(5) *Closure.* Courts-martial shall be open to the public unless (1) there is a substantial probability that an overriding interest will be prejudiced if the proceedings remain open; (2) closure is no broader than necessary to protect the overriding interest; (3) reasonable alternatives to closure were considered and found inadequate; and (4) the military judge makes case-specific findings on the record justifying closure.

(6) *Right of victim to be reasonably protected from the accused* A victim of an alleged offense committed by the accused has the right to be reasonably protected from the accused.

Discussion

The military judge is responsible for protecting both the accused's right to, and the public's interest in, a public trial. A court-martial session is "closed" when no member of the public is permitted to attend. A court-martial is not "closed" merely because the exclusion of certain individuals results in there being no spectators present, as long as the exclusion is not so broad as to effectively bar everyone who might attend the sessions and is put into place for a proper purpose.

A session may be closed over the objection of the accused or the public upon meeting the constitutional standard set forth in this Rule. *See also* Mil. R. Evid. 412(c), 505(i), and 513(e)(2).

The accused may waive his right to a public trial. The fact that the prosecution and defense jointly seek to have a session closed does not, however, automatically justify closure, for the public has a right in attending courts-martial. Opening trials to public scrutiny reduces the chance of arbitrary and capricious decisions and enhances public confidence in the court-martial process.

The most likely reason for a defense request to close court-martial proceedings is to minimize the potentially adverse effect of publicity on the trial. For example, a pretrial Article 39(a) hearing at which the admissibility of a confession will be litigated may, under some circumstances, be closed, in accordance with this Rule, in order to prevent disclosure to the public (and hence to potential members) of the very evidence that may be excluded.

When such publicity may be a problem, a session should be closed only as a last resort.

There are alternative means of protecting the proceedings from harmful effects of publicity, including a thorough *voir dire* (*see* R.C.M. 912), and, if necessary, a continuance to allow the harmful effects of publicity to dissipate (*see* R.C.M. 906(b)(1)). Alternatives that may occasionally be appropriate and are usually preferable to closing a session include: directing members not to read, listen to, or watch any accounts concerning the case; issuing a protective order (*see* R.C.M. 806(d)); selecting members from recent arrivals in the command, or from outside the immediate area (*see* R.C.M. 503(a)(3)); changing the place of trial (*see* R.C.M. 906(b)(11)); or sequestering the members.

(c) *Photography and broadcasting prohibited.* Video and audio recording and the taking of photographs—except for the purpose of preparing the record of trial—in the courtroom during the proceedings and radio or television broadcasting of proceedings from the courtroom shall not be permitted. However, the military judge may, as a matter of discretion permit contemporaneous closed-circuit video or audio transmission to permit viewing or hearing by an accused removed under R.C.M. 804 or by spectators when courtroom facilities are inadequate to accommodate a reasonable number of spectators.

(d) *Protective orders.* The military judge may, upon request of any party or *sua sponte*, issue an appropriate protective order, in writing, to prevent parties and witnesses from making extrajudicial statements that present a substantial likelihood of material prejudice to a fair trial by impartial members. For purposes of this subsection, "military judge" does not include the president of a special court-martial without a military judge.

Discussion

A protective order may proscribe extrajudicial statements by counsel, parties, and witnesses that might divulge prejudicial matter not of public record in the case. Other appropriate matters may also be addressed by such a protective order. Before issuing a protective order, the military judge must consider whether other available remedies would effectively mitigate the adverse effects that any publicity might create, and consider such an order's likely effectiveness in ensuring an impartial court-martial panel. A military judge should not issue a protective order without first providing notice to the parties and an opportunity to be heard. The military judge must state on the record the reasons for issuing the protective order. If the reasons for issuing the order change, the military judge may reconsider the continued necessity for a protective order.

Rule 807. Oaths

(a) *Definition.* "Oath" includes "affirmation."

Discussion

An affirmation is the same as an oath, except in an affirmation the words "so help you God" are omitted.

(b) *Oaths in courts-martial.*

(1) *Who must be sworn.*

(A) *Court-martial personnel.* The military judge, members of a general or special court-martial, trial counsel, assistant trial counsel, defense counsel, associate defense counsel, assistant defense counsel, reporter, interpreter, and escort shall take an oath to perform their duties faithfully. For purposes of this rule, "defense counsel," "associate defense counsel," and "assistant defense counsel," include detailed and individual military and civilian counsel.

Discussion

Article 42(a) provides that regulations of the Secretary concerned shall prescribe: the form of the oath; the time and place of the taking thereof; the manner of recording it; and whether the oath shall be taken for all cases in which the duties are to be performed or in each case separately. In the case of certified legal personnel (Article 26(b); Article 27(b)) these regulations may provide for the administration of an oath on a one-time basis. *See also* R.C.M. 813 and 901 concerning the point in the proceedings at which it is ordinarily determined whether the required oaths have been taken or are then administered.

(B) *Witnesses.* Each witness before a court-martial shall be examined on oath.

Discussion

See R.C.M. 307 concerning the requirement for an oath in preferral of charges. *See* R.C.M. 405 and 702 concerning the requirements for an oath in Article 32 preliminary hearings and depositions.

An accused making an unsworn statement is not a "witness." *See* R.C.M. 1001(c)(2)(C).

A victim of an offense of which the accused has been found guilty is not a "witness" when making an unsworn statement during the presentencing phase of a court-martial. *See* R.C.M. 1001A.

---

(2) *Procedure for administering oaths.* Any procedure which appeals to the conscience of the person to whom the oath is administered and which binds that person to speak the truth, or, in the case of one other than a witness, properly to perform certain duties, is sufficient.

Discussion

When the oath is administered in a session to the military judge, members, or any counsel, all persons in the courtroom should stand. In those rare circumstances in which the trial counsel testifies as a witness, the military judge administers the oath.

Unless otherwise prescribed by the Secretary concerned the forms below may be used, as appropriate, to administer an oath.

(A) *Oath for military judge.* When the military judge is not previously sworn, the trial counsel will administer the following oath to the military judge:

"Do you (swear) (affirm) that you will faithfully and impartially perform, according to your conscience and the laws applicable to trial by court-martial, all the duties incumbent upon you as military judge of this court-martial (,so help you God)?"

(B) *Oath for members.* The following oath, as appropriate, will be administered to the members by the trial counsel:

"Do you (swear) (affirm) that you will answer truthfully the questions concerning whether you should serve as a member of this court-martial; that you will faithfully and impartially try, according to the evidence, your conscience, and the laws applicable to trial by court-martial, the case of the accused now before this court; and that you will not disclose or discover the vote or opinion of any particular member of the court (upon a challenge or) upon the findings or sentence unless required to do so in due course of law (,so help you God)?"

(C) *Oaths for counsel.* When counsel for either side, including any associate or assistant, is not previously sworn the following oath, as appropriate, will be administered by the military judge:

"Do you (swear) (affirm) that you will faithfully perform all the duties of (trial) (assistant trial) (defense)(associate defense) (assistant defense) counsel in the case now in hearing (,so help you God)?"

(D) *Oath for reporter.* The trial counsel will administer the following oath to every reporter of a court-martial who has not been previously sworn:

"Do you (swear) (affirm) that you will faithfully perform the duties of reporter to this court-martial (,so help you God)?"

(E) *Oath for interpreter.* The trial counsel or the summary court-martial shall administer the following oath to every interpreter in the trial of any case before a court-martial:

"Do you (swear) (affirm) that in the case now in hearing you will interpret truly the testimony you are called upon to interpret (,so help you God)?"

(F) *Oath for witnesses.* The trial counsel or the summary court-martial will administer the following oath to each witness before the witness first testifies in a case:

"Do you (swear) (affirm) that the evidence you shall give in the case now in hearing shall be the truth, the whole truth, and nothing but the truth (,so help you God)?"

(G) *Oath for escort.* The escort on views or inspections by the court-martial will, before serving, take the following oath, which will be administered by the trial counsel:

"Do you (swear) (affirm) that you will escort the court-martial and will well and truly point out to them (the place in which the offense charged in this case is alleged to have been committed) (_____); and that you will not speak to the members concerning (the alleged offense) (_____), except to describe (the place aforesaid) (_____) (,so help you God)?"

See Article 136 concerning persons authorized to administer oaths.

Rule 808. Record of trial

The trial counsel of a general or special court-martial shall take such action as may be necessary to ensure that a record which will meet the requirements of R.C.M. 1103 can be prepared.

Discussion

Except in a special court-martial not authorized to adjudge a bad-conduct discharge, confinement for more than six months, or forfeiture of pay for more than six months, the trial counsel should ensure that a qualified court reporter is detailed to the court-martial. Trial counsel should also ensure that all exhibits and other documents relating to the case are properly maintained for later inclusion in the record. See also R.C.M. 1103(j) as to the use of videotapes, audiotapes, and similar recordings for the record of trial. Because of the potential requirement for a verbatim transcript, all proceedings, including sidebar conferences, arguments, and rulings and instructions by the military judge, should be recorded.

Where there is recorder failure or loss of court reporter's notes, the record should be reconstructed as completely as possible. See also R.C.M. 1103(f). If the interruption is discovered during trial, the military judge should summarize or reconstruct the portion of the proceedings which has not been recorded and then proceed anew and repeat the proceedings from the point where the interruption began.

See R.C.M. 1305 concerning the record of trial in summary courts-martial.

See DD Forms 490 (Record of Trial), 491 (Summarized Record of Trial), and 491–1 (Summarized Record of Trial-Article 39(a) Session).

Rule 809. Contempt proceedings

(a) *In general.* Courts-martial may exercise contempt power under Article 48.

Discussion

Article 48 makes punishable "direct" contempt, as well as "indirect" or "constructive" contempt. "Direct" contempt is that which is committed in the presence of the court-martial or its immediate proximity. "Presence" includes those places outside the courtroom itself, such as waiting areas, deliberation rooms, and other places set aside for the use of the court-martial while it is in session. "Indirect" or "constructive" contempt is non-compliance with lawful writs, processes, orders, rules, decrees, or commands of the court-martial. A "direct" or "indirect" contempt may

be actually seen or heard by the court-martial, in which case it may be punished summarily. See subsection (b)(1) of this Rule. A "direct" or "indirect" contempt may also be a contempt not actually observed by the court-martial, for example, when an unseen person makes loud noises, whether inside or outside the courtroom, which impede the orderly progress of the proceedings. In such a case the procedures for punishing contempt are more extensive. See subsection (b)(2) of this Rule.

The words "any person," as used in Article 48, include all persons, whether or not subject to military law, except the military judge and foreign nationals outside the territorial limits of the United States who are not subject to the code. The military judge may order the offender removed whether or not contempt proceedings are held. It may be appropriate to warn a person whose conduct is improper that persistence in a course of behavior may result in removal or punishment for contempt. See R.C.M. 804, 806.

Each finding of contempt may be separately punished.

A person subject to the code who commits contempt may be tried by court-martial or otherwise disciplined under Article 134 for such misconduct in addition to or instead of punishment for contempt. See paragraph 108, Part IV; see also Article 98. The 2011 amendment of Article 48 expanded the contempt power of military courts to enable them to enforce orders, such as discovery orders or protective orders regarding evidence, against military or civilian attorneys. Persons not subject to military jurisdiction under Article 2, having been duly subpoenaed, may be prosecuted in Federal civilian court under Article 47 for neglect or refusal to appear or refusal to qualify as a witness or to testify or to produce evidence.

(b) *Method of disposition.*

(1) *Summary disposition.* When conduct constituting contempt is directly witnessed by the court-martial, the conduct may be punished summarily.

(2) *Disposition upon notice and hearing.* When the conduct apparently constituting contempt is not directly witnessed by the court-martial, the alleged offender shall be brought before the court-martial and informed orally or in writing of the alleged contempt. The alleged offender shall be given a reasonable opportunity to present evidence, including calling witnesses. The alleged offender shall have the right to be represented by counsel and shall be so advised. The contempt must be proved beyond a reasonable doubt before it may be punished.

(c) *Procedure.* The military judge shall in all cases determine whether to punish for contempt and, if so, what the punishment shall be. The military judge shall also determine when during the court-martial the contempt proceedings shall be conducted; however, if the court-martial is composed of members, the military judge shall conduct the contempt proceedings outside the members' presence. The military judge may punish summarily under subsection (b)(1) only if the military judge recites the facts for the record and states that they were directly witnessed by the military judge in the actual presence of the court-martial. Otherwise, the provisions of subsection (b)(2) shall apply.

(d) *Record; review.* A record of the contempt proceedings shall be part of the record of the court-martial during which it occurred. If the person was held in contempt, then a separate record of the contempt proceedings shall be prepared and forwarded to the convening authority for review. The convening authority may approve or disapprove all or part of the sentence. The action of the convening authority is not subject to further review or appeal.

(e) *Sentence.* A sentence of confinement pursuant to a finding of contempt shall begin to run when it is adjudged unless deferred, suspended, or disapproved by the convening authority. The place of confinement for a civilian or military person who is held in contempt and is to be punished by confinement shall be designated by the convening authority. A fine does not become effective until ordered executed by the convening authority. The military judge may delay announcing the sentence after a finding of contempt to permit the person involved to continue to participate in the proceedings.

Discussion

The immediate commander of the person held in contempt, or, in the case of a civilian, the convening authority should be notified immediately so that the necessary action on the sentence may be taken. *See* R.C.M. 1101.

(f) *Informing person held in contempt.* The person held in contempt shall be informed by the convening authority in writing of the holding and sentence, if any, of the court-martial and of the action of the convening authority upon the sentence.

Discussion

Copies of this communication should be furnished to such other persons including the immediate commander of the offender as may be concerned with the execution of the punishment. A copy shall be included with the record of both the trial and the contempt proceeding.

Rule 810. Procedures for rehearings, new trials, and other trials

(a) *In general.*

(1) *Rehearings in full and new or other trials.* In rehearings which require findings on all charges and specifications referred to a court-martial and in new or other trials, the procedure shall be the same as in an original trial except as otherwise provided in this rule.

(2) *Rehearings on sentence only.* In a rehearing on sentence only, the procedure shall be the same as in an original trial, except that the portion of the procedure which ordinarily occurs after challenges and through and including the findings is omitted, and except as otherwise provided in this rule.

(A) *Contents of the record.* The contents of the record of the original trial consisting of evidence properly admitted on the merits relating to each offense of which the accused stands convicted but not sentenced may be established by any party whether or not testimony so read is otherwise admissible under Mil. R. Evid. 804(b)(1) and whether or not it was given through an interpreter.

Discussion

Matters excluded from the record of the original trial on the merits or improperly admitted on the merits must not be brought to the attention of the members as a part of the original record of trial.

(B) *Plea.* The accused at a rehearing only on sentence may not withdraw any plea of guilty upon which findings of guilty are based. However, if such a plea is found to be improvident, the rehearing shall be suspended and the matter reported to the authority ordering the rehearing.

(3) *Combined rehearings.* When a rehearing on sentence is combined with a trial on the merits of one or more specifications referred to the court-martial, whether or not such specifications are being tried for the first time or reheard, the trial will proceed first on the merits, without reference to the offenses being reheard on sentence only. After findings on the merits are announced, the members, if any, shall be advised of the offenses on which the rehearing on sentence has been directed. Additional challenges for cause may be permitted, and the sentencing procedure shall be the same as at an original

trial, except as otherwise provided in this rule. A single sentence shall be adjudged for all offenses.

(b) *Composition.*

(1) *Members.* No member of the court-martial which previously heard the case may sit as a member of the court-martial at any rehearing, new trial, or other trial of the same case.

(2) *Military judge.* The military judge at a rehearing may be the same military judge who presided over a previous trial of the same case. The existence or absence of a request for trial by military judge alone at a previous hearing shall have no effect on the composition of a court-martial on rehearing.

(3) *Accused's election.* The accused at a rehearing or new or other trial shall have the same right to request enlisted members or trial by military judge alone as the accused would have at an original trial.

Discussion

See R.C.M. 902; 903.

(c) *Examination of record of former proceedings.* No member may, upon a rehearing or upon a new or other trial, examine the record of any former proceedings in the same case except:

(1) When permitted to do so by the military judge after such matters have been received in evidence; or

(2) That the president of a special court-martial without a military judge may examine that part of the record of former proceedings which relates to errors committed at the former proceedings when necessary to decide the admissibility of offered evidence or other questions of law, and such a part of the record may be read to the members when necessary for them to consider a matter subject to objection by any member.

Discussion

See R.C.M. 801(e)(2).

When a rehearing is ordered, the trial counsel should be provided a record of the former proceedings, accompanying documents, and any decision or review relating to the case, as well as a statement of the reason for the rehearing.

(d) *Sentence limitations.*

(1) *In general.* Sentences at rehearings, new trials, or other trials shall be adjudged within the limitations set forth in R.C.M. 1003. Except as otherwise provided in subsection (d)(2) of this rule, offenses on which a rehearing, new trial, or other trial has been ordered shall not be the basis for an approved sentence in excess of or more severe than the sentence ultimately approved by the convening or higher authority following the previous trial or hearing, unless the sentence prescribed for the offense is mandatory. When a rehearing or sentencing is combined with trial on new charges, the maximum punishment that may be approved by the convening authority shall be the maximum punishment under R.C.M. 1003 for the offenses being reheard as limited above, plus the total maximum punishment under R.C.M. 1003 for any new charges of which the accused has been found guilty. In the case of an "other trial" no sentence limitations apply if the original trial was invalid because a summary or special court-martial improperly tried an offense involving a mandatory punishment or one otherwise considered capital.

Discussion

At a rehearing, the trier of fact is not bound by the sentence previously adjudged or approved. The members should not be advised of the sentence limitation under this rule. See R.C.M. 1005(e)(1). An appropriate sentence on a retried or reheard offense should be adjudged without regard to any credit to which the accused may be entitled. See R.C.M. 103(2) and R.C.M. 103(3) as to when a rehearing may be a capital case.

---

(2) *Pretrial agreement.* If, after the earlier court-martial, the sentence was approved in accordance with a pretrial agreement and at the rehearing the accused fails to comply with the pretrial agreement, by failing to enter a plea of guilty or otherwise, the approved sentence resulting at a rehearing of the affected charges and specifications may include any otherwise lawful punishment not in excess of or more serious than lawfully adjudged at the earlier court-martial.

(e) *Definition.* "Other trial" means another trial of a case in which the original proceedings were declared invalid because of lack of jurisdiction or failure of a charge to state an offense.

Rule 811. Stipulations

(a) *In general.* The parties may make an oral or written stipulation to any fact, the contents of a document, or the expected testimony of a witness.

(b) *Authority to reject.* The military judge may, in the interest of justice, decline to accept a stipulation.

Discussion

Although the decision to stipulate should ordinarily be left to the parties, the military judge should not accept a stipulation if there is any doubt of the accused's or any other party's understanding of the nature and effect of the stipulation. The military judge should also refuse to accept a stipulation which is unclear or ambiguous. A stipulation of fact which amounts to a complete defense to any offense charged should not be accepted nor, if a plea of not guilty is outstanding, should one which practically amounts to a confession, except as described in the discussion under subsection (c) of this rule. If a stipulation is rejected, the parties may be entitled to a continuance.

(c) *Requirements.* Before accepting a stipulation in evidence, the military judge must be satisfied that the parties consent to its admission.

Discussion

Ordinarily, before accepting any stipulation the military judge should inquire to ensure that the accused understands the right not to stipulate, understands the stipulation, and consents to it.

If the stipulation practically amounts to a confession to an offense to which a not guilty plea is outstanding, it may not be accepted unless the military judge ascertains: (A) from the accused that the accused understands the right not to stipulate and that the stipulation will not be accepted without the accused's consent; that the accused understands the contents and effect of the stipulation; that a factual basis exists for the stipulation; and that the accused, after consulting with counsel, consents to the stipulation; and (B) from the accused and counsel for each party whether there are any agreements between the parties in connection with the stipulation, and, if so, what the terms of such agreements are.

A stipulation practically amounts to a confession when it is the equivalent of a guilty plea, that is, when it establishes, directly or by reasonable inference, every element of a charged offense and when the defense does not present evidence to contest any potential remaining issue of the merits. Thus, a stipulation which tends to establish, by reasonable inference, every element of a charged offense does not practically amount to a confession if the defense contests an issue going to guilt which is not foreclosed by the stipulation. For example, a stipulation of fact that contraband drugs were discovered in a vehicle owned by the accused would normally practically amount to a confession if no other evidence were presented on the issue, but would not if the defense presented evidence to show that the accused was unaware of the presence of the drugs. Whenever a stipulation establishes the elements of a charged offense, the military judge should conduct an inquiry as described above.

If, during an inquiry into a confessional stipulation the military judge discovers that there is a pretrial agreement, the military judge must conduct an inquiry into the pretrial agreement. *See* R.C.M. 910(f). *See also* R.C.M. 705.

(d) *Withdrawal.* A party may withdraw from an agreement to stipulate or from a stipulation at any time before a stipulation is accepted; the stipulation may not then be accepted. After a stipulation has been accepted a party may withdraw from it only if permitted to do so in the discretion of the military judge.

Discussion

If a party withdraws from an agreement to stipulate or from a stipulation, before or after it has been accepted, the opposing party may be entitled to a continuance to obtain proof of the matters which were to have been stipulated.

If a party is permitted to withdraw from a stipulation previously accepted, the stipulation must be disregarded by the court-martial, and an instruction to that effect should be given.

(e) *Effect of stipulation.* Unless properly withdrawn or ordered stricken from the record, a stipulation of fact that has been accepted is binding on the court-martial and may not be contradicted by the parties thereto. The contents of a stipulation of expected testimony or of a document's contents may be attacked, contradicted, or explained in the same way as if the witness had actually so testified or the document had been actually admitted. The fact that the parties so stipulated does not admit the truth of the indicated testimony or document's contents, nor does it add anything to the evidentiary nature of the testimony or document. The Military Rules of Evidence apply to the contents of stipulations.

(f) *Procedure.* When offered, a written stipulation shall be presented to the military judge and shall be included in the record whether accepted or not. Once accepted, a written stipulation of expected testimony shall be read to the members, if any, but shall not be presented to them; a written stipulation of fact or of a document's contents may be read to the members, if any, presented to them, or both. Once accepted, an oral stipulation shall be announced to the members, if any.

Rule 812. Joint and common trials

In joint trials and in common trials, each accused

shall be accorded the rights and privileges as if tried separately.

Discussion

See R.C.M. 307(c)(5) concerning preparing charges and specifications for joint trials. *See* R.C.M. 601(e)(3) concerning referral of charges for joint or common trials, and the distinction between the two. *See* R.C.M. 906(b)(9) concerning motions to sever and other appropriate motions in joint or common trials.

In a joint or common trial, each accused may be represented by separate counsel, make challenges for cause, make peremptory challenges (*see* R.C.M. 912), cross-examine witnesses, elect whether to testify, introduce evidence, request that the membership of the court include enlisted persons, if an enlisted accused, and, if a military judge has been detailed, request trial by military judge alone.

Where different elections are made (and, when necessary, approved) as to court-martial composition a severance is necessary. Thus, if one co-accused elects to be tried by a court-martial composed of officers, and a second requests that enlisted members be detailed to the court, and a third submits a request for trial by military judge alone, which request is approved, three separate trials must be conducted.

In a joint or common trial, evidence which is admissible against only one or some of the joint or several accused may be considered only against the accused concerned. For example, when a stipulation is accepted which was made by only one or some of the accused, the stipulation does not apply to those accused who did not join it. *See also* Mil. R. Evid. 306. In such instances the members must be instructed that the stipulation or evidence may be considered only with respect to the accused with respect to whom it is accepted.

Rule 813. Announcing personnel of the court-martial and accused

(a) *Opening sessions.* When the court-martial is cal- led to order for the first time in a case, the military judge shall ensure that the following is announced:

(1) The order, including any amendment, by which the court-martial is convened;

(2) The name, rank, and unit or address of the accused;

(3) The name and rank of the military judge, if one has been detailed;

(4) The names and ranks of the members, if any, who are present;

(5) The names and ranks of members who are absent, if presence of members is required;

(6) The names and ranks (if any) of counsel who are present;

(7) The names and ranks (if any) of counsel who are absent; and

(8) The name and rank (if any) of any detailed court reporter.

(b) *Later proceedings.* When the court-martial is called to order after a recess or adjournment or after it has been closed for any reason, the military judge shall ensure that the record reflects whether all parties and members who were present at the time of the adjournment or recess, or at the time the court-martial closed, are present.

(c) *Additions, replacement, and absences of personnel.* Whenever there is a replacement of the military judge, any member, or counsel, either through the appearance of new personnel or personnel previously absent or through the absence of personnel previously present, the military judge shall ensure the record reflects the change and the reason for it.

CHAPTER IX. TRIAL PROCEDURES THROUGH FINDINGS

Rule 901. Opening session

(a) *Call to order.* A court-martial is in session when the military judge so declares.

Discussion

The military judge should examine the charge sheet, convening order, and any amending orders before calling the initial session to order.

Article 35 provides that in time of peace, no proceedings, including Article 39(a) sessions, may be conducted over the accused's objection until five days have elapsed from the service of charges on the accused in the case of a general court-martial. The period is three days for a special court-martial. In computing these periods, the date of service and the date of the proceedings are excluded. Holidays and Sundays are not excluded. Failure to object waives the right to the waiting period, but if it appears that the waiting period has not elapsed, the military judge should bring this to the attention of the defense and secure an affirmative waiver on the record.

(b) *Announcement of parties.* After the court-martial is called to order, the presence or absence of the parties, military judge, and members shall be announced.

Discussion

If the orders detailing the military judge and counsel have not been reduced to writing, an oral announcement of such detailing is required. *See* R.C.M. 503(b) and (c).

(c) *Swearing reporter and interpreter.* After the personnel have been accounted for as required in subsection (b) of this rule, the trial counsel shall announce whether the reporter and interpreter, if any is present, have been properly sworn. If not sworn, the reporter and interpreter, if any, shall be sworn.

Discussion

See R.C.M. 807 concerning the oath to be administered to a court reporter or interpreter. If a reporter or interpreter is replaced at any time during trial, this should be noted for the record, and the procedures in this subsection should be repeated.

(d) *Counsel.*

(1) *Trial counsel.* The trial counsel shall announce the legal qualifications and status as to oaths of the members of the prosecution and whether any member of the prosecution has acted in any manner which might tend to disqualify that counsel.

(2) *Defense counsel.* The detailed defense counsel shall announce the legal qualifications and status as to oaths of the detailed members of the defense and whether any member of the defense has acted in any manner which might tend to disqualify that counsel. Any defense counsel not detailed shall state that counsel's legal qualifications, and whether that counsel has acted in any manner which might tend to disqualify the counsel.

(3) *Disqualification.* If it appears that any counsel may be disqualified, the military judge shall decide the matter and take appropriate action.

Discussion

Counsel may be disqualified because of lack of necessary qualifications, or because of duties or actions which are inconsistent with the role of counsel. *See* R.C.M. 502(d) concerning qualifications of counsel.

If it appears that any counsel may be disqualified, the military judge should conduct an inquiry or hearing. If any detailed counsel is disqualified, the appropriate authority should be informed. If any defense counsel is disqualified, the accused should be so informed.

If the disqualification of trial or defense counsel is one which the accused may waive, the accused should be so informed by the military judge, and given the opportunity to decide whether to waive the disqualification. In the case of defense counsel, if the disqualification is not waivable or if the accused elects not to waive the disqualification, the accused should be informed of the choices available and given the opportunity to exercise such options.

If any counsel is disqualified, the military judge should ensure that the accused is not prejudiced by any actions of the disqualified counsel or any break in representation of the accused.

Disqualification of counsel is not a jurisdictional defect; such error must be tested for prejudice.

If the membership of the prosecution or defense changes at any time during the proceedings, the procedures in this subsection should be repeated as to the new counsel. In addition, the military judge should ascertain on the record whether the accused objects to a change of defense counsel. *See* R.C.M. 505(d)(2) and 506(c).

---

(4) *Inquiry.* The military judge shall, in open session:

(A) Inform the accused of the rights to be represented by military counsel detailed to the defense; or by individual military counsel requested by the accused, if such military counsel is reasonably available; and by civilian counsel, either alone or in association with military counsel, if such civilian counsel is provided at no expense to the United States;

(B) Inform the accused that, if afforded individual military counsel, the accused may request retention of detailed counsel as associate counsel, which request may be granted or denied in the sole discretion of the authority who detailed the counsel;

(C) Ascertain from the accused whether the accused understands these rights;

(D) Promptly inquire, whenever two or more accused in a joint or common trial are represented by the same detailed or individual military or civilian counsel, or by civilian counsel who are associated in the practice of law, with respect to such joint representation and shall personally advise each accused of the right to effective assistance of counsel, including separate representation. Unless it appears that there is good cause to believe no conflict of interest is likely to arise, the military judge shall take appropriate measures to protect each accused's right to counsel; and

Discussion

Whenever it appears that any defense counsel may face a conflict of interest, the military judge should inquire into the matter, advise the accused of the right to effective assistance of counsel, and ascertain the accused's choice of counsel. When defense counsel is aware of a potential conflict of interest, counsel should discuss the matter with the accused. If the accused elects to waive such conflict, counsel should inform the military judge of the matter at an Article 39(a) session so that an appropriate record can be made.

(E) Ascertain from the accused by whom the accused chooses to be represented.

(5) *Unsworn counsel.* The military judge shall administer the oath to any counsel not sworn.

Discussion

See R.C.M. 807.

(e) *Presence of members.* In cases in which a military judge has been detailed, the procedures described in R.C.M. 901 through 903, 904 when authorized by the Secretary concerned, and 905 through 910 shall be conducted without members present in accordance with R.C.M. 803.

Rule 902. Disqualification of military judge

(a) *In general.* Except as provided in subsection (e) of this rule, a military judge shall disqualify himself or herself in any proceeding in which that military judge's impartiality might reasonably be questioned.

(b) *Specific grounds.* A military judge shall also disqualify himself or herself in the following circumstances:

(1) Where the military judge has a personal bias or prejudice concerning a party or personal knowledge of disputed evidentiary facts concerning the proceeding.

(2) Where the military judge has acted as counsel, preliminary hearing officer, investigating officer, legal officer, staff judge advocate, or convening authority as to any offense charged or in the same case generally.

(3) Where the military judge has been or will be a witness in the same case, is the accuser, has forwarded charges in the case with a personal recommendation as to disposition, or, except in the performance of duties as military judge in a previous trial of the same or a related case, has expressed an opinion concerning the guilt or innocence of the accused.

(4) Where the military judge is not eligible to act because the military judge is not qualified under R.C.M. 502(c) or not detailed under R.C.M. 503(b).

(5) Where the military judge, the military judge's spouse, or a person within the third degree of relationship to either of them or a spouse of such person:

(A) Is a party to the proceeding;

(B) Is known by the military judge to have an interest, financial or otherwise, that could be substantially affected by the outcome of the proceeding; or

(C) Is to the military judge's knowledge likely to be a material witness in the proceeding.

Discussion

A military judge should inform himself or herself about his or her financial interests, and make a reasonable effort to inform himself or herself about the financial interests of his or her spouse and minor children living in his or her household.

(c) *Definitions.* For the purposes of this rule the

following words or phrases shall have the meaning indicated—

(1) "Proceeding" includes pretrial, trial, post-trial, appellate review, or other stages of litigation.

(2) The "degree of relationship" is calculated according to the civil law system.

Discussion

Relatives within the third degree of relationship are children, grandchildren, great grandchildren, parents, grandparents, great grandparents, brothers, sisters, uncles, aunts, nephews, and nieces.

---

(3) "Military judge" does not include the president of a special court-martial without a military judge.

(d) *Procedure.*

(1) The military judge shall, upon motion of any party or *sua sponte*, decide whether the military judge is disqualified.

Discussion

There is no peremptory challenge against a military judge. A military judge should carefully consider whether any of the grounds for disqualification in this rule exist in each case. The military judge should broadly construe grounds for challenge but should not step down from a case unnecessarily.

Possible grounds for disqualification should be raised at the earliest reasonable opportunity. They may be raised at any time, and an earlier adverse ruling does not bar later consideration of the same issue, as, for example, when additional evidence is discovered.

---

(2) Each party shall be permitted to question the military judge and to present evidence regarding a possible ground for disqualification before the military judge decides the matter.

Discussion

Nothing in this rule prohibits the military judge from reasonably limiting the presentation of evidence, the scope of questioning, and argument on the subject so as to ensure that only matters material to the central issue of the military judge's possible disqualification are considered, thereby, preventing the proceedings from becoming a forum for unfounded opinion, speculation or innuendo.

---

(3) Except as provided under subsection (e) of this rule, if the military judge rules that the military judge is disqualified, the military judge shall recuse himself or herself.

(e) *Waiver.* No military judge shall accept from the

parties to the proceeding a waiver of any ground for disqualification enumerated in subsection (b) of this rule. Where the ground for disqualification arises only under subsection (a) of this rule, waiver may be accepted provided it is preceded by a full disclosure on the record of the basis for disqualification.

Rule 903. Accused's elections on composition of court-martial

(a) *Time of elections.*

(1) *Request for enlisted members.* Before the end of the initial Article 39(a) session or, in the absence of such a session, before assembly, the military judge shall ascertain, as applicable, whether an enlisted accused elects to be tried by a court-martial including enlisted members. The military judge may, as a matter of discretion, permit the accused to defer requesting enlisted members until any time before assembly, which time may be determined by the military judge.

(2) *Request for trial by military judge alone.* Before the end of the initial Article 39(a) session, or, in the absence of such a session, before assembly, the military judge shall ascertain, as applicable, whether in a noncapital case, the accused requests trial by the military judge alone. The accused may defer requesting trial by military judge alone until any time before assembly.

Discussion

Only an enlisted accused may request that enlisted members be detailed to a court-martial. Trial by military judge alone is not permitted in capital cases (*see* R.C.M. 201(f)(1)(C)) or in special courts-martial in which no military judge has been detailed.

(b) *Form of election.*

(1) *Request for enlisted members.* A request for the membership of the court-martial to include enlisted persons shall be in writing and signed by the accused or shall be made orally on the record.

(2) *Request for trial by military judge alone.* A request for trial by military judge alone shall be in writing and signed by the accused or shall be made orally on the record.

(c) *Action on election.*

(1) *Request for enlisted members.* Upon notice of a timely request for enlisted members by an enlisted accused, the convening authority shall detail enlisted members to the court-martial in accordance with

R.C.M. 503 or prepare a detailed written statement explaining why physical conditions or military exigencies prevented this. The trial of the general issue shall not proceed until this is done.

(2) *Request for military judge alone.* Upon receipt of a timely request for trial by military judge alone the military judge shall:

(A) Ascertain whether the accused has consulted with defense counsel and has been informed of the identity of the military judge and of the right to trial by members; and

Discussion

Ordinarily the military judge should inquire personally of the accused to ensure that the accused's waiver of the right to trial by members is knowing and understanding. Failure to do so is not error, however, where such knowledge and understanding otherwise appear on the record.

DD Form 1722 (Request for Trial Before Military Judge Alone (Art.16, UCMJ)) should normally be used for the purpose of requesting trial by military judge alone under this rule, if a written request is used.

(B) Approve or disapprove the request, in the military judge's discretion.

Discussion

A timely request for trial by military judge alone should be granted unless there is substantial reason why, in the interest of justice, the military judge should not sit as factfinder. The military judge may hear arguments from counsel before acting on the request. The basis for denial of a request must be made a matter of record.

(3) *Other.* In the absence of a request for enlisted members or a request for trial by military judge alone, trial shall be by a court-martial composed of officers.

Discussion

Ordinarily if no request for enlisted members or trial by military judge alone is submitted, the military judge should inquire whether such a request will be made (*see* subsection (a)(1) of this rule) unless these elections are not available to the accused.

(d) *Right to withdraw request.*

(1) *Enlisted members.* A request for enlisted members may be withdrawn by the accused as a matter of right any time before the end of the initial

Article 39(a) session, or, in the absence of such a session, before assembly.

(2) *Military judge.* A request for trial by military judge alone may be withdrawn by the accused as a matter of right any time before it is approved, or even after approval, if there is a change of the military judge.

Discussion

Withdrawal of a request for enlisted members or trial by military judge alone should be shown in the record.

(e) *Untimely requests.* Failure to request, or failure to withdraw a request for enlisted members or trial by military judge alone in a timely manner shall waive the right to submit or to withdraw such a request. However, the military judge may until the beginning of the introduction of evidence on the merits, as a matter of discretion, approve an untimely request or withdrawal of a request.

Discussion

In exercising discretion whether to approve an untimely request or withdrawal of a request, the military judge should balance the reason for the request (for example, whether it is a mere change of tactics or results from a substantial change of circumstances) against any expense, delay, or inconvenience which would result from granting the request.

(f) *Scope.* For purposes of this rule, "military judge" does not include the president of a special court-martial without a military judge.

Rule 904. Arraignment

Arraignment shall be conducted in a court-martial session and shall consist of reading the charges and specifications to the accused and calling on the accused to plead. The accused may waive the reading.

Discussion

Arraignment is complete when the accused is called upon to plead; the entry of pleas is not part of the arraignment.

When authorized by regulations of the Secretary concerned, the arraignment should be conducted at an Article 39(a) session when a military judge has been detailed. The accused may not be arraigned at a conference under R.C.M. 802.

Once the accused has been arraigned, no additional charges against that accused may be referred to that court-martial for trial with the previously referred charges. See R.C.M. 601(e)(2).

The defense should be asked whether it has any motions to make before pleas are entered. Some motions ordinarily must be made before a plea is entered. *See* R.C.M. 905(b).

Rule 905. Motions generally

(a) *Definitions and form.* A motion is an application to the military judge for particular relief. Motions may be oral or, at the discretion of the military judge, written. A motion shall state the grounds upon which it is made and shall set forth the ruling or relief sought. The substance of a motion, not its form or designation, shall control.

Discussion

Motions may be motions to suppress [(*see* R.C.M. 905(b)(3))]; motions for appropriate relief (*see* R.C.M. 906); motions to dismiss (*see* R.C.M. 907); or motions for findings of not guilty (*see* R.C.M. 917).

(b) *Pretrial motions.* Any defense, objection, or request which is capable of determination without the trial of the general issue of guilt may be raised before trial. The following must be raised before a plea is entered:

(1) Defenses or objections based on defects (other than jurisdictional defects) in the preferral, forwarding, or referral of charges, or in the preliminary hearing;

Discussion

Such nonjurisdictional defects include unsworn charges, inadequate Article 32 preliminary hearing, and inadequate pretrial advice. *See* R.C.M. 307; 401–407; 601–604.

---

(2) Defenses or objections based on defects in the charges and specifications (other than any failure to show jurisdiction or to charge an offense, which objections shall be resolved by the military judge at any time during the pendency of the proceedings);

Discussion

See R.C.M. 307; 906(b)(3).

---

(3) Motions to suppress evidence;

Discussion

Mil. R. Evid. 304(d), 311(d), and 321(c) deal with the admissibility of confessions and admissions, evidence obtained from unlawful searches and seizures, and eyewitness identification,

respectively. Questions concerning the admissibility of evidence on other grounds may be raised by objection at trial or by motions *in limine. See* R.C.M. 906(b)(13); Mil. R. Evid. 103(c); 104(a) and (c).

---

(4) Motions for discovery under R.C.M. 701 or for production of witnesses or evidence;

Discussion

See also R.C.M. 703; 1001(e).

---

(5) Motions for severance of charges or accused; or

Discussion

See R.C.M. 812; 906(b)(9) and (10).

---

(6) Objections based on denial of request for individual military counsel or for retention of detailed defense counsel when individual military counsel has been granted.

Discussion

See R.C.M. 506(b); 906(b)(2).

(c) *Burden of proof.*

(1) *Standard.* Unless otherwise provided in this Manual, the burden of proof on any factual issue the resolution of which is necessary to decide a motion shall be by a preponderance of the evidence.

Discussion

See Mil. R. Evid. 104(a) concerning the applicability of the Military Rules of Evidence to certain preliminary questions.

---

(2) *Assignment.*

(A) Except as otherwise provided in this Manual the burden of persuasion on any factual issue the resolution of which is necessary to decide a motion shall be on the moving party.

Discussion

See, for example, subsection (c)(2)(B) of this rule, R.C.M. 908 and Mil. R. Evid. 304(e), 311(e), and 321(d) for provisions specifically assigning the burden of proof.

(B) In the case of a motion to dismiss for lack

of jurisdiction, denial of the right to speedy trial under R.C.M. 707, or the running of the statute of limitations, the burden of persuasion shall be upon the prosecution.

(d) *Ruling on motions.* A motion made before pleas are entered shall be determined before pleas are entered unless, if otherwise not prohibited by this Manual, the military judge for good cause orders that determination be deferred until trial of the general issue or after findings, but no such determination shall be deferred if a party's right to review or appeal is adversely affected. Where factual issues are involved in determining a motion, the military judge shall state the essential findings on the record.

Discussion

When trial cannot proceed further as the result of dismissal or other rulings on motions, the court-martial should adjourn and a record of the proceedings should be prepared for the convening authority. *See* R.C.M. 908(b)(4) regarding automatic stay of certain rulings and orders subject to appeal under that rule. Notwithstanding the dismissal of some specifications, trial may proceed in the normal manner as long as one or more charges and specifications remain. The promulgating orders should reflect the action taken by the court-martial on each charge and specification, including any which were dismissed by the military judge on a motion. *See* R.C.M. 1114.

(e) *Effect of failure to raise defenses or objections.* Failure by a party to raise defenses or objections or to make motions or requests which must be made before pleas are entered under subsection (b) of this rule shall constitute waiver. The military judge for good cause shown may grant relief from the waiver. Other motions, requests, defenses, or objections, except lack of jurisdiction or failure of a charge to allege an offense, must be raised before the court-martial is adjourned for that case and, unless otherwise provided in this Manual, failure to do so shall constitute waiver.

Discussion

See also R.C.M. 910(j) concerning matters waived by a plea of guilty.

(f) *Reconsideration.* On request of any party or *sua sponte,* the military judge may, prior to authentication of the record of trial, reconsider any ruling,

other than one amounting to a finding of not guilty, made by the military judge.

Discussion

Subsection (f) permits the military judge to reconsider any ruling that affects the legal sufficiency of any finding of guilt or the sentence. *See* R.C.M. 917(d) for the standard to be used to determine the legal sufficiency of evidence. *See also* R.C.M. 1102 concerning procedures for post-trial reconsideration. Different standards may apply depending on the nature of the ruling. *See United States v. Scaff,* 29 M.J. 60 (C.M.A. 1989).

(g) *Effect of final determinations.* Any matter put in issue and finally determined by a court-martial, reviewing authority, or appellate court which had jurisdiction to determine the matter may not be disputed by the United States in any other court-martial of the same accused, except that, when the offenses charged at one court-martial did not arise out of the same transaction as those charged at the court-martial at which the determination was made, a determination of law and the application of law to the facts may be disputed by the United States. This rule also shall apply to matters which were put in issue and finally determined in any other judicial proceeding in which the accused and the United States or a Federal governmental unit were parties.

Discussion

See also R.C.M. 907(b)(2)(C). Whether a matter has been finally determined in another judicial proceeding with jurisdiction to decide it, and whether such determination binds the United States in another proceeding are interlocutory questions. *See* R.C.M. 801(e). It does not matter whether the earlier proceeding ended in an acquittal, conviction, or otherwise, as long as the determination is final. Except for a ruling which is, or amounts to, a finding of not guilty, a ruling ordinarily is not final until action on the court-martial is completed. *See* Article 76; R.C.M. 1209. The accused is not bound in a court-martial by rulings in another court-martial. *But see* Article 3(b); R.C.M. 202.

The determination must have been made by a court-martial, reviewing authority, or appellate court, or by another judicial body, such as a United States court. A pretrial determination by a convening authority is not a final determination under this rule, although some decisions by a convening authority may bind the Government under other rules. *See,* for example, R.C.M. 601, 604, 704, 705.

The United States is bound by a final determination by a court of competent jurisdiction even if the earlier determination is erroneous, except when the offenses charged at the second proceeding arose out of a different transaction from those charged at the first and the ruling at the first proceeding was based on an incorrect determination of law.

A final determination in one case may be the basis for a motion to dismiss or a motion for appropriate relief in another case, depending on the circumstances. The nature of the earlier determination and the grounds for it will determine its effect in other proceedings.

Examples:

(1) The military judge dismissed a charge for lack of personal jurisdiction, on grounds that the accused was only 16 years old at the time of enlistment and when the offenses occurred. At a second court-martial of the same accused for a different offense, the determination in the first case would require dismissal of the new charge unless the prosecution could show that since that determination the accused had effected a valid enlistment or constructive enlistment. *See* R.C.M. 202. Note, however, that if the initial ruling had been based on an error of law (for example, if the military judge had ruled the enlistment invalid because the accused was 18 at the time of enlistment) this would not require dismissal in the second court-martial for a different offense.

(2) The accused was tried in United States district court for assault on a Federal officer. The accused defended solely on the basis of alibi and was acquitted. The accused is then charged in a court-martial with assault on a different person at the same time and place as the assault on a Federal officer was alleged to have occurred. The acquittal of the accused in Federal district court would bar conviction of the accused in the court-martial. In cases of this nature, the facts of the first trial must be examined to determine whether the finding of the first trial is logically inconsistent with guilt in the second case.

(3) At a court-martial for larceny, the military judge excluded evidence of a statement made by the accused relating to the larceny and other uncharged offenses because the statement was obtained by coercion. At a second court-martial for an unrelated offense, the statement excluded at the first trial would be inadmissible, based on the earlier ruling, if the first case had become final. If the earlier ruling had been based on an incorrect interpretation of law, however, the issue of admissibility could be litigated anew at the second proceeding.

(4) At a court-martial for absence without authority, the charge and specification were dismissed for failure to state an offense. At a later court-martial for the same offense, the earlier dismissal would be grounds for dismissing the same charge and specification, but would not bar further proceedings on a new specification not containing the same defect as the original specification.

(h) *Written motions.* Written motions may be submitted to the military judge after referral and when appropriate they may be supported by affidavits, with service and opportunity to reply to the opposing party. Such motions may be disposed of before arraignment and without a session. Upon request, either party is entitled to an Article 39(a) session to present oral argument or have an evidentiary hearing concerning the disposition of written motions.

(i) *Service.* Written motions shall be served on all other parties. Unless otherwise directed by the military judge, the service shall be made upon counsel for each party.

(j) *Application to convening authority.* Except as otherwise provided in this Manual, any matters which may be resolved upon motion without trial of the general issue of guilt may be submitted by a party to the convening authority before trial for decision. Submission of such matter to the convening authority is not, except as otherwise provided in this Manual, required, and is, in any event, without prejudice to the renewal of the issue by timely motion before the military judge.

(k) *Production of statements on motion to suppress.* Except as provided in this subsection, R.C.M. 914 shall apply at a hearing on a motion to suppress evidence under subsection (b)(3) of this rule. For purposes of this subsection, a law enforcement officer shall be deemed a witness called by the Government, and upon a claim of privilege the military judge shall excise portions of the statement containing privileged matter.

Rule 906. Motions for appropriate relief

(a) *In general.* A motion for appropriate relief is a request for a ruling to cure a defect which deprives a party of a right or hinders a party from preparing for trial or presenting its case.

(b) *Grounds for appropriate relief.* The following may be requested by motion for appropriate relief. This list is not exclusive.

(1) *Continuances.* A continuance may be granted only by the military judge.

Discussion

The military judge should, upon a showing of reasonable cause, grant a continuance to any party for as long and as often as is just. Article 40. Whether a request for a continuance should be granted is a matter within the discretion of the military judge. Reasons for a continuance may include: insufficient opportunity to prepare for trial; unavailability of an essential witness; the interest of Government in the order of trial of related cases; and illness of an accused, counsel, military judge, or member. *See also* R.C.M. 602; 803.

---

(2) *Record of denial of individual military counsel or of denial of request to retain detailed counsel when a request for individual military counsel granted.* If a request for military counsel was denied, which denial was upheld on appeal (if available) or if a request to retain detailed counsel was denied when the accused is represented by individual military counsel, and if the accused so requests, the

military judge shall ensure that a record of the matter is included in the record of trial, and may make findings. The trial counsel may request a continuance to inform the convening authority of those findings. The military judge may not dismiss the charges or otherwise effectively prevent further proceedings based on this issue. However, the military judge may grant reasonable continuances until the requested military counsel can be made available if the unavailability results from temporary conditions or if the decision of unavailability is in the process of review in administrative channels.

(3) Correction of defects in the Article 32 preliminary hearing or pretrial advice.

Discussion

See R.C.M. 405; 406. If the motion is granted, the military judge should ordinarily grant a continuance so the defect may be corrected.

---

(4) *Amendment of charges or specifications.* A charge or specification may not be amended over the accused's objection unless the amendment is minor within the meaning of R.C.M. 603(a).

Discussion

See also R.C.M. 307.

An amendment may be appropriate when a specification is unclear, redundant, inartfully drafted, misnames an accused, or is laid under the wrong article. A specification may be amended by striking surplusage, or substituting or adding new language. Surplusage may include irrelevant or redundant details or aggravating circumstances which are not necessary to enhance the maximum authorized punishment or to explain the essential facts of the offense. When a specification is amended after the accused has entered a plea to it, the accused should be asked to plead anew to the amended specification. A bill of particulars (*see* subsection (b)(6) of this rule) may also be used when a specification is indefinite or ambiguous.

If a specification, although stating an offense, is so defective that the accused appears to have been misled, the accused should be given a continuance upon request, or, in an appropriate case (*see* R.C.M. 907(b)(3)), the specification may be dismissed.

---

(5) Severance of a duplicitous specification into two or more specifications.

Discussion

Each specification may state only one offense. R.C.M. 307(c)(4). A duplicitous specification is one which alleges two or more separate offenses. Lesser included offenses (*see* paragraph 3, Part IV) are not separate, nor is a continuing offense involving sepa-

rate acts. The sole remedy for a duplicitous specification is severance of the specification into two or more specifications, each of which alleges a separate offense contained in the duplicitous specification. However, if the duplicitousness is combined with or results in other defects, such as misleading the accused, other remedies may be appropriate. See subsection (b)(3) of this rule. *See also* R.C.M. 907(b)(3).

---

(6) *Bill of particulars.* A bill of particulars may be amended at any time, subject to such conditions as justice permits.

Discussion

The purposes of a bill of particulars are to inform the accused of the nature of the charge with sufficient precision to enable the accused to prepare for trial, to avoid or minimize the danger of surprise at the time of trial, and to enable the accused to plead the acquittal or conviction in bar of another prosecution for the same offense when the specification itself is too vague and indefinite for such purposes.

A bill of particulars should not be used to conduct discovery of the Government's theory of a case, to force detailed disclosure of acts underlying a charge, or to restrict the Government's proof at trial.

A bill of particulars need not be sworn because it is not part of the specification. A bill of particulars cannot be used to repair a specification which is otherwise not legally sufficient.

---

(7) Discovery and production of evidence and witnesses.

Discussion

See R.C.M. 701 concerning discovery. *See* R.C.M. 703, 914 and 1001(e) concerning production of evidence and witnesses.

---

(8) *Relief from pretrial confinement.* Upon a motion for release from pretrial confinement, a victim of an alleged offense committed by the accused has the right to reasonable, accurate, and timely notice of the motion and any hearing, the right to confer with trial counsel, and the right to be reasonably heard. Inability to reasonably afford a victim these rights shall not delay the proceedings. The right to be heard under this rule includes the right to be heard through counsel.

Discussion

See R.C.M. 305(j).

---

(9) Severance of multiple accused, if it appears that an accused or the Government is prejudiced by

a joint or common trial. In a common trial, a severance shall be granted whenever any accused, other than the moving accused, faces charges unrelated to those charged against the moving accused.

Discussion

A motion for severance is a request that one or more accused against whom charges have been referred to a joint or common trial be tried separately. Such a request should be granted if good cause is shown. For example, a severance may be appropriate when: the moving party wishes to use the testimony of one or more of the coaccused or the spouse of a coaccused; a defense of a coaccused is antagonistic to the moving party; or evidence as to any other accused will improperly prejudice the moving accused.

If a severance is granted by the military judge, the military judge will decide which accused will be tried first. *See* R.C.M. 801(a)(1). In the case of joint charges, the military judge will direct an appropriate amendment of the charges and specifications.

See also R.C.M. 307(c)(5); 601(e)(3); 604; 812.

(10) Severance of offenses, but only to prevent manifest injustice.

Discussion

Ordinarily, all known charges should be tried at a single court-martial. Joinder of minor and major offenses, or of unrelated offenses is not alone a sufficient ground to sever offenses. For example, when an essential witness as to one offense is unavailable, it might be appropriate to sever that offense to prevent violation of the accused's right to a speedy trial.

(11) *Change of place of trial.* The place of trial may be changed when necessary to prevent prejudice to the rights of the accused or for the convenience of the Government if the rights of the accused are not prejudiced thereby.

Discussion

A change of the place of trial may be necessary when there exists in the place where the court-martial is pending so great a prejudice against the accused that the accused cannot obtain a fair and impartial trial there, or to obtain compulsory process over an essential witness.

When it is necessary to change the place of trial, the choice of places to which the court-martial will be transferred will be left to the convening authority, as long as the choice is not inconsistent with the ruling of the military judge.

(12) *Unreasonable multiplication of charges.* The military judge may provide a remedy, as provided below, if he or she finds there has been an unreasonable multiplication of charges as applied to findings or sentence.

(i) *As applied to findings.* Charges that arise from substantially the same transaction, while not legally multiplicious, may still be unreasonably multiplied as applied to findings. When the military judge finds, in his or her discretion, that the offenses have been unreasonably multiplied, the appropriate remedy shall be dismissal of the lesser offenses or merger of the offenses into one specification.

(ii) *As applied to sentence.* Where the military judge finds that the nature of the harm requires a remedy that focuses more appropriately on punishment than on findings, he or she may find that there is an unreasonable multiplication of charges as applied to sentence. If the military judge makes such a finding, the maximum punishment for those offenses determined to be unreasonably multiplied shall be the maximum authorized punishment of the offense carrying the greatest maximum punishment.

Discussion

Unreasonable multiplication of charges as applied to findings and sentence is a limitation on the military's discretion to charge separate offenses and does not have a foundation in the Constitution. The concept is based on reasonableness and the prohibition against prosecutorial overreaching. In contrast, multiplicity is grounded in the Double Jeopardy Clause of the Fifth Amendment. It prevents an accused from being twice punished for one offense if it is contrary to the intent of Congress. *See* R.C.M. 907(b)(3). Therefore, a motion for relief from unreasonable multiplication of charges as applied to findings and sentence differs from a motion to dismiss on the grounds of multiplicity.

The following non-exhaustive factors should be considered when determining whether two or more offenses are unreasonably multiplied: whether the specifications are aimed at distinctly separate criminal acts; whether they represent or exaggerate the accused's criminality; whether they unreasonably increase his or her exposure to punishment; and whether they suggest prosecutorial abuse of discretion in drafting of the specifications. Because prosecutors are permitted to charge in the alternative based on exigencies of proof, a ruling on this motion ordinarily should be deferred until after findings are entered.

(13) Preliminary ruling on admissibility of evidence.

Discussion

See Mil. R. Evid. 104(c)

A request for a preliminary ruling on admissibility is a request that certain matters which are ordinarily decided during trial of the general issue be resolved before they arise, outside the presence of members. The purpose of such a motion is to avoid the prejudice which may result from bringing inadmissible matters to the attention of court members.

Whether to rule on an evidentiary question before it arises during trial is a matter within the discretion of the military judge. *But see* R.C.M. 905(b)(3) and (d); and Mil. R. Evid. 304(e)(2); 311(e)(2); 321(d)(2). Reviewability of preliminary rulings will be controlled by the Supreme Court's decision in *Luce v. United States*, 469 U.S. 38 (1984).

---

(14) Motions relating to mental capacity or responsibility of the accused.

Discussion

See R.C.M. 706, 909, and 916(k) regarding procedures and standards concerning the mental capacity or responsibility of the accused.

Rule 907. Motions to dismiss

(a) *In general.* A motion to dismiss is a request to terminate further proceedings as to one or more charges and specifications on grounds capable of resolution without trial of the general issue of guilt.

Discussion

Dismissal of a specification terminates the proceeding with respect to that specification unless the decision to dismiss is reconsidered and reversed by the military judge. *See* R.C.M. 905(f). Dismissal of a specification on grounds stated in subsection (b)(1) or (b)(3)(A) below does not ordinarily bar a later court-martial for the same offense if the grounds for dismissal no longer exist. *See also* R.C.M. 905(g) and subsection (b)(2) below.

See R.C.M. 916 concerning defenses.

(b) *Grounds for dismissal.* Grounds for dismissal include the following—

(1) *Nonwaivable grounds.* A charge or specification shall be dismissed at any stage of the proceedings if the court-martial lacks jurisdiction to try the accused for the offense.

Discussion

See R.C.M. 201-203.

---

(2) *Waivable grounds.* A charge or specification shall be dismissed upon motion made by the accused before the final adjournment of the court-martial in that case if:

(A) Dismissal is required under R.C.M. 707;

(B) The statute of limitations (Article 43) has run, provided that, if it appears that the accused is unaware of the right to assert the statute of limitations in bar of trial, the military judge shall inform the accused of this right;

Discussion

Except for certain offenses for which there is either: no limitation as to time; or child abuse offenses for which a time limitation has been enacted and applies that is based upon the life of a child abuse victim, *see* Article 43(a) and (b)(2) , a person charged with an offense under the code may not be tried by court-martial over objection if sworn charges have not been received by the officer exercising summary court-martial jurisdiction over the command within five years. *See* Article 43(b). This period may be tolled (Article 43(c) and (d)), extended (Article 43(e) and (g)), or suspended (Article 43(f)) under certain circumstances. The prosecution bears the burden of proving that the statute of limitations has been tolled, extended, or suspended if it appears that is has run.

Some offenses are continuing offenses and any period of the offense occurring within the statute of limitations is not barred. Absence without leave, desertion, and fraudulent enlistment are not continuing offenses and are committed, respectively, on the day the person goes absent, deserts, or first receives pay or allowances under the enlistment.

When computing the statute of limitations, periods in which the accused was fleeing from justice or periods when the accused was absent without leave or in desertion are excluded. The military judge must determine by a preponderance, as an interlocutory matter, whether the accused was absent without authority or fleeing from justice. It would not be necessary that the accused be charged with the absence offense. In cases where the accused is charged with both an absence offense and a non-absence offense, but is found not guilty of the absence offense, the military judge would reconsider, by a preponderance, his or her prior determination whether that period of time is excludable.

If sworn charges have been received by an officer exercising summary court-martial jurisdiction over the command within the period of the statute, minor amendments (*see* R.C.M. 603(a)) may be made in the specification after the statute of limitations has run. However, if new charges are drafted or a major amendment made (*see* R.C.M. 603(d)) after the statute of limitations has run, prosecution is barred. The date of receipt of sworn charges is excluded when computing the appropriate statutory period. The date of the offense is included in the computation of the elapsed time. Article 43(g) allows the government time to reinstate charges dismissed as defective or insufficient for any cause. The government would have up to six months to reinstate the charges if the original period of limitations has expired or will expire within six months of the dismissal.

In some cases, the issue whether the statute of limitations has run will depend on the findings on the general issue of guilt. For example, where the date of an offense is in dispute, a finding by the court-martial that the offense occurred at an earlier time may affect a determination as to the running of the statute of limitations.

When the statute of limitations has run as to a lesser included offense, but not as to the charged offense, *see* R.C.M.

920(e)(2) with regard to instructions on the lesser offense.

(C) The accused has previously been tried by court-martial or federal civilian court for the same offense, provided that:

(i) No court-martial proceeding is a trial in the sense of this rule unless presentation of evidence on the general issue of guilt has begun;

(ii) No court-martial proceeding which has been terminated under R.C.M. 604(b) or R.C.M. 915 shall bar later prosecution for the same offense or offenses, if so provided in those rules;

(iii) No court-martial proceeding in which an accused has been found guilty of any charge or specification is a trial in the sense of this rule until the finding of guilty has become final after review of the case has been fully completed; and

(iv) No court-martial proceeding which lacked jurisdiction to try the accused for the offense is a trial in the sense of this rule.

(D) Prosecution is barred by:

(i) A pardon issued by the President;

Discussion

A pardon may grant individual or general amnesty.

(ii) Immunity from prosecution granted by a person authorized to do so;

Discussion

See R.C.M. 704.

(iii) Constructive condonation of desertion established by unconditional restoration to duty without trial of a deserter by a general court-martial convening authority who knew of the desertion; or

(iv) Prior punishment under Articles 13 or 15 for the same offense, if that offense was minor.

Discussion

See Articles 13 and 15(f). *See* paragraph 1e of Part V for a definition of "minor" offenses.

(E) The specification fails to state an offense.

Discussion

See R.C.M. 307(c).

---

(3) *Permissible grounds.* A specification may be dismissed upon timely motion by the accused if one of the following is applicable:

(A) *Defective.* When the specification is so defective that it substantially misled the accused, and the military judge finds that, in the interest of justice, trial should proceed on any remaining charges and specifications without undue delay; or

(B) *Multiplicity.* When the specification is multiplicious with another specification, is unnecessary to enable the prosecution to meet the exigencies of proof through trial, review, and appellate action, and should be dismissed in the interest of justice. A charge is multiplicious if the proof of such charge also proves every element of another charge.

Discussion

Multiplicity is a legal concept, arising from the Double Jeopardy Clause of the Fifth Amendment, which provides that no person shall be put in jeopardy twice for the same offense. Absent legislative intent to the contrary, an accused cannot be convicted and punished for violations of two or more statutes if those violations arise from a single act. Where Congress intended to impose multiple punishments for the same act, imposition of such sentence does not violate the Constitution.

Multiplicity differs from unreasonable multiplication of charges. If two offenses are not multiplicious, they nonetheless may constitute an unreasonable multiplication of charges as applied to findings or sentence. *See* R.C.M. 906(b)(12). Unreasonable multiplication of charges is a limitation on the military's discretion to charge separate offenses. It does not have a foundation in the Constitution; it is based on reasonableness and the prohibition against prosecutorial overreaching. The military judge is to determine, in his or her discretion, whether the charges constitute unreasonable multiplication of charges as applied to findings or sentencing. *See* R.C.M. 906(b)(12).

To determine if two charges are multiplicious, the practitioner should first determine whether they are based on separate acts. If so, the charges are not multiplicious because separate acts may be charged and punished separately. If the charges are based upon a single act, the practitioner should next determine if Congress intended to impose multiple convictions and punishments for the same act. When there is no overt expression of congressional intent in the relevant statutes, such intent may be inferred based on the elements of the charged statutes and their relationship to each other or other principles of statutory interpretation. If each statute contains an element not contained in the other, it may be inferred that Congress intended they be charged and punished separately. Likewise, if each statute contains the same elements, it may be inferred that Congress did not intend they be charged and punished separately. A lesser included offense will always be multiplicious if charged separately, but offenses do not have to be lesser included to be multiplicious.

Ordinarily, a specification should not be dismissed for multiplicity before trial. The less serious of any multiplicious specifications shall be dismissed after findings have been reached. Due consideration must be given, however, to possible post-trial or appellate action with regard to the remaining specification.

Rule 908. Appeal by the United States

(a) *In general.* In a trial by a court-martial over which a military judge presides and in which a punitive discharge may be adjudged, the United States may appeal an order or ruling that terminates the proceedings with respect to a charge or specification, or excludes evidence that is substantial proof of a fact material in the proceedings, or directs the disclosure of classified information, or that imposes sanctions for nondisclosure of classified information. The United States may also appeal a refusal by the military judge to issue a protective order sought by the United States to prevent the disclosure of classified information or to enforce such an order that has previously been issued by the appropriate authority. However, the United States may not appeal an order or ruling that is, or amounts to, a finding of not guilty with respect to the charge or specification.

(b) *Procedure.*

(1) *Delay.* After an order or ruling which may be subject to an appeal by the United States, the court-martial may not proceed, except as to matters unaffected by the ruling or order, if the trial counsel requests a delay to determine whether to file notice of appeal under this rule. Trial counsel is entitled to no more than 72 hours under this subsection.

(2) *Decision to appeal.* The decision whether to file notice of appeal under this rule shall be made within 72 hours of the ruling or order to be appealed. If the Secretary concerned so prescribes, the trial counsel shall not file notice of appeal unless authorized to do so by a person designated by the Secretary concerned.

(3) *Notice of appeal.* If the United States elects to appeal, the trial counsel shall provide the military judge with written notice to this effect not later than 72 hours after the ruling or order. Such notice shall identify the ruling or order to be appealed and the charges and specifications affected. Trial counsel shall certify that the appeal is not taken for the purpose of delay and (if the order or ruling appealed is one which excludes evidence) that the evidence excluded is substantial proof of a fact material in the proceeding.

(4) *Effect on the court-martial.* Upon written notice to the military judge under subsection (b)(3) of this rule, the ruling or order that is the subject of the appeal is automatically stayed and no session of the court-martial may proceed pending disposition by the Court of Criminal Appeals of the appeal, except that solely as to charges and specifications not affected by the ruling or order:

(A) Motions may be litigated, in the discretion of the military judge, at any point in the proceedings;

(B) When trial on the merits has not begun,

(i) a severance may be granted upon request of all the parties;

(ii) a severance may be granted upon request of the accused and when appropriate under R.C.M. 906(b)(10); or

(C) When trial on the merits has begun but has not been completed, a party may, on that party's request and in the discretion of the military judge, present further evidence on the merits.

(5) *Record.* Upon written notice to the military judge under subsection (b)(3) of this rule, trial counsel shall cause a record of the proceedings to be prepared. Such record shall be verbatim and complete to the extent necessary to resolve the issues appealed. R.C.M. 1103(g), (h), and (i) shall apply and the record shall be authenticated in accordance with R.C.M. 1104(a). The military judge or the Court of Criminal Appeals may direct that additional parts of the proceeding be included in the record; R.C.M. 1104(d) shall not apply to such additions.

(6) *Forwarding.* Upon written notice to the military judge under subsection (b)(3) of this rule, trial counsel shall promptly and by expeditious means forward the appeal to a representative of the Government designated by the Judge Advocate General. The matter forwarded shall include: a statement of the issues appealed; the record of the proceedings or, if preparation of the record has not been completed, a summary of the evidence; and such other matters as the Secretary concerned may prescribe. The person designated by the Judge Advocate General shall promptly decide whether to file the appeal with the Court of Criminal Appeals and notify the trial counsel of that decision.

(7) *Appeal filed.* If the United States elects to file an appeal, it shall be filed directly with the Court of Criminal Appeals, in accordance with the rules of that court.

(8) *Appeal not filed.* If the United States elects not to file an appeal, trial counsel promptly shall notify the military judge and the other parties.

(9) *Pretrial confinement of accused pending appeal.* If an accused is in pretrial confinement at the time the United States files notice of its intent to appeal under subsection (3) above, the commander, in determining whether the accused should be confined pending the outcome of an appeal by the United States, should consider the same factors which would authorize the imposition of pretrial confinement under R.C.M. 305(h)(2)(B).

(c) *Appellate proceedings.*

(1) *Appellate counsel.* The parties shall be represented before appellate courts in proceedings under this rule as provided in R.C.M. 1202. Appellate Government counsel shall diligently prosecute an appeal under this rule.

(2) *Court of Criminal Appeals.* An appeal under Article 62 shall, whenever practicable, have priority over all other proceedings before the Court of Criminal Appeals. In determining an appeal under Article 62, the Court of Criminal Appeals may take action only with respect to matters of law.

(3) *Action following decision of Court of Criminal Appeals.* After the Court of Criminal Appeals has decided any appeal under Article 62, the accused may petition for review by the Court of Appeals for the Armed Forces, or the Judge Advocate General may certify a question to the Court of Appeals for the Armed Forces. The parties shall be notified of the decision of the Court of Criminal Appeals promptly. If the decision is adverse to the accused, the accused shall be notified of the decision and of the right to petition the Court of Appeals for the Armed Forces for review within 60 days orally on the record at the court-martial or in accordance with R.C.M. 1203(d). If the accused is notified orally on the record, trial counsel shall forward by expeditious means a certificate that the accused was so notified to the Judge Advocate General, who shall forward a copy to the clerk of the Court of Appeals for the Armed Forces when required by the Court. If the decision by the Court of Criminal Appeals permits it, the court-martial may proceed as to the affected charges and specifications pending further review by the Court of Appeals for the Armed Forces or the Supreme Court, unless either court orders the proceedings stayed. Unless the case is reviewed by the Court of Appeals for the Armed Forces, it shall be returned to the military judge or the convening authority for appropriate action in accordance with the decision of the Court of Criminal Appeals. If the case is reviewed by the Court of Appeals for the Armed Forces, R.C.M. 1204 and 1205 shall apply.

(d) *Military judge.* For purposes of this rule, "military judge" does not include the president of a special court-martial without a military judge.

Rule 909. Capacity of the accused to stand trial by court-martial

(a) *In general.* No person may be brought to trial by court-martial if that person is presently suffering from a mental disease or defect rendering him or her mentally incompetent to the extent that he or she is unable to understand the nature of the proceedings against them or to conduct or cooperate intelligently in the defense of the case.

Discussion

See also R.C.M. 916(k).

(b) *Presumption of capacity.* A person is presumed to have the capacity to stand trial unless the contrary is established.

(c) *Determination before referral.* If an inquiry pursuant to R.C.M. 706 conducted before referral concludes that an accused is suffering from a mental disease or defect that renders him or her mentally incompetent to stand trial, the convening authority before whom the charges are pending for disposition may disagree with the conclusion and take any action authorized under R.C.M. 401, including referral of the charges to trial. If that convening authority concurs with the conclusion, he or she shall forward the charges to the general court-martial convening authority. If, upon receipt of the charges, the general court-martial convening authority similarly concurs, then he or she shall commit the accused to the custody of the Attorney General. If the general court-martial convening authority does not concur, that authority may take any action that he or she deems appropriate in accordance with R.C.M. 407, including referral of the charges to trial.

(d) *Determination after referral.* After referral, the military judge may conduct a hearing to determine the mental capacity of the accused, either *sua sponte* or upon request of either party. If an inquiry pursuant to R.C.M. 706 conducted before or after referral concludes that an accused is suffering from a mental disease or defect that renders him or her mentally incompetent to stand trial, the military judge shall conduct a hearing to determine the mental capacity of the accused. Any such hearing shall be conducted in accordance with paragraph (e) of this rule.

(e) *Incompetence determination hearing.*

(1) *Nature of issue.* The mental capacity of the accused is an interlocutory question of fact.

(2) *Standard.* Trial may proceed unless it is established by a preponderance of the evidence that the accused is presently suffering from a mental disease or defect rendering him or her mentally incompetent to the extent that he or she is unable to understand the nature of the proceedings or to conduct or cooperate intelligently in the defense of the case. In making this determination, the military judge is not bound by the rules of evidence except with respect to privileges.

(3) If the military judge finds the accused is incompetent to stand trial, the judge shall report this finding to the general court-martial convening authority, who shall commit the accused to the custody of the Attorney General

(f) *Hospitalization of the accused.* An accused who is found incompetent to stand trial under this rule shall be hospitalized by the Attorney General as provided in section 4241(d) of title 18, United States Code. If notified that the accused has recovered to such an extent that he or she is able to understand the nature of the proceedings and to conduct or cooperate intelligently in the defense of the case, then the general court-martial convening authority shall promptly take custody of the accused. If, at the end of the period of hospitalization, the accused's mental condition has not so improved, action shall be taken in accordance with section 4246 of title 18, United States Code.

Discussion

Under section 4241(d) of title 18, the initial period of hospitalization for an incompetent accused shall not exceed four months. However, in determining whether there is a substantial probability the accused will attain the capacity to permit the trial to proceed

in the foreseeable future, the accused may be hospitalized for an additional reasonable period of time. This additional period of time ends either when the accused's mental condition is improved so that trial may proceed, or when the pending charges against the accused are dismissed. If charges are dismissed solely due to the accused's mental condition, the accused is subject to hospitalization as provided in section 4246 of title 18.

(g) *Excludable delay.* All periods of commitment shall be excluded as provided by R.C.M. 707(c). The 120-day time period under R.C.M. 707 shall begin anew on the date the general court-martial convening authority takes custody of the accused at the end of any period of commitment.

Rule 910. Pleas

(a) *Alternatives.*

(1) *In general.* An accused may plead as follows: guilty; not guilty to an offense as charged, but guilty of a named lesser included offense; guilty with exceptions, with or without substitutions, not guilty of the exceptions, but guilty of the substitutions, if any; or, not guilty. A plea of guilty may not be received as to an offense for which the death penalty may be adjudged by the court-martial.

Discussion

See paragraph 3, Part IV, concerning lesser included offenses. When the plea is to a lesser included offense without the use of exceptions and substitutions, the defense counsel should provide a written revised specification to be included in the record as an appellate exhibit.

A plea of guilty to a lesser included offense does not bar the prosecution from proceeding on the offense as charged. *See also* subsection (g) of this rule.

A plea of guilty does not prevent the introduction of evidence, either in support of the factual basis for the plea, or, after findings are entered, in aggravation. *See* R.C.M. 1001(b)(4).

----

(2) *Conditional pleas.* With the approval of the military judge and the consent of the Government, an accused may enter a conditional plea of guilty, reserving the right, on further review or appeal, to review of the adverse determination of any specified pretrial motion. If the accused prevails on further review or appeal, the accused shall be allowed to withdraw the plea of guilty. The Secretary concerned may prescribe who may consent for Government; unless otherwise prescribed by the Secretary concerned, the trial counsel may consent on behalf of the Government.

(b) *Refusal to plead; irregular plea.* If an accused fails or refuses to plead, or makes an irregular plea, the military judge shall enter a plea of not guilty for the accused.

Discussion

An irregular plea includes pleas such as guilty without criminality or guilty to a charge but not guilty to all specifications thereunder. When a plea is ambiguous, the military judge should have it clarified before proceeding further.

(c) *Advice to accused.* Before accepting a plea of guilty, the military judge shall address the accused personally and inform the accused of, and determine that the accused understands, the following:

(1) The nature of the offense to which the plea is offered, the mandatory minimum penalty, if any, provided by law, and the maximum possible penalty provided by law;

Discussion

The elements of each offense to which the accused has pleaded guilty should be described to the accused. *See also* subsection (e) of this rule.

---

(2) In a general or special court-martial, if the accused is not represented by counsel, that the accused has the right to be represented by counsel at every stage of the proceedings;

Discussion

In a general or special court-martial, if the accused is not represented by counsel, a plea of guilty should not be accepted.

---

(3) That the accused has the right to plead not guilty or to persist in that plea if already made, and that the accused has the right to be tried by a court-martial, and that at such trial the accused has the right to confront and cross-examine witnesses against the accused, and the right against self-incrimination;

(4) That if the accused pleads guilty, there will not be a trial of any kind as to those offenses to which the accused has so pleaded, so that by pleading guilty the accused waives the rights described in subsection (c)(3) of this Rule; and

(5) That if the accused pleads guilty, the military judge will question the accused about the offenses to which the accused has pleaded guilty, and, if the accused answers these questions under oath, on the record, and in the presence of counsel, the accused's answers may later be used against the accused in a prosecution for perjury or false statement.

Discussion

The advice in subsection (5) is inapplicable in a court-martial in which the accused is not represented by counsel.

(d) *Ensuring that the plea is voluntary.* The military judge shall not accept a plea of guilty without first, by addressing the accused personally, determining that the plea is voluntary and not the result of force or threats or of promises apart from a plea agreement under R.C.M. 705. The military judge shall also inquire whether the accused's willingness to plead guilty results from prior discussions between the convening authority, a representative of the convening authority, or trial counsel, and the accused or defense counsel.

(e) *Determining accuracy of plea.* The military judge shall not accept a plea of guilty without making such inquiry of the accused as shall satisfy the military judge that there is a factual basis for the plea. The accused shall be questioned under oath about the offenses.

Discussion

A plea of guilty must be in accord with the truth. Before the plea is accepted, the accused must admit every element of the offense(s) to which the accused pleaded guilty. Ordinarily, the elements should be explained to the accused. If any potential defense is raised by the accused's account of the offense or by other matter presented to the military judge, the military judge should explain such a defense to the accused and should not accept the plea unless the accused admits facts which negate the defense. If the statute of limitations would otherwise bar trial for the offense, the military judge should not accept a plea of guilty to it without an affirmative waiver by the accused. *See* R.C.M. 907(b)(2)(B).

The accused need not describe from personal recollection all the circumstances necessary to establish a factual basis for the plea. Nevertheless the accused must be convinced of, and able to describe all the facts necessary to establish guilt. For example, an accused may be unable to recall certain events in an offense, but may still be able to adequately describe the offense based on witness statements or similar sources which the accused believes to be true.

The accused should remain at the counsel table during questioning by the military judge.

(f) *Plea agreement inquiry.*

(1) *In general.* A plea agreement may not be accepted if it does not comply with R.C.M. 705.

(2) *Notice.* The parties shall inform the military judge if a plea agreement exists.

Discussion

The military judge should ask whether a plea agreement exists. *See* subsection (d) of this rule. Even if the military judge fails to so inquire or the accused answers incorrectly, counsel have an obligation to bring any agreements or understandings in connection with the plea to the attention of the military judge.

(3) *Disclosure.* If a plea agreement exists, the military judge shall require disclosure of the entire agreement before the plea is accepted, provided that in trial before military judge alone the military judge ordinarily shall not examine any sentence limitation contained in the agreement until after the sentence of the court-martial has been announced.

(4) *Inquiry.* The military judge shall inquire to ensure:

(A) That the accused understands the agreement; and

(B) That the parties agree to the terms of the agreement.

Discussion

If the plea agreement contains any unclear or ambiguous terms, the military judge should obtain clarification from the parties. If there is doubt about the accused's understanding of any terms in the agreement, the military judge should explain those terms to the accused.

(g) *Findings.* Findings based on a plea of guilty may be entered immediately upon acceptance of the plea at an Article 39(a) session unless:

(1) Such action is not permitted by regulations of the Secretary concerned;

(2) The plea is to a lesser included offense and the prosecution intends to proceed to trial on the offense as charged; or

(3) Trial is by a special court-martial without a military judge, in which case the president of the court-martial may enter findings based on the pleas without a formal vote except when subsection (g)(2) of this rule applies.

Discussion

If the accused has pleaded guilty to some offenses but not to

others, the military judge should ordinarily defer informing the members of the offenses to which the accused has pleaded guilty until after findings on the remaining offenses have been entered. *See* R.C.M. 913(a), Discussion and R.C.M. 920(e), Discussion, paragraph 3.

(h) *Later action.*

(1) *Withdrawal by the accused.* If after acceptance of the plea but before the sentence is announced the accused requests to withdraw a plea of guilty and substitute a plea of not guilty or a plea of guilty to a lesser included offense, the military judge may as a matter of discretion permit the accused to do so.

(2) *Statements by accused inconsistent with plea.* If after findings but before the sentence is announced the accused makes a statement to the court-martial, in testimony or otherwise, or presents evidence which is inconsistent with a plea of guilty on which a finding is based, the military judge shall inquire into the providence of the plea. If, following such inquiry, it appears that the accused entered the plea improvidently or through lack of understanding of its meaning and effect a plea of not guilty shall be entered as to the affected charges and specifications.

Discussion

When the accused withdraws a previously accepted plea for guilty or a plea of guilty is set aside, counsel should be given a reasonable time to prepare to proceed. In a trial by military judge alone, recusal of the military judge or disapproval of the request for trial by military judge alone will ordinarily be necessary when a plea is rejected or withdrawn after findings; in trial with members, a mistrial will ordinarily be necessary.

(3) *Pretrial agreement inquiry.* After sentence is announced the military judge shall inquire into any parts of a pretrial agreement which were not previously examined by the military judge. If the military judge determines that the accused does not understand the material terms of the agreement, or that the parties disagree as to such terms, the military judge shall conform, with the consent of the Government, the agreement to the accused's understanding or permit the accused to withdraw the plea.

Discussion

See subsection (f)(3) of this rule.

(i) *Record of proceedings.* A verbatim record of the guilty plea proceedings shall be made in cases in which a verbatim record is required under R.C.M. 1103. In other special courts-martial, a summary of the explanation and replies shall be included in the record of trial. As to summary courts-martial, *see* R.C.M. 1305.

(j) *Waiver.* Except as provided in subsection (a)(2) of this rule, a plea of guilty which results in a finding of guilty waives any objection, whether or not previously raised, insofar as the objection relates to the factual issue of guilt of the offense(s) to which the plea was made.

Rule 911. Assembly of the court-martial

The military judge shall announce the assembly of the court-martial.

Discussion

When trial is by a court-martial with members, the court-martial is ordinarily assembled immediately after the members are sworn. The members are ordinarily sworn at the first session at which they appear, as soon as all parties and personnel have been announced. The members are seated with the president, who is the senior member, in the center, and the other members alternately to the president's right and left according to rank. If the rank of a member is changed, or if the membership of the court-martial changes, the members should be reseated accordingly.

When trial is by military judge alone, the court-martial is ordinarily assembled immediately following approval of the request for trial by military judge alone.

Assembly of the court-martial is significant because it marks the point after which: substitution of the members and military judge may no longer take place without good cause (*see* Article 29; R.C.M. 505; 902; 912); the accused may no longer, as a matter of right, request trial by military judge alone or withdraw such a request previously approved (*see* Article 16; R.C.M. 903(a)(2)(d)); and the accused may no longer request, even with the permission of the military judge, or withdraw from a request for, enlisted members (*see* Article 25(c)(1); R.C.M. 903(a)(1)(d)).

Rule 912. Challenge of selection of members; examination and challenges of members

(a) *Pretrial matters.*

(1) *Questionnaires.* Before trial the trial counsel may, and shall upon request of the defense counsel, submit to each member written questions requesting the following information:

(A) Date of birth;

(B) Sex;

(C) Race;

(D) Marital status and sex, age, and number of dependents;

(E) Home of record;

(F) Civilian and military education, including, when available, major areas of study, name of school or institution, years of education, and degrees received;

(G) Current unit to which assigned;

(H) Past duty assignments;

(I) Awards and decorations received;

(J) Date of rank; and

(K) Whether the member has acted as accuser, counsel, preliminary hearing officer, investigating officer, convening authority, or legal officer or staff judge advocate for the convening authority in the case, or has forwarded the charges with a recommendation as to disposition.

Discussion

Using questionnaires before trial may expedite voir dire and may permit more informed exercise of challenges.

If the questionnaire is marked or admitted as an exhibit at the court-martial it must be attached to or included in the record of trial. *See* R.C.M. 1103(b)(2)(D)(iv) and (b)(3)(B).

---

(2) *Other materials.* A copy of any written materials considered by the convening authority in selecting the members detailed to the court-martial shall be provided to any party upon request, except that such materials pertaining solely to persons who were not selected for detail as members need not be provided unless the military judge, for good cause, so directs.

(b) *Challenge of selection of members.*

(1) *Motion.* Before the examination of members under subsection (d) of this rule begins, or at the next session after a party discovered or could have discovered by the exercise of diligence, the grounds therefor, whichever is earlier, that party may move to stay the proceedings on the ground that members were selected improperly.

Discussion

See R.C.M. 502(a) and 503(a) concerning selection of members. Members are also improperly selected when, for example, a certain group or class is arbitrarily excluded from consideration as members.

---

(2) *Procedure.* Upon a motion under subsection (b)(1) of this rule containing an offer of proof of matters which, if true, would constitute improper selection of members, the moving party shall be entitled to present evidence, including any written materials considered by the convening authority in selecting the members. Any other party may also present evidence on the matter. If the military judge determines that the members have been selected improperly, the military judge shall stay any proceedings requiring the presence of members until members are properly selected.

(3) *Waiver.* Failure to make a timely motion under this subsection shall waive the improper selection unless it constitutes a violation of R.C.M. 501(a), 502(a)(1), or 503(a)(2).

(c) *Stating grounds for challenge.* The trial counsel shall state any ground for challenge for cause against any member of which the trial counsel is aware.

(d) *Examination of members.* The military judge may permit the parties to conduct the examination of members or may personally conduct the examination. In the latter event the military judge shall permit the parties to supplement the examination by such further inquiry as the military judge deems proper or the military judge shall submit to the members such additional questions by the parties as the military judge deems proper. A member may be questioned outside the presence of other members when the military judge so directs.

Discussion

Examination of the members is called "voir dire." If the members have not already been placed under oath for the purpose of voir dire (*see* R.C.M. 807(b)(2) Discussion (B)), they should be sworn before they are questioned.

The opportunity for voir dire should be used to obtain information for the intelligent exercise of challenges; counsel should not purposely use voir dire to present factual matter which will not be admissible or to argue the case.

The nature and scope of the examination of members is within the discretion of the military judge. Members may be questioned individually or collectively. Ordinarily, the military judge should permit counsel to personally question the members. Trial counsel ordinarily conducts an inquiry before the defense. Whether trial counsel will question all the members before the defense begins or whether some other procedure will be followed depends on the circumstances. For example, when members are

questioned individually outside the presence of other members, each party would ordinarily complete questioning that member before another member is questioned. The military judge and each party may conduct additional questioning, after initial questioning by a party, as necessary.

Ordinarily the members should be asked whether they are aware of any ground for challenge against them. This may expedite further questioning. The members should be cautioned, however, not to disclose information in the presence of other members which might disqualify them.

(e) *Evidence.* Any party may present evidence relating to whether grounds for challenge exist against a member.

(f) *Challenges and removal for cause.*

(1) *Grounds.* A member shall be excused for cause whenever it appears that the member:

(A) Is not competent to serve as a member under Article 25(a), (b), or (c);

(B) Has not been properly detailed as a member of the court-martial;

(C) Is an accuser as to any offense charged;

(D) Will be a witness in the court-martial;

(E) Has acted as counsel for any party as to any offense charged;

(F) Has been an investigating or preliminary hearing officer as to any offense charged;

(G) Has acted in the same case as convening authority or as the legal officer or staff judge advocate to the convening authority;

(H) Will act in the same case as reviewing authority or as the legal officer or staff judge advocate to the reviewing authority;

(I) Has forwarded charges in the case with a personal recommendation as to disposition;

(J) Upon a rehearing or new or other trial of the case, was a member of the court-martial which heard the case before;

(K) Is junior to the accused in grade or rank, unless it is established that this could not be avoided;

(L) Is in arrest or confinement;

(M) Has formed or expressed a definite opinion as to the guilt or innocence of the accused as to any offense charged;

(N) Should not sit as a member in the interest of having the court-martial free from substantial doubt as to legality, fairness, and impartiality.

Discussion

Examples of matters which may be grounds for challenge under subsection (N) are that the member: has a direct personal interest in the result of the trial; is closely related to the accused, a counsel, or a witness in the case; has participated as a member or counsel in the trial of a closely related case; has a decidedly friendly or hostile attitude toward a party; or has an inelastic opinion concerning an appropriate sentence for the offenses charged.

---

(2) *When made.*

(A) *Upon completion of examination.* Upon completion of any examination under subsection (d) of this rule and the presentation of evidence, if any, on the matter, each party shall state any challenges for cause it elects to make.

(B) *Other times.* A challenge for cause may be made at any other time during trial when it becomes apparent that a ground for challenge may exist. Such examination of the member and presentation of evidence as may be necessary may be made in order to resolve the matter.

(3) *Procedure.* Each party shall be permitted to make challenges outside the presence of the members. The party making a challenge shall state the grounds for it. Ordinarily the trial counsel shall enter any challenges for cause before the defense counsel. The military judge shall rule finally on each challenge. When a challenge for cause is granted, the member concerned shall be excused. The burden of establishing that grounds for a challenge exist is upon the party making the challenge. A member successfully challenged shall be excused.

(4) *Waiver.* The grounds for challenge in subsection (f)(1)(A) of this rule may not be waived except that membership of enlisted members in the same unit as the accused may be waived. Membership of enlisted members in the same unit as the accused and any other ground for challenge is waived if the party knew of or could have discovered by the exercise of diligence the ground for challenge and failed to raise it in a timely manner. Notwithstanding the absence of a challenge or waiver of a challenge by the parties, the military judge may, in the interest of justice, excuse a member against whom a challenge for cause would lie. When a challenge for cause has been denied the successful use of a peremptory challenge by either party, excusing the challenged member from further participation in the court-martial, shall preclude further consideration of the challenge of that excused member upon later review. Further, failure by the challenging party to exercise a peremptory challenge against any member shall constitute waiver of further consideration of the challenge upon later review.

Discussion

See also Mil. R. Evid. 606(b) when a member may be a witness.

(g) *Peremptory challenges.*

(1) *Procedure.* Each party may challenge one member peremptorily. Any member so challenged shall be excused. No party may be required to exercise a peremptory challenge before the examination of members and determination of any challenges for cause has been completed. Ordinarily the trial counsel shall enter any peremptory challenge before the defense.

Discussion

Generally, no reason is necessary for a peremptory challenge. *But see Batson v. Kentucky* 476 U.S. 79 (1986); *United States v. Curtis*, 33 M.J. 101 (C.M.A. 1991), *cert. denied*, 112 S.Ct. 1177 (1992); *United States v. Moore*, 28 M.J. 366 (C.M.A. 1989); *United States v. Santiago-Davilla*, 26 M.J. 380 (C.M.A. 1988).

---

(2) *Waiver.* Failure to exercise a peremptory challenge when properly called upon to do so shall waive the right to make such a challenge. The military judge may, for good cause shown, grant relief from the waiver, but a peremptory challenge may not be made after the presentation of evidence before the members has begun. However, nothing in this subsection shall bar the exercise of a previously unexercised peremptory challenge against a member newly detailed under R.C.M. 505(c)(2)(B), even if presentation of evidence on the merits has begun.

Discussion

When the membership of the court-martial has been reduced below a quorum (*see* R.C.M. 501) or, when enlisted members have been requested, the fraction of enlisted members has been reduced below one-third, the proceedings should be adjourned and the convening authority notified so that new members may be detailed. *See* R.C.M. 505. *See also* R.C.M. 805(d) concerning other procedures when new members are detailed.

(h) *Special courts-martial without a military judge.* In a special court-martial without a military judge, the procedures in this rule shall apply, except that challenges shall be made in the presence of the members and a ruling on any challenge for cause shall be decided by a majority vote of the members upon secret written ballot in closed session. The challenged member shall not be present at the closed session at which the challenge is decided. A tie vote on a challenge disqualifies the member challenged. Before closing, the president shall give such instructions as may be necessary to resolve the challenge. Each challenge shall be decided separately, and all unexcused members except the challenged member shall participate. When only three members are present and one is challenged, the remaining two may decide the challenge. When the president is challenged, the next senior member shall act as president for purposes of deciding the challenge.

(i) *Definitions.*

(1) *Military judge.* For purpose of this rule, "military judge" does not include the president of a special court-martial without a military judge.

(2) *Witness.* For purposes of this rule, "witness" includes one who testifies at a court-martial and anyone whose declaration is received in evidence for any purpose, including written declarations made by affidavit or otherwise.

Discussion

For example, a person who by certificate has attested or otherwise authenticated an official record or other writing introduced in evidence is a witness.

(3) *Preliminary hearing officer.* For purposes of this rule, "preliminary hearing officer" includes any person who has examined charges under R.C.M. 405 and any person who was counsel for a member of a court of inquiry, or otherwise personally has conducted an investigation of the general matter involving the offenses charged.

Rule 913. Presentation of the case on the merits

(a) *Preliminary instructions.* The military judge may give such preliminary instructions as may be appropriate. If mixed pleas have been entered, the military judge should ordinarily defer informing the members of the offenses to which the accused pleaded guilty until after the findings on the remaining contested offenses have been entered.

Discussion

Preliminary instructions may include a description of the duties of members, procedures to be followed in the court-martial, and other appropriate matters.

Exceptions to the rule requiring the military judge to defer informing the members of an accused's prior pleas of guilty include cases in which the accused has specifically requested, on the record, that the military judge instruct the members of the prior pleas of guilty and cases in which a plea of guilty was to a lesser included offense within the contested offense charged in the specification. *See* R.C.M. 910(g), Discussion and R.C.M. 920(e), Discussion, paragraph 3.

(b) *Opening statements.* Each party may make one opening statement to the court-martial before presentation of evidence has begun. The defense may elect to make its statement after the prosecution has rested, before the presentation of evidence for the defense. The military judge may, as a matter of discretion, permit the parties to address the court-martial at other times.

Discussion

Counsel should confine their remarks to evidence they expect to be offered which they believe in good faith will be available and admissible and a brief statement of the issues in the case.

(c) *Presentation of evidence.* Each party shall have full opportunity to present evidence.

(1) *Order of presentation.* Ordinarily the following sequence shall be followed:

(A) Presentation of evidence for the prosecution;

(B) Presentation of evidence for the defense;

(C) Presentation of prosecution evidence in rebuttal;

(D) Presentation of defense evidence in surrebuttal;

(E) Additional rebuttal evidence in the discretion of the military judge; and

(F) Presentation of evidence requested by the military judge or members.

Discussion

See R.C.M. 801(a) and Mil. R. Evid. 611 concerning control by the military judge over the order of proceedings.

(2) *Taking testimony.* The testimony of witnesses

shall be taken orally in open session, unless otherwise provided in this Manual.

Discussion

Each witness must testify under oath. *See* R.C.M. 807(b)(1)(B); Mil. R. Evid. 603. After a witness is sworn, the witness should be identified for the record (full name, rank, and unit, if military, or full name and address, if civilian). The party calling the witness conducts direct examination of the witness, followed by cross-examination of the witness by the opposing party. Redirect and re-cross-examination are conducted as necessary, followed by any questioning by the military judge and members. *See* Mil. R. Evid. 611; 614.

All documentary and real evidence (except marks or wounds on a person's body) should be marked for identification when first referred to in the proceedings and should be included in the record of trial whether admitted in evidence or not. *See* R.C.M. 1103(b)(2)(C), (c). "Real evidence" include physical objects, such as clothing, weapons, and marks or wounds on a person's body. If it is impracticable to attach an item of real evidence to the record, the item should be clearly and accurately described by testimony, photographs, or other means so that it may be considered on review. Similarly, when documentary evidence is used, if the document cannot be attached to the record (as in the case of an original official record or a large map), a legible copy or accurate extract should be included in the record. When a witness points to or otherwise refers to certain parts of a map, photograph, diagram, chart, or other exhibit, the place to which the witness pointed or referred should be clearly identified for the record, either by marking the exhibit or by an accurate description of the witness' actions with regard to the exhibit.

(3) *Views and inspections.* The military judge may, as a matter of discretion, permit the court-martial to view or inspect premises or a place or an article or object. Such a view or inspection shall take place only in the presence of all parties, the members (if any), and the military judge. A person familiar with the scene may be designated by the military judge to escort the court-martial. Such person shall perform the duties of escort under oath. The escort shall not testify, but may point out particular features prescribed by the military judge. Any statement made at the view or inspection by the escort, a party, the military judge, or any member shall be made part of the record.

Discussion

A view or inspection should be permitted only in extraordinary circumstances. The fact that a view or inspection has been made does not necessarily preclude the introduction in evidence of photographs, diagrams, maps, or sketches of the place or item viewed, if these are otherwise admissible.

(4) *Evidence subject to exclusion.* When offered evidence would be subject to exclusion upon objection, the military judge may, as a matter of discretion, bring the matter to the attention of the parties and may, in the interest of justice, exclude the evidence without an objection by a party.

Discussion

The military judge should not exclude evidence which is not objected to by a party except in extraordinary circumstances. Counsel should be permitted to try the case and present the evidence without unnecessary interference by the military judge. *See also* Mil. R. Evid. 103.

(5) *Reopening case.* The military judge may, as a matter of discretion, permit a party to reopen its case after it has rested.

Rule 914. Production of statements of witnesses

(a) *Motion for production.* After a witness other than the accused has testified on direct examination, the military judge, on motion of a party who did not call the witness, shall order the party who called the witness to produce, for examination and use by the moving party, any statement of the witness that relates to the subject matter concerning which the witness has testified, and that is:

(1) In the case of a witness called by the trial counsel, in the possession of the United States; or

(2) In the case of a witness called by the defense, in the possession of the accused or defense counsel.

Discussion

See also R.C.M. 701 (Discovery).

Counsel should anticipate legitimate demands for statements under this and similar rules and avoid delays in the proceedings by voluntary disclosure before arraignment.

This rule does not apply to preliminary hearings under Article 32.

As to procedures for certain government information as to which a privilege is asserted, *see* Mil. R. Evid. 505; 506.

(b) *Production of entire statement.* If the entire contents of the statement relate to the subject matter concerning which the witness has testified, the military judge shall order that the statement be delivered to the moving party.

(c) *Production of excised statement.* If the party who called the witness claims that the statement contains matter that does not relate to the subject matter concerning which the witness has testified, the military judge shall order that it be delivered to the military judge. Upon inspection, the military judge shall excise the portions of the statement that do not relate to the subject matter concerning which the witness has testified, and shall order that the statement, with such material excised, be delivered to the moving party. Any portion of a statement that is withheld from an accused over objection shall be preserved by the trial counsel, and, in the event of a conviction, shall be made available to the reviewing authorities for the purpose of determining the correctness of the decision to excise the portion of the statement.

(d) *Recess for examination of the statement.* Upon delivery of the statement to the moving party, the military judge may recess the trial for the examination of the statement and preparation for its use in the trial.

(e) *Remedy for failure to produce statement.* If the other party elects not to comply with an order to deliver a statement to the moving party, the military judge shall order that the testimony of the witness be disregarded by the trier of fact and that the trial proceed, or, if it is the trial counsel who elects not to comply, shall declare a mistrial if required in the interest of justice.

(f) *Definition.* As used in this rule, a "statement" of a witness means:

(1) A written statement made by the witness that is signed or otherwise adopted or approved by the witness;

(2) A substantially verbatim recital of an oral statement made by the witness that is recorded contemporaneously with the making of the oral statement and contained in a stenographic, mechanical, electrical, or other recording or a transcription thereof; or

(3) A statement, however taken or recorded, or a transcription thereof, made by the witness to a Federal grand jury.

Rule 914A. Use of remote live testimony of a child

(a) *General procedures.* A child shall be allowed to testify out of the presence of the accused after the military judge has determined that the requirements of Mil. R. Evid. 611(d)(3) have been satisfied. The procedure used to take such testimony will be determined by the military judge based upon the exigencies of the situation. At a minimum, the following procedures shall be observed:

(1) The witness shall testify from a remote location outside the courtroom;

(2) Attendance at the remote location shall be limited to the child, counsel for each side (not including an accused pro se), equipment operators, and other persons, such as an attendant for the child, whose presence is deemed necessary by the military judge;

(3) Sufficient monitors shall be placed in the courtroom to allow viewing and hearing of the testimony by the military judge, the accused, the members, the court reporter and the public;

(4) The voice of the military judge shall be transmitted into the remote location to allow control of the proceedings; and

(5) The accused shall be permitted private, contemporaneous communication with his counsel.

(b) *Definition.* As used in this rule, "remote live testimony" includes, but is not limited to, testimony by videoteleconference, closed circuit television, or similar technology.

(c) *Prohibitions.* The procedures described above shall not be used where the accused elects to absent himself from the courtroom pursuant to R.C.M. 804(c).

Discussion

For purposes of this rule, unlike R.C.M. 914B, remote means or similar technology does not include receiving testimony by telephone where the parties cannot see and hear each other.

Rule 914B. Use of remote testimony

(a) *General procedures.* The military judge shall determine the procedures used to take testimony via remote means. At a minimum, all parties shall be able to hear each other, those in attendance at the remote site shall be identified, and the accused shall be permitted private, contemporaneous communication with his counsel.

(b) *Definition.* As used in this rule, testimony via "remote means" includes, but is not limited to, testimony by videoteleconference, closed circuit television, telephone, or similar technology.

Discussion

This rule applies for all witness testimony other than child witness testimony specifically covered by Mil. R. Evid. 611(d) and R.C.M. 914A. When utilizing testimony via remote means, military justice practitioners are encouraged to consult the procedure used in *In re San Juan Dupont Plaza Hotel Fire Litigation*, 129 F.R.D. 424 (D.P.R. 1989) and to read *United States v. Gigante*, 166 F.3d 75 (2d Cir. 1999), cert. denied, 528 U.S. 1114 (2000).

Rule 915. Mistrial

(a) *In general.* The military judge may, as a matter of discretion, declare a mistrial when such action is manifestly necessary in the interest of justice because of circumstances arising during the proceedings which cast substantial doubt upon the fairness of the proceedings. A mistrial may be declared as to some or all charges, and as to the entire proceedings or as to only the proceedings after findings.

Discussion

The power to grant a mistrial should be used with great caution, under urgent circumstances, and for plain and obvious reasons. As examples, a mistrial may be appropriate when inadmissible matters so prejudicial that a curative instruction would be inadequate are brought to the attention of the members or when members engage in prejudicial misconduct. Also a mistrial is appropriate when the proceedings must be terminated because of a legal defect, such as a jurisdictional defect, which can be cured; for example, when the referral is jurisdictionally defective. *See also* R.C.M. 905(g) concerning the effect of rulings in one proceeding on later proceedings.

(b) *Procedure.* On motion for a mistrial or when it otherwise appears that grounds for a mistrial may exist, the military judge shall inquire into the views of the parties on the matter and then decide the matter as an interlocutory question.

Discussion

Except in a special court-martial without a military judge, the hearing on a mistrial should be conducted out of the presence of the members.

(c) *Effect of declaration of mistrial.*

(1) *Withdrawal of charges.* A declaration of a mistrial shall have the effect of withdrawing the affected charges and specifications from the court-martial.

Discussion

Upon declaration of a mistrial, the affected charges are returned to the convening authority who may refer them anew or otherwise dispose of them. *See* R.C.M. 401-407.

---

(2) *Further proceedings.* A declaration of a mistrial shall not prevent trial by another court-martial on the affected charges and specifications except when the mistrial was declared after jeopardy attached and before findings, and the declaration was:

(A) An abuse of discretion and without the consent of the defense; or

(B) The direct result of intentional prosecutorial misconduct designed to necessitate a mistrial.

Rule 916. Defenses

(a) *In general.* As used in this rule, "defenses" includes any special defense which, although not denying that the accused committed the objective acts constituting the offense charged, denies, wholly or partially, criminal responsibility for those acts.

Discussion

Special defenses are also called "affirmative defenses."

"Alibi" and "good character" are not special defenses, as they operate to deny that the accused committed one or more of the acts constituting the offense. As to evidence of the accused's good character, *see* Mil. R. Evid. 404(a)(1). *See* R.C.M. 701(b)(1) concerning notice of alibi.

(b) *Burden of proof.*

(1) *General rule.* Except as listed below in paragraphs (2) and (3), the prosecution shall have the burden of proving beyond a reasonable doubt that the defense did not exist.

(2) *Lack of mental responsibility.* The accused has the burden of proving the defense of lack of mental responsibility by clear and convincing evidence.

(3) *Mistake of fact as to age.* In the defense of mistake of fact as to age as described in Article 120b(d)(2) in a prosecution of a child sexual offense, the accused has the burden of proving mistake of fact as to age by a preponderance of the evidence.

Discussion

A defense may be raised by evidence presented by the defense, the prosecution, or the court-martial. For example, in a prosecution for assault, testimony by prosecution witnesses that the victim brandished a weapon toward the accused may raise a defense of self-defense. *See* subsection (e) below. More than one defense may be raised as to a particular offense. The defenses need not necessarily be consistent.

See R.C.M. 920(e)(3) concerning instructions on defenses.

(c) *Justification.* A death, injury, or other act caused or done in the proper performance of a legal duty is justified and not unlawful.

Discussion

The duty may be imposed by statute, regulation, or order. For example, the use of force by a law enforcement officer when reasonably necessary in the proper execution of a lawful apprehension is justified because the duty to apprehend is imposed by lawful authority. Also, killing an enemy combatant in battle is justified.

(d) *Obedience to orders.* It is a defense to any offense that the accused was acting pursuant to orders unless the accused knew the orders to be unlawful or a person of ordinary sense and understanding would have known the orders to be unlawful.

Discussion

Ordinarily the lawfulness of an order is finally decided by the military judge. *See* R.C.M. 801(e). An exception might exist when the sole issue is whether the person who gave the order in fact occupied a certain position at the time.

An act performed pursuant to a lawful order is justified. *See* subsection (c) of this rule. An act performed pursuant to an unlawful order is excused unless the accused knew it to be unlawful or a person of ordinary sense and understanding would have known it to be unlawful.

(e) *Self-defense.*

(1) *Homicide or assault cases involving deadly force.* It is a defense to a homicide, assault involving deadly force, or battery involving deadly force that the accused:

(A) Apprehended, on reasonable grounds, that death or grievous bodily harm was about to be inflicted wrongfully on the accused; and

(B) Believed that the force the accused used was necessary for protection against death or grievous bodily harm.

Discussion

The words "involving deadly force" described the factual circumstances of the case, not specific assault offenses. If the accused is charged with simple assault, battery or any form of aggravated assault, or if simple assault, battery or any form of aggravated assault is in issue as a lesser included offense, the accused may rely on this subsection if the test specified in subsections (A) and (B) is satisfied.

The test for the first element of self-defense is objective. Thus, the accused's apprehension of death or grievous bodily harm must have been one which a reasonable, prudent person would have held under the circumstances. Because this test is objective, such matters as intoxication or emotional instability of the accused are irrelevant. On the other hand, such matters as the relative height, weight, and general build of the accused and the alleged victim, and the possibility of safe retreat are ordinarily among the circumstances which should be considered in determining the reasonableness of the apprehension of death or grievous bodily harm.

The test for the second element is entirely subjective. The accused is not objectively limited to the use of reasonable force. Accordingly, such matters as the accused's emotional control, education, and intelligence are relevant in determining the accused's actual belief as to the force necessary to repel the attack.

See also Mil. R. Evid. 404(a)(2) as to evidence concerning the character of the victim.

---

(2) *Certain aggravated assault cases.* It is a defense to assault with a dangerous weapon or means likely to produce death or grievous bodily harm that the accused:

(A) Apprehended, on reasonable grounds, that bodily harm was about to be inflicted wrongfully on the accused; and

(B) In order to deter the assailant, offered but did not actually apply or attempt to apply such means or force as would be likely to cause death or grievous bodily harm.

Discussion

The principles in the discussion of subsection (e)(1) of this rule concerning reasonableness of the apprehension of bodily harm apply here.

If, as a result of the accused's offer of a means or force likely to produce grievous bodily harm, the victim was killed or injured unintentionally by the accused, this aspect of self-defense may operate in conjunction with the defense of accident (*see* subsection (f) of this rule) to excuse the accused's acts. The death or injury must have been an unintended and unexpected result of the accused's exercise of the right of self-defense.

---

(3) *Other assaults.* It is a defense to any assault punishable under Article 90, 91, or 128 and not listed in subsections (e)(1) or (2) of this rule that the accused:

(A) Apprehended, upon reasonable grounds,

that bodily harm was about to be inflicted wrongfully on the accused; and

(B) Believed that the force that accused used was necessary for protection against bodily harm, provided that the force used by the accused was less than force reasonably likely to produce death or grievous bodily harm.

Discussion

The principles in the discussion under subsection (e)(1) apply here.

If, in using only such force as the accused was entitled to use under this aspect of self-defense, death or serious injury to the victim results, this aspect of self-defense may operate in conjunction with the defense of accident (*see* subsection (f) of this rule) to excuse the accused's acts. The death or serious injury must have been an unintended and unexpected result of the accused's proper exercise of the right of self-defense.

---

(4) *Loss of right to self-defense.* The right to self-defense is lost and the defenses described in subsections (e)(1), (2), and (3) of this rule shall not apply if the accused was an aggressor, engaged in mutual combat, or provoked the attack which gave rise to the apprehension, unless the accused had withdrawn in good faith after the aggression, combat, or provocation and before the offense alleged occurred.

Discussion

A person does not become an aggressor or provocateur merely because that person approaches another to seek an interview, even if the approach is not made in a friendly manner. For example, one may approach another and demand an explanation of offensive words or redress of a complaint. If the approach is made in a nonviolent manner, the right to self-defense is not lost.

Failure to retreat, when retreat is possible, does not deprive the accused of the right to self-defense if the accused was lawfully present. The availability of avenues of retreat is one factor which may be considered in addressing the reasonableness of the accused's apprehension of bodily harm and the sincerity of the accused's belief that the force used was necessary for self-protection.

---

(5) *Defense of another.* The principles of self-defense under subsection (e)(1) through (4) of this rule apply to defense of another. It is a defense to homicide, attempted homicide, assault with intent to kill, or any assault under Article 90, 91, or 128 that the accused acted in defense of another, provided that the accused may not use more force than the person

defended was lawfully entitled to use under the circumstances.

Discussion

The accused acts at the accused's peril when defending another. Thus, if the accused goes to the aid of an apparent assault victim, the accused is guilty of any assault the accused commits on the apparent assailant if, unbeknownst to the accused, the apparent victim was in fact the aggressor and not entitled to use self-defense.

(f) *Accident.* A death, injury, or other event which occurs as the unintentional and unexpected result of doing a lawful act in a lawful manner is an accident and excusable.

Discussion

The defense of accident is not available when the act which caused the death, injury, or event was a negligent act.

(g) *Entrapment.* It is a defense that the criminal design or suggestion to commit the offense originated in the Government and the accused had no predisposition to commit the offense.

Discussion

The "Government" includes agents of the Government and persons cooperating with them (for example, informants). The fact that persons acting for the Government merely afford opportunities or facilities for the commission of the offense does not constitute entrapment. Entrapment occurs only when the criminal conduct is the product of the creative activity of law enforcement officials.

When the defense of entrapment is raised, evidence of uncharged misconduct by the accused of a nature similar to that charged is admissible to show predisposition. *See* Mil. R. Evid. 404(b).

(h) *Coercion or duress.* It is a defense to any offense except killing an innocent person that the accused's participation in the offense was caused by a reasonable apprehension that the accused or another innocent person would be immediately killed or would immediately suffer serious bodily injury if the accused did not commit the act. The apprehension must reasonably continue throughout the commission of the act. If the accused has any reasonable opportunity to avoid committing the act without subjecting the accused or another innocent person to the harm threatened, this defense shall not apply.

Discussion

The immediacy of the harm necessary may vary with the circumstances. For example, a threat to kill a person's wife the next day may be immediate if the person has no opportunity to contact law enforcement officials or otherwise protect the intended victim or avoid committing the offense before then.

(i) *Inability.* It is a defense to refusal or failure to perform a duty that the accused was, through no fault of the accused, not physically or financially able to perform the duty.

Discussion

The test of inability is objective in nature. The accused's opinion that a physical impairment prevented performance of the duty will not suffice unless the opinion is reasonable under all the circumstances.

If the physical or financial inability of the accused occurred through the accused's own fault or design, it is not a defense. For example, if the accused, having knowledge of an order to get a haircut, spends money on other nonessential items, the accused's inability to pay for the haircut would not be a defense.

(j) *Ignorance or mistake of fact.*

(1) *Generally.* Except as otherwise provided in this subsection, it is a defense to an offense that the accused held, as a result of ignorance or mistake, an incorrect belief of the true circumstances such that, if the circumstances were as the accused believed them, the accused would not be guilty of the offense. If the ignorance or mistake goes to an element requiring premeditation, specific intent, willfulness, or knowledge of a particular fact, the ignorance or mistake need only have existed in the mind of the accused. If the ignorance or mistake goes to any other element requiring only general intent or knowledge, the ignorance or mistake must have existed in the mind of the accused and must have been reasonable under all the circumstances. However, if the accused's knowledge or intent is immaterial as to an element, then ignorance or mistake is not a defense.

(2) *Child Sexual Offenses.* It is a defense to a prosecution for Article 120b(b), sexual assault of a child, and Article 120b(c), sexual abuse of a child, that, at the time of the offense, the accused reasonably believed that the child had attained the age of 16 years, if the child had in fact attained at least the age

of 12 years. The accused must prove this defense by a preponderance of the evidence.

Discussion

Examples of ignorance or mistake which need only exist in fact include: ignorance of the fact that the person assaulted was an officer; belief that property allegedly stolen belonged to the accused; belief that a controlled substance was really sugar.

Examples of ignorance or mistake which must be reasonable as well as actual include: belief that the accused charged with unauthorized absence had permission to go; belief that the accused had a medical "profile" excusing shaving as otherwise required by regulation. Some offenses require special standards of conduct (see, for example, paragraph 68, Part IV, Dishonorable failure to maintain sufficient funds); the element of reasonableness must be applied in accordance with the standards imposed by such offenses.

Examples of offenses in which the accused's intent or knowledge is immaterial include: any rape of a child, or any sexual assault or sexual abuse of a child when the child is under 12 years old. However, such ignorance or mistake may be relevant in extenuation and mitigation.

See subsection (l)(1) of this rule concerning ignorance or mistake of law.

(k) *Lack of mental responsibility.*

(1) *Lack of mental responsibility.* It is an affirmative defense to any offense that, at the time of the commission of the acts constituting the offense, the accused, as a result of a severe mental disease or defect, was unable to appreciate the nature and quality or the wrongfulness of his or her acts. Mental disease or defect does not otherwise constitute a defense.

Discussion

See R.C.M. 706 concerning sanity inquiries; R.C.M. 909 concerning the capacity of the accused to stand trial; and R.C.M. 1102A concerning any post-trial hearing for an accused found not guilty only by reason of lack of mental responsibility.

---

(2) *Partial mental responsibility.* A mental condition not amounting to a lack of mental responsibility under subsection (k)(1) of this rule is not an affirmative defense.

Discussion

Evidence of a mental condition not amounting to a lack of mental responsibility may be admissible as to whether the accused entertained a state of mind necessary to be proven as an element of the offense. The defense must notify the trial counsel before the beginning of trial on the merits if the defense intends to introduce expert testimony as to the accused's mental condition. *See* R.C.M. 701(b)(2).

(3) *Procedure.*

(A) *Presumption.* The accused is presumed to have been mentally responsible at the time of the alleged offense. This presumption continues until the accused establishes, by clear and convincing evidence, that he or she was not mentally responsible at the time of the alleged offense.

Discussion

The accused is presumed to be mentally responsible, and this presumption continues throughout the proceedings unless the finder of fact determines that the accused has proven lack of mental responsibility by clear and convincing evidence. *See* subsection (b) of this rule.

(B) *Inquiry.* If a question is raised concerning the mental responsibility of the accused, the military judge shall rule finally whether to direct an inquiry under R.C.M. 706. In a special court-martial without a military judge, the president shall rule finally except to the extent that the question is one of fact, in which case the president rules subject to objection by any member.

Discussion

See R.C.M. 801(e)(3) for the procedures for voting on rulings of the president of a special court-martial without a military judge.

If an inquiry is directed, priority should be given to it.

(C) *Determination.* The issue of mental responsibility shall not be considered as an interlocutory question.

(l) *Not defenses generally.*

(1) *Ignorance or mistake of law.* Ignorance or mistake of law, including general orders or regulations, ordinarily is not a defense.

Discussion

For example, ignorance that it is a crime to possess marijuana is not a defense to wrongful possession of marijuana.

Ignorance or mistake of law may be a defense in some limited circumstances. If the accused, because of a mistake as to a separate nonpenal law, lacks the criminal intent or state of mind necessary to establish guilt, this may be a defense. For example, if the accused, under mistaken belief that the accused is entitled to take an item under property law, takes an item, this mistake of law (as to the accused's legal right) would, if genuine, be a

defense to larceny. On the other hand, if the accused disobeyed an order, under the actual but mistaken belief that the order was unlawful, this would not be a defense because the accused's mistake was as to the order itself, and not as to a separate nonpenal law. Also, mistake of law may be a defense when the mistake results from reliance on the decision or pronouncement of an authorized public official or agency. For example, if an accused, acting on the advice of an official responsible for administering benefits that the accused is entitled to those benefits, applies for and receives those benefits, the accused may have a defense even though the accused was not legally eligible for the benefits. On the other hand, reliance on the advice of counsel that a certain course of conduct is legal is not, of itself, a defense.

(2) *Voluntary intoxication.* Voluntary intoxication, whether caused by alcohol or drugs, is not a defense. However, evidence of any degree of voluntary intoxication may be introduced for the purpose of raising a reasonable doubt as to the existence of actual knowledge, specific intent, willfulness, or a premeditated design to kill, if actual knowledge, specific intent, willfulness, or premeditated design to kill is an element of the offense.

Discussion

Intoxication may reduce premeditated murder to unpremeditated murder, but it will not reduce murder to manslaughter or any other lesser offense. *See* paragraph 43c(2)(c), Part IV.

Although voluntary intoxication is not a defense, evidence of voluntary intoxication may be admitted in extenuation.

Rule 917. Motion for a finding of not guilty

(a) *In general.* The military judge, on motion by the accused or *sua sponte*, shall enter a finding of not guilty of one or more offenses charged after the evidence on either side is closed and before findings on the general issue of guilt are announced if the evidence is insufficient to sustain a conviction of the offense affected. If a motion for a finding of not guilty at the close of the prosecution's case is denied, the defense may offer evidence on that offense without having reserved the right to do so.

(b) *Form of motion.* The motion shall specifically indicate wherein the evidence is insufficient.

(c) *Procedure.* Before ruling on a motion for a finding of not guilty, whether made by counsel or *sua sponte*, the military judge shall give each party an opportunity to be heard on the matter.

Discussion

The military judge ordinarily should permit the trial counsel to reopen the case as to the insufficiency specified in the motion.

See R.C.M. 801(e)(2) and (3) for additional procedures to be followed in a special court-martial without a military judge. *See* R.C.M. 1102(b)(2) for the military judge's authority, upon motion or sua sponte, to enter finding of not guilty after findings but prior to authentication of the record.

(d) *Standard.* A motion for a finding of not guilty shall be granted only in the absence of some evidence which, together with all reasonable inferences and applicable presumptions, could reasonably tend to establish every essential element of an offense charged. The evidence shall be viewed in the light most favorable to the prosecution, without an evaluation of the credibility of witnesses.

(e) *Motion as to greater offense.* A motion for a finding of not guilty may be granted as to part of a specification and, if appropriate, the corresponding charge, as long as a lesser offense charged is alleged in the portion of the specification as to which the motion is not granted. In such cases, the military judge shall announce that a finding of not guilty has been granted as to specified language in the specification and, if appropriate, corresponding charge. In cases before members, the military judge shall instruct the members accordingly, so that any findings later announced will not be inconsistent with the granting of the motion.

(f) *Effect of ruling.* A ruling granting a motion for a finding of not guilty is final when announced and may not be reconsidered. Such a ruling is a finding of not guilty of the affected specification, or affected portion thereof, and, when appropriate, of the corresponding charge. A ruling denying a motion for a finding of not guilty may be reconsidered at any time prior to authentication of the record of trial.

(g) *Effect of denial on review.* If all the evidence admitted before findings, regardless by whom offered, is sufficient to sustain findings of guilty, the findings need not be set aside upon review solely because the motion for finding of not guilty should have been granted upon the state of the evidence when it was made.

Rule 918. Findings

(a) *General findings.* The general findings of a court-martial state whether the accused is guilty of each offense charged. If two or more accused are tried together, separate findings as to each shall be made.

(1) *As to a specification.* General findings as to a specification may be: guilty; not guilty of an offense as charged, but guilty of a named lesser included offense; guilty with exceptions, with or without substitutions, not guilty of the exceptions, but guilty of the substitutions, if any; not guilty only by reason of lack of mental responsibility; or, not guilty. Exceptions and substitutions may not be used to substantially change the nature of the offense or to increase the seriousness of the offense or the maximum punishment for it.

Discussion

Exceptions and Substitutions. One or more words or figures may be excepted from a specification and, when necessary, others substituted, if the remaining language of the specification, with or without substitutions, states an offense by the accused which is punishable by the court-martial. Changing the date or place of the offense may, but does not necessarily, change the nature or identity of an offense.

If A and B are joint accused and A is convicted but B is acquitted of an offense charged, A should be found guilty by excepting the name of B from the specification as well as any other words indicating the offense was a joint one.

Lesser Included Offenses. If the evidence fails to prove the offense charged but does prove an offense necessarily included in the offense charged, the fact finder may find the accused not guilty of the offense charged but guilty of the lesser included offense. *See* paragraph 3 of Part IV concerning lesser included offenses.

Offenses arising from the same act or transaction. The accused may be found guilty of two or more offenses arising from the same act or transaction, whether or not the offenses are separately punishable. *But see* R.C.M. 906(b)(12); 907(b)(3)(B); 1003(c)(1)(C).

---

(2) *As to a charge.* General findings as to a charge may be: guilty; not guilty, but guilty of a violation of Article _____; not guilty only by reason of lack of mental responsibility; or not guilty.

Discussion

Where there are two or more specifications under one charge, conviction of any of those specifications requires a finding of guilty of the corresponding charge. Under such circumstances any findings of not guilty as to the other specifications do not affect that charge. If the accused is found guilty of one specification and of a lesser included offense prohibited by a different Article as to another specification under the same charge, the findings as to the corresponding charge should be: "Of the Charge as to specification 1: Guilty; as to specification 2: not guilty, but guilty of a violation of Article _____."

An attempt should be found as a violation of Article 80 unless the attempt is punishable under Articles 85, 94, 100, 104, or 128, in which case it should be found as a violation of that Article.

A court-martial may not find an offense as a violation of an article under which it was not charged solely for the purpose of increasing the authorized punishment or for the purpose of adjudging less than the prescribed mandatory punishment.

(b) *Special findings.* In a trial by court-martial composed of military judge alone, the military judge shall make special findings upon request by any party. Special findings may be requested only as to matters of fact reasonably in issue as to an offense and need be made only as to offenses of which the accused was found guilty. Special findings may be requested at any time before general findings are announced. Only one set of special findings may be requested by a party in a case. If the request is for findings on specific matters, the military judge may require that the request be written. Special findings may be entered orally on the record at the court-martial or in writing during or after the court-martial, but in any event shall be made before authentication and included in the record of trial.

Discussion

Special findings ordinarily include findings as to the elements of the offenses of which the accused has been found guilty, and any affirmative defense relating thereto.

See also R.C.M. 905(d); Mil. R. Evid. 304(d)(4); 311(d)(4); 321(f) concerning other findings to be made by the military judge.

Members may not make special findings.

(c) *Basis of findings.* Findings may be based on direct or circumstantial evidence. Only matters properly before the court-martial on the merits of the case may be considered. A finding of guilty of any offense may be reached only when the factfinder is satisfied that guilt has been proved beyond a reasonable doubt.

Discussion

Direct evidence is evidence which tends directly to prove or disprove a fact in issue (for example, an element of the offense charged). Circumstantial evidence is evidence which tends directly to prove not a fact in issue but some other fact or circumstance from which, either alone or together with other facts or circumstances, one may reasonably infer the existence or non-

existence of a fact in issue. There is no general rule for determining or comparing the weight to be given to direct or circumstantial evidence.

A reasonable doubt is a doubt based on reason and common sense. A reasonable doubt is not mere conjecture; it is an honest, conscientious doubt suggested by the evidence, or lack of it, in the case. An absolute or mathematical certainty is not required. The rule as to reasonable doubt extends to every element of the offense. It is not necessary that each particular fact advanced by the prosecution which is not an element be proved beyond a reasonable doubt.

The factfinder should consider the inherent probability or improbability of the evidence, using common sense and knowledge of human nature, and should weigh the credibility of witnesses. A fact finder may properly believe one witness and disbelieve others whose testimony conflicts with that of the one. A factfinder may believe part of the testimony of a witness and disbelieve other parts.

Findings of guilty may not be based solely on the testimony of a witness other than the accused which is self-contradictory, unless the contradiction is adequately explained by the witness. Even if apparently credible and corroborated, the testimony of an accomplice should be considered with great caution.

Rule 919. Argument by counsel on findings

(a) *In general.* After the closing of evidence, trial counsel shall be permitted to open the argument. The defense counsel shall be permitted to reply. Trial counsel shall then be permitted to reply in rebuttal.

(b) *Contents.* Arguments may properly include reasonable comment on the evidence in the case, including inferences to be drawn therefrom, in support of a party's theory of the case.

Discussion

The military judge may exercise reasonable control over argument. *See* R.C.M. 801(a)(3).

Argument may include comment about the testimony, conduct, motives, interests, and biases of witnesses to the extent supported by the evidence. Counsel should not express a personnel belief or opinion as to the truth or falsity of any testimony or evidence or the guilt or innocence of the accused, nor should counsel make arguments calculated to inflame passions or prejudices. In argument counsel may treat the testimony of witnesses as conclusively establishing the facts related by the witnesses. Counsel may not cite legal authorities or the facts of other cases when arguing to members on findings.

Trial counsel may not comment on the accused's exercise of the right against self-incrimination or the right to counsel. *See* Mil. R. Evid. 512. Trial counsel may not argue that the prosecution's evidence is unrebutted if the only rebuttal could come from the accused. When the accused is on trial for several offenses and testifies only as to some of the offenses, trial counsel may not comment on the accused's failure to testify as to the others. When the accused testifies on the merits regarding an offense charged, trial counsel may comment on the accused's failure in that testimony to deny or explain specific incriminating facts that the evidence for the prosecution tends to establish regarding that offense.

Trial counsel may not comment on the failure of the defense to call witnesses or of the accused to testify at the Article 32 preliminary hearing or upon the probable effect of the court-martial's findings on relations between the military and civilian communities.

The rebuttal argument of trial counsel is generally limited to matters argued by the defense. If trial counsel is permitted to introduce new matter in closing argument, the defense should be allowed to reply in rebuttal. However, this will not preclude trial counsel from presenting a final argument.

(c) *Waiver of objection to improper argument.* Failure to object to improper argument before the military judge begins to instruct the members on findings shall constitute waiver of the objection.

Discussion

If an objection that an argument is improper is sustained, the military judge should immediately instruct the members that the argument was improper and that they must disregard it. In extraordinary cases improper argument may require a mistrial. *See* R.C.M. 915. The military judge should be alert to improper argument and take appropriate action when necessary.

Rule 920. Instructions on findings

(a) *In general.* The military judge shall give the members appropriate instructions on findings.

Discussion

Instructions consist of a statement of the issues in the case and an explanation of the legal standards and procedural requirements by which the members will determine findings. Instructions should be tailored to fit the circumstances of the case, and should fairly and adequately cover the issues presented.

(b) *When given.* Instructions on findings shall be given before or after arguments by counsel, or at both times, and before the members close to deliberate on findings, but the military judge may, upon request of the members, any party, or *sua sponte*, give additional instructions at a later time.

Discussion

After members have reached a finding on a specification, instructions may not be given on an offense included therein which was not described in an earlier instruction unless the finding is illegal. This is true even if the finding has not been announced. When

instructions are to be given is a matter within the sole discretion of the military trial judge.

(c) *Requests for instructions.* At the close of the evidence or at such other time as the military judge may permit, any party may request that the military judge instruct the members on the law as set forth in the request. The military judge may require the requested instruction to be written. Each party shall be given the opportunity to be heard on any proposed instruction on findings before it is given. The military judge shall inform the parties of the proposed action on such requests before their closing arguments.

Discussion

Requests for and objections to instructions should be resolved at an Article 39(a) session. *But see* R.C.M 801(e)(3); 803.

If an issue has been raised, ordinarily the military judge must instruct on the issue when requested to do so. The military judge is not required to give the specific instruction requested by counsel, however, as long as the issue is adequately covered in the instructions.

The military judge should not identify the source of any instruction when addressing the members.

All written requests for instructions should be marked as appellate exhibits, whether or not they are given.

(d) *How given.* Instructions on findings shall be given orally on the record in the presence of all parties and the members. Written copies of the instructions, or, unless a party objects, portions of them, may also be given to the members for their use during deliberations.

Discussion

A copy of any written instructions delivered to the members should be marked as an appellate exhibit.

(e) *Required instructions.* Instructions on findings shall include:

(1) A description of the elements of each offense charged, unless findings on such offenses are unnecessary because they have been entered pursuant to a plea of guilty;

(2) A description of the elements of each lesser included offense in issue, unless trial of a lesser included offense is barred by the statute of limitations (Article 43) and the accused refuses to waive the bar;

(3) A description of any special defense under R.C.M. 916 in issue;

(4) A direction that only matters properly before the court-martial may be considered;

(5) A charge that—

(A) The accused must be presumed to be innocent until the accused's guilt is established by legal and competent evidence beyond reasonable doubt;

(B) In the case being considered, if there is a reasonable doubt as to the guilt of the accused, the doubt must be resolved in favor of the accused and the accused must be acquitted;

(C) If, when a lesser included offense is in issue, there is a reasonable doubt as to the degree of guilt of the accused, the finding must be in a lower degree as to which there is not reasonable doubt; and

(D) The burden of proof to establish the guilt of the accused is upon the Government. [When the issue of lack of mental responsibility is raised, add: The burden of proving the defense of lack of mental responsibility by clear and convincing evidence is upon the accused. When the issue of mistake of fact under R.C.M. 916(j)(2) is raised, add: The accused has the burden of proving the defense of mistake of fact as to age by a preponderance of the evidence.]

(6) Directions on the procedures under R.C.M. 921 for deliberations and voting; and

(7) Such other explanations, descriptions, or directions as may be necessary and which are properly requested by a party or which the military judge determines, *sua sponte*, should be given.

Discussion

A matter is "in issue" when some evidence, without regard to its source or credibility, has been admitted upon which members might rely if they choose. An instruction on a lesser included offense is proper when an element from the charged offense which distinguishes thatoffense from the lesser offense is in dispute.

See R.C.M. 918(c) and discussion as to reasonable doubt and other matters relating to the basis for findings which may be the subject of an instruction.

Other matters which may be the subject of instruction in appropriate cases included: inferences (*see* the explanations in Part IV concerning inferences relating to specific offenses); the limited purpose for which evidence was admitted (regardless of whether such evidence was offered by the prosecution of defense) (*see* Mil. R. Evid. 105); the effect of character evidence (*see* Mil. R. Evid. 404; 405); the effect of judicial notice (*see* Mil. R. Evid. 201, 201A); the weight to be given a pretrial statement (*see* Mil. R. Evid. 340(e)); the effect of stipulations (*see* R.C.M. 811); that,

when a guilty plea to a lesser included offense has been accepted, the members should accept as proved the matters admitted by the plea, but must determine whether the remaining elements are established; that a plea of guilty to one offense may not be the basis for inferring the existence of a fact or element of another offense; the absence of the accused from trial should not be held against the accused; and that no adverse inferences may be drawn from an accused's failure to testify (*see* Mil. R. Evid. 301(g)).

The military judge may summarize and comment upon evidence in the case in instructions. In doing so, the military judge should present an accurate, fair, and dispassionate statement of what the evidence shows; not depart from an impartial role; not assume as true the existence or nonexistence of a fact in issue when the evidence is conflicting or disputed, or when there is no evidence to support the matter; and make clear that the members must exercise their independent judgment as to the facts.

(f) *Waiver.* Failure to object to an instruction or to omission of an instruction before the members close to deliberate constitutes waiver of the objection in the absence of plain error. The military judge may require the party objecting to specify of what respect the instructions given were improper. The parties shall be given the opportunity to be heard on any objection outside the presence of the members.

Rule 921. Deliberations and voting on findings

(a) *In general.* After the military judge instructs the members on findings, the members shall deliberate and vote in a closed session. Only the members shall be present during deliberations and voting. Superiority in rank shall not be used in any manner in an attempt to control the independence of members in the exercise of their judgment.

(b) *Deliberations.* Deliberations properly include full and free discussion of the merits of the case. Unless otherwise directed by the military judge, members may take with them in deliberations their notes, if any, any exhibits admitted in evidence, and any written instructions. Members may request that the court-martial be reopened and that portions of the record be read to them or additional evidence introduced. The military judge may, in the exercise of discretion, grant such request.

(c) *Voting.*

(1) *Secret ballot.* Voting on the findings for each charge and specification shall be by secret written ballot. All members present shall vote.

(2) *Numbers of votes required to convict.*

(A) *Death penalty mandatory.* A finding of

guilty of an offense for which the death penalty is mandatory results only if all members present vote for a finding of guilty.

Discussion

Article 106 is the only offense under the code for which the death penalty is mandatory.

(B) *Other offenses.* As to any offense for which the death penalty is not mandatory, a finding of guilty results only if at least two-thirds of the members present vote for a finding of guilty.

Discussion

In computing the number of votes required to convict, any fraction of a vote is rounded up to the next whole number. For example, if there are five members, the concurrence of at least four would be required to convict. The military judge should instruct the members on the specific number of votes required to convict.

---

(3) *Acquittal.* If fewer than two-thirds of the members present vote for a finding of guilty—or, when the death penalty is mandatory, if fewer than all the members present vote for a finding of guilty—a finding of not guilty has resulted as to the charge or specification on which the vote was taken.

(4) *Not guilty only by reason of lack of mental responsibility.* When the defense of lack of mental responsibility is in issue under R.C.M. 916(k)(1), the members shall first vote on whether the prosecution has proven the elements of the offense beyond a reasonable doubt. If at least two-thirds of the members present (all members for offenses where the death penalty is mandatory) vote for a finding of guilty, then the members shall vote on whether the accused has proven lack of mental responsibility. If a majority of the members present concur that the accused has proven lack of mental responsibility by clear and convincing evidence, a finding of not guilty only by reason of lack of mental responsibility results. If the vote on lack of mental responsibility does not result in a finding of not guilty only by reason of lack of mental responsibility, then the defense of lack of mental responsibility has been rejected and the finding of guilty stands.

Discussion

If lack of mental responsibility is in issue with regard to more

than one specification, the members should determine the issue of lack of mental responsibility on each specification separately.

---

(5) *Included offenses.* Members shall not vote on a lesser included offense unless a finding of not guilty of the offense charged has been reached. If a finding of not guilty of an offense charged has been reached the members shall vote on each included offense on which they have been instructed, in order of severity beginning with the most severe. The members shall continue the vote on each included offense on which they have been instructed until a finding of guilty results or findings of not guilty have been reached as to each such offense.

(6) *Procedure for voting.*

(A) *Order.* Each specification shall be voted on separately before the corresponding charge. The order of voting on several specifications under a charge or on several charges shall be determined by the president unless a majority of the members object.

(B) *Counting votes.* The junior member shall collect the ballots and count the votes. The president shall check the count and inform the other members of the result.

Discussion

Once findings have been reached, they may be reconsidered only in accordance with R.C.M. 924.

(d) *Action after findings are reached.* After the members have reached findings on each charge and specification before them, the court-martial shall be opened and the president shall inform the military judge that findings have been reached. The military judge may, in the presence of the parties, examine any writing which the president intends to read to announce the findings and may assist the members in putting the findings in proper form. Neither that writing nor any oral or written clarification or discussion concerning it shall constitute announcement of the findings.

Discussion

Ordinarily a findings worksheet should be provided to the members as an aid to putting the findings in proper form. *See* Appendix 10 for a format for findings. If the military judge examines any writing by the members or otherwise assists them to put findings in proper form, this must be done in an open session and counsel should be given the opportunity to examine such a writing and to be heard on any instructions the military judge may give. *See* Article 39(b).

The president should not disclose any specific number of votes for or against any finding.

Rule 922. Announcement of findings

(a) *In general.* Findings shall be announced in the presence of all parties promptly after they have been determined.

Discussion

See Appendix 10. A finding of an offense about which no instructions were given is not proper.

(b) *Findings by members.* The president shall announce the findings by the members.

   (1) If a finding is based on a plea of guilty, the president shall so state.

   (2) In a capital case, if a finding of guilty is unanimous with respect to a capital offense, the president shall so state. This provision shall not apply during reconsideration under R.C.M. 924(a) of a finding of guilty previously announced in open court unless the prior finding was announced as unanimous.

Discussion

If the findings announced are ambiguous, the military judge should seek clarification. *See also* R.C.M. 924. A nonunanimous finding of guilty as to a capital offense may be reconsidered, but not for the purpose of rendering a unanimous verdict in order to authorize a capital sentencing proceeding. The president shall not make a statement regarding unanimity with respect to reconsideration of findings as to an offense in which the prior findings were not unanimous.

(c) *Findings by military judge.* The military judge shall announce the findings when trial is by military judge alone or when findings may be entered upon R.C.M. 910(g).

(d) *Erroneous announcement.* If an error was made in the announcement of the findings of the court-martial, the error may be corrected by a new announcement in accordance with this rule. The error must be discovered and the new announcement made before the final adjournment of the court-martial in the case.

Discussion

See R.C.M. 1102 concerning the action to be taken if the error in the announcement is discovered after final adjournment.

(e) *Polling prohibited.* Except as provided in Mil. R. Evid. 606, members may not be questioned about their deliberations and voting.

Rule 923. Impeachment of findings

Findings which are proper on their face may be impeached only when extraneous prejudicial information was improperly brought to the attention of a member, outside influence was improperly brought to bear upon any member, or unlawful command influence was brought to bear upon any member.

Discussion

Deliberations of the members ordinarily are not subject to disclosure. *See* Mil. R. Evid. 606. Unsound reasoning by a member, misconception of the evidence, or misapplication of the law is not a proper basis for challenging the findings. However, when a showing of a ground for impeaching the verdict has been made, members may be questioned about such a ground. The military judge determines, as an interlocutory matter, whether such an inquiry will be conducted and whether a finding has been impeached.

Rule 924. Reconsideration of findings

(a) *Time for reconsideration.* Members may reconsider any finding reached by them before such finding is announced in open session.

(b) *Procedure.* Any member may propose that a finding be reconsidered. If such a proposal is made in a timely manner the question whether to reconsider shall be determined in closed session by secret written ballot. Any finding of not guilty shall be reconsidered if a majority vote for reconsideration. Any finding of guilty shall be reconsidered if more than one-third of the members vote for reconsideration. When the death penalty is mandatory, a request by any member for reconsideration of a guilty finding requires reconsideration. Any finding of not guilty only by reason of lack of mental responsibility shall be reconsidered on the issue of the finding of guilty of the elements if more than one-third of the members vote for reconsideration, and on the issue of mental responsibility if a majority vote for reconsideration. If a vote to reconsider a finding succeeds, the procedures in R.C.M. 921 shall apply.

Discussion

After the initial secret ballot vote on a finding in closed session, no other vote may be taken on that finding unless a vote to reconsider succeeds.

─────────────

(c) *Military judge sitting alone.* In trial by military judge alone, the military judge may reconsider any finding of guilty at any time before announcement of sentence and may reconsider the issue of the finding of guilty of the elements in a finding of not guilty only by reason of lack of mental responsibility at any time before announcement of sentence or authentication of the record of trial in the case of a complete acquittal.

CHAPTER X. SENTENCING

Rule 1001. Presentencing procedure

(a) *In general.*

(1) *Procedure.* After findings of guilty have been announced, the prosecution and defense may present matter pursuant to this rule to aid the court-martial in determining an appropriate sentence. Such matter shall ordinarily be presented in the following sequence—

(A) Presentation by trial counsel of:

(i) service data relating to the accused taken from the charge sheet;

(ii) personal data relating to the accused and of the character of the accused's prior service as reflected in the personnel records of the accused;

(iii) evidence of prior convictions, military or civilian;

(iv) evidence of aggravation; and

(v) evidence of rehabilitative potential.

(B) Victim's right to be reasonably heard. *See* R.C.M. 1001A.

(C) Presentation by the defense of evidence in extenuation or mitigation or both.

(D) Rebuttal.

(E) Argument by trial counsel on sentence.

(F) Argument by defense counsel on sentence.

(G) Rebuttal arguments in the discretion of the military judge.

(2) *Adjudging sentence.* A sentence shall be adjudged in all cases without unreasonable delay.

(3) *Advice and inquiry.* The military judge shall personally inform the accused of the right to present matters in extenuation and mitigation, including the right to make a sworn or unsworn statement or to remain silent, and shall ask whether the accused chooses to exercise those rights.

(b) *Matter to be presented by the prosecution.*

(1) *Service data from the charge sheet.* Trial counsel shall inform the court-martial of the data on the charge sheet relating to the pay and service of the accused and the duration and nature of any pretrial restraint. In the discretion of the military judge, this may be done by reading the material from the charge sheet or by giving the court-martial a written statement of such matter. If the defense objects to the data as being materially inaccurate or incomplete, or containing specified objectionable matter, the military judge shall determine the issue. Objections not asserted are waived.

(2) *Personal data and character of prior service of the accused.* Under regulations of the Secretary concerned, trial counsel may obtain and introduce from the personnel records of the accused evidence of the accused's marital status; number of dependents, if any; and character of prior service. Such evidence includes copies of reports reflecting the past military efficiency, conduct, performance, and history of the accused and evidence of any disciplinary actions including punishments under Article 15.

"Personnel records of the accused" includes any records made or maintained in accordance with departmental regulations that reflect the past military efficiency, conduct, performance, and history of the accused. If the accused objects to a particular document as inaccurate or incomplete in a specified respect, or as containing matter that is not admissible under the Military Rules of Evidence, the matter shall be determined by the military judge. Objections not asserted are waived.

(3) *Evidence of prior convictions of the accused.*

(A) *In general.* The trial counsel may introduce evidence of military or civilian convictions of the accused. For purposes of this rule, there is a "conviction" in a court-martial case when a sentence has been adjudged. In a civilian case, a "conviction" includes any disposition following an initial judicial determination or assumption of guilt, such as when guilt has been established by guilty plea, trial, or plea of nolo contendere, regardless of the subsequent disposition, sentencing procedure, or final judgment. However, a "civilian conviction" does not include a diversion from the judicial process without a finding or admission of guilt; expunged convictions; juvenile adjudications; minor traffic violations; foreign convictions; tribal court convictions; or convictions reversed, vacated, invalidated or pardoned because of errors of law or because of subsequently discovered evidence exonerating the accused.

Discussion

A vacation of a suspended sentence (*see* R.C.M. 1109) is not a conviction and is not admissible as such, but may be admissible under subsection (b)(2) of this rule as reflective of the character of the prior service of the accused.

Whether a civilian conviction is admissible is left to the

discretion of the military judge. As stated in the rule, a civilian "conviction" includes any disposition following an initial judicial determination or assumption of guilt regardless of the sentencing procedure and the final judgment following probation or other sentence. Therefore, convictions may be admissible regardless of whether a court ultimately suspended judgment upon discharge of the accused following probation, permitted withdrawal of the guilty plea, or applies some other form of alternative sentencing. Additionally, the term "conviction" need not be taken to mean a final judgment of conviction and sentence.

(B) *Pendency of appeal.* The pendency of an appeal therefrom does not render evidence of a conviction inadmissible except that a conviction by summary court-martial or special court-martial without a military judge may not be used for purposes of this rule until review has been completed pursuant to Article 64 or Article 66, if applicable. Evidence of the pendency of an appeal is admissible.

(C) *Method of proof.* Previous convictions may be proved by any evidence admissible under the Military Rules of Evidence.

Discussion

Normally, previous convictions may be proved by use of the personnel records of the accused, by the record of the conviction, or by the order promulgating the result of trial. *See* DD Form 493 (Extract of Military Records of Previous Convictions).

---

(4) *Evidence in aggravation.* The trial counsel may present evidence as to any aggravating circumstances directly relating to or resulting from the offenses of which the accused has been found guilty. Evidence in aggravation includes, but is not limited to, evidence of financial, social, psychological, and medical impact on or cost to any person or entity who was the victim of an offense committed by the accused and evidence of significant adverse impact on the mission, discipline, or efficiency of the command directly and immediately resulting from the accused's offense. In addition, evidence in aggravation may include evidence that the accused intentionally selected any victim or any property as the object of the offense because of the actual or perceived race, color, religion, national origin, ethnicity, gender, disability, or sexual orientation of any person. Except in capital cases a written or oral deposition taken in accordance with R.C.M. 702 is admissible in aggravation.

Discussion

See also R.C.M. 1004 concerning aggravating circumstances in capital cases.

---

(5) *Evidence of rehabilitative potential.* Rehabilitative potential refers to the accused's potential to be restored, through vocational, correctional, or therapeutic training or other corrective measures to a useful and constructive place in society.

(A) *In general.* The trial counsel may present, by testimony or oral deposition in accordance with R.C.M. 702(g)(1), evidence in the form of opinions concerning the accused's previous performance as a servicemember and potential for rehabilitation.

(B) *Foundation for opinion.* The witness or deponent providing opinion evidence regarding the accused's rehabilitative potential must possess sufficient information and knowledge about the accused to offer a rationally-based opinion that is helpful to the sentencing authority. Relevant information and knowledge include, but are not limited to, information and knowledge about the accused's character, performance of duty, moral fiber, determination to be rehabilitated, and nature and severity of the offense or offenses.

Discussion

See generally Mil. R. Evid. 701, Opinion testimony by lay witnesses. *See also* Mil. R. Evid. 703, Bases of opinion testimony by experts, if the witness or deponent is testifying as an expert. The types of information and knowledge reflected in this subparagraph are illustrative only.

(C) *Bases for opinion.* An opinion regarding the accused's rehabilitative potential must be based upon relevant information and knowledge possessed by the witness or deponent, and must relate to the accused's personal circumstances. The opinion of the witness or deponent regarding the severity or nature of the accused's offense or offenses may not serve as the principal basis for an opinion of the accused's rehabilitative potential.

(D) *Scope of opinion.* An opinion offered under this rule is limited to whether the accused has rehabilitative potential and to the magnitude or quality of any such potential. A witness may not offer an opinion regarding the appropriateness of a punitive discharge or whether the accused should be returned to the accused's unit.

Discussion

On direct examination, a witness or deponent may respond affirmatively or negatively regarding whether the accused has rehabilitative potential. The witness or deponent may also opine succinctly regarding the magnitude or quality of the accused rehabilitative potential; for example, the witness or deponent may opine that the accused has "great" or "little" rehabilitative potential. The witness or deponent, however, generally may not further elaborate on the accused's rehabilitative potential, such as describing the particular reasons for forming the opinion.

(E) *Cross-examination.* On cross-examination, inquiry is permitted into relevant and specific instances of conduct.

(F) *Redirect.* Notwithstanding any other provision in this rule, the scope of opinion testimony permitted on redirect may be expanded, depending upon the nature and scope of the cross-examination.

Discussion

For example, on redirect a witness or deponent may testify regarding specific instances of conduct when the cross-examination of the witness or deponent concerned specific instances of misconduct. Similarly, for example, on redirect a witness or deponent may offer an opinion on matters beyond the scope of the accused's rehabilitative potential if an opinion about such matters was elicited during cross-examination of the witness or deponent and is otherwise admissible.

(c) *Matter to be presented by the defense.*

(1) *In general.* The defense may present matters in rebuttal of any material presented by the prosecution and may present matters in extenuation and mitigation regardless whether the defense offered evidence before findings.

(A) *Matter in extenuation.* Matter in extenuation of an offense serves to explain the circumstances surrounding the commission of an offense, including those reasons for committing the offense which do not constitute a legal justification or excuse.

(B) *Matter in mitigation.* Matter in mitigation of an offense is introduced to lessen the punishment to be adjudged by the court-martial, or to furnish grounds for a recommendation of clemency. It includes the fact that nonjudicial punishment under Article 15 has been imposed for an offense growing out of the same act or omission that constitutes the offense of which the accused has been found guilty, particular acts of good conduct or bravery and evidence of the reputation or record of the accused in the service for efficiency, fidelity, subordination, temperance, courage, or any other trait that is desirable in a servicemember.

(2) *Statement by the accused.*

(A) *In general.* The accused may testify, make an unsworn statement, or both in extenuation, in mitigation or to rebut matters presented by the prosecution, or for all three purposes whether or not the accused testified prior to findings. The accused may limit such testimony or statement to any one or more of the specifications of which the accused has been found guilty. This subsection does not permit the filing of an affidavit of the accused.

(B) *Testimony of the accused.* The accused may give sworn oral testimony under this paragraph and shall be subject to cross-examination concerning it by the trial counsel or examination on it by the court-martial, or both.

(C) *Unsworn statement.* The accused may make an unsworn statement and may not be cross-examined by the trial counsel upon it or examined upon it by the court-martial. The prosecution may, however, rebut any statements of facts therein. The unsworn statement may be oral, written, or both, and may be made by the accused, by counsel, or both.

Discussion

An unsworn statement ordinarily should not include what is properly argument, but inclusion of such matter by the accused when personally making an oral statement normally should not be grounds for stopping the statement.

---

(3) *Rules of evidence relaxed.* The military judge may, with respect to matters in extenuation or mitigation or both, relax the rules of evidence. This may include admitting letters, affidavits, certificates of military and civil officers, and other writings of similar authenticity and reliability.

(d) *Rebuttal and surrebuttal.* The prosecution may rebut matters presented by the defense. The defense in surrebuttal may then rebut any rebuttal offered by the prosecution. Rebuttal and surrebuttal may continue, in the discretion of the military judge. If the Military Rules of Evidence were relaxed under subsection (c)(3) of this rule, they may be relaxed during rebuttal and surrebuttal to the same degree.

(e) *Production of witnesses.*

(1) *In general.* During the presentence proceedings, there shall be much greater latitude than on the merits to receive information by means other than testimony presented through the personal appearance of witnesses. Whether a witness shall be produced to testify during presentence proceedings is a matter within the discretion of the military judge, subject to the limitations in subsection (e)(2) of this rule.

Discussion

See R.C.M. 703 concerning the procedures for production of witnesses.

---

(2) *Limitations.* A witness may be produced to testify during presentence proceedings through a subpoena or travel orders at Government expense only if—

(A) The testimony expected to be offered by the witness is necessary for consideration of a matter of substantial significance to a determination of an appropriate sentence, including evidence necessary to resolve an alleged inaccuracy or dispute as to a material fact;

(B) The weight or credibility of the testimony is of substantial significance to the determination of an appropriate sentence;

(C) The other party refuses to enter into a stipulation of fact containing the matters to which the witness is expected to testify, except in an extraordinary case when such a stipulation of fact would be an insufficient substitute for the testimony;

(D) Other forms of evidence, such as oral depositions, written interrogatories, former testimony, or testimony by remote means would not be sufficient to meet the needs of the court-martial in the determination of an appropriate sentence; and

(E) The significance of the personal appearance of the witness to the determination of an appropriate sentence, when balanced against the practical difficulties of producing the witness, favors production of the witness. Factors to be considered include the costs of producing the witness, the timing of the request for production of the witness, the potential delay in the presentencing proceeding that may be caused by the production of the witness, and the

likelihood of significant interference with military operational deployment, mission accomplishment, or essential training.

Discussion

The procedures for receiving testimony via remote means and the definition thereof are contained in R.C.M. 914B.

(f) *Additional matters to be considered.* In addition to matters introduced under this rule, the court-martial may consider—

(1) That a plea of guilty is a mitigating factor; and

(2) Any evidence properly introduced on the merits before findings, including:

(A) Evidence of other offenses or acts of misconduct even if introduced for a limited purpose; and

(B) Evidence relating to any mental impairment or deficiency of the accused.

Discussion

The fact that the accused is of low intelligence or that, because of a mental or neurological condition the accused's ability to adhere to the right is diminished, may be extenuating. On the other hand, in determining the severity of a sentence, the court-martial may consider evidence tending to show that an accused has little regard for the rights of others.

(g) *Argument.* After introduction of matters relating to sentence under this rule, counsel for the prosecution and defense may argue for an appropriate sentence. Trial counsel may not in argument purport to speak for the convening authority or any higher authority, or refer to the views of such authorities or any policy directive relative to punishment or to any punishment or quantum of punishment greater than that court-martial may adjudge. Trial counsel may, however, recommend a specific lawful sentence and may also refer to generally accepted sentencing philosophies, including rehabilitation of the accused, general deterrence, specific deterrence of misconduct by the accused, and social retribution. Failure to object to improper argument before the military judge begins to instruct the members on sentencing shall constitute waiver of the objection.

Discussion

A victim, victim's counsel, or designee has no right to present argument under this rule.

Rule 1001A. Crime victims and presentencing

(a) *In general.* A crime victim of an offense of which the accused has been found guilty has the right to be reasonably heard at a sentencing hearing relating to that offense. A victim under this rule is not considered a witness for purposes of Article 42(b). Trial counsel shall ensure the victim is aware of the opportunity to exercise that right. If the victim exercises the right to be reasonably heard, the victim shall be called by the court-martial. This right is independent of whether the victim testified during findings or is called to testify under R.C.M. 1001.

(b) *Definitions.*

(1) *Crime victim.* For purposes of this rule, a "crime victim" is an individual who has suffered direct physical, emotional, or pecuniary harm as a result of the commission of an offense of which the accused was found guilty.

(2) *Victim impact.* For the purposes of this rule, "victim impact" includes any financial, social, psychological, or medical impact on the victim directly relating to or arising from the offense of which the accused has been found guilty.

(3) *Mitigation.* For the purposes of this rule, "mitigation" includes a matter to lessen the punishment to be adjudged by the court-martial or to furnish grounds for a recommendation of clemency.

(4) *Right to be reasonably heard.*

(A) *Capital cases.* In capital cases, for purposes of this rule, the "right to be reasonably heard" means the right to make a sworn statement.

(B) *Non-capital cases.* In non-capital cases, for purposes of this rule, the "right to be reasonably heard" means the right to make a sworn or unsworn statement.

(c) *Content of statement.* The content of statements made under subsections (d) and (e) of this rule may include victim impact or matters in mitigation.

(d) *Sworn statement.* The victim may give a sworn statement under this rule and shall be subject to cross-examination concerning the statement by the trial counsel or defense counsel or examination on the statement by the court-martial, or all or any of the three. When a victim is under 18 years of age, incompetent, incapacitated, or deceased, the sworn statement may be made by the victim's designee appointed under R.C.M. 801(a)(6). Additionally, a victim under 18 years of age may elect to make a sworn statement.

(e) *Unsworn statement.* The victim may make an unsworn statement and may not be cross-examined by the trial counsel or defense counsel upon it or examined upon it by the court-martial. The prosecution or defense may, however, rebut any statements of facts therein. The unsworn statement may be oral, written, or both. When a victim is under 18 years of age, incompetent, incapacitated, or deceased, the unsworn statement may be made by the victim's designee appointed under R.C.M. 801(a)(6). Additionally, a victim under 18 years of age may elect to make an unsworn statement.

(1) *Procedure for presenting unsworn statement.* After the announcement of findings, a victim who would like to present an unsworn statement shall provide a copy to the trial counsel, defense counsel, and military judge. The military judge may waive this requirement for good cause shown.

Discussion

When the military judge waives the notice requirement under this rule, the military judge may conduct a session under Article 39(a) to ascertain the content of the victim's anticipated unsworn statement.

---

(2) Upon good cause shown, the military judge may permit the victim's counsel to deliver all or part of the victim's unsworn statement.

Discussion

If there are numerous victims, the military judge may reasonably limit the form of the statements provided.

A victim's unsworn statement should not exceed what is permitted under R.C.M. 1001A(c) and may not include a recommendation of a specific sentence. Upon objection by either party or *sua sponte*, a military judge may stop or interrupt a victim's unsworn statement that includes matters outside the scope of R.C.M. 1001A(c). A victim, victim's counsel, or designee has no separate right to present argument under R.C.M. 1001(g).

Rule 1002. Sentence determination

(a) *Generally.* Subject to limitations in this Manual,

the sentence to be adjudged is a matter within the discretion of the court-martial; except when a mandatory minimum sentence is prescribed by the code, a court-martial may adjudge any punishment authorized in this Manual, including the maximum punishment or any lesser punishment, or may adjudge a sentence of no punishment.

(b) *Unitary Sentencing.* Sentencing by a court-martial is unitary. The court-martial will adjudge a single sentence for all the offenses of which the accused was found guilty. A court-martial may not impose separate sentences for each finding of guilty, but may impose only a single, unitary sentence covering all of the guilty findings in their entirety.

Discussion

See R.C.M. 1003 concerning authorized punishments and limitations on punishments. *See also* R.C.M. 1004 in capital cases.

Rule 1003. Punishments

(a) *In general.* Subject to the limitations in this Manual, the punishments authorized in this rule may be adjudged in the case of any person found guilty of an offense by a court-martial.

Discussion

"Any person" includes officers, enlisted persons, person in custody of the armed forces serving a sentence imposed by a court-martial, and, insofar as the punishments are applicable, any other person subject to the code. *See* R.C.M. 202.

(b) *Authorized punishments.* Subject to the limitations in this Manual, a court-martial may adjudge only the following punishments:

(1) *Reprimand.* A court-martial shall not specify the terms or wording of a reprimand. A reprimand, if approved, shall be issued, in writing, by the convening authority;

Discussion

A reprimand adjudged by a court-martial is a punitive censure.

---

(2) *Forfeiture of pay and allowances.* Unless a total forfeiture is adjudged, a sentence to forfeiture shall state the exact amount in whole dollars to be forfeited each month and the number of months the forfeitures will last.

Allowances shall be subject to forfeiture only when the sentence includes forfeiture of all pay and allowances. The maximum authorized amount of a partial forfeiture shall be determined by using the basic pay, retired pay, or retainer pay, as applicable, or, in the case of reserve component personnel on inactive-duty, compensation for periods of inactive-duty training, authorized by the cumulative years of service of the accused, and, if no confinement is adjudged, any sea or hardship duty pay. If the sentence also includes reduction in grade, expressly or by operation of law, the maximum forfeiture shall be based on the grade to which the accused is reduced.

Discussion

A forfeiture deprives the accused of the amount of pay (and allowances) specified as it accrues. Forfeitures accrue to the United States.

Forfeitures of pay and allowances adjudged as part of a court-martial sentence, or occurring by operation of Article 58b are effective 14 days after the sentence is adjudged or when the sentence is approved by the convening authority, whichever is earlier.

"Basic pay" does not include pay for special qualifications, such as diving pay, or incentive pay such as flying, parachuting, or duty on board a submarine.

Forfeiture of pay and allowances under Article 58b is not a part of the sentence, but is an administrative result thereof.

At general courts-martial, if both a punitive discharge and confinement are adjudged, then the operation of Article 58b results in total forfeiture of pay and allowances during that period of confinement. If only confinement is adjudged, then if that confinement exceeds six months, the operation of Article 58b results in total forfeiture of pay and allowances during that period of confinement. If only a punitive discharge is adjudged, Article 58b has no effect on pay and allowances. A death sentence results in total forfeiture of pay and allowances.

At a special court-martial, if a bad-conduct discharge and confinement are adjudged, then the operation of Article 58b results in a forfeiture of two-thirds of pay only (not allowances) during that period of confinement. If only confinement is adjudged, and that confinement exceeds six months, then the operation of Article 58b results in a forfeiture of two-thirds of pay only (not allowances) during the period of confinement. If only a bad conduct discharge is adjudged, Article 58b has no effect on pay.

If the sentence, as approved by the convening authority or other competent authority, does not result in forfeitures by the operation of Article 58b, then only adjudged forfeitures are effective.

Article 58b has no effect on summary courts-martial.

---

(3) *Fine.* Any court-martial may adjudge a fine in lieu of or in addition to forfeitures. In the case of a

member of the armed forces, summary and special courts-martial may not adjudge any fine or combination of fine and forfeitures in excess of the total amount of forfeitures that may be adjudged in that case. In the case of a person serving with or accompanying an armed force in the field, a summary court-martial may not adjudge a fine in excess of two-thirds of one month of the highest rate of enlisted pay, and a special court-martial may not adjudge a fine in excess of two-thirds of one year of the highest rate of officer pay. To enforce collection, a fine may be accompanied by a provision in the sentence that, in the event the fine is not paid, the person fined shall, in addition to any period of confinement adjudged, be further confined until a fixed period considered an equivalent punishment to the fine has expired. The total period of confinement so adjudged shall not exceed the jurisdictional limitations of the court-martial;

Discussion

A fine is in the nature of a judgment and, when ordered executed, makes the accused immediately liable to the United States for the entire amount of money specified in the sentence. A fine normally should not be adjudged against a member of the armed forces unless the accused was unjustly enriched as a result of the offense of which convicted. In the case of a civilian subject to military law, a fine, rather than a forfeiture, is the proper monetary penalty to be adjudged, regardless of whether unjust enrichment is present.

See R.C.M. 1113(e)(3) concerning imposition of confinement when the accused fails to pay a fine.

Where the sentence adjudged at a special court-martial includes a fine, see R.C.M. 1107(d)(5) for limitations on convening authority action on the sentence.

---

(4) *Reduction in pay grade.* Except as provided in R.C.M. 1301(d), a court-martial may sentence an enlisted member to be reduced to the lowest or any intermediate pay grade;

Discussion

Reduction under Article 58a is not a part of the sentence but is an administrative result thereof.

---

(5) *Restriction to specified limits.* Restriction may be adjudged for no more than 2 months for each month of authorized confinement and in no case for more than 2 months. Confinement and restriction may be adjudged in the same case, but they may not together exceed the maximum authorized period of confinement, calculating the equivalency at the rate specified in this subsection;

Discussion

Restriction does not exempt the person on whom it is imposed from any military duty. Restriction and hard labor without confinement may be adjudged in the same case provided they do not exceed the maximum limits for each. *See* subsection (c)(1)(A)(ii) of this rule. The sentence adjudged should specify the limits of the restriction.

---

(6) *Hard labor without confinement.* Hard labor without confinement may be adjudged for no more than 1-1/2 months for each month of authorized confinement and in no case for more than three months. Hard labor without confinement may be adjudged only in the cases of enlisted members. The court-martial shall not specify the hard labor to be performed. Confinement and hard labor without confinement may be adjudged in the same case, but they may not together exceed the maximum authorized period of confinement, calculating the equivalency at the rate specified in this subsection.

Discussion

Hard labor without confinement is performed in addition to other regular duties and does not excuse or relieve a person from performing regular duties. Ordinarily, the immediate commander of the accused will designate the amount and character of the labor to be performed. Upon completion of the daily assignment, the accused should be permitted to take leave or liberty to which entitled.

See R.C.M. 1301(d) concerning limitations on hard labor without confinement in summary courts-martial.

---

(7) *Confinement.* The place of confinement shall not be designated by the court-martial. When confinement for life is authorized, it may be with or without eligibility for parole. A court-martial shall not adjudge a sentence to solitary confinement or to confinement without hard labor;

Discussion

The authority executing a sentence to confinement may require hard labor whether or not the words "at hard labor" are included in the sentence. *See* Article 58(b). To promote uniformity, the words "at hard labor" should be omitted in a sentence to confinement.

---

(8) *Punitive separation.* A court-martial may not

adjudge an administrative separation from the service. There are three types of punitive separation.

(A) *Dismissal.* Dismissal applies only to commissioned officers, commissioned warrant officers, cadets, and midshipmen and may be adjudged only by a general court-martial. Regardless of the maximum punishment specified for an offense in Part IV of this Manual, a dismissal may be adjudged for any offense of which a commissioned officer, commissioned warrant officer, cadet, or midshipman has been found guilty;

(B) *Dishonorable discharge.* A dishonorable discharge applies only to enlisted persons and warrant officers who are not commissioned and may be adjudged only by a general court-martial. Regardless of the maximum punishment specified for an offense in Part IV of this Manual, a dishonorable discharge may be adjudged for any offense of which a warrant officer who is not commissioned has been found guilty. A dishonorable discharge should be reserved for those who should be separated under conditions of dishonor, after having been convicted of offenses usually recognized in civilian jurisdictions as felonies, or of offenses of a military nature requiring severe punishment; and

Discussion

See also subsection (d)(1) of this rule regarding when a dishonorable discharge is authorized as an additional punishment.
See Article 56a.

(C) *Bad conduct discharge.* A bad-conduct discharge applies only to enlisted persons and may be adjudged by a general court-martial and by a special court-martial which has met the requirements of R.C.M. 201(f)(2)(B). A bad-conduct discharge is less severe than a dishonorable discharge and is designed as a punishment for bad-conduct rather than as a punishment for serious offenses of either a civilian or military nature. It is also appropriate for an accused who has been convicted repeatedly of minor offenses and whose punitive separation appears to be necessary;

Discussion

See also subsections (d)(2) and (3) of this rule regarding when a bad-conduct discharge is authorized as an additional punishment.

---

(9) *Death.* Death may be adjudged only in accordance with R.C.M. 1004; and

(10) *Punishments under the law of war.* In cases tried under the law of war, a general court-martial may adjudge any punishment not prohibited by the law of war.

(c) *Limits on punishments.*

(1) *Based on offenses.*

(A) *Offenses listed in Part IV.*

(i) *Maximum punishment.* The maximum limits for the authorized punishments of confinement, forfeitures and punitive discharge (if any) are set forth for each offense listed in Part IV of this Manual. These limitations are for each separate offense, not for each charge. When a dishonorable discharge is authorized, a bad-conduct discharge is also authorized.

(ii) *Other punishments.* Except as otherwise specifically provided in this Manual, the types of punishments listed in subsections (b)(1), (3), (4), (5), (6) and (7) of this rule may be adjudged in addition to or instead of confinement, forfeitures, a punitive discharge (if authorized), and death (if authorized).

(B) *Offenses not listed Part IV.*

(i) *Included or related offenses.* For an offense not listed in Part IV of this Manual which is included in or closely related to an offense listed therein the maximum punishment shall be that of the offense listed; however if an offense not listed is included in a listed offense, and is closely related to another or is equally closely related to two or more listed offenses, the maximum punishment shall be the same as the least severe of the listed offenses.

(ii) *Not included or related offenses.* An offense not listed in Part IV and not included in or closely related to any offense listed therein is punishable as authorized by the United States Code, or as authorized by the custom of the service. When the United States Code provides for confinement for a specified period or not more than a specified period the maximum punishment by court-martial shall include confinement for that period. If the period is 1 year or longer, the maximum punishment by court-martial also includes a dishonorable discharge and forfeiture of all pay and allowances; if 6 months or more, a bad-conduct discharge and forfeiture of all pay and allowances; if less than 6 months, forfeiture of two-thirds pay per month for the authorized period of confinement.

(C) *Multiple Offenses.* When the accused is found guilty of two or more offenses, the maximum authorized punishment may be imposed for each separate offense, unless the military judge finds that the offenses are either multiplicious or unreasonably multiplied.

(i) *Multiplicity.* A charge is multiplicious and must be dismissed if the proof of such charge also proves every element of another charged offense.

(ii) *Unreasonable Multiplication.* If the military judge finds that there is an unreasonable multiplication of charges as applied to sentence, the maximum punishment for those offenses shall be the maximum authorized punishment for the offense carrying the greatest maximum punishment. The military judge may either merge the offenses for sentencing, or dismiss one or more of the charges.

Discussion

See also R.C.M. 906(b)(12); 907(b)(3)(B).

Even if charges are not multiplicious, a military judge may rule on a motion that the prosecutor abused his discretion under R.C.M. 307(c)(4) or a motion that an unreasonable multiplication of charges requires relief under R.C.M. 1003(b)(1). Rather than the "single impulse" test previously noted in this Discussion, "[t]he better approach is to allow the military judge, in his or her discretion, to merge the offenses for sentencing purposes..." by determining whether the Quiroz test is fulfilled. *United States v. Campbell*, 71 M.J. 19 (C.A.A.F. 2012). (citing *United States v. Quiroz*, 55 M.J. 334, 338 (C.A.A.F. 2001).

Multiplicity is addressed in R.C.M. 907(b)(3)(B). Unreasonable multiplication of charges is addressed in R.C.M. 906(b)(12).

---

(2) *Based on rank of accused.*

(A) *Commissioned or warrant officers, cadets, and midshipmen.*

(i) A commissioned or warrant officer or a cadet, or midshipman may not be reduced in grade by any court-martial. However, in time of war or national emergency the Secretary concerned, or such Under Secretary or Assistant Secretary as may be designated by the Secretary concerned, may commute a sentence of dismissal to reduction to any enlisted grade.

(ii) Only a general court-martial may sentence a commissioned or warrant officer or a cadet, or midshipman to confinement.

(iii) A commissioned or warrant officer or a cadet or midshipman may not be sentenced to hard labor without confinement.

(iv) Only a general court-martial, upon conviction of any offense in violation of the Code, may sentence a commissioned or warrant officer or a cadet or midshipman to be separated from the service with a punitive separation. In the case of commissioned officers, cadets, midshipmen, and commissioned warrant officers, the separation shall be by dismissal. In the case of all other warrant officers, the separation shall by dishonorable discharge.

(B) *Enlisted persons. See* subsection (b)(9) of this rule and R.C.M. 1301(d).

(3) *Based on reserve status in certain circumstances.*

(A) *Restriction on liberty.* A member of a reserve component whose order to active duty is approved pursuant to Article 2(d)(5) may be required to serve any adjudged restriction on liberty during that period of active duty. Other members of a reserve component ordered to active duty pursuant to Article 2(d)(1) or tried by summary court-martial while on inactive duty training may not—

(i) by sentenced to confinement; or

(ii) be required to serve a court-martial punishment consisting of any other restriction on liberty except during subsequent periods of inactive-duty training or active duty.

(B) *Forfeiture.* A sentence to forfeiture of pay of a member not retained on active duty after completion of disciplinary proceedings may be collected from active duty and inactive-duty training pay during subsequent periods of duty.

Discussion

For application of this subsection, *see* R.C.M. 204. At the conclusion of nonjudicial punishment proceedings or final adjournment of the court-martial, the reserve component member who was ordered to active duty for the purpose of conducting disciplinary proceedings should be released from active duty within one working day unless the order to active duty was approved by the Secretary concerned and confinement or other restriction on liberty was adjudged. Unserved punishments may be carried over to subsequent periods of inactive-duty training or active duty.

---

(4) *Based on status as a person serving with or accompanying an armed force in the field.* In the case of a person serving with or accompanying an armed force in the field, no court-martial may ad-

judge forfeiture of pay and allowances, reduction in pay grade, hard labor without confinement, or a punitive separation.

(5) *Based on other rules.* The maximum limits on punishments in this rule may be further limited by other Rules of Courts-martial.

Discussion

The maximum punishment may be limited by: the jurisdictional limits of the court-martial (*see* R.C.M. 201(f) and 1301(d)); the nature of the proceedings (*see* R.C.M. 810(d) (sentence limitations in rehearings, new trials, and other trials)); and by instructions by a convening authority (*see* R.C.M. 601(e)(1)). *See also* R.C.M. 1107(d)(4) concerning limits on the maximum punishment which may be approved depending on the nature of the record.

(d) *Circumstances permitting increased punishments.*

(1) *Three or more convictions.* If an accused is found guilty of an offense or offenses for none of which a dishonorable discharge is otherwise authorized, proof of three or more previous convictions adjudged by a court-martial during the year next preceding the commission of any offense of which the accused stands convicted shall authorize a dishonorable discharge and forfeiture of all pay and allowances and, if the confinement otherwise authorized is less than 1 year, confinement for 1 year. In computing the 1-year period preceding the commission of any offense, periods of unauthorized absence shall be excluded. For purposes of this subsection, the court-martial convictions must be final.

(2) *Two or more convictions.* If an accused is found guilty of an offense or offenses for none of which a dishonorable or bad-conduct discharge is otherwise authorized, proof of two or more previous convictions adjudged by a court-martial during the 3 years next preceding the commission of any offense of which the accused stands convicted shall authorize a bad-conduct discharge and forfeiture of all pay and allowances and, if the confinement otherwise authorized is less than 3 months, confinement for 3 months. In computing the 3 year period preceding the commission of any offense, periods of unauthorized absence shall be excluded. For purposes of this subsection the court-martial convictions must be final.

(3) *Two or more offenses.* If an accused is found guilty of two or more offenses for none of which a dishonorable or bad-conduct discharge is otherwise authorized, the fact that the authorized confinement for these offenses totals 6 months or more shall, in addition, authorize a bad-conduct discharge and forfeiture of all pay and allowances.

Discussion

All of these increased punishments are subject to all other limitations on punishments set forth elsewhere in this rule. Convictions by summary court-martial may not be used to increase the maximum punishment under this rule. However they may be admitted and considered under R.C.M. 1001.

Rule 1004. Capital cases

(a) *In general.* Death may be adjudged only when:

(1) Death is expressly authorized under Part IV of this Manual for an offense of which the accused has been found guilty or is authorized under the law of war for an offense of which the accused has been found guilty under the law of war; and

(2) The accused was convicted of such an offense by the concurrence of all the members of the court-martial present at the time the vote was taken; and

(3) The requirements of subsections (b) and (c) of this rule have been met.

(b) *Procedure.* In addition to the provisions in R.C.M. 1001, the following procedures shall apply in capital cases—

(1) *Notice.*

(A) *Referral.* The convening authority shall indicate that the case is to be tried as a capital case by including a special instruction in the referral block of the charge sheet. Failure to include this special instruction at the time of the referral shall not bar the convening authority from later adding the required special instruction, provided:

(i) that the convening authority has otherwise complied with the notice requirement of subsection (B); and

(ii) that if the accused demonstrates specific prejudice from such failure to include the special instruction, a continuance or a recess is an adequate remedy.

(B) *Arraignment.* Before arraignment, trial counsel shall give the defense written notice of which aggravating factors under subsection (c) of this rule the prosecution intends to prove. Failure to provide timely notice under this subsection of any aggravating factors under subsection (c) of this rule shall not bar later notice and proof of such additional aggravating factors unless the accused demonstrates specific prejudice from such failure and that a continuance or a recess is not an adequate remedy.

(2) *Evidence of aggravating factors.* Trial counsel may present evidence in accordance with R.C.M. 1001(b)(4) tending to establish one or more of the aggravating factors in subsection (c) of this rule.

Discussion

See also subsection (b)(5) of this rule.

---

(3) *Evidence in extenuation and mitigation.* The accused shall be given broad latitude to present evidence in extenuation and mitigation.

Discussion

See R.C.M. 1001(c).

---

(4) *Necessary findings.* Death may not be adjudged unless—

(A) The members find that at least one of the aggravating factors under subsection (c) existed;

(B) Notice of such factor was provided in accordance with paragraph (1) of this subsection and all members concur in the finding with respect to such factor; and

(C) All members concur that any extenuating or mitigating circumstances are substantially outweighed by any aggravating circumstances admissible under R.C.M. 1001(b)(4), including the factors under subsection (c) of this rule.

(5) *Basis for findings.* The findings in subsection (b)(4) of this rule may be based on evidence introduced before or after findings under R.C.M. 921, or both.

(6) *Instructions.* In addition to the instructions required under R.C.M. 1005, the military judge shall instruct the members of such aggravating factors under subsection (c) of this rule as may be in issue in the case, and on the requirements and procedures under subsections (b)(4), (5), (7), and (8) of this rule. The military judge shall instruct the members that they must consider all evidence in extenuation and mitigation before they may adjudge death.

(7) *Voting.* In closed session, before voting on a sentence, the members shall vote by secret written ballot separately on each aggravating factor under subsection (c) of this rule on which they have been instructed. Death may not be adjudged unless all members concur in a finding of the existence of at least one such aggravating factor. After voting on all the aggravating factors on which they have been instructed, the members shall vote on a sentence in accordance with R.C.M. 1006.

(8) *Announcement.* If death is adjudged, the president shall, in addition to complying with R.C.M. 1007, announce which aggravating factors under subsection (c) of this rule were found by the members.

(c) *Aggravating factors.* Death may be adjudged only if the members find, beyond a reasonable doubt, one or more of the following aggravating factors:

(1) That the offense was committed before or in the presence of the enemy, except that this factor shall not apply in the case of a violation of Article 118 or 120;

Discussion

See paragraph 23, Part IV, for a definition of "before or in the presence of the enemy."

---

(2) That in committing the offense the accused—

(A) Knowingly created a grave risk of substantial damage to the national security of the United States; or

(B) Knowingly created a grave risk of substantial damage to a mission, system, or function of the United States, provided that this subparagraph shall apply only if substantial damage to the national security of the United States would have resulted had the intended damage been effected;

(3) That the offense caused substantial damage to the national security of the United States, whether or not the accused intended such damage, except that this factor shall not apply in case of a violation of Article 118 or 120;

(4) That the offense was committed in such a way or under circumstances that the life of one or more persons other than the victim was unlawfully and substantially endangered, except that this factor shall not apply to a violation of Articles 104, 106a, or 120;

(5) That the accused committed the offense with the intent to avoid hazardous duty;

(6) That, only in the case of a violation of Article 118 or 120, the offense was committed in time of war and in territory in which the United States or an ally of the United States was then an occupying power or in which the armed forces of the United States were then engaged in active hostilities;

(7) That, only in the case of a violation of Article 118(1):

(A) The accused was serving a sentence of confinement for 30 years or more or for life at the time of the murder;

(B) The murder was committed: while the accused was engaged in the commission or attempted commission of any robbery, rape, rape of a child, sexual assault, sexual assault of a child, aggravated sexual contact, sexual abuse of a child, aggravated arson, forcible sodomy, burglary, kidnapping, mutiny, sedition, or piracy of an aircraft or vessel; or while the accused was engaged in the commission or attempted commission of any offense involving the wrongful distribution, manufacture, or introduction or possession, with intent to distribute, of a controlled substance; or, while the accused was engaged in flight or attempted flight after the commission or attempted commission of any such offense.

(C) The murder was committed for the purpose of receiving money or a thing of value;

(D) The accused procured another by means of compulsion, coercion, or a promise of an advantage, a service, or a thing of value to commit the murder;

(E) The murder was committed with the intent to avoid or to prevent lawful apprehension or effect an escape from custody or confinement;

(F) The victim was the President of the United States, the President-elect, the Vice President, or, if there was no Vice President, the officer in the order of succession to the office of President of the United States, the Vice-President-elect, or any individual who is acting as President under the Constitution and laws of the United States, any Member of Congress (including a Delegate to, or Resident Commissioner in, the Congress) or Member-of-Congress elect, justice or judge of the United States, a chief of state or head of government (or the political equivalent) of a foreign nation, or a foreign official (as such term is defined in section 1116(b)(3)(A) of title 18, United States Code), if the official was on official business at the time of the offense and was in the United States or in a place described in Mil. R. Evid.315(c)(2), 315(c)(3);

(G) The accused then knew that the victim was any of the following persons in the execution of office: a commissioned, warrant, noncommissioned, or petty officer of the armed services of the United States; a member of any law enforcement or security activity or agency, military or civilian, including correctional custody personnel; or any firefighter;

(H) The murder was committed with intent to obstruct justice;

(I) The murder was preceded by the intentional infliction of substantial physical harm or prolonged, substantial mental or physical pain and suffering to the victim. For purposes of this section, "substantial physical harm" means fractures or dislocated bones, deep cuts, torn members of the body, serious damage to internal organs, or other serious bodily injuries. The term "substantial physical harm" does not mean minor injuries, such as a black eye or bloody nose. The term "substantial mental or physical pain or suffering" is accorded its common meaning and includes torture.

(J) The accused has been found guilty in the same case of another violation of Article 118;

(K) The victim of the murder was under 15 years of age.

(8) That only in the case of a violation of Article 118(4), the accused was the actual perpetrator of the killing or was a principal whose participation in the burglary, forcible sodomy, rape, rape of a child, sexual assault, sexual assault of a child, aggravated sexual contact, sexual abuse of a child, robbery, or aggravated arson was major and who manifested a reckless indifference for human life.

Discussion

Conduct amounts to "reckless indifference" when it evinces a wanton disregard of consequences under circumstances involving grave danger to the life of another, although no harm is necessarily intended. The accused must have had actual knowledge of the grave danger to others or knowledge of circumstances that would cause a reasonable person to realize the highly dangerous character of such conduct. In determining whether participation in the offense was major, the accused's presence at the scene and the extent to which the accused aided, abetted, assisted, encouraged, or advised the other participants should be considered. *See United States v. Berg*, 31 M.J. 38 (C.M.A. 1990); *United States v. McMonagle* 38 M.J. 53 (C.M.A. 1993).

(9) That, in addition to the offense for which the accused is eligible for the death penalty, the accused has also been convicted of a sexual offense in which:

(A) Under Article 120b, the victim was under the age of 12; or

(B) Under Articles 120 or 120b, the accused maimed or attempted to kill the victim;

(10) That, only in the case of a violation of the law of war, death is authorized under the law of war for the offense;

(11) That, only in the case of a violation of Article 104 or 106a:

(A) The accused has been convicted of another offense involving espionage or treason for which either a sentence of death or imprisonment for life was authorized by statute; or

(B) That in committing the offense, the accused knowingly created a grave risk of death to a person other than the individual who was the victim.

For purposes of this rule, "national security" means the national defense and foreign relations of the United States and specifically includes: a military or defense advantage over any foreign nation or group of nations; a favorable foreign relations position; or a defense posture capable of successfully resisting hostile or destructive action from within or without.

Discussion

Examples of substantial damage of the national security of the United States include: impeding the performance of a combat mission or operation; impeding the performance of an important mission in a hostile fire or imminent danger pay area (*see* 37 U.S.C. § 310(a)); and disclosing military plans, capabilities, or intelligence such as to jeopardize any combat mission or operation of the armed services of the United States or its allies or to materially aid an enemy of the United States.

(d) *Spying.* If the accused has been found guilty of spying under Article 106, subsections (a)(2), (b), and (c) of this rule and R.C.M. 1006 and 1007 shall not apply. Sentencing proceedings in accordance with R.C.M. 1001 shall be conducted, but the military judge shall announce that by operation of law a sentence of death has been adjudged.

(e) *Other penalties.* Except for a violation of Article 106, when death is an authorized punishment for an offense, all other punishments authorized under R.C.M. 1003 are also authorized for that offense, including confinement for life, with or without eligibility for parole, and may be adjudged in lieu of the death penalty, subject to limitations specifically prescribed in this Manual. A sentence of death includes a dishonorable discharge or dismissal as appropriate. Confinement is a necessary incident of a sentence of death, but not a part of it.

Discussion

A sentence of death may not be ordered executed until approved by the President. *See* R.C.M. 1207. A sentence to death which has been finally ordered executed will be carried out in the manner prescribed by the Secretary concerned. *See* R.C.M. 1113(e)(1).

Rule 1005. Instructions on sentence

(a) *In general.* The military judge shall give the members appropriate instructions on sentence.

Discussion

Instructions should be tailored to the facts and circumstances of the individual case.

(b) *When given.* Instructions on sentence shall be given after arguments by counsel and before the members close to deliberate on sentence, but the military judge may, upon request of the members, any party, or *sua sponte*, give additional instructions at a later time.

(c) *Requests for instructions.* After presentation of matters relating to sentence or at such other time as the military judge may permit, any party may request that the military judge instruct the members on the law as set forth in the request. The military judge may require the requested instruction to be written. Each party shall be given the opportunity to be heard on any proposed instruction on sentence before it is given. The military judge shall inform the parties of the proposed action on such requests before their closing arguments on sentence.

Discussion

Requests for and objections to instructions should be resolved at an Article 39(a) session. *But see* R.C.M. 801(c)(1)(C); 803.

The military judge is not required to give the specific instruction requested by counsel if the matter is adequately covered in the instructions.

The military judge should not identify the source of any instruction when addressing the members.

All written requests for instructions should be marked as

appellate exhibits, whether or not they are given.

(d) *How given.* Instructions on sentence shall be given orally on the record in the presence of all parties and the members. Written copies of the instructions, or unless a party objects, portions of them, may also be given to the members for their use during deliberations.

Discussion

A copy of any written instructions delivered to the members should be marked as an appellate exhibit.

(e) *Required instructions.* Instructions on sentence shall include:

(1) A statement of the maximum authorized punishment that may be adjudged and of the mandatory minimum punishment, if any;

Discussion

The maximum punishment that may be adjudged is the lowest of the total permitted by the applicable paragraph(s) in Part IV for each separate offense of which the accused was convicted (*see also* R.C.M. 1003 concerning additional limits on punishments and additional punishments which may be adjudged) or the jurisdictional limit of the court-martial (*see* R.C.M. 201(f) and R.C.M. 1301(d)). *See also* Discussion to R.C.M. 810(d). The military judge may upon request or when otherwise appropriate instruct on lesser punishments. *See* R.C.M. 1003. If an additional punishment is authorized under R.C.M. 1003(d), the members must be informed of the basis for the increased punishment.

A carefully drafted sentence worksheet ordinarily should be used and should include reference to all authorized punishments in the case.

---

(2) A statement of the effect any sentence announced including a punitive discharge and confinement, or confinement in excess of six months, will have on the accused's entitlement to pay and allowances;

(3) A statement of the procedures for deliberation and voting on the sentence set out in R.C.M. 1006;

Discussion

See also R.C.M. 1004 concerning additional instructions required in capital cases.

---

(4) A statement informing the members that they are solely responsible for selecting an appropriate sentence and may not rely on the possibility of any mitigating action by the convening or higher authority; and

Discussion

See also R.C.M. 1002.

---

(5) A statement that the members should consider all matters in extenuation, mitigation, and aggravation, whether introduced before or after findings, and matters introduced under R.C.M. 1001(b)(1), (2), (3) and (5).

Discussion

For example, tailored instructions on sentencing should bring attention to the reputation or record of the accused in the service for good conduct, efficiency, fidelity, courage, bravery, or other traits of good character, and any pretrial restraint imposed on the accused.

(f) *Waiver.* Failure to object to an instruction or to omission of an instruction before the members close to deliberate on the sentence constitutes waiver of the objection in the absence of plain error. The military judge may require the party objecting to specify in what respect the instructions were improper. The parties shall be given the opportunity to be heard on any objection outside the presence of the members.

Rule 1006. Deliberations and voting on sentence

(a) *In general.* The members shall deliberate and vote after the military judge instructs the members on sentence. Only the members shall be present during deliberations and voting. Superiority in rank shall not be used in any manner to control the independence of members in the exercise of their judgment.

(b) *Deliberations.* Deliberations may properly include full and free discussion of the sentence to be imposed in the case. Unless otherwise directed by the military judge, members may take with them in deliberations their notes, if any, any exhibits admitted in evidence, and any written instructions. Members may request that the court-martial be reopened and that portions of the record be read to them or additional evidence introduced. The military judge may, in the exercise of discretion, grant such requests.

(c) *Proposal of sentences.* Any member may propose a sentence. Each proposal shall be in writing and shall contain the complete sentence proposed. The junior member shall collect the proposed sentences and submit them to the president.

Discussion

A proposal should state completely each kind and, where appropriate, amount of authorized punishment proposed by that member. For example, a proposal of confinement for life would state whether it is with or without eligibility for parole. *See* R.C.M.1003(b).

(d) *Voting.*

(1) *Duty of members.* Each member has the duty to vote for a proper sentence for the offenses of which the court-martial found the accused guilty, regardless of the member's vote or opinion as to the guilt of the accused.

(2) *Secret ballot.* Proposed sentences shall be voted on by secret written ballot.

(3) *Procedure.*

(A) *Order.* All members shall vote on each proposed sentence in its entirety beginning with the least severe and continuing, as necessary, with the next least severe, until a sentence is adopted by the concurrence of the number of members required under subsection (d)(4) of this rule. The process of proposing sentences and voting on them may be repeated as necessary until a sentence is adopted.

(B) *Counting votes.* The junior member shall collect the ballots and count the votes. The president shall check the count and inform the other members of the result.

Discussion

A sentence adopted by the required number of members may be reconsidered only in accordance with R.C.M. 1009.

(4) *Number of votes required.*

(A) *Death.* A sentence which includes death may be adjudged only if all members present vote for that sentence.

Discussion

See R.C.M. 1004.

(B) *Confinement for life, with or without eligi-*

bility for parole, or more than 10 years. A sentence that includes confinement for life, with or without eligibility for parole, or more than 10 years may be adjudged only if at least three-fourths of the members present vote for that sentence.

(C) *Other.* A sentence other than those described in subsection (d)(4)(A) or (B) of this rule may be adjudged only if at least two-thirds of the members present vote for that sentence.

Discussion

In computing the number of votes required to adopt a sentence, any fraction of a vote is rounded up to the next whole number. For example, if there are seven members, at least six would have to concur to impose a sentence requiring a three-fourths vote, while at least five would have to concur to impose a sentence requiring a two-thirds vote.

(5) *Mandatory sentence.* When a mandatory minimum is prescribed under Article 118 the members shall vote on a sentence in accordance with this rule.

(6) *Effect of failure to agree.* If the required number of members do not agree on a sentence after a reasonable effort to do so, a mistrial may be declared as to the sentence and the case shall be returned to the convening authority, who may order a rehearing on sentence only or order that a sentence of no punishment be imposed.

(e) *Action after a sentence is reached.* After the members have agreed upon a sentence, the court-martial shall be opened and the president shall inform the military judge that a sentence has been reached. The military judge may, in the presence of the parties, examine any writing which the president intends to read to announce the sentence and may assist the members in putting the sentence in proper form. Neither that writing nor any oral or written clarification or discussion concerning it shall constitute announcement of the sentence.

Discussion

Ordinarily a sentence worksheet should be provided to the members as an aid to putting the sentence in proper form. *See* Appendix 11 for a format for forms of sentences. If a sentence worksheet has been provided, the military judge should examine it before the president announces the sentence. If the military judge intends to instruct the members after such examination, counsel should be permitted to examine the worksheet and to be heard on any instructions the military judge may give.

The president should not disclose any specific number of votes for or against any sentence.

If the sentence is ambiguous or apparently illegal, *see*

R.C.M. 1009.

Rule 1007. Announcement of sentence

(a) *In general.* The sentence shall be announced by the president or, in a court-martial composed of a military judge alone, by the military judge, in the presence of all parties promptly after it has been determined.

Discussion

See Appendix 11.

An element of a sentence adjudged by members about which no instructions were given and which is not listed on a sentence worksheet is not proper.

(b) *Erroneous announcement.* If the announced sentence is not the one actually determined by the court-martial, the error may be corrected by a new announcement made before the record of trial is authenticated and forwarded to the convening authority. This action shall not constitute reconsideration of the sentence. If the court-martial has been adjourned before the error is discovered, the military judge may call the court-martial into session to correct the announcement.

Discussion

For procedures governing reconsideration of the sentence, *see* R.C.M. 1009. *See also* R.C.M. 1102 concerning the action to be taken if the error in the announcement is discovered after the record is authenticated and forwarded to the convening authority.

(c) *Polling prohibited.* Except as provided in Mil. R. Evid. 606, members may not otherwise be questioned about their deliberations and voting.

Rule 1008. Impeachment of sentence

A sentence which is proper on its face may be impeached only when extraneous prejudicial information was improperly brought to the attention of a member, outside influence was improperly brought to bear upon any member, or unlawful command influence was brought to bear upon any member.

Discussion

See R.C.M. 923 Discussion concerning impeachment of findings.

Rule 1009. Reconsideration of sentence

(a) *Reconsideration.* Subject to this rule, a sentence may be reconsidered at any time before such sentence is announced in open session of the court.

(b) *Exceptions.*

(1) If the sentence announced in open session was less than the mandatory minimum prescribed for an offense of which the accused has been found guilty, the court that announced the sentence may reconsider such sentence upon reconsideration in accordance with subsection (e) of this rule.

(2) If the sentence announced in open session exceeds the maximum permissible punishment for the offense or the jurisdictional limitation of the court-martial, the sentence may be reconsidered after announcement in accordance with subsection (e) of this rule.

(c) *Clarification of sentence.* A sentence may be clarified at any time prior to action of the convening authority on the case.

(1) *Sentence adjudged by the military judge.* When a sentence adjudged by the military judge is ambiguous, the military judge shall call a session for clarification as soon as practical after the ambiguity is discovered.

(2) *Sentence adjudged by members.* When a sentence adjudged by members is ambiguous, the military judge shall bring the matter to the attention of the members if the matter is discovered before the court-martial is adjourned. If the matter is discovered after adjournment, the military judge may call a session for clarification by the members who adjudged the sentence as soon as practical after the ambiguity is discovered.

(d) *Action by the convening authority.* When a sentence adjudged by the court-martial is ambiguous, the convening authority may return the matter to the court-martial for clarification. When a sentence adjudged by the court-martial is apparently illegal, the convening authority may return the matter to the court-martial for reconsideration or may approve a sentence no more severe than the legal, unambiguous portions of the adjudged sentence.

(e) *Reconsideration procedure.* Any member of the

court-martial may propose that a sentence reached by the members be reconsidered.

(1) *Instructions.* When a sentence has been reached by members and reconsideration has been initiated, the military judge shall instruct the members on the procedure for reconsideration.

(2) *Voting.* The members shall vote by secret written ballot in closed session whether to reconsider a sentence already reached by them.

(3) *Number of votes required.*

(A) *With a view to increasing.* Subject to subsection (b) of this rule, members may reconsider a sentence with a view of increasing it only if at least a majority vote for reconsideration.

(B) *With a view to decreasing.* Members may reconsider a sentence with a view to decreasing it only if:

(i) In the case of a sentence which includes death, at least one member votes to reconsider;

(ii) In the case of a sentence which includes confinement for life, with or without eligibility for parole, or more than 10 years, more than one-fourth of the members vote to reconsider; or;

(iii) In the case of any other sentence, more than one-third of the members vote to reconsider.

Discussion

After a sentence has been adopted by secret ballot vote in closed session, no other vote may be taken on the sentence unless a vote to reconsider succeeds.

For example, if six of nine (two-thirds) members adopt a sentence, a vote of at least five would be necessary to reconsider to increase it; four would have to vote to reconsider in order to decrease it. If seven of nine (three-fourths) members is required to adopt a sentence, a vote of at least five would be necessary to reconsider to increase it, while three would be necessary to reconsider to decrease it.

(4) *Successful vote.* If a vote to reconsider a sentence succeeds, the procedures in R.C.M. 1006 shall apply.

Rule 1010. Notice concerning post-trial and appellate rights

In each general and special court-martial, prior to adjournment, the military judge shall ensure that the defense counsel has informed the accused orally and in writing of:

(a) The right to submit matters to the convening authority to consider before taking action;

(b) The right to appellate review, as applicable, and the effect of waiver or withdrawal of such right;

(c) The right to apply for relief from the Judge Advocate General if the case is neither reviewed by a Court of Criminal Appeals nor reviewed by the Judge Advocate General under R.C.M. 1201(b)(1); and

(d) The right to the advice and assistance of counsel in the exercise of the foregoing rights or any decision to waive them.

The written advice to the accused concerning post-trial and appellate rights shall be signed by the accused and the defense counsel and inserted in the record of trial as an appellate exhibit.

Discussion

The post-trial duties of the defense counsel concerning the appellate rights of the accused are set forth in paragraph (E)(iv) of the Discussion accompanying R.C.M. 502(d)(6). The defense counsel shall explain the appellate rights to the accused and prepare the written document of such advisement prior to or during trial.

Rule 1011. Adjournment

The military judge may adjourn the court-martial at the end of the trial of an accused or proceed to trial of other cases referred to that court-martial. Such an adjournment may be for a definite or indefinite period.

Discussion

A court-martial and its personnel have certain powers and responsibilities following the trial. *See,* for example, R.C.M. 502(d)(5) Discussion (F); 502(d)(6) Discussion (E); 808; 1007; 1009; Chapter XI.

CHAPTER XI. POST-TRIAL PROCEDURE

Rule 1101. Report of result of trial; post-trial restraint; deferment of confinement, forfeitures and reduction in grade; waiver of Article 58b forfeitures

(a) *Report of the result of trial.* After final adjournment of the court-martial in a case, the trial counsel shall promptly notify the accused's immediate commander, the convening authority or the convening authority's designee, and, if appropriate, the officer in charge of the confinement facility of the findings and sentence.

(b) *Post-trial confinement.*

(1) *In general.* An accused may be placed in post-trial confinement if the sentence adjudged by the court-martial includes death or confinement.

(2) *Who may order confinement.* Unless limited by superior authority, a commander of the accused may order the accused into post-trial confinement when post-trial confinement is authorized under subsection (b)(1) of this rule. A commander authorized to order post-trial confinement under this subsection may delegate this authority to the trial counsel.

Discussion

The commander may release the accused, order confinement, or order other appropriate restraint. Regardless whether the accused is ordered into confinement, a sentence to confinement begins to run on the date it is adjudged unless it is deferred under subsection (c) of this rule. *See* Article 57.

_____

(3) *Confinement on other grounds.* Nothing in this rule shall prohibit confinement of a person after a court-martial on proper grounds other than the offenses for which the accused was tried at the court-martial.

Discussion

See R.C.M. 304, 305, and paragraph 5b(2), Part V, for other grounds for confinement.

_____

(c) *Deferment of confinement, forfeitures or reduction in grade.*

(1) *In general.* Deferment of a sentence to confinement, forfeitures, or reduction in grade is a postponement of the running of the sentence.

Discussion

Deferment is not suspension of the sentence or a form of clemency.

_____

(2) *Who may defer.* The convening authority or, if the accused is no longer in the convening authority's jurisdiction, the officer exercising general court-martial jurisdiction over the command to which the accused is assigned, may, upon written application of the accused, at any time after the adjournment of the court-martial, defer the accused's service of a sentence to confinement, forfeitures, or reduction in grade that has not been ordered executed.

(3) *Action on deferment request.* The authority acting on the deferment request may, in that authority's discretion, defer service of a sentence to confinement, forfeitures, or reduction in grade. The accused shall have the burden of showing that the interests of the accused and the community in deferral outweigh the community's interests in imposition of the punishment on its effective date. Factors that the authority acting on a deferment request may consider in determining whether to grant the deferment request include, where applicable: the probability of the accused's flight; the probability of the accused's commission of other offenses, intimidation of witnesses, or interference with the administration of justice; the nature of the offenses (including the effect on the victim) of which the accused was convicted; the sentence adjudged; the command's immediate need for the accused; the effect of deferment on good order and discipline in the command; the accused's character, mental condition, family situation, and service record. The decision of the authority acting on the deferment request shall be subject to judicial review only for abuse of discretion. The action of the authority acting on the deferment request shall be in writing and a copy shall be provided to the accused.

Discussion

The deferment request and the action on the request must be attached to the record of trial. *See* R.C.M. 1103(b)(3)(D). If the request for deferment is denied, the basis for the denial should be in writing and attached to the record of trial.

_____

(4) *Orders.* The action granting deferment shall be

reported in the convening authority's action under R.C.M. 1107(f)(4)(E) and shall include the date of the action on the request when it occurs prior to or concurrently with the action. Action granting deferment after the convening authority's action under R.C.M. 1107 shall be reported in orders under R.C.M. 1114 and included in the record of trial.

(5) *Restraint when deferment is granted.* When deferment of confinement is granted, no form of restraint or other limitation on the accused's liberty may be ordered as a substitute form of punishment. An accused may, however, be restricted to specified limits or conditions may be placed on the accused's liberty during the period of deferment for any other proper reason, including a ground for restraint under R.C.M. 304.

(6) *End of deferment.* Deferment of a sentence to confinement, forfeitures, or reduction in grade ends when:

(A) The convening authority takes action under R.C.M. 1107, unless the convening authority specifies in the action that service of confinement after the action is deferred;

(B) The confinement, forfeitures, or reduction in grade are suspended;

(C) The deferment expires by its own terms; or

(D) The deferment is otherwise rescinded in accordance with subsection (c)(7) of this rule. Deferment of confinement may not continue after the conviction is final under R.C.M. 1209.

Discussion

When the sentence is ordered executed, forfeitures or reduction in grade may be suspended, but may not be deferred; deferral of confinement may continue after action in accordance with R.C.M. 1107. A form of punishment cannot be both deferred and suspended at the same time. When deferment of confinement, forfeitures, or reduction in grade ends, the sentence to confinement, forfeitures, or reduction in grade begins to run or resumes running, as appropriate. When the convening authority has specified in the action that confinement will be deferred after the action, the deferment may not be terminated, except under subsections (6)(B), (C), or (D), until the conviction is final under R.C.M. 1209.

See R.C.M. 1203 for deferment of a sentence to confinement pending review under Article 67(a)(2).

---

(7) *Rescission of deferment.*

(A) *Who may rescind.* The authority who granted the deferment or, if the accused is no longer within that authority's jurisdiction, the officer exercising general court-martial jurisdiction over the command to which the accused is assigned, may rescind the deferment.

(B) *Action.* Deferment of confinement, forfeitures, or reduction in grade may be rescinded when additional information is presented to a proper authority which, when considered with all other information in the case, that authority finds, in that authority's discretion, is grounds for denial of deferment under subsection (c)(3) of this rule. The accused shall promptly be informed of the basis for the rescission and of the right to submit written matters in the accused's behalf and to request that the rescission be reconsidered. However, the accused may be required to serve the sentence to confinement, forfeitures, or reduction in grade pending this action.

(C) *Execution.* When deferment of confinement is rescinded after the convening authority's action under R.C.M. 1107, the confinement may be ordered executed. However, no such order to rescind a deferment of confinement may be issued within 7 days of notice of the rescission of a deferment of confinement to the accused under subsection (c)(7)(B) of this rule, to afford the accused an opportunity to respond. The authority rescinding the deferment may extend this period for good cause shown. The accused shall be credited with any confinement actually served during this period.

(D) *Orders.* Rescission of a deferment before or concurrently with the initial action in the case shall be reported in the action under R.C.M. 1107(f)(4)(E), which action shall include the dates of the granting of the deferment and the rescission. Rescission of a deferment of confinement after the convening authority's action shall be reported in supplementary orders in accordance with R.C.M. 1114 and shall state whether the approved period of confinement is to be executed or whether all or part of it is to be suspended.

Discussion

See Appendix 16 for forms.

(d) *Waiving forfeitures resulting from a sentence to confinement to provide for dependent support.*

(1) With respect to forfeiture of pay and allowances resulting only by operation of law and not adjudged by the court, the convening authority may

waive, for a period not to exceed six months, all or part of the forfeitures for the purpose of providing support to the accused's dependent(s). The convening authority may waive and direct payment of any such forfeitures when they become effective by operation of Article 57(a).

(2) Factors that may be considered by the convening authority in determining the amount of forfeitures, if any, to be waived include, but are not limited to, the length of the accused's confinement, the number and age(s) of the accused's family members, whether the accused requested waiver, any debts owed by the accused, the ability of the accused's family members to find employment, and the availability of transitional compensation for abused dependents permitted under 10 U.S.C. 1059.

(3) For the purposes of this Rule, a "dependent" means any person qualifying as a "dependent" under 37 U.S.C. 401.

Discussion

Forfeitures resulting by operation of law, rather than those adjudged as part of a sentence, may be waived for six months or for the duration of the period of confinement, whichever is less. The waived forfeitures are paid as support to dependent(s) designated by the convening authority. When directing waiver and payment, the convening authority should identify by name the dependent(s) to whom the payments will be made and state the number of months for which the waiver and payment shall apply. In cases where the amount to be waived and paid is less than the jurisdictional limit of the court, the monthly dollar amount of the waiver and payment should be stated.

Rule 1102. Post-trial sessions

(a) *In general.* Post-trial sessions may be proceedings in revision or Article 39(a) sessions. Such sessions may be directed by the military judge or the convening authority in accordance with this rule.

(b) *Purpose.*

(1) *Proceedings in revision.* Proceedings in revision may be directed to correct an apparent error, omission, or improper or inconsistent action by the court-martial, which can be rectified by reopening the proceedings without material prejudice to the accused.

Discussion

Because the action at a proceeding in revision is corrective, a

proceeding in revision may not be conducted for the purpose of presenting additional evidence.

Examples when a proceeding in revision is appropriate include: correction of an ambiguous or apparently illegal action by the court-martial; inquiry into the terms of a pretrial agreement; and inquiry to establish the accused's awareness of certain rights.

See also R.C.M. 1104(d) concerning correction of the record by certificate of correction.

---

(2) *Article 39(a) sessions.* An Article 39(a) session under this rule may be called, upon motion of either party or *sua sponte* by the military judge, for the purpose of inquiring into, and, when appropriate, resolving any matter that arises after trial and that substantially affects the legal sufficiency of any findings of guilty or the sentence. The military judge may also call an Article 39(a) session, upon motion of either party or sua sponte, to reconsider any trial ruling that substantially affects the legal sufficiency of any findings of guilty or the sentence. The military judge may, *sua sponte*, at any time prior to authentication of the record of trial, enter a finding of not guilty of one or more offenses charged, or may enter a finding of not guilty of a part of a specification as long as a lesser offense charged is alleged in the remaining portion of the specification. Prior to entering such a finding or findings, the military judge shall give each party an opportunity to be heard on the matter in a post-trial Article 39(a) session.

Discussion

For example, an Article 39(a) session may be called to permit a military judge to reconsider a trial ruling, or to examine allegations of misconduct by a counsel, a member, or a witness. *See* R.C.M. 917(d) for the standard to be used to determine the legal sufficiency of evidence.

(c) *Matters not subject to post-trial sessions.* Post-trial session may not be directed:

(1) For reconsideration of a finding of not guilty of any specification, or a ruling which amounts to a finding of not guilty;

(2) For reconsideration of a finding of not guilty of any charge, unless the record shows a finding of guilty under a specification laid under that charge, which sufficiently alleges a violation of some article of the code; or

(3) For increasing the severity of the sentence

unless the sentence prescribed for the offense is mandatory.

(d) *When directed.* The military judge may direct a post-trial session any time before the record is authenticated. The convening authority may direct a post-trial session any time before the convening authority takes initial action on the case or at such later time as the convening authority is authorized to do so by a reviewing authority.

(e) *Procedure.*

(1) *Personnel.* The requirements of R.C.M. 505 and 805 shall apply at post-trial sessions except that—

(A) For a proceeding in revision, if trial was before members and the matter subject to the proceeding in revision requires the presence of members:

(i) The absence of any members does not invalidate the proceedings if, in the case of a general court-martial, at least five members are present, or, in the case of a special court-martial, at least three members are present; and

(ii) A different military judge may be detailed, subject to R.C.M. 502(c) and 902, if the military judge who presided at the earlier proceedings is not reasonably available.

(B) For an Article 39(a) session, a different military judge may be detailed, subject to R.C.M. 502(c) and 902, for good cause.

(2) *Action.* The military judge shall take such action as may be appropriate, including appropriate instructions when members are present. The members may deliberate in closed session, if necessary, to determine what corrective action, if any, to take. Prior to the military judge *sua sponte* entering a finding of not guilty of one or more offenses charged or entering a finding of not guilty of a part of a specification as long as a lesser offense charged is alleged in the remaining portion of the specification, the military judge shall give each party an opportunity to be heard on the matter.

(3) *Record.* All post-trial sessions, except any deliberations by the members, shall be held in open session. The record of the post-trial sessions shall be prepared, authenticated, and served in accordance with R.C.M. 1103 and 1104 and shall be included in the record of the prior proceedings.

Rule 1102A. Post-trial hearing for person found not guilty only by reason of lack of mental responsibility

(a) *In general.* The military judge shall conduct a hearing not later than forty days following the finding that an accused is not guilty only by reason of a lack of mental responsibility.

(b) *Psychiatric or psychological examination and report.* Prior to the hearing, the military judge or convening authority shall order a psychiatric or psychological examination of the accused, with the resulting psychiatric or psychological report transmitted to the military judge for use in the post-trial hearing.

(c) *Post-trial hearing.*

(1) The accused shall be represented by defense counsel and shall have the opportunity to testify, present evidence, call witnesses on his or her behalf, and to confront and cross-examine witnesses who appear at the hearing.

(2) The military judge is not bound by the rules of evidence except with respect to privileges.

(3) An accused found not guilty only by reason of a lack of mental responsibility of an offense involving bodily injury to another, or serious damage to the property of another, or involving a substantial risk of such injury or damage, has the burden of proving by clear and convincing evidence that his or her release would not create a substantial risk of bodily injury to another person or serious damage to property of another due to a present mental disease or defect. With respect to any other offense, the accused has the burden of such proof by a preponderance of the evidence.

(4) If, after the hearing, the military judge finds the accused has satisfied the standard specified in subsection (3) of this section, the military judge shall inform the general court-martial convening authority of this result and the accused shall be released. If, however, the military judge finds after the hearing that the accused has not satisfied the standard specified in subsection (3) of this section, then the military judge shall inform the general court-martial convening authority of this result and that authority may commit the accused to the custody of the Attorney General.

Rule 1103. Preparation of record of trial

(a) *In general.* Each general, special, and summary

court-martial shall keep a separate record of the proceedings in each case brought before it.

(b) *General courts-martial.*

(1) *Responsibility for preparation.* The trial counsel shall:

(A) Under the direction of the military judge, cause the record of trial to be prepared; and

(B) Under regulations prescribed by the Secretary concerned, cause to be retained stenographic or other notes or mechanical or electronic recordings from which the record of trial was prepared.

(2) *Contents.*

(A) *In general.* The record of trial in each general court-martial shall be separate, complete, and independent of any other document.

(B) *Verbatim transcript required.* Except as otherwise provided in subsection (j) of this rule, the record of trial shall include a verbatim transcript of all sessions except sessions closed for deliberations and voting when:

(i) The sentence adjudged includes confinement for twelve months or more or any punishment that may not be adjudged by a special court-martial; or

(ii) A bad-conduct discharge has been adjudged.

Discussion

A verbatim transcript includes: all proceedings including sidebar conferences, arguments of counsel, and rulings and instructions by the military judge; matter which the military judge orders stricken from the record or disregarded; and when a record is amended in revision proceedings (*see* R.C.M. 1102), the part of the original record changed and the changes made, without physical alteration of the original record. Conferences under R.C.M. 802 need not be recorded, but matters agreed upon at such conferences must be included in the record. If testimony is given through an interpreter, a verbatim transcript must so reflect.

(C) *Verbatim transcript not required.* If a verbatim transcript is not required under subsection (b)(2)(B) of this rule, a summarized report of the proceedings may be prepared instead of a verbatim transcript.

Discussion

See also R.C.M. 910(i) concerning guilty plea inquiries.

(D) *Other matters.* In addition to the matter re-

quired under subsection (b)(2)(B) or (b)(2)(C) of this rule, a complete record shall include:

(i) The original charge sheet or a duplicate;

(ii) A copy of the convening order and any amending order(s);

(iii) The request, if any, for trial by military judge alone, or that the membership of the court-martial include enlisted persons, and, when applicable, any statement by the convening authority required under R.C.M. 201(f)(2)(B)(ii) or 503(a)(2);

(iv) The original dated, signed action by the convening authority; and

(v) Exhibits, or, with the permission of the military judge, copies, photographs, or descriptions of any exhibits which were received in evidence and any appellate exhibits.

(3) *Matters attached to the record.* The following matters shall be attached to the record:

(A) If not used as exhibits—

(i) The report of preliminary hearing under Article 32, if any;

(ii) The staff judge advocate's pretrial advice under Article 34, if any;

(iii) If the trial was a rehearing or new or other trial of the case, the record of the former hearing(s); and

(iv) Written special findings, if any, by the military judge.

(B) Exhibits or, with the permission of the military judge, copies, photographs, or descriptions of any exhibits which were marked for and referred to on the record but not received in evidence;

(C) Any matter filed by the accused under R.C.M. 1105, or any written waiver of the right to submit such matter;

(D) Any deferment request and the action on it;

(E) Explanation for any substitute authentication under R.C.M. 1104(a)(2)(B);

(F) Explanation for any failure to serve the record of trial on the accused under R.C.M. 1104(b);

(G) The post-trial recommendation of the staff judge advocate or legal officer and proof of service on defense counsel in accordance with R.C.M. 1106(f)(1);

(H) Any response by defense counsel to the post-trial review;

(I) Recommendations and other papers relative to clemency;

(J) Any statement why it is impracticable for the convening authority to act;

(K) Conditions of suspension, if any, and proof of service on probationer under R.C.M. 1108;

(L) Any waiver or withdrawal of appellate review under R.C.M. 1110; and

(M) Records of any proceedings in connection with vacation of suspension under R.C.M. 1109.

(N) Documents pertaining to the receipt of the record of trial by the victim pursuant to subsection (g)(3) of this rule.

Discussion

Per R.C.M. 1114(f), consult service regulations for distribution of promulgating orders.

(c) *Special courts-martial.*

(1) *Involving a bad-conduct discharge, confinement for more than six months, or forfeiture of pay for more than six months.* The requirements of subsections (b)(1), (b)(2)(A), (b)(2)(B), (b)(2)(D), and (b)(3) of this rule shall apply in a special court-martial in which a bad-conduct discharge, confinement for more than six months, or forfeiture of pay for more than six months, has been adjudged.

(2) *All other special courts-martial.* If the special court-martial resulted in findings of guilty but a bad-conduct discharge, confinement for more than six months, or forfeiture of pay for more than six months, was not adjudged, the requirements of subsections (b)(1), (b)(2)(D), and (b)(3)(A)-(F) and (I)-(M) of this rule shall apply.

(d) *Summary courts-martial.* The summary court-martial record of trial shall be prepared as prescribed in R.C.M. 1305.

(e) *Acquittal; courts-martial resulting in findings of not guilty only by reason of lack of mental responsibility; termination prior to findings; termination after findings.* Notwithstanding subsections (b), (c), and (d) of this rule, if proceedings resulted in an acquittal of all charges and specifications or in a finding of not guilty only by reason of lack of mental responsibility of all charges and specifications, or if the proceedings were terminated by withdrawal, mistrial, or dismissal before findings, or if the proceedings were terminated after findings by ap-

proval of an administrative discharge in lieu of court-martial, the record may consist of the original charge sheet, a copy of the convening order and amending orders (if any), and sufficient information to establish jurisdiction over the accused and the offenses (if not shown on the charge sheet). The convening authority or higher authority may prescribe additional requirements.

Discussion

The notes or recordings of court-martial proceedings described in this subsection should be retained if reinstitution and re-referral of the affected charges is likely or when they may be necessary for the trial of another accused in a related case. *See* R.C.M. 905(g) and 914.

(f) *Loss of notes or recordings of the proceedings.* If, because of loss of recordings or notes, or other reasons, a verbatim transcript cannot be prepared when required by subsection (b)(2)(B) or (c)(1) of this rule, a record which meets the requirements of subsection (b)(2)(C) of this rule shall be prepared, and the convening authority may:

(1) Approve only so much of the sentence that could be adjudged by a special court-martial, except that a bad-conduct discharge, confinement for more than six months, or forfeiture of two-thirds pay per month for more than six months, may not be approved; or

(2) Direct a rehearing as to any offense of which the accused was found guilty if the finding is supported by the summary of the evidence contained in the record, provided that the convening authority may not approve any sentence imposed at such a rehearing more severe than or in excess of that adjudged by the earlier court-martial.

(g) *Copies of the record of trial.*

(1) *General and special courts-martial.*

(A) *In general.* In general and special courts-martial that require a verbatim transcript under subsections (b) or (c) of this rule and are subject to a review by a Court of Criminal Appeals under Article 66, the trial counsel shall cause to be prepared an original record of trial.

Discussion

An original record of trial includes any record of the proceedings recorded in a form that satisfies the definition of a "writing" in R.C.M. 103. Any requirement to prepare a printed record of trial pursuant to this rule, either in lieu of or in addition to a record of trial recorded or compiled in some other format, including electronic or digital formats, is subject to service regulation.

(B) *Additional copies.* The convening or higher authority may direct that additional copies of the record of trial of any general or special court-martial be prepared.

(2) *Summary courts-martial.* Copies of the summary court-martial record of trial shall be prepared as prescribed in R.C.M. 1305(b).

(3) *Cases involving sexual offenses.*

(A) *"Victim" defined.* For the purposes of this rule, a victim is a person who suffered a direct physical, emotional, or pecuniary harm as a result of matters set forth in a charge or specification; and is named in a specification under Article 120, Article 120b, Article 120c, Article 125, or any attempt to commit such offense in violation of Article 80.

(B) *Scope; qualifying victim.* In a general or special court-martial, a copy of the record of trial shall be given free of charge to a victim as defined in subparagraph (A) for a specification identified in subparagraph (A) that resulted in any finding under R.C.M. 918 (a)(1). If a victim is a minor, a copy of the record of trial shall instead be provided to the parent or legal guardian of the victim.

Discussion

This rule is not intended to limit the Services' discretion to provide records of trial to other individuals.

(C) *Notice.* In accordance with regulations of the Secretary concerned, and no later than authentication of the record, trial counsel shall cause each qualifying victim to be notified of the opportunity to receive a copy of the record of trial. Qualifying victims may decline receipt of such documents in writing and any written declination shall be attached to the original record of trial.

(D) *Documents to be provided.* For purposes of this subsection, the record of trial shall consist of documents described in subsection (b)(2) of this rule, except for proceedings described in subsection (e) of this rule, in which case the record of trial shall consist of items described in subsection (e). Matters attached to the record as described in subsection (b)(3) of this rule are not required to be provided.

Discussion

Subsections (b)(3)(N) and (g)(3) of this rule were added to implement Article 54(e), in compliance with the National Defense Authorization Act for Fiscal Year 2012 (P.L. 112-81, § 586). Service of a copy of the record of trial on a victim is prescribed in R.C.M. 1104 (b)(1)(E).

(h) *Security classification.* If the record of trial contains matter which must be classified under applicable security regulations, the trial counsel shall cause a proper security classification to be assigned to the record of trial and on each page thereof on which classified material appears.

Discussion

See R.C.M. 1104(b)(1)(D) concerning the disposition of records of trial requiring security protection.

(i) *Examination and correction before authentication.*

(1) *General and special courts-martial.*

(A) *Examination and correction by trial counsel.* In general and special courts-martial, the trial counsel shall examine the record of trial before authentication and cause those changes to be made which are necessary to report the proceedings accurately. The trial counsel shall not change the record after authentication.

Discussion

The trial counsel may personally correct and initial the necessary changes or, if major changes are necessary, direct the reporter to rewrite the entire record or the portion of the record which is defective.

The trial counsel must ensure that the reporter makes a true, complete, and accurate record of the proceedings such that the record will meet the applicable requirements of this rule.

(B) *Examination by defense counsel.* Except when unreasonable delay will result, the trial counsel shall permit the defense counsel to examine the record before authentication.

Discussion

If the defense counsel discovers errors or omissions in the record, the defense counsel may suggest to the trial counsel appropriate changes to make the record accurate, forward for attachment to the record under Article 38(c) any objections to the record, or bring any suggestions for correction of the record to the attention of the person who authenticates the record.

The defense counsel should be granted reasonable access to the reporter's notes and tapes to facilitate the examination of the record.

A suitable notation that the defense counsel has examined the record should be made on the authentication page. *See* Appendix 13 or 14 for sample forms.

———————

(2) *Summary courts-martial.* The summary court-martial shall examine and correct the summary court-martial record of trial as prescribed in R.C.M. 1305(a).

(j) *Videotape and similar records.*

(1) *Recording proceedings.* If authorized by regulations of the Secretary concerned, general and special courts-martial may be recorded by videotape, audiotape, or similar material from which sound and visual images may be reproduced to accurately depict the entire court-martial. Such means of recording may be used in lieu of recording by a qualified court reporter, when one is required, subject to this rule.

(2) *Preparation of written record.* When the court-martial, or any part of it, is recorded by videotape, audiotape, or similar material under subsection (j)(1) of this rule, a transcript or summary in writing (as defined in R.C.M. 103), as required in subsection (b)(2)(A), (b)(2)(B), (b)(2)(C), or (c) of this rule, as appropriate, shall be prepared in accordance with this rule and R.C.M. 1104 before the record is forwarded under R.C.M. 1104(e), unless military exigencies prevent transcription.

(3) *Military exigency.* If military exigency prevents preparation of a written transcript or summary, as required, and when the court-martial has been recorded by videotape, audiotape, or similar material under subsection (j)(1) of this rule, the videotape, audiotape, or similar material, together with the matters in subsections (b)(2)(D) and (b)(3) of this rule shall be authenticated and forwarded in accordance with R.C.M. 1104, provided that in such case the convening authority shall cause to be attached to the record a statement of the reasons why a written record could not be prepared, and provided further that in such case the defense counsel shall be given reasonable opportunity to listen to or to view and listen to the recording whenever defense counsel is otherwise entitled to examine the record under these rules. Subsection (g) of this rule shall not apply in case of military exigency under this subsection.

(4) *Further review.*

(A) *Cases reviewed by the Court of Criminal Appeals.* Before review, if any, by a Court of Criminal Appeals of a case in which the record includes an authenticated recording prepared under subsection (j)(3) of this rule, a complete written transcript shall be prepared and certified as accurate in accordance with regulations of the Secretary concerned. The authenticated recording shall be retained for examination by appellate authorities.

(B) *Cases not reviewed by the Court of Criminal Appeals.* In cases in which the record includes an authenticated recording prepared under subsection (j)(3) of this rule, a written record shall be prepared under such circumstances as the Secretary concerned may prescribe.

(5) *Accused's copy.* When a record includes an authenticated recording under subsection (j)(3) of this rule, the Government shall, in order to comply with R.C.M. 1104(b):

(A) Provide the accused with a duplicate copy of the videotape, audiotape, or similar matter and copies of any written contents of and attachments to the record, and give the accused reasonable opportunity to use such viewing equipment as is necessary to listen to or view and listen to the recording; or

(B) With the written consent of the accused, defer service of the record until a written record is prepared under subsection (4) of this rule.

Rule 1103A. Sealed exhibits and proceedings.

(a) *In general.* If the report of preliminary hearing or record of trial contains exhibits, proceedings, or other matter ordered sealed by the preliminary hearing officer or military judge, counsel for the government or trial counsel shall cause such materials to be sealed so as to prevent unauthorized viewing or disclosure. Counsel for the government or trial counsel shall ensure that such materials are properly marked, including an annotation that the material was sealed by order of the preliminary hearing officer or military judge, and inserted at the appropriate place in the original record of trial. Copies of the report of preliminary hearing or record of trial shall contain appropriate annotations that matters were sealed by order of the preliminary hearing officer or military judge and have been inserted in the report of preliminary hearing or original record of trial. This Rule shall be implemented in a manner consistent with Executive Order 13526, concerning classified national security information.

(b) *Examination of sealed exhibits and proceedings.* Except as provided in the following subsections to this rule, sealed exhibits may not be examined.

(1) *Prior to referral.* The following individuals may examine sealed materials only if necessary for proper fulfillment of their responsibilities under the UCMJ, the MCM, governing directives, instructions, regulations, applicable rules for practice and procedure, or rules of professional responsibility: the judge advocate advising the convening authority who directed the Article 32 preliminary hearing; the convening authority who directed the Article 32 preliminary hearing; the staff judge advocate to the general court-martial convening authority; and the general court-martial convening authority.

(2) *Prior to authentication.* Prior to authentication of the record by the military judge, sealed materials may not be examined in the absence of an order from the military judge based on good cause shown.

(3) *Authentication through action.* After authentication and prior to disposition of the record of trial pursuant to Rule for Courts-Martial 1111, sealed materials may not be examined in the absence of an order from the military judge upon a showing of good cause at a post-trial Article 39a session directed by the Convening Authority.

Discussion

A convening authority who has granted clemency based upon review of sealed materials in the record of trial is not permitted to disclose the contents of the sealed materials when providing a written explanation of the reason for such action, as directed under R.C.M. 1107.

---

(4) *Reviewing and appellate authorities.*

(A) Reviewing and appellate authorities may examine sealed matters when those authorities determine that such action is reasonably necessary to a proper fulfillment of their responsibilities under the Uniform Code of Military Justice, the Manual for Courts-Martial, governing directives, instructions, regulations, applicable rules for practice and procedure, or rules of professional responsibility.

(B) Reviewing and appellate authorities shall

not, however, disclose sealed matter or information in the absence of:

(i) Prior authorization of the Judge Advocate General in the case of review under Rule for Courts-Martial 1201(b); or

(ii) Prior authorization of the appellate court before which a case is pending review under Rules for Courts-Martial 1203 and 1204.

(C) In those cases in which review is sought or pending before the United States Supreme Court, authorization to disclose sealed materials or information shall be obtained under that Court's rules of practice and procedure.

(D) The authorizing officials in paragraph (B)(ii) above may place conditions on authorized disclosures in order to minimize the disclosure.

(E) For purposes of this rule, reviewing and appellate authorities are limited to:

(i) Judge advocates reviewing records pursuant to Rule for Courts-Martial 1112;

(ii) Officers and attorneys in the office of the Judge Advocate General reviewing records pursuant to Rule for Courts-Martial 1201(b);

(iii) Appellate government counsel;

(iv) Appellate defense counsel;

(v) Appellate judges of the Courts of Criminal Appeals and their professional staffs;

(vi) The judges of the United States Court of Appeals for the Armed Forces and their professional staffs;

(vii) The Justices of the United States Supreme Court and their professional staffs; and

(viii) Any other court of competent jurisdiction.

(5) *Examination of sealed matters.* For the purpose of this rule, "examination" includes reading, viewing, photocopying, photographing, disclosing, or manipulating the sealed matters in any way.

Rule 1104. Records of trial: Authentication; service; loss; correction; forwarding

(a) *Authentication.*

(1) *In general.* A record is authenticated by the signature of a person specified in this rule who thereby declares that the record accurately reports the proceedings. An electronic record of trial may be authenticated with the electronic signature of the military judge or other authorized person. Service of

an authenticated electronic copy of the record of trial with a means to review the record of trial satisfies the requirement of service under R.C.M. 1105(c) and 1305(d). No person may be required to authenticate a record of trial if that person is not satisfied that it accurately reports the proceedings.

(2) *General and special courts-martial.*

(A) *Authentication by the military judge.* In special courts-martial in which a bad-conduct discharge, confinement for more than six months, or forfeiture of pay for more than six months, has been adjudged and in general courts-martial, except as provided in subsection (a)(2)(B) of this rule, the military judge present at the end of the proceedings shall authenticate the record of trial, or that portion over which the military judge presided. If more than one military judge presided over the proceedings, each military judge shall authenticate the record of the proceedings over which that military judge presided, except as provided in subsection (a)(2)(B) of this rule. The record of trial of special courts-martial in which a bad-conduct discharge, confinement for more than six months, or forfeiture of pay for more than six months, was not adjudged shall be authenticated in accordance with regulations of the Secretary concerned.

(B) *Substitute authentication.* If the military judge cannot authenticate the record of trial because of the military judge's death, disability, or absence, the trial counsel present at the end of the proceedings shall authenticate the record of trial. If the trial counsel cannot authenticate the record of trial because of the trial counsel's death, disability, or absence, a member shall authenticate the record of trial. In a court-martial composed of a military judge alone, or as to sessions without members, the court reporter shall authenticate the record of trial when this duty would fall upon a member under this subsection. A person authorized to authenticate a record under this subsection may authenticate the record only as to those proceedings at which that person was present.

Discussion

See Appendix 13 or 14 for sample forms.

Substitute authentication is authorized only in emergencies. A brief, temporary absence of the military judge from the situs of the preparation of the record of trial does not justify a substitute authentication. Prolonged absence, including permanent change of station, ordinarily justifies substitute authentication.

The person who authenticates the record of trial instead of the military judge should attach to the record of trial an explanation for the substitute authentication. *See* R.C.M. 1103(b)(3) (E).

---

(3) *Summary courts-martial.* The summary court-martial shall authenticate the summary court-martial record of trial as prescribed in R.C.M. 1305(a).

(b) *Service.*

(1) *General and special courts-martial.*

(A) *Service of record of trial on accused.* In each general and special court-martial, except as provided in subsection (b)(1)(C) or (D) of this rule, the trial counsel shall cause a copy of the record of trial to be served on the accused as soon as the record of trial is authenticated.

(B) *Proof of service of record of trial on accused.* The trial counsel shall cause the accused's receipt for the copy of the record of trial to be attached to the original record of trial. If it is impracticable to secure a receipt from the accused before the original record of trial is forwarded to the convening authority, the trial counsel shall prepare a certificate indicating that a copy of the record of trial has been transmitted to the accused, including the means of transmission and the address, and cause the certificate to be attached to the original record of trial. In such a case the accused's receipt shall be forwarded to the convening authority as soon as it is obtained.

(C) *Substitute service.* If it is impracticable to serve the record of trial on the accused because of the transfer of the accused to a distant place, the unauthorized absence of the accused, or military exigency, or if the accused so requests on the record at the court-martial or in writing, the accused's copy of the record shall be forwarded to the accused's defense counsel, if any. Trial counsel shall attach a statement to the record explaining why the accused was not served personally. If the accused has more than one counsel, R.C.M. 1106(f)(2) shall apply. If the accused has no counsel and if the accused is absent without authority, the trial counsel shall prepare an explanation for the failure to serve the record. The explanation and the accused's copy of the record shall be forwarded with the original record. The accused shall be provided with a copy of the record as soon as practicable.

Discussion

See Appendix 13 or 14 for sample forms.

(D) *Classified information.*

(i) *Forwarding to convening authority.* If the copy of the record of trial prepared for the accused contains classified information, the trial counsel, unless directed otherwise by the convening authority, shall forward the accused's copy to the convening authority, before it is served on the accused.

(ii) *Responsibility of the convening authority.* The convening authority shall:

(a) cause any classified information to be deleted or withdrawn from the accused's copy of the record of trial;

(b) cause a certificate indicating that classified information has been deleted or withdrawn to be attached to the record of trial; and

(c) cause the expurgated copy of the record of trial and the attached certificate regarding classified information to be served on the accused as provided in subsections (b)(1)(A) and (B) of this rule except that the accused's receipt shall show that the accused has received an expurgated copy of the record of trial.

(iii) *Contents of certificate.* The certificate regarding deleted or withdrawn classified information shall indicate:

(a) that the original record of trial may be inspected in the Office of the Judge Advocate General concerned under such regulations as the Secretary concerned may prescribe;

(b) the pages of the record of trial from which matter has been deleted;

(c) the pages of the record of trial which have been entirely deleted; and

(d) the exhibits which have been withdrawn.

Discussion

See R.C.M. 1103(h) concerning classified information.

(E) *Victims of sexual assault.* Qualifying victims, as defined in R.C.M. 1103 (g)(3)(A), shall be served a copy of the record of trial in the same manner as the accused under subsection (b) of this rule. In accordance with regulations of the Secretary concerned:

(i) A copy of the record of trial shall be provided to each qualifying victim as soon as it is authenticated or, if the victim requests, at a time thereafter. The victim's receipt of the record of trial, including any delay in receiving it, shall be documented and attached to the original record of trial.

(ii) A copy of the convening authority's action as described in R.C.M. 1103(b)(2)(D)(iv) shall be provided to each qualifying victim as soon as each document is prepared. If the victim makes a request in writing, service of the record of trial may be delayed until the action is available.

(iii) Classified information pursuant to subsection (b)(1)(D) of this rule, sealed matters pursuant to R.C.M. 1103A, or other portions of the record the release of which would unlawfully violate the privacy interests of any party, to include those afforded by 5 U.S.C.§552a, the Privacy Act of 1974, shall not be provided. Matters attached to the record as described in R.C.M. 1103 (b)(3) are not required to be provided.

Discussion

Subsection (b)(1)(E) of this rule was added to implement Article 54(e) in compliance with the National Defense Authorization Act for Fiscal Year 2012 (P.L. 112-81, § 586). The content of the victim's record of trial is prescribed in R.C.M. 1103(g)(3)(D).

Promulgating orders are to be distributed in accordance with R.C.M. 1114(f).

---

(2) *Summary courts-martial.* The summary court-martial record of trial shall be disposed of as provided in R.C.M. 1305(d). Subsection (b)(1)(D) of this rule shall apply if classified information is included in the record of trial of a summary court-martial.

(c) *Loss of record.* If the authenticated record of trial is lost or destroyed, the trial counsel shall, if practicable, cause another record of trial to be prepared for authentication. The new record of trial shall become the record of trial in the case if the requirements of R.C.M. 1103 and this rule are met.

(d) *Correction of record after authentication; certificate of correction.*

(1) *In general.* A record of trial found to be incomplete or defective after authentication may be corrected to make it accurate. A record of trial may be returned to the convening authority by superior competent authority for correction under this rule.

Discussion

The record of trial is corrected with a certificate of correction. *See* Appendix 13 or 14 for a form for a certificate of correction. A certificate of correction may be used only to make the record of trial correspond to the actual proceedings. If the members were not sworn, for example, the error cannot be cured by a certificate of correction. If the members were sworn but the record did not so reflect, the record could be corrected.

---

(2) *Procedure.* An authenticated record of trial believed to be incomplete or defective may be returned to the military judge or summary court-martial for a certificate of correction. The military judge or summary court-martial shall give notice of the proposed correction to all parties and permit them to examine and respond to the proposed correction before authenticating the certificate of correction. All parties shall be given reasonable access to any original reporter's notes or tapes of the proceedings.

Discussion

The type of opportunity to respond depends on the nature and scope of the proposed correction. In many instances an adequate opportunity can be provided by allowing the respective parties to present affidavits and other documentary evidence to the person authenticating the certificate of correction or by a conference telephone call among the authenticating person, the parties, and the reporter. In other instances, an evidentiary hearing with witnesses may be required. The accused need not be present at any hearing on a certificate of correction.

---

(3) *Authentication of certificate of correction; service on the accused.* The certificate of correction shall be authenticated as provided in subsection (a) of this rule and a copy served on the accused as provided in subsection (b) of this rule. The certificate of correction and the accused's receipt for the certificate of correction shall be attached to each copy of the record of trial required to be prepared under R.C.M. 1103(g).

(e) *Forwarding.* After every court-martial, including a rehearing and new and other trials, the authenticated record shall be forwarded to the convening authority for initial review and action, provided that in case of a special court-martial in which a bad-conduct discharge or confinement for one year was adjudged or a general court-martial, the convening authority shall refer the record to the staff judge advocate or legal officer for recommendation under

R.C.M. 1106 before the convening authority takes action.

Rule 1105. Matters submitted by the accused

[Note: R.C.M. 1105(b)(1) and (b)(2)(C) apply to offenses committed on or after 24 June 2014.]

(a) *In general.* After a sentence is adjudged in any court-martial, the accused may submit matters to the convening authority in accordance with this rule.

(b) *Matters which may be submitted.*

(1) The accused may submit to the convening authority any matters that may reasonably tend to affect the convening authority's decision whether to disapprove any findings of guilty or to approve the sentence, except as may be limited by R.C.M. 1107(b)(3)(C). The convening authority is only required to consider written submissions.

(2) Submissions are not subject to the Military Rules of Evidence and may include:

(A) Allegations of errors affecting the legality of the findings or sentence;

(B) Portions or summaries of the record and copies of documentary evidence offered or introduced at trial;

(C) Matters in mitigation that were not available for consideration at the court-martial, except as may be limited by R.C.M. 1107(b)(3)(B); and

Discussion

For example, post-trial conduct of the accused, such as providing restitution to the victim of the accused's offense in accordance with Article 6b(a)(6), or exemplary behavior, might be appropriate.

(D) Clemency recommendations by any member, the military judge, or any other person. The defense may ask any person for such a recommendation.

Discussion

A clemency recommendation should state reasons for the recommendation and should specifically indicate the amount and character of the clemency recommended.

A clemency recommendation by a member should not disclose the vote or opinion of any member expressed in deliberations. Except as provided in R.C.M. 923 and 1008 and Mil. R. Evid. 606(b), a clemency recommendation does not impeach the findings or the sentence. If the sentencing authority makes a clemency recommendation in conjunction with the announced sentence, *see* R.C.M. 1106(d)(3).

Although only written submissions must be considered, the convening authority may consider any submission by the accused, including, but not limited to, videotapes, photographs, and oral presentations.

(c) *Time periods.*

(1) *General and special courts-martial.* After a general or special court-martial, the accused may submit matters under this rule within the later of 10 days after a copy of the authenticated record of trial or, if applicable, the recommendation of the staff judge advocate or legal officer, or an addendum to the recommendation containing new matter is served on the accused. If, within the 10-day period, the accused shows that additional time is required for the accused to submit such matters, the convening authority or that authority's staff judge advocate may, for good cause, extend the 10-day period for not more than 20 additional days; however, only the convening authority may deny a request for such an extension.

(2) *Summary courts-martial.* After a summary court-martial, the accused may submit matters under this rule within 7 days after the sentence is announced. If the accused shows that additional time is required for the accused to submit such comments, the convening authority may, for good cause, extend the period in which comments may be submitted for up to 20 additional days.

(3) *Post-trial sessions.* A post-trial session under R.C.M. 1102 shall have no effect on the running of any time period in this rule, except when such session results in the announcement of a new sentence, in which case the period shall run from that announcement.

(4) *Good cause.* For purposes of this rule, good cause for an extension ordinarily does not include the need for securing matters which could reasonably have been presented at the court-martial.

(d) *Waiver.*

(1) *Failure to submit matters.* Failure to submit matters within the time prescribed by this rule shall be deemed a waiver of the right to submit such matters.

(2) *Submission of matters.* Submission of any matters under this rule shall be deemed a waiver of the right to submit additional matters unless the right to submit additional matters within the prescribed time limits is expressly reserved in writing.

(3) *Written waiver.* The accused may expressly waive, in writing, the right to submit matters under this rule. Once filed, such waiver may not be revoked.

(4) *Absence of accused.* If, as a result of the unauthorized absence of the accused, the record cannot be served on the accused in accordance with R.C.M. 1104(b)(1) and if the accused has no counsel to receive the record, the accused shall be deemed to have waived the right to submit matters under this rule within the time limit which begins upon service on the accused of the record of trial.

Discussion

The accused is not required to raise objections to the trial proceedings in order to preserve them for later review.

Rule 1105A. Matters submitted by a crime victim

(a) *In general.* A crime victim of an offense tried by any court-martial shall have the right to submit a written statement to the convening authority after the sentence is adjudged.

(b) *"Crime victim" defined.* For purposes of this rule, a crime victim is a person who has suffered direct physical, emotional, or pecuniary harm as a result of the commission of an offense of which the accused was found guilty, and on which the convening authority is taking action under R.C.M. 1107. When a victim is under 18 years of age, incompetent, incapacitated, or deceased, the term includes one of the following (in order of precedence): a spouse, legal guardian, parent, child, sibling, or similarly situated family member. For a victim that is an institutional entity, the term includes an authorized representative of the entity.

(c) *Format of statement.* The statement shall be in writing, and signed by the crime victim. Statements may include photographs, but shall not include video, audio, or other media.

Discussion

Statements should be submitted to the convening authority's staff judge advocate or legal officer, or, in the case of a summary court-martial, to the summary court-martial officer.

(d) *Timing of statement.*

(1) *General and special courts-martial.* The crime victim shall submit the statement to the convening authority's staff judge advocate or legal officer no later than 10 days after the later of:

(A) if the victim is entitled to a copy of the record of proceedings in accordance with Article 54(e), the date on which the victim receives an authenticated copy of the record of trial or waives the right to receive such a copy; or

(B) the date on which the recommendation of the staff judge advocate or legal officer is served on the victim.

(2) *Summary courts-martial.* The crime victim shall submit the statement to the summary court-martial officer no later than 7 days after the sentence is announced.

(3) *Extensions.* If a victim shows that additional time is required for submission of matters, the convening authority or other person taking action, for good cause, may extend the submission period for not more than an additional 20 days.

(e) *Notice.* Subject to such regulations as the Secretary concerned may prescribe, trial counsel or the summary court-martial officer shall make reasonable efforts to inform crime victims of their rights under this rule, and shall advise such crime victims on the manner in which their statements may be submitted.

(f) *Waiver.*

(1) *Failure to submit a statement.* Failure to submit a statement within the time prescribed by this rule shall be deemed a waiver of the right to submit such a statement.

(2) *Submission of a statement.* Submission of a statement under this rule shall be deemed a waiver of the right to submit an additional statement.

(3) *Written waiver.* A crime victim may expressly waive, in writing, the right to submit a statement under this rule. Once filed, such waiver may not be revoked.

Rule 1106. Recommendation of the staff judge advocate or legal officer

(a) *In general.* Before the convening authority takes action under R.C.M. 1107 on a record of trial by general court-martial, on a record of trial by special court-martial that includes a sentence to a bad-conduct discharge or confinement for one year, or on a record of trial by special court-martial in which a victim is entitled to submit a statement pursuant to R.C.M. 1105A, that convening authority's staff judge advocate or legal officer shall, except as provided in subsection (c) of this rule, forward to the convening authority a recommendation under this rule.

(b) *Disqualification.* No person who has acted as member, military judge, trial counsel, assistant trial counsel, defense counsel, associate or assistant defense counsel, or preliminary hearing officer in any case may later act as a staff judge advocate or legal officer to any reviewing or convening authority in the same case.

Discussion

The staff judge advocate or legal officer may also be ineligible when, for example, the staff judge advocate or legal officer; served as the defense counsel in a companion case; testified as to a contested matter (unless the testimony is clearly uncontroverted); has other than an official interest in the same case; or must review that officer's own pretrial action (such as the pretrial advice under Article 34; *see* R.C.M. 406) when the sufficiency or correctness of the earlier action has been placed in issue.

(c) *When the convening authority has no staff judge advocate.*

(1) *When the convening authority does not have a staff judge advocate or legal officer or that person is disqualified.* If the convening authority does not have a staff judge advocate or legal officer, or if the person serving in that capacity is disqualified under subsection (b) of this rule or otherwise, the convening authority shall:

(A) Request the assignment of another staff judge advocate or legal officer to prepare a recommendation under this rule; or

(B) Forward the record for action to any officer exercising general court-martial jurisdiction as provided in R.C.M. 1107(a).

(2) *When the convening authority has a legal officer but wants the recommendation of a staff judge advocate.* If the convening authority has a legal officer but no staff judge advocate, the convening authority may, as a matter of discretion, request designation of a staff judge advocate to prepare the recommendation.

(d) *Form and content of recommendation.*

(1) The purpose of the recommendation of the staff judge advocate or legal officer is to assist the convening authority to decide what action to take on

the sentence in the exercise of command preroga- tive. The staff judge advocate or legal officer shall use the record of trial in the preparation of the rec- ommendation, and may also use the personnel re- cords of the accused or other matters in advising the convening authority whether clemency is warranted.

(2) *Form.* The recommendation of the staff judge advocate or legal officer shall be a concise written communication.

(3) *Required contents.* Except as provided in sub- section (e), the staff judge advocate or legal advisor shall provide the convening authority with a copy of the report of results of the trial, setting forth the findings, sentence, and confinement credit to be ap- plied; a copy or summary of the pretrial agreement, if any; a copy of any statement submitted by a crime victim pursuant to R.C.M. 1105A; any recommenda- tion for clemency by the sentencing authority made in conjunction with the announced sentence; and the staff judge advocate's concise recommendation.

Discussion

The recommendation required by this rule need not include information regarding other recommendations for clemency. It may include a summary of clemency actions authorized under R.C.M. 1107. *See* R.C.M. 1105(b)(2)(D) (pertaining to clemency recommendations that may be submitted by the accused to the convening authority).

---

(4) *Legal errors.* The staff judge advocate or legal officer is not required to examine the record for legal errors. However, when the recommendation is prepared by a staff judge advocate, the staff judge advocate shall state whether, in the staff judge advo- cate's opinion, corrective action on the findings or sentence should be taken when an allegation of legal error is raised in matters submitted under R.C.M. 1105 or when otherwise deemed appropriate by the staff judge advocate. The response may consist of a statement of agreement or disagreement with the matter raised by the accused. An analysis or ration- ale for the staff judge advocate's statement, if any, concerning legal error is not required.

(5) *Optional matters.* The recommendation of the staff judge advocate or legal officer may include, in addition to matters included under subsection (d)(3) and (4) of this rule, any additional matters deemed appropriate by the staff judge advocate or legal offi-

cer. Such matter may include matters outside the record.

Discussion

See R.C.M. 1107(b)(3)(B)(iii) if matters adverse to the accused from outside the record are included.

---

(6) *Effect of error.* In case of error in the recom- mendation not otherwise waived under subsection (f)(6) of this rule, appropriate corrective action shall be taken by appellate authorities without returning the case for further action by a convening authority.

(e) *No findings of guilty; findings of not guilty only by reason of lack of mental responsibility.* If the proceedings resulted in an acquittal or in a finding of not guilty only by reason of lack of mental re- sponsibility of all charges and specifications, or if, after the trial began, the proceedings were termi- nated without findings and no further action is con- templated, a recommendation under this rule is not required.

(f) *Service of recommendation on defense counsel, accused, and victim; defense response.*

(1) *Service of recommendation on defense coun- sel, accused, and victim.* Before forwarding the rec- ommendation and the record of trial to the convening authority for action under R.C.M. 1107, the staff judge advocate or legal officer shall cause a copy of the recommendation to be served on the counsel for the accused. A separate copy will be served on the accused. If it is impracticable to serve the recommendation on the accused for reasons in- cluding the transfer of the accused to a different place, the unauthorized absence of the accused, or military exigency, or if the accused so requests on the record at the court-martial or in writing, the accused's copy shall be forwarded to the accused's defense counsel. A statement shall be attached to the record explaining why the accused was not served personally. If the accused was found guilty of any offense that resulted in direct physical, emotional, or pecuniary harm to a victim or victims, a separate copy of the recommendation will be served on that victim or those victims. When a victim is under 18 years of age, incompetent, incapacitated, deceased, or otherwise unavailable, service shall be made on one of the following (in order of precedence): the victim's attorney, spouse, legal guardian, parent, child, sibling, or similarly situated family member.

For a victim that is an institutional entity, service shall be made on an authorized representative of the entity.

Discussion

The method of service and the form of the proof of service are not prescribed and may be by any appropriate means. *See* R.C.M. 1103(b)(3)(G). For example, a certificate of service, attached to the record of trial, would be appropriate when the accused is served personally.

(2) *Counsel for the accused.* The accused may, at trial or in writing to the staff judge advocate or legal officer before the recommendation has been served under this rule, designate which counsel (detailed, individual military, or civilian) will be served with the recommendation. In the absence of such designation, the staff judge advocate or legal officer shall cause the recommendation to be served in the following order of precedence, as applicable, on: (1) civilian counsel; (2) individual military counsel; or (3) detailed defense counsel. If the accused has not retained civilian counsel and the detailed defense counsel and individual military counsel, if any, have been relieved or are not reasonably available to represent the accused, substitute military counsel to represent the accused shall be detailed by an appropriate authority. Substitute counsel shall enter into an attorney-client relationship with the accused before examining the recommendation and preparing any response.

Discussion

When the accused is represented by more than one counsel, the military judge should inquire of the accused and counsel before the end of the court-martial as to who will act for the accused under this rule.

(3) *Record of trial.* The staff judge advocate or legal officer shall, upon request of counsel for the accused served with the recommendation, provide that counsel with a copy of the record of trial for use while preparing the response to the recommendation.

(4) *Response.* Counsel for the accused may submit, in writing, corrections or rebuttal to any matter in the recommendation and its enclosures believed to be erroneous, inadequate, or misleading, and may comment on any other matter.

Discussion

See also R.C.M. 1105.

(5) *Time period.* Counsel for the accused shall be given 10 days from service of the record of trial under R.C.M. 1104(b) or receipt of the recommendation, whichever is later, in which to submit comments on the recommendation. The convening authority may, for good cause, extend the period in which comments may be submitted for up to 20 additional days.

(6) *Waiver.* Failure of counsel for the accused to comment on any matter in the recommendation or matters attached to the recommendation in a timely manner shall waive later claim of error with regard to such matter in the absence of plain error.

Discussion

The accused is not required to raise objections to the trial proceedings in order to preserve them for later review.

(7) *New matter in addendum to recommendation.* The staff judge advocate or legal officer may supplement the recommendation after the accused and counsel for the accused have been served with the recommendation and given an opportunity to comment. When new matter is introduced after the accused and counsel for the accused have examined the recommendation, however, the accused and counsel for the accused must be served with the new matter and given 10 days from service of the addendum in which to submit comments. Substitute service of the accused's copy of the addendum upon counsel for the accused is permitted in accordance with the procedures outlined in subparagraph (f)(1) of this rule.

Discussion

"New matter" includes discussion of the effect of new decisions on issues in the case, matter from outside the record of trial, and issues not previously discussed. "New matter" does not ordinarily include any discussion by the staff judge advocate or legal officer of the correctness of the initial defense comments on the recommendation. The method of service and the form of the proof of service are not prescribed and may be by any appropriate means. *See* R.C.M. 1103(b)(3)(G). For example, a certificate of service, attached to the record of trial, would be appropriate when the accused is served personally. If a victim statement, submitted under R.C.M. 1105A, is served on the accused prior to service of the recommendation, then that statement shall not be considered a "new matter" when it is again served on the accused as an enclosure to the recommendation.

Rule 1107. Action by convening authority

[Note: Subsections (b)-(f) of R.C.M. 1107 apply to offenses committed on or after 24 June 2014; however, if at least one offense resulting in a finding of guilty in a case occurred prior to 24 June 2014, or includes a date range where the earliest date in the range for that offense is before 24 June 2014, then the prior version of R.C.M. 1107 applies to all offenses in the case, except that mandatory minimum sentences under Article 56(b) and applicable rules under R.C.M. 1107(d)(1)(D)-(E) still apply.]

(a) *Who may take action.* The convening authority shall take action on the sentence and, in the discretion of the convening authority, the findings, unless it is impracticable. If it is impracticable for the convening authority to act, the convening authority shall, in accordance with such regulations as the Secretary concerned may prescribe, forward the case to an officer exercising general court-martial jurisdiction who may take action under this rule.

Discussion

The convening authority may not delegate the function of taking action on the findings or sentence. The convening authority who convened the court-martial may take action on the case regardless whether the accused is a member of or present in the convening authority's command.

It would be impracticable for the convening authority to take initial action when, for example, a command has been decommissioned or inactivated before the convening authority's action; when a command has been alerted for immediate overseas movement; or when the convening authority is disqualified because the convening authority has other than an official interest in the case or because a member of the court-martial which tried the accused later became the convening authority.

If the convening authority forwards the case to an officer exercising general court-martial jurisdiction for initial review and action, the record should include a statement of the reasons why the convening authority did not act.

(b) *General considerations.*

(1) *Discretion of convening authority.* Any action to be taken on the findings and sentence is within the sole discretion of the convening authority. The convening authority is not required to review the case for legal errors or factual sufficiency.

Discussion

The action is taken in the interests of justice, discipline, mission requirements, clemency, and other appropriate reasons. If errors

are noticed by the convening authority, the convening authority may take corrective action under this rule to the extent that the convening authority is empowered by Article 60.

---

(2) *When action may be taken.* The convening authority may take action only after the applicable time periods under R.C.M. 1105(c) have expired or the accused has waived the right to present matters under R.C.M. 1105(d), whichever is earlier, subject to regulations of the Secretary concerned.

(3) *Matters considered.*

(A) *Required matters.* Before taking action, the convening authority shall consider:

(i) The result of trial;

Discussion

See R.C.M. 1101(a).

(ii) The recommendation of the staff judge advocate or legal officer under R.C.M. 1106, if applicable; and

(iii) Any matters submitted by the accused under R.C.M. 1105 or, if applicable, R.C.M. 1106(f);

(iv) Any statement submitted by a crime victim pursuant to R.C.M. 1105A and subsection (C) of this rule.

(B) *Additional matters.* Before taking action the convening authority may consider:

(i) The record of trial, subject to the provisions of R.C.M. 1103A and subsection (C) of this rule;

(ii) The personnel records of the accused; and

(iii) Such other matters as the convening authority deems appropriate. However, if the convening authority considers matters adverse to the accused from outside the record, with knowledge of which the accused is not chargeable, the accused shall be notified and given an opportunity to rebut.

(C) *Prohibited matters.* The convening authority shall not consider any matters that relate to the character of a victim unless such matters were presented as evidence at trial and not excluded at trial.

(4) *When proceedings resulted in finding of not guilty or not guilty only by reason of lack of mental responsibility, or there was a ruling amounting to a finding of not guilty.* The convening authority shall

not take action disapproving a finding of not guilty, a finding of not guilty only by reason of lack of mental responsibility, or a ruling amounting to a finding of not guilty. When an accused is found not guilty only by reason of lack of mental responsibility, the convening authority, however, shall commit the accused to a suitable facility pending a hearing and disposition in accordance with R.C.M. 1102A.

Discussion

Commitment of the accused to the custody of the Attorney General for hospitalization is discretionary.

(5) *Action when accused lacks mental capacity.* The convening authority may not approve a sentence while the accused lacks mental capacity to understand and to conduct or cooperate intelligently in the post-trial proceedings. In the absence of substantial evidence to the contrary, the accused is presumed to have the capacity to understand and to conduct or cooperate intelligently in the post-trial proceedings. If a substantial question is raised as to the requisite mental capacity of the accused, the convening authority may direct an examination of the accused in accordance with R.C.M. 706 before deciding whether the accused lacks mental capacity, but the examination may be limited to determining the accused's present capacity to understand and cooperate in the post-trial proceedings. The convening authority may approve the sentence unless it is established, by a preponderance of the evidence—including matters outside the record of trial—that the accused does not have the requisite mental capacity.

(c) *Action on findings.* Action on the findings is not required. However, the convening authority may take action subject to the following limitations:

(1) Where a court-martial includes a finding of guilty for an offense listed in subparagraph (c)(1)(A) of this rule, the convening authority may not take the actions listed in subparagraph (c)(1)(B) of this rule:

(A) *Offenses*

(i) Article 120(a) or (b), Article 120b, or Article 125;

(ii) Offenses for which the maximum sentence of confinement that may be adjudged exceeds two years without regard to the jurisdictional limits of the court; or

(iii) Offenses where the adjudged sentence for the case includes dismissal, dishonorable discharge, bad-conduct discharge, or confinement for more than six months.

(B) *Prohibited actions*

(i) Dismiss a charge or specification by setting aside a finding of guilty thereto; or

(ii) Change a finding of guilty to a charge or specification to a finding of guilty to an offense that is a lesser included offense of the offense stated in the charge or specification.

(2) The convening authority may direct a rehearing in accordance with subsection (e) of this rule.

Discussion

The military follows a unitary sentencing model where the court-martial may impose only a single, unitary sentence covering all of the offenses for which there was a finding of guilty; courts-martial do not impose sentences per offense. *See* R.C.M. 1002(b). Therefore, where the adjudged sentence for the case includes dismissal, dishonorable discharge, bad-conduct discharge, or confinement for more than six months, the sentence adjudged for the entire case, and not per offense, controls when deciding what actions are available to the convening authority.

(3) For offenses other than those listed in subparagraph (c)(1)(A) of this rule:

(A) The convening authority may change a finding of guilty to a charge or specification to a finding of guilty to an offense that is a lesser included offense of the offense stated in the charge or specification; or

(B) Set aside any finding of guilty and:

(i) Dismiss the specification and, if appropriate, the charge; or

(ii) Direct a rehearing in accordance with subsection (e) of this rule.

(4) If the convening authority acts to dismiss or change any charge or specification for an offense, the convening authority shall provide, at the same time, a written explanation of the reasons for such action. The written explanation shall be made a part of the record of trial and action thereon.

(d) *Action on the sentence.*

(1) The convening authority shall take action on the sentence subject to the following:

(A) The convening authority may disapprove, commute, or suspend, in whole or in part, any portion of an adjudged sentence not explicitly prohibited by this rule, to include reduction in pay grade, forfeitures of pay and allowances, fines, reprimands, restrictions, and hard labor without confinement.

(B) Except as provided in subparagraph (d)(1)(C) of this rule, the convening authority may not disapprove, commute, or suspend, in whole or in part, that portion of an adjudged sentence that includes:

(i) confinement for more than six months; or

(ii) dismissal, dishonorable discharge, or bad-conduct discharge.

(C) *Exceptions.*

(i) *Trial counsel recommendation.* Upon the recommendation of the trial counsel, in recognition of the substantial assistance by the accused in the investigation or prosecution of another person who has committed an offense, the convening authority or another person authorized to act under this rule shall have the authority to disapprove, commute, or suspend the adjudged sentence, in whole or in part, even with respect to an offense for which a mandatory minimum sentence exists.

Discussion

The phrase "investigation or prosecution of another person who has committed an offense" includes offenses under the UCMJ or other Federal, State, local, or foreign criminal statutes.

(ii) *Pretrial agreement.* If a pretrial agreement has been entered into by the convening authority and the accused, as authorized by R.C.M. 705, the convening authority or another person authorized to act under this rule shall have the authority to approve, disapprove, commute, or suspend a sentence, in whole or in part, pursuant to the terms of the pretrial agreement. However, if a mandatory minimum sentence of a dishonorable discharge applies to an offense for which an accused has been convicted, the convening authority or another person authorized to act under this rule may commute the dishonorable discharge to a bad-conduct discharge pursuant to the terms of the pretrial agreement.

(D) If the convening authority acts to disapprove, commute, or suspend, in whole or in part, the sentence of the court-martial for an offense listed in subparagraph (c)(1)(A) of this rule, the convening authority shall provide, at the same time, a written explanation of the reasons for such action. The writ-

ten explanation shall be made a part of the record of trial and action thereon.

Discussion

A sentence adjudged by a court-martial may be approved if it was within the jurisdiction of the court-martial to adjudge (*see* R.C.M.201(f)) and did not exceed the maximum limits prescribed in Part IV and Chapter X of this Part for the offense(s) of which the accused legally has been found guilty.

When mitigating forfeitures, the duration and amounts of forfeiture may be changed as long as the total amount forfeited is not increased and neither the amount nor duration of the forfeitures exceeds the jurisdiction of the court-martial. When mitigating confinement or hard labor without confinement, the convening authority should use the equivalencies at R.C.M. 1003(b)(5)–(6), as appropriate.

Unless prohibited by this rule, the convening authority may disapprove, mitigate, or change to a less severe punishment any individual component of a sentence. For example, if an accused is found guilty of assault consummated by a battery and sentenced to a bad-conduct discharge, three months of confinement, and reduction to E-1, without a pre-trial agreement and without being able to apply the substantial assistance exception, the convening authority may disapprove or reduce any part of the sentence except the bad-conduct discharge.

---

(2) *Determining what sentence should be approved.* The convening authority shall, subject to the limitations in subsection (d)(1) above, approve that sentence that is warranted by the circumstances of the offense and appropriate for the accused.

Discussion

In determining what sentence should be approved, the convening authority should consider all relevant and permissible factors including the possibility of rehabilitation, the deterrent effect of the sentence, and all matters relating to clemency, such as pretrial confinement. *See also* R.C.M. 1001-1004.

When an accused is not serving confinement, the accused should not be deprived of more than two-thirds pay for any month as a result of one or more sentences by court-martial and other stoppages or involuntary deductions, unless requested by the accused. Since court-martial forfeitures constitute a loss of entitlement of the pay concerned, they take precedence over all debts.

---

(3) *Deferring service of a sentence to confinement.*

(A) In a case in which a court-martial sentences an accused referred to in subsection (B), below, to confinement, the convening authority may defer service of a sentence to confinement by a court-martial, without the consent of the accused, until after the accused has been permanently released to the armed forces by a state or foreign country.

(B) Subsection (A) applies to an accused who, while in custody of a state or foreign country, is temporarily returned by that state or foreign country to the armed forces for trial by court-martial; and after the court-martial, is returned to that state or foreign country under the authority of a mutual agreement or treaty, as the case may be.

(C) As used in subsection (d)(3), the term "state" means a state of the United States, the District of Columbia, a territory, and a possession of the United States.

Discussion

The convening authority's decision to postpone service of a court-martial sentence to confinement normally should be reflected in the action.

(4) *Limitations on sentence based on record of trial.* If the record of trial does not meet the requirements of R.C.M. 1103(b)(2)(B) or (c)(1), the convening authority may not approve a sentence in excess of that which may be adjudged by a special court-martial, or one that includes a bad-conduct discharge, confinement for more than six months, forfeiture of pay exceeding two-thirds pay per month, or any forfeiture of pay for more than six months.

Discussion

See also R.C.M. 1103(f).

(5) *Limitations on sentence of a special court-martial where a fine has been adjudged.* A convening authority may not approve in its entirety a sentence adjudged at a special court-martial when, if approved, the cumulative impact of the fine and forfeitures, whether adjudged or by operation of Article 58b, would exceed the jurisdictional maximum dollar amount of forfeitures that may be adjudged at that court-martial.

(e) *Ordering rehearing or other trial.*

(1) *Rehearings not permitted.* A rehearing may not be ordered by the convening authority where the adjudged sentence for the case includes a sentence of dismissal, dishonorable discharge, or bad-conduct discharge or confinement for more than six months.

Discussion

Pursuant to Article 60(c)(4)(A) and subsection (d)(1)(A) and (B) of this rule, disapproval of the sentence is not authorized where a court-martial's adjudged sentence for the case includes confinement for more than six months or a sentence of dismissal, dishonorable discharge, or bad- conduct discharge. In such cases, the convening authority may not order a rehearing because disapproval of the sentence is required for a convening authority to order a rehearing. *See* Article 60(f)(3).

(2) *Rehearings permitted.*

(A) *In general.* Subject to paragraph (e)(1) and subparagraphs (e)(2)(B) through (e)(2)(E) of this rule, the convening authority may in the convening authority's discretion order a rehearing. A rehearing may be ordered as to some or all offenses of which findings of guilty were entered and the sentence, or as to the sentence only.

(B) *When the convening authority may order a rehearing.* The convening authority may order a rehearing:

(i) *When taking action on the court-martial under this rule.* Prior to ordering a rehearing on a finding, the convening authority must disapprove the applicable finding and the sentence and state the reasons for disapproval of said finding. Prior to ordering a rehearing on the sentence, the convening authority must disapprove the sentence.

(ii) *When authorized to do so by superior competent authority.* If the convening authority finds a rehearing as to any offenses impracticable, the convening authority may dismiss those specifications and, when appropriate, charges.

(iii) *Sentence reassessment.* If a superior competent authority has approved some of the findings of guilty and has authorized a rehearing as to other offenses and the sentence, the convening authority may, unless otherwise directed, reassess the sentence based on the approved findings of guilty and dismiss the remaining charges. Reassessment is appropriate only where the convening authority determines that the accused's sentence would have been at least of a certain magnitude had the prejudicial error not been committed and the reassessed sentence is appropriate in relation to the affirmed findings of guilty.

Discussion

A sentence rehearing, rather than a reassessment, may be more appropriate in cases where a significant part of the government's case has been dismissed. The convening authority may not take any actions inconsistent with directives of superior competent authority. Where that directive is unclear, appropriate clarification should be sought from the authority issuing the original directive. For purposes of R.C.M. 1107(e)(1)(B), the term "superior competent authority" does not include superior convening authorities but rather, for example, the appropriate Judge Advocate General or a court of competent jurisdiction.

(C) *Limitations.*

(i) *Sentence approved.* A rehearing shall not be ordered if, in the same action, a sentence is approved.

(ii) *Lack of sufficient evidence.* A rehearing may not be ordered as to findings of guilty when there is a lack of sufficient evidence in the record to support the findings of guilty of the offense charged or of any lesser included offense. A rehearing may be ordered, however, if the proof of guilt consisted of inadmissible evidence for which there is available an admissible substitute. A rehearing may be ordered as to any lesser offense included in an offense of which the accused was found guilty, provided there is sufficient evidence in the record to support the lesser included offense.

Discussion

For example, if proof of absence without leave was by improperly authenticated documentary evidence admitted over the objection of the defense, the convening authority may disapprove the findings of guilty and sentence and order a rehearing if there is reason to believe that properly authenticated documentary evidence or other admissible evidence of guilt will be available at the rehearing. On the other hand, if no proof of unauthorized absence was introduced at trial, a rehearing may not be ordered.

(iii) *Rehearing on sentence only.* A rehearing on sentence only shall not be referred to a different kind of court-martial from that which made the original findings. If the convening authority determines a rehearing on sentence is impracticable, the convening authority may approve a sentence of no punishment without conducting a rehearing.

(D) *Additional charges.* Additional charges may be referred for trial together with charges as to which a rehearing has been directed.

(E) *Lesser included offenses.* If at a previous trial the accused was convicted of a lesser included offense, a rehearing may be ordered only as to that included offense or as to a lesser included offense of the included offense that resulted in a finding of guilty at the previous trial. If, however, a rehearing is ordered improperly on the original offense charged and the accused is convicted of that offense at the rehearing, the finding as to the lesser included offense of which the accused was convicted at the original trial may nevertheless be approved.

(3) *"Other" trial.* The convening or higher authority may order an "other" trial if the original proceedings were invalid because of lack of jurisdiction or failure of a specification to state an offense. The authority ordering an "other" trial shall state in the action the basis for declaring the proceedings invalid.

(f) *Contents of action and related matters.*

(1) *In general.* The convening authority shall state in writing and insert in the record of trial the convening authority's decision as to the sentence, whether any findings of guilty are disapproved, and orders as to further disposition. The action shall be signed personally by the convening authority. The convening authority's authority to sign shall appear below the signature.

Discussion

See Appendix 16 for forms.

---

(2) *Modification of initial action.* Subject to the limitations in subsections (c) and (d) of this rule, the convening authority may recall and modify any action taken by that convening authority at any time before it has been published or before the accused has been officially notified. The convening authority may also recall and modify any action at any time prior to forwarding the record for review, as long as the modification does not result in action less favorable to the accused than the earlier action. In addition, in any special court-martial, the convening authority may recall and correct an illegal, erroneous, incomplete, or ambiguous action at any time before completion of review under R.C.M. 1112, as long as the correction does not result in action less favorable to the accused than the earlier action. When so directed by a higher reviewing authority or the Judge Advocate General, the convening authority shall modify any incomplete, ambiguous, void, or inaccurate action noted in review of the record of trial under Articles 64, 66, 67, or examination of the record of trial under Article 69. The convening au-

thority shall personally sign any supplementary or corrective action. A written explanation is required for any modification of initial action that: (1) sets aside any finding of guilt or dismisses or changes any charge or specification for an offense; or (2) disapproves, commutes, or suspends, in whole or in part, the sentence. The written explanation shall be made a part of the record of trial and action thereon.

Discussion

For purposes of this rule, a record is considered to have been forwarded for review when the convening authority has either delivered it in person or has entrusted it for delivery to a third party over whom the convening authority exercises no lawful control (*e.g.*, the United States Postal Service).

(3) *Findings of guilty.* If any findings of guilty are disapproved, the action shall so state. If a rehearing is not ordered, the affected charges and specifications shall be dismissed by the convening authority in the action. If a rehearing or other trial is directed, the reasons for the disapproval shall be set forth in the action.

Discussion

If a rehearing or other trial is not directed, the reasons for disapproval need not be stated in the action, but they may be when appropriate. It may be appropriate to state them when the reasons may affect administrative disposition of the accused; for example, when the finding is disapproved because of the lack of mental responsibility of the accused or the running of the statute of limitations.

No express action is necessary to approve findings of guilty. *See* subsection (c) of this rule.

(4) *Action on sentence.*

(A) *In general.* The action shall state whether the sentence adjudged by the court-martial is approved. If only part of the sentence is approved, the action shall state which parts are approved. A rehearing may not be directed if any sentence is approved.

Discussion

See Appendix 16 for forms.
See R.C.M. 1108 concerning suspension of sentences.
See R.C.M. 1113 concerning execution of sentences.

(B) *Execution; suspension.* The action shall indicate, when appropriate, whether an approved sentence is to be executed or whether the execution of all or any part of the sentence is to be suspended. No reasons need be stated.

(C) *Place of confinement.* If the convening authority orders a sentence of confinement into execution, the convening authority shall designate the place of confinement in the action, unless otherwise prescribed by the Secretary concerned. If a sentence of confinement is ordered into execution after the initial action of the convening authority, the authority ordering the execution shall designate the place of confinement unless otherwise prescribed by the Secretary concerned.

Discussion

See R.C.M. 1113(e)(2)(C) concerning the place of confinement.

(D) *Custody or confinement pending appellate review; capital cases.* When a record of trial involves an approved sentence to death, the convening authority shall, unless any approved sentence of confinement has been ordered into execution and a place of confinement designated, provide in the action for the temporary custody or confinement of the accused pending final disposition of the case on appellate review.

(E) *Deferment of service of sentence to confinement.* Whenever the service of the sentence to confinement is deferred by the convening authority under R.C.M. 1101(c) before or concurrently with the initial action in the case, the action shall include the date on which the deferment became effective. The reason for the deferment need not be stated in the action.

(F) *Credit for illegal pretrial confinement.* When the military judge has directed that the accused receive credit under R.C.M. 305(k), the convening authority shall so direct in the action.

(G) *Reprimand.* The convening authority shall include in the action any reprimand which the convening authority has ordered executed.

Discussion

See R.C.M. 1003(b)(1) concerning reprimands.

(5) *Action on rehearing or new or other trial.*

(A) *Rehearing or other trial.* In acting on a rehearing or other trial the convening authority shall be subject to the sentence limitations prescribed in R.C.M. 810(d). Except when a rehearing or other trial is combined with a trial on additional offenses and except as otherwise provided in R.C.M. 810(d), if any part of the original sentence was suspended and the suspension was not properly vacated before the order directing the rehearing, the convening authority shall take the necessary suspension action to prevent an increase in the same type of punishment as was previously suspended. The convening authority may approve a sentence adjudged upon a rehearing or other trial regardless whether any kind or amount of the punishment adjudged at the former trial has been served or executed. However, in computing the term or amount of punishment to be actually served or executed under the new sentence, the accused shall be credited with any kind or amount of the former sentence included within the new sentence that was served or executed before the time it was disapproved or set aside. The convening authority shall, if any part of a sentence adjudged upon a rehearing or other trial is approved, direct in the action that any part or amount of the former sentence served or executed between the date it was adjudged and the date it was disapproved or set aside shall be credited to the accused. If, in the action on the record of a rehearing, the convening authority disapproves the findings of guilty of all charges and specifications which were tried at the former hearing and that part of the sentence which was based on these findings, the convening authority shall, unless a further rehearing is ordered, provide in the action that all rights, privileges, and property affected by any executed portion of the sentence adjudged at the former hearing shall be restored. The convening authority shall take the same restorative action if a court-martial at a rehearing acquits the accused of all charges and specifications which were tried at the former hearing.

(B) *New trial.* The action of the convening authority on a new trial shall, insofar as practicable, conform to the rules prescribed for rehearings and other trials in subsection (f)(5)(A) of this rule.

Discussion

See R.C.M. 810 for procedures at other trials.

In approving a sentence not in excess of or more severe than one previously approved (*see* R.C.M. 810(d)), a convening authority is prohibited from approving a punitive discharge more severe than one formerly approved, e.g., a convening authority is prohibited from approving a dishonorable discharge if a bad con-

duct discharge had formerly been approved. Otherwise, in approving a sentence not in excess of or more severe than one previously imposed, a convening authority is not limited to approving the same or lesser type of "other punishments" formerly approved.

(g) *Incomplete, ambiguous, or erroneous action.* When the action of the convening authority or of a higher authority is incomplete or ambiguous or contains error, the authority who took the incomplete, ambiguous, or erroneous action may be instructed by an authority acting under Articles 64, 66, 67, 67a, or 69 to withdraw the original action and substitute a corrected action.

(h) *Service on accused.* A copy of the convening authority's action shall be served on the accused or on defense counsel. If the action is served on defense counsel, defense counsel shall, by expeditious means, provide the accused with a copy.

Discussion

If the promulgating order is prepared promptly, service of it will satisfy subsection (h).

Rule 1108. Suspension of execution of sentence; remission

(a) *In general.* Suspension of a sentence grants the accused a probationary period during which the suspended part of an approved sentence is not executed, and upon the accused's successful completion of which the suspended part of the sentence shall be remitted. Remission cancels the unexecuted part of a sentence to which it applies.

(b) *Who may suspend and remit.*
[Note: R.C.M. 1108(b) applies to offenses committed on or after 24 June 2014; however, if at least one offense in a case occurred prior to 24 June 2014, then the prior version of R.C.M. 1108(b) applies to all offenses in the case.]

The convening authority may, after approving the sentence, suspend the execution of all or any part of the sentence of a court-martial, except for a sentence of death or as prohibited under R.C.M. 1107(d). The general court-martial convening authority over the accused at the time of the court-martial may, when taking action under R.C.M. 1112(f), suspend or remit any part of the sentence. The Secretary concerned and, when designated by the Secretary concerned, any Under Secretary, Assistant Secretary, Judge Advocate General, or commanding officer may suspend or remit any part or amount of the unexecuted part of any sentence other than a sentence approved by the President or a sentence of confinement for life without eligibility for parole that has been ordered executed. The Secretary concerned may, however, suspend or remit the unexecuted part of a sentence of confinement for life without eligibility for parole after the service of a period of confinement of not less than 20 years. The commander of the accused who has the authority to convene a court-martial of the kind that adjudged the sentence may suspend or remit any part of the unexecuted part of any sentence by summary court-martial or of any sentence by special court-martial that does not include a bad-conduct discharge regardless of whether the person acting has previously approved the sentence. The "unexecuted part of any sentence" is that part that has been approved and ordered executed but that has not actually been carried out.

Discussion

See R.C.M. 1113 (execution of sentences); R.C.M. 1201 (action by the Judge Advocate General); R.C.M. 1206 (powers and responsibilities of the Secretary).

The military judge and members of courts-martial may not suspend sentences.

The limitations on suspension of the execution of any sentence or part thereof contained in Article 60 apply to a decision by a convening authority or other person acting on the case under Article 60, as opposed to an individual remitting or suspending a sentence pursuant to a different authority, such as Article 74. *See* R.C.M. 1107(d).

(c) *Conditions of suspension.* The authority who suspends the execution of the sentence of a court-martial shall:

(1) Specify in writing the conditions of the suspension;

(2) Cause a copy of the conditions of the suspension to be served on the probationer; and

(3) Cause a receipt to be secured from the probationer for service of the conditions of the suspension.

Unless otherwise stated, an action suspending a sentence includes as a condition that the probationer not violate any punitive article of the code.

(d) *Limitations on suspension.* Suspension shall be for a stated period or until the occurrence of an anticipated future event. The period shall not be unreasonably long. The Secretary concerned may further limit by regulations the period for which the execution of a sentence may be suspended. The convening authority shall provide in the action that unless the suspension is sooner vacated, the expiration of the period of suspension shall remit the suspended portion of the sentence. An appropriate authority may, before the expiration of the period of suspension, remit any part of the sentence, including a part which has been suspended; reduce the period of suspension; or, subject to R.C.M. 1109, vacate the suspension in whole or in part.

(e) *Termination of suspension by remission.* Expiration of the period provided in the action suspending a sentence or part of a sentence shall remit the suspended portion unless the suspension is sooner vacated. Death or separation which terminates status as a person subject to the code shall result in remission of the suspended portion of the sentence.

Discussion

See R.C.M. 1109(b)(4) concerning interruption of the period of suspension.

Rule 1109. Vacation of suspension of sentence

(a) *In general.* Suspension of execution of the sentence of a court-martial may be vacated for violation of any condition of the suspension as provided in this rule.

(b) *Timeliness.*

(1) *Violation of conditions.* Vacation shall be based on a violation of the conditions of suspension which occurs within the period of suspension.

(2) *Vacation proceedings.* Vacation proceedings under this rule shall be completed within a reasonable time.

(3) *Order vacating the suspension.* The order vacating the suspension shall be issued before the expiration of the period of suspension.

Discussion

The order vacating a suspended sentence must be issued before the end of suspension even though, in certain cases, it may not be effective as an order of execution of the suspended sentence until the completion of appellate review or action by the President or the Secretary concerned. *See* R.C.M. 1113 concerning execution of sentences.

---

(4) *Interruptions to the period of suspension.* Unauthorized absence of the probationer or the commencement of proceedings under this rule to vacate suspension interrupts the running of the period of suspension.

(c) *Confinement of probationer pending vacation proceedings.*

(1) *In general.* A probationer under a suspended sentence to confinement may be confined pending action under subsection (d)(2) of this rule, in accordance with the procedures in this subsection.

(2) *Who may order confinement.* Any person who may order pretrial restraint under R.C.M. 304(b) may order confinement of a probationer under a suspended sentence to confinement.

(3) *Basis for confinement.* A probationer under a suspended sentence to confinement may be ordered into confinement upon probable cause to believe the probationer violated any conditions of the suspension.

Discussion

A determination that confinement is necessary to ensure the presence of the probationer or to prevent further misconduct is not required.

If the violation of the conditions also constitutes an offense under the code for which trial by court-martial is considered, an appropriate form of pretrial restraint may be imposed as an alternative to confinement under this rule. *See* R.C.M. 304 and 305.

---

(4) *Review of confinement.* Unless proceedings under subsection (d)(1), (e), (f), or (g) of this rule are completed within 7 days of imposition of confinement of the probationer (not including any delays requested by probationer), a preliminary hearing shall be conducted by a neutral and detached officer appointed in accordance with regulations of the Secretary concerned.

(A) *Rights of probationer.* Before the preliminary hearing, the probationer shall be notified in writing of:

(i) The time, place, and purpose of the hearing, including the alleged violation(s) of the conditions of suspension;

(ii) The right to be present at the hearing;

(iii) The right to be represented at the hearing by civilian counsel provided by the probationer or, upon request, by military counsel detailed for this purpose; and

(iv) The opportunity to be heard, to present witnesses who are reasonably available and other evidence, and the right to confront and cross-examine adverse witnesses unless the hearing officer determines that this would subject these witnesses to risk or harm. For purposes of this subsection, a witness is not reasonably available if the witness requires reimbursement by the United States for cost incurred in appearing, cannot appear without unduly delaying the proceedings or, if a military witness, cannot be excused from other important duties.

(B) *Rules of evidence.* Except for Mil. R. Evid. Section V (Privileges) and Mil. R. Evid. 302 and 305, the Military Rules of Evidence shall not apply to matters considered at the preliminary hearing under this rule.

(C) *Decision.* The hearing officer shall determine whether there is probable cause to believe that the probationer violated the conditions of the probationer's suspension. If the hearing officer determines that probable cause is lacking, the hearing officer shall issue a written order directing that the probationer be released from confinement. If the hearing officer determines that there is probable cause to believe that the probationer violated a condition of suspension, the hearing officer shall set forth this determination in a written memorandum that details therein the evidence relied upon and reasons for making the decision. The hearing officer shall forward the original memorandum or release order to the probationer's commander and forward a copy to the probationer and the officer in charge of the confinement facility.

(d) *Vacation of suspended general court-martial sentence.*

(1) *Action by officer having special court-martial jurisdiction over probationer.*

(A) *In general.* Before vacation of the suspension of any general court-martial sentence, the officer having special court-martial jurisdiction over the probationer shall personally hold a hearing on the alleged violation of the conditions of suspension. If there is no officer having special court-martial jurisdiction over the probationer who is subordinate to the officer having general court-martial jurisdiction over the probationer, the officer exercising general court-martial jurisdiction over the probationer shall personally hold a hearing under subsection (d)(1) of this rule. In such cases, subsection (d)(1)(D) of this rule shall not apply. The purpose of the hearing is for the hearing officer to determine whether there is probable cause to believe that the probationer violated a condition of the probationer's suspension.

(B) *Notice to probationer.* Before the hearing, the officer conducting the hearing shall cause the probationer to be notified in writing of:

(i) The time, place, and purpose of the hearing;

(ii) The right to be present at the hearing;

(iii) The alleged violation(s) of the conditions of suspension and the evidence expected to be relied on;

(iv) The right to be represented at the hearing by civilian counsel provided by the probationer or, upon request, by military counsel detailed for this purpose; and

(v) The opportunity to be heard, to present witnesses and other evidence, and the right to confront and cross-examine adverse witnesses unless the hearing officer determines that there is good cause for not allowing confrontation and cross-examination.

Discussion

The notice should be provided sufficiently in advance of the hearing to permit adequate preparation.

(C) *Hearing.* The procedure for the vacation hearing shall follow that prescribed in subsection (h) of this rule.

(D) *Record and recommendation.* The officer who conducts the vacation proceeding shall make a summarized record of the proceeding and forward the record and that officer's written recommendation concerning vacation to the officer exercising general court-martial jurisdiction over the probationer. This record shall include the recommendation, the evidence relied upon, and reasons for making the decision.

(E) *Release from confinement.* If the special court-martial convening authority finds there is not probable cause to believe that the probationer violated the conditions of the suspension, the special court-martial convening authority shall order the release of the probationer from any confinement or-

dered under subsection (c) of this rule. The special court-martial convening authority shall, in any event, forward the record and recommendation under subsection (d)(1)(D) of this rule.

Discussion

See Appendix 18 for a sample of a Report of Proceedings to Vacate Suspension of a General Court-Martial Sentence under Article 72, UCMJ, and R.C.M. 1109 (DD Form 455).

(2) *Action by officer exercising general court-martial jurisdiction over probationer.*

(A) *In general.* The officer exercising general court-martial jurisdiction over the probationer shall review the record produced by and the recommendation of the officer exercising special court-martial jurisdiction over the probationer, decide whether there is probable cause to believe that the probationer violated a condition of the probationer's suspension, and, if so, decide whether to vacate the suspended sentence. If the officer exercising general court-martial jurisdiction decides to vacate the suspended sentence, that officer shall prepare a written statement of the evidence relied on and the reasons for vacating the suspended sentence.

(B) *Execution.* Any unexecuted part of a suspended sentence ordered vacated under this rule shall, subject to R.C.M. 1113(c), be ordered executed.

(e) *Vacation of a suspended special court-martial sentence wherein a bad-conduct discharge or confinement for one year was not adjudged.*

(1) *In general.* Before vacating the suspension of a special court-martial punishment that does not include a bad-conduct discharge or confinement for one year, the special court-martial convening authority for the command in which the probationer is serving or assigned shall cause a hearing to be held on the alleged violation(s) of the conditions of suspension. The purpose of the hearing is for the hearing officer to determine whether there is probable cause to believe that the probationer violated the conditions of the probationer's suspension.

(2) *Notice to probationer.* The person conducting the hearing shall notify the probationer, in writing, before the hearing of the rights specified in subsection (d)(1)(B) of this rule.

(3) *Hearing.* The procedure for the vacation hear-

ing shall follow that prescribed in subsection (h) of this rule.

(4) *Authority to vacate suspension.* The special court-martial convening authority for the command in which the probationer is serving or assigned shall have the authority to vacate any punishment that the officer has the authority to order executed.

(5) *Record and recommendation.* If the hearing is not held by the commander with authority to vacate the suspension, the person who conducts the hearing shall make a summarized record of the hearing and forward the record and that officer's written recommendation concerning vacation to the commander with authority to vacate the suspension. This record shall include the recommendation, the evidence relied upon, and reasons for making the decision.

(6) *Decision.* The special court-martial convening authority shall review the record produced by and the recommendation of the person who conducted the vacation proceeding, decide whether there is probable cause to believe that the probationer violated a condition of the probationer's suspension, and, if so, decide whether to vacate the suspended sentence. If the officer exercising jurisdiction decides to vacate the suspended sentence, that officer shall prepare a written statement of the evidence relied on and the reasons for vacating the suspended sentence.

(7) *Execution.* Any unexecuted part of a suspended sentence ordered vacated under this subsection shall be ordered executed.

(f) *Vacation of a suspended special court-martial sentence that includes a bad-conduct discharge or confinement for one year.*

(1) The procedure for the vacation of a suspended approved bad-conduct discharge or of any suspended portion of an approved sentence to confinement for one year, shall follow that set forth in subsection (d) of this rule.

(2) The procedure for the vacation of a suspension of any lesser special court-martial punishment shall follow that set forth in subsection (e) of this rule.

Discussion

An officer exercising special court-martial jurisdiction may vacate any suspended punishments other than an approved suspended bad-conduct discharge or any suspended portion of an approved sentence to confinement for one year, regardless of whether they are contained in the same sentence as the bad-conduct discharge

or confinement for one year. See Appendix 18 for a sample of a Report of Proceedings to Vacate Suspension of a Special Court-Martial Sentence including a bad-conduct discharge or confinement for one year under Article 72, UCMJ, and R.C.M. 1109 (DD Form 455).

(g) *Vacation of a suspended summary court-martial sentence.*

(1) Before vacation of the suspension of a summary court-martial sentence, the summary court-martial convening authority for the command in which the probationer is serving or assigned shall cause a hearing to be held on the alleged violation(s) of the conditions of suspension. The purpose of the hearing is for the hearing officer to determine whether there is probable cause to believe that the probationer violated the conditions of the probationer's suspension.

(2) *Notice to probationer.* The person conducting the hearing shall notify the probationer before the hearing of the rights specified in subsections (d)(1)(B)(i), (ii), (iii), and (v) of this rule.

(3) *Hearing.* The procedure for the vacation hearing shall follow that prescribed in subsection (h) of this rule.

(4) *Authority to vacate suspension.* The summary court-martial convening authority for the command in which the probationer is serving or assigned shall have the authority to vacate any punishment that the officer had the authority to order executed.

(5) *Record and recommendation.* If the hearing is not held by the commander with authority to vacate the suspension, the person who conducts the vacation proceeding shall make a summarized record of the proceeding and forward the record and that officer's written recommendation concerning vacation to the commander with authority to vacate the suspension. This record shall include the recommendation, the evidence relied upon, and reasons for making the decision.

(6) *Decision.* A commander with authority to vacate the suspension shall review the record produced by and the recommendation of the person who conducted the vacation proceeding, decide whether there is probable cause to believe that the probationer violated a condition of the probationer's suspension, and, if so, decide whether to vacate the suspended sentence. If the officer exercising jurisdiction decides to vacate the suspended sentence, that officer shall prepare a written statement of the evidence

relied on and the reasons for vacating the suspended sentence.

(7) *Execution.* Any unexecuted part of a suspended sentence ordered vacated under this subsection shall be ordered executed.

(h) *Hearing procedure.*

(1) *Generally.* The hearing shall begin with the hearing officer informing the probationer of the probationer's rights. The government will then present evidence. Upon the conclusion of the government's presentation of evidence, the probationer may present evidence. The probationer shall have full opportunity to present any matters in defense, extenuation, or mitigation. Both the government and probationer shall be afforded an opportunity to cross-examine adverse witnesses. The hearing officer may also question witnesses called by the parties.

(2) *Rules of evidence.* The Military Rules of Evidence—other than Mil. R. Evid. 301, 302, 303, 305, 412, and Section V—shall not apply. Nor shall Mil. R. Evid. 412(b)(1)(C) apply. In applying these rules to a vacation hearing, the term "military judge," as used in these rules, shall mean the hearing officer, who shall assume the military judge's authority to exclude evidence from the hearing, and who shall, in discharging this duty, follow the procedures set forth in these rules. However, the hearing officer is not authorized to order production of communications covered by Mil. R. Evid. 513 or 514.

(3) *Production of witnesses and other evidence.* The procedure for the production of witnesses and other evidence shall follow that prescribed in R.C.M. 405(g), except that R.C.M. 405(g)(3)(B) shall not apply. The hearing officer shall only consider testimony and other evidence that is relevant to the limited purpose of the hearing.

(4) *Presentation of testimony.* Witness testimony may be provided in person, by video teleconference, by telephone, or by similar means of remote testimony. All testimony shall be taken under oath, except that the probationer may make an unsworn statement.

Discussion

The following oath may be given to witnesses:

"Do you (swear) (affirm) that the evidence you give shall be the truth, the whole truth, and nothing but the truth (so help you God)?"

The hearing officer is required to include in the record of the hearing, at a minimum, a summary of the substance of all testimony.

All hearing officer notes of testimony and recordings of testimony should be preserved until the end of trial.

If during the hearing any witness subject to the Code is suspected of an offense under the Code, the hearing officer should comply with the warning requirements of Mil. R. Evid. 305(c), (d), and, if necessary, (e).

Bearing in mind that the probationer and government are responsible for preparing and presenting their cases, the hearing officer may ask a witness questions relevant to the limited purpose of the hearing. When questioning a witness, the hearing officer may not depart from an impartial role and become an advocate for either side.

---

(5) *Other evidence.* If relevant to the limited purpose of the hearing, and not cumulative, a hearing officer may consider other evidence, in addition to or in lieu of witness testimony, including statements, tangible evidence, or reproductions thereof, offered by either side, that the hearing officer determines is reliable. This other evidence need not be sworn.

(6) *Presence of probationer.* The taking of evidence shall not be prevented and the probationer shall be considered to have waived the right to be present whenever the probationer:

(A) After being notified of the time and place of the proceeding is voluntarily absent; or

(B) After being warned by the hearing officer that disruptive conduct will cause removal from the proceeding, persists in conduct that is such as to justify exclusion from the proceeding.

(7) *Objections.* Any objection alleging failure to comply with these rules shall be made to the convening authority via the hearing officer. The hearing officer shall include a record of all objections in the written recommendations to the convening authority.

(8) *Access by spectators.* Vacation hearings are public proceedings and should remain open to the public whenever possible. The convening authority who directed the hearing or the hearing officer may restrict or foreclose access by spectators to all or part of the proceedings if an overriding interest exists that outweighs the value of an open hearing. Examples of overriding interests may include: preventing psychological harm or trauma to a child witness or an alleged victim of a sexual crime, protecting the safety or privacy of a witness or alleged victim, protecting classified material, and receiving evidence where a witness is incapable of testifying in an open setting. Any closure must be

narrowly tailored to achieve the overriding interest that justified the closure. Convening authorities or hearing officers must conclude that no lesser methods short of closing the hearing can be used to protect the overriding interest in the case. Convening authorities or hearing officers must conduct a case-by-case, witness-by-witness, circumstance-by-circumstance analysis of whether closure is necessary. If a convening authority or hearing officer believes closing the hearing is necessary, the convening authority or hearing officer must make specific fmdings of fact in writing that support the closure. The written findings of fact must be included in the record.

(9) *Victim's rights.* Any victim of the underlying offense for which the probationer received the suspended sentence, or any victim of the alleged offense that is the subject of the vacation hearing, has the right to reasonable, accurate, and timely notice of the vacation hearing. For purposes of this rule, the term "victim" is defined as an individual who has suffered direct physical, emotional, or pecuniary harm as a result of the commission of an offense.

Rule 1110. Waiver or withdrawal of appellate review

(a) *In general.* After any general court-martial, except one in which the approved sentence includes death, and after any special court-martial in which the approved sentence includes a bad-conduct discharge or confinement for one year, the accused may waive or withdraw appellate review.

Discussion

Appellate review is not available for special courts-martial in which a bad-conduct discharge or confinement for one year was not adjudged or approved or for summary courts-martial. Cases not subject to appellate review, or in which appellate review is waived or withdrawn, are reviewed by a judge advocate under R.C.M. 1112. Such cases may also be submitted to the Judge Advocate General for review. *See* R.C.M. 1201(b)(3). Appellate review is mandatory when the approved sentence includes death.

(b) *Right to counsel.*

(1) *In general.* The accused shall have the right to consult with counsel qualified under R.C.M. 502(d)(1) before submitting a waiver or withdrawal of appellate review.

(2) *Waiver.*

(A) *Counsel who represented the accused at the court-martial.* The accused shall have the right to consult with any civilian, individual military, or detailed counsel who represented the accused at the court-martial concerning whether to waive appellate review unless such counsel has been excused under R.C.M. 505(d)(2)(B).

(B) *Associate counsel.* If counsel who represented the accused at the court-martial has not been excused but is not immediately available to consult with the accused, because of physical separation or other reasons, associate defense counsel shall be detailed to the accused upon request by the accused. Such counsel shall communicate with counsel who represented the accused at the court-martial, and shall advise the accused concerning whether to waive appellate review.

(C) *Substitute counsel.* If counsel who represented the accused at the court-martial has been excused under R.C.M. 505(d)(2)(B), substitute defense counsel shall be detailed to advise the accused concerning waiver of appellate rights.

(3) *Withdrawal.*

(A) *Appellate defense counsel.* If the accused is represented by appellate defense counsel, the accused shall have the right to consult with such counsel concerning whether to withdraw the appeal.

(B) *Associate defense counsel.* If the accused is represented by appellate defense counsel, and such counsel is not immediately available to consult with the accused, because of physical separation or other reasons, associate defense counsel shall be detailed to the accused, upon request by the accused. Such counsel shall communicate with appellate defense counsel and shall advise the accused whether to withdraw the appeal.

(C) *No counsel.* If appellate defense counsel has not been assigned to the accused, defense counsel shall be detailed for the accused. Such counsel shall advise the accused concerning whether to withdraw the appeal. If practicable, counsel who represented the accused at the court-martial shall be detailed.

(4) *Civilian counsel.* Whether or not the accused was represented by civilian counsel at the court-martial, the accused may consult with civilian counsel, at no expense to the United States, concerning whether to waive or withdraw appellate review.

(5) *Record of trial.* Any defense counsel with

whom the accused consults under this rule shall be given reasonable opportunity to examine the record of trial.

Discussion

Ordinarily counsel may use the accused's copy of the record. If this is not possible, as when the accused and counsel are physically separated, another copy should be made available to counsel.

---

(6) *Consult.* The right to consult with counsel, as used in this rule, does not require communication in the presence of one another.

(c) *Compulsion, coercion, inducement prohibited.* No person may compel, coerce, or induce an accused by force, promises of clemency, or otherwise to waive or withdraw appellate review.

(d) *Form of waiver or withdrawal.* A waiver or withdrawal of appellate review shall:

(1) Be written;

(2) State that the accused and defense counsel have discussed the accused's right to appellate review and the effect of waiver or withdrawal of appellate review and that the accused understands these matters;

(3) State that the waiver or withdrawal is submitted voluntarily; and

(4) Be signed by the accused and by defense counsel.

Discussion

See Appendix 19 (DD Form 2330) or Appendix 20 (DD Form 2331) for samples of forms.

(e) *To whom submitted.*

(1) *Waiver.* A waiver of appellate review shall be filed with the convening authority. The waiver shall be attached to the record of trial.

(2) *Withdrawal.* A withdrawal of appellate review may be filed with the authority exercising general court-martial jurisdiction over the accused, who shall promptly forward it to the Judge Advocate General, or directly with the Judge Advocate General.

(f) *Time limit.*

(1) *Waiver.* The accused may sign a waiver of appellate review at any time after the sentence is announced. The waiver must be filed within 10 days after the accused or defense counsel is served with a copy of the action under R.C.M. 1107(h). Upon written application of the accused, the convening authority may extend this period for good cause, for not more than 30 days.

(2) *Withdrawal.* The accused may file withdrawal from appellate review at any time before such review is completed.

(g) *Effect of waiver or withdrawal; substantial compliance required.*

(1) *In general.* A waiver or withdrawal of appellate review under this rule shall bar review by the Judge Advocate General under R.C.M. 1201(b)(1) and by the Court of Criminal Appeals. Once submitted, a waiver or withdrawal in compliance with this rule may not be revoked.

(2) *Waiver.* If the accused files a timely waiver of appellate review in accordance with this rule, the record shall be forwarded for review by a judge advocate under R.C.M. 1112.

(3) *Withdrawal.* Action on a withdrawal of appellate review shall be carried out in accordance with procedures established by the Judge Advocate General, or if the case is pending before a Court of Criminal Appeals, in accordance with the rules of such court. If the appeal is withdrawn, the Judge Advocate General shall forward the record to an appropriate authority for compliance with R.C.M. 1112.

(4) *Substantial compliance required.* A purported waiver or withdrawal of an appeal which does not substantially comply with this rule shall have no effect.

Rule 1111. Disposition of the record of trial after action

(a) *General courts-martial.*

(1) *Cases forwarded to the Judge Advocate General.* A record of trial by general court-martial and the convening authority's action shall be sent directly to the Judge Advocate General concerned if the approved sentence includes death or if the accused has not waived review under R.C.M. 1110. Unless otherwise prescribed by regulations of the Secretary concerned, 10 copies of the order promulgating the result of trial as to each accused shall be forwarded with the original record of trial. Two additional copies of the record of trial shall accompany the original record if the approved sentence includes

death or if it includes dismissal of an officer, cadet, or midshipman, dishonorable or bad-conduct discharge, or confinement for one year or more and the accused has not waived appellate review. Forwarding of an authenticated electronic copy of the record of trial satisfies the requirements under this rule.

(2) *Cases forwarded to a judge advocate.* A record of trial by general court-martial and the convening authority's action shall be sent directly to a judge advocate for review under R.C.M. 1112 if the sentence does not include death and if the accused has waived appellate review under R.C.M. 1110. Unless otherwise prescribed by the Secretary concerned, 4 copies of the order promulgating the result of trial shall be forwarded with the original record of trial.

(b) *Special courts-martial.*

(1) *Cases including an approved bad-conduct discharge or confinement for one year.* If the approved sentence of a special court-martial includes a bad-conduct discharge or confinement for one year, the record shall be disposed of as provided in subsection (a) of this rule.

(2) *Other cases.* The record of trial by a special court-martial in which the approved sentence does not include a bad-conduct discharge or confinement for one year shall be forwarded directly to a judge advocate for review under R.C.M. 1112. Four copies of the order promulgating the result of trial shall be forwarded with the record of trial, unless otherwise prescribed by regulations of the Secretary concerned.

(c) *Summary courts-martial.* The convening authority shall dispose of a record of trial by summary court-martial as provided by R.C.M. 1306.

Discussion

See DD Form 494 (Court-Martial Data Sheet).

Rule 1112. Review by a judge advocate

(a) *In general.* Except as provided in subsection (b) of this rule, under regulations of the Secretary concerned, a judge advocate shall review:

(1) Each general court-martial in which the accused has waived or withdrawn appellate review under R.C.M. 1110.

(2) Each special court-martial in which the accused has waived or withdrawn appellate review

under R.C.M. 1110 or in which the approved sentence does not include a bad-conduct discharge or confinement for one year; and

(3) Each summary court-martial.

(b) *Exception.* If the accused was found not guilty or not guilty only by reason of lack of mental responsibility of all offenses or if the convening authority disapproved all findings of guilty, no review under this rule is required.

(c) *Disqualification.* No person may review a case under this rule if that person has acted in the same case as an accuser, preliminary hearing officer, member of the court-martial, military judge, or counsel, or has otherwise acted on behalf of the prosecution or defense.

(d) *Form and content of review.* The judge advocate's review shall be in writing and shall contain the following:

(1) Conclusions as to whether—

(A) The court-martial had jurisdiction over the accused and each offense as to which there is a finding of guilty which has not been disapproved;

(B) Each specification as to which there is a finding of guilty which has not been disapproved stated an offense; and

(C) The sentence was legal;

(2) A response to each allegation of error made in writing by the accused. Such allegations may be filed under R.C.M. 1105, 1106(f), or directly with the judge advocate who reviews the case; and

(3) If the case is sent for action to the officer exercising general court-martial jurisdiction under subsection (e) of this rule, a recommendation as to the appropriate action to be taken and an opinion as to whether corrective action is required as a matter of law.

Copies of the judge advocate's review under this rule shall be attached to the original and all copies of the record of trial. A copy of the review shall be forwarded to the accused.

(e) *Forwarding to officer exercising general court-martial jurisdiction.* In cases reviewed under subsection (a) of this rule, the record of trial shall be sent for action to the officer exercising general court-martial convening authority over the accused at the time the court-martial was held (or to that officer's successor) when:

(1) The judge advocate who reviewed the case recommends corrective action;

(2) The sentence approved by the convening authority includes dismissal, a dishonorable or bad-conduct discharge, or confinement for more than 6 months; or

(3) Such action is otherwise required by regulations of the Secretary concerned.

(f) *Action by officer exercising general court-martial jurisdiction.*

(1) *Action.* The officer exercising general court-martial jurisdiction who receives a record under subsection (e) of this rule may—

(A) Disapprove or approve the findings or sentence in whole or in part;

(B) Remit, commute, or suspend the sentence in whole or in part;

(C) Except where the evidence was insufficient at the trial to support the findings, order a rehearing on the findings, on the sentence, or on both; or

(D) Dismiss the charges.

Discussion

See R.C.M. 1113 concerning when the officer exercising general court-martial jurisdiction may order parts of the sentence executed. *See* R.C.M. 1114 concerning orders promulgating the action of the officer exercising general court-martial jurisdiction. *See also* Appendix 16 (Forms for actions) and Appendix 17 (Forms for court-martial orders).

---

(2) *Rehearing.* If the officer exercising general court-martial jurisdiction orders a rehearing, but the convening authority finds a rehearing impracticable, the convening authority shall dismiss the charges.

(3) *Notification.* After the officer exercising general court-martial jurisdiction has taken action, the accused shall be notified of the action and the accused shall be provided with a copy of the judge advocate's review.

(g) *Forwarding following review under this rule.*

(1) *Records forwarded to the Judge Advocate General.* If the judge advocate who reviews the case under this rule states that corrective action is required as a matter of law, and the officer exercising general court-martial jurisdiction does not take action that is at least as favorable to the accused as that recommended by the judge advocate, the record of trial and the action thereon shall be forwarded to

the Judge Advocate General concerned for review under R.C.M. 1201(b)(2).

(2) *Sentence including dismissal.* If the approved sentence includes dismissal, the record shall be forwarded to the Secretary concerned.

Discussion

A dismissal may not be ordered executed until approved by the Secretary or the Secretary's designee. *See* R.C.M. 1206.

---

(3) *Other records.* Records reviewed under this rule which are not forwarded under subsection (g)(1) of this rule shall be disposed of as prescribed by the Secretary concerned.

Discussion

A dismissal may not be ordered executed until approved by the Secretary or the Secretary's designee under R.C.M. 1206.

Rule 1113. Execution of sentences

(a) *In general.* No sentence of a court-martial may be executed unless it has been approved by the convening authority.

Discussion

An order executing the sentence directs that the sentence be carried out. Except as provided in subsections (d)(2), (3), and (5) of this rule, no part of a sentence may be carried out until it is ordered executed.

(b) *Punishments which the convening authority may order executed in the initial action.* Except as provided in subsection (c) of this rule, the convening authority may order all or part of the sentence of a court-martial executed when the convening authority takes initial action under R.C.M. 1107.

(c) *Punishments which the convening authority may not order executed in the initial action.*

(1) *Dishonorable or a bad-conduct discharge.* Except as may otherwise be prescribed by the Secretary concerned, a dishonorable or a bad-conduct discharge may be ordered executed only by:

(A) The officer who reviews the case under R.C.M. 1112(f), as part of the action approving the sentence, except when that action must be forwarded under R.C.M. 1112(g)(1); or

(B) The officer then exercising general court-martial jurisdiction over the accused.

A dishonorable or bad-conduct discharge may be ordered executed only after a final judgment within the meaning of R.C.M. 1209 has been rendered in the case. If on the date of final judgment a servicemember is not on appellate leave and more than 6 months have elapsed since approval of the sentence by the convening authority, before a dishonorable or a bad-conduct discharge may be executed, the officer exercising general court-martial jurisdiction over the servicemember shall consider the advice of that officer's staff judge advocate as to whether retention of the servicemember would be in the best interest of the service. Such advice shall include the findings and sentence as finally approved, the nature and character of duty since approval of the sentence by the convening authority, and a recommendation whether the discharge should be executed.

(2) *Dismissal of a commissioned officer, cadet, or midshipman.* Dismissal of a commissioned officer, cadet, or midshipman may be approved and ordered executed only by the Secretary concerned or such Under Secretary or Assistant Secretary as the Secretary concerned may designate.

Discussion

See R.C.M. 1206(a) concerning approval by the Secretary.

---

(3) *Sentences extending to death.* A punishment of death may be ordered executed only by the President.

Discussion

See R.C.M. 1207 concerning approval by the President.

(d) *Self-executing punishments.* Under regulations prescribed by the Secretary concerned, a dishonorable or bad conduct discharge that has been approved by an appropriate convening authority may be self-executing after final judgment at such time as:

(1) The accused has received a sentence of no confinement or has completed all confinement;

(2) The accused has been placed on excess or appellate leave; and,

(3) The appropriate official has certified that the accused's case is final. Upon completion of the cer-

tification, the official shall forward the certification to the accused's personnel office for preparation of a final discharge order and certificate.

(e) *Other considerations concerning the execution of certain sentences.*

(1) *Death.*

(A) *Manner carried out.* A sentence to death which has been finally ordered executed shall be carried out in the manner prescribed by the Secretary concerned.

(B) *Action when accused lacks mental capacity.* An accused lacking the mental capacity to understand the punishment to be suffered or the reason for imposition of the death sentence may not be put to death during any period when such incapacity exists. The accused is presumed to have such mental capacity. If a substantial question is raised as to whether the accused lacks capacity, the convening authority then exercising general court-martial jurisdiction over the accused shall order a hearing on the question. A military judge, counsel for the government, and counsel for the accused shall be detailed. The convening authority shall direct an examination of the accused in accordance with R.C.M. 706, but the examination may be limited to determining whether the accused understands the punishment to be suffered and the reason therefore. The military judge shall consider all evidence presented, including evidence provided by the accused. The accused has the burden of proving such lack of capacity by a preponderance of the evidence. The military judge shall make findings of fact, which will then be forwarded to the convening authority ordering the hearing. If the accused is found to lack capacity, the convening authority shall stay the execution until the accused regains appropriate capacity.

Discussion

A verbatim transcript of the hearing should accompany the findings of fact.

---

(2) *Confinement.*

(A) *Effective date of confinement.* Any period of confinement included in the sentence of a court-martial begins to run from the date the sentence is adjudged by the court-martial, but the following shall be excluded in computing the service of the term of confinement:

(i) Periods during which the sentence to confinement is suspended or deferred;

(ii) Periods during which the accused is in custody of civilian authorities under Article 14 from the time of the delivery to the return to military custody, if the accused was convicted in the civilian court;

(iii) Periods during which the accused is in custody of civilian or foreign authorities after the convening authority, pursuant to Article 57a.(b)(1), has postponed the service of a sentence to confinement.

Discussion

The convening authority's decision to postpone service of a court-martial sentence to confinement normally should be reflected in the action.

(iv) Periods during which the accused has escaped or is absent without authority, or is absent under a parole which proper authority has later revoked, or is erroneously released from confinement through misrepresentation or fraud on the part of the prisoner, or is erroneously released from confinement upon the prisoner's petition for a writ of habeas corpus under a court order which is later reversed; and

(v) Periods during which another sentence by court-martial to confinement is being served. When a prisoner serving a court-martial sentence to confinement is later convicted by a court-martial of another offense and sentenced to confinement, the later sentence interrupts the running of the earlier sentence. Any unremitted remaining portion of the earlier sentence will be served after the later sentence is fully executed.

(B) *Nature of the confinement.* The omission of "hard labor" from any sentence of a court-martial which has adjudged confinement shall not prohibit the authority who orders the sentence executed from requiring hard labor as part of the punishment.

(C) *Place of confinement.* The authority who orders a sentence to confinement into execution shall designate the place of confinement under regulations prescribed by the Secretary concerned, unless otherwise prescribed by the Secretary concerned. Under such regulations as the Secretary concerned may prescribe, a sentence to confinement adjudged by a court-martial or other military tribunal, regardless whether the sentence includes a punitive discharge or dismissal and regardless whether the punitive discharge or dismissal has been executed, may be ordered to be served in any place of confinement under the control of any of the armed forces or in any penal or correctional institution under the control of the United States or which the United States may be allowed to use. Persons so confined in a penal or correctional institution not under the control of one of the armed forces are subject to the same discipline and treatment as persons confined or committed by the courts of the United States or of the State, Territory, District of Columbia, or place in which the institution is situated. When the service of a sentence to confinement has been deferred and the deferment is later rescinded, the convening authority shall designate the place of confinement in the initial action on the sentence or in the order rescinding the deferment. No member of the armed forces, or person serving with or accompanying an armed force in the field, may be placed in confinement in immediate association with enemy prisoners or with other foreign nationals not subject to the code. The Secretary concerned may prescribe regulations governing the place and conditions of confinement.

Discussion

See R.C.M. 1101(c) concerning deferment of a sentence to confinement.

---

(3) *Confinement in lieu of fine.* Confinement may not be executed for failure to pay a fine if the accused demonstrates that the accused has made good faith efforts to pay but cannot because of indigency, unless the authority considering imposition of confinement determines, after giving the accused notice and opportunity to be heard, that there is no other punishment adequate to meet the Government's interest in appropriate punishment.

(4) *Restriction; hard labor without confinement.* When restriction and hard labor without confinement are included in the same sentence, they shall, unless one is suspended, be executed concurrently.

(5) *More than one sentence.* If at the time forfeitures may be ordered executed, the accused is already serving a sentence to forfeitures by another court-martial, the authority taking action may order

that the later forfeitures will be executed when the earlier sentence to forfeitures is completed.

Rule 1114. Promulgating orders

(a) *In general.*

(1) *Scope of rule.* Unless otherwise prescribed by the Secretary concerned, orders promulgating the result of trial and the actions of the convening or higher authorities on the record shall be prepared, issued, and distributed as prescribed in this rule.

(2) *Purpose.* A promulgating order publishes the result of the court-martial and the convening authority's action and any later action taken on the case.

(3) *Summary courts-martial.* An order promulgating the result of a trial by summary court-martial need not be issued.

Discussion

See R.C.M. 1306(b)(2) concerning summary courts-martial.

---

(4) *Self-executing final orders.* An order promulgating a self-executing dishonorable or bad conduct discharge need not be issued. The original action by a convening authority approving a discharge and certification by the appropriate official that the case is final may be forwarded to the accused's personnel office for preparation of a discharge order and certificate.

(b) *By whom issued.*

(1) *Initial orders.* The order promulgating the result of trial and the initial action of the convening authority shall be issued by the convening authority.

(2) *Orders issued after the initial action.* Any action taken on the case subsequent to the initial action shall be promulgated in supplementary orders. The subsequent action and the supplementary order may be the same document if signed personally by the appropriate convening or higher authority.

(A) *When the President or the Secretary concerned has taken final action.* General court-martial orders publishing the final result in cases in which the President or the Secretary concerned has taken final action shall be promulgated as prescribed by regulations of the Secretary concerned.

(B) *Other cases.* In cases other than those in subsection (b)(2)(A) of this rule, the final action

may be promulgated by an appropriate convening authority.

(c) *Contents.*

(1) *In general.* The order promulgating the initial action shall set forth: the type of court-martial and the command by which it was convened; the charges and specifications, or a summary thereof, on which the accused was arraigned; the accused's pleas; the findings or other disposition of each charge and specification; the sentence, if any; and the action of the convening authority, or a summary thereof. Supplementary orders shall recite, verbatim, the action or order of the appropriate authority, or a summary thereof.

(2) *Dates.* A promulgating order shall bear the date of the initial action, if any, of the convening authority. An order promulgating an acquittal, a court-martial terminated before findings, a court-martial resulting in a finding of not guilty only by reason of lack of mental responsibility of all charges and specifications, or action on the findings or sentence taken after the initial action of the convening authority shall bear the date of its publication. A promulgating order shall state the date the sentence was adjudged, the date on which the acquittal was announced, or the date on which the proceedings were otherwise terminated.

Discussion

See Appendix 17 for sample forms for promulgating orders.

---

(3) *Order promulgated regardless of the result of trial or nature of the action.* An order promulgating the result of trial by general or special court-martial shall be issued regardless of the result and regardless of the action of the convening or higher authorities.

(d) *Orders containing classified information.* When an order contains information which must be classified, only the order retained in the unit files and those copies which accompany the record of trial shall be complete and contain the classified information. The order shall be assigned the appropriate security classification. Asterisks shall be substituted for the classified information in the other copies of the order.

(e) *Authentication.* The promulgating order shall be authenticated by the signature of the convening or other competent authority acting on the case, or a person acting under the direction of such authority.

A promulgating order prepared in compliance with this rule shall be presumed authentic.

(f) *Distribution.* Promulgating orders shall be distributed as provided in regulations of the Secretary concerned.

CHAPTER XII. APPEALS AND REVIEW

Rule 1201. Action by the Judge Advocate General

(a) *Cases required to be referred to a Court of Criminal Appeals.* The Judge Advocate General shall refer to a Court of Criminal Appeals the record in each trial by court-martial:

(1) In which the sentence, as approved, extends to death; or

(2) In which—

(A) The sentence, as approved, extends to dismissal of a commissioned officer, cadet, or midshipman, dishonorable or bad-conduct discharge, or confinement for 1 year or longer; and

(B) The accused has not waived or withdrawn appellate review.

Discussion

See R.C.M. 1110 concerning waiver or withdrawal of appellate review.

See also subsection (b)(1) of this rule concerning cases reviewed by the Judge Advocate General which may be referred to a Court of Criminal Appeals.

See R.C.M. 1203 concerning review by the Court of Criminal Appeals and the powers and responsibilities of the Judge Advocate General after such review. *See* R.C.M. 1202 concerning appellate counsel.

(b) *Cases reviewed by the Judge Advocate General.*

(1) *Mandatory examination of certain general courts-martial.* Except when the accused has waived the right to appellate review or withdrawn such review, the record of trial by a general court-martial in which there has been a finding of guilty and a sentence, the appellate review of which is not provided for in subsection (a) of this rule, shall be examined in the office of the Judge Advocate General. If any part of the findings or sentence is found unsupported in law, or if reassessment of the sentence is appropriate, the Judge Advocate General may modify or set aside the findings or sentence or both. If the Judge Advocate General so directs, the record shall be reviewed by a Court of Criminal Appeals in accordance with R.C.M. 1203. If the case is forwarded to a Court of Criminal Appeals, the accused shall be informed and shall have the rights under R.C.M. 1202(b)(2).

Discussion

A case forwarded to a Court of Criminal Appeals under this subsection is subject to review by the Court of Appeals for the Armed Forces upon petition by the accused under Article 67(a)(3) or when certified by the Judge Advocate General under Article 67(a)(2).

---

(2) *Mandatory review of cases forwarded under R.C.M. 1112(g)(1).* The Judge Advocate General shall review each case forwarded under R.C.M. 1112(g)(1). On such review, the Judge Advocate General may vacate or modify, in whole or part, the findings or sentence, or both, of a court-martial on the ground of newly discovered evidence, fraud on the court-martial, lack of jurisdiction over the accused or the offense, error prejudicial to the substantial rights of the accused, or the appropriateness of the sentence.

(3) *Review by the Judge Advocate General after final review.*

(A) *In general.* Notwithstanding R.C.M. 1209, the Judge Advocate General may, *sua sponte* or upon application of the accused or a person with authority to act for the accused, vacate or modify, in whole or in part, the findings, sentence, or both of a court-martial which has been finally reviewed, but has not been reviewed either by a Court of Criminal Appeals or by the Judge Advocate General under subsection (b)(1) of this rule, on the ground of newly discovered evidence, fraud on the court-martial, lack of jurisdiction over the accused or the offense, error prejudicial to the substantial rights of the accused, or the appropriateness of the sentence.

Discussion

See R.C.M. 1210 concerning petition for new trial. Review of a case by a Judge Advocate General under this subsection is not part of appellate review within the meaning of Article 76 or R.C.M. 1209.

Review of a finding of not guilty only by reason of lack of mental responsibility under this rule may not extend to the determination of lack of mental responsibility. Thus, modification of a finding of not guilty only by reason of lack of mental responsibility under this rule is limited to changing the finding to not guilty or not guilty only by reason of lack of mental responsibility of a lesser included offense.

(B) *Procedure.* Each Judge Advocate General shall provide procedures for considering all cases properly submitted under subsection (b)(3) of this rule and may prescribe the manner by which an application for relief under subsection (b)(3) of this rule may be made and, if submitted by a person other than the accused, may require that the applicant show authority to act on behalf of the accused.

Discussion

See R.C.M. 1114 concerning orders promulgating action under this rule.

(C) *Time limits on applications.* Any application for review by the Judge Advocate General under Article 69 must be made on or before the last day of the two year period beginning on the date the sentence is approved by the convening authority or the date the findings are announced for cases which do not proceed to sentencing, unless the accused establishes good cause for failure to file within that time.

(4) *Rehearing.* If the Judge Advocate General sets aside the findings or sentence, the Judge Advocate General may, except when the setting aside is based on lack of sufficient evidence in the record to support the findings, order a rehearing. If the Judge Advocate General sets aside the findings and sentence and does not order a rehearing, the Judge Advocate General shall order that the charges be dismissed. If the Judge Advocate General orders a rehearing but the convening authority finds a rehearing impractical, the convening authority shall dismiss the charges.

(c) *Remission and suspension.* The Judge Advocate General may, when so authorized by the Secretary concerned under Article 74, at any time remit or suspend the unexecuted part of any sentence, other than a sentence approved by the President.

Rule 1202. Appellate counsel

(a) *In general.* The Judge Advocate General concerned shall detail one or more commissioned officers as appellate Government counsel and one or more commissioned officers as appellate defense counsel who are qualified under Article 27(b)(1).

(b) *Duties.*

(1) *Appellate Government counsel.* Appellate Government counsel shall represent the United States before the Court of Criminal Appeals or the United States Court of Appeals for the Armed Forces when directed to do so by the Judge Advocate General concerned. Appellate Government counsel may represent the United States before the United States Supreme Court when requested to do so by the Attorney General.

(2) *Appellate defense counsel.* Appellate defense counsel shall represent the accused before the Court of Criminal Appeals, the Court of Appeals for the Armed Forces, or the Supreme Court when the accused is a party in the case before such court and:

(A) The accused requests to be represented by appellate defense counsel;

(B) The United States is represented by counsel; or

(C) The Judge Advocate General has sent the case to the United States Court of Appeals for the Armed Forces. Appellate defense counsel is authorized to communicate directly with the accused. The accused is a party in the case when named as a party in pleadings before the court or, even if not so named, when the military judge is named as respondent in a petition by the Government for extraordinary relief from a ruling in favor of the accused at trial.

Discussion

For a discussion of the duties of the trial defense counsel concerning post-trial and appellate matters, *see* R.C.M. 502(d)(6) Discussion (E). Appellate defense counsel may communicate with trial defense counsel concerning the case. *See also* Mil. R. Evid. 502 (privileges).

If all or part of the findings and sentence are affirmed by the Court of Criminal Appeals, appellate defense counsel should advise the accused whether the accused should petition for further review in the United States Court of Appeals for the Armed Forces and concerning which issues should be raised.

The accused may be represented by civilian counsel before the Court of Criminal Appeals, the Court of Appeals for the Armed Forces, and the Supreme Court. Such counsel will not be provided at the expense of the United States. Civilian counsel may represent the accused before these courts in addition to or instead of military counsel.

If, after any decision of the Court of Appeals for the Armed Forces, the accused may apply for a writ of certiorari (*see* R.C.M. 1205), appellate defense counsel should advise the accused whether to apply for review by the Supreme Court and which issues might be raised. If authorized to do so by the accused, appellate defense counsel may prepare and file a petition for a writ of certiorari on behalf of the accused.

The accused has no right to select appellate defense counsel. Under some circumstances, however, the accused may be entitled to request that the detailed appellate defense counsel be replaced by another appellate defense counsel.

See also R.C.M. 1204(b)(1) concerning detailing counsel with respect to the right to petition the Court of Appeals for the Armed Forces for review.

Rule 1203. Review by a Court of Criminal Appeals

(a) *In general.* Each Judge Advocate General shall establish a Court of Criminal Appeals composed of appellate military judges.

Discussion

See Article 66 concerning the composition of the Courts of Criminal Appeals, the qualifications of appellate military judges, the grounds for their ineligibility, and restrictions upon the official relationship of the members of the court to other members. Uniform rules of court for the Courts of Criminal Appeals are prescribed by the Judge Advocates General.

(b) *Cases reviewed by a Court of Criminal Appeals.* A Court of Criminal Appeals shall review cases referred to it by the Judge Advocate General under R.C.M. 1201(a) or (b)(1).

Discussion

See R.C.M. 1110 concerning withdrawal of a case pending before a Court of Criminal Appeals.

See R.C.M. 908 concerning procedures for interlocutory appeals by the Government.

In cases referred to it under R.C.M. 1201, a Court of Criminal Appeals may act only with respect to the findings and sentence as approved by proper authority. It may affirm only such findings of guilty or such part of a finding of guilty as includes an included offense, as it finds correct in law and fact and determines on the basis of the entire record should be approved. A Court of Criminal Appeals has generally the same powers as the convening authority to modify a sentence (*see* R.C.M. 1107), but it may not suspend all or part of a sentence. However, it may reduce the period of a suspension prescribed by a convening authority. It may not defer service of a sentence to confinement. (*see* R.C.M. 1101(c)). It may, however, review a decision by a convening authority concerning deferral, to determine whether that decision was an abuse of the convening authority's discretion.

In considering the record of a case referred to it under R.C.M. 1201, a Court of Criminal Appeals may weigh the evidence, judge the credibility of witnesses, and determine controverted questions of fact, recognizing that the court-martial saw and heard the evidence. A finding or sentence of a court-martial may not be held incorrect on the ground of an error of law unless the error materially prejudices the substantial rights of the accused. Article 59(a).

If a Court of Criminal Appeals sets aside any findings of guilty or the sentence, it may, except as to findings set aside for lack of sufficient evidence in the record to support the findings, order an appropriate type of rehearing or reassess the sentence as appropriate. *See* R.C.M. 810 concerning rehearings. If the Court of Criminal Appeals sets aside all the findings and the sentence and does not order a rehearing, it must order the charges dismissed. *See* Articles 59(a) and 66.

A Court of Criminal Appeals may on petition for extraordinary relief issue all writs necessary or appropriate in aid of its jurisdiction and agreeable to the usages and principles of law. Any party may petition a Court of Criminal Appeals for extraordinary relief.

(c) *Action on cases reviewed by a Court of Criminal Appeals.*

(1) *Forwarding by the Judge Advocate General to the Court of Appeals for the Armed Forces.* The Judge Advocate General may forward the decision of the Court of Criminal Appeals to the Court of Appeals for the Armed Forces for review with respect to any matter of law. In such a case, the Judge Advocate General shall cause a copy of the decision of the Court of Criminal Appeals and the order forwarding the case to be served on the accused and on appellate defense counsel. While a review of a forwarded case is pending, the Secretary concerned may defer further service of a sentence to confinement that has been ordered executed in such a case.

(2) *Action when sentence is set aside.* In a case reviewed by it under this rule in which the Court of Criminal Appeals has set aside the sentence and which is not forwarded to the Court of Appeals for the Armed Forces under subsection (c)(1) of this rule, the Judge Advocate General shall instruct an appropriate convening authority to take action in accordance with the decision of the Court of Criminal Appeals. If the Court of Criminal Appeals has ordered a rehearing, the record shall be sent to an appropriate convening authority. If that convening authority finds a rehearing impracticable that convening authority may dismiss the charges.

Discussion

If charges are dismissed, *see* R.C.M. 1208 concerning restoration of rights, privileges, and property. *See* R.C.M. 1114 concerning promulgating orders.

---

(3) *Action when sentence is affirmed in whole or part.*

(A) *Sentence requiring approval by the Presi-*

dent. If the Court of Criminal Appeals affirms any sentence which includes death, the Judge Advocate General shall transmit the record of trial and the decision of the Court of Criminal Appeals directly to the Court of Appeals for the Armed Forces when any period for reconsideration provided by the rules of the Courts of Criminal Appeals has expired.

(B) *Other cases.* If the Court of Criminal Appeals affirms any sentence other than one which includes death, the Judge Advocate General shall cause a copy of the decision of the Court of Criminal Appeals to be served on the accused in accordance with subsection (d) of this rule.

(4) *Remission or suspension.* If the Judge Advocate General believes that a sentence as affirmed by the Court of Criminal Appeals, other than one which includes death, should be remitted or suspended in whole or part, the Judge Advocate General may, before taking action under subsections (c)(1) or (3) of this rule, transmit the record of trial and the decision of the Court of Criminal Appeals to the secretary concerned with a recommendation for action under Article 74 or may take such action as may be authorized by the Secretary concerned under Article 74(a).

Discussion

See R.C.M. 1201(c); 1206.

(5) *Action when accused lacks mental capacity.* An appellate authority may not affirm the proceedings while the accused lacks mental capacity to understand and to conduct or cooperate intelligently in the appellate proceedings. In the absence of substantial evidence to the contrary, the accused is presumed to have the capacity to understand and to conduct or cooperate intelligently in the appellate proceedings. If a substantial question is raised as to the requisite mental capacity of the accused, the appellate authority may direct that the record be forwarded to an appropriate authority for an examination of the accused in accordance with R.C.M. 706, but the examination may be limited to determining the accused's present capacity to understand and cooperate in the appellate proceedings. The order of the appellate authority will instruct the appropriate authority as to permissible actions that may be taken to dispose of the matter. If the record is thereafter returned to the appellate authority, the appellate

authority may affirm part or all of the findings or sentence unless it is established, by a preponderance of the evidence—including matters outside the record of trial—that the accused does not have the requisite mental capacity. If the accused does not have the requisite mental capacity, the appellate authority shall stay the proceedings until the accused regains appropriate capacity, or take other appropriate action. Nothing in this subsection shall prohibit the appellate authority from making a determination in favor of the accused which will result in the setting aside of a conviction.

(d) *Notification to accused.*

(1) *Notification of decision.* The accused shall be notified of the decision of the Court of Criminal Appeals in accordance with regulations of the Secretary concerned.

Discussion

The accused may be notified personally, or a copy of the decision may be sent, after service on appellate counsel of record, if any, by first class certified mail to the accused at an address provided by the accused or, if no such address has been provided by the accused, at the latest address listed for the accused in the accused's official service record.

If the Judge Advocate General has forwarded the case to the Court of Appeals for the Armed Forces, the accused should be so notified. *See* subsection (c)(1) of this rule.

(2) *Notification of right to petition the Court of Appeals for the Armed Forces for review.* If the accused has the right to petition the Court of Appeals for the Armed Forces for review, the accused shall be provided with a copy of the decision of the Court of Criminal Appeals bearing an endorsement notifying the accused of this right. The endorsement shall inform the accused that such a petition:

(A) May be filed only within 60 days from the time the accused was in fact notified of the decision of the Court of Criminal Appeals or the mailed copy of the decision was postmarked, whichever is earlier; and

(B) May be forwarded through the officer immediately exercising general court-martial jurisdiction over the accused and through the appropriate Judge Advocate General or filed directly with the Court of Appeals for the Armed Forces.

Discussion

See Article 67(c).
See also R.C.M. 1204(b).

The accused may petition the Court of Appeals for the Armed Forces for review, as to any matter of law, of any decision of the Court of Criminal Appeals except: (1) a case which was referred to the Court of Criminal Appeals by the Judge Advocate General under R.C.M. 1201(b)(1); (2) a case in which the Court of Criminal Appeals has set aside the sentence; and (3) a case in which the sentence includes death (because review by the Court of Appeals for the Armed Forces is mandatory).

The placing of a petition for review in proper military channels divests the Court of Criminal Appeals of jurisdiction over the case, and jurisdiction is thereby conferred on the Court of Appeals for the Armed Forces. *See* R.C.M. 1113 concerning action to be taken if the accused does not file or the Court of Appeals for the Armed Forces denies a petition for review.

---

(3) *Receipt by the accused—disposition.* When the accused has the right to petition the Court of Appeals for the Armed Forces for review, the receipt of the accused for the copy of the decision of the Court of Criminal Appeals, a certificate of service on the accused, or the postal receipt for delivery of certified mail shall be transmitted in duplicate by expeditious means to the appropriate Judge Advocate General. If the accused is personally served, the receipt or certificate of service shall show the date of service. The Judge Advocate General shall forward one copy of the receipt, certificate, or postal receipt to the clerk of the Court of Appeals for the Armed Forces when required by the court.

(e) *Cases not reviewed by the Court of Appeals for the Armed Forces.* If the decision of the Court of Criminal Appeals is not subject to review by the Court of Appeals for the Armed Forces, or if the Judge Advocate General has not forwarded the case to the Court of Appeals for the Armed Forces and the accused has not filed or the Court of Appeals for the Armed Forces has denied a petition for review, the Judge Advocate General shall—

(1) If the sentence affirmed by the Court of Criminal Appeals includes a dismissal, transmit the record, the decision of the Court of Criminal Appeals, and the Judge Advocate General's recommendation to the Secretary concerned for action under R.C.M. 1206; or

(2) If the sentence affirmed by the Court of Criminal Appeals does not include a dismissal, notify the convening authority, the officer exercising general court-martial jurisdiction over the accused, or the Secretary concerned, as appropriate, who, subject to R.C.M. 1113(c)(1), may order into execution any

unexecuted sentence affirmed by the Court of Criminal Appeals or take other action, as authorized.

Discussion

See R.C.M. 1113, 1206, and Article 74(a) concerning the authority of the Secretary and others to take action.

(f) *Scope.* Except as otherwise expressly provided in this rule, this rule does not apply to appeals by the Government under R.C.M. 908.

(g) *Article 6b(e) petition for writ of mandamus.* The Judge Advocates General shall establish the means by which the petitions for writs of mandamus described in Article 6b(e) are forwarded to the Courts of Criminal Appeals in accordance with their rule-making functions of Article 66(f).

Rule 1204. Review by the Court of Appeals for the Armed Forces

(a) *Cases reviewed by the Court of Appeals for the Armed Forces.* Under such rules as it may prescribe, the Court of Appeals for the Armed Forces shall review the record in all cases:

(1) In which the sentence, as affirmed by a Court of Criminal Appeals, extends to death;

(2) Reviewed by a Court of Criminal Appeals which the Judge Advocate General orders sent to the Court of Appeals for the Armed Forces for review; and

(3) Reviewed by a Court of Criminal Appeals, except those referred to it by the Judge Advocate General under R.C.M. 1201(b)(1), in which, upon petition by the accused and on good cause shown, the Court of Appeals for the Armed Forces has granted a review.

Discussion

See Article 67(a) concerning the composition of the Court of Appeals for the Armed Forces. In any case reviewed by it, the Court of Appeals for the Armed Forces may act only with respect to the findings and sentence as approved by the convening authority and as affirmed or set aside as incorrect in law by the Court of Criminal Appeals. *See* Article 67(d) and (e). The rules of practice and procedure before the Court of Appeals for the Armed Forces are published in the Military Justice Reporter.

The Court of Appeals for the Armed Forces may entertain petitions for extraordinary relief and may issue all writs necessary or appropriate in aid of its jurisdiction and agreeable to the usages and principles of law. Any party may petition the Court of Appeals for the Armed Forces for extraordinary relief. However, in the interest of judicial economy, such petitions usually should be filed with and adjudicated before the appropriate Court of Criminal Appeals prior to submission to the Court of Appeals for the Armed Forces.

(b) *Petition by the accused for review by the Court of Appeals for the Armed Forces.*

(1) *Counsel.* When the accused is notified of the right to forward a petition for review by the Court of Appeals for the Armed Forces, if requested by the accused, associate counsel qualified under R.C.M. 502(d)(1) shall be detailed to advise and assist the accused in connection with preparing a petition for further appellate review.

Discussion

If reasonably available, the counsel who conducted the defense at trial may perform these duties. The counsel detailed to represent the accused should communicate with the appellate defense counsel representing the accused. *See* R.C.M. 1202.

(2) *Forwarding petition.* The accused shall file any petition for review by the Court of Appeals for the Armed Forces under subsection (a)(3) of this rule directly with the Court of Appeals for the Armed Forces.

Discussion

See Article 67(c) and R.C.M. 1203(d)(2) concerning notifying the accused of the right to petition the Court of Appeals for the Armed Forces for review and the time limits for submitting a petition. *See also* the rules of the Court of Appeals for the Armed Forces concerning when the time for filing a petition begins to run and when a petition is now timely.

(c) *Action on decision by the Court of Appeals for the Armed Forces.*

(1) *In general.* After it has acted on a case, the Court of Appeals for the Armed Forces may direct the Judge Advocate General to return the record to the Court of Criminal Appeals for further proceedings in accordance with the decision of the court. Otherwise, unless the decision is subject to review by the Supreme Court, or there is to be further action by the President or the Secretary concerned, the Judge Advocate General shall instruct the convening authority to take action in accordance with that decision. If the Court has ordered a rehearing, but the convening authority to whom the record is

transmitted finds a rehearing impracticable, the convening authority may dismiss the charges.

Discussion

See R.C.M. 1114 concerning final orders in the case. *See also* R.C.M. 1206 and Article 74(a).

(2) *Sentence requiring approval of the President.*

(A) If the Court of Appeals for the Armed Forces has affirmed a sentence that must be approved by the President before it may be executed, the Judge Advocate General shall transmit the record of trial, the decision of the Court of Criminal Appeals, the decision of the Court of Appeals for the Armed Forces, and the recommendation of the Judge Advocate General to the Secretary concerned.

(B) If the Secretary concerned is the Secretary of a military department, the Secretary concerned shall forward the material received under paragraph (A) to the Secretary of Defense, together with the recommendation of the Secretary concerned. The Secretary of Defense shall forward the material, with the recommendation of the Secretary concerned and the recommendation of the Secretary of Defense, to the President for the action of the President.

(C) If the Secretary concerned is the Secretary of Homeland Security, the Secretary concerned shall forward the material received under paragraph (A) to the President, together with the recommendation of the Secretary concerned, for the action of the President.

Discussion

See Article 71(a) and R.C.M. 1207.

(3) *Sentence requiring approval of the Secretary concerned.* If the Court of Appeals for the Armed Forces has affirmed a sentence which requires approval of the Secretary concerned before it may be executed, the Judge Advocate General shall follow the procedure in R.C.M. 1203(e)(1).

Discussion

See Article 71(b) and R.C.M. 1206.

(4) *Decision subject to review by the Supreme Court.* If the decision of the Court of Appeals for the Armed Forces is subject to review by the

Supreme Court, the Judge Advocate General shall take no action under subsections (c)(1), (2), or (3) of this rule until: (A) the time for filing a petition for a writ of certiorari with the Supreme Court has expired; or (B) the Supreme Court has denied any petitions for writ of certiorari filed in the case. After (A) or (B) has occurred, the Judge Advocate General shall take action under subsection (c)(1), (2), or (3). If the Supreme Court grants a writ of certiorari, the Judge Advocate General shall take action under R.C.M. 1205(b).

Rule 1205. Review by the Supreme Court

(a) *Cases subject to review by the Supreme Court.* Under 28 U.S.C. § 1259 and Article 67(h), decisions of the Court of Appeals for the Armed Forces may be reviewed by the Supreme Court by writ of certiorari in the following cases:

(1) Cases reviewed by the Court of Appeals for the Armed Forces under Article 67(b)(1);

(2) Cases certified to the Court of Appeals for the Armed Forces by the Judge Advocate General under Article 67(b)(2);

(3) Cases in which the Court of Appeals for the Armed Forces granted a petition for review under Article 67(b)(3); and

(4) Cases other than those described in subsections (a)(1), (2), and (3) of this rule in which the Court of Appeals for the Armed Forces granted relief.

The Supreme Court may not review by writ of certiorari any action of the Court of Appeals for the Armed Forces in refusing to grant a petition for review.

(b) *Action by the Supreme Court.* After the Supreme Court has taken action, other than denial of a petition for writ of certiorari, in any case, the Judge Advocate General shall, unless the case is returned to the Court of Appeals for the Armed Forces for further proceedings, forward the case to the President or the Secretary concerned in accordance with R.C.M. 1204(c)(2) or (3) when appropriate, or instruct the convening authority to take action in accordance with the decision.

Rule 1206. Powers and responsibilities of the Secretary

(a) *Sentences requiring approval by the Secretary.*

II-186

No part of a sentence extending to dismissal of a commissioned officer, cadet, or midshipman may be executed until approved by the Secretary concerned or such Under Secretary or Assistant Secretary as may be designated by the Secretary.

Discussion

See Article 71(b).

(b) *Remission and suspension.*

(1) *In general.* The Secretary concerned and, when designated by the Secretary concerned, any Under Secretary, Assistant Secretary, Judge Advocate General, or commander may remit or suspend any part or amount of the unexecuted part of any sentence, including all uncollected forfeitures, other than a sentence approved by the President.

(2) *Substitution of discharge.* The Secretary concerned may, for good cause, substitute an administrative discharge for a discharge or dismissal executed in accordance with the sentence of a court-martial.

(3) *Sentence commuted by the President.* When the President has commuted a death sentence to a lesser punishment, the Secretary concerned may remit or suspend any remaining part or amount of the unexecuted portion of the sentence of a person convicted by a military tribunal under the Secretary's jurisdiction.

Rule 1207. Sentences requiring approval by the President

No part of a court-martial sentence extending to death may be executed until approved by the President.

Discussion

See Article 71(a). *See also* R.C.M. 1203 and 1204 concerning review by the Court of Criminal Appeals and Court of Appeals for the Armed Forces in capital cases.

Rule 1208. Restoration

(a) *New trial.* All rights, privileges, and property affected by an executed portion of a court-martial sentence—except an executed dismissal or discharge—which has not again been adjudged upon a new trial or which, after the new trial, has not been sustained upon the action of any reviewing authority, shall be restored. So much of the findings and so much of the sentence adjudged at the earlier trial shall be set aside as may be required by the findings and sentence at the new trial. Ordinarily, action taken under this subsection shall be announced in the court-martial order promulgating the final results of the proceedings.

Discussion

See Article 75(b) and (c) concerning the action to be taken on an executed dismissal or discharge which is not imposed at a new trial.

(b) *Other cases.* In cases other than those in subsection (a) of this rule, all rights, privileges, and property affected by an executed part of a court-martial sentence which has been set aside or disapproved by any competent authority shall be restored unless a new trial, other trial, or rehearing is ordered and such executed part is included in a sentence imposed at the new trial, other trial, or rehearing. Ordinarily, any restoration shall be announced in the court-martial order promulgating the final results of the proceedings.

Discussion

See R.C.M. 1114 concerning promulgating orders.

Rule 1209. Finality of courts-martial

(a) *When a conviction is final.* A court-martial conviction is final when:

(1) Review is completed by a Court of Criminal Appeals and—

(A) The accused does not file a timely petition for review by the Court of Appeals for the Armed Forces and the case is not otherwise under review by that court;

(B) A petition for review is denied or otherwise rejected by the Court of Appeals for the Armed Forces; or

(C) Review is completed in accordance with the judgment of the Court of Appeals for the Armed Forces and—

(i) A petition for a writ of certiorari is not filed within the time limits prescribed by the Supreme Court,

(ii) A petition for writ of certiorari is denied or otherwise rejected by the Supreme Court, or

(iii) Review is otherwise completed in accordance with the judgment of the Supreme Court; or

Discussion

See R.C.M. 1201, 1203, 1204, and 1205 concerning cases subject to review by a Court of Criminal Appeals, the Court of Appeals for the Armed Forces, and the Supreme Court. *See also* R.C.M. 1110.

---

(2) In cases not reviewed by a Court of Criminal Appeals—

(A) The findings and sentence have been found legally sufficient by a judge advocate and, when action by such officer is required, have been approved by the officer exercising general court-martial jurisdiction over the accused at the time the court-martial was convened (or that officer's successor); or

(B) The findings and sentence have been affirmed by the Judge Advocate General when review by the Judge Advocate General is required under R.C.M. 1112(g)(1) or 1201(b)(1).

(b) *Effect of finality.* The appellate review of records of trial provided by the code, the proceedings, findings, and sentences of courts-martial as approved, reviewed, or affirmed as required by the code, and all dismissals and discharges carried into execution under sentences by courts-martial following approval, review, or affirmation as required by the code, are final and conclusive. Orders publishing the proceedings of courts-martial and all action taken pursuant to those proceedings are binding upon all departments, courts, agencies, and officers of the United States, subject only to action upon a petition for a new trial under Article 73, to action by the Judge Advocate General under Article 69(b), to action by the Secretary concerned as provided in Article 74, and the authority of the President.

Rule 1210. New trial

(a) *In general.* At any time within 2 years after approval by the convening authority of a court-martial sentence, the accused may petition the Judge Advocate General for a new trial on the ground of newly discovered evidence or fraud on the court-martial. A petition may not be submitted after the death of the accused. A petition for a new trial of the facts may not be submitted on the basis of newly discovered evidence when the petitioner was found guilty of the relevant offense pursuant to a guilty plea.

(b) *Who may petition.* A petition for a new trial may be submitted by the accused personally, or by accused's counsel, regardless whether the accused has been separated from the service.

(c) *Form of petition.* A petition for a new trial shall be written and shall be signed under oath or affirmation by the accused, by a person possessing the power of attorney of the accused for that purpose, or by a person with the authorization of an appropriate court to sign the petition as the representative of the accused. The petition shall contain the following information, or an explanation why such matters are not included:

(1) The name, service number, and current address of the accused;

(2) The date and location of the trial;

(3) The type of court-martial and the title or position of the convening authority;

(4) The request for the new trial;

(5) The sentence or a description thereof as approved or affirmed, with any later reduction thereof by clemency or otherwise;

(6) A brief description of any finding or sentence believed to be unjust;

(7) A full statement of the newly discovered evidence or fraud on the court-martial which is relied upon for the remedy sought;

(8) Affidavits pertinent to the matters in subsection (c)(6) of this rule; and

(9) The affidavit of each person whom the accused expects to present as a witness in the event of a new trial. Each such affidavit should set forth briefly the relevant facts within the personal knowledge of the witness.

(d) *Effect of petition.* The submission of a petition for a new trial does not stay the execution of a sentence.

(e) *Who may act on petition.* If the accused's case is pending before a Court of Criminal Appeals or the Court of Appeals for the Armed Forces, the Judge Advocate General shall refer the petition to the appropriate court for action. Otherwise, the Judge Advocate General of the armed force which reviewed the previous trial shall act on the petition, except that petitions submitted by persons who, at the time of trial and sentence from which the petitioner seeks relief, were members of the Coast Guard, and who, and who were members of the Coast Guard at the time the petition is submitted, shall be acted on in the Department in which the Coast Guard is serving at the time the petition is so submitted.

(f) *Grounds for new trial.*

(1) *In general.* A new trial may be granted only on grounds of newly discovered evidence or fraud on the court-martial.

(2) *Newly discovered evidence.* A new trial shall not be granted on the grounds of newly discovered evidence unless the petition shows that:

(A) The evidence was discovered after the trial;

(B) The evidence is not such that it would have been discovered by the petitioner at the time of trial in the exercise of due diligence; and

(C) The newly discovered evidence, if considered by a court-martial in the light of all other pertinent evidence, would probably produce a substantially more favorable result for the accused.

(3) *Fraud on court-martial.* No fraud on the court-martial warrants a new trial unless it had a substantial contributing effect on a finding of guilty or the sentence adjudged.

Discussion

Examples of fraud on a court-martial which may warrant granting a new trial are: confessed or proved perjury in testimony or forgery of documentary evidence which clearly had a substantial contributing effect on a finding of guilty and without which there probably would not have been a finding of guilty of the offense; willful concealment by the prosecution from the defense of evidence favorable to the defense which, if presented to the court-martial, would probably have resulted in a finding of not guilty; and willful concealment of a material ground for challenge of the military judge or any member or of the disqualification of counsel or the convening authority, when the basis for challenge or disqualification was not known to the defense at the time of trial (*see* R.C.M. 912).

(g) *Action on the petition.*

(1) *In general.* The authority considering the petition may cause such additional investigation to be made and such additional information to be secured as that authority believes appropriate. Upon written request, and in its discretion, the authority consider-

ing the petition may permit oral argument on the matter.

(2) *Courts of Criminal Appeals; Court of Appeals for the Armed Forces.* The Courts of Criminal Appeals and the Court of Appeals for the Armed Forces shall act on a petition for a new trial in accordance with their respective rules.

(3) *The Judge Advocates General.* When a petition is considered by the Judge Advocate General, any hearing may be before the Judge Advocate General or before an officer or officers designated by the Judge Advocate General. If the Judge Advocate General believes meritorious grounds for relief under Article 74 have been established but that a new trial is not appropriate, the Judge Advocate General may act under Article 74 if authorized to do so, or transmit the petition and related papers to the Secretary concerned with a recommendation. The Judge Advocate General may also, in cases which have been finally reviewed but have not been reviewed by a Court of Criminal Appeals, act under Article 69.

Discussion

See also R.C.M. 1201(b)(3).

(h) *Action when new trial is granted.*

(1) *Forwarding to convening authority.* When a petition for a new trial is granted, the Judge Advocate General shall select and forward the case to a convening authority for disposition.

(2) *Charges at new trial.* At a new trial, the accused may not be tried for any offense of which the accused was found not guilty or upon which the accused was not tried at the earlier court-martial.

Discussion

See also R.C.M. 810 concerning additional special rules which apply at a new trial. In other respects a new trial is conducted like any other court-martial.

---

(3) *Action by convening authority.* The convening authority's action on the record of a new trial is the same as in other courts-martial.

(4) *Disposition of record.* The disposition of the record of a new trial is the same as for other courts-martial.

(5) *Court-martial orders.* Court-martial orders promulgating the final action taken as a result of a new trial, including any restoration of rights, privileges, and property, shall be promulgated in accordance with R.C.M. 1114.

Discussion

See Article 75 and R.C.M. 1208 concerning restoration of rights when the executed portion of a sentence is not sustained in a new trial or action following it.

---

(6) *Action by persons charged with execution of the sentence.* Persons charged with the administrative duty of executing a sentence adjudged upon a new trial after it has been ordered executed shall credit the accused with any executed portion or amount of the original sentence included in the new sentence in computing the term or amount of punishment actually to be executed pursuant to the sentence.

CHAPTER XIII. SUMMARY COURTS-MARTIAL

Rule 1301. Summary courts-martial generally

(a) *Composition.* A summary court-martial is composed of one commissioned officer on active duty. Unless otherwise prescribed by the Secretary concerned a summary court-martial shall be of the same armed force as the accused. Summary courts-martial shall be conducted in accordance with the regulations of the military service to which the accused belongs. Whenever practicable, a summary court-martial should be an officer whose grade is not below lieutenant of the Navy or Coast Guard or captain of the Army, Air Force, or Marine Corps. When only one commissioned officer is present with a command or detachment, that officer shall be the summary court-martial of that command or detachment. When more than one commissioned officer is present with a command or detachment, the convening authority may not be the summary court-martial of that command or detachment.

(b) *Function.* The function of the summary court-martial is to promptly adjudicate minor offenses under a simple procedure. The summary court-martial shall thoroughly and impartially inquire into both sides of the matter and shall ensure that the interests of both the Government and the accused are safeguarded and that justice is done. A summary court-martial may seek advice from a judge advocate or legal officer on questions of law, but the summary court-martial may not seek advice from any person on factual conclusions which should be drawn from evidence or the sentence which should be imposed, as the summary court-martial has the independent duty to make these determinations.

Discussion

For a definition of "minor offenses," *see* paragraph 1e, Part V.

(c) *Jurisdiction.*
[Note: R.C.M. 1301(c) applies to offenses committed on or after 24 June 2014.]

(1) Subject to Chapter II, summary courts-martial have the power to try persons subject to the code, except commissioned officers, warrant officers, cadets, aviation cadets, and midshipmen, for any noncapital offense made punishable by the code.

Discussion

See R.C.M. 103(3) for a definition of capital offenses.

---

(2) Notwithstanding subsection (c)(1) of this rule, summary courts-martial do not have jurisdiction over offenses under Articles 120(a), 120(b), 120b(a), 120b(b), forcible sodomy under Article 125, and attempts thereof under Article 80. Such offenses shall not be referred to a summary court-martial.

Discussion

Pursuant to the National Defense Authorization Act for Fiscal Year 2014, only a general court-martial has jurisdiction to try penetrative sex offenses under subsections (a) and (b) of Article 120, subsections (a) and (b) of Article 120b, Article 125, and attempts to commit such penetrative sex offenses under Article 80.

(d) *Punishments.*

(1) *Limitations—amount.* Subject to R.C.M. 1003, summary courts-martial may adjudge any punishment not forbidden by the code except death, dismissal, dishonorable or bad-conduct discharge, confinement for more than 1 month, hard labor without confinement for more than 45 days, restriction to specified limits for more than 2 months, or forfeiture of more than two-thirds of 1 month's pay.

Discussion

The maximum penalty which can be adjudged in a summary court-martial is confinement for 30 days, forfeiture of two-thirds pay per month for one month, and reduction to the lowest pay grade. *See* subsection (2) below for additional limits on enlisted persons serving in pay grades above the fourth enlisted pay grade.

A summary court-martial may not suspend all or part of a sentence, although the summary court-martial may recommend to the convening authority that all or part of a sentence be suspended. If a sentence includes both reduction in grade and forfeitures, the maximum forfeiture is calculated at the reduced pay grade. *See also* R.C.M. 1003 concerning other punishments which may be adjudged, the effects of certain types of punishment, and combination of certain types of punishment. The summary court-martial should ascertain the effect of Article 58a in that armed force.

---

(2) *Limitations—pay grade.* In the case of enlisted members above the fourth enlisted pay grade, summary courts-martial may not adjudge confinement,

hard labor without confinement, or reduction except to the next pay grade.

Discussion

The provisions of this subsection apply to an accused in the fifth enlisted pay grade who is reduced to the fourth enlisted pay grade by the summary court-martial.

(e) *Counsel.* The accused at a summary court-martial does not have the right to counsel. If the accused has civilian counsel provided by the accused and qualified under R.C.M. 502(d)(3), that counsel shall be permitted to represent the accused at the summary court-martial if such appearance will not unreasonably delay the proceedings and if military exigencies do not preclude it.

Discussion

Neither the Constitution nor any statute establishes any right to counsel at summary courts-martial. Therefore, it is not error to deny an accused the opportunity to be represented by counsel at a summary court-martial. However, appearance of counsel is not prohibited. The detailing authority may, as a matter of discretion, detail, or otherwise make available, a military attorney to represent the accused at a summary court-martial.

(f) *Power to obtain witnesses and evidence.* A summary court-martial may obtain evidence pursuant to R.C.M. 703.

Discussion

The summary court-martial must obtain witnesses for the prosecution and the defense pursuant to the standards in R.C.M. 703. The summary court-martial rules on any request by the accused for witnesses or evidence in accordance with the procedure in R.C.M. 703(c) and (f).

(g) *Secretarial limitations.* The Secretary concerned may prescribe procedural or other rules for summary courts-martial not inconsistent with this Manual or the code.

Rule 1302. Convening a summary court-martial

(a) *Who may convene summary courts-martial.* Unless limited by competent authority summary courts-martial may be convened by:

(1) Any person who may convene a general or special court-martial;

(2) The commander of a detached company or other detachment of the Army;

(3) The commander of a detached squadron or other detachment of the Air Force;

(4) The commander or officer in charge of any other command when empowered by the Secretary concerned; or

(5) A superior competent authority to any of the above.

(b) *When convening authority is accuser.* If the convening authority or the summary court-martial is the accuser, it is discretionary with the convening authority whether to forward the charges to a superior authority with a recommendation to convene the summary court-martial. If the convening authority or the summary court-martial is the accuser, the jurisdiction of the summary court-martial is not affected.

(c) *Procedure.* After the requirements of Chapters III and IV of this Part have been satisfied, summary courts-martial shall be convened in accordance with R.C.M. 504(d)(2). The convening order may be by notation signed by the convening authority on the charge sheet. Charges shall be referred to summary courts-martial in accordance with R.C.M. 601.

Discussion

When the convening authority is the summary court-martial because the convening authority is the only commissioned officer present with the command or detachment, *see* R.C.M. 1301(a), that fact should be noted on the charge sheet.

Rule 1303. Right to object to trial by summary court-martial

No person who objects thereto before arraignment may be tried by summary court-martial even if that person also refused punishment under Article 15 and demanded trial by court-martial for the same offenses.

Discussion

If the accused objects to trial by summary court-martial, the convening authority may dispose of the case in accordance with R.C.M. 401.

Rule 1304. Trial procedure

(a) *Pretrial duties.*

(1) *Examination of file.* The summary court-mar-

tial shall carefully examine the charge sheet, allied papers, and immediately available personnel records of the accused before trial.

Discussion

"Personnel records" are those personnel records of the accused which are maintained locally and are immediately available. "Allied papers" in a summary court-martial include convening orders, investigative reports, correspondence relating to the case, and witness statements.

———

(2) *Report of irregularity.* The summary court-martial shall report to the convening authority any substantial irregularity in the charge sheet, allied papers, or personnel records.

Discussion

The summary court-martial should examine the charge sheet, allied papers, and personnel records to ensure that they are complete and free from errors or omissions which might affect admissibility. The summary court-martial should check the charges and specifications to ensure that each alleges personal jurisdiction over the accused (*see* R.C.M. 202) and an offense under the code (*see* R.C.M. 203 and Part IV). Substantial defects or errors in the charges and specifications must be reported to the convening authority, since such defects cannot be corrected except by preferring and referring the affected charge and specification anew in proper form. A defect or error is substantial if correcting it would state an offense not otherwise stated, or include an offense, person, or matter not fairly included in the specification as preferred. *See* subsection (3) below concerning minor errors.

———

(3) *Correction and amendment.* The summary court-martial may, subject to R.C.M. 603, correct errors on the charge sheet and amend charges and specifications. Any such corrections or amendments shall be initialed.

(b) *Summary court-martial procedure.*

Discussion

A sample guide is at Appendix 9. The summary court-martial should review and become familiar with the guide used before proceeding.

———

(1) *Preliminary proceeding.* After complying with R.C.M. 1304(a), the summary court-martial shall hold a preliminary proceeding during which the accused shall be given a copy of the charge sheet and informed of the following:

(A) The general nature of the charges;

(B) The fact that the charges have been referred to a summary court-martial for trial and the date of referral;

(C) The identity of the convening authority;

(D) The name(s) of the accuser(s);

(E) The names of the witnesses who could be called to testify and any documents or physical evidence which the summary court-martial expects to introduce into evidence;

(F) The accused's right to inspect the allied papers and immediately available personnel records;

(G) That during the trial the summary court-martial will not consider any matters, including statements previously made by the accused to the officer detailed as summary court-martial unless admitted in accordance with the Military Rules of Evidence;

(H) The accused's right to plead not guilty or guilty;

(I) The accused's right to cross-examine witnesses and have the summary court-martial cross-examine witnesses on behalf of the accused;

(J) The accused's right to call witnesses and produce evidence with the assistance of the summary court-martial as necessary;

(K) The accused's right to testify on the merits, or to remain silent with the assurance that no adverse inference will be drawn by the summary court-martial from such silence;

(L) If any findings of guilty are announced, the accused's rights to remain silent, to make an unsworn statement, oral or written or both, and to testify, and to introduce evidence in extenuation or mitigation;

(M) The maximum sentence which the summary court-martial may adjudge if the accused is found guilty of the offense or offenses alleged; and

(N) The accused's right to object to trial by summary court-martial.

(2) *Trial proceeding.*

(A) *Objection to trial.* The summary court-martial shall give the accused a reasonable period of time to decide whether to object to trial by summary court-martial. The summary court-martial shall thereafter record the response. If the accused objects to trial by summary court-martial, the summary court-martial shall return the charge sheet, allied papers, and personnel records to the convening authority. If the accused fails to object to trial by summary court-martial, trial shall proceed.

(B) *Arraignment.* After complying with R.C.M. 1304(b)(1) and (2)(A), the summary court-martial shall read and show the charges and specifications to the accused and, if necessary, explain them. The accused may waive the reading of the charges. The summary court-martial shall then ask the accused to plead to each specification and charge.

(C) *Motions.* Before receiving pleas the summary court-martial shall allow the accused to make motions to dismiss or for other relief. The summary court-martial shall take action on behalf of the accused, if requested by the accused, or if it appears necessary in the interests of justice.

(D) *Pleas.*

(i) *Not guilty pleas.* When a not guilty plea is entered, the summary court-martial shall proceed to trial.

(ii) *Guilty pleas.* If the accused pleads guilty to any offense, the summary court-martial shall comply with R.C.M. 910.

(iii) *Rejected guilty pleas.* If the summary court-martial is in doubt that the accused's pleas of guilty are voluntarily and understandingly made, or if at any time during the trial any matter inconsistent with pleas of guilty arises, which inconsistency cannot be resolved, the summary court-martial shall enter not guilty pleas as to the affected charges and specifications.

(iv) *No plea.* If the accused refuses to plead, the summary court-martial shall enter not guilty pleas.

(v) *Changed pleas.* The accused may change any plea at any time before findings are announced. The accused may change pleas from guilty to not guilty after findings are announced only for good cause.

(E) *Presentation of evidence.*

(i) The Military Rules of Evidence (Part III) apply to summary courts-martial.

(ii) The summary court-martial shall arrange for the attendance of necessary witnesses for the prosecution and defense, including those requested by the accused.

Discussion

See R.C.M. 703. Ordinarily witnesses should be excluded from the courtroom until called to testify. *See* Mil. R. Evid. 615.

(iii) Witnesses for the prosecution shall be called first and examined under oath. The accused shall be permitted to cross-examine these witnesses. The summary court-martial shall aid the accused in cross-examination if such assistance is requested or appears necessary in the interests of justice. The witnesses for the accused shall then be called and similarly examined under oath.

(iv) The summary court-martial shall obtain evidence which tends to disprove the accused's guilt or establishes extenuating circumstances.

Discussion

See R.C.M. 703 and 1001.

(F) *Findings and sentence.*

(i) The summary court-martial shall apply the principles in R.C.M. 918 in determining the findings. The summary court-martial shall announce the findings to the accused in open session.

(ii) The summary court-martial shall follow the procedures in R.C.M. 1001 and apply the principles in the remainder of Chapter X in determining a sentence. The summary court-martial shall announce the sentence to the accused in open session.

(iii) If the sentence includes confinement, the summary court-martial shall advise the accused of the right to apply to the convening authority for deferment of the service of the confinement.

(iv) If the accused is found guilty, the summary court-martial shall advise the accused of the rights under R.C.M. 1306(a) and (d) after the sentence is announced.

(v) The summary court-martial shall, as soon as practicable, inform the convening authority of the findings, sentence, recommendations, if any, for suspension of the sentence, and any deferment request.

(vi) If the sentence includes confinement, the summary court-martial shall cause the delivery of the accused to the accused's commanding officer or the commanding officer's designee.

Discussion

If the accused's immediate commanding officer is not the convening authority, the summary court-martial should ensure that the immediate commanding officer is informed of the findings, sentence, and any recommendations pertaining thereto. *See* R.C.M. 1101 concerning post-trial confinement.

Rule 1305. Record of trial

(a) *In general.* The record of trial of a summary court-martial shall be prepared as prescribed in subsection (b) of this rule. The convening or higher authority may prescribe additional requirements for the record of trial.

Discussion

See Appendix 15 for a sample of a Record of Trial by Summary Court-Martial (DD Form 2329).

Any petition submitted under R.C.M. 1306(a) should be appended to the record of trial.

(b) *Contents.* The summary court-martial shall prepare a written record of trial, which shall include:

(1) The pleas, findings, and sentence, and if the accused was represented by counsel at the summary court-martial, a notation to that effect;

(2) The fact that the accused was advised of the matters set forth in R.C.M. 1304(b)(1);

(3) If the summary court-martial is the convening authority, a notation to that effect.

(c) *Authentication.* The summary court-martial shall authenticate the record by signing the record of trial. An electronic record of trial may be authenticated with the electronic signature of the summary court-martial.

Discussion

"Authentication" means attesting that the record accurately reports the proceedings. *See* R.C.M. 1104(a).

(d) *Forwarding copies of the record.*

(1) *Accused's copy.*

(A) *Service.* The summary court-martial shall cause a copy of the record of trial to be served on the accused as soon as it is authenticated. Service of an authenticated electronic copy of the record of trial with a means to review the record of trial satisfies the requirement of service under this rule.

(B) *Receipt.* The summary court-martial shall cause the accused's receipt for the copy of the re-

cord of trial to be obtained and attached to the original record of trial or shall attach to the original record of trial a certificate that the accused was served a copy of the record. If the record of trial was not served on the accused personally, the summary court-martial shall attach a statement explaining how and when such service was accomplished. If the accused was represented by counsel, such counsel may be served with the record of trial.

(C) *Classified information.* If classified information is included in the record of trial of a summary court-martial, R.C.M. 1104(b)(1)(D) shall apply.

(2) *Forwarding to the convening authority.* The original and one copy of the record of trial shall be forwarded to the convening authority after compliance with subsection (d)(1) of this rule.

(3) *Further disposition.* After compliance with R.C.M. 1306(b) and (c), the record of trial shall be disposed of under regulations prescribed by the Secretary concerned.

Rule 1306. Post-trial procedure

(a) *Matters submitted.*

(1) *By a crime victim.* After a sentence is adjudged, a crime victim may submit a written statement to the convening authority in accordance with R.C.M. 1105A. A statement submitted by a crime victim shall be immediately served on the accused.

(2) *By the accused.* After a sentence is adjudged, the accused may submit written matters to the convening authority in accordance with R.C.M. 1105.

(b) *Convening authority's action.*

(1) *Who shall act.* Except as provided herein, the convening authority shall take action in accordance with R.C.M. 1107. The convening authority shall not take action before the period prescribed in R.C.M. 1105(c)(2) has expired, unless the right to submit matters has been waived under R.C.M. 1105(d).

(2) *Action.* The action of the convening authority shall be shown on all copies of the record of trial except that provided the accused if the accused has retained that copy. An order promulgating the result of a trial by summary court-martial need not be issued. A copy of the action shall be forwarded to the accused.

(3) *Signature.* The action on the record of trial shall be signed by the convening authority. The ac-

tion on an electronic record of trial may be signed with the electronic signature of the convening authority.

(4) *Subsequent action.* Any action taken on a summary court-martial after the initial action by the convening authority shall be in writing, signed by the authority taking the action, and promulgated in appropriate orders.

Discussion

See R.C.M. 1114 concerning promulgating orders.

(c) *Review by a judge advocate.* Unless otherwise prescribed by regulations of the Secretary concerned, the original record of the summary court-martial shall be reviewed by a judge advocate in accordance with R.C.M. 1112.

(d) *Review by the Judge Advocate General.* The accused may request review of a final conviction by summary court-martial by the Judge Advocate General in accordance with R.C.M. 1201(b)(3).

PART III
MILITARY RULES OF EVIDENCE

SECTION I
GENERAL PROVISIONS

Rule 101. Scope

(a) *Scope.* These rules apply to courts-martial proceedings to the extent and with the exceptions stated in Mil. R. Evid. 1101.

(b) *Sources of Law.* In the absence of guidance in this Manual or these rules, courts-martial will apply:

(1) First, the Federal Rules of Evidence and the case law interpreting them; and

(2) Second, when not inconsistent with subdivision (b)(1), the rules of evidence at common law.

(c) *Rule of Construction.* Except as otherwise provided in these rules, the term "military judge" includes the president of a special court-martial without a military judge and a summary court-martial officer.

Discussion

Discussion was added to these rules in 2013. The Discussion itself does not have the force of law, even though it may describe legal requirements derived from other sources. It is in the nature of treatise, and may be used as secondary authority. If a matter is included in a rule, it is intended that the matter be binding, unless it is clearly expressed as precatory. The Discussion will be revised from time to time as warranted by changes in applicable law. *See* Composition of the Manual for Courts-Martial in Appendix 21.

Practitioners should also refer to the Analysis of the Military Rules of Evidence contained in Appendix 22 of this Manual. The Analysis is similar to Committee Notes accompanying the Federal Rules of Evidence and is intended to address the basis of the rule, deviation from the Federal Rules of Evidence, relevant precedent, and drafters' intent.

Rule 102. Purpose

These rules should be construed so as to administer every proceeding fairly, eliminate unjustifiable expense and delay, and promote the development of evidence law, to the end of ascertaining the truth and securing a just determination.

Rule 103. Rulings on evidence

(a) *Preserving a Claim of Error.* A party may claim error in a ruling to admit or exclude evidence only if the error materially prejudices a substantial right of the party and:

(1) if the ruling admits evidence, a party, on the record:

(A) timely objects or moves to strike; and

(B) states the specific ground, unless it was apparent from the context; or

(2) if the ruling excludes evidence, a party informs the military judge of its substance by an offer of proof, unless the substance was apparent from the context.

(b) *Not Needing to Renew an Objection or Offer of Proof.* Once the military judge rules definitively on the record admitting or excluding evidence, either before or at trial, a party need not renew an objection or offer of proof to preserve a claim of error for appeal.

(c) *Review of Constitutional Error.* The standard provided in subdivision (a)(2) does not apply to errors implicating the United States Constitution as it applies to members of the Armed Forces, unless the error arises under these rules and subdivision (a)(2) provides a standard that is more advantageous to the accused than the constitutional standard.

(d) *Military Judge's Statement about the Ruling; Directing an Offer of Proof.* The military judge may make any statement about the character or form of the evidence, the objection made, and the ruling. The military judge may direct that an offer of proof be made in question-and-answer form.

(e) *Preventing the Members from Hearing Inadmissible Evidence.* In a court-martial composed of a military judge and members, to the extent practicable, the military judge must conduct a trial so that inadmissible evidence is not suggested to the members by any means.

(f) *Taking Notice of Plain Error.* A military judge may take notice of a plain error that materially prejudices a substantial right, even if the claim of error was not properly preserved.

Rule 104. Preliminary questions

(a) *In General.* The military judge must decide any

preliminary question about whether a witness is available or qualified, a privilege exists, a continuance should be granted, or evidence is admissible. In so deciding, the military judge is not bound by evidence rules, except those on privilege.

(b) *Relevance that Depends on a Fact.* When the relevance of evidence depends on whether a fact exists, proof must be introduced sufficient to support a finding that the fact does exist. The military judge may admit the proposed evidence on the condition that the proof be introduced later. A ruling on the sufficiency of evidence to support a finding of fulfillment of a condition of fact is the sole responsibility of the military judge, except where these rules or this Manual provide expressly to the contrary.

(c) *Conducting a Hearing so that the Members Cannot Hear It.* Except in cases tried before a special court-martial without a military judge, the military judge must conduct any hearing on a preliminary question so that the members cannot hear it if:

(1) the hearing involves the admissibility of a statement of the accused under Mil. R. Evid. 301-306;

(2) the accused is a witness and so requests; or

(3) justice so requires.

(d) *Cross-Examining the Accused.* By testifying on a preliminary question, the accused does not become subject to cross-examination on other issues in the case.

(e) *Evidence Relevant to Weight and Credibility.* This rule does not limit a party's right to introduce before the members evidence that is relevant to the weight or credibility of other evidence.

Rule 105. Limiting evidence that is not admissible against other parties or for other purposes

If the military judge admits evidence that is admissible against a party or for a purpose – but not against another party or for another purpose – the military judge, on timely request, must restrict the evidence to its proper scope and instruct the members accordingly.

Rule 106. Remainder of or related writings or recorded statements

If a party introduces all or part of a writing or recorded statement, an adverse party may require the

introduction, at that time, of any other part – or any other writing or recorded statement – that in fairness ought to be considered at the same time.

SECTION II
JUDICIAL NOTICE

Rule 201. Judicial notice of adjudicative facts

(a) *Scope.* This rule governs judicial notice of an adjudicative fact only, not a legislative fact.

(b) *Kinds of Facts that May Be Judicially Noticed.* The military judge may judicially notice a fact that is not subject to reasonable dispute because it:

(1) is generally known universally, locally, or in the area pertinent to the event; or

(2) can be accurately and readily determined from sources whose accuracy cannot reasonably be questioned.

(c) *Taking Notice.* The military judge:

(1) may take judicial notice whether requested or not; or

(2) must take judicial notice if a party requests it and the military judge is supplied with the necessary information.

The military judge must inform the parties in open court when, without being requested, he or she takes judicial notice of an adjudicative fact essential to establishing an element of the case.

(d) *Timing.* The military judge may take judicial notice at any stage of the proceeding.

(e) *Opportunity to Be Heard.* On timely request, a party is entitled to be heard on the propriety of taking judicial notice and the nature of the fact to be noticed. If the military judge takes judicial notice before notifying a party, the party, on request, is still entitled to be heard.

(f) *Instructing the Members.* The military judge must instruct the members that they may or may not accept the noticed fact as conclusive.

Rule 202. Judicial notice of law

(a) *Domestic Law.* The military judge may take judicial notice of domestic law. If a domestic law is a fact that is of consequence to the determination of the action, the procedural requirements of Mil. R. Evid. 201 – except Rule 201(f) – apply.

(b) *Foreign Law.* A party who intends to raise an

issue concerning the law of a foreign country must give reasonable written notice. The military judge, in determining foreign law, may consider any relevant material or source, in accordance with Mil. R. Evid. 104. Such a determination is a ruling on a question of law.

SECTION III

EXCLUSIONARY RULES AND RELATED MATTERS CONCERNING SELF-INCRIMINATION, SEARCH AND SEIZURE, AND EYEWITNESS IDENTIFICATION

Rule 301. Privilege concerning compulsory self-incrimination

(a) *General Rule.* An individual may claim the most favorable privilege provided by the Fifth Amendment to the United States Constitution, Article 31, or these rules. The privileges against self-incrimination are applicable only to evidence of a testimonial or communicative nature.

(b) *Standing.* The privilege of a witness to refuse to respond to a question that may tend to incriminate the witness is a personal one that the witness may exercise or waive at his or her discretion.

(c) *Limited Waiver.* An accused who chooses to testify as a witness waives the privilege against self-incrimination only with respect to the matters about which he or she testifies. If the accused is on trial for two or more offenses and on direct examination testifies about only one or some of the offenses, the accused may not be cross-examined as to guilt or innocence with respect to the other offenses unless the cross-examination is relevant to an offense concerning which the accused has testified. This waiver is subject to Mil. R. Evid. 608(b).

Discussion

A military judge is not required to provide Article 31 warnings. If a witness who seems uninformed of the privileges under this rule appears likely to incriminate himself or herself, the military judge may advise the witness of the right to decline to make any answer that might tend to incriminate the witness and that any self-incriminating answer the witness might make can later be used as evidence against the witness. Counsel for any party or for the witness may ask the military judge to so advise a witness if such a request is made out of the hearing of the witness and the members, if present. Failure to so advise a witness does not make the testimony of the witness inadmissible.

(d) *Exercise of the Privilege.* If a witness states that the answer to a question may tend to incriminate him or her, the witness cannot be required to answer unless the military judge finds that the facts and circumstances are such that no answer the witness might make to the question would tend to incriminate the witness or that the witness has, with respect to the question, waived the privilege against self-incrimination. A witness may not assert the privilege if he or she is not subject to criminal penalty as a result of an answer by reason of immunity, running of the statute of limitations, or similar reason.

(1) *Immunity Requirements.* The minimum grant of immunity adequate to overcome the privilege is that which under either R.C.M. 704 or other proper authority provides that neither the testimony of the witness nor any evidence obtained from that testimony may be used against the witness at any subsequent trial other than in a prosecution for perjury, false swearing, the making of a false official statement, or failure to comply with an order to testify after the military judge has ruled that the privilege may not be asserted by reason of immunity.

(2) *Notification of Immunity or Leniency.* When a prosecution witness before a court-martial has been granted immunity or leniency in exchange for testimony, the grant must be reduced to writing and must be served on the accused prior to arraignment or within a reasonable time before the witness testifies. If notification is not made as required by this rule, the military judge may grant a continuance until notification is made, prohibit or strike the testimony of the witness, or enter such other order as may be required.

(e) *Waiver of the Privilege.* A witness who answers a self-incriminating question without having asserted the privilege against self-incrimination may be required to answer questions relevant to the disclosure, unless the questions are likely to elicit additional self-incriminating information.

(1) If a witness asserts the privilege against self-incrimination on cross-examination, the military judge, upon motion, may strike the direct testimony of the witness in whole or in part, unless the matters to which the witness refuses to testify are purely collateral.

(2) Any limited waiver of the privilege under subdivision (e) applies only at the trial in which the answer is given, does not extend to a rehearing or

new or other trial, and is subject to Mil. R. Evid. 608(b).

(f) *Effect of Claiming the Privilege.*

(1) *No Inference to Be Drawn.* The fact that a witness has asserted the privilege against self-incrimination cannot be considered as raising any inference unfavorable to either the accused or the government.

(2) *Pretrial Invocation Not Admissible.* The fact that the accused during official questioning and in exercise of rights under the Fifth Amendment to the United States Constitution or Article 31 remained silent, refused to answer a certain question, requested counsel, or requested that the questioning be terminated, is not admissible against the accused.

(3) *Instructions Regarding the Privilege.* When the accused does not testify at trial, defense counsel may request that the members of the court be instructed to disregard that fact and not to draw any adverse inference from it. Defense counsel may request that the members not be so instructed. Defense counsel's election will be binding upon the military judge except that the military judge may give the instruction when the instruction is necessary in the interests of justice.

Rule 302. Privilege concerning mental examination of an accused

(a) *General rule.* The accused has a privilege to prevent any statement made by the accused at a mental examination ordered under R.C.M. 706 and any derivative evidence obtained through use of such a statement from being received into evidence against the accused on the issue of guilt or innocence or during sentencing proceedings. This privilege may be claimed by the accused notwithstanding the fact that the accused may have been warned of the rights provided by Mil. R. Evid. 305 at the examination.

(b) *Exceptions.*

(1) There is no privilege under this rule when the accused first introduces into evidence such statements or derivative evidence.

(2) If the court-martial has allowed the defense to present expert testimony as to the mental condition of the accused, an expert witness for the prosecution may testify as to the reasons for his or her conclusions, but such testimony may not extend to state-

ments of the accused except as provided in subdivision (b)(1).

(c) *Release of Evidence from an R.C.M. 706 Examination.* If the defense offers expert testimony concerning the mental condition of the accused, the military judge, upon motion, must order the release to the prosecution of the full contents, other than any statements made by the accused, of any report prepared pursuant to R.C.M. 706. If the defense offers statements made by the accused at such examination, the military judge, upon motion, may order the disclosure of such statements made by the accused and contained in the report as may be necessary in the interests of justice.

(d) *Noncompliance by the Accused.* The military judge may prohibit an accused who refuses to cooperate in a mental examination authorized under R.C.M. 706 from presenting any expert medical testimony as to any issue that would have been the subject of the mental examination.

(e) *Procedure.* The privilege in this rule may be claimed by the accused only under the procedure set forth in Mil. R. Evid. 304 for an objection or a motion to suppress.

Rule 303. Degrading questions

Statements and evidence are inadmissible if they are not material to the issue and may tend to degrade the person testifying.

Rule 304. Confessions and admissions

(a) *General rule.* If the accused makes a timely motion or objection under this rule, an involuntary statement from the accused, or any evidence derived therefrom, is inadmissible at trial except as provided in subdivision (e).

(1) *Definitions.* As used in this rule:

(A) "Involuntary statement" means a statement obtained in violation of the self-incrimination privilege or Due Process Clause of the Fifth Amendment to the United States Constitution, Article 31, or through the use of coercion, unlawful influence, or unlawful inducement.

(B) "Confession" means an acknowledgment of guilt.

(C) "Admission" means a self-incriminating statement falling short of an acknowledgment of guilt, even if it was intended by its maker to be exculpatory.

(2) Failure to deny an accusation of wrongdoing is not an admission of the truth of the accusation if at the time of the alleged failure the person was under investigation or was in confinement, arrest, or custody for the alleged wrongdoing.

(b) *Evidence Derived from a Statement of the Accused.* When the defense has made an appropriate and timely motion or objection under this rule, evidence allegedly derived from a statement of the accused may not be admitted unless the military judge finds by a preponderance of the evidence that:

(1) the statement was made voluntarily,

(2) the evidence was not obtained by use of the accused's statement, or

(3) the evidence would have been obtained even if the statement had not been made.

(c) *Corroboration of a Confession or Admission.*

(1) An admission or a confession of the accused may be considered as evidence against the accused on the question of guilt or innocence only if independent evidence, either direct or circumstantial, has been admitted into evidence that would tend to establish the trustworthiness of the admission or confession.

(2) Other uncorroborated confessions or admissions of the accused that would themselves require corroboration may not be used to supply this independent evidence. If the independent evidence raises an inference of the truth of the admission or confession, then it may be considered as evidence against the accused. Not every element or fact contained in the confession or admission must be independently proven for the confession or admission to be admitted into evidence in its entirety.

(3) Corroboration is not required for a statement made by the accused before the court by which the accused is being tried, for statements made prior to or contemporaneously with the act, or for statements offered under a rule of evidence other than that pertaining to the admissibility of admissions or confessions.

(4) *Quantum of Evidence Needed.* The independent evidence necessary to establish corroboration need not be sufficient of itself to establish beyond a reasonable doubt the truth of facts stated in the admission or confession. The independent evidence need raise only an inference of the truth of the admission or confession. The amount and type of evidence introduced as corroboration is a factor to be considered by the trier of fact in determining the weight, if any, to be given to the admission or confession.

(5) *Procedure.* The military judge alone is to determine when adequate evidence of corroboration has been received. Corroborating evidence must be introduced before the admission or confession is introduced unless the military judge allows submission of such evidence subject to later corroboration.

(d) *Disclosure of Statements by the Accused and Derivative Evidence.* Before arraignment, the prosecution must disclose to the defense the contents of all statements, oral or written, made by the accused that are relevant to the case, known to the trial counsel, and within the control of the Armed Forces, and all evidence derived from such statements, that the prosecution intends to offer against the accused.

(e) *Limited Use of an Involuntary Statement.* A statement obtained in violation of Article 31 or Mil. R. Evid. 305(b)-(c) may be used only:

(1) to impeach by contradiction the in-court testimony of the accused; or

(2) in a later prosecution against the accused for perjury, false swearing, or the making of a false official statement.

(f) *Motions and Objections.*

(1) Motions to suppress or objections under this rule, or Mil. R. Evid. 302 or 305, to any statement or derivative evidence that has been disclosed must be made by the defense prior to submission of a plea. In the absence of such motion or objection, the defense may not raise the issue at a later time except as permitted by the military judge for good cause shown. Failure to so move or object constitutes a waiver of the objection.

(2) If the prosecution seeks to offer a statement made by the accused or derivative evidence that was not disclosed before arraignment, the prosecution must provide timely notice to the military judge and defense counsel. The defense may object at that time, and the military judge may make such orders as are required in the interests of justice.

(3) The defense may present evidence relevant to the admissibility of evidence as to which there has been an objection or motion to suppress under this rule. An accused may testify for the limited purpose

of denying that the accused made the statement or that the statement was made voluntarily.

(A) Prior to the introduction of such testimony by the accused, the defense must inform the military judge that the testimony is offered under subdivision (f)(3).

(B) When the accused testifies under subdivision (f)(3), the accused may be cross-examined only as to the matter on which he or she testifies. Nothing said by the accused on either direct or cross-examination may be used against the accused for any purpose other than in a prosecution for perjury, false swearing, or the making of a false official statement.

(4) *Specificity.* The military judge may require the defense to specify the grounds upon which the defense moves to suppress or object to evidence. If defense counsel, despite the exercise of due diligence, has been unable to interview adequately those persons involved in the taking of a statement, the military judge may make any order required in the interests of justice, including authorization for the defense to make a general motion to suppress or general objection.

(5) *Rulings.* The military judge must rule, prior to plea, upon any motion to suppress or objection to evidence made prior to plea unless, for good cause, the military judge orders that the ruling be deferred for determination at trial or after findings. The military judge may not defer ruling if doing so adversely affects a party's right to appeal the ruling. The military judge must state essential findings of fact on the record when the ruling involves factual issues.

(6) *Burden of Proof.* When the defense has made an appropriate motion or objection under this rule, the prosecution has the burden of establishing the admissibility of the evidence. When the military judge has required a specific motion or objection under subdivision (f)(4), the burden on the prosecution extends only to the grounds upon which the defense moved to suppress or object to the evidence.

(7) *Standard of Proof.* The military judge must find by a preponderance of the evidence that a statement by the accused was made voluntarily before it may be received into evidence. When trial is by a special court-martial without a military judge, a determination by the president of the court that a statement was made voluntarily is subject to objection by any member of the court. When such objection is

made, it will be resolved pursuant to R.C.M. 801(e)(3)(C).

(8) *Effect of Guilty Plea.* Except as otherwise expressly provided in R.C.M. 910(a)(2), a plea of guilty to an offense that results in a finding of guilty waives all privileges against self-incrimination and all motions and objections under this rule with respect to that offense regardless of whether raised prior to plea.

(g) *Weight of the Evidence.* If a statement is admitted into evidence, the military judge must permit the defense to present relevant evidence with respect to the voluntariness of the statement and must instruct the members to give such weight to the statement as it deserves under all the circumstances.

(h) *Completeness.* If only part of an alleged admission or confession is introduced against the accused, the defense, by cross-examination or otherwise, may introduce the remaining portions of the statement.

(i) *Evidence of an Oral Statement.* A voluntary oral confession or admission of the accused may be proved by the testimony of anyone who heard the accused make it, even if it was reduced to writing and the writing is not accounted for.

(j) *Refusal to Obey an Order to Submit a Body Substance.* If an accused refuses a lawful order to submit for chemical analysis a sample of his or her blood, breath, urine or other body substance, evidence of such refusal may be admitted into evidence on:

(1) A charge of violating an order to submit such a sample; or

(2) Any other charge on which the results of the chemical analysis would have been admissible.

Rule 305. Warnings about rights

(a) *General rule.* A statement obtained in violation of this rule is involuntary and will be treated under Mil. R. Evid. 304.

(b) *Definitions.* As used in this rule:

(1) "Person subject to the code" means a person subject to the Uniform Code of Military Justice as contained in Chapter 47 of Title 10, United States Code. This term includes, for purposes of subdivision (c) of this rule, a knowing agent of any such person or of a military unit.

(2) "Interrogation" means any formal or informal questioning in which an incriminating response ei-

ther is sought or is a reasonable consequence of such questioning.

(3) "Custodial interrogation" means questioning that takes place while the accused or suspect is in custody, could reasonably believe himself or herself to be in custody, or is otherwise deprived of his or her freedom of action in any significant way.

(c) *Warnings Concerning the Accusation, Right to Remain Silent, and Use of Statements.*

(1) *Article 31 Rights Warnings.* A statement obtained from the accused in violation of the accused's rights under Article 31 is involuntary and therefore inadmissible against the accused except as provided in subdivision (d). Pursuant to Article 31, a person subject to the code may not interrogate or request any statement from an accused or a person suspected of an offense without first:

(A) informing the accused or suspect of the nature of the accusation;

(B) advising the accused or suspect that the accused or suspect has the right to remain silent; and

(C) advising the accused or suspect that any statement made may be used as evidence against the accused or suspect in a trial by court-martial.

(2) *Fifth Amendment Right to Counsel.* If a person suspected of an offense and subjected to custodial interrogation requests counsel, any statement made in the interrogation after such request, or evidence derived from the interrogation after such request, is inadmissible against the accused unless counsel was present for the interrogation.

(3) *Sixth Amendment Right to Counsel.* If an accused against whom charges have been preferred is interrogated on matters concerning the preferred charges by anyone acting in a law enforcement capacity, or the agent of such a person, and the accused requests counsel, or if the accused has appointed or retained counsel, any statement made in the interrogation, or evidence derived from the interrogation, is inadmissible unless counsel was present for the interrogation.

(4) *Exercise of Rights.* If a person chooses to exercise the privilege against self-incrimination, questioning must cease immediately. If a person who is subjected to interrogation under the circumstances described in subdivisions (c)(2) or (c)(3) of this rule chooses to exercise the right to counsel, questioning must cease until counsel is present.

(d) *Presence of Counsel.* When a person entitled to counsel under this rule requests counsel, a judge advocate or an individual certified in accordance with Article 27(b) will be provided by the United States at no expense to the person and without regard to the person's indigency and must be present before the interrogation may proceed. In addition to counsel supplied by the United States, the person may retain civilian counsel at no expense to the United States. Unless otherwise provided by regulations of the Secretary concerned, an accused or suspect does not have a right under this rule to have military counsel of his or her own selection.

(e) *Waiver.*

(1) *Waiver of the Privilege Against Self-Incrimination.* After receiving applicable warnings under this rule, a person may waive the rights described therein and in Mil. R. Evid. 301 and make a statement. The waiver must be made freely, knowingly, and intelligently. A written waiver is not required. The accused or suspect must affirmatively acknowledge that he or she understands the rights involved, affirmatively decline the right to counsel, and affirmatively consent to making a statement.

(2) *Waiver of the Right to Counsel.* If the right to counsel is applicable under this rule and the accused or suspect does not affirmatively decline the right to counsel, the prosecution must demonstrate by a preponderance of the evidence that the individual waived the right to counsel.

(3) *Waiver After Initially Invoking the Right to Counsel.*

(A) *Fifth Amendment Right to Counsel.* If an accused or suspect subjected to custodial interrogation requests counsel, any subsequent waiver of the right to counsel obtained during a custodial interrogation concerning the same or different offenses is invalid unless the prosecution can demonstrate by a preponderance of the evidence that:

(i) the accused or suspect initiated the communication leading to the waiver; or

(ii) the accused or suspect has not continuously had his or her freedom restricted by confinement, or other means, during the period between the request for counsel and the subsequent waiver.

(B) *Sixth Amendment Right to Counsel.* If an accused or suspect interrogated after preferral of charges as described in subdivision (c)(1) requests counsel, any subsequent waiver of the right to counsel obtained during an interrogation concerning the same offenses is invalid unless the prosecution can demonstrate by a preponderance of the evidence that the accused or suspect initiated the communication leading to the waiver.

(f) *Standards for Nonmilitary Interrogations.*

(1) *United States Civilian Interrogations.* When a person subject to the code is interrogated by an official or agent of the United States, of the District of Columbia, or of a State, Commonwealth, or possession of the United States, or any political subdivision of such a State, Commonwealth, or possession, the person's entitlement to rights warnings and the validity of any waiver of applicable rights will be determined by the principles of law generally recognized in the trial of criminal cases in the United States district courts involving similar interrogations.

(2) *Foreign Interrogations.* Warnings under Article 31 and the Fifth and Sixth Amendments to the United States Constitution are not required during an interrogation conducted outside of a State, district, Commonwealth, territory, or possession of the United States by officials of a foreign government or their agents unless such interrogation is conducted, instigated, or participated in by military personnel or their agents or by those officials or agents listed in subdivision (f)(1). A statement obtained from a foreign interrogation is admissible unless the statement is obtained through the use of coercion, unlawful influence, or unlawful inducement. An interrogation is not "participated in" by military personnel or their agents or by the officials or agents listed in subdivision (f)(1) merely because such a person was present at an interrogation conducted in a foreign nation by officials of a foreign government or their agents, or because such a person acted as an interpreter or took steps to mitigate damage to property or physical harm during the foreign interrogation.

Rule 306. Statements by one of several accused

When two or more accused are tried at the same trial, evidence of a statement made by one of them which is admissible only against him or her or only against some but not all of the accused may not be received in evidence unless all references inculpating an accused against whom the statement is inadmissible are deleted effectively or the maker of the statement is subject to cross-examination.

Rule 311. Evidence obtained from unlawful searches and seizures

(a) *General rule.* Evidence obtained as a result of an unlawful search or seizure made by a person acting in a governmental capacity is inadmissible against the accused if:

(1) the accused makes a timely motion to suppress or an objection to the evidence under this rule;

(2) the accused had a reasonable expectation of privacy in the person, place, or property searched; the accused had a legitimate interest in the property or evidence seized when challenging a seizure; or the accused would otherwise have grounds to object to the search or seizure under the Constitution of the United States as applied to members of the Armed Forces; and

(3) exclusion of the evidence results in appreciable deterrence of future unlawful searches or seizures and the benefits of such deterrence outweigh the costs to the justice system.

(b) *Definition.* As used in this rule, a search or seizure is "unlawful" if it was conducted, instigated, or participated in by:

(1) military personnel or their agents and was in violation of the Constitution of the United States as applied to members of the Armed Forces, a federal statute applicable to trials by court-martial that requires exclusion of evidence obtained in violation thereof, or Mil. R. Evid. 312-317;

(2) other officials or agents of the United States, of the District of Columbia, or of a State, Commonwealth, or possession of the United States or any political subdivision of such a State, Commonwealth, or possession, and was in violation of the Constitution of the United States, or is unlawful under the principles of law generally applied in the trial of criminal cases in the United States district courts involving a similar search or seizure; or

(3) officials of a foreign government or their agents, where evidence was obtained as a result of a foreign search or seizure that subjected the accused to gross and brutal maltreatment. A search or seizure is not "participated in" by a United States military or civilian official merely because that person is present at a search or seizure conducted in a foreign nation by officials of a foreign government or their agents, or because that person acted as an interpreter or took steps to mitigate damage to property or physical harm during the foreign search or seizure.

(c) *Exceptions.*

(1) *Impeachment.* Evidence that was obtained as a result of an unlawful search or seizure may be used to impeach by contradiction the in-court testimony of the accused.

(2) *Inevitable Discovery.* Evidence that was obtained as a result of an unlawful search or seizure may be used when the evidence would have been obtained even if such unlawful search or seizure had not been made.

(3) *Good Faith Execution of a Warrant or Search Authorization.* Evidence that was obtained as a result of an unlawful search or seizure may be used if:

(A) the search or seizure resulted from an authorization to search, seize or apprehend issued by an individual competent to issue the authorization under Mil. R. Evid. 315(d) or from a search warrant or arrest warrant issued by competent civilian authority;

(B) the individual issuing the authorization or warrant had a substantial basis for determining the existence of probable cause; and

(C) the officials seeking and executing the authorization or warrant reasonably and with good faith relied on the issuance of the authorization or warrant. Good faith is to be determined using an objective standard.

(4) *Reliance on Statute.* Evidence that was obtained as a result of an unlawful search or seizure may be used when the official seeking the evidence acts in objectively reasonable reliance on a statute later held violative of the Fourth Amendment.

(d) *Motions to Suppress and Objections.*

(1) *Disclosure.* Prior to arraignment, the prosecution must disclose to the defense all evidence seized from the person or property of the accused, or believed to be owned by the accused, or evidence derived therefrom, that it intends to offer into evidence against the accused at trial.

(2) *Time Requirements.*

(A) When evidence has been disclosed prior to arraignment under subdivision (d)(1), the defense must make any motion to suppress or objection under this rule prior to submission of a plea. In the absence of such motion or objection, the defense may not raise the issue at a later time except as permitted by the military judge for good cause shown. Failure to so move or object constitutes a waiver of the motion or objection.

(B) If the prosecution intends to offer evidence described in subdivision (d)(1) that was not disclosed prior to arraignment, the prosecution must provide timely notice to the military judge and to counsel for the accused. The defense may enter an objection at that time and the military judge may make such orders as are required in the interest of justice.

(3) *Specificity.* The military judge may require the defense to specify the grounds upon which the defense moves to suppress or object to evidence described in subdivision (d)(1). If defense counsel, despite the exercise of due diligence, has been unable to interview adequately those persons involved in the search or seizure, the military judge may enter any order required by the interests of justice, including authorization for the defense to make a general motion to suppress or a general objection.

(4) *Challenging Probable Cause.*

(A) *Relevant Evidence.* If the defense challenges evidence seized pursuant to a search warrant or search authorization on the ground that the warrant or authorization was not based upon probable cause, the evidence relevant to the motion is limited to evidence concerning the information actually presented to or otherwise known by the authorizing officer, except as provided in subdivision (d)(4)(B).

(B) *False Statements.* If the defense makes a substantial preliminary showing that a government agent included a false statement knowingly and intentionally or with reckless disregard for the truth in the information presented to the authorizing officer, and if the allegedly false statement is necessary to the finding of probable cause, the defense, upon request, is entitled to a hearing. At the hearing, the defense has the burden of establishing by a preponderance of the evidence the allegation of knowing and intentional falsity or reckless disregard for the truth. If the defense meets its burden, the prosecution has the burden of proving by a preponderance of the evidence, with the false information set aside, that the remaining information presented to the authorizing officer is sufficient to establish probable cause. If the prosecution does not meet its burden, the objection or motion must be granted unless the search is otherwise lawful under these rules.

(5) *Burden and Standard of Proof.*

(A) *In general.* When the defense makes an appropriate motion or objection under subdivision (d), the prosecution has the burden of proving by a preponderance of the evidence that the evidence was not obtained as a result of an unlawful search or seizure, that the evidence would have been obtained even if the unlawful search or seizure had not been made, that the evidence was obtained by officials who reasonably and with good faith relied on the issuance of an authorization to search, seize, or apprehend or a search warrant or an arrest warrant; that the evidence was obtained by officials in objectively reasonable reliance on a statute later held violative of the Fourth Amendment; or that the deterrence of future unlawful searches or seizures is not appreciable or such deterrence does not outweigh the costs to the justice system of excluding the evidence.

(B) *Statement Following Apprehension.* In addition to subdivision (d)(5)(A), a statement obtained from a person apprehended in a dwelling in violation R.C.M. 302(d)(2) and (e), is admissible if the prosecution shows by a preponderance of the evidence that the apprehension was based on probable cause, the statement was made at a location outside the dwelling subsequent to the apprehension, and the statement was otherwise in compliance with these rules.

(C) *Specific Grounds of Motion or Objection.* When the military judge has required the defense to make a specific motion or objection under subdivision (d)(3), the burden on the prosecution extends only to the grounds upon which the defense moved to suppress or objected to the evidence.

(6) *Defense Evidence.* The defense may present evidence relevant to the admissibility of evidence as to which there has been an appropriate motion or objection under this rule. An accused may testify for the limited purpose of contesting the legality of the search or seizure giving rise to the challenged evidence. Prior to the introduction of such testimony by the accused, the defense must inform the military judge that the testimony is offered under subdivision (d). When the accused testifies under subdivision (d), the accused may be cross-examined only as to the matter on which he or she testifies. Nothing said by the accused on either direct or cross-examination may be used against the accused for any purpose other than in a prosecution for perjury, false swearing, or the making of a false official statement.

(7) *Rulings.* The military judge must rule, prior to plea, upon any motion to suppress or objection to evidence made prior to plea unless, for good cause, the military judge orders that the ruling be deferred for determination at trial or after findings. The military judge may not defer ruling if doing so adversely affects a party's right to appeal the ruling. The military judge must state essential findings of fact on the record when the ruling involves factual issues.

(8) *Informing the Members.* If a defense motion or objection under this rule is sustained in whole or in part, the court-martial members may not be informed of that fact except when the military judge must instruct the members to disregard evidence.

(e) *Effect of Guilty Plea.* Except as otherwise expressly provided in R.C.M. 910(a)(2), a plea of guilty to an offense that results in a finding of guilty waives all issues under the Fourth Amendment to the Constitution of the United States and Mil. R. Evid. 311-317 with respect to the offense, whether or not raised prior to plea.

Rule 312. Body views and intrusions

(a) *General rule.* Evidence obtained from body views and intrusions conducted in accordance with this rule is admissible at trial when relevant and not otherwise inadmissible under these rules.

(b) *Visual examination of the body.*

(1) *Consensual Examination.* Evidence obtained from a visual examination of the unclothed body is admissible if the person consented to the inspection in accordance with Mil. R. Evid. 314(e).

(2) *Involuntary Examination.* Evidence obtained from an involuntary display of the unclothed body, including a visual examination of body cavities, is admissible only if the inspection was conducted in a reasonable fashion and authorized under the following provisions of the Military Rules of Evidence:

(A) inspections and inventories under Mil. R. Evid. 313;

(B) searches under Mil. R. Evid. 314(b) and 314(c) if there is a reasonable suspicion that weapons, contraband, or evidence of crime is concealed on the body of the person to be searched;

(C) searches incident to lawful apprehension under Mil. R. Evid. 314(g);

(D) searches within a jail, confinement facility, or similar facility under Mil. R. Evid. 314(h) if reasonably necessary to maintain the security of the institution or its personnel;

(E) emergency searches under Mil. R. Evid. 314(i); and

(F) probable cause searches under Mil. R. Evid. 315.

Discussion

An examination of the unclothed body under this rule should be conducted whenever practicable by a person of the same sex as that of the person being examined; however, failure to comply with this requirement does not make an examination an unlawful search within the meaning of Mil. R. Evid. 311.

(c) *Intrusion into Body Cavities.*

(1) *Mouth, Nose, and Ears.* Evidence obtained from a reasonable nonconsensual physical intrusion into the mouth, nose, and ears is admissible under the same standards that apply to a visual examination of the body under subdivision (b).

(2) *Other Body Cavities.* Evidence obtained from nonconsensual intrusions into other body cavities is admissible only if made in a reasonable fashion by a person with appropriate medical qualifications and if:

(A) at the time of the intrusion there was probable cause to believe that a weapon, contraband, or other evidence of crime was present;

(B) conducted to remove weapons, contraband, or evidence of crime discovered under subdivisions (b) or (c)(2)(A) of this rule;

(C) conducted pursuant to Mil. R. Evid. 316(c)(5)(C);

(D) conducted pursuant to a search warrant or search authorization under Mil. R. Evid. 315; or

(E) conducted pursuant to Mil. R. Evid. 314(h) based on a reasonable suspicion that the individual is concealing a weapon, contraband, or evidence of crime.

(d) *Extraction of Body Fluids.* Evidence obtained from nonconsensual extraction of body fluids is admissible if seized pursuant to a search warrant or a search authorization under Mil. R. Evid. 315. Evidence obtained from nonconsensual extraction of body fluids made without such a warrant or authorization is admissible, notwithstanding Mil. R. Evid. 315(g), only when probable cause existed at the time of extraction to believe that evidence of crime would be found and that the delay necessary to obtain a search warrant or search authorization could have resulted in the destruction of the evidence. Evidence obtained from nonconsensual extraction of body fluids is admissible only when executed in a reasonable fashion by a person with appropriate medical qualifications.

(e) *Other Intrusive Searches.* Evidence obtained from a nonconsensual intrusive search of the body, other than searches described in subdivisions (c) or (d), conducted to locate or obtain weapons, contraband, or evidence of crime is admissible only if obtained pursuant to a search warrant or search authorization under Mil. R. Evid. 315 and conducted in a reasonable fashion by a person with appropriate medical qualifications in such a manner so as not to endanger the health of the person to be searched.

Discussion

Compelling a person to ingest substances for the purposes of locating the property described above or to compel the bodily elimination of such property is a search within the meaning of this section.

(f) *Intrusions for Valid Medical Purposes.* Evidence or contraband obtained in the course of a medical examination or an intrusion conducted for a valid medical purpose is admissible. Such an examination or intrusion may not, for the purpose of obtaining evidence or contraband, exceed what is necessary for the medical purpose.

Discussion

Nothing in this rule will be deemed to interfere with the lawful authority of the Armed Forces to take whatever action may be necessary to preserve the health of a service member.

(g) *Medical Qualifications.* The Secretary concerned may prescribe appropriate medical qualifications for persons who conduct searches and seizures under this rule.

Rule 313. Inspections and inventories in the Armed Forces

(a) *General Rule.* Evidence obtained from lawful inspections and inventories in the Armed Forces is admissible at trial when relevant and not otherwise inadmissible under these rules. An unlawful weapon, contraband, or other evidence of a crime discovered during a lawful inspection or inventory may be seized and is admissible in accordance with this rule.

(b) *Lawful Inspections.* An "inspection" is an examination of the whole or part of a unit, organization, installation, vessel, aircraft, or vehicle, including an examination conducted at entrance and exit points, conducted as an incident of command the primary purpose of which is to determine and to ensure the security, military fitness, or good order and discipline of the unit, organization, installation, vessel, aircraft, or vehicle. Inspections must be conducted in a reasonable fashion and, if applicable, must comply with Mil. R. Evid. 312. Inspections may utilize any reasonable natural or technological aid and may be conducted with or without notice to those inspected.

(1) *Purpose of Inspections.* An inspection may include, but is not limited to, an examination to determine and to ensure that any or all of the following requirements are met: that the command is properly equipped, functioning properly, maintaining proper standards of readiness, sea or airworthiness, sanitation and cleanliness; and that personnel are present, fit, and ready for duty. An order to produce body fluids, such as urine, is permissible in accordance with this rule.

(2) *Searches for Evidence.* An examination made for the primary purpose of obtaining evidence for use in a trial by court-martial or in other disciplinary proceedings is not an inspection within the meaning of this rule.

(3) *Examinations to Locate and Confiscate Weapons or Contraband.*

(A) An inspection may include an examination to locate and confiscate unlawful weapons and other contraband provided that the criteria set forth in subdivision (b)(3)(B) are not implicated.

(B) The prosecution must prove by clear and convincing evidence that the examination was an inspection within the meaning of this rule if a purpose of an examination is to locate weapons or contraband, and if:

(i) the examination was directed immediately following a report of a specific offense in the unit, organization, installation, vessel, aircraft, or vehicle and was not previously scheduled;

(ii) specific individuals are selected for examination; or

(iii) persons examined are subjected to sub-

stantially different intrusions during the same examination.

(c) *Lawful Inventories.* An "inventory" is a reasonable examination, accounting, or other control measure used to account for or control property, assets, or other resources. It is administrative and not prosecutorial in nature, and if applicable, the inventory must comply with Mil. R. Evid. 312. An examination made for the primary purpose of obtaining evidence for use in a trial by court-martial or in other disciplinary proceedings is not an inventory within the meaning of this rule.

Rule 314. Searches not requiring probable cause

(a) *General Rule.* Evidence obtained from reasonable searches not requiring probable cause is admissible at trial when relevant and not otherwise inadmissible under these rules or the Constitution of the United States as applied to members of the Armed Forces.

(b) *Border Searches.* Evidence from a border search for customs or immigration purposes authorized by a federal statute is admissible.

(c) *Searches Upon Entry to or Exit from United States Installations, Aircraft, and Vessels Abroad.* In addition to inspections under Mil. R. Evid. 313(b), evidence is admissible when a commander of a United States military installation, enclave, or aircraft on foreign soil, or in foreign or international airspace, or a United States vessel in foreign or international waters, has authorized appropriate personnel to search persons or the property of such persons upon entry to or exit from the installation, enclave, aircraft, or vessel to ensure the security, military fitness, or good order and discipline of the command. A search made for the primary purpose of obtaining evidence for use in a trial by court-martial or other disciplinary proceeding is not authorized by subdivision (c).

Discussion

Searches under subdivision (c) may not be conducted at a time or in a manner contrary to an express provision of a treaty or agreement to which the United States is a party; however, failure to comply with a treaty or agreement does not render a search unlawful within the meaning of Mil. R. Evid. 311.

(d) *Searches of Government Property.* Evidence

resulting from a search of government property without probable cause is admissible under this rule unless the person to whom the property is issued or assigned has a reasonable expectation of privacy therein at the time of the search. Normally a person does not have a reasonable expectation of privacy in government property that is not issued for personal use. Wall or floor lockers in living quarters issued for the purpose of storing personal possessions normally are issued for personal use, but the determination as to whether a person has a reasonable expectation of privacy in government property issued for personal use depends on the facts and circumstances at the time of the search.

(e) *Consent Searches.*

(1) *General Rule.* Evidence of a search conducted without probable cause is admissible if conducted with lawful consent.

(2) *Who May Consent.* A person may consent to a search of his or her person or property, or both, unless control over such property has been given to another. A person may grant consent to search property when the person exercises control over that property.

Discussion

Where a co-occupant of property is physically present at the time of the requested search and expressly states his refusal to consent to the search, a warrantless search is unreasonable as to that co-occupant and evidence from the search is inadmissible as to that co-occupant. *Georgia v. Randolph*, 547 U.S. 103 (2006).

---

(3) *Scope of Consent.* Consent may be limited in any way by the person granting consent, including limitations in terms of time, place, or property, and may be withdrawn at any time.

(4) *Voluntariness.* To be valid, consent must be given voluntarily. Voluntariness is a question to be determined from all the circumstances. Although a person's knowledge of the right to refuse to give consent is a factor to be considered in determining voluntariness, the prosecution is not required to demonstrate such knowledge as a prerequisite to establishing a voluntary consent. Mere submission to the color of authority of personnel performing law enforcement duties or acquiescence in an announced or indicated purpose to search is not a voluntary consent.

(5) *Burden and Standard of Proof.* The prosecution must prove consent by clear and convincing evidence. The fact that a person was in custody while granting consent is a factor to be considered in determining the voluntariness of consent, but it does not affect the standard of proof.

(f) *Searches Incident to a Lawful Stop.*

(1) *Lawfulness.* A stop is lawful when conducted by a person authorized to apprehend under R.C.M. 302(b) or others performing law enforcement duties and when the person making the stop has information or observes unusual conduct that leads him or her reasonably to conclude in light of his or her experience that criminal activity may be afoot. The stop must be temporary and investigatory in nature.

(2) *Stop and Frisk.* Evidence is admissible if seized from a person who was lawfully stopped and who was frisked for weapons because he or she was reasonably suspected to be armed and dangerous. Contraband or evidence that is located in the process of a lawful frisk may be seized.

Discussion

Subdivision (f)(2) requires that the official making the stop have a reasonable suspicion based on specific and articulable facts that the person being frisked is armed and dangerous. Officer safety is a factor, and the officer need not be absolutely certain that the individual detained is armed for the purposes of frisking or patting down that person's outer clothing for weapons. The test is whether a reasonably prudent person in similar circumstances would be warranted in a belief that his or her safety was in danger. The purpose of a frisk is to search for weapons or other dangerous items, including but not limited to: firearms, knives, needles, or razor blades. A limited search of outer clothing for weapons serves to protect both the officer and the public; therefore, a frisk is reasonable under the Fourth Amendment.

---

(3) *Vehicles.* Evidence is admissible if seized in the course of a search for weapons in the areas of the passenger compartment of a vehicle in which a weapon may be placed or hidden, so long as the person lawfully stopped is the driver or a passenger and the official who made the stop has a reasonable suspicion that the person stopped is dangerous and may gain immediate control of a weapon.

Discussion

The scope of the search is similar to the "stop and frisk" defined in subdivision (f)(2) of this rule. During the search for weapons, the official may seize any item that is immediately apparent as contraband or as evidence related to the offense serving as the basis for the stop. As a matter of safety, the official may, after conducting a lawful stop of a vehicle, order the driver and any passengers out of the car without any additional suspicion or justification.

(g) *Searches Incident to Apprehension.*

(1) *General Rule.* Evidence is admissible if seized in a search of a person who has been lawfully apprehended or if seized as a result of a reasonable protective sweep.

(2) *Search for Weapons and Destructible Evidence.* A lawful search incident to apprehension may include a search for weapons or destructible evidence in the area within the immediate control of a person who has been apprehended. 'Immediate control' means that area in which the individual searching could reasonably believe that the person apprehended could reach with a sudden movement to obtain such property.

Discussion

The scope of the search for weapons is limited to that which is necessary to protect the arresting official. The official may not search a vehicle for weapons if there is no possibility that the arrestee could reach into the searched area, for example, after the arrestee is handcuffed and removed from the vehicle. The scope of the search is broader for destructible evidence related to the offense for which the individual is being arrested. Unlike a search for weapons, the search for destructible offense-related evidence may take place after the arrestee is handcuffed and removed from a vehicle. If, however, the official cannot expect to find destructible offense-related evidence, this exception does not apply.

---

(3) *Protective Sweep for Other Persons.*

(A) *Area of Potential Immediate Attack.* Apprehending officials may, incident to apprehension, as a precautionary matter and without probable cause or reasonable suspicion, look in closets and other spaces immediately adjoining the place of apprehension from which an attack could be immediately launched.

(B) *Wider Protective Sweep.* When an apprehension takes place at a location in which another person might be present who might endanger the apprehending officials or others in the area of the apprehension, a search incident to arrest may lawfully include a reasonable examination of those spaces where a person might be found. Such a reasonable examination is lawful under subdivision (g) if the apprehending official has a reasonable suspicion based on specific and articulable facts that the

area to be examined harbors an individual posing a danger to those in the area of the apprehension.

(h) *Searches within Jails, Confinement Facilities, or Similar Facilities.* Evidence obtained from a search within a jail, confinement facility, or similar facility is admissible even if conducted without probable cause provided that it was authorized by persons with authority over the institution.

(i) *Emergency Searches to Save Life or for Related Purposes.* Evidence obtained from emergency searches of persons or property conducted to save life, or for a related purpose, is admissible provided that the search was conducted in a good faith effort to render immediate medical aid, to obtain information that will assist in the rendering of such aid, or to prevent immediate or ongoing personal injury.

(j) *Searches of Open Fields or Woodlands.* Evidence obtained from a search of an open field or woodland is admissible provided that the search was not unlawful within the meaning of Mil. R. Evid. 311.

Rule 315. Probable cause searches

(a) *General rule.* Evidence obtained from reasonable searches conducted pursuant to a search warrant or search authorization, or under the exigent circumstances described in this rule, is admissible at trial when relevant and not otherwise inadmissible under these rules or the Constitution of the United States as applied to members of the Armed Forces.

Discussion

Although military personnel should adhere to procedural guidance regarding the conduct of searches, violation of such procedural guidance does not render evidence inadmissible unless the search is unlawful under these rules or the Constitution of the United States as applied to members of the Armed Forces. For example, if the person whose property is to be searched is present during a search conducted pursuant to a search authorization granted under this rule, the person conducting the search should notify him or her of the fact of authorization and the general substance of the authorization. Such notice may be made prior to or contemporaneously with the search. Property seized should be inventoried at the time of a seizure or as soon thereafter as practicable. A copy of the inventory should be given to a person from whose possession or premises the property was taken. Failure to provide notice, make an inventory, furnish a copy thereof, or otherwise comply with this guidance does not render a search or seizure unlawful within the meaning of Mil. R. Evid. 311.

(b) *Definitions.* As used in these rules:

(1) "Search authorization" means express permission, written or oral, issued by competent military authority to search a person or an area for specified property or evidence or for a specific person and to seize such property, evidence, or person. It may contain an order directing subordinate personnel to conduct a search in a specified manner.

(2) "Search warrant" means express permission to search and seize issued by competent civilian authority.

(c) *Scope of Search Authorization.* A search authorization may be valid under this rule for a search of:

(1) the physical person of anyone subject to military law or the law of war wherever found;

(2) military property of the United States or of nonappropriated fund activities of an Armed force of the United States wherever located;

(3) persons or property situated on or in a military installation, encampment, vessel, aircraft, vehicle, or any other location under military control, wherever located; or

(4) nonmilitary property within a foreign country.

Discussion

If nonmilitary property within a foreign country is owned, used, occupied by, or in the possession of an agency of the United States other than the Department of Defense, a search should be conducted in coordination with an appropriate representative of the agency concerned, although failure to obtain such coordination would not render a search unlawful within the meaning of Mil. R. Evid. 311. If other nonmilitary property within a foreign country is to be searched, the search should be conducted in accordance with any relevant treaty or agreement or in coordination with an appropriate representative of the foreign country, although failure to obtain such coordination or noncompliance with a treaty or agreement would not render a search unlawful within the meaning of Mil. R. Evid. 311.

(d) *Who May Authorize.* A search authorization under this rule is valid only if issued by an impartial individual in one of the categories set forth in subdivisions (d)(1) and (d)(2). An otherwise impartial authorizing official does not lose impartiality merely because he or she is present at the scene of a search or is otherwise readily available to persons who may seek the issuance of a search authorization; nor does such an official lose impartial character merely because the official previously and impartially authorized investigative activities when such previous authorization is similar in intent or function to a

pretrial authorization made by the United States district courts.

(1) *Commander.* A commander or other person serving in a position designated by the Secretary concerned as either a position analogous to an officer in charge or a position of command, who has control over the place where the property or person to be searched is situated or found, or, if that place is not under military control, having control over persons subject to military law or the law of war; or

(2) *Military Judge or Magistrate.* A military judge or magistrate if authorized under regulations prescribed by the Secretary of Defense or the Secretary concerned.

(e) *Who May Search.*

(1) *Search Authorization.* Any commissioned officer, warrant officer, petty officer, noncommissioned officer, and, when in the execution of guard or police duties, any criminal investigator, member of the Air Force security forces, military police, or shore patrol, or person designated by proper authority to perform guard or police duties, or any agent of any such person, may conduct or authorize a search when a search authorization has been granted under this rule or a search would otherwise be proper under subdivision (g).

(2) *Search Warrants.* Any civilian or military criminal investigator authorized to request search warrants pursuant to applicable law or regulation is authorized to serve and execute search warrants. The execution of a search warrant affects admissibility only insofar as exclusion of evidence is required by the Constitution of the United States or an applicable federal statute.

(f) *Basis for Search Authorizations.*

(1) *Probable Cause Requirement.* A search authorization issued under this rule must be based upon probable cause.

(2) *Probable Cause Determination.* Probable cause to search exists when there is a reasonable belief that the person, property, or evidence sought is located in the place or on the person to be searched. A search authorization may be based upon hearsay evidence in whole or in part. A determination of probable cause under this rule will be based upon any or all of the following:

(A) written statements communicated to the authorizing official;

(B) oral statements communicated to the

authorizing official in person, via telephone, or by other appropriate means of communication; or

(C) such information as may be known by the authorizing official that would not preclude the officer from acting in an impartial fashion. The Secretary of Defense or the Secretary concerned may prescribe additional requirements through regulation.

(g) *Exigencies.* Evidence obtained from a probable cause search is admissible without a search warrant or search authorization when there is a reasonable belief that the delay necessary to obtain a search warrant or search authorization would result in the removal, destruction, or concealment of the property or evidence sought. Military operational necessity may create an exigency by prohibiting or preventing communication with a person empowered to grant a search authorization.

Rule 316. Seizures

(a) *General rule.* Evidence obtained from reasonable seizures is admissible at trial when relevant and not otherwise inadmissible under these rules or the Constitution of the United States as applied to members of the Armed Forces.

(b) *Apprehension.* Apprehension is governed by R.C.M. 302.

(c) *Seizure of Property or Evidence.*

(1) *Based on Probable Cause.* Evidence is admissible when seized based on a reasonable belief that the property or evidence is an unlawful weapon, contraband, evidence of crime, or might be used to resist apprehension or to escape.

(2) *Abandoned Property.* Abandoned property may be seized without probable cause and without a search warrant or search authorization. Such seizure may be made by any person.

(3) *Consent.* Property or evidence may be seized with consent consistent with the requirements applicable to consensual searches under Mil. R. Evid. 314.

(4) *Government Property.* Government property may be seized without probable cause and without a search warrant or search authorization by any person listed in subdivision (d), unless the person to whom the property is issued or assigned has a reasonable expectation of privacy therein, as provided in Mil. R. Evid. 314(d), at the time of the seizure.

(5) *Other Property.* Property or evidence not in-

cluded in subdivisions (c)(1)-(4) may be seized for use in evidence by any person listed in subdivision (d) if:

(A) *Authorization.* The person is authorized to seize the property or evidence by a search warrant or a search authorization under Mil. R. Evid. 315;

(B) *Exigent Circumstances.* The person has probable cause to seize the property or evidence and under Mil. R. Evid. 315(g) a search warrant or search authorization is not required; or

(C) *Plain View.* The person while in the course of otherwise lawful activity observes in a reasonable fashion property or evidence that the person has probable cause to seize.

(6) *Temporary Detention.* Nothing in this rule prohibits temporary detention of property on less than probable cause when authorized under the Constitution of the United States.

(d) *Who May Seize.* Any commissioned officer, warrant officer, petty officer, noncommissioned officer, and, when in the execution of guard or police duties, any criminal investigator, member of the Air Force security forces, military police, or shore patrol, or individual designated by proper authority to perform guard or police duties, or any agent of any such person, may seize property pursuant to this rule.

(e) *Other Seizures.* Evidence obtained from a seizure not addressed in this rule is admissible provided that its seizure was permissible under the Constitution of the United States as applied to members of the Armed Forces.

Rule 317. Interception of wire and oral communications

(a) *General rule.* Wire or oral communications constitute evidence obtained as a result of an unlawful search or seizure within the meaning of Mil. R. Evid. 311 when such evidence must be excluded under the Fourth Amendment to the Constitution of the United States as applied to members of the Armed Forces or if such evidence must be excluded under a federal statute applicable to members of the Armed Forces.

(b) *When Authorized by Court Order* Evidence from the interception of wire or oral communications is admissible when authorized pursuant to an application to a federal judge of competent jurisdiction under the provisions of a federal statute.

Discussion

Pursuant to 18 U.S.C. § 2516(1), the Attorney General, Deputy Attorney General, Associate Attorney General, or any Assistant Attorney General, any acting Assistant Attorney General, or any Deputy Assistant Attorney General or acting Deputy Assistant Attorney General in the Criminal Division or National Security Division specially designated by the Attorney General, may authorize an application to a Federal judge of competent jurisdiction for, and such judge may grant in conformity with 18 U.S.C. § 2518, an order authorizing or approving the interception of wire or oral communications by the Federal Bureau of Investigation, or a Federal agency having responsibility for the investigation of the offense as to which the application is made, for purposes of obtaining evidence concerning the offenses enumerated in 18 U.S.C. § 2516(1), to the extent such offenses are punishable under the Uniform Code of Military Justice.

(c) *Regulations.* Notwithstanding any other provision of these rules, evidence obtained by members of the Armed Forces or their agents through interception of wire or oral communications for law enforcement purposes is not admissible unless such interception:

(1) takes place in the United States and is authorized under subdivision (b);

(2) takes place outside the United States and is authorized under regulations issued by the Secretary of Defense or the Secretary concerned; or

(3) is authorized under regulations issued by the Secretary of Defense or the Secretary concerned and is not unlawful under applicable federal statutes.

Rule 321. Eyewitness identification

(a) *General rule.* Testimony concerning a relevant out-of-court identification by any person is admissible, subject to an appropriate objection under this rule, if such testimony is otherwise admissible under these rules. The witness making the identification and any person who has observed the previous identification may testify concerning it. When in testimony a witness identifies the accused as being, or not being, a participant in an offense or makes any other relevant identification concerning a person in the courtroom, evidence that on a previous occasion the witness made a similar identification is admissible to corroborate the witness's testimony as to identity even if the credibility of the witness has not

been attacked directly, subject to appropriate objection under this rule.

(b) *When Inadmissible.* An identification of the accused as being a participant in an offense, whether such identification is made at the trial or otherwise, is inadmissible against the accused if:

(1) The identification is the result of an unlawful lineup or other unlawful identification process, as defined in subdivision (c), conducted by the United States or other domestic authorities and the accused makes a timely motion to suppress or an objection to the evidence under this rule; or

(2) Exclusion of the evidence is required by the Due Process Clause of the Fifth Amendment to the Constitution of the United States as applied to members of the Armed Forces. Evidence other than an identification of the accused that is obtained as a result of the unlawful lineup or unlawful identification process is inadmissible against the accused if the accused makes a timely motion to suppress or an objection to the evidence under this rule and if exclusion of the evidence is required under the Constitution of the United States as applied to members of the Armed Forces.

(c) *Unlawful Lineup or Identification Process.*

(1) *Unreliable.* A lineup or other identification process is unreliable, and therefore unlawful, if the lineup or other identification process is so suggestive as to create a substantial likelihood of misidentification.

(2) *In Violation of Right to Counsel.* A lineup is unlawful if it is conducted in violation of the accused's rights to counsel.

(A) *Military Lineups.* An accused or suspect is entitled to counsel if, after preferral of charges or imposition of pretrial restraint under R.C.M. 304 for the offense under investigation, the accused is required by persons subject to the code or their agents to participate in a lineup for the purpose of identification. When a person entitled to counsel under this rule requests counsel, a judge advocate or a person certified in accordance with Article 27(b) will be provided by the United States at no expense to the accused or suspect and without regard to indigency or lack thereof before the lineup may proceed. The accused or suspect may waive the rights provided in this rule if the waiver is freely, knowingly, and intelligently made.

(B) *Nonmilitary Lineups.* When a person subject to the code is required to participate in a lineup for purposes of identification by an official or agent of the United States, of the District of Columbia, or of a State, Commonwealth, or possession of the United States, or any political subdivision of such a State, Commonwealth, or possession, and the provisions of subdivision (c)(2)(A) do not apply, the person's entitlement to counsel and the validity of any waiver of applicable rights will be determined by the principles of law generally recognized in the trial of criminal cases in the United States district courts involving similar lineups.

(d) *Motions to Suppress and Objections.*

(1) *Disclosure.* Prior to arraignment, the prosecution must disclose to the defense all evidence of, or derived from, a prior identification of the accused as a lineup or other identification process that it intends to offer into evidence against the accused at trial.

(2) *Time Requirement.* When such evidence has been disclosed, any motion to suppress or objection under this rule must be made by the defense prior to submission of a plea. In the absence of such motion or objection, the defense may not raise the issue at a later time except as permitted by the military judge for good cause shown. Failure to so move constitutes a waiver of the motion or objection.

(3) *Continuing Duty.* If the prosecution intends to offer such evidence and the evidence was not disclosed prior to arraignment, the prosecution must provide timely notice to the military judge and counsel for the accused. The defense may enter an objection at that time, and the military judge may make such orders as are required in the interests of justice.

(4) *Specificity.* The military judge may require the defense to specify the grounds upon which the defense moves to suppress or object to evidence. If defense counsel, despite the exercise of due diligence, has been unable to interview adequately those persons involved in the lineup or other identification process, the military judge may enter any order required by the interests of justice, including authorization for the defense to make a general motion to suppress or a general objection.

(5) *Defense Evidence.* The defense may present evidence relevant to the issue of the admissibility of evidence as to which there has been an appropriate motion or objection under this rule. An accused may testify for the limited purpose of contesting the legality of the lineup or identification process giving rise to the challenged evidence. Prior to the introduction of such testimony by the accused, the defense must inform the military judge that the testimony is offered under subdivision (d). When the accused testifies under subdivision (d), the accused may be cross-examined only as to the matter on which he or she testifies. Nothing said by the accused on either direct or cross-examination may be used against the accused for any purpose other than in a prosecution for perjury, false swearing, or the making of a false official statement.

(6) *Burden and Standard of Proof.* When the defense has raised a specific motion or objection under subdivision (d)(3), the burden on the prosecution extends only to the grounds upon which the defense moved to suppress or object to the evidence.

(A) *Right to Counsel.*

(i) *Initial Violation of Right to Counsel at a Lineup.* When the accused raises the right to presence of counsel under this rule, the prosecution must prove by a preponderance of the evidence that counsel was present at the lineup or that the accused, having been advised of the right to the presence of counsel, voluntarily and intelligently waived that right prior to the lineup.

(ii) *Identification Subsequent to a Lineup Conducted in Violation of the Right to Counsel.* When the military judge determines that an identification is the result of a lineup conducted without the presence of counsel or an appropriate waiver, any later identification by one present at such unlawful lineup is also a result thereof unless the military judge determines that the contrary has been shown by clear and convincing evidence.

(B) *Unreliable Identification.*

(i) *Initial Unreliable Identification.* When an objection raises the issue of an unreliable identification, the prosecution must prove by a preponderance of the evidence that the identification was reliable under the circumstances.

(ii) *Identification Subsequent to an Unreliable Identification.* When the military judge determines that an identification is the result of an unreliable identification, a later identification may be admitted if the prosecution proves by clear and convincing evidence that the later identification is not the result of the inadmissible identification.

(7) *Rulings.* A motion to suppress or an objection to evidence made prior to plea under this rule will

be ruled upon prior to plea unless the military judge, for good cause, orders that it be deferred for determination at the trial of the general issue or until after findings, but no such determination will be deferred if a party's right to appeal the ruling is affected adversely. Where factual issues are involved in ruling upon such motion or objection, the military judge will state his or her essential findings of fact on the record.

(e) *Effect of Guilty Pleas.* Except as otherwise expressly provided in R.C.M. 910(a)(2), a plea of guilty to an offense that results in a finding of guilty waives all issues under this rule with respect to that offense whether or not raised prior to the plea.

SECTION IV
RELEVANCY AND ITS LIMITS

Rule 401. Test for relevant evidence

Evidence is relevant if:

(a) it has any tendency to make a fact more or less probable than it would be without the evidence; and

(b) the fact is of consequence in determining the action.

Rule 402. General admissibility of relevant evidence

(a) Relevant evidence is admissible unless any of the following provides otherwise:

(1) the United States Constitution as it applies to members of the Armed Forces;

(2) a federal statute applicable to trial by courts-martial;

(3) these rules; or

(4) this Manual.

(b) Irrelevant evidence is not admissible.

Rule 403. Excluding relevant evidence for prejudice, confusion, waste of time, or other reasons

The military judge may exclude relevant evidence if its probative value is substantially outweighed by a danger of one or more of the following: unfair prejudice, confusing the issues, misleading the members, undue delay, wasting time, or needlessly presenting cumulative evidence.

Rule 404. Character evidence; crimes or other acts

(a) *Character Evidence.*

(1) *Prohibited Uses.* Evidence of a person's character or character trait is not admissible to prove that on a particular occasion the person acted in accordance with the character or trait.

(2) *Exceptions for an Accused or Victim*

(A) The accused may offer evidence of the accused's pertinent trait and, if the evidence is admitted, the prosecution may offer evidence to rebut it. General military character is not a pertinent trait for the purposes of showing the probability of innocence of the accused for the following offenses under the UCMJ:

(i) Articles 120-123a;

(ii) Articles 125-127;

(iii) Articles 129-132;

(iv) Any other offense in which evidence of general military character of the accused is not relevant to any element of an offense for which the accused has been charged; or

(v) An attempt or conspiracy to commit one of the above offenses.

(B) Subject to the limitations in Mil. R. Evid. 412, the accused may offer evidence of an alleged victim's pertinent trait, and if the evidence is admitted, the prosecution may:

(i) offer evidence to rebut it; and

(ii) offer evidence of the accused's same trait; and

(C) in a homicide or assault case, the prosecution may offer evidence of the alleged victim's trait of peacefulness to rebut evidence that the victim was the first aggressor.

(3) *Exceptions for a Witness.* Evidence of a witness's character may be admitted under Mil R. Evid. 607, 608, and 609.

(b) *Crimes, Wrongs, or Other Acts.*

(1) *Prohibited Uses.* Evidence of a crime, wrong, or other act is not admissible to prove a person's character in order to show that on a particular occasion the person acted in accordance with the character.

(2) *Permitted Uses; Notice.* This evidence may be admissible for another purpose, such as proving motive, opportunity, intent, preparation, plan, knowledge, identity, absence of mistake, or lack of

accident. On request by the accused, the prosecution must:

(A) provide reasonable notice of the general nature of any such evidence that the prosecution intends to offer at trial; and

(B) do so before trial – or during trial if the military judge, for good cause, excuses lack of pretrial notice.

Rule 405. Methods of proving character

(a) *By Reputation or Opinion.* When evidence of a person's character or character trait is admissible, it may be proved by testimony about the person's reputation or by testimony in the form of an opinion. On cross-examination of the character witness, the military judge may allow an inquiry into relevant specific instances of the person's conduct.

(b) *By Specific Instances of Conduct.* When a person's character or character trait is an essential element of a charge, claim, or defense, the character or trait may also be proved by relevant specific instances of the person's conduct.

(c) *By Affidavit.* The defense may introduce affidavits or other written statements of persons other than the accused concerning the character of the accused. If the defense introduces affidavits or other written statements under this subdivision, the prosecution may, in rebuttal, also introduce affidavits or other written statements regarding the character of the accused. Evidence of this type may be introduced by the defense or prosecution only if, aside from being contained in an affidavit or other written statement, it would otherwise be admissible under these rules.

(d) *Definitions.* "Reputation" means the estimation in which a person generally is held in the community in which the person lives or pursues a business or profession. "Community" in the Armed Forces includes a post, camp, ship, station, or other military organization regardless of size.

Rule 406. Habit; routine practice

Evidence of a person's habit or an organization's routine practice may be admitted to prove that on a particular occasion the person or organization acted in accordance with the habit or routine practice. The military judge may admit this evidence regardless of

whether it is corroborated or whether there was an eyewitness.

Rule 407. Subsequent remedial measures

(a) When measures are taken that would have made an earlier injury or harm less likely to occur, evidence of the subsequent measures is not admissible to prove:

(1) negligence;

(2) culpable conduct;

(3) a defect in a product or its design; or

(4) a need for a warning or instruction.

(b) The military judge may admit this evidence for another purpose, such as impeachment or – if disputed – proving ownership, control, or the feasibility of precautionary measures.

Rule 408. Compromise offers and negotiations

(a) *Prohibited Uses.* Evidence of the following is not admissible – on behalf of any party – either to prove or disprove the validity or amount of a disputed claim or to impeach by a prior inconsistent statement or a contradiction:

(1) furnishing, promising, or offering – or accepting, promising to accept, or offering to accept – a valuable consideration in order to compromise the claim; and

(2) conduct or a statement made during compromise negotiations about the claim – except when the negotiations related to a claim by a public office in the exercise of its regulatory, investigative, or enforcement authority.

(b) *Exceptions.* The military judge may admit this evidence for another purpose, such as proving witness bias or prejudice, negating a contention of undue delay, or proving an effort to obstruct a criminal investigation or prosecution.

Rule 409. Offers to pay medical and similar expenses

Evidence of furnishing, promising to pay, or offering to pay medical, hospital, or similar expenses resulting from an injury is not admissible to prove liability for the injury.

Rule 410. Pleas, plea discussions, and related statements

(a) *Prohibited Uses.* Evidence of the following is not admissible against the accused who made the plea or participated in the plea discussions:

(1) a guilty plea that was later withdrawn;

(2) a nolo contendere plea;

(3) any statement made in the course of any judicial inquiry regarding either of the foregoing pleas; or

(4) any statement made during plea discussions with the convening authority, staff judge advocate, trial counsel or other counsel for the government if the discussions did not result in a guilty plea or they resulted in a later-withdrawn guilty plea.

(b) *Exceptions.* The military judge may admit a statement described in subdivision (a)(3) or (a)(4):

(1) when another statement made during the same plea or plea discussions has been introduced, if in fairness the statements ought to be considered together; or

(2) in a proceeding for perjury or false statement, if the accused made the statement under oath, on the record, and with counsel present.

(c) *Request for Administrative Disposition.* A "statement made during plea discussions" includes a statement made by the accused solely for the purpose of requesting disposition under an authorized procedure for administrative action in lieu of trial by court-martial; "on the record" includes the written statement submitted by the accused in furtherance of such request.

Rule 411. Liability Insurance

Evidence that a person was or was not insured against liability is not admissible to prove whether the person acted negligently or otherwise wrongfully. The military judge may admit this evidence for another purpose, such as proving witness bias or prejudice or proving agency, ownership, or control.

Rule 412. Sex offense cases: The victim's sexual behavior or predisposition

(a) *Evidence generally inadmissible.* The following evidence is not admissible in any proceeding involving an alleged sexual offense except as provided in subdivisions (b) and (c):

(1) Evidence offered to prove that any alleged victim engaged in other sexual behavior.

(2) Evidence offered to prove any alleged victim's sexual predisposition.

(b) *Exceptions.*

(1) In a proceeding, the following evidence is admissible, if otherwise admissible under these rules:

(A) evidence of specific instances of sexual behavior by the alleged victim offered to prove that a person other than the accused was the source of semen, injury, or other physical evidence;

(B) evidence of specific instances of sexual behavior by the alleged victim with respect to the person accused of the sexual misconduct offered by the accused to prove consent or by the prosecution; and

(C) evidence the exclusion of which would violate the constitutional rights of the accused.

(c) *Procedure to determine admissibility.*

(1) A party intending to offer evidence under subsection (b) must—

(A) file a written motion at least 5 days prior to entry of pleas specifically describing the evidence and stating the purpose for which it is offered unless the military judge, for good cause shown, requires a different time for filing or permits filing during trial; and

(B) serve the motion on the opposing party and the military judge and notify the alleged victim or, when appropriate, the alleged victim's guardian or representative.

(2) Before admitting evidence under this rule, the military judge must conduct a hearing, which shall be closed. At this hearing, the parties may call witnesses, including the alleged victim, and offer relevant evidence. The alleged victim must be afforded a reasonable opportunity to attend and be heard. However, the hearing may not be unduly delayed for this purpose. The right to be heard under this rule includes the right to be heard through counsel, including Special Victims' Counsel under section 1044e of title 10, United States Code. In a case before a court-martial composed of a military judge and members, the military judge shall conduct the hearing outside the presence of the members pursuant to Article 39(a). The motion, related papers, and the record of the hearing must be sealed in accordance with R.C.M. 1103A and remain under

seal unless the military judge or an appellate court orders otherwise.

(3) If the military judge determines on the basis of the hearing described in paragraph (2) of this subsection that the evidence that the accused seeks to offer is relevant for a purpose under subsection (b) and that the probative value of such evidence outweighs the danger of unfair prejudice to the alleged victim's privacy, such evidence shall be admissible under this rule to the extent an order made by the military judge specifies evidence that may be offered and areas with respect to which the alleged victim may be examined or cross-examined. Such evidence is still subject to challenge under Mil. R. Evid. 403.

(d) For purposes of this rule, the term "sexual offense" includes any sexual misconduct punishable under the Uniform Code of Military Justice, federal law or state law. "Sexual behavior" includes any sexual behavior not encompassed by the alleged offense. The term "sexual predisposition" refers to an alleged victim's mode of dress, speech, or lifestyle that does not directly refer to sexual activities or thoughts but that may have a sexual connotation for the factfinder.

Rule 413. Similar crimes in sexual offense cases

(a) *Permitted Uses.* In a court-martial proceeding for a sexual offense, the military judge may admit evidence that the accused committed any other sexual offense. The evidence may be considered on any matter to which it is relevant.

(b) *Disclosure to the Accused.* If the prosecution intends to offer this evidence, the prosecution must disclose it to the accused, including any witnesses' statements or a summary of the expected testimony. The prosecution must do so at least 5 days prior to entry of pleas or at a later time that the military judge allows for good cause.

(c) *Effect on Other Rules.* This rule does not limit the admission or consideration of evidence under any other rule.

(d) *Definition.* As used in this rule, "sexual offense" means an offense punishable under the Uniform Code of Military Justice, or a crime under federal or state law (as "state" is defined in 18 U.S.C. § 513), involving:

(1) any conduct prohibited by Article 120;

(2) any conduct prohibited by 18 U.S.C. chapter 109A;

(3) contact, without consent, between any part of the accused's body, or an object held or controlled by the accused, and another person's genitals or anus;

(4) contact, without consent, between the accused's genitals or anus and any part of another person's body;

(5) contact with the aim of deriving sexual pleasure or gratification from inflicting death, bodily injury, or physical pain on another person; or

(6) an attempt or conspiracy to engage in conduct described in subdivisions (d)(1)-(5).

Rule 414. Similar crimes in child-molestation cases

(a) *Permitted Uses.* In a court-martial proceeding in which an accused is charged with an act of child molestation, the military judge may admit evidence that the accused committed any other offense of child molestation. The evidence may be considered on any matter to which it is relevant.

(b) *Disclosure to the Accused.* If the prosecution intends to offer this evidence, the prosecution must disclose it to the accused, including witnesses' statements or a summary of the expected testimony. The prosecution must do so at least 5 days prior to entry of pleas or at a later time that the military judge allows for good cause.

(c) *Effect on Other Rules.* This rule does not limit the admission or consideration of evidence under any other rule.

(d) *Definitions.* As used in this rule:

(1) "Child" means a person below the age of 16; and

(2) "Child molestation" means an offense punishable under the Uniform Code of Military Justice, or a crime under federal law or under state law (as "state" is defined in 18 U.S.C. § 513), that involves:

(A) any conduct prohibited by Article 120 and committed with a child, or prohibited by Article 120b.

(B) any conduct prohibited by 18 U.S.C. chapter 109A and committed with a child;

(C) any conduct prohibited by 18 U.S.C. chapter 110;

(D) contact between any part of the accused's

body, or an object held or controlled by the accused, and a child's genitals or anus;

(E) contact between the accused's genitals or anus and any part of a child's body;

(F) contact with the aim of deriving sexual pleasure or gratification from inflicting death, bodily injury, or physical pain on a child; or

(G) an attempt or conspiracy to engage in conduct described in subdivisions (d)(2)(A)-(F).

SECTION V
PRIVILEGES

Rule 501. Privilege in general

(a) A person may not claim a privilege with respect to any matter except as required by or provided for in:

(1) the United States Constitution as applied to members of the Armed Forces;

(2) a federal statute applicable to trials by courts-martial;

(3) these rules;

(4) this Manual; or

(5) the principles of common law generally recognized in the trial of criminal cases in the United States district courts under rule 501 of the Federal Rules of Evidence, insofar as the application of such principles in trials by courts-martial is practicable and not contrary to or inconsistent with the Uniform Code of Military Justice, these rules, or this Manual.

(b) A claim of privilege includes, but is not limited to, the assertion by any person of a privilege to:

(1) refuse to be a witness;

(2) refuse to disclose any matter;

(3) refuse to produce any object or writing; or

(4) prevent another from being a witness or disclosing any matter or producing any object or writing.

(c) The term "person" includes an appropriate representative of the Federal Government, a State, or political subdivision thereof, or any other entity claiming to be the holder of a privilege.

(d) Notwithstanding any other provision of these rules, information not otherwise privileged does not become privileged on the basis that it was acquired by a medical officer or civilian physician in a professional capacity.

Rule 502. Lawyer-client privilege

(a) *General Rule.* A client has a privilege to refuse to disclose and to prevent any other person from disclosing confidential communications made for the purpose of facilitating the rendition of professional legal services to the client:

(1) between the client or the client's representative and the lawyer or the lawyer's representative;

(2) between the lawyer and the lawyer's representative;

(3) by the client or the client's lawyer to a lawyer representing another in a matter of common interest;

(4) between representatives of the client or between the client and a representative of the client; or

(5) between lawyers representing the client.

(b) *Definitions.* As used in this rule:

(1) "Client" means a person, public officer, corporation, association, organization, or other entity, either public or private, who receives professional legal services from a lawyer, or who consults a lawyer with a view to obtaining professional legal services from the lawyer.

(2) "Lawyer" means a person authorized, or reasonably believed by the client to be authorized, to practice law; or a member of the Armed Forces detailed, assigned, or otherwise provided to represent a person in a court-martial case or in any military investigation or proceeding. The term "lawyer" does not include a member of the Armed Forces serving in a capacity other than as a judge advocate, legal officer, or law specialist as defined in Article 1, unless the member:

(A) is detailed, assigned, or otherwise provided to represent a person in a court-martial case or in any military investigation or proceeding;

(B) is authorized by the Armed Forces, or reasonably believed by the client to be authorized, to render professional legal services to members of the Armed Forces; or

(C) is authorized to practice law and renders professional legal services during off-duty employment.

(3) "Lawyer's representative" means a person employed by or assigned to assist a lawyer in providing professional legal services.

(4) A communication is "confidential" if not intended to be disclosed to third persons other than those to whom disclosure is in furtherance of the rendition of professional legal services to the client or those reasonably necessary for the transmission of the communication.

(c) *Who May Claim the Privilege.* The privilege may be claimed by the client, the guardian or conservator of the client, the personal representative of a deceased client, or the successor, trustee, or similar representative of a corporation, association, or other organization, whether or not in existence. The lawyer or the lawyer's representative who received the communication may claim the privilege on behalf of the client. The authority of the lawyer to do so is presumed in the absence of evidence to the contrary.

(d) *Exceptions.* There is no privilege under this rule under any of the following circumstances:

(1) *Crime or Fraud.* If the communication clearly contemplated the future commission of a fraud or crime or if services of the lawyer were sought or obtained to enable or aid anyone to commit or plan to commit what the client knew or reasonably should have known to be a crime or fraud;

(2) *Claimants through Same Deceased Client.* As to a communication relevant to an issue between parties who claim through the same deceased client, regardless of whether the claims are by testate or intestate succession or by inter vivos transaction;

(3) *Breach of Duty by Lawyer or Client.* As to a communication relevant to an issue of breach of duty by the lawyer to the client or by the client to the lawyer;

(4) *Document Attested by the Lawyer.* As to a communication relevant to an issue concerning an attested document to which the lawyer is an attesting witness; or

(5) *Joint Clients.* As to a communication relevant to a matter of common interest between two or more clients if the communication was made by any of them to a lawyer retained or consulted in common, when offered in an action between any of the clients.

Rule 503. Communications to clergy

(a) *General Rule.* A person has a privilege to refuse to disclose and to prevent another from disclosing a confidential communication by the person to a clergyman or to a clergyman's assistant, if such commu-

nication is made either as a formal act of religion or as a matter of conscience.

(b) *Definitions.* As used in this rule:

(1) "Clergyman" means a minister, priest, rabbi, chaplain, or other similar functionary of a religious organization, or an individual reasonably believed to be so by the person consulting the clergyman.

(2) "Clergyman's assistant" means a person employed by or assigned to assist a clergyman in his capacity as a spiritual advisor.

(3) A communication is "confidential" if made to a clergyman in the clergyman's capacity as a spiritual adviser or to a clergyman's assistant in the assistant's official capacity and is not intended to be disclosed to third persons other than those to whom disclosure is in furtherance of the purpose of the communication or to those reasonably necessary for the transmission of the communication.

(c) *Who May Claim the Privilege.* The privilege may be claimed by the person, guardian, or conservator, or by a personal representative if the person is deceased. The clergyman or clergyman's assistant who received the communication may claim the privilege on behalf of the person. The authority of the clergyman or clergyman's assistant to do so is presumed in the absence of evidence to the contrary.

Rule 504. Marital privilege

(a) *Spousal Incapacity.* A person has a privilege to refuse to testify against his or her spouse. There is no privilege under subdivision (a) when, at the time of the testimony, the parties are divorced, or the marriage has been annulled.

(b) *Confidential Communication Made During the Marriage.*

(1) *General Rule.* A person has a privilege during and after the marital relationship to refuse to disclose, and to prevent another from disclosing, any confidential communication made to the spouse of the person while they were married and not separated as provided by law.

(2) *Who May Claim the Privilege.* The privilege may be claimed by the spouse who made the communication or by the other spouse on his or her behalf. The authority ofthe latter spouse to do so is presumed in the absence of evidence of a waiver. The privilege will not prevent disclosure of the communication at the request of the spouse to whom the communication was made if that spouse is an ac-

cused regardless of whether the spouse who made the communication objects to its disclosure.

(c) *Exceptions.*

(1) *To Confidential Communications Only.* Where both parties have been substantial participants in illegal activity, those communications between the spouses during the marriage regarding the illegal activity in which they have jointly participated are not marital communications for purposes of the privilege in subdivision (b) and are not entitled to protection under the privilege in subdivision (b).

(2) *To Spousal Incapacity and Confidential Communications.* There is no privilege under subdivisions (a) or (b):

(A) In proceedings in which one spouse is charged with a crime against the person or property of the other spouse or a child of either, or with a crime against the person or property of a third person committed in the course of committing a crime against the other spouse;

(B) When the marital relationship was entered into with no intention of the parties to live together as spouses, but only for the purpose of using the purported marital relationship as a sham, and with respect to the privilege in subdivision (a), the relationship remains a sham at the time the testimony or statement of one of the parties is to be introduced against the other, or with respect to the privilege in subdivision (b), the relationship was a sham at the time of the communication; or

(C) In proceedings in which a spouse is charged, in accordance with Article 133 or 134, with importing the other spouse as an alien for prostitution or other immoral purpose in violation of 8 U.S.C. § 1328 with transporting the other spouse in interstate commerce for prostitution, immoral purposes, or another offense in violation of 18 U.S.C. §§ 2421-2424; or with violation of such other similar statutes under which such privilege may not be claimed in the trial of criminal cases in the United States district courts.

(d) *Definitions.* As used in this rule:

(1) "A child of either" means a biological child, adopted child, or ward of one of the spouses and includes a child who is under the permanent or temporary physical custody of one of the spouses, regardless of the existence of a legal parent-child relationship. For purposes of this rule only, a child is:

(A) an individual under the age of 18; or

(B) an individual with a mental handicap who functions under the age of 18.

(2) "Temporary physical custody" means a parent has entrusted his or her child with another. There is no minimum amount of time necessary to establish temporary physical custody, nor is a written agreement required. Rather, the focus is on the parent's agreement with another for assuming parental responsibility for the child. For example, temporary physical custody may include instances where a parent entrusts another with the care of his or her child for recurring care or during absences due to temporary duty or deployments.

(3) As used in this rule, a communication is "confidential" if made privately by any person to the spouse of the person and is not intended to be disclosed to third persons other than those reasonably necessary for transmission of the communication.

Rule 505. Classified information

(a) *General Rule.* Classified information must be protected and is privileged from disclosure if disclosure would be detrimental to the national security. Under no circumstances may a military judge order the release of classified information to any person not authorized to receive such information. The Secretary of Defense may prescribe security procedures for protection against the compromise of classified information submitted to courts-martial and appellate authorities.

(b) *Definitions.* As used in this rule:

(1) "Classified information" means any information or material that has been determined by the United States Government pursuant to an executive order, statute, or regulations, to require protection against unauthorized disclosure for reasons of national security, and any restricted data, as defined in 42 U.S.C. §2014(y).

(2) "National security" means the national defense and foreign relations of the United States.

(3) "In camera hearing" means a session under Article 39(a) from which the public is excluded.

(4) "In camera review" means an inspection of documents or other evidence conducted by the military judge alone in chambers and not on the record.

(5) "Ex parte" means a discussion between the military judge and either the defense counsel or prosecution, without the other party or the public

present. This discussion can be on or off the record, depending on the circumstances. The military judge will grant a request for an ex parte discussion or hearing only after finding that such discussion or hearing is necessary to protect classified information or other good cause. Prior to granting a request from one party for an ex parte discussion or hearing, the military judge must provide notice to the opposing party on the record. If the ex parte discussion is conducted off the record, the military judge should later state on the record that such ex parte discussion took place and generally summarize the subject matter of the discussion, as appropriate.

(c) *Access to Evidence.* Any information admitted into evidence pursuant to any rule, procedure, or order by the military judge must be provided to the accused.

(d) *Declassification.* Trial counsel should, when practicable, seek declassification of evidence that may be used at trial, consistent with the requirements of national security. A decision not to declassify evidence under this section is not subject to review by a military judge or upon appeal.

(e) *Action Prior to Referral of Charges*

(1) Prior to referral of charges, upon a showing by the accused that the classified information sought is relevant and necessary to an element of the offense or a legally cognizable defense, the convening authority must respond in writing to a request by the accused for classified information if the privilege in this rule is claimed for such information. In response to such a request, the convening authority may:

(A) delete specified items of classified information from documents made available to the accused;

(B) substitute a portion or summary of the information for such classified documents;

(C) substitute a statement admitting relevant facts that the classified information would tend to prove;

(D) provide the document subject to conditions that will guard against the compromise of the information disclosed to the accused; or

(E) withhold disclosure if actions under (A) through (D) cannot be taken without causing identifiable damage to the national security.

(2) An Article 32 preliminary hearing officer may not rule on any objection by the accused to the release of documents or information protected by this rule.

(3) Any objection by the accused to the withholding of information or to the conditions of disclosure must be raised through a motion for appropriate relief at a pretrial conference.

(f) *Actions after Referral of Charges.*

(1) *Pretrial Conference.* At any time after referral of charges, any party may move for a pretrial conference under Article 39(a) to consider matters relating to classified information that may arise in connection with the trial. Following such a motion, or when the military judge recognizes the need for such conference, the military judge must promptly hold a pretrial conference under Article 39(a).

(2) *Ex Parte Permissible.* Upon request by either party and with a showing of good cause, the military judge must hold such conference ex parte to the extent necessary to protect classified information from disclosure.

(3) *Matters to be Established at Pretrial Conference.*

(A) *Timing of Subsequent Actions.* At the pretrial conference, the military judge must establish the timing of:

(i) requests for discovery;

(ii) the provision of notice required by subdivision (i) of this rule; and

(iii) established by subdivision (j) of this rule.

(B) *Other Matters.* At the pretrial conference, the military judge may also consider any matter that relates to classified information or that may promote a fair and expeditious trial.

(4) *Convening Authority Notice and Action.* If a claim of privilege has been made under this rule with respect to classified information that apparently contains evidence that is relevant and necessary to an element of the offense or a legally cognizable defense and is otherwise admissible in evidence in the court-martial proceeding, the matter must be reported to the convening authority. The convening authority may:

(A) institute action to obtain the classified information for the use by the military judge in making a determination under subdivision (j);

(B) dismiss the charges;

(C) dismiss the charges or specifications or both to which the information relates; or

(D) take such other action as may be required in the interests of justice.

(5) *Remedies.* If, after a reasonable period of time, the information is not provided to the military judge in circumstances where proceeding with the case without such information would materially prejudice a substantial right of the accused, the military judge must dismiss the charges or specifications or both to which the classified information relates.

(g) *Protective Orders.* Upon motion of the trial counsel, the military judge must issue an order to protect against the disclosure of any classified information that has been disclosed by the United States to any accused in any court-martial proceeding or that has otherwise been provided to, or obtained by, any such accused in any such court-martial proceeding. The terms of any such protective order may include, but are not limited to, provisions.

(1) prohibiting the disclosure of the information except as authorized by the military judge;

(2) requiring storage of material in a manner appropriate for the level of classification assigned to the documents to be disclosed;

(3) requiring controlled access to the material during normal business hours and at other times upon reasonable notice;

(4) mandating that all persons requiring security clearances will cooperate with investigatory personnel in any investigations that are necessary to obtain a security clearance;

(5) requiring the maintenance of logs regarding access by all persons authorized by the military judge to have access to the classified information in connection with the preparation of the defense;

(6) regulating the making and handling of notes taken from material containing classified information; or

(7) requesting the convening authority to authorize the assignment of government security personnel and the provision of government storage facilities.

(h) *Discovery and Access by the Accused.*

(1) *Limitations.*

(A) *Government Claim of Privilege.* In a court-martial proceeding in which the government seeks to delete, withhold, or otherwise obtain other relief with respect to the discovery of or access to any classified information, the trial counsel must submit a declaration invoking the United States' classified information privilege and setting forth the damage to the national security that the discovery of or access to such information reasonably could be expected to cause. The declaration must be signed by the head, or designee, of the executive or military department or government agency concerned.

(B) *Standard for Discovery or Access by the Accused.* Upon the submission of a declaration under subdivision (h)(1)(A), the military judge may not authorize the discovery of or access to such classified information unless the military judge determines that such classified information would be noncumulative and relevant to a legally cognizable defense, rebuttal of the prosecution's case, or to sentencing. If the discovery of or access to such classified information is authorized, it must be addressed in accordance with the requirements of subdivision (h)(2).

(2) *Alternatives to Full Discovery.*

(A) *Substitutions and Other Alternatives.* The military judge, in assessing the accused's right to discover or access classified information under subdivision (h), may authorize the government:

(i) to delete or withhold specified items of classified information;

(ii) to substitute a summary for classified information; or

(iii) to substitute a statement admitting relevant facts that the classified information or material would tend to prove, unless the military judge determines that disclosure of the classified information itself is necessary to enable the accused to prepare for trial.

(B) *In Camera Review.* The military judge must, upon the request of the prosecution, conduct an in camera review of the prosecution's motion and any materials submitted in support thereof and must not disclose such information to the accused.

(C) *Action by Military Judge.* The military judge must grant the request of the trial counsel to substitute a summary or to substitute a statement admitting relevant facts, or to provide other relief in accordance with subdivision (h)(2)(A), if the military judge finds that the summary, statement, or other relief would provide the accused with substantially the same ability to make a defense as would discovery of or access to the specific classified information.

(3) *Reconsideration.* An order of a military judge authorizing a request of the trial counsel to substitute, summarize, withhold, or prevent access to classified information under subdivision (h) is not subject to a motion for reconsideration by the accused, if such order was entered pursuant to an ex parte showing under subdivision (h).

(i) *Disclosure by the Accused.*

(1) *Notification to Trial Counsel and Military Judge.* If an accused reasonably expects to disclose, or to cause the disclosure of, classified information in any manner in connection with any trial or pretrial proceeding involving the prosecution of such accused, the accused must, within the time specified by the military judge or, where no time is specified, prior to arraignment of the accused, notify the trial counsel and the military judge in writing.

(2) *Content of Notice.* Such notice must include a brief description of the classified information.

(3) *Continuing Duty to Notify.* Whenever the accused learns of additional classified information the accused reasonably expects to disclose, or to cause the disclosure of, at any such proceeding, the accused must notify trial counsel and the military judge in writing as soon as possible thereafter and must include a brief description of the classified information.

(4) *Limitation on Disclosure by Accused.* The accused may not disclose, or cause the disclosure of, any information known or believed to be classified in connection with a trial or pretrial proceeding until:

(A) notice has been given under subdivision (i); and

(B) the government has been afforded a reasonable opportunity to seek a determination pursuant to the procedure set forth in subdivision (j).

(5) *Failure to comply.* If the accused fails to comply with the requirements of subdivision (i), the military judge:

(A) may preclude disclosure of any classified information not made the subject of notification; and

(B) may prohibit the examination by the accused of any witness with respect to any such information.

(j) *Procedure for Use of Classified Information in Trials and Pretrial Proceedings.*

(1) *Hearing on Use of Classified Information.*

(A) *Motion for Hearing.* Within the time specified by the military judge for the filing of a motion under this rule, either party may move for a hearing concerning the use at any proceeding of any classified information. Upon a request by either party, the military judge must conduct such a hearing and must rule prior to conducting any further proceedings.

(B) *Request for In Camera Hearing.* Any hearing held pursuant to subdivision (j) (or any portion of such hearing specified in the request of a knowledgeable United States official) must be held in camera if a knowledgeable United States official possessing authority to classify information submits to the military judge a declaration that a public proceeding may result in the disclosure of classified information.

(C) *Notice to Accused.* Before the hearing, trial counsel must provide the accused with notice of the classified information that is at issue. Such notice must identify the specific classified information at issue whenever that information previously has been made available to the accused by the United States. When the United States has not previously made the information available to the accused in connection with the case the information may be described by generic category, in such forms as the military judge may approve, rather than by identification of the specific information of concern to the United States.

(D) *Standard for Disclosure.* Classified information is not subject to disclosure under subdivision (j) unless the information is relevant and necessary to an element of the offense or a legally cognizable defense and is otherwise admissible in evidence. In presentencing proceedings, relevant and material classified information pertaining to the appropriateness of, or the appropriate degree of, punishment must be admitted only if no unclassified version of such information is available.

(E) *Written Findings.* As to each item of classified information, the military judge must set forth in writing the basis for the determination.

(2) *Alternatives to Full Disclosure.*

(A) *Motion by the Prosecution.* Upon any determination by the military judge authorizing the disclosure of specific classified information under the procedures established by subdivision (j), the trial counsel may move that, in lieu of the disclosure of such specific classified information, the military judge order:

(i) the substitution for such classified information of a statement admitting relevant facts that the specific classified information would tend to prove;

(ii) the substitution for such classified information of a summary of the specific classified information; or

(iii) any other procedure or redaction limiting the disclosure of specific classified information.

(B) *Declaration of Damage to National Security.* The trial counsel may, in connection with a motion under subdivision (j), submit to the military judge a declaration signed by the head, or designee, of the executive or military department or government agency concerned certifying that disclosure of classified information would cause identifiable damage to the national security of the United States and explaining the basis for the classification of such information. If so requested by the trial counsel, the military judge must examine such declaration during an in camera review.

(C) *Hearing.* The military judge must hold a hearing on any motion under subdivision (j). Any such hearing must be held in camera at the request of a knowledgeable United States official possessing authority to classify information.

(D) *Standard for Use of Alternatives.* The military judge must grant such a motion of the trial counsel if the military judge finds that the statement, summary, or other procedure or redaction will provide the accused with substantially the same ability to make his or her defense as would disclosure of the specific classified information.

(3) *Sealing of Records of In Camera Hearings.* If at the close of an in camera hearing under subdivision (j) (or any portion of a hearing under subdivision (j) that is held in camera), the military judge determines that the classified information at issue may not be disclosed or elicited at the trial or pretrial proceeding, the record of such in camera hearing must be sealed in accordance with R.C.M. 1103A and preserved for use in the event of an appeal. The accused may seek reconsideration of the military judge's determination prior to or during trial.

(4) *Remedies.*

(A) If the military judge determines that alternatives to full disclosure may not be used and the prosecution continues to object to disclosure of the information, the military judge must issue any order that the interests of justice require, including but not limited to, an order:

(i) striking or precluding all or part of the testimony of a witness;

(ii) declaring a mistrial;

(iii) finding against the government on any issue as to which the evidence is relevant and material to the defense;

(iv) dismissing the charges, with or without prejudice; or

(v) dismissing the charges or specifications or both to which the information relates.

(B) The government may avoid the sanction for nondisclosure by permitting the accused to disclose the information at the pertinent court-martial proceeding.

(5) *Disclosure of Rebuttal Information.* Whenever the military judge determines that classified information may be disclosed in connection with a trial or pretrial proceeding, the military judge must, unless the interests of fairness do not so require, order the prosecution to provide the accused with the information it expects to use to rebut the classified information.

(A) *Continuing Duty.* The military judge may place the prosecution under a continuing duty to disclose such rebuttal information.

(B) *Sanction for Failure to Comply.* If the prosecution fails to comply with its obligation under subdivision (j), the military judge:

(i) may exclude any evidence not made the subject of a required disclosure; and

(ii) may prohibit the examination by the prosecution of any witness with respect to such information.

(6) *Disclosure at Trial of Previous Statements by a Witness.*

(A) *Motion for Production of Statements in Possession of the Prosecution.* After a witness called by the trial counsel has testified on direct examination, the military judge, on motion of the accused, may order production of statements of the witness in the possession of the prosecution that relate to the subject matter as to which the witness has testified.

This paragraph does not preclude discovery or assertion of a privilege otherwise authorized.

(B) *Invocation of Privilege by the Government.* If the government invokes a privilege, the trial counsel may provide the prior statements of the witness to the military judge for in camera review to the extent necessary to protect classified information from disclosure.

(C) *Action by Military Judge.* If the military judge finds that disclosure of any portion of the statement identified by the government as classified would be detrimental to the national security in the degree required to warrant classification under the applicable Executive Order, statute, or regulation, that such portion of the statement is consistent with the testimony of the witness, and that the disclosure of such portion is not necessary to afford the accused a fair trial, the military judge must excise that portion from the statement. If the military judge finds that such portion of the statement is inconsistent with the testimony of the witness or that its disclosure is necessary to afford the accused a fair trial, the military judge must, upon the request of the trial counsel, consider alternatives to disclosure in accordance with subdivision (j)(2).

(k) *Introduction into Evidence of Classified Information.*

(1) *Preservation of Classification Status.* Writings, recordings, and photographs containing classified information may be admitted into evidence in court-martial proceedings under this rule without change in their classification status.

(A) *Precautions.* The military judge in a trial by court-martial, in order to prevent unnecessary disclosure of classified information, may order admission into evidence of only part of a writing, recording, or photograph, or may order admission into evidence of the whole writing, recording, or photograph with excision of some or all of the classified information contained therein, unless the whole ought in fairness be considered.

(B) *Classified Information Kept Under Seal.* The military judge must allow classified information offered or accepted into evidence to remain under seal during the trial, even if such evidence is disclosed in the court-martial proceeding, and may, upon motion by the government, seal exhibits containing classified information in accordance with R.C.M. 1103A for any period after trial as necessary

to prevent a disclosure of classified information when a knowledgeable United States official possessing authority to classify information submits to the military judge a declaration setting forth the damage to the national security that the disclosure of such information reasonably could be expected to cause.

(2) *Testimony.*

(A) *Objection by Trial Counsel.* During the examination of a witness, trial counsel may object to any question or line of inquiry that may require the witness to disclose classified information not previously found to be admissible.

(B) *Action by Military Judge.* Following an objection under subdivision (k), the military judge must take such suitable action to determine whether the response is admissible as will safeguard against the compromise of any classified information. Such action may include requiring trial counsel to provide the military judge with a proffer of the witness's response to the question or line of inquiry and requiring the accused to provide the military judge with a proffer of the nature of the information sought to be elicited by the accused. Upon request, the military judge may accept an ex parte proffer by trial counsel to the extent necessary to protect classified information from disclosure.

(3) *Closed session.* The military judge may, subject to the requirements of the United States Constitution, exclude the public during that portion of the presentation of evidence that discloses classified information.

(l) *Record of Trial.* If under this rule any information is withheld from the accused, the accused objects to such withholding, and the trial is continued to an adjudication of guilt of the accused, the entire unaltered text of the relevant documents as well as the prosecution's motion and any materials submitted in support thereof must be sealed in accordance with R.C.M. 1103A and attached to the record of trial as an appellate exhibit. Such material must be made available to reviewing authorities in closed proceedings for the purpose of reviewing the determination of the military judge. The record of trial with respect to any classified matter will be prepared under R.C.M. 1103(h) and 1104(b)(1)(D).

Discussion

In addition to the Sixth Amendment right of an accused to a public trial, the Supreme Court has held that the press and general public have a constitutional right under the First Amendment to access to criminal trials. *United States v. Hershey*, 20 M.J. 433, 436 (C.M.A. 1985) (citing *Richmond Newspapers, Inc. v. Virginia*, 448 U.S. 555 (1980)). The test that must be met before closure of a criminal trial to the public is set out in *Press-Enterprise Co. v. Superior Court*, 464 U.S. 501 (1984), to wit: the presumption of openness "may be overcome only by an overriding interest based on findings that closure is essential to preserve higher values and is narrowly tailored to serve that interest." *Id.* at 510. The military judge must consider reasonable alternatives to closure and must make adequate findings supporting the closure to aid in review.

Rule 506. Government information other than classified information

(a) *Protection of Government Information.* Except where disclosure is required by a federal statute, government information is privileged from disclosure if disclosure would be detrimental to the public interest.

(b) *Scope.* "Government information" includes official communication and documents and other information within the custody or control of the Federal Government. This rule does not apply to classified information (Mil. R. Evid. 505) or to the identity of an informant (Mil. R. Evid. 507).

(c) *Definitions.* As used in this rule:

(1) "In camera hearing" means a session under Article 39(a) from which the public is excluded.

(2) "In camera review" means an inspection of documents or other evidence conducted by the military judge alone in chambers and not on the record.

(3) "Ex parte" means a discussion between the military judge and either the defense counsel or prosecution, without the other party or the public present. This discussion can be on or off the record, depending on the circumstances. The military judge will grant a request for an ex parte discussion or hearing only after finding that such discussion or hearing is necessary to protect government information or other good cause. Prior to granting a request from one party for an ex parte discussion or hearing, the military judge must provide notice to the opposing party on the record. If the ex parte discussion is conducted off the record, the military judge should later state on the record that such ex parte discussion took place and generally summarize the subject matter of the discussion, as appropriate.

(d) *Who May Claim the Privilege.* The privilege may be claimed by the head, or designee, of the executive or military department or government agency concerned. The privilege for records and information of the Inspector General may be claimed by the immediate superior of the inspector general officer responsible for creation of the records or information, the Inspector General, or any other superior authority. A person who may claim the privilege may authorize a witness or the trial counsel to claim the privilege on his or her behalf. The authority of a witness or the trial counsel to do so is presumed in the absence of evidence to the contrary.

(e) *Action Prior to Referral of Charges.*

(1) Prior to referral of charges, upon a showing by the accused that the government information sought is relevant and necessary to an element of the offense or a legally cognizable defense, the convening authority must respond in writing to a request by the accused for government information if the privilege in this rule is claimed for such information. In response to such a request, the convening authority may:

(A) delete specified items of government information claimed to be privileged from documents made available to the accused;

(B) substitute a portion or summary of the information for such documents;

(C) substitute a statement admitting relevant facts that the government information would tend to prove;

(D) provide the document subject to conditions similar to those set forth in subdivision (g) of this rule; or

(E) withhold disclosure if actions under subdivisions (e)(1)(1)-(4) cannot be taken without causing identifiable damage to the public interest.

(2) Any objection by the accused to withholding of information or to the conditions of disclosure must be raised through a motion for appropriate relief at a pretrial conference.

(f) *Action After Referral of Charges.*

(1) *Pretrial Conference.* At any time after referral of charges, any party may move for a pretrial conference under Article 39(a) to consider matters relating to government information that may arise in connection with the trial. Following such a motion, or when the military judge recognizes the need for such conference, the military judge must promptly hold a pretrial conference under Article 39(a).

(2) *Ex Parte Permissible.* Upon request by either

party and with a showing of good cause, the military judge must hold such conference ex parte to the extent necessary to protect government information from disclosure.

(3) *Matters to be Established at Pretrial Conference.*

(A) *Timing of Subsequent Actions.* At the pretrial conference, the military judge must establish the timing of:

(i) requests for discovery;

(ii) the provision of notice required by subdivision (i) of this rule; and

(iii) the initiation of the procedure established by subdivision (j) of this rule.

(B) *Other Matters.* At the pretrial conference, the military judge may also consider any matter which relates to government information or which may promote a fair and expeditious trial.

(4) *Convening Authority Notice and Action.* If a claim of privilege has been made under this rule with respect to government information that apparently contains evidence that is relevant and necessary to an element of the offense or a legally cognizable defense and is otherwise admissible in evidence in the court-martial proceeding, the matter must be reported to the convening authority. The convening authority may:

(A) institute action to obtain the information for use by the military judge in making a determination under subdivision (j);

(B) dismiss the charges;

(C) dismiss the charges or specifications or both to which the information relates; or

(D) take such other action as may be required in the interests of justice.

(5) *Remedies.* If after a reasonable period of time the information is not provided to the military judge in circumstances where proceeding with the case without such information would materially prejudice a substantial right of the accused, the military judge must dismiss the charges or specifications or both to which the information relates.

(g) *Protective Orders.* Upon motion of the trial counsel, the military judge must issue an order to protect against the disclosure of any government information that has been disclosed by the United States to any accused in any court-martial proceeding or that has otherwise been provided to, or obtained by, any such accused in any such court-martial proceeding. The terms of any such protective order may include, but are not limited to, provisions:

(1) prohibiting the disclosure of the information except as authorized by the military judge;

(2) requiring storage of the material in a manner appropriate for the nature of the material to be disclosed;

(3) requiring controlled access to the material during normal business hours and at other times upon reasonable notice;

(4) requiring the maintenance of logs recording access by persons authorized by the military judge to have access to the government information in connection with the preparation of the defense;

(5) regulating the making and handling of notes taken from material containing government information; or

(6) requesting the convening authority to authorize the assignment of government security personnel and the provision of government storage facilities.

(h) *Discovery and Access by the Accused.*

(1) *Limitations.*

(A) *Government Claim of Privilege.* In a court-martial proceeding in which the government seeks to delete, withhold, or otherwise obtain other relief with respect to the discovery of or access to any government information subject to a claim of privilege, the trial counsel must submit a declaration invoking the United States' government information privilege and setting forth the detriment to the public interest that the discovery of or access to such information reasonably could be expected to cause. The declaration must be signed by a knowledgeable United States official as described in subdivision (d) of this rule.

(B) *Standard for Discovery or Access by the Accused.* Upon the submission of a declaration under subdivision (h)(1)(A), the military judge may not authorize the discovery of or access to such government information unless the military judge determines that such government information would be noncumulative, relevant, and helpful to a legally cognizable defense, rebuttal of the prosecution's case, or to sentencing. If the discovery of or access to such government information is authorized, it must be addressed in accordance with the requirements of subdivision (h)(2).

(2) *Alternatives to Full Disclosure.*

(A) *Substitutions and Other Alternatives.* The military judge, in assessing the accused's right to discover or access government information under subdivision (h), may authorize the government:

(i) to delete or withhold specified items of government information;

(ii) to substitute a summary for government information; or

(iii) to substitute a statement admitting relevant facts that the government information or material would tend to prove, unless the military judge determines that disclosure of the government information itself is necessary to enable the accused to prepare for trial.

(B) *In Camera Review.* The military judge must, upon the request of the prosecution, conduct an in camera review of the prosecution's motion and any materials submitted in support thereof and must not disclose such information to the accused.

(C) *Action by Military Judge.* The military judge must grant the request of the trial counsel to substitute a summary or to substitute a statement admitting relevant facts, or to provide other relief in accordance with subdivision (h)(2)(A), if the military judge finds that the summary, statement, or other relief would provide the accused with substantially the same ability to make a defense as would discovery of or access to the specific government information.

(i) *Disclosure by the Accused.*

(1) *Notification to Trial Counsel and Military Judge.* If an accused reasonably expects to disclose, or to cause the disclosure of, government information subject to a claim of privilege in any manner in connection with any trial or pretrial proceeding involving the prosecution of such accused, the accused must, within the time specified by the military judge or, where no time is specified, prior to arraignment of the accused, notify the trial counsel and the military judge in writing.

(2) *Content of Notice.* Such notice must include a brief description of the government information.

(3) *Continuing Duty to Notify.* Whenever the accused learns of additional government information the accused reasonably expects to disclose, or to cause the disclosure of, at any such proceeding, the accused must notify trial counsel and the military judge in writing as soon as possible thereafter and

must include a brief description of the government information.

(4) *Limitation on Disclosure by Accused.* The accused may not disclose, or cause the disclosure of, any information known or believed to be subject to a claim of privilege in connection with a trial or pretrial proceeding until:

(A) notice has been given under subdivision (i); and

(B) the government has been afforded a reasonable opportunity to seek a determination pursuant to the procedure set forth in subdivision (j).

(5) *Failure to Comply.* If the accused fails to comply with the requirements of subdivision (i), the military judge:

(A) may preclude disclosure of any government information not made the subject of notification; and

(B) may prohibit the examination by the accused of any witness with respect to any such information.

(j) *Procedure for Use of Government Information Subject to a Claim of Privilege in Trials and Pretrial Proceedings.*

(1) *Hearing on Use of Government Information.*

(A) *Motion for Hearing.* Within the time specified by the military judge for the filing of a motion under this rule, either party may move for an in camera hearing concerning the use at any proceeding of any government information that may be subject to a claim of privilege. Upon a request by either party, the military judge must conduct such a hearing and must rule prior to conducting any further proceedings.

(B) *Request for In Camera Hearing.* Any hearing held pursuant to subdivision (j) must be held in camera if a knowledgeable United States official described in subdivision (d) of this rule submits to the military judge a declaration that disclosure of the information reasonably could be expected to cause identifiable damage to the public interest.

(C) *Notice to Accused.* Subject to subdivision (j)(2) below, the prosecution must disclose government information claimed to be privileged under this rule for the limited purpose of litigating, in camera, the admissibility of the information at trial. The military judge must enter an appropriate protective order to the accused and all other appropriate trial participants concerning the disclosure of the information according to subdivision (g), above. The accused may not disclose any information provided under subdivision (j) unless, and until, such information has been admitted into evidence by the military judge. In the in camera hearing, both parties may have the opportunity to brief and argue the admissibility of the government information at trial.

(D) *Standard for Disclosure.* Government information is subject to disclosure at the court-martial proceeding under subdivision (j) if the party making the request demonstrates a specific need for information containing evidence that is relevant to the guilt or innocence or to punishment of the accused, and is otherwise admissible in the court-martial proceeding.

(E) *Written Findings.* As to each item of government information, the military judge must set forth in writing the basis for the determination.

(2) *Alternatives to Full Disclosure.*

(A) *Motion by the Prosecution.* Upon any determination by the military judge authorizing disclosure of specific government information under the procedures established by subdivision (j), the prosecution may move that, in lieu of the disclosure of such information, the military judge order:

(i) the substitution for such government information of a statement admitting relevant facts that the specific government information would tend to prove;

(ii) the substitution for such government information of a summary of the specific government information; or

(iii) any other procedure or redaction limiting the disclosure of specific government information.

(B) *Hearing.* The military judge must hold a hearing on any motion under subdivision (j). At the request of the trial counsel, the military judge will conduct an in camera hearing.

(C) *Standard for Use of Alternatives.* The military judge must grant such a motion of the trial counsel if the military judge finds that the statement, summary, or other procedure or redaction will provide the accused with substantially the same ability to make his or her defense as would disclosure of the specific government information.

(3) *Sealing of Records of In Camera Hearings.* If at the close of an in camera hearing under subdivision (j) (or any portion of a hearing under subdivision (j) that is held in camera), the military judge

determines that the government information at issue may not be disclosed or elicited at the trial or pretrial proceeding, the record of such in camera hearing must be sealed in accordance with R.C.M. 1103A and preserved for use in the event of an appeal. The accused may seek reconsideration of the military judge's determination prior to or during trial.

(4) *Remedies.*

(A) If the military judge determines that alternatives to full disclosure may not be used and the prosecution continues to object to disclosure of the information, the military judge must issue any order that the interests of justice require, including but not limited to, an order:

(i) striking or precluding all or part of the testimony of a witness;

(ii) declaring a mistrial;

(iii) finding against the government on any issue as to which the evidence is relevant and necessary to the defense;

(iv) dismissing the charges, with or without prejudice; or

(v) dismissing the charges or specifications or both to which the information relates.

(B) The government may avoid the sanction for nondisclosure by permitting the accused to disclose the information at the pertinent court-martial proceeding.

(5) *Disclosure of Rebuttal Information.* Whenever the military judge determines that government information may be disclosed in connection with a trial or pretrial proceeding, the military judge must, unless the interests of fairness do not so require, order the prosecution to provide the accused with the information it expects to use to rebut the government information.

(A) *Continuing Duty.* The military judge may place the prosecution under a continuing duty to disclose such rebuttal information.

(B) *Sanction for Failure to Comply.* If the prosecution fails to comply with its obligation under subdivision (j), the military judge may make such ruling as the interests of justice require, to include:

(i) excluding any evidence not made the subject of a required disclosure; and

(ii) prohibiting the examination by the prosecution of any witness with respect to such information.

(k) *Appeals of Orders and Rulings.* In a court-martial in which a punitive discharge may be adjudged, the government may appeal an order or ruling of the military judge that terminates the proceedings with respect to a charge or specification, directs the disclosure of government information, or imposes sanctions for nondisclosure of government information. The government may also appeal an order or ruling in which the military judge refuses to issue a protective order sought by the United States to prevent the disclosure of government information, or to enforce such an order previously issued by appropriate authority. The government may not appeal an order or ruling that is, or amounts to, a finding of not guilty with respect to the charge or specification.

(l) *Introduction into Evidence of Government Information Subject to a Claim of Privilege.*

(1) *Precautions.* The military judge in a trial by court-martial, in order to prevent unnecessary disclosure of government information after there has been a claim of privilege under this rule, may order admission into evidence of only part of a writing, recording, or photograph or admit into evidence the whole writing, recording, or photograph with excision of some or all of the government information contained therein, unless the whole ought in fairness to be considered.

(2) *Government Information Kept Under Seal.* The military judge must allow government information offered or accepted into evidence to remain under seal during the trial, even if such evidence is disclosed in the court-martial proceeding, and may, upon motion by the prosecution, seal exhibits containing government information in accordance with R.C.M. 1103A for any period after trial as necessary to prevent a disclosure of government information when a knowledgeable United States official described in subdivision (d) submits to the military judge a declaration setting forth the detriment to the public interest that the disclosure of such information reasonably could be expected to cause.

(3) *Testimony.*

(A) *Objection by Trial Counsel.* During examination of a witness, trial counsel may object to any question or line of inquiry that may require the witness to disclose government information not previously found admissible if such information has

been or is reasonably likely to be the subject of a claim of privilege under this rule.

(B) *Action by Military Judge.* Following such an objection, the military judge must take such suitable action to determine whether the response is admissible as will safeguard against the compromise of any government information. Such action may include requiring trial counsel to provide the military judge with a proffer of the witness's response to the question or line of inquiry and requiring the accused to provide the military judge with a proffer of the nature of the information sought to be elicited by the accused. Upon request, the military judge may accept an ex parte proffer by trial counsel to the extent necessary to protect government information from disclosure.

(m) *Record of Trial.* If under this rule any information is withheld from the accused, the accused objects to such withholding, and the trial is continued to an adjudication of guilt of the accused, the entire unaltered text of the relevant documents as well as the prosecution's motion and any materials submitted in support thereof must be sealed in accordance with R.C.M. 1103A and attached to the record of trial as an appellate exhibit. Such material must be made available to reviewing authorities in closed proceedings for the purpose of reviewing the determination of the military judge.

Rule 507. Identity of informants

(a) *General Rule.* The United States or a State or subdivision thereof has a privilege to refuse to disclose the identity of an informant. Unless otherwise privileged under these rules, the communications of an informant are not privileged except to the extent necessary to prevent the disclosure of the informant's identity.

(b) *Definitions.* As used in this rule:

(1) "Informant" means a person who has furnished information relating to or assisting in an investigation of a possible violation of law to a person whose official duties include the discovery, investigation, or prosecution of crime.

(2) "In camera review" means an inspection of documents or other evidence conducted by the military judge alone in chambers and not on the record.

(c) *Who May Claim the Privilege.* The privilege may be claimed by an appropriate representative of the United States, regardless of whether information was furnished to an officer of the United States or a State or subdivision thereof. The privilege may be claimed by an appropriate representative of a State or subdivision if the information was furnished to an officer thereof, except the privilege will not be allowed if the prosecution objects.

(d) *Exceptions.*

(1) *Voluntary Disclosures; Informant as a Prosecution Witness.* No privilege exists under this rule:

(A) if the identity of the informant has been disclosed to those who would have cause to resent the communication by a holder of the privilege or by the informant's own action; or

(B) if the informant appears as a witness for the prosecution.

(2) *Informant as a Defense Witness.* If a claim of privilege has been made under this rule, the military judge must, upon motion by the accused, determine whether disclosure of the identity of the informant is necessary to the accused's defense on the issue of guilt or innocence. Whether such a necessity exists will depend on the particular circumstances of each case, taking into consideration the offense charged, the possible defense, the possible significance of the informant's testimony, and other relevant factors. If it appears from the evidence in the case or from other showing by a party that an informant may be able to give testimony necessary to the accused's defense on the issue of guilt or innocence, the military judge may make any order required by the interests of justice.

(3) *Informant as a Witness regarding a Motion to Suppress Evidence.* If a claim of privilege has been made under this rule with respect to a motion under Mil. R. Evid. 311, the military judge must, upon motion of the accused, determine whether disclosure of the identity of the informant is required by the United States Constitution as applied to members of the Armed Forces. In making this determination, the military judge may make any order required by the interests of justice.

(e) *Procedures.*

(1) *In Camera Review.* If the accused has articulated a basis for disclosure under the standards set forth in this rule, the prosecution may ask the military judge to conduct an in camera review of affidavits or other evidence relevant to disclosure.

(2) *Order by the Military Judge.* If a claim of privilege has been made under this rule, the military judge may make any order required by the interests of justice.

(3) *Action by the Convening Authority.* If the military judge determines that disclosure of the identity of the informant is required under the standards set forth in this rule, and the prosecution elects not to disclose the identity of the informant, the matter must be reported to the convening authority. The convening authority may institute action to secure disclosure of the identity of the informant, terminate the proceedings, or take such other action as may be appropriate under the circumstances.

(4) *Remedies.* If, after a reasonable period of time disclosure is not made, the military judge, sua sponte or upon motion of either counsel and after a hearing if requested by either party, may dismiss the charge or specifications or both to which the information regarding the informant would relate if the military judge determines that further proceedings would materially prejudice a substantial right of the accused.

Rule 508. Political vote

A person has a privilege to refuse to disclose the tenor of the person's vote at a political election conducted by secret ballot unless the vote was cast illegally.

Rule 509. Deliberations of courts and juries

Except as provided in Mil. R. Evid. 606, the deliberations of courts, courts-martial, military judges, and grand and petit juries are privileged to the extent that such matters are privileged in trial of criminal cases in the United States district courts, but the results of the deliberations are not privileged.

Rule 510. Waiver of privilege by voluntary disclosure

(a) A person upon whom these rules confer a privilege against disclosure of a confidential matter or communication waives the privilege if the person or the person's predecessor while holder of the privilege voluntarily discloses or consents to disclosure of any significant part of the matter or communication under such circumstances that it would be inappropriate to allow the claim of privilege. This rule does not apply if the disclosure is itself a privileged communication.

(b) Unless testifying voluntarily concerning a privileged matter or communication, an accused who testifies in his or her own behalf or a person who testifies under a grant or promise of immunity does not, merely by reason of testifying, waive a privilege to which he or she may be entitled pertaining to the confidential matter or communication.

Rule 511. Privileged matter disclosed under compulsion or without opportunity to claim privilege

(a) *General Rule.* Evidence of a statement or other disclosure of privileged matter is not admissible against the holder of the privilege if disclosure was compelled erroneously or was made without an opportunity for the holder of the privilege to claim the privilege.

(b) *Use of Communications Media.* The telephonic transmission of information otherwise privileged under these rules does not affect its privileged character. Use of electronic means of communication other than the telephone for transmission of information otherwise privileged under these rules does not affect the privileged character of such information if use of such means of communication is necessary and in furtherance of the communication.

Rule 512. Comment upon or inference from claim of privilege; instruction

(a) *Comment or Inference Not Permitted.*

(1) The claim of a privilege by the accused whether in the present proceeding or upon a prior occasion is not a proper subject of comment by the military judge or counsel for any party. No inference may be drawn therefrom.

(2) The claim of a privilege by a person other than the accused whether in the present proceeding or upon a prior occasion normally is not a proper subject of comment by the military judge or counsel for any party. An adverse inference may not be drawn there from except when determined by the military judge to be required by the interests of justice.

(b) *Claiming a Privilege Without the Knowledge of the Members.* In a trial before a court-martial with members, proceedings must be conducted, to the extent practicable, so as to facilitate the making of claims of privilege without the knowledge of the members. Subdivision (b) does not apply to a special court-martial without a military judge.

(c) *Instruction.* Upon request, any party against whom the members might draw an adverse inference from a claim of privilege is entitled to an instruction that no inference may be drawn there from except as provided in subdivision (a)(2).

Rule 513. Psychotherapist—patient privilege

(a) *General Rule.* A patient has a privilege to refuse to disclose and to prevent any other person from disclosing a confidential communication made between the patient and a psychotherapist or an assistant to the psychotherapist, in a case arising under the Uniform Code of Military Justice, if such communication was made for the purpose of facilitating diagnosis or treatment of the patient's mental or emotional condition.

(b) *Definitions.* As used in this rule:

(1) "Patient" means a person who consults with or is examined or interviewed by a psychotherapist for purposes of advice, diagnosis, or treatment of a mental or emotional condition.

(2) "Psychotherapist" means a psychiatrist, clinical psychologist, clinical social worker, or other mental health professional who is licensed in any State, territory, possession, the District of Columbia, or Puerto Rico to perform professional services as such, or who holds credentials to provide such services as such, or who holds credentials to provide such services from any military health care facility, or is a person reasonably believed by the patient to have such license or credentials.

(3) "Assistant to a psychotherapist" means a person directed by or assigned to assist a psychotherapist in providing professional services, or is reasonably believed by the patient to be such.

(4) A communication is "confidential" if not intended to be disclosed to third persons other than those to whom disclosure is in furtherance of the rendition of professional services to the patient or those reasonably necessary for such transmission of the communication.

(5) "Evidence of a patient's records or communications" means testimony of a psychotherapist, or assistant to the same, or patient records that pertain to communications by a patient to a psychotherapist, or assistant to the same, for the purposes of diagno-

sis or treatment of the patient's mental or emotional condition.

(c) *Who May Claim the Privilege.* The privilege may be claimed by the patient or the guardian or conservator of the patient. A person who may claim the privilege may authorize trial counsel or defense counsel to claim the privilege on his or her behalf. The psychotherapist or assistant to the psychotherapist who received the communication may claim the privilege on behalf of the patient. The authority of such a psychotherapist, assistant, guardian, or conservator to so assert the privilege is presumed in the absence of evidence to the contrary.

(d) *Exceptions.* There is no privilege under this rule:

(1) when the patient is dead;

(2) when the communication is evidence of child abuse or of neglect, or in a proceeding in which one spouse is charged with a crime against a child of either spouse;

(3) when federal law, state law, or service regulation imposes a duty to report information contained in a communication;

(4) when a psychotherapist or assistant to a psychotherapist believes that a patient's mental or emotional condition makes the patient a danger to any person, including the patient;

(5) if the communication clearly contemplated the future commission of a fraud or crime or if the services of the psychotherapist are sought or obtained to enable or aid anyone to commit or plan to commit what the patient knew or reasonably should have known to be a crime or fraud;

(6) when necessary to ensure the safety and security of military personnel, military dependents, military property, classified information, or the accomplishment of a military mission;

(7) when an accused offers statements or other evidence concerning his mental condition in defense, extenuation, or mitigation, under circumstances not covered by R.C.M. 706 or Mil. R. Evid. 302. In such situations, the military judge may, upon motion, order disclosure of any statement made by the accused to a psychotherapist as may be necessary in the interests of justice; or

(e) *Procedure to Determine Admissibility of Patient Records or Communications.*

(1) In any case in which the production or admission of records or communications of a patient other than the accused is a matter in dispute, a party may seek an interlocutory ruling by the military judge. In order to obtain such a ruling, the party must:

(A) file a written motion at least 5 days prior to entry of pleas specifically describing the evidence and stating the purpose for which it is sought or offered, or objected to, unless the military judge, for good cause shown, requires a different time for filing or permits filing during trial; and

(B) serve the motion on the opposing party, the military judge and, if practical, notify the patient or the patient's guardian, conservator, or representative that the motion has been filed and that the patient has an opportunity to be heard as set forth in subdivision (e)(2).

(2) Before ordering the production or admission of evidence of a patient's records or communication, the military judge must conduct a hearing, which shall be closed. At the hearing, the parties may call witnesses, including the patient, and offer other relevant evidence. The patient must be afforded a reasonable opportunity to attend the hearing and be heard. However, the hearing may not be unduly delayed for this purpose. The right to be heard under this rule includes the right to be heard through counsel, including Special Victims' Counsel under section 1044e of title 10, United States Code. In a case before a court-martial composed of a military judge and members, the military judge must conduct the hearing outside the presence of the members.

(3) The military judge may examine the evidence or a proffer thereof in camera, if such examination is necessary to rule on the production or admissibility of protected records or communications. Prior to conducting an in camera review, the military judge must find by a preponderance of the evidence that the moving party showed:

(A) a specific factual basis demonstrating a reasonable likelihood that the records or communications would yield evidence admissible under an exception to the privilege;

(B) that the requested information meets one of the enumerated exceptions under subsection (d) of this rule;

(C) that the information sought is not merely cumulative of other information available; and

(D) that the party made reasonable efforts to obtain the same or substantially similar information through non-privileged sources.

(4) Any production or disclosure permitted by the military judge under this rule must be narrowly tailored to only the specific records or communications, or portions of such records or communications, that meet the requirements for one of the enumerated exceptions to the privilege under subsection (d) above and are included in the stated purpose for which the records or communications are sought under subsection (e)(1)(A) above.

(5) To prevent unnecessary disclosure of evidence of a patient's records or communications, the military judge may issue protective orders or may admit only portions of the evidence.

(6) The motion, related papers, and the record of the hearing must be sealed in accordance with R.C.M. 1103A and must remain under seal unless the military judge or an appellate court orders otherwise.

Rule 514. Victim advocate-victim and Department of Defense Safe Helpline staff-victim privilege.

(a) *General rule.* A victim has a privilege to refuse to disclose and to prevent any other person from disclosing a confidential communication made between the alleged victim and a victim advocate or between the alleged victim and Department of Defense Safe Helpline staff, in a case arising under the UCMJ, if such communication was made for the purpose of facilitating advice or assistance to the alleged victim.

(b) *Definitions.* As used in this rule:

(1) "Victim" means any person who is alleged to have suffered direct physical or emotional harm as the result of a sexual or violent offense.

(2) "Victim advocate" means a person who:

(A) is designated in writing as a victim advocate in accordance with service regulation;

(B) is authorized to perform victim advocate duties in accordance with service regulation and is acting in the performance of those duties; or

(C) is certified as a victim advocate pursuant to federal or state requirements.

(3) "Department of Defense Safe Helpline staff" are persons who are designated by competent authority in writing as Department of Defense Safe Helpline staff.

(4) A communication is "confidential" if made in the course of the victim advocate-victim relationship or Department of Defense Safe Helpline staff-victim relationship and not intended to be disclosed to third persons other than those to whom disclosure is made in furtherance of the rendition of advice or assistance to the alleged victim or those reasonably necessary for such transmission of the communication.

(5) "Evidence of a victim's records or communications" means testimony of a victim advocate or Department of Defense Safe Helpline staff, or records that pertain to communications by a victim to a victim advocate or Department of Defense Safe Helpline staff, for the purposes of advising or providing assistance to the victim.

(c) *Who may claim the privilege.* The privilege may be claimed by the victim or the guardian or conservator of the victim. A person who may claim the privilege may authorize trial counsel or a counsel representing the victim to claim the privilege on his or her behalf. The victim advocate or Department of Defense Safe Helpline staff who received the communication may claim the privilege on behalf of the victim. The authority of such a victim advocate, Department of Defense Safe Helpline staff, guardian, conservator, or a counsel representing the victim to so assert the privilege is presumed in the absence of evidence to the contrary.

(d) *Exceptions.* There is no privilege under this rule:

(1) when the victim is dead;

(2) When federal law, state law, Department of Defense regulation, or service regulation imposes a duty to report information contained in a communication;

(3) When a victim advocate or Department of Defense Safe Helpline staff believes that a victim's mental or emotional condition makes the victim a danger to any person, including the victim;

(4) If the communication clearly contemplated the future commission of a fraud or crime, or if the services of the victim advocate or Department of Defense Safe Helpline staff are sought or obtained to enable or aid anyone to commit or plan to commit what the victim knew or reasonably should have known to be a crime or fraud;

(5) when necessary to ensure the safety and security of military personnel, military dependents, military property, classified information, or the accomplishment of a military mission; or

(6) when admission or disclosure of a communication is constitutionally required.

(e) *Procedure to Determine Admissibility of Victim Records or Communications.*

(1) In any case in which the production or admission of records or communications of a victim is a matter in dispute, a party may seek an interlocutory ruling by the military judge. In order to obtain such a ruling, the party must:

(A) file a written motion at least 5 days prior to entry of pleas specifically describing the evidence and stating the purpose for which it is sought or offered, or objected to, unless the military judge, for good cause shown, requires a different time for filing or permits filing during trial; and

(B) serve the motion on the opposing party, the military judge and, if practicable, notify the victim or the victim's guardian, conservator, or representative that the motion has been filed and that the victim has an opportunity to be heard as set forth in subdivision (e)(2).

(2) Before ordering the production or admission of evidence of a victim's records or communication, the military judge must conduct a hearing, which shall be closed. At the hearing, the parties may call witnesses, including the victim, and offer other relevant evidence. The victim must be afforded a reasonable opportunity to attend the hearing and be heard. However, the hearing may not be unduly delayed for this purpose. The right to be heard under this rule includes the right to be heard through counsel, including Special Victims' Counsel under section 1044e of title 10, United States Code. In a case before a court-martial composed of a military judge and members, the military judge must conduct the hearing outside the presence of the members.

(3) The military judge may examine the evidence, or a proffer thereof, in camera if such examination is necessary to rule on the production or admissibility of protected records or communications. Prior to conducting an in camera review, the military judge must find by a preponderance of the evidence that the moving party showed:

(A) a specific factual basis demonstrating a reasonable likelihood that the records or communications would yield evidence admissible under an exception to the privilege;

(B) that the requested information meets one of the enumerated exceptions under subsection (d) of this rule;

(C) that the information sought is not merely cumulative of other information available; and

(D) that the party made reasonable efforts to obtain the same or substantially similar information through non-privileged sources.

(4) Any production or disclosure permitted by the military judge under this rule must be narrowly tailored to only the specific records or communications, or portions of such records or communications, that meet the requirements for one of the enumerated exceptions to the privilege under subsection (d) of this rule and are included in the stated purpose for which the records or communications are sought under subsection (e)(1)(A) of this rule.

(5) To prevent unnecessary disclosure of evidence of a victim's records or communications, the military judge may issue protective orders or may admit only portions of the evidence.

(6) The motion, related papers, and the record of the hearing must be sealed in accordance with R.C.M. 1103A and must remain under seal unless the military judge or an appellate court orders otherwise.

SECTION VI
WITNESSES

Rule 601. Competency to testify in general

Every person is competent to be a witness unless these rules provide otherwise.

Rule 602. Need for personal knowledge

A witness may testify to a matter only if evidence is introduced sufficient to support a finding that the witness has personal knowledge of the matter. Evidence to prove personal knowledge may consist of the witness's own testimony. This rule does not apply to a witness's expert testimony under Mil. R. Evid. 703.

Rule 603. Oath or affirmation to testify truthfully

Before testifying, a witness must give an oath or affirmation to testify truthfully. It must be in a form designed to impress that duty on the witness's conscience.

Rule 604. Interpreter

An interpreter must be qualified and must give an oath or affirmation to make a true translation.

Rule 605. Military judge's competency as a witness.

(a) The presiding military judge may not testify as a witness at any proceeding of that court-martial. A party need not object to preserve the issue.

(b) This rule does not preclude the military judge from placing on the record matters concerning docketing of the case.

Rule 606. Member's competency as a witness.

(a) *At the Trial by Court-Martial.* A member of a court-martial may not testify as a witness before the other members at any proceeding of that court-martial. If a member is called to testify, the military judge must – except in a special court-martial without a military judge – give the opposing party an opportunity to object outside the presence of the members.

(b) *During an Inquiry into the Validity of a Finding or Sentence.*

(1) *Prohibited Testimony or Other Evidence.* During an inquiry into the validity of a finding or sentence, a member of a court-martial may not testify about any statement made or incident that occurred during the deliberations of that court-martial; the effect of anything on that member's or another member's vote; or any member's mental processes concerning the finding or sentence. The military judge may not receive a member's affidavit or evidence of a member's statement on these matters.

(2) *Exceptions.* A member may testify about whether:

(A) extraneous prejudicial information was improperly brought to the members' attention;

(B) unlawful command influence or any other outside influence was improperly brought to bear on any member; or

(C) a mistake was made in entering the finding or sentence on the finding or sentence forms.

Rule 607. Who may impeach a witness.

Any party, including the party that called the witness, may attack the witness's credibility.

Rule 608. A witness's character for truthfulness or untruthfulness.

(a) *Reputation or Opinion Evidence.* A witness's credibility may be attacked or supported by testimony about the witness's reputation for having a character for truthfulness or untruthfulness, or by testimony in the form of an opinion about that character. Evidence of truthful character is admissible only after the witness's character for truthfulness has been attacked.

(b) *Specific Instances of Conduct.* Except for a criminal conviction under Mil. R. Evid. 609, extrinsic evidence is not admissible to prove specific instances of a witness's conduct in order to attack or support the witness's character for truthfulness. The military judge may, on cross-examination, allow them to be inquired into if they are probative of the character for truthfulness or untruthfulness of:

(1) the witness; or

(2) another witness whose character the witness being cross-examined has testified about. By testifying on another matter, a witness does not waive any privilege against self-incrimination for testimony that relates only to the witness's character for truthfulness.

(c) *Evidence of Bias.* Bias, prejudice, or any motive to misrepresent may be shown to impeach the witness either by examination of the witness or by evidence otherwise adduced.

Rule 609. Impeachment by evidence of a criminal conviction.

(a) *In General.* The following rules apply to attacking a witness's character for truthfulness by evidence of a criminal conviction:

(1) For a crime that, in the convicting jurisdiction, was punishable by death, dishonorable discharge, or by imprisonment for more than one year, the evidence:

(A) must be admitted, subject to Mil. R. Evid.

403, in a court-martial in which the witness is not the accused; and

(B) must be admitted in a court-martial in which the witness is the accused, if the probative value of the evidence outweighs its prejudicial effect to that accused; and

(2) For any crime regardless of the punishment, the evidence must be admitted if the court can readily determine that establishing the elements of the crime required proving – or the witness's admitting – a dishonest act or false statement.

(3) In determining whether a crime tried by court-martial was punishable by death, dishonorable discharge, or imprisonment in excess of one year, the maximum punishment prescribed by the President under Article 56 at the time of the conviction applies without regard to whether the case was tried by general, special, or summary court-martial.

(b) *Limit on Using the Evidence After 10 Years.* Subdivision (b) applies if more than 10 years have passed since the witness's conviction or release from confinement for it, whichever is later. Evidence of the conviction is admissible only if:

(1) its probative value, supported by specific facts and circumstances, substantially outweighs its prejudicial effect; and

(2) the proponent gives an adverse party reasonable written notice of the intent to use it so that the party has a fair opportunity to contest its use.

(c) *Effect of a Pardon, Annulment, or Certificate of Rehabilitation.* Evidence of a conviction is not admissible if:

(1) the conviction has been the subject of a pardon, annulment, certificate of rehabilitation, or other equivalent procedure based on a finding that the person has been rehabilitated, and the person has not been convicted of a later crime punishable by death, dishonorable discharge, or imprisonment for more than one year; or

(2) the conviction has been the subject of a pardon, annulment, or other equivalent procedure based on a finding of innocence.

(d) *Juvenile Adjudications.* Evidence of a juvenile adjudication is admissible under this rule only if:

(1) the adjudication was of a witness other than the accused;

(2) an adult's conviction for that offense would be admissible to attack the adult's credibility; and

(3) admitting the evidence is necessary to fairly determine guilt or innocence.

(e) *Pendency of an Appeal.* A conviction that satisfies this rule is admissible even if an appeal is pending, except that a conviction by summary court-martial or special court-martial without a military judge may not be used for purposes of impeachment until review has been completed under Article 64 or Article 66, if applicable. Evidence of the pendency is also admissible.

(f) *Definition.* For purposes of this rule, there is a "conviction" in a court-martial case when a sentence has been adjudged.

Rule 610. Religious beliefs or opinions.

Evidence of a witness's religious beliefs or opinions is not admissible to attack or support the witness's credibility.

Rule 611. Mode and order of examining witnesses and presenting evidence.

(a) *Control by the Military Judge; Purposes.* The military judge should exercise reasonable control over the mode and order of examining witnesses and presenting evidence so as to:

(1) make those procedures effective for determining the truth;

(2) avoid wasting time; and

(3) protect witnesses from harassment or undue embarrassment.

(b) *Scope of Cross-Examination.* Cross-examination should not go beyond the subject matter of the direct examination and matters affecting the witness's credibility. The military judge may allow inquiry into additional matters as if on direct examination.

(c) *Leading Questions.* Leading questions should not be used on direct examination except as necessary to develop the witness's testimony. Ordinarily, the military judge should allow leading questions:

(1) on cross-examination; and

(2) when a party calls a hostile witness or a witness identified with an adverse party.

(d) *Remote live testimony of a child.*

(1) In a case involving domestic violence or the abuse of a child, the military judge must, subject to the requirements of subdivision (d)(3) of this rule, allow a child victim or witness to testify from an

area outside the courtroom as prescribed in R.C.M. 914A.

(2) *Definitions.* As used in this rule:

(A) "Child" means a person who is under the age of 16 at the time of his or her testimony.

(B) "Abuse of a child" means the physical or mental injury, sexual abuse or exploitation, or negligent treatment of a child.

(C) "Exploitation" means child pornography or child prostitution.

(D) "Negligent treatment" means the failure to provide, for reasons other than poverty, adequate food, clothing, shelter, or medical care so as to endanger seriously the physical health of the child.

(E) "Domestic violence" means an offense that has as an element the use, or attempted or threatened use of physical force against a person by a current or former spouse, parent, or guardian of the victim; by a person with whom the victim shares a child in common; by a person who is cohabiting with or has cohabited with the victim as a spouse, parent, or guardian; or by a person similarly situated to a spouse, parent, or guardian of the victim.

(3) Remote live testimony will be used only where the military judge makes the following three findings on the record:

(A) that it is necessary to protect the welfare of the particular child witness;

(B) that the child witness would be traumatized, not by the courtroom generally, but by the presence of the defendant; and

(C) that the emotional distress suffered by the child witness in the presence of the defendant is more than *de minimis.*

(4) Remote live testimony of a child will not be used when the accused elects to absent himself from the courtroom in accordance with R.C.M. 804(d).

(5) In making a determination under subdivision (d)(3), the military judge may question the child in chambers, or at some comfortable place other than the courtroom, on the record for a reasonable period of time, in the presence of the child, a representative of the prosecution, a representative of the defense, and the child's attorney or guardian ad litem.

Rule 612. Writing used to refresh a witness's memory.

(a) *Scope.* This rule gives an adverse party certain options when a witness uses a writing to refresh memory:

(1) while testifying; or

(2) before testifying, if the military judge decides that justice requires the party to have those options.

(b) *Adverse Party's Options; Deleting Unrelated Matter.* An adverse party is entitled to have the writing produced at the hearing, to inspect it, to cross-examine the witness about it, and to introduce in evidence any portion that relates to the witness's testimony. If the producing party claims that the writing includes unrelated or privileged matter, the military judge must examine the writing in camera, delete any unrelated or privileged portion, and order that the rest be delivered to the adverse party. Any portion deleted over objection must be preserved for the record.

(c) *Failure to Produce or Deliver the Writing.* If a writing is not produced or is not delivered as ordered, the military judge may issue any appropriate order. If the prosecution does not comply, the military judge must strike the witness's testimony or – if justice so requires – declare a mistrial.

(d) *No Effect on Other Disclosure Requirements.* This rule does not preclude disclosure of information required to be disclosed under other provisions of these rules or this Manual.

Rule 613. Witness's prior statement.

(a) *Showing or Disclosing the Statement During Examination.* When examining a witness about the witness's prior statement, a party need not show it or disclose its contents to the witness. The party must, on request, show it or disclose its contents to an adverse party's attorney.

(b) *Extrinsic Evidence of a Prior Inconsistent Statement.* Extrinsic evidence of a witness's prior inconsistent statement is admissible only if the witness is given an opportunity to explain or deny the statement and an adverse party is given an opportunity to examine the witness about it, or if justice so requires. Subdivision (b) does not apply to an opposing party's statement under Mil R. Evid. 801(d)(2).

Rule 614. Court-martial's calling or examining a witness.

(a) *Calling.* The military judge may – sua sponte or at the request of the members or the suggestion of a party – call a witness. Each party is entitled to cross-examine the witness. When the members wish to call or recall a witness, the military judge must determine whether the testimony would be relevant and not barred by any rule or provision of this Manual.

(b) *Examining.* The military judge or members may examine a witness regardless of who calls the witness. Members must submit their questions to the military judge in writing. Following the opportunity for review by both parties, the military judge must rule on the propriety of the questions, and ask the questions in an acceptable form on behalf of the members. When the military judge or the members call a witness who has not previously testified, the military judge may conduct the direct examination or may assign the responsibility to counsel for any party.

(c) *Objections.* Objections to the calling of witnesses by the military judge or the members or to the interrogation by the military judge or the members may be made at the time or at the next available opportunity when the members are not present.

Rule 615. Excluding witnesses.

At a party's request, the military judge must order witnesses excluded so that they cannot hear other witnesses' testimony, or the military judge may do so *sua sponte*. This rule does not authorize excluding:

(a) the accused;

(b) a member of an Armed service or an employee of the United States after being designated as a representative of the United States by the trial counsel;

(c) a person whose presence a party shows to be essential to presenting the party's case;

(d) a person authorized by statute to be present; or

(e) A victim of an offense from the trial of an accused for that offense, unless the military judge, after receiving clear and convincing evidence, determines that testimony by the victim would be materially altered if the victim heard other testimony at that hearing or proceeding.

SECTION VII
OPINIONS AND EXPERT TESTIMONY

Rule 701. Opinion testimony by lay witnesses.

If a witness is not testifying as an expert, testimony in the form of an opinion is limited to one that is:

(a) rationally based on the witness's perception;

(b) helpful to clearly understanding the witness's testimony or to determining a fact in issue; and

(c) not based on scientific, technical, or other specialized knowledge within the scope of Mil. R. Evid. 702.

Rule 702. Testimony by expert witnesses.

A witness who is qualified as an expert by knowledge, skill, experience, training, or education may testify in the form of an opinion or otherwise if:

(a) the expert's scientific, technical, or other specialized knowledge will help the trier of fact to understand the evidence or to determine a fact in issue;

(b) the testimony is based on sufficient facts or data;

(c) the testimony is the product of reliable principles and methods; and

(d) the expert has reliably applied the principles and methods to the facts of the case.

Rule 703. Bases of an expert's opinion testimony

An expert may base an opinion on facts or data in the case that the expert has been made aware of or personally observed. If experts in the particular field would reasonably rely on those kinds of facts or data in forming an opinion on the subject, they need not be admissible for the opinion to be admitted. If the facts or data would otherwise be inadmissible, the proponent of the opinion may disclose them to the members of a court-martial only if the military judge finds that their probative value in helping the members evaluate the opinion substantially outweighs their prejudicial effect.

Rule 704. Opinion on an ultimate issue

An opinion is not objectionable just because it embraces an ultimate issue.

Rule 705. Disclosing the facts or data underlying an expert's opinion

Unless the military judge orders otherwise, an expert may state an opinion – and give the reasons for it – without first testifying to the underlying facts or data. The expert may be required to disclose those facts or data on cross-examination.

Rule 706. Court-appointed expert witnesses

(a) *Appointment Process.* The trial counsel, the defense counsel, and the court-martial have equal opportunity to obtain expert witnesses under Article 46 and R.C.M. 703.

(b) *Compensation.* The compensation of expert witnesses is governed by R.C.M. 703.

(c) *Accused's Choice of Experts.* This rule does not limit an accused in calling any expert at the accused's own expense.

Rule 707. Polygraph examinations

(a) *Prohibitions.* Notwithstanding any other provision of law, the result of a polygraph examination, the polygraph examiner's opinion, or any reference to an offer to take, failure to take, or taking of a polygraph examination is not admissible.

(b) *Statements Made During a Polygraph Examination.* This rule does not prohibit admission of an otherwise admissible statement made during a polygraph examination.

SECTION VIII
HEARSAY

Rule 801. Definitions that apply to this section; exclusions from hearsay

(a) *Statement.* "Statement" means a person's oral assertion, written assertion, or nonverbal conduct, if the person intended it as an assertion.

(b) *Declarant.* "Declarant" means the person who made the statement.

(c) *Hearsay.* "Hearsay" means a statement that:

(1) the declarant does not make while testifying at the current trial or hearing; and

(2) a party offers in evidence to prove the truth of the matter asserted in the statement.

(d) *Statements that Are Not Hearsay.* A statement that meets the following conditions is not hearsay:

(1) *A Declarant-Witness's Prior Statement.* The declarant testifies and is subject to cross-examination about a prior statement, and the statement:

(A) is inconsistent with the declarant's testimony and was given under penalty of perjury at a trial, hearing, or other proceeding or in a deposition;

(B) is consistent with the declarant's testimony and is offered:

(i) to rebut an express or implied charge that the declarant recently fabricated it or acted from a recent improper influence or motive in so testifying; or

(ii) to rehabilitate the declarant's credibility as a witness when attacked on another ground; or

(C) identifies a person as someone the declarant perceived earlier.

(2) *An Opposing Party's Statement.* The statement is offered against an opposing party and:

(A) was made by the party in an individual or representative capacity;

(B) is one the party manifested that it adopted or believed to be true;

(C) was made by a person whom the party authorized to make a statement on the subject;

(D) was made by the party's agent or employee on a matter within the scope of that relationship and while it existed; or

(E) was made by the party's co-conspirator during and in furtherance of the conspiracy.
The statement must be considered but does not by itself establish the declarant's authority under (C); the existence or scope of the relationship under (D); or the existence of the conspiracy or participation in it under (E).

Rule 802. The rule against hearsay

Hearsay is not admissible unless any of the following provides otherwise:

(a) a federal statute applicable in trial by courts-martial; or

(b) these rules.

Rule 803. Exceptions to the rule against hearsay – regardless of whether the declarant is available as a witness

The following are not excluded by the rule against

hearsay, regardless of whether the declarant is available as a witness:

(1) *Present Sense Impression.* A statement describing or explaining an event or condition, made while or immediately after the declarant perceived it.

(2) *Excited Utterance.* A statement relating to a startling event or condition, made while the declarant was under the stress of excitement that it caused.

(3) *Then-Existing Mental, Emotional, or Physical Condition.* A statement of the declarant's then-existing state of mind (such as motive, intent, or plan) or emotional, sensory, or physical condition (such as mental feeling, pain, or bodily health), but not including a statement of memory or belief to prove the fact remembered or believed unless it relates to the validity or terms of the declarant's will.

(4) *Statement Made for Medical Diagnosis or Treatment.* A statement that -

(A) is made for – and is reasonably pertinent to – medical diagnosis or treatment; and

(B) describes medical history; past or present symptoms or sensations; their inception; or their general cause.

(5) *Recorded Recollection.* A record that:

(A) is on a matter the witness once knew about but now cannot recall well enough to testify fully and accurately;

(B) was made or adopted by the witness when the matter was fresh in the witness's memory; and

(C) accurately reflects the witness's knowledge. If admitted, the record may be read into evidence but may be received as an exhibit only if offered by an adverse party.

(6) *Records of a Regularly Conducted Activity.* A record of an act, event, condition, opinion, or diagnosis if:

(A) the record was made at or near the time by – or from information transmitted by – someone with knowledge;

(B) the record was kept in the course of a regularly conducted activity of a uniformed service, business, institution, association, profession, organization, occupation, or calling of any kind, whether or not conducted for profit;

(C) making the record was a regular practice of that activity;

(D) all these conditions are shown by the testimony of the custodian or another qualified witness, or by a certification that complies with Mil. R. Evid. 902(11) or with a statute permitting certification in a criminal proceeding in a court of the United States; and

(E) the opponent does not show that the source of information or the method or circumstance of preparation indicate a lack of trustworthiness. Records of regularly conducted activities include, but are not limited to, enlistment papers, physical examination papers, fingerprint cards, forensic laboratory reports, chain of custody documents, morning reports and other personnel accountability documents, service records, officer and enlisted qualification records, logs, unit personnel diaries, individual equipment records, daily strength records of prisoners, and rosters of prisoners.

(7) *Absence of a Record of a Regularly Conducted Activity.* Evidence that a matter is not included in a record described in paragraph (6) if:

(A) the evidence is admitted to prove that the matter did not occur or exist;

(B) a record was regularly kept for a matter of that kind; and

(C) the opponent does not show that the possible source of the information or other circumstances indicate a lack of trustworthiness.

(8) *Public Records.* A record or statement of a public office if:

(A) it sets out:

(i) the office's activities;

(ii) a matter observed while under a legal duty to report, but not including a matter observed by law-enforcement personnel and other personnel acting in a law enforcement capacity; or

(iii) against the government, factual findings from a legally authorized investigation; and

(B) the opponent does not show that the source of information or other circumstances indicate a lack of trustworthiness. Notwithstanding subdivision (8)(A)(ii), the following are admissible as a record of a fact or event if made by a person within the scope of the person's official duties and those duties included a duty to know or to ascertain through appropriate and trustworthy channels of information the truth of the fact or event and to record such fact or event: enlistment papers, physical examination papers, fingerprint cards, forensic laboratory reports, chain of custody documents, morning reports and other personnel accountability documents, service records, officer and enlisted qualification records, court-martial conviction records, logs, unit personnel diaries, individual equipment records, daily strength records of prisoners, and rosters of prisoners.

(9) *Public Records of Vital Statistics.* A record of a birth, death, or marriage, if reported to a public office in accordance with a legal duty.

(10) *Absence of a Public Record.* Testimony – or a certification under Rule 902 – that a diligent search failed to disclose a public record or statement if:

(A) the testimony or certification is admitted to prove that

(i) the record or statement does not exist; or

(ii) a matter did not occur or exist, if a public office regularly kept a record or statement for a matter of that kind; and

(B) a counsel for the government who intends to offer a certification provides written notice of that intent at least 14 days before trial, and the accused does not object in writing within 7 days of receiving the notice — unless the military judge sets a different time for the notice or the objection.

(11) *Records of Religious Organizations Concerning Personal or Family History.* A statement of birth, legitimacy, ancestry, marriage, divorce, death, relationship by blood or marriage, or similar facts of personal or family history, contained in a regularly kept record of a religious organization.

(12) *Certificates of Marriage, Baptism, and Similar Ceremonies.* A statement of fact contained in a certificate:

(A) made by a person who is authorized by a religious organization or by law to perform the act certified;

(B) attesting that the person performed a marriage or similar ceremony or administered a sacrament; and

(C) purporting to have been issued at the time of the act or within a reasonable time after it.

(13) *Family Records.* A statement of fact about personal or family history contained in a family record, such as a Bible, genealogy, chart, engraving on a ring, inscription on a portrait, or engraving on an urn or burial marker.

(14) *Records of Documents that Affect an Interest in Property.* The record of a document that purports to establish or affect an interest in property if:

(A) the record is admitted to prove the content of the original recorded document, along with its signing and its delivery by each person who purports to have signed it;

(B) the record is kept in a public office; and

(C) a statute authorizes recording documents of that kind in that office.

(15) *Statements in Documents that Affect an Interest in Property.* A statement contained in a document that purports to establish or affect an interest in property if the matter stated was relevant to the document's purpose unless later dealings with the property are inconsistent with the truth of the statement or the purport of the document.

(16) *Statements in Ancient Documents.* A statement in a document that is at least 20 years old and whose authenticity is established.

(17) *Market Reports and Similar Commercial Publications.* Market quotations, lists (including government price lists), directories, or other compilations that are generally relied on by the public or by persons in particular occupations.

(18) *Statements in Learned Treatises, Periodicals, or Pamphlets.* A statement contained in a treatise, periodical, or pamphlet if:

(A) the statement is called to the attention of an expert witness on cross-examination or relied on by the expert on direct examination; and

(B) the publication is established as a reliable authority by the expert's admission or testimony, by another expert's testimony, or by judicial notice.
If admitted, the statement may be read into evidence but not received as an exhibit.

(19) *Reputation Concerning Personal or Family History.* A reputation among a person's family by blood, adoption, or marriage – or among a person's associates or in the community – concerning the person's birth, adoption, legitimacy, ancestry, marriage, divorce, death, relationship by blood, adoption, or marriage, or similar facts of personal or family history, age, ancestry, or other similar fact of the person's personal or family history.

(20) *Reputation Concerning Boundaries or General History.* A reputation in a community – arising before the controversy – concerning boundaries of land in the community or customs that affect the land, or concerning general historical events important to that community, State, or nation.

(21) *Reputation Concerning Character.* A reputa-

tion among a person's associates or in the community concerning the person's character.

(22) *Judgment of a Previous Conviction.* Evidence of a final judgment of conviction if:

(A) the judgment was entered after a trial or guilty plea, but not a nolo contendere plea;

(B) the conviction was for a crime punishable by death, dishonorable discharge, or by imprisonment for more than a year;

(C) the evidence is admitted to prove any fact essential to the judgment; and

(D) when offered by the prosecution for a purpose other than impeachment, the judgment was against the accused.

The pendency of an appeal may be shown but does not affect admissibility. In determining whether a crime tried by court-martial was punishable by death, dishonorable discharge, or imprisonment for more than one year, the maximum punishment prescribed by the President under Article 56 of the Uniform of Military Justice at the time of the conviction applies without regard to whether the case was tried by general, special, or summary court-martial.

(23) *Judgments Involving Personal, Family, or General History, or a Boundary.* A judgment that is admitted to prove a matter of personal, family, or general history, or boundaries, if the matter:

(A) was essential to the judgment; and

(B) could be proved by evidence of reputation.

Rule 804. Exceptions to the rule against hearsay – when the declarant is unavailable as a witness

(a) *Criteria for Being Unavailable.* A declarant is considered to be unavailable as a witness if the declarant:

(1) is exempted from testifying about the subject matter of the declarant's statement because the military judge rules that a privilege applies;

(2) refuses to testify about the subject matter despite the military judge's order to do so;

(3) testifies to not remembering the subject matter;

(4) cannot be present or testify at the trial or hearing because of death or a then-existing infirmity, physical illness, or mental illness; or

(5) is absent from the trial or hearing and the statement's proponent has not been able, by process or other reasonable means, to procure:

(A) the declarant's attendance, in the case of a hearsay exception under subdivision (b)(1) or (b)(5);

(B) the declarant's attendance or testimony, in the case of a hearsay exception under subdivision (b)(2), (b)(3), or (b)(4); or

(6) is unavailable within the meaning of Article 49(d)(2).

Subdivision (a) does not apply if the statement's proponent procured or wrongfully caused the declarant's unavailability as a witness in order to prevent the declarant from attending or testifying.

(b) *The Exceptions.* The following are exceptions to the rule against hearsay, and are not excluded by that rule if the declarant is unavailable as a witness:

(1) *Former Testimony.* Testimony that:

(A) was given by a witness at a trial, hearing, or lawful deposition, whether given during the current proceeding or a different one; and

(B) is now offered against a party who had an opportunity and similar motive to develop it by direct, cross-, or redirect examination. Subject to the limitations in Articles 49 and 50, a record of testimony given before a court-martial, court of inquiry, military commission, other military tribunal, or preliminary hearing under Article 32 is admissible under subdivision (b)(1) if the record of the testimony is a verbatim record.

(2) *Statement under the Belief of Imminent Death.* In a prosecution for any offense resulting in the death of the alleged victim, a statement that the declarant, while believing the declarant's death to be imminent, made about its cause or circumstances.

(3) *Statement against Interest.* A statement that:

(A) a reasonable person in the declarant's position would have made only if the person believed it to be true because, when made, it was so contrary to the declarant's proprietary or pecuniary interest or had so great a tendency to invalidate the declarant's claim against someone else or to expose the declarant to civil or criminal liability; and

(B) is supported by corroborating circumstances that clearly indicate its trustworthiness, if it tends to expose the declarant to criminal liability and is offered to exculpate the accused.

(4) *Statement of Personal or Family History.* A statement about:

(A) the declarant's own birth, adoption, legitimacy, ancestry, marriage, divorce, relationship by blood or marriage, or similar facts of personal or family history, even though the declarant had no way of acquiring personal knowledge about that fact; or

(B) another person concerning any of these facts, as well as death, if the declarant was related to the person by blood, adoption, or marriage or was so intimately associated with the person's family that the declarant's information is likely to be accurate.

(5) *Other Exceptions.* [Transferred to Mil.R.Evid. 807]

(6) *Statement Offered against a Party that Wrongfully Caused the Declarant's Unavailability.* A statement offered against a party that wrongfully caused or acquiesced in wrongfully causing the declarant's unavailability as a witness, and did so intending that result.

Rule 805. Hearsay within hearsay

Hearsay within hearsay is not excluded by the rule against hearsay if each part of the combined statements conforms with an exception or exclusion to the rule.

Rule 806. Attacking and supporting the declarant's credibility

When a hearsay statement – or a statement described in Mil. R. Evid. 801(d)(2)(C), (D), or (E) – has been admitted in evidence, the declarant's credibility may be attacked, and then supported, by any evidence that would be admissible for those purposes if the declarant had testified as a witness. The military judge may admit evidence of the declarant's inconsistent statement or conduct, regardless of when it occurred or whether the declarant had an opportunity to explain or deny it. If the party against whom the statement was admitted calls the declarant as a witness, the party may examine the declarant on the statement as if on cross-examination.

Rule 807. Residual exception.

(a) *In General.* Under the following circumstances, a hearsay statement is not excluded by the rule against hearsay even if the statement is not specifically covered by a hearsay exception in Mil. R. Evid. 803 or 804:

(1) the statement has equivalent circumstantial guarantees of trustworthiness;

(2) it is offered as evidence of a material fact;

(3) it is more probative on the point for which it is offered than any other evidence that the proponent can obtain through reasonable efforts; and

(4) admitting it will best serve the purposes of these rules and the interests of justice.

(b) *Notice.* The statement is admissible only if, before the trial or hearing, the proponent gives an adverse party reasonable notice of the intent to offer the statement and its particulars, including the declarant's name and address, so that the party has a fair opportunity to meet it.

SECTION IX
AUTHENTICATION AND IDENTIFICATION

Rule 901. Authenticating or identifying evidence

(a) *In General.* To satisfy the requirement of authenticating or identifying an item of evidence, the proponent must produce evidence sufficient to support a finding that the item is what the proponent claims it is.

(b) *Examples.* The following are examples only – not a complete list – of evidence that satisfies the requirement:

(1) *Testimony of a Witness with Knowledge.* Testimony that an item is what it is claimed to be.

(2) *Nonexpert Opinion about Handwriting.* A nonexpert's opinion that handwriting is genuine, based on a familiarity with it that was not acquired for the current litigation.

(3) *Comparison by an Expert Witness or the Trier of Fact.* A comparison with an authenticated specimen by an expert witness or the trier of fact.

(4) *Distinctive Characteristics and the Like.* The appearance, contents, substance, internal patterns, or other distinctive characteristics of the item, taken together with all the circumstances.

(5) *Opinion about a Voice.* An opinion identifying a person's voice – whether heard firsthand or through mechanical or electronic transmission or recording – based on hearing the voice at any time

under circumstances that connect it with the alleged speaker.

(6) *Evidence about a Telephone Conversation.* For a telephone conversation, evidence that a call was made to the number assigned at the time to:

(A) a particular person, if circumstances, including self-identification, show that the person answering was the one called; or

(B) a particular business, if the call was made to a business and the call related to business reasonably transacted over the telephone.

(7) *Evidence about Public Records.* Evidence that:

(A) a document was recorded or filed in a public office as authorized by law; or

(B) a purported public record or statement is from the office where items of this kind are kept.

(8) *Evidence about Ancient Documents or Data Compilations.* For a document or data compilation, evidence that it:

(A) is in a condition that creates no suspicion about its authenticity;

(B) was in a place where, if authentic, it would likely be; and

(C) is at least 20 years old when offered.

(9) *Evidence about a Process or System.* Evidence describing a process or system and showing that it produces an accurate result.

(10) *Methods Provided by a Statute or Rule.* Any method of authentication or identification allowed by a federal statute, a rule prescribed by the Supreme Court, or an applicable regulation prescribed pursuant to statutory authority.

Rule 902. Evidence that Is self-authenticating

The following items of evidence are self-authenticating; they require no extrinsic evidence of authenticity in order to be admitted:

(1) *Domestic Public Documents that are Sealed and Signed.* A document that bears:

(A) a seal purporting to be that of the United States; any State, district, Commonwealth, territory, or insular possession of the United States; the former Panama Canal Zone; the Trust Territory of the Pacific Islands; a political subdivision of any of these entities; or a department, agency, or officer of any entity named above; and

(B) a signature purporting to be an execution or attestation.

(2) *Domestic Public Documents that are Not Sealed but are Signed and Certified.* A document that bears no seal if:

(A) it bears the signature of an officer or employee of an entity named in subdivision (1)(A) above; and

(B) another public officer who has a seal and official duties within that same entity certifies under seal – or its equivalent – that the signer has the official capacity and that the signature is genuine.

(3) *Foreign Public Documents.* A document that purports to be signed or attested by a person who is authorized by a foreign country's law to do so. The document must be accompanied by a final certification that certifies the genuineness of the signature and official position of the signer or attester – or of any foreign official whose certificate of genuineness relates to the signature or attestation or is in a chain of certificates of genuineness relating to the signature or attestation. The certification may be made by a secretary of a United States embassy or legation; by a consul general, vice consul, or consular agent of the United States; or by a diplomatic or consular official of the foreign country assigned or accredited to the United States. If all parties have been given a reasonable opportunity to investigate the document's authenticity and accuracy, the military judge may, for good cause, either:

(A) order that it be treated as presumptively authentic without final certification; or

(B) allow it to be evidenced by an attested summary with or without final certification.

(4) *Certified Copies of Public Records.* A copy of an official record – or a copy of a document that was recorded or filed in a public office as authorized by law – if the copy is certified as correct by:

(A) the custodian or another person authorized to make the certification; or

(B) a certificate that complies with subdivision (1), (2), or (3) above, a federal statute, a rule prescribed by the Supreme Court, or an applicable regulation prescribed pursuant to statutory authority.

(4a) *Documents or Records of the United States Accompanied by Attesting Certificates.* Documents or records kept under the authority of the United States by any department, bureau, agency, office, or court thereof when attached to or accompanied by an attesting certificate of the custodian of the document or record without further authentication.

(5) *Official Publications.* A book, pamphlet, or other publication purporting to be issued by a public authority.

(6) *Newspapers and Periodicals.* Printed material purporting to be a newspaper or periodical.

(7) *Trade Inscriptions and the Like.* An inscription, sign, tag, or label purporting to have been affixed in the course of business and indicating origin, ownership, or control.

(8) *Acknowledged Documents.* A document accompanied by a certificate of acknowledgment that is lawfully executed by a notary public or another officer who is authorized to take acknowledgments.

(9) *Commercial Paper and Related Documents.* Commercial paper, a signature on it, and related documents, to the extent allowed by general commercial law.

(10) *Presumptions under a Federal Statute or Regulation.* A signature, document, or anything else that a federal statute, or an applicable regulation prescribed pursuant to statutory authority, declares to be presumptively or prima facie genuine or authentic.

(11) *Certified Domestic Records of a Regularly Conducted Activity.* The original or a copy of a domestic record that meets the requirements of Mil. R. Evid. 803(6)(A)-(C), as shown by a certification of the custodian or another qualified person that complies with a federal statute or a rule prescribed by the Supreme Court. Before the trial or hearing, or at a later time that the military judge allows for good cause, the proponent must give an adverse party reasonable written notice of the intent to offer the record and must make the record and certification available for inspection so that the party has a fair opportunity to challenge them.

Rule 903. Subscribing witness's testimony

A subscribing witness's testimony is necessary to authenticate a writing only if required by the law of the jurisdiction that governs its validity.

SECTION X
CONTENTS OF WRITINGS, RECORDINGS, AND PHOTOGRAPHS

Rule 1001. Definitions that apply to this section

In this section:

(a) A "writing" consists of letters, words, numbers, or their equivalent set down in any form.

(b) A "recording" consists of letters, words, numbers, or their equivalent recorded in any manner.

(c) A "photograph" means a photographic image or its equivalent stored in any form.

(d) An "original" of a writing or recording means the writing or recording itself or any counterpart intended to have the same effect by the person who executed or issued it. For electronically stored information, "original" means any printout or other output readable by sight if it accurately reflects the information. An "original" of a photograph includes the negative or a print from it.

(e) A "duplicate" means a counterpart produced by a mechanical, photographic, chemical, electronic, or other equivalent process or technique that accurately reproduces the original.

Rule 1002. Requirement of the original

An original writing, recording, or photograph is required in order to prove its content unless these rules, this Manual, or a federal statute provides otherwise.

Rule 1003. Admissibility of duplicates

A duplicate is admissible to the same extent as the original unless a genuine question is raised about the original's authenticity or the circumstances make it unfair to admit the duplicate.

Rule 1004. Admissibility of other evidence of content

An original is not required and other evidence of the content of a writing, recording, or photograph is admissible if:

(a) *Originals lost or destroyed.* all the originals are lost or destroyed, and not by the proponent acting in bad faith;

(b) *Original not obtainable.* an original cannot be obtained by any available judicial process;

(c) *Original in possession of opponent.* the party against whom the original would be offered had control of the original; was at that time put on notice, by pleadings or otherwise, that the original would be a subject of proof at the trial or hearing; and fails to produce it at the trial or hearing; or

(d) *Collateral matters.* the writing, recording, or photograph is not closely related to a controlling issue.

Rule 1005. Copies of public records to prove content

The proponent may use a copy to prove the content of an official record – or of a document that was recorded or filed in a public office as authorized by law – if these conditions are met: the record or document is otherwise admissible; and the copy is certified as correct in accordance with Mil. R. Evid. 902(4) or is testified to be correct by a witness who has compared it with the original. If no such copy can be obtained by reasonable diligence, then the proponent may use other evidence to prove the content.

Rule 1006. Summaries to prove content

The proponent may use a summary, chart, or calculation to prove the content of voluminous writings, recordings, or photographs that cannot be conveniently examined in court. The proponent must make the originals or duplicates available for examination or copying, or both, by other parties at a reasonable time or place. The military judge may order the proponent to produce them in court.

Rule 1007. Testimony or statement of a party to prove content

The proponent may prove the content of a writing, recording, or photograph by the testimony, deposition, or written statement of the party against whom the evidence is offered. The proponent need not account for the original.

Rule 1008. Functions of the military judge and the members

Ordinarily, the military judge determines whether the proponent has fulfilled the factual conditions for admitting other evidence of the content of a writing, recording, or photograph under Mil. R. Evid. 1004 or 1005. When a court-martial is composed of a military judge and members, the members determine – in accordance with Mil. R. Evid. 104(b) – any issue about whether:

(a) an asserted writing, recording, or photograph ever existed;

(b) another one produced at the trial or hearing is the original; or

(c) other evidence of content accurately reflects the content.

SECTION XI
MISCELLANEOUS RULES

Rule 1101. Applicability of these rules

(a) *In General.* Except as otherwise provided in this Manual, these rules apply generally to all courts-martial, including summary courts-martial, Article 39(a) sessions, limited factfinding proceedings ordered on review, proceedings in revision, and contempt proceedings other than contempt proceedings in which the judge may act summarily.

(b) *Rules Relaxed.* The application of these rules may be relaxed in presentencing proceedings as provided under R.C.M. 1001 and otherwise as provided in this Manual.

(c) *Rules on Privilege.* The rules on privilege apply at all stages of a case or proceeding.

(d) *Exceptions.* These rules – except for Mil. R. Evid. 412 and those on privilege – do not apply to the following:

(1) the military judge's determination, under Rule 104(a), on a preliminary question of fact governing admissibility;

(2) preliminary hearings under Article 32;

(3) proceedings for vacation of suspension of sentence under Article 72; and

(4) miscellaneous actions and proceedings related to search authorizations, pretrial restraint, pretrial confinement, or other proceedings authorized under the Uniform Code of Military Justice or this Manual that are not listed in subdivision (a).

Rule 1102. Amendments

(a) *General Rule.* Amendments to the Federal Rules of Evidence – other than Articles III and V – will amend parallel provisions of the Military Rules of Evidence by operation of law 18 months after the effective date of such amendments, unless action to the contrary is taken by the President.

(b) *Rules Determined Not to Apply.* The President has determined that the following Federal Rules of Evidence do not apply to the Military Rules of Evidence: Rules 301, 302, 415, and 902(12).

Rule 1103. Title

These rules may be cited as the Military Rules of Evidence.

PART IV
PUNITIVE ARTICLES
(Statutory text of each Article is in bold)

Discussion

[Note: To state an offense under Article 134, practitioners should expressly allege at least one of the three terminal elements, i.e., that the alleged conduct was: prejudicial to good order and discipline; service discrediting; or a crime or offense not capital. *See United States v. Fosler*, 70 M.J. 225 (C.A.A.F. 2011); *United States v. Ballan*, 71 M.J. 28 (C.A.A.F. 2012). *See also* paragraph 60c(6)(a) in this part and R.C.M. 307(c)(3).]

[Note: In 2010, the Court of Appeals for the Armed Forces examined Article 79 and clarified the legal test for lesser included offenses. *United States v. Jones*, 68 M.J. 465 (C.A.A.F. 2010). An offense under Article 79 is "necessarily included" in the offense charged only if the elements of the lesser offense are a subset of the elements of the greater offense alleged. *See* discussion following paragraph 3b(1)(c) in this part and the related analysis in Appendix 23 of this Manual.]

Part IV of the Manual addresses the punitive articles, 10 U.S.C. §§ 877-934. Part IV is organized by paragraph beginning with Article 77; therefore, each paragraph number is associated with an article. For example, paragraph 45 addresses Article 120, Rape and sexual assault generally. Article 77, Principals, and Article 79, Lesser included offenses, are located in the punitive article subchapter of Title 10 but are not chargeable offenses as such.

Other than Articles 77 and 79, the punitive articles of the code are discussed using the following sequence:

    a. Text of the article
    b. Elements of the offense or offenses
    c. Explanation
    d. Lesser included offenses
    e. Maximum punishment
    f. Sample specifications

Lesser included offenses are established in subparagraph d of each paragraph of Part IV and are defined and explained under Article 79. Practitioners are advised, however, to read and comply with *United States v. Jones*, 68 M.J. 465 (C.A.A.F. 2010). *See* note above.

Sample specifications are provided in subparagraph f of each paragraph in Part IV and are meant to serve as a guide. The specifications may be varied in form and content as necessary. R.C.M. 307 prescribes rules for preferral of charges and for drafting specifications. The discussion under that rule explains how to allege violations under the code using the format of charge and specification; however, practitioners are advised to read and comply with *United States v. Fosler*, 70 M.J. 225 (C.A.A.F. 2011) and *United States v. Jones*, 68 M.J. 465 (C.A.A.F. 2010). *See* two notes above and R.C.M. 307(c)(3).

The term "elements," as used in Part IV, includes both the statutory elements of the offense and any aggravating factors listed under the President's authority which increases the maximum permissible punishment when specified aggravating factors are pleaded and proven.

The prescriptions of maximum punishments in subparagraph e of each paragraph of Part IV must be read in conjunction with R.C.M. 1003, which prescribes additional punishments that may be available and additional limitations on punishments.

---

1. Article 77—Principals

a. *Text of statute.*

Any person punishable under this chapter who—

(1) commits an offense punishable by this chapter, or aids, abets, counsels, commands, or procures its commission; or

(2) causes an act to be done which if directly performed by him would be punishable by this chapter; is a principal.

b. *Explanation.*

(1) *Purpose.* Article 77 does not define an offense. Its purpose is to make clear that a person need not personally perform the acts necessary to constitute an offense to be guilty of it. A person who aids, abets, counsels, commands, or procures the commission of an offense, or who causes an act to be done which, if done by that person directly, would be an offense is equally guilty of the offense as one who commits it directly, and may be punished to the same extent.

Article 77 eliminates the common law distinctions between principal in the first degree ("perpetrator"); principal in the second degree (one who aids, counsels, commands, or encourages the commission of an offense and who is present at the scene of the crime—commonly known as an "aider and abettor"); and accessory before the fact (one who aids, counsels, commands, or encourages the commission of an offense and who is not present at the scene of the crime). All of these are now "principals."

(2) *Who may be liable for an offense.*

(a) *Perpetrator.* A perpetrator is one who actually commits the offense, either by the perpetrator's own hand, or by causing an offense to be committed by knowingly or intentionally inducing or setting in motion acts by an animate or inanimate agency or instrumentality which result in the commission of an offense. For example, a person who knowingly conceals contraband drugs in an automobile, and then induces another person, who is unaware and has no reason to know of the presence of drugs, to drive the automobile onto a military installation, is, although not present in the automobile, guilty of wrongful introduction of drugs onto a military installation. (On these facts, the driver would be guilty of no crime.) Similarly, if, upon orders of a superior, a soldier shot a person who appeared to the soldier to be an enemy, but was known to the superior as a friend, the superior would be guilty of murder (but the soldier would be guilty of no offense).

(b) *Other Parties.* If one is not a perpetrator, to be guilty of an offense committed by the perpetrator, the person must:

(i) Assist, encourage, advise, instigate, counsel, command, or procure another to commit, or assist, encourage, advise, counsel, or command another in the commission of the offense; and

(ii) Share in the criminal purpose or design.

One who, without knowledge of the criminal venture or plan, unwittingly encourages or renders assistance to another in the commission of an offense is not guilty of a crime. *See* the parentheticals in the examples in paragraph 1b(2)(a) above. In some circumstances, inaction may make one liable as a party, where there is a duty to act. If a person (for example, a security guard) has a duty to interfere in the commission of an offense, but does not interfere, that person is a party to the crime *if* such a noninterference is intended to and does operate as an aid or encouragement to the actual perpetrator.

(3) *Presence.*

(a) *Not necessary.* Presence at the scene of the crime is not necessary to make one a party to the crime and liable as a principal. For example, one who, knowing that a person intends to shoot another person and intending that such an assault be carried out, provides the person with a pistol, is guilty of assault when the offense is committed, even though not present at the scene.

(b) *Not sufficient.* Mere presence at the scene of a crime does not make one a principal unless the requirements of paragraph 1b(2)(a) or (b) have been met.

(4) *Parties whose intent differs from the perpetrator's.* When an offense charged requires proof of a specific intent or particular state of mind as an element, the evidence must prove that the accused had that intent or state of mind, whether the accused is charged as a perpetrator or an "other party" to

crime. It is possible for a party to have a state of mind more or less culpable than the perpetrator of the offense. In such a case, the party may be guilty of a more or less serious offense than that committed by the perpetrator. For example, when a homicide is committed, the perpetrator may act in the heat of sudden passion caused by adequate provocation and be guilty of manslaughter, while the party who, without such passion, hands the perpetrator a weapon and encourages the perpetrator to kill the victim, would be guilty of murder. On the other hand, if a party assists a perpetrator in an assault on a person who, known only to the perpetrator, is an officer, the party would be guilty only of assault, while the perpetrator would be guilty of assault on an officer.

(5) *Responsibility for other crimes.* A principal may be convicted of crimes committed by another principal if such crimes are likely to result as a natural and probable consequence of the criminal venture or design. For example, the accused who is a party to a burglary is guilty as a principal not only of the offense of burglary, but also, if the perpetrator kills an occupant in the course of the burglary, of murder. (*See also* paragraph 5 concerning liability for offenses committed by co-conspirators.)

(6) *Principals independently liable.* One may be a principal, even if the perpetrator is not identified or prosecuted, or is acquitted.

(7) *Withdrawal.* A person may withdraw from a common venture or design and avoid liability for any offenses committed after the withdrawal. To be effective, the withdrawal must meet the following requirements:

(a) It must occur before the offense is committed;

(b) The assistance, encouragement, advice, instigation, counsel, command, or procurement given by the person must be effectively countermanded or negated; and

(c) The withdrawal must be clearly communicated to the would-be perpetrators or to appropriate law enforcement authorities in time for the perpetrators to abandon the plan or for law enforcement authorities to prevent the offense.

2. Article 78—Accessory after the fact

a. *Text of statute.*

Any person subject to this chapter who, know-

ing that an offense punishable by this chapter has been committed, receives, comforts, or assists the offender in order to hinder or prevent his apprehension, trial, or punishment shall be punished as a court-martial may direct.

b. *Elements.*

(1) That an offense punishable by the code was committed by a certain person;

(2) That the accused knew that this person had committed such offense;

(3) That thereafter the accused received, comforted, or assisted the offender; and

(4) That the accused did so for the purpose of hindering or preventing the apprehension, trial, or punishment of the offender.

c. *Explanation.*

(1) *In general.* The assistance given a principal by an accessory after the fact is not limited to assistance designed to effect the escape or concealment of the principal, but also includes acts performed to conceal the commission of the offense by the principal (for example, by concealing evidence of the offense).

(2) *Failure to report offense.* The mere failure to report a known offense will not make one an accessory after the fact. Such failure may violate a general order or regulation, however, and thus constitute an offense under Article 92. *See* paragraph 16. If the offense involved is a serious offense, failure to report it may constitute the offense of misprision of a serious offense, under Article 134. *See* paragraph 95.

(3) *Offense punishable by the code.* The term "offense punishable by this chapter" in the text of the article means any offense described in the code.

(4) *Status of principal.* The principal who committed the offense in question need not be subject to the code, but the offense committed must be punishable by the code.

(5) *Conviction or acquittal of principal.* The prosecution must prove that a principal committed the offense to which the accused is allegedly an accessory after the fact. However, evidence of the conviction or acquittal of the principal in a separate trial is not admissible to show that the principal did or did not commit the offense. Furthermore, an accused may be convicted as an accessory after the fact despite the acquittal in a separate trial of the principal whom the accused allegedly comforted, received, or assisted.

(6) *Accessory after the fact not a lesser included offense.* The offense of being an accessory after the fact is not a lesser included offense of the primary offense.

(7) *Actual knowledge.* Actual knowledge is required but may be proved by circumstantial evidence.

d. *Lesser included offenses.* See paragraph 3 of this part and Appendix 12A.

e. *Maximum punishment.* Any person subject to the code who is found guilty as an accessory after the fact to an offense punishable by the code shall be subject to the maximum punishment authorized for the principal offense, except that in no case shall the death penalty nor more than one-half of the maximum confinement authorized for that offense be adjudged, nor shall the period of confinement exceed 10 years in any case, including offenses for which life imprisonment may be adjudged.

f. *Sample specification.*

In that _____ (personal jurisdiction data), knowing that (at/on board—location), on or about _____ 20 ___ , had committed an offense punishable by the Uniform Code of Military Justice, to wit: _____ , did, (at/on board—location) (subject-matter jurisdiction data, if required), on or about _____ 20 ___ , in order to (hinder) (prevent) the (apprehension) (trial) (punishment) of the said _____ , (receive) (comfort) (assist) the said _____ by _____ .

3. Article 79—Conviction of lesser included offenses

a. *Text of statute.*

An accused may be found guilty of an offense necessarily included in the offense charged or of an attempt to commit either the offense charged or an offense necessarily included therein.

b. *Explanation.*

(1) *In general.* A lesser offense is "necessarily included" in a charged offense when the elements of the lesser offense are a subset of the elements of the charged offense, thereby putting the accused on notice to defend against the lesser offense in addition to the offense specifically charged. A lesser offense may be "necessarily included" when:

(a) All of the elements of the lesser offense are

included in the greater offense, and the common elements are identical (for example, larceny as a lesser included offense of robbery);

(b) All of the elements of the lesser offense are included in the greater offense, but at least one element is a subset by being legally less serious (for example, housebreaking as a lesser included offense of burglary); or

(c) All of the elements of the lesser offense are "included and necessary" parts of the greater offense, but the mental element is a subset by being legally less serious (for example, wrongful appropriation as a lesser included offense of larceny).

Discussion

The "elements test" is the proper method for determining lesser included offenses. *See United States v. Jones*, 68 M.J. 465 (C.A.A.F. 2010); *Schmuck v. United States*, 489 U.S. 705 (1989); Appendix 23 of this Manual, Art. 79. Paragraph 3.b.(1) was amended to comport with the elements test, which requires that the elements of the lesser offense must be a subset of the elements of the charged offense. The elements test does not require identical statutory language, and use of normal principles of statutory interpretation is permitted. The elements test is necessary to safeguard the due process requirement of notice to a criminal defendant.

---

(2) *Sua sponte duty.* A military judge must instruct panel members on lesser included offenses reasonably raised by the evidence.

(3) *Multiple lesser included offenses.* When the offense charged is a compound offense comprising two or more lesser included offenses, an accused may be found guilty of any or all of the offenses included in the offense charged. For example, robbery includes both larceny and assault. Therefore, in a proper case, a court-martial may find an accused not guilty of robbery, but guilty of wrongful appropriation and assault.

(4) *Findings of guilty to a lesser included offense.* A court-martial may find an accused not guilty of the offense charged, but guilty of a lesser included offense by the process of exception and substitution. The court-martial may except (that is, delete) the words in the specification that pertain to the offense charged and, if necessary, substitute language appropriate to the lesser included offense. For example, the accused is charged with murder in violation of Article 118, but found guilty of voluntary man-

slaughter in violation of Article 119. Such a finding may be worded as follows:

Of the Specification: Guilty, except the word "murder" substituting therefor the words "willfully and unlawfully kill," of the excepted word, not guilty, of the substituted words, guilty.

Of the Charge: Not guilty, but guilty of a violation of Article 119.

If a court-martial finds an accused guilty of a lesser included offense, the finding as to the charge shall state a violation of the specific punitive article violated and not a violation of Article 79.

(5) *Specific lesser included offenses.* Specific lesser included offenses, if any, are listed for each offense in Appendix 12A, but the list is merely guidance to practitioners, is not all-inclusive, and is not binding on military courts.

Discussion

Practitioners must consider lesser included offenses on a case-by-case basis. *See United States v. Jones*, 68 M.J. 465 (C.A.A.F. 2010); *United States v. Alston*, 69 M.J. 214 (C.A.A.F. 2010); discussion following paragraph 3.b.(1)(c) above. The lesser included offenses listed in Appendix 12A were amended in 2016 to comport with the elements test; however, practitioners must analyze each lesser included offense on a case-by-case basis. *See* Appendix 23 of this Manual, Art. 79.

---

4. Article 80—Attempts

a. *Text of statute.*

(a) **An act, done with specific intent to commit an offense under this chapter, amounting to more than mere preparation and tending, even though failing, to effect its commission, is an attempt to commit that offense.**

(b) **Any person subject to this chapter who attempts to commit any offense punishable by this chapter shall be punished as a court-martial may direct, unless otherwise specifically prescribed.**

(c) **Any person subject to this chapter may be convicted of an attempt to commit an offense although it appears on the trial that the offense was consummated.**

b. *Elements.*

(1) That the accused did a certain overt act;

(2) That the act was done with the specific intent to commit a certain offense under the code;

(3) That the act amounted to more than mere preparation; and

(4) That the act apparently tended to effect the commission of the intended offense.

c. *Explanation.*

(1) *In general.* To constitute an attempt there must be a specific intent to commit the offense accompanied by an overt act which directly tends to accomplish the unlawful purpose.

(2) *More than preparation.* Preparation consists of devising or arranging the means or measures necessary for the commission of the offense. The overt act required goes beyond preparatory steps and is a direct movement toward the commission of the offense. For example, a purchase of matches with the intent to burn a haystack is not an attempt to commit arson, but it is an attempt to commit arson to applying a burning match to a haystack, even if no fire results. The overt act need not be the last act essential to the consummation of the offense. For example, an accused could commit an overt act, and then voluntarily decide not to go through with the intended offense. An attempt would nevertheless have been committed, for the combination of a specific intent to commit an offense, plus the commission of an overt act directly tending to accomplish it, constitutes the offense of attempt. Failure to complete the offense, whatever the cause, is not a defense.

(3) *Factual impossibility.* A person who purposely engages in conduct which would constitute the offense if the attendant circumstances were as that person believed them to be is guilty of an attempt. For example, if A, without justification or excuse and with intent to kill B, points a gun at B and pulls the trigger, A is guilty of attempt to murder, even though, unknown to A, the gun is defective and will not fire. Similarly, a person who reaches into the pocket of another with the intent to steal that person's billfold is guilty of an attempt to commit larceny, even though the pocket is empty.

(4) *Voluntary abandonment.* It is a defense to an attempt offense that the person voluntarily and completely abandoned the intended crime, solely because of the person's own sense that it was wrong, prior to the completion of the crime. The voluntary abandonment defense is not allowed if the abandonment results, in whole or in part, from other reasons, for example, the person feared detection or apprehension, decided to await a better opportunity for success, was unable to complete the crime, or encountered unanticipated difficulties or unexpected resistance. A person who is entitled to the defense of voluntary abandonment may nonetheless be guilty of a lesser included, completed offense. For example, a person who voluntarily abandoned an attempted armed robbery may nonetheless be guilty of assault with a dangerous weapon.

(5) *Solicitation.* Soliciting another to commit an offense does not constitute an attempt. *See* paragraph 6 for a discussion of Article 82, solicitation.

(6) *Attempts not under Article 80.* While most attempts should be charged under Article 80, the following attempts are specifically addressed by some other article, and should be charged accordingly:

(a) Article 85—desertion

(b) Article 94—mutiny or sedition.

(c) Article 100—subordinate compelling

(d) Article 104—aiding the enemy

(e) Article 106a—espionage

(f) Article 119a—attempting to kill an unborn child

(g) Article 128—assault

(7) *Regulations.* An attempt to commit conduct which would violate a lawful general order or regulation under Article 92 (*see* paragraph 16) should be charged under Article 80. It is not necessary in such cases to prove that the accused intended to violate the order or regulation, but it must be proved that the accused intended to commit the prohibited conduct.

d. *Lesser included offenses.* See paragraph 3 of this part and Appendix 12A.

e. *Maximum punishment.* Any person subject to the code who is found guilty of an attempt under Article 80 to commit any offense punishable by the code shall be subject to the same maximum punishment authorized for the commission of the offense attempted, except that in no case shall the death penalty be adjudged, and in no case, other than attempted murder, shall confinement exceeding 20 years be adjudged. Except in the cases of attempts of Article 120(a) or (b), rape or sexual assault of a child under Article 120b(a) or (b), and forcible sodomy under Article 125, mandatory minimum puilishment provisions shall not apply.

f. *Sample specification.*

In that _____ (personal jurisdiction data) did, (at/on board—location) (subject-matter jurisdiction data, if required), on or about _____ 20 __ , attempt to (describe offense with sufficient detail to include expressly or by necessary implication every element).

5. Article 81—Conspiracy

a. *Text of statute.*

(a) Any person subject to this chapter who conspires with any other person to commit an offense under this chapter shall, if one or more of the conspirators does an act to effect the object of the conspiracy, be punished as a court-martial may direct.

(b) Any person subject to this chapter who conspires with any other person to commit an offense under the law of war, and who knowingly performs an overt act to effect the object of the conspiracy, shall be punished, if death results to one or more of the victims, by death or such other punishment as a court-martial or military commission may direct, and, if death does not result to any of the victims, by such punishment, other than death, as a court-martial or military commission may direct.

b. *Elements.*

(1) *Conspiracy.*

(a) That the accused entered into an agreement with one or more persons to commit an offense under the UCMJ; and

(b) That, while the agreement continued to exist, and while the accused remained a party to the agreement, the accused or at least one of the co-conspirators performed an overt act for the purpose of bringing about the object of the conspiracy.

(2) *Conspiracy when offense is an offense under the law of war resulting in the death of one or more victims.*

(a) That the accused entered into an agreement with one or more persons to commit an offense under the law of war;

(b) That, while the agreement continued to exist, and while the accused remained a party to the agreement, the accused knowingly performed an overt act for the purpose of bringing about the object of the conspiracy; and

(c) That death resulted to one or more victims.

c. *Explanation.*

(1) *Co-conspirators.* Two or more persons are required in order to have a conspiracy. Knowledge of the identity of co-conspirators and their particular connection with the criminal purpose need not be established. The accused must be subject to the code, but the other co-conspirators need not be. A person may be guilty of conspiracy although incapable of committing the intended offense. For example, a bedridden conspirator may knowingly furnish the car to be used in a robbery. The joining of another conspirator after the conspiracy has been established does not create a new conspiracy or affect the status of the other conspirators. However, the conspirator who joined an existing conspiracy can be convicted of this offense only if, at or after the time of joining the conspiracy, an overt act in furtherance of the object of the agreement is committed.

(2) *Agreement.* The agreement in a conspiracy need not be in any particular form or manifested in any formal words. It is sufficient if the minds of the parties arrive at a common understanding to accomplish the object of the conspiracy, and this may be shown by the conduct of the parties. The agreement need not state the means by which the conspiracy is to be accomplished or what part each conspirator is to play.

(3) *Object of the agreement.* The object of the agreement must, at least in part, involve the commission of one or more offenses under the code. An agreement to commit several offenses is ordinarily but a single conspiracy. Some offenses require two or more culpable actors acting in concert. There can be no conspiracy where the agreement exists only between the persons necessary to commit such an offense. Examples include dueling, bigamy, incest, adultery, and bribery.

(4) *Overt act.*

(a) The overt act must be independent of the agreement to commit the offense; must take place at the time of or after the agreement; must be done by one or more of the conspirators, but not necessarily the accused; and must be done to effectuate the object of the agreement.

(b) The overt act need not be in itself criminal, but it must be a manifestation that the agreement is being executed. Although committing the intended offense may constitute the overt act, it is not essential that the object offense be committed. Any overt act is enough, no matter how preliminary or preparatory in nature, as long as it is a manifestation that the agreement is being executed.

(c) An overt act by one conspirator becomes

the act of all without any new agreement specifically directed to that act and each conspirator is equally guilty even though each does not participate in, or have knowledge of, all of the details of the execution of the conspiracy.

(5) *Liability for offenses.* Each conspirator is liable for all offenses committed pursuant to the conspiracy by any of the co-conspirators while the conspiracy continues and the person remains a party to it.

(6) *Withdrawal.* A party to the conspiracy who abandons or withdraws from the agreement to commit the offense before the commission of an overt act by any conspirator is not guilty of conspiracy. An effective withdrawal or abandonment must consist of affirmative conduct which is wholly inconsistent with adherence to the unlawful agreement and which shows that the party has severed all connection with the conspiracy. A conspirator who effectively abandons or withdraws from the conspiracy after the performance of an overt act by one of the conspirators remains guilty of conspiracy and of any offenses committed pursuant to the conspiracy up to the time of the abandonment or withdrawal. However, a person who has abandoned or withdrawn from the conspiracy is not liable for offenses committed thereafter by the remaining conspirators. The withdrawal of a conspirator from the conspiracy does not affect the status of the remaining members.

(7) *Factual impossibility.* It is not a defense that the means adopted by the conspirators to achieve their object, if apparently adapted to that end, were actually not capable of success, or that the conspirators were not physically able to accomplish their intended object.

(8) *Conspiracy as a separate offense.* A conspiracy to commit an offense is a separate and distinct offense from the offense which is the object of the conspiracy, and both the conspiracy and the consummated offense which was its object may be charged, tried, and punished. The commission of the intended offense may also constitute the overt act which is an element of the conspiracy to commit that offense.

(9) *Special conspiracies under Article 134.* The United States Code prohibits conspiracies to commit certain specific offenses which do not require an overt act. These conspiracies should be charged under Article 134. Examples include conspiracies to impede or injure any Federal officer in the discharge

of duties under 18 U.S.C. § 372, conspiracies against civil rights under 18 U.S.C. § 241, and certain drug conspiracies under 21 U.S.C. § 846. *See* paragraph 60c(4)(c)(ii).

d. *Lesser included offenses.* See paragraph 3 of this part and Appendix 12A.

e. *Maximum punishment.* Any person subject to the code who is found guilty of conspiracy shall be subject to the maximum punishment authorized for the offense that is the object of the conspiracy. However, with the exception noted below, if death is an authorized punishment for the offense that is the object of the conspiracy, the maximum punishment shall be dishonorable discharge, forfeiture of all pay and allowances, and confinement for life without eligibility for parole. If the offense that is the object of the conspiracy is an offense under the law of war, the person knowingly performed an overt act for the purpose of bringing about the object of the conspiracy, and death results to one or more victims, the death penalty shall be an available punishment.

f. *Sample specification.*

(1) *Conspiracy.*

In that _____ (personal jurisdiction data), did, (at/on board—location) (subject-matter jurisdiction data, if required), on or about _____ 20 __ , conspire with _____ (and _____) to commit an offense under the Uniform Code of Military Justice, to wit: (larceny of _____ , of a value of (about) $ _____ , the property of _____), and in order to effect the object of the conspiracy the said _____ (and _____) did _____ .

(2) *Conspiracy when offense is an offense under the law of war resulting in the death of one or more victims.*

In that _____ (personal jurisdiction data), did, (at/on board—location) (subject-matter jurisdiction data, if required), on or about _____ 20 __ , conspire with _____ (and _____) to commit an offense under the law of war, to wit: (murder of _____), and in order to effect the object of the conspiracy the said _____ knowingly did _____ resulting in the death of _____ .

6. Article 82—Solicitation

a. *Text of statute.*

(a) **Any person subject to this chapter who so-**

licits or advises another or other to desert in violation of section 885 of this title (Article 85) or mutiny in violation of section 894 of this title (Article 94) shall, if the offense solicited or advised is attempted or committed, be punished with the punishment provided for the commission of the offense, but, if the offense solicited or advised is not committed or attempted, he shall be punished as a court-martial may direct.

(b) Any person subject to this chapter who solicits or advises another or others to commit an act of misbehavior before the enemy in violation of section 899 of this title (Article 99) or sedition in violation of section 894 of this title (Article 94) shall, if the offense solicited or advised is committed, be punished with the punishment provided for the commission of the offense, but, if the offense solicited or advised is not committed, he shall be punished as a court-martial may direct.

b. *Elements.*

(1) That the accused solicited or advised a certain person or persons to commit any of the four offenses named in Article 82; and

(2) That the accused did so with the intent that the offense actually be committed.
[Note: If the offense solicited or advised was attempted or committed, add the following element]

(3) That the offense solicited or advised was (committed) (attempted) as the proximate result of the solicitation.

c. *Explanation.*

(1) *Instantaneous offense.* The offense is complete when a solicitation is made or advice is given with the specific wrongful intent to influence another or others to commit any of the four offenses named in Article 82. It is not necessary that the person or persons solicited or advised agree to or act upon the solicitation or advice.

(2) *Form of solicitation.* Solicitation may be by means other than word of mouth or writing. Any act or conduct which reasonably may be construed as a serious request or advice to commit one of the four offenses named in Article 82 may constitute solicitation. It is not necessary that the accused act alone in the solicitation or in the advising; the accused may act through other persons in committing this offense.

(3) *Solicitations in violation of Article 134.* Solicitation to commit offenses other than violations of the four offenses named in Article 82 may be

charged as violations of Article 134. *See* paragraph 105. However, some offenses require, as an element of proof, some act of solicitation by the accused. These offenses are separate and distinct from solicitations under Articles 82 and 134. When the accused's act of solicitation constitutes, by itself, a separate offense, the accused should be charged with that separate, distinct offense—for example, pandering (*see* paragraph 97) and obstruction of justice (*see* paragraph 96) in violation of Article 134.

d. *Lesser included offenses.* See paragraph 3 of this part and Appendix 12A.

e. *Maximum punishment.* If the offense solicited or advised is committed or (in the case of soliciting desertion or mutiny) attempted, then the accused shall be punished with the punishment provided for the commission of the offense solicited or advised. If the offense solicited or advised is not committed or (in the case of soliciting desertion or mutiny) attempted, then the following punishment may be imposed:

(1) To desert—Dishonorable discharge, forfeiture of all pay and allowances, and confinement for 3 years.

(2) To mutiny—Dishonorable discharge, forfeiture of all pay and allowances, and confinement for 10 years.

(3) To commit an act of misbehavior before the enemy—Dishonorable discharge, forfeiture of all pay and allowances, and confinement for 10 years.

(4) To commit an act of sedition—Dishonorable discharge, forfeiture of all pay and allowances, and confinement for 10 years.

f. *Sample specifications.*

(1) *For soliciting desertion (Article 85) or mutiny (Article 94).*

In that _____ (personal jurisdiction data), did, (at/on board—location), on or about _____ 20 __ , (a time of war) by (here state the manner and form of solicitation or advice), (solicit) (advise) _____ (and _____) to (desert in violation of Article 85) (mutiny in violation of Article 94) [*and, as a result of such (solicitation) (advice), the offense (solicited) (advised) was, on or about _____ , 20 __ , (at/on board—location), (attempted) (committed) by _____ (and _____)].

[*Note: This language should be added to the end of the specification if the offense solicited or advised is actually committed.]

(2) *For soliciting an act of misbehavior before the enemy (Article 99) or sedition (Article 94).*

In that _____ (personal jurisdiction data) did, (at/on board—location), on or about _____ 20 ___ , (a time of war) by (here state the manner and form of solicitation or advice), (solicit) (advise), _____ (and _____) to commit (an act of misbehavior before the enemy in violation of Article 99) (sedition in violation of Article 94) [*and, as a result of such (solicitation) (advice), the offense (solicited) (advised) was, on or about _____ 20 ___ , (at/on board—location), committed by _____ (and _____)].

[*Note: This language should be added to the end of the specification if the offense solicited or advised is actually committed.]

7. Article 83—Fraudulent enlistment, appointment, or separation

a. *Text of statute.*

Any person who—

(1) procures his own enlistment or appointment in the armed forces by knowingly false representation or deliberate concealment as to his qualifications for that enlistment or appointment and receives pay or allowances thereunder; or

(2) procures his own separation from the armed forces by knowingly false representation or deliberate concealment as to his eligibility for that separation;

shall be punished as a court-martial may direct.

b. *Elements.*

(1) *Fraudulent enlistment or appointment.*

(a) That the accused was enlisted or appointed in an armed force;

(b) That the accused knowingly misrepresented or deliberately concealed a certain material fact or facts regarding qualifications of the accused for enlistment or appointment;

(c) That the accused's enlistment or appointment was obtained or procured by that knowingly false representation or deliberate concealment; and

(d) That under this enlistment or appointment that accused received pay or allowances or both.

(2) *Fraudulent separation.*

(a) That the accused was separated from an armed force;

(b) That the accused knowingly misrepresented or deliberately concealed a certain material fact or facts about the accused's eligibility for separation; and

(c) That the accused's separation was obtained or procured by that knowingly false representation or deliberate concealment.

c. *Explanation.*

(1) *In general.* A fraudulent enlistment, appointment, or separation is one procured by either a knowingly false representation as to any of the qualifications prescribed by law, regulation, or orders for the specific enlistment, appointment, or separation, or a deliberate concealment as to any of those disqualifications. Matters that may be material to an enlistment, appointment, or separation include any information used by the recruiting, appointing, or separating officer in reaching a decision as to enlistment, appointment, or separation in any particular case, and any information that normally would have been so considered had it been provided to that officer.

(2) *Receipt of pay or allowances.* A member of the armed forces who enlists or accepts an appointment without being regularly separated from a prior enlistment or appointment should be charged under Article 83 only if that member has received pay or allowances under the fraudulent enlistment or appointment. Acceptance of food, clothing, shelter, or transportation from the government constitutes receipt of allowances. However, whatever is furnished the accused while in custody, confinement, arrest, or other restraint pending trial for fraudulent enlistment or appointment is not considered an allowance. The receipt of pay or allowances may be proved by circumstantial evidence.

(3) *One offense.* One who procures one's own enlistment, appointment, or separation by several misrepresentations or concealment as to qualifications for the one enlistment, appointment, or separation so procured, commits only one offense under Article 83.

d. *Lesser included offenses.* See paragraph 3 of this part and Appendix 12A.

e. *Maximum punishment.*

(1) *Fraudulent enlistment or appointment.* Dishonorable discharge, forfeiture of all pay and allowances, and confinement for 2 years.

(2) *Fraudulent separation.* Dishonorable discharge, forfeiture of all pay and allowances, and confinement for 5 years.

f. *Sample specifications.*

(1) *For fraudulent enlistment or appointment.*

In that _____ (personal jurisdiction data), did, (at/on board—location), on or about _____ 20 ___ , by means of (knowingly false representations that (here state the fact or facts material to qualification for enlistment or appointment which were represented), when in fact (here state the true fact of facts)) (deliberate concealment of the fact that (here state the fact or facts disqualifying the accused for enlistment or appointment which were concealed)), procure himself/herself to be (enlisted as a _____) (appointed as a _____) in the (here state the armed force in which the accused procured the enlistment or appointment), and did thereafter, (at/on board—location), receive (pay) (allowances) (pay and allowances) under the enlistment) (appointment) so procured.

(2) *For fraudulent separation.*

In that _____ (personal jurisdiction data), did, (at/on board—location), on or about _____ 20 ___ , by means of (knowingly false representations that (here state the fact or facts material to eligibility for separation which were represented), when in fact (here state the true fact or facts)) (deliberate concealment of the fact that (here state the fact or facts concealed which made the accused ineligible for separation)), procure himself/herself to be separated from the (here state the armed force from which the accused procured his/her separation).

8. Article 84—Effecting unlawful enlistment, appointment, or separation

a. *Text of statute.*

Any person subject to this chapter who effects an enlistment or appointment in or a separation from the armed forces of any person who is known to him to be ineligible for that enlistment, appointment, or separation because it is prohibited by law, regulation, or order shall be punished as a court-martial may direct.

b. *Elements.*

(1) That the accused effected the enlistment, appointment, or separation of the person named;

(2) That this person was ineligible for this enlistment, appointment, or separation because it was prohibited by law, regulation, or order; and

(3) That the accused knew of the ineligibility at the time of the enlistment, appointment, or separation.

c. *Explanation.* It must be proved that the enlistment, appointment, or separation was prohibited by law, regulation, or order when effected and that the accused then knew that the person enlisted, appointed, or separated was ineligible for the enlistment, appointment, or separation.

d. *Lesser included offenses.* See paragraph 3 of this part and Appendix 12A.

e. *Maximum punishment.* Dishonorable discharge, forfeiture of all pay and allowances, and confinement for 5 years.

f. *Sample specification.*

In that _____ (personal jurisdiction data), did, (at/on board—location), on or about _____ 20 ___ , effect (the (enlistment) (appointment) of _____ as a _____ in (here state the armed force in which the person was enlisted or appointed)) (the separation of _____ from (here state the armed force from which the person was separated)), then well knowing that the said _____ was ineligible for such (enlistment) (appointment) (separation) because (here state facts whereby the enlistment, appointment, or separation was prohibited by law, regulation, or order).

9. Article 85—Desertion

a. *Text of statute.*

(a) **Any member of the armed forces who—**

(1) **without authority goes or remains absent from his unit, organization, or place of duty with intent to remain away therefrom permanently;**

(2) **quits his unit, organization, or place of duty with intent to avoid hazardous duty or to shirk important service; or**

(3) **without being regularly separated from one of the armed forces enlists or accepts an appointment in the same or another one of the armed forces without fully disclosing the fact that he has not been regularly separated, or enters any foreign armed service except when authorized by the United States; is guilty of desertion.**

(b) **Any commissioned officer of the armed forces who, after tender of his resignation and before notice of its acceptance, quits his post or proper duties without leave and with intent to remain away therefrom permanently is guilty of desertion.**

(c) **Any person found guilty of desertion or attempt to desert shall be punished, if the offense is committed in time of war, by death or such other punishment as a court-martial may direct, but if the desertion or attempt to desert occurs at any other time, by such punishment, other than death, as a court-martial may direct.**

[Note: Paragraph 9a(a)(3) above has been held not to state a separate offense by the United States Court of Military Appeals in *United States v. Huff*, 22 C.M.R. 37 (1956)]

b. *Elements.*

(1) *Desertion with intent to remain away permanently.*

(a) That the accused absented himself or herself from his or her unit, organization, or place of duty;

(b) That such absence was without authority;

(c) That the accused, at the time the absence began or at some time during the absence, intended to remain away from his or her unit, organization, or place of duty permanently; and

(d) That the accused remained absent until the date alleged.
[Note: If the absence was terminated by apprehension, add the following element]

(e) That the accused's absence was terminated by apprehension.

(2) *Desertion with intent to avoid hazardous duty or to shirk important service.*

(a) That the accused quit his or her unit, organization, or other place of duty;

(b) That the accused did so with the intent to avoid a certain duty or shirk a certain service;

(c) That the duty to be performed was hazardous or the service important;

(d) That the accused knew that he or she would be required for such duty or service; and

(e) That the accused remained absent until the date alleged.

(3) *Desertion before notice of acceptance of resignation.*

(a) That the accused was a commissioned officer of an armed force of the United States, and had tendered his or her resignation;

(b) That before he or she received notice of the acceptance of the resignation, the accused quit his or her post or proper duties;

(c) That the accused did so with the intent to remain away permanently from his or her post or proper duties; and

(d) That the accused remained absent until the date alleged.
[Note: If the absence was terminated by apprehension, add the following element]

(e) That the accused's absence was terminated by apprehension.

(4) *Attempted desertion.*

(a) That the accused did a certain overt act;

(b) That the act was done with the specific intent to desert;

(c) That the act amounted to more than mere preparation; and

(d) That the act apparently tended to effect the commission of the offense of desertion.

c. *Explanation.*

(1) *Desertion with intent to remain away permanently.*

(a) *In general.* Desertion with intent to remain away permanently is complete when the person absents himself or herself without authority from his or her unit, organization, or place of duty, with the intent to remain away therefrom permanently. A prompt repentance and return, while material in extenuation, is no defense. It is not necessary that the person be absent entirely from military jurisdiction and control.

(b) *Absence without authority* —inception, duration, termination. *See* paragraph 10c.

(c) *Intent to remain away permanently.*

(i) The intent to remain away permanently from the unit, organization, or place of duty may be formed any time during the unauthorized absence. The intent need not exist throughout the absence, or for any particular period of time, as long as it exists at some time during the absence.

(ii) The accused must have intended to remain away permanently from the unit, organization, or place of duty. When the accused had such an intent, it is no defense that the accused also intended to report for duty elsewhere, or to enlist or accept an appointment in the same or a different armed force.

(iii) The intent to remain away permanently

may be established by circumstantial evidence. Among the circumstances from which an inference may be drawn that an accused intended to remain absent permanently are: that the period of absence was lengthy; that the accused attempted to, or did, dispose of uniforms or other military property; that the accused purchased a ticket for a distant point or was arrested, apprehended, or surrendered a considerable distance from the accused's station; that the accused could have conveniently surrendered to military control but did not; that the accused was dissatisfied with the accused's unit, ship, or with military service; that the accused made remarks indicating an intention to desert; that the accused was under charges or had escaped from confinement at the time of the absence; that the accused made preparations indicative of an intent not to return (for example, financial arrangements); or that the accused enlisted or accepted an appointment in the same or another armed force without disclosing the fact that the accused had not been regularly separated, or entered any foreign armed service without being authorized by the United States. On the other hand, the following are included in the circumstances which may tend to negate an inference that the accused intended to remain away permanently: previous long and excellent service; that the accused left valuable personal property in the unit or on the ship; or that the accused was under the influence of alcohol or drugs during the absence. These lists are illustrative only.

(iv) Entries on documents, such as personnel accountability records, which administratively refer to an accused as a "deserter" are not evidence of intent to desert.

(v) Proof of, or a plea of guilty to, an unauthorized absence, even of extended duration, does not, without more, prove guilt of desertion.

(d) *Effect of enlistment or appointment in the same or a different armed force.* Article 85a(3) does not state a separate offense. Rather, it is a rule of evidence by which the prosecution may prove intent to remain away permanently. Proof of an enlistment or acceptance of an appointment in a service without disclosing a preexisting duty status in the same or a different service provides the basis from which an inference of intent to permanently remain away from the earlier unit, organization, or place of duty may be drawn. Furthermore, if a person, without being regularly separated from one of the armed forces, enlists or accepts an appointment in the same or

another armed force, the person's presence in the military service under such an enlistment or appointment is not a return to military control and does not terminate any desertion or absence without authority from the earlier unit or organization, unless the facts of the earlier period of service are known to military authorities. If a person, while in desertion, enlists or accepts an appointment in the same or another armed force, and deserts while serving the enlistment or appointment, the person may be tried and convicted for each desertion.

(2) *Quitting unit, organization, or place of duty with intent to avoid hazardous duty or to shirk important service.*

(a) *Hazardous duty or important service.* "Hazardous duty" or "important service" may include service such as duty in a combat or other dangerous area; embarkation for certain foreign or sea duty; movement to a port of embarkation for that purpose; entrainment for duty on the border or coast in time of war or threatened invasion or other disturbances; strike or riot duty; or employment in aid of the civil power in, for example, protecting property, or quelling or preventing disorder in times of great public disaster. Such services as drill, target practice, maneuvers, and practice marches are not ordinarily "hazardous duty or important service." Whether a duty is hazardous or a service is important depends upon the circumstances of the particular case, and is a question of fact for the court-martial to decide.

(b) *Quits.* "Quits" in Article 85 means "goes absent without authority."

(c) *Actual knowledge.* Article 85 *a*(2) requires proof that the accused actually knew of the hazardous duty or important service. Actual knowledge may be proved by circumstantial evidence.

(3) *Attempting to desert.* Once the attempt is made, the fact that the person desists, voluntarily or otherwise, does not cancel the offense. The offense is complete, for example, if the person, intending to desert, hides in an empty freight car on a military reservation, intending to escape by being taken away in the car. Entering the car with the intent to desert is the overt act. For a more detailed discussion of attempts, *see* paragraph 4. For an explanation concerning intent to remain away permanently, *see* paragraph 9c(1)(c).

(4) *Prisoner with executed punitive discharge.* A prisoner whose dismissal or dishonorable or bad-

conduct discharge has been executed is not a "member of the armed forces" within the meaning of Articles 85 or 86, although the prisoner may still be subject to military law under Article 2(*a*)(7). If the facts warrant, such a prisoner could be charged with escape from confinement under Article 95 or an offense under Article 134.

d. *Lesser included offenses.* See paragraph 3 of this part and Appendix 12A.

e. *Maximum punishment.*

(1) *Completed or attempted desertion with intent to avoid hazardous duty or to shirk important service.* Dishonorable discharge, forfeiture of all pay and allowances, and confinement for 5 years.

(2) *Other cases of completed or attempted desertion.*

(a) *Terminated by apprehension.* Dishonorable discharge, forfeiture of all pay and allowances, and confinement for 3 years.

(b) *Terminated otherwise.* Dishonorable discharge, forfeiture of all pay and allowances, and confinement for 2 years.

(3) *In time of war.* Death or such other punishment as a court-martial may direct.

f. *Sample specifications.*

(1) *Desertion with intent to remain away permanently.*

In that _____ (personal jurisdiction data), did, on or about _____ 20 ___ , (a time of war) without authority and with intent to remain away therefrom permanently, absent himself/herself from his/her (unit) (organization) (place of duty), to wit: _____ , located at (_____), and did remain so absent in desertion until (he/she was apprehended) on or about _____ 20 ___ .

(2) *Desertion with intent to avoid hazardous duty or shirk important service.*

In that _____ (personal jurisdiction data), did, on or about _____ 20 ___ , (a time of war) with intent to (avoid hazardous duty) (shirk important service), namely: _____ , quit his/her (unit) (organization) (place of duty), to wit: _____ , located at (_____), and did remain so absent in desertion until on or about _____ 20 ___ .

(3) *Desertion prior to acceptance of resignation.*

In that _____ (personal jurisdiction data) having tendered his/her resignation and prior to due notice of the acceptance of the same, did, on or about _____ 20 ___ , (a time of war) without leave and with intent to remain away therefrom permanently, quit his/her (post) (proper duties), to wit: _____ , and did remain so absent in desertion until (he/she was apprehended) on or about _____ 20 ___ .

(4) *Attempted desertion.*

In that _____ (personal jurisdiction data), did (at/on board—location), on or about _____ 20 ___ , (a time of war) attempt to (absent himself/herself from his/her (unit) (organization) (place of duty) to wit: _____ , without authority and with intent to remain away therefrom permanently) (quit his/her (unit) (organization) (place of duty), to wit: _____ , located at _____ , with intent to (avoid hazardous duty) (shirk important service) namely _____) (_____).

10. Article 86—Absence without leave

a. *Text of statute.*

Any member of the armed forces who, without authority—

(1) fails to go to his appointed place of duty at the time prescribed;

(2) goes from that place; or

(3) absents himself or remains absent from his unit, organization, or place of duty at which he is required to be at the time prescribed;

shall be punished as a court-martial may direct.

b. *Elements.*

(1) *Failure to go to appointed place of duty.*

(a) That a certain authority appointed a certain time and place of duty for the accused;

(b) That the accused knew of that time and place; and

(c) That the accused, without authority, failed to go to the appointed place of duty at the time prescribed.

(2) *Going from appointed place of duty.*

(a) That a certain authority appointed a certain time and place of duty for the accused;

(b) That the accused knew of that time and place; and

(c) That the accused, without authority, went from the appointed place of duty after having reported at such place.

(3) *Absence from unit, organization, or place of duty.*

(a) That the accused absented himself or herself from his or her unit, organization, or place of duty at which he or she was required to be;

(b) That the absence was without authority from anyone competent to give him or her leave; and

(c) That the absence was for a certain period of time.
[Note: if the absence was terminated by apprehension, add the following element]

(d) That the absence was terminated by apprehension.

(4) *Abandoning watch or guard.*

(a) That the accused was a member of a guard, watch, or duty;

(b) That the accused absented himself or herself from his or her guard, watch, or duty section;

(c) That absence of the accused was without authority; and
[Note: If the absence was with intent to abandon the accused's guard, watch, or duty section, add the following element]

(d) That the accused intended to abandon his or her guard, watch, or duty section.

(5) *Absence from unit, organization, or place of duty with intent to avoid maneuvers or field exercises.*

(a) That the accused absented himself or herself from his or her unit, organization, or place of duty at which he or she was required to be;

(b) That the absence of the accused was without authority;

(c) That the absence was for a certain period of time;

(d) That the accused knew that the absence would occur during a part of a period of maneuvers or field exercises; and

(e) That the accused intended to avoid all or part of a period of maneuvers or field exercises.

c. *Explanation.*

(1) *In general.* This article is designed to cover every case not elsewhere provided for in which any member of the armed forces is through the member's own fault not at the place where the member is required to be at a prescribed time. It is not necessary that the person be absent entirely from military jurisdiction and control. The first part of this article—relating to the appointed place of duty—applies whether the place is appointed as a rendezvous for several or for one only.

(2) *Actual knowledge.* The offenses of failure to go to and going from appointed place of duty require proof that the accused actually knew of the appointed time and place of duty. The offense of absence from unit, organization, or place of duty with intent to avoid maneuvers or field exercises requires proof that the accused actually knew that the absence would occur during a part of a period of maneuvers or field exercises. Actual knowledge may be proved by circumstantial evidence.

(3) *Intent.* Specific intent is not an element of unauthorized absence. Specific intent is an element for certain aggravated unauthorized absences.

(4) *Aggravated forms of unauthorized absence.* There are variations of unauthorized absence under Article 86(3) which are more serious because of aggravating circumstances such as duration of the absence, a special type of duty from which the accused absents himself or herself, and a particular specific intent which accompanies the absence. These circumstances are not essential elements of a violation of Article 86. They simply constitute special matters in aggravation. The following are aggravated unauthorized absences:

(a) Unauthorized absence for more than 3 days (duration).

(b) Unauthorized absence for more than 30 days (duration).

(c) Unauthorized absence from a guard, watch, or duty (special type of duty).

(d) Unauthorized absence from guard, watch, or duty section with the intent to abandon it (special type of duty and specific intent).

(e) Unauthorized absence with the intent to avoid maneuvers or field exercises (special type of duty and specific intent).

(5) *Control by civilian authorities.* A member of the armed forces turned over to the civilian authorities upon request under Article 14 (*see* R.C.M. 106) is not absent without leave while held by them under that delivery. When a member of the armed forces, being absent with leave, or absent without leave, is held, tried, and acquitted by civilian authorities, the member's status as absent with leave, or absent without leave, is not thereby changed, regardless how long held. The fact that a member of the armed forces is convicted by the civilian authorities, or adjudicated to be a juvenile offender, or the case is "diverted" out of the regular criminal process for a probationary period does not excuse any un-

authorized absence, because the member's inability to return was the result of willful misconduct. If a member is released by the civilian authorities without trial, and was on authorized leave at the time of arrest or detention, the member may be found guilty of unauthorized absence only if it is proved that the member actually committed the offense for which detained, thus establishing that the absence was the result of the member's own misconduct.

(6) *Inability to return.* The status of absence without leave is not changed by an inability to return through sickness, lack of transportation facilities, or other disabilities. But the fact that all or part of a period of unauthorized absence was in a sense enforced or involuntary is a factor in extenuation and should be given due weight when considering the initial disposition of the offense. When, however, a person on authorized leave, without fault, is unable to return at the expiration thereof, that person has not committed the offense of absence without leave.

(7) *Determining the unit or organization of an accused.* A person undergoing transfer between activities is ordinarily considered to be attached to the activity to which ordered to report. A person on temporary additional duty continues as a member of the regularly assigned unit and if the person is absent from the temporary duty assignment, the person becomes absent without leave from both units, and may be charged with being absent without leave from either unit.

(8) *Duration.* Unauthorized absence under Article 86(3) is an instantaneous offense. It is complete at the instant an accused absents himself or herself without authority. Duration of the absence is a matter in aggravation for the purpose of increasing the maximum punishment authorized for the offense. Even if the duration of the absence is not over 3 days, it is ordinarily alleged in an Article 86(3) specification. If the duration is not alleged or if alleged but not proved, an accused can be convicted of and punished for only 1 day of unauthorized absence.

(9) *Computation of duration.* In computing the duration of an unauthorized absence, any one continuous period of absence found that totals not more than 24 hours is counted as 1 day; any such period that totals more than 24 hours and not more than 48 hours is counted as 2 days, and so on. The hours of departure and return on different dates are assumed to be the same if not alleged and proved. For exam-

ple, if an accused is found guilty of unauthorized absence from 0600 hours, 4 April, to 1000 hours, 7 April of the same year (76 hours), the maximum punishment would be based on an absence of 4 days. However, if the accused is found guilty simply of unauthorized absence from 4 April to 7 April, the maximum punishment would be based on an absence of 3 days.

(10) *Termination—methods of return to military control.*

(a) *Surrender to military authority.* A surrender occurs when a person presents himself or herself to any military authority, whether or not a member of the same armed force, notifies that authority of his or her unauthorized absence status, and submits or demonstrates a willingness to submit to military control. Such a surrender terminates the unauthorized absence.

(b) *Apprehension by military authority.* Apprehension by military authority of a known absentee terminates an unauthorized absence.

(c) *Delivery to military authority.* Delivery of a known absentee by anyone to military authority terminates the unauthorized absence.

(d) *Apprehension by civilian authorities at the request of the military.* When an absentee is taken into custody by civilian authorities at the request of military authorities, the absence is terminated.

(e) *Apprehension by civilian authorities without prior military request.* When an absentee is in the hands of civilian authorities for other reasons and these authorities make the absentee available for return to military control, the absence is terminated when the military authorities are informed of the absentee's availability.

(11) *Findings of more than one absence under one specification.* An accused may properly be found guilty of two or more separate unauthorized absences under one specification, provided that each absence is included within the period alleged in the specification and provided that the accused was not misled. If an accused is found guilty of two or more unauthorized absences under a single specification, the maximum authorized punishment shall not exceed that authorized if the accused had been found guilty as charged in the specification.

d. *Lesser included offenses.* See paragraph 3 of this part and Appendix 12A.

e. *Maximum punishment.*

(1) *Failing to go to, or going from, the appointed place of duty.* Confinement for 1 month and forfeiture of two-thirds pay per month for 1 month.

(2) *Absence from unit, organization, or other place of duty.*

(a) For not more than 3 days. Confinement for 1 month and forfeiture of two-thirds pay per month for 1 month.

(b) For more than 3 days but not more than 30 days. Confinement for 6 months and forfeiture of two-thirds pay per month for 6months.

(c) For more than 30 days. Dishonorable discharge, forfeiture of all pay and allowances, and confinement for 1 year.

(d) For more than 30 days and terminated by apprehension. Dishonorable discharge, forfeiture of all pay and allowances, and confinement for 18 months.

(3) *From guard or watch.* Confinement for 3 months and forfeiture of two-thirds pay per month for 3 months.

(4) *From guard or watch with intent to abandon.* Bad-conduct discharge, forfeiture of all pay and allowances, and confinement for 6 months.

(5) *With intent to avoid maneuvers or field exercises.* Bad-conduct discharge, forfeiture of all pay and allowances, and confinement for 6 months.

f. *Sample specifications.*

(1) *Failing to go or leaving place of duty.* In that _____ (personal jurisdiction data), did (at/on board—location), on or about _____ 20 __ , without authority, (fail to go at the time prescribed to) (go from) his/her appointed place of duty, to wit: (here set forth the appointed place of duty).

(2) *Absence from unit, organization, or place of duty.* In that _____ (personal jurisdiction data), did, on or about _____ 20 __ , without authority, absent himself/herself from his/her (unit) (organization) (place of duty at which he/she was required to be), to wit: _____ , located at _____ , and did remain so absent until (he/she was apprehended) on or about _____ 20 __ .

(3) *Absence from unit, organization, or place of duty with intent to avoid maneuvers or field exercises.* In that _____ (personal jurisdiction data), did, on or about _____ 20 __ , without authority and with intent to avoid (maneuvers) (field exercises), absent himself/herself from his/her (unit) (organiza-

tion) (place of duty at which he/she was required to be), to wit: _____ located at (_____), and did remain so absent until on or about _____ 20 __ .

(4) *Abandoning watch or guard.* In that _____ (personal jurisdiction data), being a member of the _____ (guard) (watch) (duty section), did, (at/on board-location), on or about _____ 20 __ , without authority, go from his/her (guard) (watch) (duty section) (with intent to abandon the same).

11. Article 87—Missing movement

a. *Text of statute.*

Any person subject to this chapter who through neglect or design misses the movement of a ship, aircraft, or unit with which he is required in the course of duty to move shall be punished as a court-martial may direct.

b. *Elements.*

(1) That the accused was required in the course of duty to move with a ship, aircraft or unit;

(2) That the accused knew of the prospective movement of the ship, aircraft or unit;

(3) That the accused missed the movement of the ship, aircraft or unit; and

(4) That the accused missed the movement through design or neglect.

c. *Explanation.*

(1) *Movement.* "Movement" as used in Article 87 includes a move, transfer, or shift of a ship, aircraft, or unit involving a substantial distance and period of time. Whether a particular movement is substantial is a question to be determined by the court-martial considering all the circumstances. Changes which do not constitute a "movement" include practice marches of a short duration with a return to the point of departure, and minor changes in location of ships, aircraft, or units, as when a ship is shifted from one berth to another in the same shipyard or harbor or when a unit is moved from one barracks to another on the same post.

(2) *Mode of movement.*

(a) *Unit.* If a person is required in the course of duty to move with a unit, the mode of travel is not important, whether it be military or commercial, and includes travel by ship, train, aircraft, truck, bus, or walking. The word "unit" is not limited to any specific technical category such as those listed in a table of organization and equipment, but also includes units which are created before the movement with the intention that they have organizational continuity upon arrival at their destination regardless of their technical designation, and units intended to be disbanded upon arrival at their destination.

(b) *Ship, aircraft.* If a person is assigned as a crew member or is ordered to move as a passenger aboard a particular ship or aircraft, military or chartered, then missing the particular sailing or flight is essential to establish the offense of missing movement.

(3) *Design.* "Design" means on purpose, intentionally, or according to plan and requires specific intent to miss the movement.

(4) *Neglect.* "Neglect" means the omission to take such measures as are appropriate under the circumstances to assure presence with a ship, aircraft, or unit at the time of a scheduled movement, or doing some act without giving attention to its probable consequences in connection with the prospective movement, such as a departure from the vicinity of the prospective movement to such a distance as would make it likely that one could not return in time for the movement.

(5) *Actual knowledge.* In order to be guilty of the offense, the accused must have actually known of the prospective movement that was missed. Knowledge of the exact hour or even of the exact date of the scheduled movement is not required. It is sufficient if the approximate date was known by the accused as long as there is a causal connection between the conduct of the accused and the missing of the scheduled movement. Knowledge may be proved by circumstantial evidence.

(6) *Proof of absence.* That the accused actually missed the movement may be proved by documentary evidence, as by a proper entry in a log or a morning report. This fact may also be proved by the testimony of personnel of the ship, aircraft, or unit (or by other evidence) that the movement occurred at a certain time, together with evidence that the accused was physically elsewhere at that time.

d. *Lesser included offenses.* See paragraph 3 of this part and Appendix 12A.

e. *Maximum punishment.*

(1) *Design.* Dishonorable discharge, forfeiture of all pay and allowances, and confinement for 2 years.

(2) *Neglect.* Bad-conduct discharge, forfeiture of all pay and allowances, and confinement for 1 year.

f. *Sample specification.*

In that _____ (personal jurisdiction data), did, (at/on board—location), on or about _____ 20 ___ , through (neglect) (design) miss the movement of (Aircraft No. _____) (Flight _____) (the USS _____) (Company A, 1st Battalion, 7th Infantry) (_____) with which he/she was required in the course of duty to move.

12. Article 88—Contempt toward officials

a. *Text of statute.*

Any commissioned officer who uses contemptuous words against the President, the Vice President, Congress, the Secretary of Defense, the Secretary of a military department, the Secretary of Homeland Security, or the Governor or legislature of any State, Territory, Commonwealth, or possession in which he is on duty or present shall be punished as a court-martial may direct.

b. *Elements.*

(1) That the accused was a commissioned officer of the United States armed forces;

(2) That the accused used certain words against an official or legislature named in the article;

(3) That by an act of the accused these words came to the knowledge of a person other than the accused; and

(4) That the words used were contemptuous, either in themselves or by virtue of the circumstances under which they were used.
[Note: If the words were against a Governor or legislature, add the following element]

(5) That the accused was then present in the State, Territory, Commonwealth, or possession of the Governor or legislature concerned.

c. *Explanation.* The official or legislature against whom the words are used must be occupying one of the offices or be one of the legislatures named in Article 88 at the time of the offense. Neither "Congress" nor "legislature" includes its members individually. "Governor" does not include "lieutenant governor." It is immaterial whether the words are used against the official in an official or private capacity. If not personally contemptuous, adverse criticism of one of the officials or legislatures named in the article in the course of a political discussion, even though emphatically expressed, may not be charged as a violation of the article. Similarly, expressions of opinion made in a purely private conversation should not ordinarily be charged. Giving broad circulation to a written publication containing contemptuous words of the kind made punishable by this article, or the utterance of contemptuous words of this kind in the presence of military subordinates, aggravates the offense. The truth or falsity of the statements is immaterial.

d. *Lesser included offenses.* See paragraph 3 of this part and Appendix 12A.

e. *Maximum punishment.* Dismissal, forfeiture of all pay and allowances, and confinement for 1 year.

f. *Sample specification.*

In that _____ (personal jurisdiction data), did, (at/on board—location), on or about _____ 20 ___ , [use (orally and publicly) (_____) the following contemptuous words] [in a contemptuous manner, use (orally and publicly) (_____) the following words] against the [(President) (Vice President) (Congress) (Secretary of _____)] [(Governor) (legislature) of the (State of _____) (Territory of _____) (_____), a (State) (Territory) (_____) in which he/she, the said _____ , was then (on duty), (present)], to wit: " _____ ," or words to that effect.

13. Article 89—Disrespect toward a superior commissioned officer

a. *Text of statute.*

Any person subject to this chapter who behaves with disrespect toward his superior commissioned officer shall be punished as a court-martial may direct.

b. *Elements.*

(1) That the accused did or omitted certain acts or used certain language to or concerning a certain commissioned officer;

(2) That such behavior or language was directed toward that officer;

(3) That the officer toward whom the acts, omissions, or words were directed was the superior commissioned officer of the accused;

(4) That the accused then knew that the commissioned officer toward whom the acts, omissions, or words were directed was the accused's superior commissioned officer; and

(5) That, under the circumstances, the behavior or language was disrespectful to that commissioned officer.

c. *Explanation.*

(1) *Superior commissioned officer.*

(a) *Accused and victim in same uniformed service.* If the accused and the victim are in the same uniformed service, the victim is a "superior commissioned officer" of the accused when either superior in rank or command to the accused; however, the victim is not a "superior commissioned officer" of the accused if the victim is inferior in command, even though superior in rank.

(b) *Accused and victim in different uniformed service.* If the accused and the victim are in different uniformed services, the victim is a "superior commissioned officer" of the accused when the victim is a commissioned officer and superior in the chain of command over the accused or when the victim, not a medical officer or a chaplain, is senior in grade to the accused and both are detained by a hostile entity so that recourse to the normal chain of command is prevented. The victim is not a "superior commissioned officer" of the accused merely because the victim is superior in grade to the accused.

(c) *Execution of office.* It is not necessary that the "superior commissioned officer" be in the execution of office at the time of the disrespectful behavior.

(2) *Knowledge.* If the accused did not know that the person against whom the acts or words were directed was the accused's superior commissioned officer, the accused may not be convicted of a violation of this article. Knowledge may be proved by circumstantial evidence.

(3) *Disrespect.* Disrespectful behavior is that which detracts from the respect due the authority and person of a superior commissioned officer. It may consist of acts or language, however expressed, and it is immaterial whether they refer to the superior as an officer or as a private individual. Disrespect by words may be conveyed by abusive epithets or other contemptuous or denunciatory language. Truth is no defense. Disrespect by acts includes neglecting the customary salute, or showing a marked disdain, indifference, insolence, impertinence, undue familiarity, or other rudeness in the presence of the superior officer.

(4) *Presence.* It is not essential that the disrespectful behavior be in the presence of the superior, but ordinarily one should not be held accountable

under this article for what was said or done in a purely private conversation.

(5) *Special defense—unprotected victim.* A superior commissioned officer whose conduct in relation to the accused under all the circumstances departs substantially from the required standards appropriate to that officer's rank or position under similar circumstances loses the protection of this article. That accused may not be convicted of being disrespectful to the officer who has so lost the entitlement to respect protected by Article 89.

d. *Lesser included offenses.* See paragraph 3 of this part and Appendix 12A.

e. *Maximum punishment.* Bad-conduct discharge, forfeiture of all pay and allowances, and confinement for 1 year.

f. *Sample specification.*

In that _____ (personal jurisdiction data), did, (at/on board—location), on or about _____ 20 ___, behave himself/herself with disrespect toward _____ , his/her superior commissioned officer, then known by the said _____ to be his/her superior commissioned officer, by (saying to him/her " _____ ," or words to that effect) (contemptuously turning from and leaving him/her while he/she, the said _____ , was talking to him/her, the said _____) (_____).

14. Article 90—Assaulting or willfully disobeying superior commissioned officer

a. *Text of statute.*

Any person subject to this chapter who—

(1) strikes his superior commissioned officer or draws or lifts up any weapon or offers any violence against him while he is in the execution of his office; or

(2) willfully disobeys a lawful command of his superior commissioned officer;
shall be punished, if the offense is committed in time of war, by death or such other punishment as a court-martial may direct, and if the offense is committed at any other time, by such punishment, other than death, as a court-martial may direct.

b. *Elements.*

(1) *Striking or assaulting superior commissioned officer.*

(a) That the accused struck, drew, or lifted up a weapon against, or offered violence against, a certain commissioned officer;

(b) That the officer was the superior commissioned officer of the accused;

(c) That the accused then knew that the officer was the accused's superior commissioned officer; and

(d) That the superior commissioned officer was then in the execution of office.

(2) *Disobeying superior commissioned officer.*

(a) That the accused received a lawful command from a certain commissioned officer;

(b) That this officer was the superior commissioned officer of the accused;

(c) That the accused then knew that this officer was the accused's superior commissioned officer; and

(d) That the accused willfully disobeyed the lawful command.

c. *Explanation.*

(1) *Striking or assaulting superior commissioned officer.*

(a) *Definitions.*

(i) *Superior commissioned officer.* The definitions in paragraph 13c(1)(*a*) and (*b*) apply here and in subparagraph c(2).

(ii) *Strikes.* "Strikes" means an intentional blow, and includes any offensive touching of the person of an officer, however slight.

(iii) *Draws or lifts up any weapon against.* The phrase "draws or lifts up any weapon against" covers any simple assault committed in the manner stated. The drawing of any weapon in an aggressive manner or the raising or brandishing of the same in a threatening manner in the presence of and at the superior is the sort of act proscribed. The raising in a threatening manner of a firearm, whether or not loaded, of a club, or of anything by which a serious blow or injury could be given is included in "lifts up."

(iv) *Offers any violence against.* The phrase "offers any violence against" includes any form of battery or of mere assault not embraced in the preceding more specific terms "strikes" and "draws or lifts up." If not executed, the violence must be physically attempted or menaced. A mere threatening in words is not an offering of violence in the sense of this article.

(b) *Execution of office.* An officer is in the execution of office when engaged in any act or service required or authorized by treaty, statute, regulation, the order of a superior, or military usage. In general, any striking or use of violence against any superior officer by a person over whom it is the duty of that officer to maintain discipline at the time, would be striking or using violence against the officer in the execution of office. The commanding officer on board a ship or the commanding officer of a unit in the field is generally considered to be on duty at all times.

(c) *Knowledge.* If the accused did not know the officer was the accused's superior commissioned officer, the accused may not be convicted of this offense. Knowledge may be proved by circumstantial evidence.

(d) *Defenses.* In a prosecution for striking or assaulting a superior commissioned officer in violation of this article, it is a defense that the accused acted in the proper discharge of some duty, or that the victim behaved in a manner toward the accused such as to lose the protection of this article (*see* paragraph 13c(5)). For example, if the victim initiated an unlawful attack on the accused, this would deprive the victim of the protection of this article, and, in addition, could excuse any lesser included offense of assault as done in self-defense, depending on the circumstances (*see* paragraph 54c; R.C.M. 916(*e*)).

(2) *Disobeying superior commissioned officer.*

(a) *Lawfulness of the order.*

(i) *Inference of lawfulness.* An order requiring the performance of a military duty or act may be inferred to be lawful and it is disobeyed at the peril of the subordinate. This inference does not apply to a patently illegal order, such as one that directs the commission of a crime.

(ii) *Determination of lawfulness.* The lawfulness of an order is a question of law to be determined by the military judge.

(iii) *Authority of issuing officer.* The commissioned officer issuing the order must have authority to give such an order. Authorization may be based on law, regulation, or custom of the service.

(iv) *Relationship to military duty.* The order must relate to military duty, which includes all activities reasonably necessary to accomplish a military mission, or safeguard or promote the morale, disci-

pline, and usefulness of members of a command and directly connected with the maintenance of good order in the service. The order may not, without such a valid military purpose, interfere with private rights or personal affairs. However, the dictates of a person's conscience, religion, or personal philosophy cannot justify or excuse the disobedience of an otherwise lawful order. Disobedience of an order which has for its sole object the attainment of some private end, or which is given for the sole purpose of increasing the penalty for an offense which it is expected the accused may commit, is not punishable under this article.

(v) *Relationship to statutory or constitutional rights.* The order must not conflict with the statutory or constitutional rights of the person receiving the order.

(b) *Personal nature of the order.* The order must be directed specifically to the subordinate. Violations of regulations, standing orders or directives, or failure to perform previously established duties are not punishable under this article, but may violate Article 92.

(c) *Form and transmission of the order.* As long as the order is understandable, the form of the order is immaterial, as is the method by which it is transmitted to the accused.

(d) *Specificity of the order.* The order must be a specific mandate to do or not to do a specific act. An exhortation to "obey the law" or to perform one's military duty does not constitute an order under this article.

(e) *Knowledge.* The accused must have actual knowledge of the order and of the fact that the person issuing the order was the accused's superior commissioned officer. Actual knowledge may be proved by circumstantial evidence.

(f) *Nature of the disobedience.* "Willful disobedience" is an intentional defiance of authority. Failure to comply with an order through heedlessness, remissness, or forgetfulness is not a violation of this article but may violate Article 92.

(g) *Time for compliance.* When an order requires immediate compliance, an accused's declared intent not to obey and the failure to make any move to comply constitutes disobedience. Immediate compliance is required for any order that does not explicitly or implicitly indicate that delayed compliance is authorized or directed. If an order requires performance in the future, an accused's present statement of intention to disobey the order does not constitute disobedience of that order, although carrying out that intention may.

(3) *Civilians and discharged prisoners.* A discharged prisoner or other civilian subject to military law (*see* Article 2) and under the command of a commissioned officer is subject to the provisions of this article.

d. *Lesser included offenses.* See paragraph 3 of this part and Appendix 12A.

e. *Maximum punishment.*

(1) *Striking, drawing, or lifting up any weapon or offering any violence to superior commissioned officer in the execution of office.* Dishonorable discharge, forfeiture of all pay and allowances, and confinement for 10 years.

(2) *Willfully disobeying a lawful order of superior commissioned officer.* Dishonorable discharge, forfeiture of all pay and allowances, and confinement for 5 years.

(3) *In time of war.* Death or such other punishment as a court-martial may direct.

f. *Sample specifications.*

(1) *Striking superior commissioned officer.*

In that _____ (personal jurisdiction data), did, (at/on board—location) (subject-matter jurisdiction data, if required), on or about _____ 20 __ , (a time of war) strike _____ , his/her superior commissioned officer, then known by the said _____ to be his/her superior commissioned officer, who was then in the execution of his/her office, (in) (on) the _____ with (*a*) (his/her) _____ .

(2) *Drawing or lifting up a weapon against superior commissioned officer.*

In that _____ (personal jurisdiction data), did, (at/on board—location) (subject-matter jurisdiction data, if required), on or about _____ 20 __ , (a time of war) (draw) lift up) a weapon, to wit: a _____ , against _____ , his/her superior commissioned officer, then known by the said _____ to be his/her superior commissioned officer, who was then in the execution of his/her office.

(3) *Offering violence to superior commissioned officer.*

In that _____ (personal jurisdiction data), did, (at/on board—location) (subject-matter jurisdic-

tion data, if required), on or about _____ 20 __ , (a time of war) offer violence against _____ , his/her superior commissioned officer, then known by the said _____ to be his/her superior commissioned officer, who was then in the execution of his/her office, by _____ .

(4) *Willful disobedience of superior commissioned officer.*

In that _____ (personal jurisdiction data), having received a lawful command from _____ , his/her superior commissioned officer, then known by the said _____ to be his/her superior commissioned officer, to _____ , or words to that effect, did, (at/on board—location), on or about _____ 20 __ , willfully disobey the same.

15. Article 91—Insubordinate conduct toward warrant officer, noncommissioned officer, or petty officer

a. *Text of statute.*

Any warrant officer or enlisted member who—

(1) strikes or assaults a warrant officer, noncommissioned officer, or petty officer, while that officer is in the execution of his office;

(2) willfully disobeys the lawful order of a warrant officer, noncommissioned officer, or petty officer; or

(3) treats with contempt or is disrespectful in language or deportment toward a warrant officer, noncommissioned officer, or petty officer while that officer is in the execution of his office; shall be punished as a court-martial may direct.

b. *Elements.*

(1) *Striking or assaulting warrant, noncommissioned, or petty officer.*

(a) That the accused was a warrant officer or enlisted member;

(b) That the accused struck or assaulted a certain warrant, noncommissioned, or petty officer;

(c) That the striking or assault was committed while the victim was in the execution of office; and

(d) That the accused then knew that the person struck or assaulted was a warrant, noncommissioned, or petty officer.

[Note: If the victim was the superior noncommissioned or petty officer of the accused, add the following elements]

(e) That the victim was the superior noncommissioned, or petty officer of the accused; and

(f) That the accused then knew that the person

struck or assaulted was the accused's superior non-commissioned, or petty officer.

(2) *Disobeying a warrant, noncommissioned, or petty officer.*

(a) That the accused was a warrant officer or enlisted member;

(b) That the accused received a certain lawful order from a certain warrant, noncommissioned, or petty officer;

(c) That the accused then knew that the person giving the order was a warrant, noncommissioned, or petty officer;

(d) That the accused had a duty to obey the order; and

(e) That the accused willfully disobeyed the order.

(3) *Treating with contempt or being disrespectful in language or deportment toward a warrant, noncommissioned, or petty officer.*

(a) That the accused was a warrant officer or enlisted member;

(b) That the accused did or omitted certain acts, or used certain language;

(c) That such behavior or language was used toward and within sight or hearing of a certain warrant, noncommissioned, or petty officer;

(d) That the accused then knew that the person toward whom the behavior or language was directed was a warrant, noncommissioned, or petty officer;

(e) That the victim was then in the execution of office; and

(f) That under the circumstances the accused, by such behavior or language, treated with contempt or was disrespectful to said warrant, noncommissioned, or petty officer.

[Note: If the victim was the superior noncommissioned, or petty officer of the accused, add the following elements]

(g) That the victim was the superior noncommissioned, or petty officer of the accused; and

(h) That the accused then knew that the person toward whom the behavior or language was directed was the accused's superior noncommissioned, or petty officer.

c. *Explanation.*

(1) *In general.* Article 91 has the same general objects with respect to warrant, noncommissioned, and petty officers as Articles 89 and 90 have with respect to commissioned officers, namely, to ensure obedience to their lawful orders, and to protect them from violence, insult, or disrespect. Unlike Articles 89 and 90, however, this article does not require a superior-subordinate relationship as an element of any of the offenses denounced. This article does not protect an acting noncommissioned officer or acting petty officer, nor does it protect military police or members of the shore patrol who are not warrant, noncommissioned, or petty officers.

(2) *Knowledge.* All of the offenses prohibited by Article 91 require that the accused have actual knowledge that the victim was a warrant, noncommissioned, or petty officer. Actual knowledge may be proved by circumstantial evidence.

(3) *Striking or assaulting a warrant, noncommissioned, or petty officer.* For a discussion of "strikes" and "in the execution of office," *see* paragraph 14c. For a discussion of "assault," see paragraph 54c. An assault by a prisoner who has been discharged from the service, or by any other civilian subject to military law, upon a warrant, noncommissioned, or petty officer should be charged under Article 128 or 134.

(4) *Disobeying a warrant, noncommissioned, or petty officer. See* paragraph 14c(2) for a discussion of lawfulness, personal nature, form, transmission, and specificity of the order, nature of the disobedience, and time for compliance with the order.

(5) *Treating with contempt or being disrespectful in language or deportment toward a warrant, noncommissioned, or petty officer.* "Toward" requires that the behavior and language be within the sight or hearing of the warrant, noncommissioned, or petty officer concerned. For a discussion of "in the execution of his office," *see* paragraph 14c. For a discussion of disrespect, *see* paragraph 13c.

d. *Lesser included offenses.* See paragraph 3 of this part and Appendix 12A.

e. *Maximum punishment.*

(1) *Striking or assaulting warrant officer.* Dishonorable discharge, forfeiture of all pay and allowances, and confinement for 5 years.

(2) *Striking or assaulting superior noncommissioned or petty officer.* Dishonorable discharge, forfeiture of all pay and allowances, and confinement for 3 years.

(3) *Striking or assaulting other noncommissioned or petty officer.* Dishonorable discharge, forfeiture of all pay and allowances, and confinement for 1 year.

(4) *Willfully disobeying the lawful order of a warrant officer.* Dishonorable discharge, forfeiture of all pay and allowances, and confinement for 2 years.

(5) *Willfully disobeying the lawful order of a noncommissioned or petty officer.* Bad-conduct discharge, forfeiture of all pay and allowances, and confinement for 1 year.

(6) *Contempt or disrespect to warrant officer.* Bad-conduct discharge, forfeiture of all pay and allowances, and confinement for 9 months.

(7) *Contempt or disrespect to superior noncommissioned or petty officer.* Bad-conduct discharge, forfeiture of all pay and allowances, and confinement for 6 months.

(8) *Contempt or disrespect to other noncommissioned or petty officer.* Forfeiture of two-thirds pay per month for 3 months, and confinement for 3 months.

f. *Sample specifications.*

(1) *Striking or assaulting warrant, noncommissioned, or petty officer.*

In that _____ (personal jurisdiction data), did, (at/on board—location) (subject-matter jurisdiction data, if required), on or about _____ 20 ___ , (strike) (assault) _____ , a _____ officer, then known to the said _____ to be a (superior) _____ officer who was then in the execution of his/her office, by _____ him/her (in) (on) (the _____) with (a) _____ (his/her) _____ .

(2) *Willful disobedience of warrant, noncommissioned, or petty officer.*

In that _____ (personal jurisdiction data), having received a lawful order from _____ , a _____ officer, then known by the said _____ to be a _____ officer, to _____ , an order which it was his/her duty to obey, did (at/on board—location), on or about _____ 20 ___ , willfully disobey the same.

(3) *Contempt or disrespect toward warrant, noncommissioned, or petty officer.*

In that _____ (personal jurisdiction data) (at/on board—location), on or about _____ 20 ___ , [did treat with contempt] [was disrespectful in (language) (deportment) toward] _____ , a _____ officer, then known by the said _____ to be a (superior) _____ officer, who was then in the execution of his/her office, by

(saying to him/her, " _____ ," or words to that effect) (spitting at his/her feet) (_____)

16. Article 92—Failure to obey order or regulation

a. *Text of statute.*

Any person subject to this chapter who—

(1) **violates or fails to obey any lawful general order or regulation;**

(2) **having knowledge of any other lawful order issued by a member of the armed forces, which it is his duty to obey, fails to obey the order; or**

(3) **is derelict in the performance of his duties; shall be punished as a court-martial may direct.**

b. *Elements.*

(1) *Violation of or failure to obey a lawful general order or regulation.*

(a) That there was in effect a certain lawful general order or regulation;

(b) That the accused had a duty to obey it; and

(c) That the accused violated or failed to obey the order or regulation.

(2) *Failure to obey other lawful order.*

(a) That a member of the armed forces issued a certain lawful order;

(b) That the accused had knowledge of the order;

(c) That the accused had a duty to obey the order; and

(d) That the accused failed to obey the order.

(3) *Dereliction in the performance of duties.*

(a) That the accused had certain duties;

(b) That the accused knew or reasonably should have known of the duties; and

(c) That the accused was (willfully) (through neglect or culpable inefficiency) derelict in the performance of those duties.

[Note: In cases where the dereliction of duty resulted in death or grievous bodily harm, add the following as applicable]

(d) That such dereliction of duty resulted in death or grievous bodily harm to a person other than the accused.

c. *Explanation.*

(1) *Violation of or failure to obey a lawful general order or regulation.*

(a) *Authority to issue general orders and regulations.* General orders or regulations are those orders or regulations generally applicable to an armed force which are properly published by the President or the Secretary of Defense, of Homeland Security, or of a military department, and those orders or regulations generally applicable to the command of the officer issuing them throughout the command or a particular subdivision thereof which are issued by:

(i) an officer having general court-martial jurisdiction;

(ii) a general or flag officer in command; or

(iii) a commander superior to (i) or (ii).

(b) *Effect of change of command on validity of order.* A general order or regulation issued by a commander with authority under Article 92(1) retains its character as a general order or regulation when another officer takes command, until it expires by its own terms or is rescinded by separate action, even if it is issued by an officer who is a general or flag officer in command and command is assumed by another officer who is not a general or flag officer.

(c) *Lawfulness.* A general order or regulation is lawful unless it is contrary to the Constitution, the laws of the United States, or lawful superior orders or for some other reason is beyond the authority of the official issuing it. *See* the discussion of lawfulness in paragraph 14c(2)(a).

(d) *Knowledge.* Knowledge of a general order or regulation need not be alleged or proved, as knowledge is not an element of this offense and a lack of knowledge does not constitute a defense.

(e) *Enforceability.* Not all provisions in general orders or regulations can be enforced under Article 92(1). Regulations which only supply general guidelines or advice for conducting military functions may not be enforceable under Article 92(1).

(2) *Violation of or failure to obey other lawful order.*

(a) *Scope.* Article 92(2) includes all other lawful orders which may be issued by a member of the armed forces, violations of which are not chargeable under Article 90, 91, or 92(1). It includes the violation of written regulations which are not general regulations. *See also* subparagraph (1)(e) above as applicable.

(b) *Knowledge.* In order to be guilty of this offense, a person must have had actual knowledge of the order or regulation. Knowledge of the order may be proved by circumstantial evidence.

(c) *Duty to obey order.*

(i) *From a superior.* A member of one armed force who is senior in rank to a member of another armed force is the superior of that member with authority to issue orders which that member has a duty to obey under the same circumstances as a commissioned officer of one armed force is the superior commissioned officer of a member of another armed force for the purposes of Articles 89 and 90. *See* paragraph 13c(1).

(ii) *From one not a superior.* Failure to obey the lawful order of one not a superior is an offense under Article 92(2), provided the accused had a duty to obey the order, such as one issued by a sentinel or a member of the armed forces police. *See* paragraph 15b(2) if the order was issued by a warrant, noncommissioned, or petty officer in the execution of office.

(3) *Dereliction in the performance of duties.*

(a) *Duty.* A duty may be imposed by treaty, statute, regulation, lawful order, standard operating procedure, or custom of the service.

(b) *Knowledge.* Actual knowledge of duties may be proved by circumstantial evidence. Actual knowledge need not be shown if the individual reasonably should have known of the duties. This may be demonstrated by regulations, training or operating manuals, customs of the service, academic literature or testimony, testimony of persons who have held similar or superior positions, or similar evidence.

(c) *Derelict.* A person is derelict in the performance of duties when that person willfully or negligently fails to perform that person's duties or when that person performs them in a culpably inefficient manner. "Willfully" means intentionally. It refers to the doing of an act knowingly and purposely, specifically intending the natural and probable consequences of the act. "Negligently" means an act or omission of a person who is under a duty to use due care which exhibits a lack of that degree of care which a reasonably prudent person would have exercised under the same or similar circumstances. "Culpable inefficiency" is inefficiency for which there is no reasonable or just excuse.

(d) *Ineptitude.* A person is not derelict in the performance of duties if the failure to perform those duties is caused by ineptitude rather than by willfulness, negligence, or culpable inefficiency, and may not be charged under this article, or otherwise punished. For example, a recruit who has tried earnestly during rifle training and throughout record firing is not derelict in the performance of duties if the recruit fails to qualify with the weapon.

(e) *Grievous bodily harm.* "Grievous bodily harm" means serious bodily injury. It does not include minor injuries, such as a black eye or a bloody nose, but does include fractured or dislocated bones, deep cuts, torn members of the body, serious damage to internal organs, and other serious bodily injuries.

(f) Where the dereliction of duty resulted in death or grievous bodily harm, an intent to cause death or grievous bodily harm is not required.

d. *Lesser included offenses.* See paragraph 3 of this part and Appendix 12A.

e. *Maximum punishment.*

(1) *Violation of or failure to obey lawful general order or regulation.* Dishonorable discharge, forfeiture of all pay and allowances, and confinement for 2 years.

(2) *Violation of or failure to obey other lawful order.* Bad-conduct discharge, forfeiture of all pay and allowances, and confinement for 6 months.

[Note: For (1) and (2), above, the punishment set forth does not apply in the following cases: if in the absence of the order or regulation which was violated or not obeyed the accused would on the same facts be subject to conviction for another specific offense for which a lesser punishment is prescribed; or if the violation or failure to obey is a breach of restraint imposed as a result of an order. In these instances, the maximum punishment is that specifically prescribed elsewhere for that particular offense.]

(3) *Dereliction in the performance of duties.*

(A) *Through neglect or culpable inefficiency.* Forfeiture of two-thirds pay per month for 3 months and confinement for 3 months.

(B) *Through neglect or culpable inefficiency resulting in death or grievous bodily harm.* Bad-conduct discharge, forfeiture of all pay and allowances, and confinement for 18 months.

(C) *Willful.* Bad-conduct discharge, forfeiture of all pay and allowances, and confinement for 6 months.

(D) *Willful dereliction of duty resulting in death or grievous bodily harm.* Dishonorable discharge, forfeiture of all pay and allowances, and confinement for 2 years.

[Note: For (1) and (2) above, the punishment set forth does not apply in the following cases: if, in the absence of the order or regulation that was violated or not obeyed, the accused would on the same facts be subject to conviction for another specific offense for which a lesser punishment is prescribed; or if the violation or failure to obey is a breach of restraint imposed as a result of an order. In these instances, the maximum punishment is that specifically prescribed elsewhere for that particular offense.]

Discussion

If the dereliction of duty resulted in death, the accused may also be charged under Article 119 or Article 134 (negligent homicide), as applicable.

---

f. *Sample specifications.*

(1) *Violation or failure to obey lawful general order or regulation.*

In that _____ (personal jurisdiction data), did, (at/on board—location) (subject-matter jurisdiction data, if required), on or about _____ 20 ___ , (violate) (fail to obey) a lawful general (order) (regulation), to wit: (paragraph _____ , (Army) (Air Force) Regulation _____ , dated _____ 20 ___) (Article _____ , U.S. Navy Regulations, dated _____ 20 ___) (General Order No. ___ , U.S. Navy, dated _____ 20 ___) (_____), by (wrongfully) _____ .

(2) *Violation or failure to obey other lawful written order.*

In that _____ (personal jurisdiction data), having knowledge of a lawful order issued by _____ , to wit: (paragraph _____ , (_____ the Combat Group Regulation No. _____) (USS _____ , Regulation _____), dated _____) (_____), an order which it was his/her duty to obey, did, (at/on board—location) (subject-matter jurisdiction data, if required), on or about _____ 20 ___ , fail to obey the same by (wrongfully) _____ .

(3) *Failure to obey other lawful order.*

In that _____ , (personal jurisdiction data) having knowledge of a lawful order issued by _____ (to submit to certain medical treatment) (to _____) (not to _____) (_____), an order which it was his/her duty to obey, did (at/on board—location) (subject-matter jurisdiction data, if required), on or about _____ 20 _____ , fail to obey the same (by (wrongfully) _____ .)

(4) *Dereliction in the performance of duties.*

In that _____ , (personal jurisdiction data), who (knew) (should have known) of his/her duties (at/on board—location) (subject-matter jurisdiction data, if required), (on or about _____ 20 _____) (from about _____ 20 _____ to about _____ 20 _____), was derelict in the performance of those duties in that he/she (negligently) (willfully) (by culpable inefficiency) failed _____ , as it was his/her duty to do (, and that such dereliction of duty resulted in (grievous bodily harm, to wit: (broken leg) (deep cut) (fractured skull) to) (the death of) _____).

17. Article 93—Cruelty and maltreatment

a. *Text of statute.*

Any person subject to this chapter who is guilty of cruelty toward, or oppression or maltreatment of, any person subject to his orders shall be punished as a court-martial may direct.

b. *Elements.*

(1) That a certain person was subject to the orders of the accused; and

(2) That the accused was cruel toward, or oppressed, or maltreated that person.

c. *Explanation.*

(1) *Nature of victim.* "Any person subject to his orders" means not only those persons under the direct or immediate command of the accused but extends to all persons, subject to the code or not, who by reason of some duty are required to obey the lawful orders of the accused, regardless whether the accused is in the direct chain of command over the person.

(2) *Nature of act.* The cruelty, oppression, or maltreatment, although not necessarily physical, must be measured by an objective standard. Assault, improper punishment, and sexual harassment may constitute this offense. Sexual harassment includes influencing, offering to influence, or threatening the career, pay, or job of another person in exchange for sexual favors, and deliberate or repeated offensive comments or gestures of a sexual nature. The imposition of necessary or proper duties and the exaction of their performance does not constitute this offense

even though the duties are arduous or hazardous or both.

d. *Lesser included offenses.* See paragraph 3 of this part and Appendix 12A.

e. *Maximum punishment.* Dishonorable discharge, forfeiture of all pay and allowances, and confinement for 2 years.

f. *Sample specification.*

In that _____ (personal jurisdiction data), (at/on board—location) (subject-matter jurisdiction data, if required), on or about _____ 20 _____ , (was cruel toward) (did (oppress) (maltreat)) _____ , a person subject to his/her orders, by (kicking him/her in the stomach) (confining him/her for twenty-four hours without water) (_____).

18. Article 94—Mutiny and sedition

a. *Text of statute.*

Any person subject to this chapter who—

(1) with intent to usurp or override lawful military authority, refuse, in concert with any other person, to obey orders or otherwise do his duty or creates any violence or disturbance is guilty of mutiny;

(2) with intent to cause the overthrow or destruction of lawful civil authority, creates, in concert with any other person, revolt, violence, or other disturbance against that authority is guilty of sedition;

(3) fails to do his utmost to prevent and suppress a mutiny or sedition being committed in his presence, or fails to take all reasonable means to inform his superior commissioned officer or commanding officer of a mutiny or sedition which he knows or has reason to believe is taking place, is guilty of a failure to suppress or report a mutiny or sedition.

(b) A person who is found guilty of attempted mutiny, mutiny, sedition, or failure to suppress or report a mutiny or sedition shall be punished by death or such other punishment as a court-martial may direct.

b. *Elements.*

(1) *Mutiny by creating violence or disturbance.*

(a) That the accused created violence or a disturbance; and

(b) That the accused created this violence or

disturbance with intent to usurp or override lawful military authority.

(2) *Mutiny by refusing to obey orders or perform duty.*

(a) That the accused refused to obey orders or otherwise do the accused's duty;

(b) That the accused in refusing to obey orders or perform duty acted in concert with another person or persons; and

(c) That the accused did so with intent to usurp or override lawful military authority.

(3) *Sedition.*

(a) That the accused created revolt, violence, or disturbance against lawful civil authority;

(b) That the accused acted in concert with another person or persons; and

(c) That the accused did so with the intent to cause the overthrow or destruction of that authority.

(4) *Failure to prevent and suppress a mutiny or sedition.*

(a) That an offense of mutiny or sedition was committed in the presence of the accused; and

(b) That the accused failed to do the accused's utmost to prevent and suppress the mutiny or sedition.

(5) *Failure to report a mutiny or sedition.*

(a) That an offense of mutiny or sedition occurred;

(b) That the accused knew or had reason to believe that the offense was taking place; and

(c) That the accused failed to take all reasonable means to inform the accused's superior commissioned officer or commander of the offense.

(6) *Attempted mutiny.*

(a) That the accused committed a certain overt act;

(b) That the act was done with specific intent to commit the offense of mutiny;

(c) That the act amounted to more than mere preparation; and

(d) That the act apparently tended to effect the commission of the offense of mutiny.

c. *Explanation.*

(1) *Mutiny.* Article 94(*a*)(1) defines two types of mutiny, both requiring an intent to usurp or override military authority.

(a) *Mutiny by creating violence or disturbance.* Mutiny by creating violence or disturbance may be committed by one person acting alone or by more than one acting together.

(b) *Mutiny by refusing to obey orders or perform duties.* Mutiny by refusing to obey orders or perform duties requires collective insubordination and necessarily includes some combination of two or more persons in resisting lawful military authority. This concert of insubordination need not be preconceived, nor is it necessary that the insubordination be active or violent. It may consist simply of a persistent and concerted refusal or omission to obey orders, or to do duty, with an insubordinate intent, that is, with an intent to usurp or override lawful military authority. The intent may be declared in words or inferred from acts, omissions, or surrounding circumstances.

(2) *Sedition.* Sedition requires a concert of action in resistance to civil authority. This differs from mutiny by creating violence or disturbance. *See* subparagraph c(1)(*a*) above.

(3) *Failure to prevent and suppress a mutiny or sedition.* "Utmost" means taking those measures to prevent and suppress a mutiny or sedition which may properly be called for by the circumstances, including the rank, responsibilities, or employment of the person concerned. "Utmost" includes the use of such force, including deadly force, as may be reasonably necessary under the circumstances to prevent and suppress a mutiny or sedition.

(4) *Failure to report a mutiny or sedition.* Failure to "take all reasonable means to inform" includes failure to take the most expeditious means available. When the circumstances known to the accused would have caused a reasonable person in similar circumstances to believe that a mutiny or sedition was occurring, this may establish that the accused had such "reason to believe" that mutiny or sedition was occurring. Failure to report an impending mutiny or sedition is not an offense in violation of Article 94. *But see* paragraph 16c(3) (dereliction of duty).

(5) *Attempted mutiny.* For a discussion of attempts, see paragraph 4.

d. *Lesser included offenses.* See paragraph 3 of this part and Appendix 12A.

e. *Maximum punishment.* For all offenses under Article 94, death or such other punishment as a court-martial may direct.

f. *Sample specifications.*

(1) *Mutiny by creating violence or disturbance.*

In that _____ (personal jurisdiction data), with intent to (usurp) (override) (usurp and override) lawful military authority, did, (at/on board—location) (subject-matter jurisdiction data, if required), on or about _____ 20 ___, create (violence) (a disturbance) by (attacking the officers of the said ship) (barricading himself/herself in Barracks T7, firing his/her rifle at _____ , and exhorting other persons to join him/her in defiance of _____) (_____).

(2) *Mutiny by refusing to obey orders or perform duties.*

In that _____ (personal jurisdiction data), with intent to (usurp) (override) (usurp and override) lawful military authority, did, (at/on board— location) on or about _____ 20 ___, refuse, in concert with _____ (and _____) (others whose names are unknown), to (obey the orders of _____ to _____) (perform his/her duty as _____).

(3) *Sedition.*

In that _____ (personal jurisdiction data), with intent to cause the (overthrow) (destruction) (overthrow and destruction) of lawful civil authority, to wit: _____ , did, (at/on board—location) (subject-matter jurisdiction data, if required), on or about _____ 20 ___, in concert with (_____) and (_____) (others whose names are unknown), create (revolt) (violence) (a disturbance) against such authority by (entering the Town Hall of _____ and destroying property and records therein) (marching upon and compelling the surrender of the police of _____) (_____).

(4) *Failure to prevent and suppress a mutiny or sedition.*

In that _____ (personal jurisdiction data), did, (at/on board—location) (subject-matter jurisdiction data, if required), on or about _____ 20 ___, fail to do his/her utmost to prevent and suppress a (mutiny) (sedition) among the (soldiers) (sailors) (airmen) (marines) (_____) of _____ , which (mutiny) (sedition) was being committed in his/her presence, in that (he/she took no means to compel the dispersal of the assembly) (he/she made no effort to assist _____ who was attempting to quell the mutiny) (_____).

(5) *Failure to report a mutiny or sedition.*

In that _____ (personal jurisdiction data), did, (at/on board—location) (subject-matter jurisdiction data, if required), on or about _____ 20 ___, fail to take all reasonable means to inform his/her superior commissioned officer or his/her commander of a (mutiny) (sedition) among the (soldiers) (sailors) (airmen) (marines) (_____) of _____ , which (mutiny) (sedition) he/she, the said _____ (knew) (had reason to believe) was taking place.

(6) *Attempted mutiny.*

In that _____ (personal jurisdiction data), with intent to (usurp) (override) (usurp and override) lawful military authority, did, (at/on board— location) (subject-matter jurisdiction data, if required), on or about _____ 20 ___, attempt to (create (violence) (a disturbance) by _____) (_____).

19. Article 95—Resistance, flight, breach of arrest, and escape

a. *Text of statute.*

Any person subject to this chapter who—

(1) **resists apprehension;**

(2) **flees from apprehension;**

(3) **breaks arrest; or**

(4) **escapes from custody or confinement;**

shall be punished as a court-martial may direct.

b. *Elements.*

(1) *Resisting apprehension.*

(a) That a certain person attempted to apprehend the accused;

(b) That said person was authorized to apprehend the accused; and

(c) That the accused actively resisted the apprehension.

(2) *Flight from apprehension.*

(a) That a certain person attempted to apprehend the accused;

(b) That said person was authorized to apprehend the accused; and

(c) That the accused fled from the apprehension.

(3) *Breaking arrest.*

(a) That a certain person ordered the accused into arrest;

(b) That said person was authorized to order the accused into arrest; and

(c) That the accused went beyond the limits of arrest before being released from that arrest by proper authority.

(4) *Escape from custody.*

(a) That a certain person apprehended the accused;

(b) That said person was authorized to apprehend the accused; and

(c) That the accused freed himself or herself from custody before being released by proper authority.

(5) *Escape from confinement.*

(a) That a certain person ordered the accused into confinement;

(b) That said person was authorized to order the accused into confinement; and

(c) That the accused freed himself or herself from confinement before being released by proper authority.

[Note: If the escape was post-trial confinement, add the following element]

(d) That the confinement was the result of a court-martial conviction.

c. *Explanation.*

(1) *Resisting apprehension.*

(a) *Apprehension.* Apprehension is the taking of a person into custody. *See* R.C.M. 302.

(b) *Authority to apprehend. See* R.C.M. 302(*b*) concerning who may apprehend. Whether the status of a person authorized that person to apprehend the accused is a question of law to be decided by the military judge. Whether the person who attempted to make an apprehension had such a status is a question of fact to be decided by the factfinder.

(c) *Nature of the resistance.* The resistance must be active, such as assaulting the person attempting to apprehend. Mere words of opposition, argument, or abuse, and attempts to escape from custody after the apprehension is complete, do not constitute the offense of resisting apprehension although they may constitute other offenses.

(d) *Mistake.* It is a defense that the accused held a reasonable belief that the person attempting to apprehend did not have authority to do so. However, the accused's belief at the time that no basis exists for the apprehension is not a defense.

(e) *Illegal apprehension.* A person may not be convicted of resisting apprehension if the attempted apprehension is illegal, but may be convicted of other offenses, such as assault, depending on all the circumstances. An attempted apprehension by a person authorized to apprehend is presumed to be legal in the absence of evidence to the contrary. Ordinarily the legality of an apprehension is a question of law to be decided by the military judge.

(2) *Flight from apprehension.* The flight must be active, such as running or driving away.

(3) *Breaking arrest.*

(a) *Arrest.* There are two types of arrest: pretrial arrest under Article 9 (*see* R.C.M. 304) and arrest under Article 15 (*see* paragraph 5c(3), Part V, MCM). This article prohibits breaking any arrest.

(b) *Authority to order arrest. See* R.C.M. 304(b) and paragraphs 2 and 5b, Part V, MCM concerning authority to order arrest.

(c) *Nature of restraint imposed by arrest.* In arrest, the restraint is moral restraint imposed by orders fixing the limits of arrest.

(d) *Breaking.* Breaking arrest is committed when the person in arrest infringes the limits set by orders. The reason for the infringement is immaterial. For example, innocence of the offense with respect to which an arrest may have been imposed is not a defense.

(e) *Illegal arrest.* A person may not be convicted of breaking arrest if the arrest is illegal. An arrest ordered by one authorized to do so is presumed to be legal in the absence of some evidence to the contrary. Ordinarily, the legality of an arrest is a question of law to be decided by the military judge.

(4) *Escape from custody.*

(a) *Custody.* "Custody" is restraint of free locomotion imposed by lawful apprehension. The restraint may be physical or, once there has been a submission to apprehension or a forcible taking into custody, it may consist of control exercised in the presence of the prisoner by official acts or orders. Custody is temporary restraint intended to continue until other restraint (arrest, restriction, confinement) is imposed or the person is released.

(b) *Authority to apprehend. See* subparagraph (1)(*b*) above.

(c) *Escape.* For a discussion of escape, *see* subparagraph c(5)(*c*), below.

(d) *Illegal custody.* A person may not be convicted of this offense if the custody was illegal. An apprehension effected by one authorized to apprehend is presumed to be lawful in the absence of evidence to the contrary. Ordinarily, the legality of an apprehension is a question of law to be decided by the military judge.

(e) *Correctional custody. See* paragraph 70.

(5) *Escape from confinement.*

(a) *Confinement.* Confinement is physical restraint imposed under R.C.M. 305, 1101, or paragraph 5b, Part V, MCM. For purposes of the element of post-trial confinement (subparagraph b(5)(d), above) and increased punishment therefrom (subparagraph e(4), below), the confinement must have been imposed pursuant to an adjudged sentence of a court-martial and not as a result of pretrial restraint or nonjudicial punishment.

(b) *Authority to order confinement. See* R.C.M. 304(b); 1101; and paragraphs 2 and 5b, Part V, MCM concerning who may order confinement.

(c) *Escape.* An escape may be either with or without force or artifice, and either with or without the consent of the custodian. However, where a prisoner is released by one with apparent authority to do so, the prisoner may not be convicted of escape from confinement. *See also* paragraph 20c(1)(b). Any completed casting off of the restraint of confinement, before release by proper authority, is an escape, and lack of effectiveness of the restraint imposed is immaterial. An escape is not complete until the prisoner is momentarily free from the restraint. If the movement toward escape is opposed, or before it is completed, an immediate pursuit follows, there is no escape until opposition is overcome or pursuit is eluded.

(d) *Status when temporarily outside confinement facility.* A prisoner who is temporarily escorted outside a confinement facility for a work detail or other reason by a guard, who has both the duty and means to prevent that prisoner from escaping, remains in confinement.

(e) *Legality of confinement.* A person may not be convicted of escape from confinement if the confinement is illegal. Confinement ordered by one authorized to do so is presumed to be lawful in the absence of evidence to the contrary. Ordinarily, the legality of confinement is a question of law to be decided by the military judge.

d. *Lesser included offenses.* See paragraph 3 of this part and Appendix 12A.

e. *Maximum punishment.*

(1) *Resisting apprehension.* Bad-conduct discharge, forfeiture of all pay and allowances, and confinement for 1 year.

(2) *Flight from apprehension.* Bad-conduct discharge, forfeiture of all pay and allowances, and confinement for 1 year.

(3) *Breaking arrest.* Bad-conduct discharge, forfeiture of all pay and allowances, and confinement for 6 months.

(4) *Escape from custody, pretrial confinement, or confinement on bread and water or diminished rations imposed pursuant to Article 15.* Dishonorable discharge, forfeiture of all pay and allowances, and confinement for 1 year.

(5) *Escape from post-trial confinement.* Dishonorable discharge, forfeiture of all pay and allowances, and confinement for 5 years.

f. *Sample specifications.*

(1) *Resisting apprehension.*

In that _____ (personal jurisdiction data), did, (at/on board—location) (subject-matter jurisdiction data, if required), on or about _____ 20 ___ , resist being apprehended by _____ , (an armed force policeman) (_____), a person authorized to apprehend the accused.

(2) *Flight from apprehension.*

In that _____ (personal jurisdiction data), did, (at/on board—location) (subject-matter jurisdiction data, if required), on or about _____ 20 ___ , flee apprehension by _____ , (an armed force policeman) (_____), a person authorized to apprehend the accused.

(3) *Breaking arrest.*

In that _____ (personal jurisdiction data), having been placed in arrest (in quarters) (in his/her company area) (_____) by a person authorized to order the accused into arrest, did, (at/on board—location) on or about _____ 20 ___ , break said arrest.

(4) *Escape from custody.*

In that _____ (personal jurisdiction data), did, (at/on board—location) (subject-matter jurisdiction data, if required), on or about _____ 20 ___ , escape from the custody of _____ , a person authorized to apprehend the accused.

(5) *Escape from confinement.*

In that _____ (personal jurisdiction data), having been placed in (post-trial) confinement in (place of confinement), by a person authorized to order said accused into confinement did, (at/on board—location) (subject-matter jurisdiction data, if required), on or about _____ 20 ___ , escape from confinement.

20. Article 96—Releasing prisoner without proper authority

a. *Text of statute.*

Any person subject to this chapter who, without proper authority, releases any prisoner committed to his charge, or who through neglect or design suffers any such prisoner to escape, shall be punished as a court-martial may direct, whether or not the prisoner was committed in strict compliance with law.

b. *Elements.*

(1) *Releasing a prisoner without proper authority.*

(a) That a certain prisoner was committed to the charge of the accused; and

(b) That the accused released the prisoner without proper authority.

(2) *Suffering a prisoner to escape through neglect.*

(a) That a certain prisoner was committed to the charge of the accused;

(b) That the prisoner escaped;

(c) That the accused did not take such care to prevent the escape as a reasonably careful person, acting in the capacity in which the accused was acting, would have taken in the same or similar circumstances; and

(d) That the escape was the proximate result of the neglect.

(3) *Suffering a prisoner to escape through design.*

(a) That a certain prisoner was committed to the charge of the accused;

(b) That the design of the accused was to suffer the escape of that prisoner; and

(c) That the prisoner escaped as a result of the carrying out of the design of the accused.

c. *Explanation.*

(1) *Releasing a prisoner without proper authority.*

(a) *Prisoner.* "Prisoner" includes a civilian or military person who has been confined.

(b) *Release.* The release of a prisoner is removal of restraint by the custodian rather than by the prisoner.

(c) *Authority to release.* See R.C.M. 305(*g*) as to who may release pretrial prisoners. Normally, the lowest authority competent to order release of a post-trial prisoner is the commander who convened the court-martial which sentenced the prisoner or the officer exercising general court-martial jurisdiction over the prisoner. *See also* R.C.M. 1101.

(d) *Committed.* Once a prisoner has been confined, the prisoner has been "committed" in the sense of Article 96, and only a competent authority (*see* subparagraph (c)) may order release, regardless of failure to follow procedures prescribed by the code, this Manual, or other law.

(2) *Suffering a prisoner to escape through neglect.*

(a) *Suffer.* "Suffer" means to allow or permit; not to forbid or hinder.

(b) *Neglect.* "Neglect" is a relative term. It is the absence of conduct which would have been taken by a reasonably careful person in the same or similar circumstances.

(c) *Escape.* Escape is defined in paragraph 19.c.(4)(c).

(d) *Status of prisoner after escape not a defense.* After escape, the fact that a prisoner returns, is captured, killed, or otherwise dies is not a defense.

(3) *Suffering a prisoner to escape through design.* An escape is suffered through design when it is intended. Such intent may be inferred from conduct so wantonly devoid of care that the only reasonable inference which may be drawn is that the escape was contemplated as a probable result.

d. *Lesser included offenses.* See paragraph 3 of this part and Appendix 12A.

e. *Maximum punishment.*

(1) *Releasing a prisoner without proper authority.* Dishonorable discharge, forfeiture of all pay and allowances, and confinement for 2 years.

(2) *Suffering a prisoner to escape through neglect.* Bad-conduct discharge, forfeiture of all pay and allowances, and confinement for 1 year.

(3) *Suffering a prisoner to escape through design.*

Dishonorable discharge, forfeiture of all pay and allowances, and confinement for 2 years.

f. *Sample specifications.*

(1) *Releasing a prisoner without proper authority.*

In that _____ (personal jurisdiction data), did, (at/on board—location), on or about _____ 20 ___ , without proper authority, release _____ , a prisoner committed to his/her charge.

(2) *Suffering a prisoner to escape through neglect or design.*

In that _____ (personal jurisdiction data), did, (at/on board—location), on or about _____ 20 ___ , through (neglect) (design), suffer _____ , a prisoner committed to his/her charge, to escape.

21. Article 97—Unlawful detention

a. *Text of statute.*

Any person subject to this chapter who, except as provided by law, apprehends, arrests, or confines any person shall be punished as a court-martial may direct.

b. *Elements.*

(1) That the accused apprehended, arrested, or confined a certain person; and

(2) That the accused unlawfully exercised the accused's authority to do so.

c. *Explanation.*

(1) *Scope.* This article prohibits improper acts by those empowered by the code to arrest, apprehend, or confine. *See* Articles 7 and 9; R.C.M. 302, 304, 305, and 1101, and paragraphs 2 and 5b, Part V. It does not apply to private acts of false imprisonment or unlawful restraint of another's freedom of movement by one not acting under such a delegation of authority under the code.

(2) *No force required.* The apprehension, arrest, or confinement must be against the will of the person restrained, but force is not required.

(3) *Defense.* A reasonable belief held by the person imposing restraint that it is lawful is a defense.

d. *Lesser included offenses.* See paragraph 3 of this part and Appendix 12A.

e. *Maximum punishment.* Dishonorable discharge, forfeiture of all pay and allowances, and confinement for 3 years.

f. *Sample specification.*

In that _____ (personal jurisdiction data), did, (at/on board—location), on or about _____ 20 ___ , unlawfully (apprehend _____) (place _____ in arrest) (confine _____ in _____).

22. Article 98—Noncompliance with procedural rules

a. *Text of statute.*

Any person subject to this chapter who—

(1) is responsible for unnecessary delay in the disposition of any case of a person accused of an offense under this chapter; or

(2) Knowingly and intentionally fails to enforce or comply with any provision of this chapter regulating the proceedings before, during, or after trial of an accused; shall be punished as a court-martial may direct.

b. *Elements.*

(1) *Unnecessary delay in disposing of case.*

(a) That the accused was charged with a certain duty in connection with the disposition of a case of a person accused of an offense under the code;

(b) That the accused knew that the accused was charged with this duty;

(c) That delay occurred in the disposition of the case;

(d) That the accused was responsible for the delay; and

(e) That, under the circumstances, the delay was unnecessary.

(2) *Knowingly and intentionally failing to enforce or comply with provisions of the code.*

(a) That the accused failed to enforce or comply with a certain provision of the code regulating a proceeding before, during, or after a trial;

(b) That the accused had the duty of enforcing or complying with that provision of the code;

(c) That the accused knew that the accused was charged with this duty; and

(d) That the accused's failure to enforce or comply with that provision was intentional.

c. *Explanation.*

(1) *Unnecessary delay in disposing of case.* The purpose of section (1) of Article 98 is to ensure expeditious disposition of cases of persons accused of offenses under the code. A person may be respon-

sible for delay in the disposition of a case only when that person's duties require action with respect to the disposition of that case.

(2) *Knowingly and intentionally failing to enforce or comply with provisions of the code.* Section (2) of Article 98 does not apply to errors made in good faith before, during, or after trial. It is designed to punish intentional failure to enforce or comply with the provisions of the code regulating the proceedings before, during, and after trial. Unlawful command influence under Article 37 may be prosecuted under this Article. *See also* Article 31 and R.C.M. 104.

d. *Lesser included offenses.* See paragraph 3 of this part and Appendix 12A.

e. *Maximum punishment.*

(1) *Unnecessary delay in disposing of case.* Bad-conduct discharge, forfeiture of all pay and allowances, and confinement for 6 months.

(2) *Knowingly and intentionally failing to enforce or comply with provisions of the code.* Dishonorable discharge, forfeiture of all pay and allowances, and confinement for 5 years.

f. *Sample specifications.*

(1) *Unnecessary delay in disposing of case.*

In that _____ (personal jurisdiction data), being charged with the duty of ((investigating) (taking immediate steps to determine the proper disposition of) charges preferred against _____ , a person accused of an offense under the Uniform Code of Military Justice) (_____), was, (at/on board—location), on or about _____ 20 ___ , responsible for unnecessary delay in (investigating said charges) (determining the proper disposition of said charges (_____), in that he/she (did _____) (failed to _____) (_____).

(2) *Knowingly and intentionally failing to enforce or comply with provisions of the code.*

In that _____ (personal jurisdiction data), being charged with the duty of _____ , did, (at/on board—location), on or about _____ 20 ___ , knowingly and intentionally fail to (enforce) (comply with) Article _____ , Uniform Code of Military Justice, in that he/she _____ .

23. Article 99—Misbehavior before the enemy

a. *Text of statute.*

Any member of the armed forces who before or in the presence of the enemy—

(1) runs away;

(2) shamefully abandons, surrenders, or delivers up any command, unit, place, or military property which it is his duty to defend;

(3) through disobedience, neglect, or intentional misconduct endangers the safety of any such command, unit, place, or military property;

(4) casts away his arms or ammunition;

(5) is guilty of cowardly conduct;

(6) quits his place of duty to plunder or pillage;

(7) causes false alarms in any command, unit, or place under control of the armed forces;

(8) willfully fails to do his utmost to encounter, engage, capture, or destroy any enemy troops, combatants, vessels, aircraft, or any other thing, which it is his duty so to encounter, engage, capture, or destroy; or

(9) does not afford all practicable relief and assistance to any troops, combatants, vessels, or aircraft of the armed forces belonging to the United States or their allies when engaged in battle; shall be punished by death or such other punishment as a court-martial may direct.

b. *Elements.*

(1) *Running away.*

(a) That the accused was before or in the presence of the enemy;

(b) That the accused misbehaved by running away; and

(c) That the accused intended to avoid actual or impending combat with the enemy by running away.

(2) *Shamefully abandoning, surrendering, or delivering up command.*

(a) That the accused was charged by orders or circumstances with the duty to defend a certain command, unit, place, ship, or military property;

(b) That, without justification, the accused shamefully abandoned, surrendered, or delivered up that command, unit, place, ship, or military property; and

(c) That this act occurred while the accused was before or in the presence of the enemy.

(3) *Endangering safety of a command, unit, place, ship, or military property.*

(a) That it was the duty of the accused to defend a certain command, unit, place, ship, or certain military property;

(b) That the accused committed certain disobedience, neglect, or intentional misconduct;

(c) That the accused thereby endangered the safety of the command, unit, place, ship, or military property; and

(d) That this act occurred while the accused was before or in the presence of the enemy.

(4) *Casting away arms or ammunition.*

(a) That the accused was before or in the presence of the enemy; and

(b) That the accused cast away certain arms or ammunition.

(5) *Cowardly conduct.*

(a) That the accused committed an act of cowardice;

(b) That this conduct occurred while the accused was before or in the presence of the enemy; and

(c) That this conduct was the result of fear.

(6) *Quitting place of duty to plunder or pillage.*

(a) That the accused was before or in the presence of the enemy;

(b) That the accused quit the accused's place of duty; and

(c) That the accused's intention in quitting was to plunder or pillage public or private property.

(7) *Causing false alarms.*

(a) That an alarm was caused in a certain command, unit, or place under control of the armed forces of the United States;

(b) That the accused caused the alarm;

(c) That the alarm was caused without any reasonable or sufficient justification or excuse; and

(d) That this act occurred while the accused was before or in the presence of the enemy.

(8) *Willfully failing to do utmost to encounter enemy.*

(a) That the accused was serving before or in the presence of the enemy;

(b) That the accused had a duty to encounter, engage, capture, or destroy certain enemy troops, combatants, vessels, aircraft, or a certain other thing; and

(c) That the accused willfully failed to do the utmost to perform that duty.

(9) *Failing to afford relief and assistance.*

(a) That certain troops, combatants, vessels, or aircraft of the armed forces belonging to the United States or an ally of the United States were engaged in battle and required relief and assistance;

(b) That the accused was in a position and able to render relief and assistance to these troops, combatants, vessels, or aircraft, without jeopardy to the accused's mission;

(c) That the accused failed to afford all practicable relief and assistance; and

(d) That, at the time, the accused was before or in the presence of the enemy.

c. *Explanation.*

(1) *Running away.*

(a) *Running away.* "Running away" means an unauthorized departure to avoid actual or impending combat. It need not, however, be the result of fear, and there is no requirement that the accused literally run.

(b) *Enemy.* "Enemy" includes organized forces of the enemy in time of war, any hostile body that our forces may be opposing, such as a rebellious mob or a band of renegades, and includes civilians as well as members of military organizations. "Enemy" is not restricted to the enemy government or its armed forces. All the citizens of one belligerent are enemies of the government and all the citizens of the other.

(c) *Before the enemy.* Whether a person is "before the enemy" is a question of tactical relation, not distance. For example, a member of an antiaircraft gun crew charged with opposing anticipated attack from the air, or a member of a unit about to move into combat may be before the enemy although miles from the enemy lines. On the other hand, an organization some distance from the front or immediate area of combat which is not a part of a tactical operation then going on or in immediate prospect is not "before or in the presence of the enemy" within the meaning of this article.

(2) *Shamefully abandoning, surrendering, or delivering up of command.*

(a) *Scope.* This provision concerns primarily commanders chargeable with responsibility for defending a command, unit, place, ship or military property. Abandonment by a subordinate would ordinarily be charged as running away.

(b) *Shameful.* Surrender or abandonment without justification is shameful within the meaning of this article.

(c) *Surrender; deliver up.* "Surrender" and "deliver up" are synonymous for the purposes of this article.

(d) *Justification.* Surrender or abandonment of a command, unit, place, ship, or military property by a person charged with its can be justified only by the utmost necessity or extremity.

(3) *Endangering safety of a command, unit, place, ship, or military property.*

(a) *Neglect.* "Neglect" is the absence of conduct which would have been taken by a reasonably careful person in the same or similar circumstances.

(b) *Intentional misconduct.* "Intentional misconduct" does not include a mere error in judgment.

(4) *Casting away arms or ammunition.* Self-explanatory.

(5) *Cowardly conduct.*

(a) *Cowardice.* "Cowardice" is misbehavior motivated by fear.

(b) *Fear.* Fear is a natural feeling of apprehension when going into battle. The mere display of apprehension does not constitute this offense.

(c) *Nature of offense.* Refusal or abandonment of a performance of duty before or in the presence of the enemy as a result of fear constitutes this offense.

(d) *Defense.* Genuine and extreme illness, not generated by cowardice, is a defense.

(6) *Quitting place of duty to plunder or pillage.*

(a) *Place of duty.* "Place of duty" includes any place of duty, whether permanent or temporary, fixed or mobile.

(b) *Plunder or pillage.* "Plunder or pillage" means to seize or appropriate public or private property unlawfully.

(c) *Nature of offense.* The essence of this offense is quitting the place of duty with intent to

plunder or pillage. Merely quitting with that purpose is sufficient, even if the intended misconduct is not done.

(7) *Causing false alarms.* This provision covers spreading of false or disturbing rumors or reports, as well as the false giving of established alarm signals.

(8) *Willfully failing to do utmost to encounter enemy.* Willfully refusing a lawful order to go on a combat patrol may violate this provision.

(9) *Failing to afford relief and assistance.*

(a) *All practicable relief and assistance.* "All practicable relief and assistance" means all relief and assistance which should be afforded within the limitations imposed upon a person by reason of that person's own specific tasks or mission.

(b) *Nature of offense.* This offense is limited to a failure to afford relief and assistance to forces "engaged in battle."

d. *Lesser included offenses.* See paragraph 3 of this part and Appendix 12A.

e. *Maximum punishment.* All offenses under Article 99. Death or such other punishment as a court-martial may direct.

f. *Sample specifications.*

(1) *Running away.*

In that _____ (personal jurisdiction data), did, (at/on board—location), on or about ____ 20 __ , (before) (in the presence of) the enemy, run away (from his/her company) (and hide) (____), (and did not return until after the engagement had been concluded) (_____).

(2) *Shamefully abandoning, surrendering, or delivering up command.*

In that _____ (personal jurisdiction data), did, (at/on board—location), on or about ____ 20 __ , (before) (in the presence of) the enemy, shamefully (abandon) (surrender) (deliver up) _____ , which it was his/her duty to defend.

(3) *Endangering safety of a command, unit, place, ship, or military property.*

In that _____ (personal jurisdiction data), did, (at/on board—location), on or about ____ 20 __ , (before) (in the presence of) the enemy, endanger the safety of _____ , which it was his/her duty to defend, by (disobeying an order from _____ to engage the enemy)(neglecting his/her duty as a sentinel by engaging in a card game while on his/her post) (intentional misconduct in that he/she became drunk and fired flares, thus revealing the location of his/her unit) (_____).

(4) *Casting away arms or ammunition.*

In that _____ (personal jurisdiction data), did, (at/on board—location), on or about _____ 20 __ , (before) (in the presence of) the enemy, cast away his/her (rifle) (ammunition) (_____).

(5) *Cowardly conduct.*

In that _____ (personal jurisdiction data), (at/on board—location), on or about _____ 20 __ , (before) (in the presence of) the enemy, was guilty of cowardly conduct as a result of fear, in that _____ .

(6) *Quitting place of duty to plunder or pillage.*

In that _____ (personal jurisdiction data), did, (at/on board— location), on or about _____ 20 __ , (before) (in the presence of) the enemy, quit his/her place of duty for the purpose of (plundering) (pillaging) (plundering and pillaging).

(7) *Causing false alarms.*

In that _____ (personal jurisdiction data), did, (at/on board—location), on or about _____ 20 __ , (before) (in the presence of) the enemy, cause a false alarm in (Fort _____) (the said ship) (the camp) (_____) by (needlessly and without authority (causing the call to arms to be sounded) (sounding the general alarm)) (_____).

(8) *Willfully failing to do utmost to encounter enemy.*

In that _____ (personal jurisdiction data), being (before) (in the presence of) the enemy, did, (at/on board—location), on or about _____ 20 __ , by, (ordering his/her troops to halt their advance) (_____), willfully fail to do his/her utmost to (encounter) (engage) (capture) (destroy), as it was his/her duty to do, (certain enemy troops which were in retreat) (_____).

(9) *Failing to afford relief and assistance.*

In that _____ (personal jurisdiction data), did, (at/on board—location), on or about _____ 20 __ , (before) (in the presence of) the enemy, fail to afford all practicable relief and assistance to (the USS _____ , which was engaged in battle and had run aground, in that he/she failed to take her in tow) (certain troops of the ground forces of _____ , which were engaged in battle and were pinned down by enemy fire, in that he/she

failed to furnish air cover) (_____) as he/she properly should have done.

24. Article 100—Subordinate compelling surrender

a. *Text of statute.*

Any person subject to this chapter who compels or attempts to compel the commander of any place, vessel, aircraft, or other military property, or of any body of members of the armed forces, to give it up to an enemy or to abandon it, or who strikes the colors or flag to an enemy without proper authority, shall be punished by death or such other punishment as a court-martial may direct.

b. *Elements.*

(1) *Compelling surrender.*

(a) That a certain person was in command of a certain place, vessel, aircraft, or other military property or of a body of members of the armed forces;

(b) That the accused did an overt act which was intended to and did compel that commander to give it up to the enemy or abandon it; and

(c) That the place, vessel, aircraft, or other military property or body of members of the armed forces was actually given up to the enemy or abandoned.

(2) *Attempting to compel surrender.*

(a) That a certain person was in command of a certain place, vessel, aircraft, or other military property or of a body of members of the armed forces;

(b) That the accused did a certain overt act;

(c) That the act was done with the intent to compel that commander to give up to the enemy or abandon the place, vessel, aircraft, or other military property or body of members of the armed forces;

(d) That the act amounted to more than mere preparation; and

(e) That the act apparently tended to bring about the compelling of surrender or abandonment.

(3) *Striking the colors or flag.*

(a) That there was an offer of surrender to an enemy;

(b) That this offer was made by striking the colors or flag to the enemy or in some other manner;

(c) That the accused made or was responsible for the offer; and

(d) That the accused did not have proper authority to make the offer.

c. *Explanation.*

(1) *Compelling surrender.*

(a) *Nature of offense.* The offenses under this article are similar to mutiny or attempted mutiny designed to bring about surrender or abandonment. Unlike some cases of mutiny, however, concert of action is not an essential element of the offenses under this article. The offense is not complete until the place, military property, or command is actually abandoned or given up to the enemy.

(b) *Surrender.* "Surrender" and "to give it up to an enemy" are synonymous.

(c) *Acts required.* The surrender or abandonment must be compelled or attempted to be compelled by acts rather than words.

(2) *Attempting to compel surrender.* The offense of attempting to compel a surrender or abandonment does not require actual abandonment or surrender, but there must be some act done with this purpose in view, even if it does not accomplish the purpose.

(3) *Striking the colors or flag.*

(a) *In general.* To "strike the colors or flag" is to haul down the colors or flag in the face of the enemy or to make any other offer of surrender. It is traditional wording for an act of surrender.

(b) *Nature of offense.* The offense is committed when one assumes the authority to surrender a military force or position when not authorized to do so either by competent authority or by the necessities of battle. If continued battle has become fruitless and it is impossible to communicate with higher authority, those facts will constitute proper authority to surrender. The offense may be committed whenever there is sufficient contact with the enemy to give the opportunity of making an offer of surrender and it is not necessary that an engagement with the enemy be in progress. It is unnecessary to prove that the offer was received by the enemy or that it was rejected or accepted. The sending of an emissary charged with making the offer or surrender is an act sufficient to prove the offer, even though the emissary does not reach the enemy.

(4) *Enemy.* For a discussion of "enemy," *see* paragraph 23c(1)(*b*).

d. *Lesser included offenses.* See paragraph 3 of this part and Appendix 12A.

e. *Maximum punishment.* All offenses under Article 100. Death or such other punishment as a court-martial may direct.

f. *Sample specifications.*

(1) *Compelling surrender or attempting to compel surrender.*

In that _____ (personal jurisdiction data), did, (at/on board—location), on or about _____ 20 __ , (attempt to) compel _____ , the commander of _____ , (to give up to the enemy) (to abandon) said _____ , by _____ .

(2) *Striking the colors or flag.*

In that _____ (personal jurisdiction data), did, (at/on board—location), on or about _____ 20 __ , without proper authority, offer to surrender to the enemy by (striking the (colors) (flag)) (_____).

25. Article 101—Improper use of countersign

a. *Text of statute.*

Any person subject to this chapter who in time of war discloses the parole or countersign to any person not entitled to receive it or who gives to another who is entitled to receive and use the parole or countersign a different parole or countersign from that which, to his knowledge, he was authorized and required to give, shall be punished by death or such other punishment as a court-martial may direct.

b. *Elements.*

(1) *Disclosing the parole or countersign to one not entitled to receive it.*

(a) That, in time of war, the accused disclosed the parole or countersign to a person, identified or unidentified; and

(b) That this person was not entitled to receive it.

(2) *Giving a parole or countersign different from that authorized.*

(a) That, in time of war, the accused knew that the accused was authorized and required to give a certain parole or countersign; and

(b) That the accused gave to a person entitled to receive and use this parole or countersign a different parole or countersign from that which the accused was authorized and required to give.

c. *Explanation.*

(1) *Countersign.* A countersign is a word, signal,

or procedure given from the principal headquarters of a command to aid guards and sentinels in their scrutiny of persons who apply to pass the lines. It consists of a secret challenge and a password, signal, or procedure.

(2) *Parole.* A parole is a word used as a check on the countersign; it is given only to those who are entitled to inspect guards and to commanders of guards.

(3) *Who may receive countersign.* The class of persons entitled to receive the countersign or parole will expand and contract under the varying circumstances of war. Who these persons are will be determined largely, in any particular case, by the general or special orders under which the accused was acting. Before disclosing such a word, a person subject to military law must determine at that person's peril that the recipient is a person authorized to receive it.

(4) *Intent, motive, negligence, mistake, ignorance not defense.* The accused's intent or motive in disclosing the countersign or parole is immaterial to the issue of guilt, as is the fact that the disclosure was negligent or inadvertent. It is no defense that the accused did not know that the person to whom the countersign or parole was given was not entitled to receive it.

(5) *How accused received countersign or parole.* It is immaterial whether the accused had received the countersign or parole in the regular course of duty or whether it was obtained in some other way.

(6) *In time of war.* See R.C.M. 103(19).

d. *Lesser included offenses.* See paragraph 3 of this part and Appendix 12A.

e. *Maximum punishment.* Death or such other punishment as a court-martial may direct.

f. *Sample specifications.*

(1) *Disclosing the parole or countersign to one not entitled to receive it.*

In that _____ (personal jurisdiction data), did, (at/on board—location), on or about _____ 20 __, a time of war, disclose the (parole) (countersign), to wit: _____ , to _____ , a person who was not entitled to receive it.

(2) *Giving a parole or countersign different from that authorized.*

In that _____ (personal jurisdiction data), did, (at/on board—location), on or about _____ 20 __, a time of war, give to _____ , a person entitled to receive and use the (parole) (coun-

tersign), a (parole) (countersign), namely: _____ which was different from that which, to his/her knowledge, he/she was authorized and required to give, to wit: _____ .

26. Article 102—Forcing a safeguard

a. *Text of statute.*

Any person subject to this chapter who forces a safeguard shall suffer death or such other punishment as a court-martial may direct.

b. *Elements.*

(1) that a safeguard had been issued or posted for the protection of a certain person or persons, place, or property;

(2) That the accused knew or should have known of the safeguard; and

(3) That the accused forced the safeguard.

c. *Explanation.*

(1) *Safeguard.* A safeguard is a detachment, guard, or detail posted by a commander for the protection of persons, places, or property of the enemy, or of a neutral affected by the relationship of belligerent forces in their prosecution of war or during circumstances amounting to a state of belligerency. The term also includes a written order left by a commander with an enemy subject or posted upon enemy property for the protection of that person or property. A safeguard is not a device adopted by a belligerent to protect its own property or nationals or to ensure order within its own forces, even if those forces are in a theater of combat operations, and the posting of guards or of off-limits signs does not establish a safeguard unless a commander takes those actions to protect enemy or neutral persons or property. The effect of a safeguard is to pledge the honor of the nation that the person or property shall be respected by the national armed forces.

(2) *Forcing a safeguard.* "Forcing a safeguard" means to perform an act or acts in violation of the protection of the safeguard.

(3) *Nature of offense.* Any trespass on the protection of the safeguard will constitute an offense under this article, whether the safeguard was imposed in time of war or in circumstances amounting to a state of belligerency short of a formal state of war.

(4) *Knowledge.* Actual knowledge of the safeguard is not required. It is sufficient if an accused should have known of the existence of the safeguard.

d. *Lesser included offenses.* See paragraph 3 of this part and Appendix 12A.

e. *Maximum punishment.* Death or such other punishment as a court-martial may direct.

f. *Sample specification.* In that _____ (personal jurisdiction data), did, (at/on board—location), on or about _____ 20 ___ , force a safeguard, (known by him/her to have been placed over the premises occupied by _____ at _____ by (overwhelming the guard posted for the protection of the same) (_____)) (_____).

27. Article 103—Captured or abandoned property

a. *Text of statute.*

(a) **All persons subject to this chapter shall secure all public property taken from the enemy for the service of the United States, and shall give notice and turn over to the proper authority without delay all captured or abandoned property in their possession, custody, or control.**

(b) **Any person subject to this chapter who—**

(1) **fails to carry out the duties prescribed in subsection (*a*);**

(2) **buys, sells, trades, or in any way deals in or disposes of captured or abandoned property, whereby he receives or expects any profit, benefit, or advantage to himself or another directly or indirectly connected with himself; or**

(3) **engages in looting or pillaging;**
shall be punished as a court-martial may direct.

b. *Elements.*

(1) *Failing to secure public property taken from the enemy.*

(a) That certain public property was taken from the enemy;

(b) That this property was of a certain value; and

(c) That the accused failed to do what was reasonable under the circumstances to secure this property for the service of the United States.

(2) *Failing to report and turn over captured or abandoned property.*

(a) That certain captured or abandoned public or private property came into the possession, custody, or control of the accused;

(b) That this property was of a certain value; and

(c) That the accused failed to give notice of its receipt and failed to turn over to proper authority, without delay, the captured or abandoned public or private property.

(3) *Dealing in captured or abandoned property.*

(a) That the accused bought, sold, traded, or otherwise dealt in or disposed of certain public or private captured or abandoned property;

(b) That this property was of certain value; and

(c) That by so doing the accused received or expected some profit, benefit, or advantage to the accused or to a certain person or persons connected directly or indirectly with the accused.

(4) *Looting or pillaging.*

(a) That the accused engaged in looting, pillaging, or looting and pillaging by unlawfully seizing or appropriating certain public or private property;

(b) That this property was located in enemy or occupied territory, or that it was on board a seized or captured vessel; and

(c) That this property was:

(i) left behind, owned by, or in the custody of the enemy, an occupied state, an inhabitant of an occupied state, or a person under the protection of the enemy or occupied state, or who, immediately prior to the occupation of the place where the act occurred, was under the protection of the enemy or occupied state; or

(ii) part of the equipment of a seized or captured vessel; or

(iii) owned by, or in the custody of the officers, crew, or passengers on board a seized or captured vessel.

c. *Explanation.*

(1) *Failing to secure public property taken from the enemy.*

(a) *Nature of property.* Unlike the remaining offenses under this article, failing to secure public property taken from the enemy involves only public property. Immediately upon its capture from the enemy public property becomes the property of the United States. Neither the person who takes it nor any other person has any private right in this property.

(b) *Nature of duty.* Every person subject to military law has an immediate duty to take such steps as are reasonably within that person's power to secure public property for the service of the United States and to protect it from destruction or loss.

(2) *Failing to report and turn over captured or abandoned property.*

(a) *Reports.* Reports of receipt of captured or abandoned property are to be made directly or through such channels as are required by current regulations, orders, or the customs of the service.

(b) *Proper authority.* "Proper authority" is any authority competent to order disposition of the property in question.

(3) *Dealing in captured or abandoned property.* "Disposed of" includes destruction or abandonment.

(4) *Looting or pillaging.* "Looting or pillaging" means unlawfully seizing or appropriating property which is located in enemy or occupied territory.

(5) *Enemy.* For a discussion of "enemy," see paragraph 23c(1)(b).

d. *Lesser included offenses.* See paragraph 3 of this part and Appendix 12A.

e. *Maximum punishment.*

(1) *Failing to secure public property taken from the enemy; failing to secure, give notice and turn over, selling, or otherwise wrongfully dealing in or disposing of captured or abandoned property:*

(a) of a value of $500.00 or less. Bad-conduct discharge, forfeiture of all pay and allowances, and confinement for 6 months.

(b) of a value of more than $500.00 or any firearm or explosive. Dishonorable discharge, forfeiture of all pay and allowances, and confinement for 5 years.

(2) *Looting or pillaging.* Any punishment, other than death, that a court-martial may direct. *See* R.C.M. 1003.

f. *Sample specifications.*

(1) *Failing to secure public property taken from the enemy.*

In that _____ (personal jurisdiction data), did, (at/on board—location), on or about _____ 20 ___, fail to secure for the service of the United States certain public property taken from the enemy, to wit: ___, of a value of (about) $ ___ .

(2) *Failing to report and turn over captured or abandoned property.*

In that _____ (personal jurisdiction data), did, (at/on board—location), on or about

_____ 20 ___, fail to give notice and turn over to proper authority without delay certain (captured) (abandoned) property which had come into his/her (possession) (custody) (control), to wit: _____ , of a value of (about), $ _____ .

(3) *Dealing in captured or abandoned property.*

In that _____ (personal jurisdiction data), did, (at/on board—location), on or about _____ 20 ___, (buy) (sell) (trade) (deal in) (dispose of) (___) certain (captured) (abandoned) property, to wit: _____ , (a firearm) (an explosive), of a value of (about) $ _____ , thereby (receiving) (expecting) a (profit) (benefit) (advantage) to (himself/herself) (_____ , his/her accomplice) (_____ , his/her brother) (_____).

(4) *Looting or pillaging.*

In that (personal jurisdiction data), did, (at/on-board—location), on or about (date), engage in (looting) (and) (pillaging) by unlawfully (seizing) (appropriating) _____ , (property which had been left behind) (the property of _____), ((an inhabitant of _____) (_____)).

28. Article 104—Aiding the enemy

a. *Text of statute.*

Any person who—

(1) aids, or attempts to aid, the enemy with arms, ammunition, supplies, money, or other things; or

(2) without proper authority, knowingly harbors or protects or gives intelligence to or communicates or corresponds with or holds any intercourse with the enemy, either directly or indirectly; shall suffer death or such other punishment as a court-martial or military commission may direct.

b. *Elements.*

(1) *Aiding the enemy.*

(a) That the accused aided the enemy; and

(b) That the accused did so with certain arms, ammunition, supplies, money, or other things.

(2) *Attempting to aid the enemy.*

(a) That the accused did a certain overt act;

(b) That the act was done with the intent to aid the enemy with certain arms, ammunition, supplies, money, or other things;

(c) That the act amounted to more than mere preparation; and

(d) That the act apparently tended to bring about the offense of aiding the enemy with certain arms, ammunition, supplies, money, or other things.

(3) *Harboring or protecting the enemy.*

(a) That the accused, without proper authority, harbored or protected a person;

(b) That the person so harbored or protected was the enemy; and

(c) That the accused knew that the person so harbored or protected was an enemy.

(4) *Giving intelligence to the enemy.*

(a) That the accused, without proper authority, knowingly gave intelligence information to the enemy; and

(b) That the intelligence information was true, or implied the truth, at least in part.

(5) *Communicating with the enemy.*

(a) That the accused, without proper authority, communicated, corresponded, or held intercourse with the enemy; and;

(b) That the accused knew that the accused was communicating, corresponding, or holding intercourse with the enemy.

c. *Explanation.*

(1) *Scope of Article 104.* This article denounces offenses by all persons whether or not otherwise subject to military law. Offenders may be tried by court-martial or by military commission.

(2) *Enemy.* For a discussion of "enemy," *see* paragraph 23c(1)(b).

(3) *Aiding or attempting to aid the enemy.* It is not a violation of this article to furnish prisoners of war subsistence, quarters, and other comforts or aid to which they are lawfully entitled.

(4) *Harboring or protecting the enemy.*

(a) *Nature of offense.* An enemy is harbored or protected when, without proper authority, that enemy is shielded, either physically or by use of any artifice, aid, or representation from any injury or misfortune which in the chance of war may occur.

(b) *Knowledge.* Actual knowledge is required, but may be proved by circumstantial evidence.

(5) *Giving intelligence to the enemy.*

(a) *Nature of offense.* Giving intelligence to the enemy is a particular case of corresponding with the enemy made more serious by the fact that the communication contains intelligence that may be useful to the enemy for any of the many reasons that make information valuable to belligerents. This intelligence may be conveyed by direct or indirect means.

(b) *Intelligence.* "Intelligence" imports that the information conveyed is true or implies the truth, at least in part.

(c) *Knowledge.* Actual knowledge is required but may be proved by circumstantial evidence.

(6) *Communicating with the enemy.*

(a) *Nature of the offense.* No unauthorized communication, correspondence, or intercourse with the enemy is permissible. The intent, content, and method of the communication, correspondence, or intercourse are immaterial. No response or receipt by the enemy is required. The offense is complete the moment the communication, correspondence, or intercourse issues from the accused. The communication, correspondence, or intercourse may be conveyed directly or indirectly. A prisoner of war may violate this Article by engaging in unauthorized communications with the enemy. *See also* paragraph 29c(3).

(b) *Knowledge.* Actual knowledge is required but may be proved by circumstantial evidence.

(c) *Citizens of neutral powers.* Citizens of neutral powers resident in or visiting invaded or occupied territory can claim no immunity from the customary laws of war relating to communication with the enemy.

d. *Lesser included offenses.* See paragraph 3 of this part and Appendix 12A.

e. *Maximum punishment.* Death or such other punishment as a court-martial or military commission may direct.

f. *Sample specifications.*

(1) *Aiding or attempting to aid the enemy.*

In that _____ (personal jurisdiction data), did, (at/on board—location), on or about _____ 20 ___, (attempt to) aid the enemy with (arms) (ammunition) (supplies) (money) (_____), by (furnishing and delivering to _____ , members of the enemy's armed forces _____) (___).

(2) *Harboring or protecting the enemy.*

In that _____ (personal jurisdiction data), did, (at/on board—location), on or about _____ 20 ___, without proper authority, knowingly (harbor) (protect) _____ , an enemy, by (concealing the said _____ in his/her house) (_____).

(3) *Giving intelligence to the enemy.*

In that _____ (personal jurisdiction data), did, (at/on board—location), on or about _____ 20 __ , without proper authority, knowingly give intelligence to the enemy, by (informing a patrol of the enemy's forces of the whereabouts of a military patrol of the United States forces) (__).

(4) *Communicating with the enemy.*

In that _____ (personal jurisdiction data), did, (at/on board—location), on or about _____ 20 __ , without proper authority, knowingly (communicate with) (correspond with) (hold intercourse with) the enemy (by writing and transmitting secretly through the lines to one _____ , whom he/she, the said _____ , knew to be (an officer of the enemy's armed forces) (____) a communication in words and figures substantially as follows, to wit: ____)) ((indirectly by publishing in ____ , a newspaper published at ____ , a communication in words and figures as follows, to wit: ____ , which communication was intended to reach the enemy)) ((____)).

29. Article 105—Misconduct as a prisoner

a. *Text of statute.*

Any person subject to this chapter who, while in the hands of the enemy in time of war—

(1) for the purpose of securing favorable treatment by his captors acts without proper authority in a manner contrary to law, custom, or regulation, to the detriment of others of whatever nationality held by the enemy as civilian or military prisoners; or

(2) while in a position of authority over such persons maltreats them without justifiable cause; shall be punished as a court-martial may direct.

b. *Elements.*

(1) *Acting without authority to the detriment of another for the purpose of securing favorable treatment.*

(a) That without proper authority the accused acted in a manner contrary to law, custom, or regulation;

(b) That the act was committed while the accused was in the hands of the enemy in time of war;

(c) That the act was done for the purpose of securing favorable treatment of the accused by the captors; and

(d) That other prisoners held by the enemy,

either military or civilian, suffered some detriment because of the accused's act.

(2) *Maltreating prisoners while in a position of authority.*

(a) That the accused maltreated a prisoner held by the enemy;

(b) That the act occurred while the accused was in the hands of the enemy in time of war;

(c) That the accused held a position of authority over the person maltreated; and

(d) That the act was without justifiable cause.

c. *Explanation.*

(1) *Enemy.* For a discussion of "enemy," *see* paragraph 23c(1)(b).

(2) *In time of war. See* R.C.M. 103(19).

(3) *Acting without authority to the detriment of another for the purpose of securing favorable treatment.*

(a) *Nature of offense.* Unauthorized conduct by a prisoner of war must be intended to result in improvement by the enemy of the accused's condition and must operate to the detriment of other prisoners either by way of closer confinement, reduced rations, physical punishment, or other harm. Examples of this conduct include reporting plans of escape being prepared by others or reporting secret food caches, equipment, or arms. The conduct of the prisoner must be contrary to law, custom, or regulation.

(b) *Escape.* Escape from the enemy is authorized by custom. An escape or escape attempt which results in closer confinement or other measures against fellow prisoners still in the hands of the enemy is not an offense under this article.

(4) *Maltreating prisoners while in a position of authority.*

(a) *Authority.* The source of authority is not material. It may arise from the military rank of the accused or—despite service regulations or customs to the contrary—designation by the captor authorities, or voluntary election or selection by other prisoners for their self-government.

(b) *Maltreatment.* The maltreatment must be real, although not necessarily physical, and it must be without justifiable cause. Abuse of an inferior by inflammatory and derogatory words may, through mental anguish, constitute this offense.

d. *Lesser included offenses.* See paragraph 3 of this part and Appendix 12A.

e. *Maximum punishment.* Any punishment other than death that a court-martial may direct. *See* R.C.M. 1003.

f. *Sample specifications.*

(1) *Acting without authority to the detriment of another for the purpose of securing favorable treatment.*

    In that _____ (personal jurisdiction data), while in the hands of the enemy, did, (at/on board—location) on or about _____ 20 ___ , a time of war, without proper authority and for the purpose of securing favorable treatment by his/her captors, (report to the commander of Camp _____ the preparations by _____ , a prisoner at said camp, to escape, as a result of which report the said _____ was placed in solitary confinement) (_____).

(2) *Maltreating prisoner while in a position of authority.*

    In that _____ (personal jurisdiction data), did, (at/on board—location), on or about _____ 20 ___ , a time of war, while in the hands of the enemy and in a position of authority over _____ , a prisoner at _____ , as (officer in charge of prisoners at _____) (_____), maltreat the said _____ by (depriving him/her of _____) (_____), without justifiable cause.

30. Article 106—Spies

a. *Text of statute.*

Any person who in time of war is found lurking as a spy or acting as a spy in or about any place, vessel, or aircraft, within the control or jurisdiction of any of the armed forces, or in or about any shipyard, any manufacturing or industrial plant, or any other place or institution engaged in work in aid of the prosecution of the war by the United States, or elsewhere, shall be tried by a general court-martial or by a military commission and on conviction shall be punished by death.

b. *Elements.*

(1) That the accused was found in, about, or in and about a certain place, vessel, or aircraft within the control or jurisdiction of an armed force of the United States, or a shipyard, manufacturing or industrial plant, or other place or institution engaged in work in aid of the prosecution of the war by the United States, or elsewhere;

(2) That the accused was lurking, acting clandestinely or under false pretenses;

(3) That the accused was collecting or attempting to collect certain information;

(4) That the accused did so with the intent to convey this information to the enemy; and

(5) That this was done in time of war.

c. *Explanation.*

(1) *In time of war. See* R.C.M. 103(19).

(2) *Enemy.* For a discussion of "enemy," *see* paragraph 23c(1)(b).

(3) *Scope of offense.* The words "any person" bring within the jurisdiction of general courts-martial and military commissions all persons of whatever nationality or status who commit spying.

(4) *Nature of offense.* A person can be a spy only when, acting clandestinely or under false pretenses, that person obtains or seeks to obtain information with the intent to convey it to a hostile party. It is not essential that the accused obtain the information sought or that it be communicated. The offense is complete with lurking or acting clandestinely or under false pretenses with intent to accomplish these objects.

(5) *Intent.* It is necessary to prove an intent to convey information to the enemy. This intent may be inferred from evidence of a deceptive insinuation of the accused among our forces, but evidence that the person had come within the lines for a comparatively innocent purpose, as to visit family or to reach friendly lines by assuming a disguise, is admissible to rebut this inference.

(6) *Persons not included under "spying."*

(a) Members of a military organization not wearing a disguise, dispatch drivers, whether members of a military organization or civilians, and persons in ships or aircraft who carry out their missions openly and who have penetrated enemy lines are not spies because, while they may have resorted to concealment, they have not acted under false pretenses.

(b) A spy who, after rejoining the armed forces to which the spy belongs, is later captured by the enemy incurs no responsibility for previous acts of espionage.

(c) A person living in occupied territory who, without lurking, or acting clandestinely or under false pretenses, merely reports what is seen or heard through agents to the enemy may be charged under

Article 104 with giving intelligence to or communicating with the enemy, but may not be charged under this article as being a spy.

d. *Lesser included offenses.* See paragraph 3 of this part and Appendix 12A.

e. *Mandatory punishment.* Death.

f. *Sample specification.*

In that _____ (personal jurisdiction data), was, (at/on board—location), on or about _____ 20 ___ , a time of war, found (lurking) (acting) as a spy (in) (about) (in and about) _____ , (a (fortification) (port) (base) (vessel) (aircraft) (_____) within the (control)(jurisdiction) (control and jurisdiction) of an armed force of the United States, to wit: _____) (a (shipyard) (manufacturing plant) (industrial plant) (_____) engaged in work in aid of the prosecution of the war by the United States) (_____), for the purpose of (collecting) (attempting to collect) information in regard to the ((numbers) (resources) (operations) (___) of the armed forces of the United States) ((military production) (___) of the United States) (___), with intent to impart the same to the enemy.

30a. Article 106a—Espionage

a. *Text of statute.*

(a)(1) **Any person subject to this chapter who, with intent or reason to believe that it is to be used to the injury of the United States or to the advantage of a foreign nation, communicates, delivers, or transmits, or attempts to communicate, deliver, or transmit, to any entity described in paragraph (2), either directly or indirectly, anything described in paragraph (3) shall be punished as a court-martial may direct, except that if the accused is found guilty of an offense that directly concerns (A) nuclear weaponry, military spacecraft or satellites, early warning systems, or other means of defense or retaliation against large scale attack, (B) war plans, (C) communications intelligence or cryptographic information, or (D) any other major weapons system or major element of defense strategy, the accused shall be punished by death or such other punishment as a court-martial may direct.**

(2) **An entity referred to in paragraph (1) is—**

(A) **a foreign government;**

(B) **a faction or party or military or naval force within a foreign country, whether recognized or unrecognized by the United States; or**

(C) **a representative, officer, agent, employee, subject, or citizen of such a government, faction, party, or force.**

(3) **A thing referred to in paragraph (1) is a document, writing, code book, signal book, sketch, photograph, photographic negative, blueprint, plan, map, model, note, instrument, appliance, or information relating to the national defense.**

(b)(1) **No person may be sentenced by court-martial to suffer death for an offense under this section (article) unless—**

(A) **the members of the court-martial unanimously find at least one of the aggravating factors set out in subsection (c); and**

(B) **the members unanimously determine that any extenuating or mitigating circumstances are substantially outweighed by any aggravating circumstances, including the aggravating factors set out under subsection (c).**

(2) **Findings under this subsection may be based on—**

(A) **evidence introduced on the issue of guilt or innocence;**

(B) **evidence introduced during the sentencing proceeding; or**

(C) **all such evidence.**

(3) **The accused shall be given broad latitude to present matters in extenuation and mitigation.**

(c) **A sentence of death may be adjudged by a court-martial for an offense under this section (article) only if the members unanimously find, beyond a reasonable doubt, one or more of the following aggravating factors:**

(1) **The accused has been convicted of another offense involving espionage or treason for which either a sentence of death or imprisonment for life was authorized by statute.**

(2) **In the commission of the offense, the accused knowingly created a grave risk of substantial damage to the national security.**

(3) **In the commission of the offense, the accused knowingly created a grave risk of death to another person.**

(4) **Any other factor that may be prescribed**

by the President by regulations under section 836 of this title (Article 36).

b. *Elements.*

(1) *Espionage.*

(a) That the accused communicated, delivered, or transmitted any document, writing, code book, signal book, sketch, photograph, photographic negative, blueprint, plan, map, model, note, instrument, appliance, or information relating to the national defense;

(b) That this matter was communicated, delivered, or transmitted to any foreign government, or to any faction or party or military or naval force within a foreign country, whether recognized or unrecognized by the United States, or to any representative, officer, agent, employee, subject or citizen thereof, either directly or indirectly; and

(c) That the accused did so with intent or reason to believe that such matter would be used to the injury of the United States or to the advantage of a foreign nation.

(2) *Attempted espionage.*

(a) That the accused did a certain overt act;

(b) That the act was done with the intent to commit the offense of espionage;

(c) That the act amounted to more than mere preparation; and

(d) That the act apparently tended to bring about the offense of espionage.

(3) *Espionage as a capital offense.*

(a) That the accused committed espionage or attempted espionage; and

(b) That the offense directly concerned (1) nuclear weaponry, military spacecraft or satellites, early warning systems, or other means of defense or retaliation against large scale attack, (2) war plans, (3) communications intelligence or cryptographic information, or (4) any other major weapons system or major element of defense strategy.

c. *Explanation.*

(1) *Intent.* "Intent or reason to believe" that the information "is to be used to the injury of the United States or to the advantage of a foreign nation" means that the accused acted in bad faith and without lawful authority with respect to information that is not lawfully accessible to the public.

(2) *National defense information.* "Instrument, appliance, or information relating to the national de-

fense" includes the full range of modern technology and matter that may be developed in the future, including chemical or biological agents, computer technology, and other matter related to the national defense.

(3) *Espionage as a capital offense.* Capital punishment is authorized if the government alleges and proves that the offense directly concerned (1) nuclear weaponry, military spacecraft or satellites, early warning systems, or other means of defense or retaliation against large scale attack, (2) war plans, (3) communications intelligence or cryptographic information, or (4) any other major weapons system or major element of defense strategy. *See* R.C.M. 1004 concerning sentencing proceedings in capital cases.

d. *Lesser included offenses.* See paragraph 3 of this part and Appendix 12A.

e. *Maximum punishment.*

(1) *Espionage as a capital offense.* Death or such other punishment as a court-martial may direct. *See* R.C.M. 1003.

(2) *Espionage or attempted espionage.* Any punishment, other than death, that a court-martial may direct. *See* R.C.M. 1003.

f. *Sample specification.*

In that _____ (personal jurisdiction data), did, (at/on board—location), on or about _____ 20 ___, with intent or reason to believe it would be used to the injury of the United States or to the advantage of _____ , a foreign nation, (attempt to) (communicate) (deliver) (transmit) _____ (description of item), (a document) (a writing) (a code book) (a sketch) (a photograph) (a photographic negative) (a blueprint) (a plan) (a map) (a model) (a note) (an instrument) (an appliance) (information) relating to the national defense, ((which directly concerned (nuclear weaponry) (military spacecraft) (military satellites) (early warning systems) (_____ , a means of defense or retaliation against a large scale attack) (war plans) (communications intelligence) (cryptographic information) (_____ , a major weapons system) (_____ , a major element of defense strategy)) to _____ ((a representative of) (an officer of) (an agent of) (an employee of) (a subject of) (a citizen of)) ((a foreign government) (a faction within a foreign country) (a party within a foreign country) (a military force within a foreign country) (a naval force within a foreign country)) (indirectly by _____).

31. Article 107—False official statements

a. *Text of statute.*

Any person subject to this chapter who, with intent to deceive, signs any false record, return, regulation, order, or other official document, knowing it to be false, or makes any other false official statement knowing it to be false, shall be punished as a court-martial may direct.

b. *Elements.*

(1) That the accused signed a certain official document or made a certain official statement;

(2) That the document or statement was false in certain particulars;

(3) That the accused knew it to be false at the time of signing it or making it; and

(4) That the false document or statement was made with the intent to deceive.

c. *Explanation.*

(1) *Official documents and statements.* Official documents and official statements include all documents and statements made in the line of duty.

(2) *Status of victim of the deception.* The rank of any person intended to be deceived is immaterial if that person was authorized in the execution of a particular duty to require or receive the statement or document from the accused. The government may be the victim of this offense.

(3) *Intent to deceive.* The false representation must be made with the intent to deceive. It is not necessary that the false statement be material to the issue inquiry. If, however, the falsity is in respect to a material matter, it may be considered as some evidence of the intent to deceive, while immateriality may tend to show an absence of this intent.

(4) *Material gain.* The expectation of material gain is not an element of this offense. Such expectation or lack of it, however, is circumstantial evidence bearing on the element of intent to deceive.

(5) *Knowledge that the document or statement was false.* The false representation must be one which the accused actually knew was false. Actual knowledge may be proved by circumstantial evidence. An honest, although erroneous, belief that a statement made is true, is a defense.

d. *Lesser included offenses.* See paragraph 3 of this part and Appendix 12A.

e. *Maximum punishment.* Dishonorable discharge, forfeiture of all pay and allowances, and confinement for 5 years.

f. *Sample specification.*

In that _____ (personal jurisdiction data), did, (at/on board—location), (subject-matter jurisdiction data, if required), on or about _____ 20 ___ , with intent to deceive, (sign an official (record) (return) (_____), to wit: _____) (make to _____ , an official statement, to wit: _____), which (record) (return) (statement) (_____) was (totally false) (false in that _____), and was then known by the said _____ to be so false.

32. Article 108—Military property of the United States—sale, loss, damage, destruction, or wrongful disposition

a. *Text of statute.*

Any person subject to this chapter who, without proper authority—

(1) sells or otherwise disposes of;

(2) willfully or through neglect damages, destroys, or loses; or

(3) willfully or through neglect suffers to be lost, damaged, destroyed, sold, or wrongfully disposed of, any military property of the United States, shall be punished as a court-martial may direct.

b. *Elements.*

(1) *Selling or otherwise disposing of military property.*

(a) That the accused sold or otherwise disposed of certain property (which was a firearm or explosive);

(b) That the sale or disposition was without proper authority;

(c) That the property was military property of the United States; and

(d) That the property was of a certain value.

(2) *Damaging, destroying, or losing military property.*

(a) That the accused, without proper authority, damaged or destroyed certain property in a certain way, or lost certain property;

(b) That the property was military property of the United States;

(c) That the damage, destruction, or loss was willfully caused by the accused or was the result of neglect by the accused; and

(d) That the property was of a certain value or the damage was of a certain amount.

(3) *Suffering military property to be lost, damaged, destroyed, sold, or wrongfully disposed of.*

(a) That certain property (which was a firearm or explosive) was lost, damaged, destroyed, sold, or wrongfully disposed of;

(b) That the property was military property of the United States;

(c) That the loss, damage, destruction, sale, or wrongful disposition was suffered by the accused, without proper authority, through a certain omission of duty by the accused;

(d) That the omission was willful or negligent; and

(e) That the property was of a certain value or the damage was of a certain amount.

c. *Explanation.*

(1) *Military property.* Military property is all property, real or personal, owned, held, or used by one of the armed forces of the United States. Military property is a term of art, and should not be confused with government property. The terms are not interchangeable. While all military property is government property, not all government property is military property. An item of government property is not military property unless the item in question meets the definition provided above. It is immaterial whether the property sold, disposed, destroyed, lost, or damaged had been issued to the accused, to someone else, or even issued at all. If it is proved by either direct or circumstantial evidence that items of individual issue were issued to the accused, it may be inferred, depending on all the evidence, that the damage, destruction, or loss proved was due to the neglect of the accused. Retail merchandise of service exchange stores is not military property under this article.

(2) *Suffering military property to be lost, damaged, destroyed, sold, or wrongfully disposed of.* "To suffer" means to allow or permit. The willful or negligent sufferance specified by this article includes: deliberate violation or intentional disregard of some specific law, regulation, or order; reckless or unwarranted personal use of the property; causing or allowing it to remain exposed to the weather, insecurely housed, or not guarded; permitting it to be consumed, wasted, or injured by other persons; or loaning it to a person, known to be irresponsible, by whom it is damaged.

(3) *Value and damage.* In the case of loss, destruction, sale, or wrongful disposition, the value of the property controls the maximum punishment which may be adjudged. In the case of damage, the amount of damage controls. As a general rule, the amount of damage is the estimated or actual cost of repair by the government agency normally employed in such work, or the cost of replacement, as shown by government price lists or otherwise, whichever is less.

d. *Lesser included offenses.* See paragraph 3 of this part and Appendix 12A.

e. *Maximum punishment.*

(1) *Selling or otherwise disposing of military property.*

(a) *Of a value of $500.00 or less.* Bad-conduct discharge, forfeiture of all pay and allowances, and confinement for 1 year.

(b) *Of a value of more than $500.00 or any firearm or explosive.* Dishonorable discharge, forfeiture of all pay and allowances, and confinement for 10 years.

(2) *Through neglect damaging, destroying, or losing, or through neglect suffering to be lost, damaged, destroyed, sold, or wrongfully disposed of, military property.*

(a) *Of a value or damage of $500.00 or less.* Confinement for 6 months, and forfeiture of two-thirds pay per month for 6 months.

(b) *Of a value or damage of more than $500.00.* Bad-conduct discharge, forfeiture of all pay and allowances, and confinement for 1 year.

(3) *Willfully damaging, destroying, or losing, or willfully suffering to be lost, damaged, destroyed, sold, or wrongfully disposed of, military property.*

(a) *Of a value or damage of $500.00 or less.* Bad-conduct discharge, forfeiture of all pay and allowances, and confinement for 1 year.

(b) *Of a value or damage of more than $500.00, or of any firearm or explosive.* Dishonorable discharge, forfeiture of all pay and allowances, and confinement for 10 years.

f. *Sample specifications.*

(1) *Selling or disposing of military property.*

In that _____ (personal jurisdiction data), did, (at/on board—location) (subject-matter jurisdiction data, if required), on or about _____ 20 ___ , without proper authority,(sell to _____) (dispose of by _____) _____ , ((a firearm) (an explosive)) of a value of (about) $ _____ , military property of the United States.

(2) *Damaging, destroying, or losing military property.*

In that _____ (personal jurisdiction data), did, (at/on board—location) (subject-matter jurisdiction data, if required), on or about _____ 20 ___ , without proper authority, ((willfully) (through neglect)) ((damage by _____) (destroy by _____)) (lose)) _____ (of a value of (about) $ _____ ,) military property of the United States (the amount of said damage being in the sum of (about) $ _____).

(3) *Suffering military property to be lost, damaged, destroyed, sold, or wrongfully disposed of.*

In that _____ (personal jurisdiction data), did, (at/on board—location) (subject-matter jurisdiction data, if required), on or about _____ 20 ___ , without proper authority, (willfully) (through neglect) suffer _____ , ((a firearm) (an explosive)) (of a value of (about) $ _____) military property of the United States, to be (lost) (damaged by _____) (destroyed by _____) (sold to _____) (wrongfully disposed of by _____) (the amount of said damage being in the sum of (about) $ _____).

33. Article 109—Property other than military property of the United States—waste, spoilage, or destruction

a. *Text of statute.*

Any person subject to this chapter who willfully or recklessly wastes, spoils, or otherwise willfully and wrongfully destroys or damages any property other than military property of the United States shall be punished as a court-martial may direct.

b. *Elements.*

(1) *Wasting or spoiling of non-military property.*

(a) That the accused willfully or recklessly wasted or spoiled certain real property in a certain manner;

(b) That the property was that of another person; and

(c) That the property was of a certain value.

(2) *Destroying or damaging non-military property.*

(a) That the accused willfully and wrongfully destroyed or damaged certain personal property in a certain manner;

(b) That the property was that of another person; and

(c) That the property was of a certain value or the damage was of a certain amount.

c. *Explanation.*

(1) *Wasting or spoiling non-military property.* This portion of Article 109 proscribes willful or reckless waste or spoliation of the real property of another. The terms "wastes" and "spoils" as used in this article refer to such wrongful acts of voluntary destruction of or permanent damage to real property as burning down buildings, burning piers, tearing down fences, or cutting down trees. This destruction in punishable whether done willfully, that is intentionally, or recklessly, that is through a culpable disregard of the foreseeable consequences of some voluntary act.

(2) *Destroying or damaging non-military property.* This portion of Article 109 proscribes the willful and wrongful destruction or damage of the personal property of another. To be destroyed, the property need not be completely demolished or annihilated, but must be sufficiently injured to be useless for its intended purpose. Damage consists of any physical injury to the property. To constitute an offense under this section, the destruction or damage of the property must have been willful and wrongful. As used in this section "willfully" means intentionally and "wrongfully" means contrary to law, regulation, lawful order, or custom. Willfulness may be proved by circumstantial evidence, such as the manner in which the acts were done.

(3) *Value and damage.* In the case of destruction, the value of the property destroyed controls the maximum punishment which may be adjudged. In the case of damage, the amount of the damage controls. As a general rule, the amount of damage is the estimated or actual cost of repair by artisans employed in this work who are available to the community wherein the owner resides, or the replacement

cost, whichever is less. *See also* paragraph 46c(1)(g).

d. *Lesser included offenses.* See paragraph 3 of this part and Appendix 12A.

e. *Maximum punishment.* Wasting, spoiling, destroying, or damaging any property other than military property of the United States of a value or damage.

(1) *Of $500.00 or less.* Bad-conduct discharge, forfeiture of all pay and allowances, and confinement for 1 year.

(2) *Of more than $500.00.* Dishonorable discharge, forfeiture of all pay and allowances, and confinement for 5 years.

f. *Sample specification.*

In that _____ (personal jurisdiction data), did, (at/on board—location) (subject-matter jurisdiction data, if required), on or about _____ 20 __ , ((willfully) recklessly) waste) ((willfully) (recklessly) spoil) (willfully and wrongfully (destroy) (damage) by _____) _____ , (of a value of (about) $ _____) (the amount of said damage being in the sum of (about $ _____), the property of _____ .

34. Article 110—Improper hazarding of vessel

a. *Text of statute.*

(a) **Any person subject to this chapter who willfully and wrongfully hazards or suffers to be hazarded any vessel of the armed forces shall suffer death or such other punishment as a court-martial may direct.**

(b) **Any person subject to this chapter who negligently hazards or suffers to be hazarded any vessel of the armed forces shall be punished as a court-martial may direct.**

b. *Elements.*

(1) That a vessel of the armed forces was hazarded in a certain manner; and

(2) That the accused by certain acts or omissions, willfully and wrongfully, or negligently, caused or suffered the vessel to be hazarded.

c. *Explanation.*

(1) *Hazard.* "Hazard" means to put in danger of loss or injury. Actual damage to, or loss of, a vessel of the armed forces by collision, stranding, running upon a shoal or a rock, or by any other cause, is conclusive evidence that the vessel was hazarded but not of the fact of culpability on the part of any particular person. "Stranded" means run aground so that the vessel is fast for a time. If the vessel "touches and goes," she is not stranded; if she "touches and sticks," she is. A shoal is a sand, mud, or gravel bank or bar that makes the water shallow.

(2) *Willfully and wrongfully.* As used in this article, "willfully" means intentionally and "wrongfully" means contrary to law, regulation, lawful order, or custom.

(3) *Negligence.* "Negligence" as used in this article means the failure to exercise the care, prudence, or attention to duties, which the interests of the government require a prudent and reasonable person to exercise under the circumstances. This negligence may consist of the omission to do something the prudent and reasonable person would have done, or the doing of something which such a person would not have done under the circumstances. No person is relieved of culpability who fails to perform such duties as are imposed by the general responsibilities of that person's grade or rank, or by the customs of the service for the safety and protection of vessels of the armed forces, simply because these duties are not specifically enumerated in a regulation or order. However, a mere error in judgment that a reasonable person might have committed under the same circumstances does not constitute an offense under this article.

(4) *Suffer.* "To suffer" means to allow or permit. A ship is willfully suffered to be hazarded by one who, although not in direct control of the vessel, knows a danger to be imminent but takes no steps to prevent it, as by a plotting officer of a ship under way who fails to report to the officer of the deck a radar target which is observed to be on a collision course with, and dangerously close to, the ship. A suffering through neglect implies an omission to take such measures as were appropriate under the circumstances to prevent a foreseeable danger.

d. *Lesser included offenses.* See paragraph 3 of this part and Appendix 12A.

e. *Maximum punishment.* Hazarding or suffering to be hazarded any vessel of the armed forces:

(1) *Willfully and wrongfully.* Death or such other punishment as a court-martial may direct.

(2) *Negligently.* Dishonorable discharge, forfeiture of all pay and allowances, and confinement for 2 years.

f. *Sample specifications.*

(1) *Hazarding or suffering to be hazarded any vessel, willfully and wrongfully.*

In that _____ (personal jurisdiction data), did, on _____ 20 ___ , while serving as _____ aboard the _____ in the vicinity of _____ , willfully and wrongfully (hazard the said vessel) (suffer the said vessel to be hazarded) by (causing the said vessel to collide with _____) (allowing the said vessel to run aground) (_____).

(2) *Hazarding of vessel, negligently.*

(a) *Example 1.*

In that _____ (personal jurisdiction data), on _____ 20 ___ , while serving in command of the _____ , making entrance to (Boston Harbor), did negligently hazard the said vessel by failing and neglecting to maintain or cause to be maintained an accurate running plot of the true position of said vessel while making said approach, as a result of which neglect the said _____ , at or about _____ , hours on the day aforesaid, became stranded in the vicinity of (Channel Buoy Number Three).

(b) *Example 2.*

In that _____ (personal jurisdiction data), on _____ 20 ___ , while serving as navigator of the _____ , cruising on special service in the _____ Ocean off the coast of _____ , notwithstanding the fact that at about midnight, _____ 20 ___ , the northeast point of _____ Island bore abeam and was about six miles distant, the said ship being then under way and making a speed of about ten knots, and well knowing the position of the said ship at the time stated, and that the charts of the locality were unreliable and the currents thereabouts uncertain, did then and there negligently hazard the said vessel by failing and neglecting to exercise proper care and attention in navigating said ship while approaching _____ Island, in that he/she neglected and failed to lay a course that would carry said ship clear of the last aforesaid island, and to change the course in due time to avoid disaster; and the said ship, as a result of said negligence on the part of said _____ , ran upon a rock off the southwest coast of _____ Island, at about _____ hours, _____ , 20 ___ , in consequence of which the said _____ was lost.

(c) *Example 3.*

In that _____ (personal jurisdiction data),

on _____ 20 ___ , while serving as navigator of the _____ and well knowing that at about sunset of said day the said ship had nearly run her estimated distance from the _____ position, obtained and plotted by him/her, to the position of _____ , and well knowing the difficulty of sighting _____ , from a safe distance after sunset, did then and there negligently hazard the said vessel by failing and neglecting to advise his/her commanding officer to lay a safe course for said ship to the northward before continuing on a westerly course, as it was the duty of said _____ to do; in consequence of which the said ship was, at about _____ hours on the day above mentioned, run upon _____ bank in the _____ Sea, about latitude ___ degrees, ___ minutes, north, and longitude ___ degrees, ___ minutes, west, and seriously injured.

(3) *Suffering a vessel to be hazarded, negligently.*

In that _____ (personal jurisdiction data), while serving as combat intelligence center officer on board the _____ , making passage from Boston to Philadelphia, and having, between _____ and _____ hours on _____ , 20 ___ , been duly informed of decreasing radar ranges and constant radar bearing indicating that the said _____ was upon a collision course approaching a radar target, did then and there negligently suffer the said vessel to be hazarded by failing and neglecting to report said collision course with said radar target to the officer of the deck, as it was his/her duty to do, and he/she, the said _____ , through negligence, did cause the said _____ to collide with the _____ at or about _____ hours on said date, with resultant damage to both vessels.

35. Article 111—Drunken or reckless operation of vehicle, aircraft, or vessel

a. *Text of statute.*

(a) Any person subject to this chapter who—

(1) operates or physically controls any vehicle, aircraft, or vessel in a reckless or wanton manner or while impaired by a substance described in section 912a(b) of this title (Article 112a(b)); or

(2) operates or is in actual physical control of any vehicle, aircraft, or vessel while drunk or when the alcohol concentration in the person's blood or breath is equal to or exceeds the appli-

cable limit under subsection (b), shall be punished as a court-martial may direct.

(b)(1) For purposes of subsection (a), the applicable limit on the alcohol concentration in a person's blood or breath is as follows:

(A) In the case of the operation or control of a vehicle, aircraft, or vessel in the United States, such limit is the lesser of—

(i) the blood alcohol content limit under the law of the State in which the conduct occurred, except as may be provided under paragraph (2) for conduct on a military installation that is in more than one State; or

(ii) the blood alcohol content limit specified in paragraph (3).

(B) In the case of the operation or control of a vehicle, aircraft, or vessel outside the United States, the applicable blood alcohol content limit is the blood alcohol content limit specified in paragraph (3) or such lower limit as the Secretary of Defense may by regulation prescribe.

(2) In the case of a military installation that is in more than one State, if those States have different blood alcohol content limits under their respective State laws, the Secretary may select one such blood alcohol content limit to apply uniformly on that installation.

(3) For purposes of paragraph (1), the blood alcohol content limit with respect to alcohol concentration in a person's blood is 0.10 grams of alcohol per 100 milliliters of blood and with respect to alcohol concentration in a person's breath is 0.10 grams of alcohol per 210 liters of breath, as shown by chemical analysis.

(4) In this subsection:

(A) The term "blood alcohol content limit" means the amount of alcohol concentration in a person's blood or breath at which operation or control of a vehicle, aircraft, or vessel is prohibited.

(B) The term "United States" includes the District of Columbia, the Commonwealth of Puerto Rico, the Virgin Islands, Guam, and American Samoa and the term "State" includes each of those jurisdictions.

b. *Elements.*

(1) That the accused was operating or in physical control of a vehicle, aircraft, or vessel; and

(2) That while operating or in physical control of a vehicle, aircraft, or vessel, the accused:

(a) did so in a wanton or reckless manner, or

(b) was drunk or impaired, or

(c) the alcohol concentration in the accused's blood or breath equaled or exceeded the applicable limit under subparagraph (b) of paragraph 35a.
[NOTE: If injury resulted add the following element]

(3) That the accused thereby caused the vehicle, aircraft, or vessel to injure a person.

c. *Explanation.*

(1) *Vehicle. See* 1 U.S.C. § 4.

(2) *Vessel. See.* 1 U.S.C. § 3.

(3) *Aircraft.* Any contrivance used or designed for transportation in the air.

(4) *Operates.* Operating a vehicle, aircraft, or vessel includes not only driving or guiding a vehicle, aircraft or vessel while it is in motion, either in person or through the agency of another, but also setting of its motive power in action or the manipulation of its controls so as to cause the particular vehicle, aircraft or vessel to move.

(5) *Physical control and actual physical control.* These terms as used in the statute are synonymous. They describe the present capability and power to dominate, direct or regulate the vehicle, vessel, or aircraft, either in person or through the agency of another, regardless of whether such vehicle, aircraft, or vessel is operated. For example, the intoxicated person seated behind the steering wheel of a vehicle with the keys of the vehicle in or near the ignition but with the engine not turned on could be deemed in actual physical control of that vehicle. However, the person asleep in the back seat with the keys in his or her pocket would not be deemed in actual physical control. Physical control necessarily encompasses operation.

(6) *Drunk or impaired.* "Drunk" and "impaired" mean any intoxication which is sufficient to impair the rational and full exercise of the mental or physical faculties. The term drunk is used in relation to intoxication by alcohol. The term impaired is used in relation to intoxication by a substance described in Article 112(a), Uniform Code of Military Justice.

(7) *Reckless.* The operation or physical control of a vehicle, vessel, or aircraft is "reckless" when it exhibits a culpable disregard of foreseeable consequences to others from the act or omission involved. Recklessness is not determined solely by reason of

the happening of an injury, or the invasion of the rights of another, nor by proof alone of excessive speed or erratic operation, but all these factors may be admissible and relevant as bearing upon the ultimate question: whether, under all the circumstances, the accused's manner of operation or physical control of the vehicle, vessel, or aircraft was of that heedless nature which made it actually or imminently dangerous to the occupants, or to the rights or safety of others. It is operating or physically controlling a vehicle, vessel, or aircraft with such a high degree of negligence that if death were caused, the accused would have committed involuntary manslaughter, at least. The nature of the conditions in which the vehicle, vessel, or aircraft is operated or controlled, the time of day or night, the proximity and number of other vehicles, vessels, or aircraft and the condition of the vehicle, vessel, or aircraft, are often matters of importance in the proof of an offense charged under this article and, where they are of importance, may properly be alleged.

(8) *Wanton.* "Wanton" includes "reckless," but in describing the operation or physical control of a vehicle, vessel, or aircraft "wanton" may, in a proper case, connote willfulness, or a disregard of probable consequences, and thus describe a more aggravated offense.

(9) *Causation.* The accused's drunken or reckless driving must be a proximate cause of injury for the accused to be guilty of drunken or reckless driving resulting in personal injury. To be proximate, the accused's actions need not be the sole cause of the injury, nor must they be the immediate cause of the injury, that is, the latest in time and space preceding the injury. A contributing cause is deemed proximate only if it plays a material role in the victim's injury.

(10) *Separate offenses.* While the same course of conduct may constitute violations of both subsections (1) and (2) of the Article, e.g., both drunken and reckless operation or physical control, this article proscribes the conduct described in both subsections as separate offenses, which may be charged separately. However, as recklessness is a relative matter, evidence of all the surrounding circumstances that made the operation dangerous, whether alleged or not, may be admissible. Thus, on a charge of reckless driving, for example, evidence of drunkenness might be admissible as establishing one aspect of the recklessness, and evidence that the

vehicle exceeded a safe speed, at a relevant prior point and time, might be admissible as corroborating other evidence of the specific recklessness charged. Similarly, on a charge of drunken driving, relevant evidence of recklessness might have probative value as corroborating other proof of drunkenness.

d. *Lesser included offenses.* See paragraph 3 of this part and Appendix 12A.

e. *Maximum punishment.*

(1) *Resulting in personal injury.* Dishonorable discharge, forfeiture of all pay and allowances, and confinement for 18 months.

(2) *No personal injury involved.* Bad-conduct discharge, forfeiture of all pay and allowances, and confinement for 6 months.

f. *Sample specification.*

In that _____ (personal jurisdiction data), did (at/on board _____ location) (subject matter jurisdiction data, if required), on or about _____ , 20 ___ , (in the motor pool area) (near the Officer's Club) (at the intersection of _____ and _____) (while in the Gulf of Mexico) (while in flight over North America) physically control [a vehicle, to wit: (a truck) (a passenger car) (_____)] [an aircraft, to wit: (an AH-64 helicopter) (an F-14A fighter) (a KC-135 tanker) (_____)] [a vessel, to wit: (the aircraft carrier USS _____) (the Coast Guard Cutter _____) (_____)], [while drunk] [while impaired by _____] [while the alcohol concentration in his (blood or breath) equaled or exceeded the applicable limit under subparagraph (b) of the text of the statute in paragraph 35 as shown by chemical analysis] [in a (reckless) (wanton) manner by (attempting to pass another vehicle on a sharp curve) (ordering that the aircraft be flown below the authorized altitude)] [and did thereby cause said (vehicle) (aircraft) (vessel) to (strike and) (injure _____)].

36. Article 112—Drunk on duty

a. *Text of statute.*

Any person subject to this chapter other than sentinel or look-out, who is found drunk on duty, shall be punished as a court-martial may direct.

b. *Elements.*

(1) That the accused was on a certain duty; and

(2) That the accused was found drunk while on this duty.

c. *Explanation.*

(1) *Drunk. See* paragraph 35c(6).

(2) *Duty.* "Duty" as used in this article means military duty. Every duty which an officer or enlisted person may legally be required by superior authority to execute is necessarily a military duty. Within the meaning of this article, when in the actual exercise of command, the commander of a post, or of a command, or of a detachment in the field is constantly on duty, as is the commanding officer on board a ship. In the case of other officers or enlisted persons, "on duty" relates to duties or routine or detail, in garrison, at a station, or in the field, and does not relate to those periods when, no duty being required of them by orders or regulations, officers and enlisted persons occupy the status of leisure known as "off duty" or "on liberty." In a region of active hostilities, the circumstances are often such that all members of a command may properly be considered as being continuously on duty within the meaning of this article. So also, an officer of the day and members of the guard, or of the watch, are on duty during their entire tour within the meaning of this article.

(3) *Nature of offense.* It is necessary that the accused be found drunk while actually on the duty alleged, and the fact the accused became drunk before going on duty, although material in extenuation, does not affect the question of guilt. If, however, the accused does not undertake the responsibility or enter upon the duty at all, the accused's conduct does not fall within the terms of this article, nor does that of a person who absents himself or herself from duty and is found drunk while so absent. Included within the article is drunkenness while on duty of an anticipatory nature such as that of an aircraft crew ordered to stand by for flight duty, or of an enlisted person ordered to stand by for guard duty.

(4) *Defenses.* If the accused is known by superior authorities to be drunk at the time a duty is assigned, and the accused is thereafter allowed to assume that duty anyway, or if the drunkenness results from an accidental over dosage administered for medicinal purposes, the accused will have a defense to this offense. *But see* paragraph 76 (incapacitation for duty).

d. *Lesser included offenses.* See paragraph 3 of this part and Appendix 12A.

e. *Maximum punishment.* Bad-conduct discharge, forfeiture of all pay and allowances, and confinement for 9 months.

f. *Sample specification.*

In that _____ (personal jurisdiction data), was, (at/on board—location), on or about _____ 20 ___ , found drunk while on duty as _____ .

37. Article 112a—Wrongful use, possession, etc., of controlled substances

a. *Text of statute.*

(a) **Any person subject to this chapter who wrongfully uses, possesses, manufactures, distributes, imports into the customs territory of the United States, exports from the United States, or introduces into an installation, vessel, vehicle, or aircraft used by or under the control of the armed forces a substance described in subsection (b) shall be punished as a court-martial may direct.**

(b) **The substances referred to in subsection (a) are the following:**

(1) **opium, heroin, cocaine, amphetamine, lysergic acid diethylamide, methamphetamine, phencyclidine, barbituric acid, and marijuana, and any compound or derivative of any such substance.**

(2) **Any substance not specified in clause (1) that is listed on a schedule of controlled substances prescribed by the President for the purposes of this article.**

(3) **Any other substance not specified in clause (1) or contained on a list prescribed by the President under clause (2) that is listed in Schedules I through V of section 202 of the Controlled Substances Act (21 U.S.C. 812).**

b. *Elements.*

(1) *Wrongful possession of controlled substance.*

(a) That the accused possessed a certain amount of a controlled substance; and

(b) That the possession by the accused was wrongful.

(2) *Wrongful use of controlled substance.*

(a) That the accused used a controlled substance; and

(b) That the use by the accused was wrongful.

(3) *Wrongful distribution of controlled substance.*

(a) That the accused distributed a certain amount of a controlled substance; and

(b) That the distribution by the accused was wrongful.

(4) *Wrongful introduction of a controlled substance.*

(a) That the accused introduced onto a vessel, aircraft, vehicle, or installation used by the armed forces or under the control of the armed forces a certain amount of a controlled substance; and

(b) That the introduction was wrongful.

(5) *Wrongful manufacture of a controlled substance.*

(a) That the accused manufactured a certain amount of a controlled substance; and

(b) That the manufacture was wrongful.

(6) *Wrongful possession, manufacture, or introduction of a controlled substance with intent to distribute.*

(a) That the accused (possessed) (manufactured) (introduced) a certain amount of a controlled substance;

(b) That the (possession) (manufacture) (introduction) was wrongful; and

(c) That the (possession) (manufacture) (introduction) was with the intent to distribute.

(7) *Wrongful importation or exportation of a controlled substance.*

(a) That the accused (imported into the customs territory of) (exported from) the United States a certain amount of a controlled substance; and

(b) That the (importation) (exportation) was wrongful.
[Note: When any of the aggravating circumstances listed in subparagraph e is alleged, it must be listed as an element.]

c. *Explanation.*

(1) *Controlled substance.* "Controlled substance" means amphetamine, cocaine, heroin, lysergic acid diethylamide, marijuana, methamphetamine, opium, phencyclidine, and barbituric acid, including phenobarbital and secobarbital. "Controlled substance" also means any substance which is included in Schedules I through V established by the Controlled Substances Act of 1970 (21 U.S.C. 812).

(2) *Possess.* "Possess" means to exercise control of something. Possession may be direct physical custody like holding an item in one's hand, or it may be constructive, as in the case of a person who hides an item in a locker or car to which that person may return to retrieve it. Possession must be knowing and conscious. Possession inherently includes the power or authority to preclude control by others. It is possible, however, for more than one person to possess an item simultaneously, as when several people share control of an item. An accused may not be convicted of possession of a controlled substance if the accused did not know that the substance was present under the accused's control. Awareness of the presence of a controlled substance may be inferred from circumstantial evidence.

(3) *Distribute.* "Distribute" means to deliver to the possession of another. "Deliver" means the actual, constructive, or attempted transfer of an item, whether or not there exists an agency relationship.

(4) *Manufacture.* "Manufacture" means the production, preparation, propagation, compounding, or processing of a drug or other substance, either directly or indirectly or by extraction from substances of natural origin, or independently by means of chemical synthesis or by a combination of extraction and chemical synthesis, and includes any packaging or repackaging of such substance or labeling or relabeling of its container. "Production," as used in this subparagraph, includes the planting, cultivating, growing, or harvesting of a drug or other substance.

(5) *Wrongfulness.* To be punishable under Article 112a, possession, use, distribution, introduction, or manufacture of a controlled substance must be wrongful. Possession, use, distribution, introduction, or manufacture of a controlled substance is wrongful if it is without legal justification or authorization. Possession, distribution, introduction, or manufacture of a controlled substance is not wrongful if such act or acts are: (A) done pursuant to legitimate law enforcement activities (for example, an informant who receives drugs as part of an undercover operation is not in wrongful possession); (B) done by authorized personnel in the performance of medical duties; or (C) without knowledge of the contraband nature of the substance (for example, a person who possesses cocaine, but actually believes it to be sugar, is not guilty of wrongful possession of cocaine). Possession, use, distribution, introduction, or manufacture of a controlled substance may be inferred to be wrongful in the absence of evidence to the contrary. The burden of going forward with evidence with respect to any such exception in any court-

martial or other proceeding under the code shall be upon the person claiming its benefit. If such an issue is raised by the evidence presented, then the burden of proof is upon the United States to establish that the use, possession, distribution, manufacture, or introduction was wrongful.

(6) *Intent to distribute.* Intent to distribute may be inferred from circumstantial evidence. Examples of evidence which may tend to support an inference of intent to distribute are: possession of a quantity of substance in excess of that which one would be likely to have for personal use; market value of the substance; the manner in which the substance is packaged; and that the accused is not a user of the substance. On the other hand, evidence that the accused is addicted to or is a heavy user of the substance may tend to negate an inference of intent to distribute.

(7) *Certain amount.* When a specific amount of a controlled substance is believed to have been possessed, distributed, introduced, or manufactured by an accused, the specific amount should ordinarily be alleged in the specification. It is not necessary to allege a specific amount, however, and a specification is sufficient if it alleges that an accused possessed, distributed, introduced, or manufactured "some," "traces of," or "an unknown quantity of" a controlled substance.

(8) *Missile launch facility.* A "missile launch facility" includes the place from which missiles are fired and launch control facilities from which the launch of a missile is initiated or controlled after launch.

(9) *Customs territory of the United States.* "Customs territory of the United States" includes only the States, the District of Columbia, and Puerto Rico.

(10) *Use.* "Use" means to inject, ingest, inhale, or otherwise introduce into the human body, any controlled substance. Knowledge of the presence of the controlled substance is a required component of use. Knowledge of the presence of the controlled substance may be inferred from the presence of the controlled substance in the accused's body or from other circumstantial evidence. This permissive inference may be legally sufficient to satisfy the government's burden of proof as to knowledge.

(11) *Deliberate ignorance.* An accused who consciously avoids knowledge of the presence of a controlled substance or the contraband nature of the

substance is subject to the same criminal liability as one who has actual knowledge.

d. *Lesser included offenses.* See paragraph 3 of this part and Appendix 12A.

e. *Maximum punishments.*

(1) *Wrongful use, possession, manufacture, or introduction of controlled substance.*

(a) *Amphetamine, cocaine, heroin, lysergic acid diethylamide, marijuana (except possession of less than 30 grams or use of marijuana), methamphetamine, opium, phencyclidine, secobarbital, and Schedule I, II, III controlled substances.* Dishonorable discharge, forfeiture of all pay and allowances, and confinement 5 years.

(b) *Marijuana (possession of less than 30 grams or use), phenobarbital, and Schedule IV and V controlled substances.* Dishonorable discharge, forfeiture of all pay and allowances, and confinement for 2 years.

(2) *Wrongful distribution, possession, manufacture, or introduction of controlled substance with intent to distribute, or wrongful importation or exportation of a controlled substance.*

(a) *Amphetamine, cocaine, heroin, lysergic acid diethylamide, marijuana, methamphetamine, opium, phencyclidine, secobarbital, and Schedule I, II, and III controlled substances.* Dishonorable discharge, forfeiture of all pay and allowances, and confinement for 15 years.

(b) *Phenobarbital and Schedule IV and V controlled substances.* Dishonorable discharge, forfeiture of all pay and allowances, and confinement for 10 years.

When any offense under paragraph 37 is committed; while the accused is on duty as a sentinel or lookout; on board a vessel or aircraft used by or under the control of the armed forces; in or at a missile launch facility used by or under the control of the armed forces; while receiving special pay under 37 U.S.C. § 310; in time of war; or in a confinement facility used by or under the control of the armed forces, the maximum period of confinement authorized for such offense shall be increased by 5 years.

f. *Sample specifications.*

(1) *Wrongful possession, manufacture, or distribution of controlled substance.*

In that _____ (personal jurisdiction data) did, (at/on board—location) (subject-matter jurisdiction data, if required), on or about _____ , 20 __ , wrongfully (possess) (distribute) (manufacture) _____ (grams) (ounces) (pounds) (_____) of _____ (a schedule (_____) controlled substance), (with the intent to distribute the said controlled substance) (while on duty as a sentinel or lookout) (while (on board a vessel/aircraft) (in or at a missile launch facility) used by the armed forces or under the control of the armed forces, to wit: _____) (while receiving special pay under 37 U.S.C. § 310) (during time of war).

(2) *Wrongful use of controlled substance.*

In that _____ (personal jurisdiction data), did, (at/on board—location) (subject-matter jurisdiction data, if required), on or about _____ , 20 ___ , wrongfully use _____ (a Schedule ___ controlled substance) (while on duty as a sentinel or lookout) (while (on board a vessel/aircraft) (in or at a missile launch facility) used by the armed forces or under the control of the armed forces, to wit: _____) (while receiving special pay under 37 U.S.C. § 310) (during time of war).

(3) *Wrongful introduction of controlled substance.*

In that _____ (personal jurisdiction data) did, (at/on board—location) on or about _____ , 20 ___ , wrongfully introduce _____ (grams) (ounces) (pounds) (_____) of _____ (a Schedule (_____) controlled substance) onto a vessel, aircraft, vehicle, or installation used by the armed forces or under control of the armed forces, to wit: _____ (with the intent to distribute the said controlled substance) (while on duty as a sentinel or lookout) (while receiving special pay under 37 U.S.C. § 310) (during a time of war).

(4) *Wrongful importation or exportation of controlled substance.*

In that _____ (personal jurisdiction data) did, (at/on board—location) on or about _____ , 20 ___ , wrongfully (import) (export) _____ (grams) (ounces) (pounds) (_____) of _____ (a Schedule (___) controlled substance) (into the customs territory of) (from) the United States (while on board a vessel/aircraft used by the armed forces or under the control of the armed forces, to wit: _____) (during time of war).

38. Article 113—Misbehavior of sentinel or lookout

a. *Text of statute.*

Any sentinel or look-out who is found drunk or sleeping upon his post, or leaves it before he is regularly relieved, shall be punished, if the offense is committed in time of war, by death or such other punishment as a court-martial may direct, but if the offense is committed at any other time, by such punishment other than death as a court-martial may direct.

b. *Elements.*

(1) That the accused was posted or on post as a sentinel or lookout;

(2) That the accused was found drunk while on post, was found sleeping while on post, or left post before being regularly relieved.
[Note: If the offense was committed in time of war or while the accused was receiving special pay under 37 U.S.C. § 310, add the following element]

(3) That the offense was committed (in time of war) (while the accused was receiving special pay under 37 U.S.C. § 310).

c. *Explanation.*

(1) *In general.* This article defines three kinds of misbehavior committed by sentinels or lookouts: being found drunk or sleeping upon post, or leaving it before being regularly relieved. This article does not include an officer or enlisted person of the guard, or of a ship's watch, not posted or performing the duties of a sentinel or lookout, nor does it include a person whose duties as a watchman or attendant do not require constant alertness.

(2) *Post.* "Post" is the area where the sentinel or lookout is required to be for the performance of duties. It is not limited by an imaginary line, but includes, according to orders or circumstances, such surrounding area as may be necessary for the proper performance of the duties for which the sentinel or lookout was posted. The offense of leaving post is not committed when a sentinel or lookout goes an immaterial distance from the post, unless it is such a distance that the ability to fully perform the duty for which posted is impaired.

(3) *On post.* A sentinel or lookout becomes "on post" after having been given a lawful order to go "on post" as a sentinel or lookout and being formally or informally posted. The fact that a sentinel or lookout is not posted in the regular way is not a

defense. It is sufficient, for example, if the sentinel or lookout has taken the post in accordance with proper instruction, whether or not formally given. A sentinel or lookout is on post within the meaning of the article not only when at a post physically defined, as is ordinarily the case in garrison or aboard ship, but also, for example, when stationed in observation against the approach of an enemy, or detailed to use any equipment designed to locate friend, foe, or possible danger, or at a designated place to maintain internal discipline, or to guard stores, or to guard prisoners while in confinement or at work.

(4) *Sentinel or lookout.* A sentinel or a lookout is a person whose duties include the requirement to maintain constant alertness, be vigilant, and remain awake, in order to observe for the possible approach of the enemy, or to guard persons, property, or a place and to sound the alert, if necessary.

(5) *Drunk.* For an explanation of "drunk," *see* paragraph 35c(3).

(6) *Sleeping.* As used in this article, "sleeping" is that condition of insentience which is sufficient sensibly to impair the full exercise of the mental and physical faculties of a sentinel or lookout. It is not necessary to show that the accused was in a wholly comatose condition. The fact that the accused's sleeping resulted from a physical incapacity caused by disease or accident is an affirmative defense. *See* R.C.M. 916(i).

d. *Lesser included offenses.* See paragraph 3 of this part and Appendix 12A.

e. *Maximum punishment.*

(1) *In time of war.* Death or such other punishment as a court-martial may direct.

(2) *While receiving special pay under 37 U.S.C. § 310.* Dishonorable discharge, forfeiture of all pay and allowances, and confinement for 10 years.

(3) *In all other places.* Dishonorable discharge, forfeiture of all pay and allowances, and confinement for 1 year.

f. *Sample specification.*

In that _____ (personal jurisdiction data), on or about _____ 20 ___ (a time of war) (at/on board—location), (while receiving special pay under 37 U.S.C. § 310), being (posted) (on post) as a (sentinel) (lookout) at (warehouse no. 7) (post no. 11) (for radar observation) (_____) (was found (drunk) (sleeping) upon his/her post) (did

leave his/her post before he/she was regularly relieved).

39. Article 114—Dueling

a. *Text of statute.*

Any person subject to this chapter who fights or promotes, or is concerned in or connives at fighting a duel, or who, having knowledge of a challenge sent or about to be sent, fails to report the fact promptly to the proper authority, shall be punished as a court-martial may direct.

b. *Elements.*

(1) *Dueling.*

(a) That the accused fought another person with deadly weapons;

(b) That the combat was for private reasons; and

(c) That the combat was by prior agreement.

(2) *Promoting a duel.*

(a) That the accused promoted a duel between certain persons; and

(b) That the accused did so in a certain manner.

(3) *Conniving at fighting a duel.*

(a) That certain persons intended to and were about to engage in a duel;

(b) That the accused had knowledge of the planned duel; and

(c) That the accused connived at the fighting of the duel in a certain manner.

(4) *Failure to report a duel.*

(a) That a challenge to fight a duel had been sent or was about to be sent;

(b) That the accused had knowledge of this challenge; and

(c) That the accused failed to report this fact promptly to proper authority.

c. *Explanation.*

(1) *Duel.* A duel is combat between two persons for private reasons fought with deadly weapons by prior agreement.

(2) *Promoting a duel.* Urging or taunting another to challenge or to accept a challenge to duel, acting as a second or as carrier of a challenge or acceptance, or otherwise furthering or contributing to the fighting of a duel are examples of promoting a duel.

(3) *Conniving at fighting a duel.* Anyone who has

knowledge that steps are being taken or have been taken toward arranging or fighting a duel and who fails to take reasonable preventive action thereby connives at the fighting of a duel.

d. *Lesser included offenses.* See paragraph 3 of this part and Appendix 12A.

e. *Maximum punishment.* For all Article 114 offenses: dishonorable discharge, forfeiture of all pay and allowances, and confinement for 1 year.

f. *Sample specifications.*

(1) *Dueling.*

In that _____ (personal jurisdiction data) (and _____), did, (at/on board—location) (subject-matter jurisdiction data, if required), on or about _____ 20 __ , fight a duel (with _____), using as weapons therefor (pistols) (swords) (_____).

(2) *Promoting a duel.*

In that _____ (personal jurisdiction data), did, (at/on board—location) (subject-matter jurisdiction data, if required), on or about _____ 20 __ , promote a duel between _____ and _____ by (telling said _____ he/she would be a coward if he/she failed to challenge said _____ to a duel) (knowingly carrying from said _____ to said _____ a challenge to fight a duel).

(3) *Conniving at fighting a duel.*

In that _____ (personal jurisdiction data), having knowledge that _____ and _____ were about to engage in a duel, did (at/on board—location) (subject-matter jurisdiction data, if required), on or about _____ 20 __ , connive at the fighting of said duel by (failing to take reasonable preventive action) (_____).

(4) *Failure to report a duel.*

In that _____ (personal jurisdiction data), having knowledge that a challenge to fight a duel (had been sent) (was about to be sent) by _____ to _____ , did, (at/on board—location) (subject-matter jurisdiction data, if required), on or about _____ 20 __ fail to report that fact promptly to the proper authority.

40. Article 115—Malingering

a. *Text of statute.*

Any person subject to this chapter who for the purpose of avoiding work, duty, or service—

(1) **feigns illness, physical disablement, mental lapse or derangement; or**

(2) **intentionally inflicts self-injury;**
shall be punished as a court-martial may direct.

b. *Elements.*

(1) That the accused was assigned to, or was aware of prospective assignment to, or availability for, the performance of work, duty, or service;

(2) That the accused feigned illness, physical disablement, mental lapse or derangement, or intentionally inflicted injury upon himself or herself; and

(3) That the accused's purpose or intent in doing so was to avoid the work, duty, or service.
[Note: If the offense was committed in time of war or in a hostile fire pay zone, add the following element]

(4) That the offense was committed (in time of war) (in a hostile fire pay zone).

c. *Explanation.*

(1) *Nature of offense.* The essence of this offense is the design to avoid performance of any work, duty, or service which may properly or normally be expected of one in the military service. Whether to avoid all duty, or only a particular job, it is the purpose to shirk which characterizes the offense. Hence, the nature or permanency of a self-inflicted injury is not material on the question of guilt, nor is the seriousness of a physical or mental disability which is a sham. Evidence of the extent of the self-inflicted injury or feigned disability may, however, be relevant as a factor indicating the presence or absence of the purpose.

Discussion

Bona fide suicide attempts should not be charged as criminal offenses. When making a determination whether the injury by the service member was a bona fide suicide attempt, the convening authority should consider factors including, but not limited to, health conditions, personal stressors, and DoD policy related to suicide prevention.

––––––––––

(2) *How injury inflicted.* The injury may be inflicted by nonviolent as well as by violent means and may be accomplished by any act or omission which produces, prolongs, or aggravates any sickness or disability. Thus, voluntary starvation which results in debility is a self-inflicted injury and when done for the purpose of avoiding work, duty, or service constitutes a violation of this article.

d. *Lesser included offenses.* See paragraph 3 of this part and Appendix 12A.

e. *Maximum punishment.*

(1) *Feigning illness, physical disablement, mental lapse, or derangement.* Dishonorable discharge, forfeiture of all pay and allowances, and confinement for 1 year.

(2) *Feigning illness, physical disablement, mental lapse, or derangement in a hostile fire pay zone or in time of war.* Dishonorable discharge, forfeiture of all pay and allowances, and confinement for 3 years.

(3) *Intentional self-inflicted injury.* Dishonorable discharge, forfeiture of all pay and allowances, and confinement for 5 years.

(4) *Intentional self-inflicted injury in a hostile fire pay zone or in time of war.* Dishonorable discharge, forfeiture of all pay and allowances, and confinement for 10 years.

f. *Sample specification.*

In that _____ (personal jurisdiction data), did, (at/on board—location) (in a hostile fire pay zone) (subject-matter jurisdiction data, if required) (on or about _____ 20 ___) (from about _____ 20 ___ to about _____ 20 ___), (a time of war) for the purpose of avoiding (his/her duty as officer of the day) (his/her duty as aircraft mechanic) (work in the mess hall) (service as an enlisted person) (_____) (feign (a headache) (a sore back) (illness) (mental lapse) (mental derangement) (___)) (intentionally injure himself/herself by _____).

41. Article 116—Riot or breach of peace

a. *Text of statute.*

Any person subject to this chapter who causes or participates in any riot or breach of the peace shall be punished as a court-martial may direct.

b. *Elements.*

(1) *Riot.*

(a) That the accused was a member of an assembly of three or more persons;

(b) That the accused and at least two other members of this group mutually intended to assist one another against anyone who might oppose them in doing an act for some private purpose;

(c) That the group or some of its members, in furtherance of such purpose, unlawfully committed a tumultuous disturbance of the peace in a violent or turbulent manner; and

(d) That these acts terrorized the public in general in that they caused or were intended to cause public alarm or terror.

(2) *Breach of the peace.*

(a) That the accused caused or participated in a certain act of a violent or turbulent nature; and

(b) That the peace was thereby unlawfully disturbed.

c. *Explanation.*

(1) *Riot.* "Riot" is a tumultuous disturbance of the peace by three or more persons assembled together in furtherance of a common purpose to execute some enterprise of a private nature by concerted action against anyone who might oppose them, committed in such a violent and turbulent manner as to cause or be calculated to cause public terror. The gravamen of the offense of riot is terrorization of the public. It is immaterial whether the act intended was lawful. Furthermore, it is not necessary that the common purpose be determined before the assembly. It is sufficient if the assembly begins to execute in a tumultuous manner a common purpose formed after it assembled.

(2) *Breach of the peace.* A "breach of the peace" is an unlawful disturbance of the peace by an outward demonstration of a violent or turbulent nature. The acts or conduct contemplated by this article are those which disturb the public tranquility or impinge upon the peace and good order to which the community is entitled. Engaging in an affray and unlawful discharge of firearms in a public street are examples of conduct which may constitute a breach of the peace. Loud speech and unruly conduct may also constitute a breach of the peace by the speaker. A speaker may also be guilty of causing a breach of the peace if the speaker uses language which can reasonably be expected to produce a violent or turbulent response and a breach of the peace results. The fact that the words are true or used under provocation is not a defense, nor is tumultuous conduct excusable because incited by others.

(3) *Community and public.* "Community" and "public" include a military organization, post, camp, ship, aircraft, or station.

d. *Lesser included offenses.* See paragraph 3 of this part and Appendix 12A.

e. *Maximum punishment.*

(1) *Riot.* Dishonorable discharge, forfeiture of all pay and allowances, and confinement for 10 years.

(2) *Breach of the peace.* Confinement for 6 months and forfeiture of two-thirds pay per month for 6 months.

f. *Sample specifications.*

(1) *Riot.*

In that _____ (personal jurisdiction data), did, (at/on board—location) (subject-matter jurisdiction data, if required), on or about _____ 20 ___, (cause) (participate in) a riot by unlawfully assembling with _____ (and _____) (and) (others to the number of about _____ whose names are unknown) for the purpose of (resisting the police of _____) (assaulting passers-by) (_____), and in furtherance of said purpose did (fight with said police) (assault certain persons, to wit: _____) (_____), to the terror and disturbance of _____ .

(2) *Breach of the peace.*

In that _____ (personal jurisdiction data), did, (at/on board—location) (subject-matter jurisdiction data, if required), on or about _____ 20 ___, (cause) (participate in) a breach of the peace by (wrongfully engaging in a fist fight in the dayroom with _____) (using the following provoking language (toward _____), to wit: " _____ ," or words to that effect) (wrongfully shouting and singing in a public place, to wit: _____) (_____).

42. Article 117—Provoking speeches or gestures

a. *Text of statute.*

Any person subject to this chapter who uses provoking or reproachful words or gestures towards any other person subject to this chapter shall be punished as a court-martial may direct.

b. *Elements.*

(1) That the accused wrongfully used words or gestures toward a certain person;

(2) That the words or gestures used were provoking or reproachful; and

(3) That the person toward whom the words or gestures were used was a person subject to the code.

c. *Explanation.*

(1) *In general.* As used in this article, "provoking" and "reproachful" describe those words or gestures which are used in the presence of the person to whom they are directed and which a rea-sonable person would expect to induce a breach of the peace under the circumstances. These words and gestures do not include reprimands, censures, reproofs and the like which may properly be administered in the interests of training, efficiency, or discipline in the armed forces.

(2) *Knowledge.* It is not necessary that the accused have knowledge that the person toward whom the words or gestures are directed is a person subject to the code.

d. *Lesser included offenses.* See paragraph 3 of this part and Appendix 12A.

e. *Maximum punishment.* Confinement for 6 months and forfeiture of two-thirds pay per month for 6 months.

f. *Sample specification.*

In that _____ (personal jurisdiction data), did, (at/on board—location) (subject-matter jurisdiction data, if required), on or about _____ 20 ___, wrongfully use (provoking) (reproachful) (words, to wit: " _____ :" or words to that effect) (and) (gestures, to wit: _____) towards (Sergeant _____ , U.S. Air Force) (_____).

43. Article 118—Murder

a. *Text of statute.*

Any person subject to this chapter who, without justification or excuse, unlawfully kills a human being, when he—

(1) has a premeditated design to kill;

(2) intends to kill or inflict great bodily harm;

(3) is engaged in an act that is inherently dangerous to another and evinces a wanton disregard of human life; or

(4) is engaged in the perpetration or attempted perpetration of burglary, sodomy, rape, rape of a child, sexual assault, sexual assault of a child, aggravated sexual contact, sexual abuse of a child, robbery or aggravated arson; is guilty of murder, and shall suffer such punishment as a court-martial may direct, except that if found guilty under clause (1) or (4), he shall suffer death or imprisonment for life as a court-martial may direct.

[Note: This statute was amended by Public Law 112-81 (FY12 NDAA), effective 28 June 2012, to reflect the modified names of sexual offenses in Articles 120 and 120b.]

b. *Elements.*

(1) *Premeditated murder.*

(a) That a certain named or described person is dead;

(b) That the death resulted from the act or omission of the accused;

(c) That the killing was unlawful; and

(d) That, at the time of the killing, the accused had a premeditated design to kill.

(2) *Intent to kill or inflict great bodily harm.*

(a) That a certain named or described person is dead;

(b) That the death resulted from the act or omission of the accused;

(c) That the killing was unlawful; and

(d) That, at the time of the killing, the accused had the intent to kill or inflict great bodily harm upon a person.

(3) *Act inherently dangerous to another.*

(a) That a certain named or described person is dead;

(b) That the death resulted from the intentional act of the accused;

(c) That this act was inherently dangerous to another and showed a wanton disregard for human life;

(d) That the accused knew that death or great bodily harm was a probable consequence of the act; and

(e) That the killing was unlawful.

(4) *During certain offenses.*

(a) That a certain named or described person is dead;

(b) That the death resulted from the act or omission of the accused;

(c) That the killing was unlawful; and

(d) That, at the time of the killing, the accused was engaged in the perpetration or attempted perpetration of burglary, sodomy, rape, rape of a child, aggravated sexual assault, aggravated sexual assault of a child, aggravated sexual contact, aggravated sexual abuse of a child, aggravated sexual contact with a child, robbery, or aggravated arson.

c. *Explanation.*

(1) *In general.* Killing a human being is unlawful when done without justification or excuse. *See* R.C.M. 916. Whether an unlawful killing constitutes murder or a lesser offense depends upon the circum-

stances. The offense is committed at the place of the act or omission although the victim may have died elsewhere. Whether death occurs at the time of the accused's act or omission, or at some time thereafter, it must have followed from an injury received by the victim which resulted from the act or omission.

(2) *Premeditated murder.*

(a) *Premeditation.* A murder is not premeditated unless the thought of taking life was consciously conceived and the act or omission by which it was taken was intended. Premeditated murder is murder committed after the formation of a specific intent to kill someone and consideration of the act intended. It is not necessary that the intention to kill have been entertained for any particular or considerable length of time. When a fixed purpose to kill has been deliberately formed, it is immaterial how soon afterwards it is put into execution. The existence of premeditation may be inferred from the circumstances.

(b) *Transferred premeditation.* When an accused with a premeditated design attempted to unlawfully kill a certain person, but, by mistake or inadvertence, killed another person, the accused is still criminally responsible for a premeditated murder, because the premeditated design to kill is transferred from the intended victim to the actual victim.

(c) *Intoxication.* Voluntary intoxication (*see* R.C.M. 916(1)(2)) not amounting to legal insanity may reduce premeditated murder (Article 118(1)) to unpremeditated murder (Article 118(2) or (3)) but it does not reduce either premeditated murder or unpremeditated murder to manslaughter (Article 119) or any other lesser offense.

(3) *Intent to kill or inflict great bodily harm.*

(a) *Intent.* An unlawful killing without premeditation is also murder when the accused had either an intent to kill or inflict great bodily harm. It may be inferred that a person intends the natural and probable consequences of an act purposely done. Hence, if a person does an intentional act likely to result in death or great bodily injury, it may be inferred that death or great bodily injury was intended. The intent need not be directed toward the person killed, or exist for any particular time before commission of the act, or have previously existed at all. It is sufficient that it existed at the time of the act or omission (except if death is inflicted in the heat of a sudden passion caused by adequate provocation— *see* paragraph 44). For example, a person committing housebreaking who strikes and kills the householder attempting to prevent flight can be guilty of murder even if the householder was not seen until the moment before striking the fatal blow.

(b) *Great bodily harm.* "Great bodily harm" means serious injury; it does not include minor injuries such as a black eye or a bloody nose, but it does include fractured or dislocated bones, deep cuts, torn members of the body, serious damage to internal organs, and other serious bodily injuries. It is synonymous with the term "grievous bodily harm."

(c) *Intoxication.* Voluntary intoxication not amounting to legal insanity does not reduce unpremeditated murder to manslaughter (Article 119) or any other lesser offense.

(4) *Act inherently dangerous to others.*

(a) *Wanton disregard of human life.* Intentionally engaging in an act inherently dangerous to another—although without an intent to cause the death of or great bodily harm to any particular person, or even with a wish that death will not be caused—may also constitute murder if the act shows wanton disregard of human life. Such disregard is characterized by heedlessness of the probable consequences of the act or omission, or indifference to the likelihood of death or great bodily harm. Examples include throwing a live grenade toward another in jest or flying an aircraft very low over one or more persons to cause alarm.

(b) *Knowledge.* The accused must know that death or great bodily harm was a probable consequence of the inherently dangerous act. Such knowledge may be proved by circumstantial evidence.

(5) *During certain offenses.*

(a) *In general.* The commission or attempted commission of any of the offenses listed in Article 118(4) is likely to result in homicide, and when an unlawful killing occurs as a consequence of the perpetration or attempted perpetration of one of these offenses, the killing is murder. Under these circumstances it is not a defense that the killing was unintended or accidental.

(b) *Separate offenses.* The perpetration or attempted perpetration of the burglary, forcible sodomy, rape, robbery, or aggravated arson may be charged separately from the homicide.

d. *Lesser included offenses.* See paragraph 3 of this part and Appendix 12A.

e. *Maximum punishment.*

(1) Article 118(1) or (4)—death. Mandatory minimum—imprisonment for life with eligibility for parole.

(2) Article 118(2) or (3)—such punishment other than death as a court-martial may direct.

f. *Sample specification.*

In that _____ (personal jurisdiction data), did, (at/on board—location) (subject-matter jurisdiction data, if required), on or about _____ 20 __ , (with premeditation) (while (perpetrating) (attempting to perpetrate) _____) murder _____ by means of (shooting him/her with a rifle) (_____).

44. Article 119—Manslaughter

a. *Text of statute.*

(a) **Any person subject to this chapter who, with an intent to kill or inflict great bodily harm, unlawfully kills a human being in the heat of sudden passion caused by adequate provocation is guilty of voluntary manslaughter and shall be punished as a court-martial may direct.**

(b) **Any person subject to this chapter who, without an intent to kill or inflict great bodily harm, unlawfully kills a human being—**

(1) **by culpable negligence; or**

(2) **while perpetrating or attempting to perpetrate an offense, other than those named in clause (4) of section 918 of this title (article 118), directly affecting the person;**
is guilty of involuntary manslaughter and shall be punished as a court-martial may direct.

b. *Elements.*

(1) *Voluntary manslaughter.*

(a) That a certain named or described person is dead;

(b) That the death resulted from the act or omission of the accused;

(c) That the killing was unlawful; and

(d) That, at the time of the killing, the accused had the intent to kill or inflict great bodily harm upon the person killed.
[Note: Add the following if applicable]

(e) That the person killed was a child under the age of 16 years.

(2) *Involuntary manslaughter.*

(a) That a certain named or described person is dead;

(b) That the death resulted from the act or omission of the accused;

(c) That the killing was unlawful; and

(d) That this act or omission of the accused constituted culpable negligence, or occurred while the accused was perpetrating or attempting to perpetrate an offense directly affecting the person other than burglary, forcible sodomy, rape, robbery, or aggravated arson.

[Note: Add the following if applicable]

(e) That the person killed was a child under the age of 16 years.

c. *Explanation.*

(1) *Voluntary manslaughter.*

(a) *Nature of offense.* An unlawful killing, although done with an intent to kill or inflict great bodily harm, is not murder but voluntary manslaughter if committed in the heat of sudden passion caused by adequate provocation. Heat of passion may result from fear or rage. A person may be provoked to such an extent that in the heat of sudden passion caused by the provocation, although not in necessary defense of life or to prevent bodily harm, a fatal blow may be struck before self-control has returned. Although adequate provocation does not excuse the homicide, it does preclude conviction of murder.

(b) *Nature of provocation.* The provocation must be adequate to excite uncontrollable passion in a reasonable person, and the act of killing must be committed under and because of the passion. However, the provocation must not be sought or induced as an excuse for killing or doing harm. If, judged by the standard of a reasonable person, sufficient cooling time elapses between the provocation and the killing, the offense is murder, even if the accused's passion persists. Examples of acts which may, depending on the circumstances, constitute adequate provocation are the unlawful infliction of great bodily harm, unlawful imprisonment, and the sight by one spouse of an act of adultery committed by the other spouse. Insulting or abusive words or gestures, a slight blow with the hand or fist, and trespass or other injury to property are not, standing alone, adequate provocation.

(c) *When committed upon a child under 16 years of age.* The maximum punishment is increased when voluntary manslaughter is committed upon a child under 16 years of age. The accused's knowl-

edge that the child was under 16 years of age at the time of the offense is not required for the increased maximum punishment.

(2) *Involuntary manslaughter.*

(a) *Culpable negligence.*

(i) *Nature of culpable negligence.* Culpable negligence is a degree of carelessness greater than simple negligence. It is a negligent act or omission accompanied by a culpable disregard for the foreseeable consequences to others of that act or omission. Thus, the basis of a charge of involuntary manslaughter may be a negligent act or omission which, when viewed in the light of human experience, might foreseeably result in the death of another, even though death would not necessarily be a natural and probable consequence of the act or omission. Acts which may amount to culpable negligence include negligently conducting target practice so that the bullets go in the direction of an inhabited house within range; pointing a pistol in jest at another and pulling the trigger, believing, but without taking reasonable precautions to ascertain, that it would not be dangerous; and carelessly leaving poisons or dangerous drugs where they may endanger life.

(ii) *Legal duty required.* When there is no legal duty to act there can be no neglect. Thus, when a stranger makes no effort to save a drowning person, or a person allows a beggar to freeze or starve to death, no crime is committed.

(b) *Offense directly affecting the person.* An "offense directly affecting the person" means one affecting some particular person as distinguished from an offense affecting society in general. Among offenses directly affecting the person are the various types of assault, battery, false imprisonment, voluntary engagement in an affray, and maiming.

(c) *When committed upon a child under 16 years of age.* The maximum punishment is increased when involuntary manslaughter is committed upon a child under 16 years of age. The accused's knowledge that the child was under 16 years of age at the time of the offense is not required for the increased maximum punishment.

d. *Lesser included offenses.* See paragraph 3 of this part and Appendix 12A.

e. *Maximum punishment.*

(1) *Voluntary manslaughter.* Dishonorable discharge, forfeiture of all pay and allowances, and confinement for 15 years.

(2) *Involuntary manslaughter.* Dishonorable discharge, forfeiture of all pay and allowances, and confinement for 10 years.

(3) *Voluntary manslaughter of a child under 16 years of age.* Dishonorable discharge, forfeiture of all pay and allowances, and confinement for 20 years.

(4) *Involuntary manslaughter of a child under 16 years of age.* Dishonorable discharge, forfeiture of all pay and allowances, and confinement for 15 years.

f. *Sample specifications.*

(1) *Voluntary manslaughter.*

In that _____ (personal jurisdiction data), did, (at/on board – location) (subject matter jurisdiction data, if required), on or about _____ 20 __ , willfully and unlawfully kill _____ , (a child under 16 years of age) by _____ him/her (in) (on) the _____ with a _____ .

(2) *Involuntary manslaughter.*

In that _____ (personal jurisdiction data), did, (at/on board location) (subject matter jurisdiction data, if required), on or about _____ (by culpable negligence) (while (perpetrating) (attempting to perpetrate) an offense directly affecting the person of _____ , to wit: (maiming) (a battery) (_____)) unlawfully kill _____ (a child under 16 years of age) by _____ him/her (in)(on) the _____ with a _____ .

44a. Article 119a—Death or injury of an unborn child

a. *Text of statute.*

(a)(1) **Any person subject to this chapter who engages in conduct that violates any of the provisions of law listed in subsection (b) and thereby causes the death of, or bodily injury (as defined in section 1365 of title 18) to, a child, who is in utero at the time the conduct takes place, is guilty of a separate offense under this section and shall, upon conviction, be punished by such punishment, other than death, as a court-martial may direct, which shall be consistent with the punishments prescribed by the President for that conduct had that injury or death occurred to the unborn child's mother.**

(2) **An offense under this section does not require proof that—**

(i) **the person engaging in the conduct had knowledge or should have had knowledge that the victim of the underlying offense was pregnant; or**

(ii) **the accused intended to cause the death of, or bodily injury to, the unborn child.**

(3) **If the person engaging in the conduct thereby intentionally kills or attempts to kill the unborn child, that person shall, instead of being punished under paragraph (1), be punished as provided under sections 880, 918, and 919(a) of this title (articles 80, 118, and 119(a)) for intentionally killing or attempting to kill a human being.**

(4) **Notwithstanding any other provision of law, the death penalty shall not be imposed for an offense under this section.**

(b) **The provisions referred to in subsection (a) are sections 918, 919(a), 919(b)(2), 920(a), 922, 924, 926, and 928 of this title (articles 118, 119(a), 119(b)(2), 120(a), 122, 124, 126, and 128).**

(c) **Nothing in this section shall be construed to permit the prosecution—**

(1) **of any person authorized by state or federal law to perform abortions for conduct relating to an abortion for which the consent of the pregnant woman, or a person authorized by law to act on her behalf, has been obtained or for which such consent is implied by law;**

(2) **of any person for any medical treatment of the pregnant woman or her unborn child; or**

(3) **of any woman with respect to her unborn child.**

(d) **As used in this section, the term "unborn child" means a child in utero, and the term "child in utero" or "child, who is in utero" means a member of the species homo sapiens, at any stage of development, who is carried in the womb.**

b. *Elements.*

(1) *Injuring an unborn child.*

(a) That the accused was engaged in the [(murder (article 118)), (voluntary manslaughter (article 119(a))), (involuntary manslaughter (article 119(b)(2))), (rape (article 120)), (robbery (article 122)), (maiming (article 124)), (assault (article 128)), of] or [burning or setting afire, as arson (article 126), of (a dwelling inhabited by) (a structure or property (known to be occupied by) (belonging to))] a woman;

(b) That the woman was then pregnant; and

(c) That the accused thereby caused bodily injury to the unborn child of that woman.

(2) *Killing an unborn child.*

(a) That the accused was engaged in the [(murder (article 118)), (voluntary manslaughter (article 119(a))), (involuntary manslaughter (article 119(b)(2))), (rape (article 120)), (robbery (article 122)), (maiming (article 124)), (assault (article 128)), of] or [burning or setting afire, as arson (article 126), of (a dwelling inhabited by) (a structure or property known to (be occupied by) (belong to))] a woman;

(b) That the woman was then pregnant; and

(c) That the accused thereby caused the death of the unborn child of that woman.

(3) *Attempting to kill an unborn child.*

(a) That the accused was engaged in the [(murder (article 118)), (voluntary manslaughter (article 119(a))), (involuntary manslaughter (article 119(b)(2))), (rape (article 120)), (robbery (article 122)), (maiming (article 124)), (assault (article 128)), of] or [burning or setting afire, as arson (article 126), of (a dwelling inhabited by) (a structure or property (known to be occupied by) (belonging to))] a woman;

(b) That the woman was then pregnant; and

(c) That the accused thereby intended and attempted to kill the unborn child of that woman.

(4) *Intentionally killing an unborn child.*

(a) That the accused was engaged in the [(murder (article 118)), (voluntary manslaughter (article 119(a))), (involuntary manslaughter (article 119(b)(2))), (rape (article 120)), (robbery (article 122)), (maiming (article 124)), (assault (article 128)), of] or [burning or setting afire, as arson (article 126), of (a dwelling inhabited by) (a structure or property (known to be occupied by) (belonging to))] a woman;

(b) That the woman was then pregnant; and

(c) That the accused thereby intentionally killed the unborn child of that woman.

c. *Explanation.*

(1) *Nature of offense.* This article makes it a separate, punishable crime to cause the death of or bodily injury to an unborn child while engaged in

arson (article 126, UCMJ); murder (article 118, UCMJ); voluntary manslaughter (article 119(a), UCMJ); involuntary manslaughter (article 119(b)(2), UCMJ); rape (article 120(a), UCMJ); robbery (article 122, UCMJ); maiming (article 124, UCMJ); or assault (article 128, UCMJ) against a pregnant woman. For all underlying offenses, except arson, this article requires that the victim of the underlying offense be the pregnant mother. For purposes of arson, the pregnant mother must have some nexus to the arson such that she sustained some "bodily injury" due to the arson. For the purposes of this article the term "woman" means a female of any age. This article does not permit the prosecution of any—

(a) person for conduct relating to an abortion for which the consent of the pregnant woman, or a person authorized by law to act on her behalf, has been obtained or for which such consent is implied by law;

(b) person for any medical treatment of the pregnant woman or her unborn child; or

(c) woman with respect to her unborn child.

(2) The offenses of "injuring an unborn child" and "killing an unborn child" do not require proof that—

(a) the person engaging in the conduct (the accused) had knowledge or should have had knowledge that the victim of the underlying offense was pregnant; or

(b) the accused intended to cause the death of, or bodily injury to, the unborn child.

(3) The offense of "attempting to kill an unborn child" requires that the accused intended by his conduct to cause the death of the unborn child (See paragraph b(3)(c) above).

(4) *Bodily injury.* For the purpose of this offense, the term "bodily injury" is that which is provided by section 1365 of title 18, to wit: a cut, abrasion, bruise, burn, or disfigurement; physical pain; illness; impairment of the function of a bodily member, organ, or mental faculty; or any other injury to the body, no matter how temporary.

(5) *Unborn child.* "Unborn child" means a child in utero or a member of the species homo sapiens who is carried in the womb, at any stage of development, from conception to birth.

d. *Lesser included offenses.* See paragraph 3 of this part and Appendix 12A.

e. *Maximum punishment.*

The maximum punishment for (1) Injuring an unborn child; (2) Killing an unborn child; (3) Attempting to kill an unborn child; or (4) Intentionally killing an unborn child is such punishment, other than death, as a court-martial may direct, but shall be consistent with the punishment had the bodily injury, death, attempt to kill, or intentional killing occurred to the unborn child's mother.

f. *Sample specifications.*

(1) *Injuring an unborn child.*

In that _____ (personal jurisdiction data), did (at/on board—location), (subject-matter jurisdiction data, if required), on or about _____ 20 __ , cause bodily injury to the unborn child of , a pregnant woman, by engaging in the [(murder) (voluntary manslaughter) (involuntary manslaughter) (rape) (robbery) (maiming) (assault) of] [(burning) (setting afire) of (a dwelling inhabited by) (a structure or property known to (be occupied by) (belong to))] that woman.

(2) *Killing an unborn child.*

In that _____ (personal jurisdiction data), did (at/on board—location), (subject-matter jurisdiction data, if required), on or about _____ 20 __ , cause the death of the unborn child of , a pregnant woman, by engaging in the [(murder) (voluntary manslaughter) (involuntary manslaughter) (rape) (robbery) (maiming) (assault) of] [(burning) (setting afire) of (a dwelling inhabited by) (a structure or property known to (be occupied by) (belong to))] that woman.

(3) *Attempting to kill an unborn child.*

In that _____ (personal jurisdiction data), did (at/on board—location), (subject-matter jurisdiction data, if required), on or about _____ 20 __ , attempt to kill the unborn child of , a pregnant woman, by engaging in the [(murder) (voluntary manslaughter) (involuntary manslaughter) (rape) (robbery) (maiming) (assault) of] [(burning) (setting afire) of (a dwelling inhabited by) (a structure or property known to (be occupied by) (belong to))] that woman.

(4) *Intentionally killing an unborn child.*

In that _____ (personal jurisdiction data), did (at/on board—location), (subject-matter jurisdiction data, if required), on or about _____ 20 __ , intentionally kill the unborn child of , a pregnant woman, by engaging in the [(murder) (voluntary manslaughter) (involuntary manslaughter) (rape)

(robbery) (maiming) (assault) of] [(burning) (setting afire) of (a dwelling inhabited by) (a structure or property known to (be occupied by) (belong to))] that woman.

45. Article 120—Rape and sexual assault generally

[Note: This statute applies to offenses committed on or after 28 June 2012. Previous versions of Article 120 are located as follows: for offenses committed on or before 30 September 2007, *see* Appendix 27; for offenses committed during the period 1 October 2007 through 27 June 2012, *see* Appendix 28.]

a. *Text of statute.*

(a) **Rape. Any person subject to this chapter who commits a sexual act upon another person by—**

(1) **using unlawful force against that other person;**

(2) **using force causing or likely to cause death or grievous bodily harm to any person;**

(3) **threatening or placing that other person in fear that any person will be subjected to death, grievous bodily harm, or kidnapping;**

(4) **first rendering that other person unconscious; or**

(5) **administering to that other person by force or threat of force, or without the knowledge or consent of that person, a drug, intoxicant, or other similar substance and thereby substantially impairing the ability of that other person to appraise or control conduct;**

is guilty of rape and shall be punished as a court-martial may direct.

(b) **Sexual Assault. Any person subject to this chapter who—**

(1) **commits a sexual act upon another person by—**

(A) **threatening or placing that other person in fear;**

(B) **causing bodily harm to that other person;**

(C) **making a fraudulent representation that the sexual act serves a professional purpose; or**

(D) **inducing a belief by any artifice, pretense, or concealment that the person is another person;**

(2) commits a sexual act upon another person when the person knows or reasonably should know that the other person is asleep, unconscious, or otherwise unaware that the sexual act is occurring; or

(3) commits a sexual act upon another person when the other person is incapable of consenting to the sexual act due to—

(A) impairment by any drug, intoxicant, or other similar substance, and that condition is known or reasonably should be known by the person; or

(B) a mental disease or defect, or physical disability, and that condition is known or reasonably should be known by the person;
is guilty of sexual assault and shall be punished as a court-martial may direct.

(c) *Aggravated Sexual Contact.* Any person subject to this chapter who commits or causes sexual contact upon or by another person, if to do so would violate subsection (a) (rape) had the sexual contact been a sexual act, is guilty of aggravated sexual contact and shall be punished as a court-martial may direct.

(d) *Abusive Sexual Contact.* Any person subject to this chapter who commits or causes sexual contact upon or by another person, if to do so would violate subsection (b) (sexual assault) had the sexual contact been a sexual act, is guilty of abusive sexual contact and shall be punished as a court-martial may direct.

(e) *Proof of Threat.* In a prosecution under this section, in proving that a person made a threat, it need not be proven that the person actually intended to carry out the threat or had the ability to carry out the threat.

(f) *Defenses.* An accused may raise any applicable defenses available under this chapter or the Rules for Court-Martial. Marriage is not a defense for any conduct in issue in any prosecution under this section.

(g) *Definitions.* In this section:

(1) *Sexual act.* The term 'sexual act' means—

(A) contact between the penis and the vulva or anus or mouth, and for purposes of this subparagraph contact involving the penis occurs upon penetration, however slight; or

(B) the penetration, however slight, of the vulva or anus or mouth of another by any part of the body or by any object, with an intent to abuse, humiliate, harass, or degrade any person or to arouse or gratify the sexual desire of any person.

(2) *Sexual contact.* The term 'sexual contact' means—

(A) touching, or causing another person to touch, either directly or through the clothing, the genitalia, anus, groin, breast, inner thigh, or buttocks of any person, with an intent to abuse, humiliate, or degrade any person; or

(B) any touching, or causing another person to touch, either directly or through the clothing, any body part of any person, if done with an intent to arouse or gratify the sexual desire of any person.
Touching may be accomplished by any part of the body.

(3) *Bodily harm.* The term 'bodily harm' means any offensive touching of another, however slight, including any nonconsensual sexual act or nonconsensual sexual contact.

(4) *Grievous bodily harm.* The term 'grievous bodily harm' means serious bodily injury. It includes fractured or dislocated bones, deep cuts, torn members of the body, serious damage to internal organs, and other severe bodily injuries. It does not include minor injuries such as a black eye or a bloody nose.

(5) *Force.* The term 'force' means—

(A) the use of a weapon;

(B) the use of such physical strength or violence as is sufficient to overcome, restrain, or injure a person; or

(C) inflicting physical harm sufficient to coerce or compel submission by the victim.

(6) *Unlawful Force.* The term 'unlawful force' means an act of force done without legal justification or excuse.

(7) *Threatening or placing that other person in fear.* The term 'threatening or placing that other person in fear' means a communication or action that is of sufficient consequence to cause a reasonable fear that non-compliance will result in the victim or another person being subjected to the wrongful action contemplated by the communication or action.

(8) *Consent.*

(A) **The term 'consent' means a freely given agreement to the conduct at issue by a competent person. An expression of lack of consent through words or conduct means there is no consent. Lack of verbal or physical resistance or submission resulting from the use of force, threat of force, or placing another person in fear does not constitute consent. A current or previous dating or social or sexual relationship by itself or the manner of dress of the person involved with the accused in the conduct at issue shall not constitute consent.**

(B) **A sleeping, unconscious, or incompetent person cannot consent. A person cannot consent to force causing or likely to cause death or grievous bodily harm or to being rendered unconscious. A person cannot consent while under threat or fear or under the circumstances described in subparagraph (C) or (D) of subsection (b)(1).**

(C) **Lack of consent may be inferred based on the circumstances of the offense. All the surrounding circumstances are to be considered in determining whether a person gave consent, or whether a person did not resist or ceased to resist only because of another person's actions.**

b. *Elements.*

(1) *Rape involving contact between penis and vulva or anus or mouth.*

(a) *By unlawful force*

(i) That the accused committed a sexual act upon another person by causing penetration, however slight, of the vulva or anus or mouth by the penis; and

(ii) That the accused did so with unlawful force.

(b) *By force causing or likely to cause death or grievous bodily harm*

(i) That the accused committed a sexual act upon another person by causing penetration, however slight, of the vulva or anus or mouth by the penis; and

(ii) That the accused did so by using force causing or likely to cause death or grievous bodily harm to any person.

(c) *By threatening or placing that other person in fear that any person would be subjected to death, grievous bodily harm, or kidnapping*

(i) That the accused committed a sexual act upon another person by causing penetration, however slight, of the vulva or anus or mouth by the penis; and

(ii) That the accused did so by threatening or placing that other person in fear that any person would be subjected to death, grievous bodily harm, or kidnapping.

(d) *By first rendering that other person unconscious*

(i) That the accused committed a sexual act upon another person by causing penetration, however slight, of the vulva or anus or mouth by the penis; and

(ii) That the accused did so by first rendering that other person unconscious.

(e) *By administering a drug, intoxicant, or other similar substance*

(i) That the accused committed a sexual act upon another person by causing penetration, however slight, of the vulva or anus or mouth by the penis; and

(ii) That the accused did so by administering to that other person by force or threat of force, or without the knowledge or permission of that person, a drug, intoxicant, or other similar substance and thereby substantially impairing the ability of that other person to appraise or control conduct.

(2) *Rape involving penetration of the vulva or anus or mouth by any part of the body or any object.*

(a) *By force*

(i) That the accused committed a sexual act upon another person by causing penetration, however slight, of the vulva or anus or mouth of another person by any part of the body or by any object;

(ii) That the accused did so with unlawful force; and

(iii) That the accused did so with an intent to abuse, humiliate, harass, or degrade any person or to arouse or gratify the sexual desire of any person.

(b) *By force causing or likely to cause death or grievous bodily harm*

(i) That the accused committed a sexual act upon another person by causing penetration, however slight, of the vulva or anus or mouth of another person by any part of the body or by any object;

(ii) That the accused did so by using force causing or likely to cause death or grievous bodily harm to any person; and

(iii) That the accused did so with an intent to abuse, humiliate, harass, or degrade any person or to arouse or gratify the sexual desire of any person.

(c) *By threatening or placing that other person in fear that any person would be subjected to death, grievous bodily harm, or kidnapping*

(i) That the accused committed a sexual act upon another person by causing penetration, however slight, of the vulva or anus or mouth of another person by any part of the body or by any object;

(ii) That the accused did so by threatening or placing that other person in fear that any person would be subjected to death, grievous bodily harm, or kidnapping; and

(iii) That the accused did so with an intent to abuse, humiliate, harass, or degrade any person or to arouse or gratify the sexual desire of any person.

(d) *By first rendering that other person unconscious*

(i) That the accused committed a sexual act upon another person by causing penetration, however slight, of the vulva or anus or mouth of another person by any part of the body or by any object;

(ii) That the accused did so by first rendering that other person unconscious; and

(iii) That the accused did so with an intent to abuse, humiliate, harass, or degrade any person or to arouse or gratify the sexual desire of any person.

(e) *By administering a drug, intoxicant, or other similar substance*

(i) That the accused committed a sexual act upon another person by causing penetration, however slight, of the vulva or anus or mouth of another person by any part of the body or by any object;

(ii) That the accused did so by administering to that other person by force or threat of force, or without the knowledge or permission of that person, a drug, intoxicant, or other similar substance and thereby substantially impairing the ability of that other person to appraise or control conduct; and

(iii) That the accused did so with an intent to abuse, humiliate, harass, or degrade any person or to arouse or gratify the sexual desire of any person.

(3) *Sexual assault involving contact between penis and vulva or anus or mouth.*

(a) *By threatening or placing that other person in fear*

(i) That the accused committed a sexual act upon another person by causing penetration, however slight, of the vulva or anus or mouth by the penis; and

(ii) That the accused did so by threatening or placing that other person in fear.

(b) *By causing bodily harm*

(i) That the accused committed a sexual act upon another person by causing penetration, however slight, of the vulva or anus or mouth by the penis; and

(ii) That the accused did so by causing bodily harm to that other person.

(c) *By fraudulent representation*

(i) That the accused committed a sexual act upon another person by causing penetration, however slight, of the vulva or anus or mouth by the penis; and

(ii) That the accused did so by making a fraudulent representation that the sexual act served a professional purpose.

(d) *By false pretense*

(i) That the accused committed a sexual act upon another person by causing penetration, however slight, of the vulva or anus or mouth by the penis; and

(ii) That the accused did so by inducing a belief by any artifice, pretense, or concealment that the accused is another person.

(e) *Of a person who is asleep, unconscious, or otherwise unaware the act is occurring*

(i) That the accused committed a sexual act upon another person by causing penetration, however slight, of the vulva or anus or mouth by the penis;

(ii) That the other person was asleep, unconscious, or otherwise unaware that the sexual act was occurring; and

(iii) That the accused knew or reasonably should have known that the other person was asleep, unconscious, or otherwise unaware that the sexual act was occurring.

(f) *When the other person is incapable of consenting*

(i) That the accused committed a sexual act upon another person by causing penetration, however slight, of the vulva or anus or mouth by the penis;

(ii) That the other person was incapable of consenting to the sexual act due to:

(A) Impairment by any drug, intoxicant or other similar substance; or

(B) A mental disease or defect, or physical disability; and

(iii) That the accused knew or reasonably should have known of the impairment, mental disease or defect, or physical disability of the other person.

(4) *Sexual assault involving penetration of the vulva or anus or mouth by any part of the body or any object.*

(a) *By threatening or placing that other person in fear*

(i) That the accused committed a sexual act upon another person by causing penetration, however slight, of the vulva or anus or mouth by any part of the body or by any object;

(ii) That the accused did so by threatening or placing that other person in fear; and

(iii) That the accused did so with an intent to abuse, humiliate, harass, or degrade any person or to arouse or gratify the sexual desire of any person.

(b) *By causing bodily harm*

(i) That the accused committed a sexual act upon another person by causing penetration, however slight, of the vulva or anus or mouth by any part of the body or by any object;

(ii) That the accused did so by causing bodily harm to that other person; and

(iii) That the accused did so with an intent to abuse, humiliate, harass, or degrade any person or to arouse or gratify the sexual desire of any person.

(c) *By fraudulent representation*

(i) That the accused committed a sexual act upon another person by causing penetration, however slight, of the vulva or anus or mouth by any part of the body or by any object;

(ii) That the accused did so by making a fraudulent representation that the sexual act served a professional purpose when it served no professional purpose; and

(iii) That the accused did so with an intent to abuse, humiliate, harass, or degrade any person or to arouse or gratify the sexual desire of any person.

(d) *By false pretense*

(i) That the accused committed a sexual act upon another person by causing penetration, however slight, of the vulva or anus or mouth by any part of the body or by any object;

(ii) That the accused did so by inducing a belief by any artifice, pretense, or concealment that the accused is another person; and

(iii) That the accused did so with an intent to abuse, humiliate, harass, or degrade any person or to arouse or gratify the sexual desire of any person.

(e) *Of a person who is asleep, unconscious, or otherwise unaware the act is occurring*

(i) That the accused committed a sexual act upon another person by causing penetration, however slight, of the vulva or anus or mouth by any part of the body or by any object;

(ii) That the other person was asleep, unconscious, or otherwise unaware that the sexual act was occurring;

(iii) That the accused knew or reasonably should have known that the other person was asleep, unconscious, or otherwise unaware that the sexual act was occurring.

(iv) That the accused did so with an intent to abuse, humiliate, harass, or degrade any person or to arouse or gratify the sexual desire of any person.

(f) *When the other person is incapable of consenting*

(i) That the accused committed a sexual act upon another person by causing penetration, however slight, of the vulva or anus or mouth by any part of the body or by any object;

(ii) That the other person was incapable of consenting to the sexual act due to:

(A) Impairment by any drug, intoxicant or other similar substance; or

(B) A mental disease or defect, or physical disability;

(iii) That the accused knew or reasonably should have known of the impairment, mental disease or defect, or physical disability of the other person; and

(iv) That the accused did so with intent to

abuse, humiliate, harass, or degrade any person or to arouse or gratify the sexual desire of any person.

(5) *Aggravated sexual contact involving the touching of the genitalia, anus, groin, breast, inner thigh, or buttocks of any person.*

(a) *By force*

(i) That the accused committed sexual contact upon another person by touching, or causing another person to touch, either directly or through the clothing, the genitalia, anus, groin, breast, inner thigh, or buttocks of any person;

(ii) That the accused did so with unlawful force; and

(iii) That the accused did so with an intent to abuse, humiliate, harass, or degrade any person or to arouse or gratify the sexual desire of any person.

(b) *By force causing or likely to cause death or grievous bodily harm*

(i) That the accused committed sexual contact upon another person by touching, or causing another person to touch, either directly or through the clothing, the genitalia, anus, groin, breast, inner thigh, or buttocks of any person;

(ii) That the accused did so by using force causing or likely to cause death or grievous bodily harm to any person; and

(iii) That the accused did so with an intent to abuse, humiliate, harass, or degrade any person or to arouse or gratify the sexual desire of any person.

(c) *By threatening or placing that other person in fear that any person would be subjected to death, grievous bodily harm, or kidnapping*

(i) That the accused committed sexual contact upon another person by touching, or causing another person to touch, either directly or through the clothing, the genitalia, anus, groin, breast, inner thigh, or buttocks of any person;

(ii) That the accused did so by threatening or placing that other person in fear that any person would be subjected to death, grievous bodily harm, or kidnapping; and

(iii) That the accused did so with an intent to abuse, humiliate, harass, or degrade any person or to arouse or gratify the sexual desire of any person.

(d) *By first rendering that other person unconscious*

(i) That the accused committed sexual contact upon another person by touching, or causing

another person to touch, either directly or through the clothing, the genitalia, anus, groin, breast, inner thigh, or buttocks of any person;

(ii) That the accused did so by first rendering that other person unconscious; and

(iii) That the accused did so with intent to abuse, humiliate, harass, or degrade any person or to arouse or gratify the sexual desire of any person.

(e) *By administering a drug, intoxicant, or other similar substance*

(i) That the accused committed sexual contact upon another person by touching, or causing another person to touch, either directly or through the clothing, the genitalia, anus, groin, breast, inner thigh, or buttocks of any person;

(ii) That the accused did so by administering to that other person by force or threat of force, or without the knowledge or permission of that person, a drug, intoxicant, or other similar substance and thereby substantially impairing the ability of that other person to appraise or control conduct; and

(iii) That the accused did so with intent to abuse, humiliate, harass, or degrade any person or to arouse or gratify the sexual desire of any person.

(6) *Aggravated sexual contact involving the touching of any body part of any person.*

(a) *By force*

(i) That the accused committed sexual contact upon another person by touching, or causing another person to touch, any body part of any person;

(ii) That the accused did so with unlawful force; and

(iii) That the accused did so with intent to arouse or gratify the sexual desire of any person.

(b) *By force causing or likely to cause death or grievous bodily harm*

(i) That the accused committed sexual contact upon another person by touching, or causing another person to touch, any body part of any person;

(ii) That the accused did so by using force causing or likely to cause death or grievous bodily harm to any person; and

(iii) That the accused did so with intent to arouse or gratify the sexual desire of any person.

(c) *By threatening or placing that other person*

in fear that any person would be subjected to death, grievous bodily harm, or kidnapping

(i) That the accused committed sexual contact upon another person by touching, or causing another person to touch, any body part of any person;

(ii) That the accused did so by threatening or placing that other person in fear that any person would be subjected to death, grievous bodily harm, or kidnapping; and

(iii) That the accused did so with intent to arouse or gratify the sexual desire of any person.

(d) *By first rendering that other person unconscious*

(i) That the accused committed sexual contact upon another person by touching, or causing another person to touch, any body part of any person;

(ii) That the accused did so by first rendering that other person unconscious; and

(iii) That the accused did so with intent to arouse or gratify the sexual desire of any person.

(e) *By administering a drug, intoxicant, or other similar substance*

(i) That the accused committed sexual contact upon another person by touching, or causing another person to touch, any body part of any person;

(ii) That the accused did so by administering to that other person by force or threat of force, or without the knowledge or permission of that person, a drug, intoxicant, or other similar substance and thereby substantially impairing the ability of that other person to appraise or control conduct; and

(iii) That the accused did so with intent to arouse or gratify the sexual desire of any person.

(7) *Abusive sexual contact involving the touching of the genitalia, anus, groin, breast, inner thigh, or buttocks of any person.*

(a) *By threatening or placing that other person in fear*

(i) That the accused committed sexual contact upon another person by touching, or causing another person to touch, either directly or through the clothing, the genitalia, anus, groin, breast, inner thigh, or buttocks of any person;

(ii) That the accused did so by threatening or placing that other person in fear; and

(iii) That the accused did so with intent to abuse, humiliate, harass, or degrade any person or to arouse or gratify the sexual desire of any person.

(b) *By causing bodily harm*

(i) That the accused committed sexual contact upon another person by touching, or causing another person to touch, either directly or through the clothing, the genitalia, anus, groin, breast, inner thigh, or buttocks of any person;

(ii) That the accused did so by causing bodily harm to that other person; and

(iii) That the accused did so with intent to abuse, humiliate, harass, or degrade any person or to arouse or gratify the sexual desire of any person.

(c) *By fraudulent representation*

(i) That the accused committed sexual contact upon another person by touching, or causing another person to touch, either directly or through the clothing, the genitalia, anus, groin, breast, inner thigh, or buttocks of any person;

(ii) That the accused did so by making a fraudulent representation that the sexual act served a professional purpose; and

(iii) That the accused did so with intent to abuse, humiliate, harass, or degrade any person or to arouse or gratify the sexual desire of any person.

(d) *By false pretense*

(i) That the accused committed sexual contact upon another person by touching, or causing another person to touch, either directly or through the clothing, the genitalia, anus, groin, breast, inner thigh, or buttocks of any person;

(ii) That the accused did so by inducing a belief by any artifice, pretense, or concealment that the accused is another person; and

(iii) That the accused did so with intent to abuse, humiliate, harass, or degrade any person or to arouse or gratify the sexual desire of any person.

(e) *Of a person who is asleep, unconscious, or otherwise unaware the act is occurring*

(i) That the accused committed sexual contact upon another person by touching, or causing another person to touch, either directly or through the clothing, the genitalia, anus, groin, breast, inner thigh, or buttocks of any person;

(ii) That the other person was asleep, unconscious, or otherwise unaware that the sexual act was occurring;

(iii) That the accused knew or reasonably should have known that the other person was asleep, unconscious, or otherwise unaware that the sexual act was occurring; and

(iv) That the accused did so with intent to abuse, humiliate, harass, or degrade any person or to arouse or gratify the sexual desire of any person.

(f) *When the other person is incapable of consenting*

(i) That the accused committed sexual contact upon another person by touching, or causing another person to touch, either directly or through the clothing, the genitalia, anus, groin, breast, inner thigh, or buttocks of any person;

(ii) That the other person was incapable of consenting to the sexual act due to:

(A) Impairment by any drug, intoxicant or other similar substance; or

(B) A mental disease or defect, or physical disability;

(iii) That the accused knew or reasonably should have known of the impairment, mental disease or defect, or physical disability of the other person; and

(iv) That the accused did so with intent to abuse, humiliate, harass, or degrade any person or to arouse or gratify the sexual desire of any person.

(8) *Abusive sexual contact involving the touching of any body part of any person.*

(a) *By threatening or placing that other person in fear*

(i) That the accused committed sexual contact upon another person by touching, or causing another person to touch, any body part of any person;

(ii) That the accused did so by threatening or placing that other person in fear; and

(iii) That the accused did so with intent to arouse or gratify the sexual desire of any person.

(b) *By causing bodily harm*

(i) That the accused committed sexual contact upon another person by touching, or causing another person to touch, any body part of any person;

(ii) That the accused did so by causing bodily harm to that other person; and

(iii) That the accused did so with intent to arouse or gratify the sexual desire of any person.

(c) *By fraudulent representation*

(i) That the accused committed sexual contact upon another person by touching, or causing another person to touch, any body part of any person;

(ii) That the accused did so by making a fraudulent representation that the sexual act served a professional purpose when it served no professional purpose; and

(iii) That the accused did so with intent to arouse or gratify the sexual desire of any person.

(d) *By false pretense*

(i) That the accused committed sexual contact upon another person by touching, or causing another person to touch, any body part of any person;

(ii) That the accused did so by inducing a belief by any artifice, pretense, or concealment that the accused is another person; and

(iii) That the accused did so with intent to arouse or gratify the sexual desire of any person.

(e) *Of a person who is asleep, unconscious, or otherwise unaware the act is occurring*

(i) That the accused committed sexual contact upon another person by touching, or causing another person to touch, any body part of any person;

(ii) That the other person was asleep, unconscious, or otherwise unaware that the sexual act was occurring;

(iii) That the accused knew or reasonably should have known that the other person was asleep, unconscious, or otherwise unaware that the sexual act was occurring; and

(iv) That the accused did so with intent to arouse or gratify the sexual desire of any person.

(f) *When the other person is incapable of consenting*

(i) That the accused committed sexual contact upon another person by touching, or causing another person to touch, any body part of any person;

(ii) That the other person was incapable of consenting to the sexual act due to:

(A) Impairment by any drug, intoxicant, or other similar substance; or

(B) A mental disease or defect, or physical disability;

(iii) That the accused knew or reasonably should have known of the impairment, mental disease or defect, or physical disability of the other person; and

(iv) That the accused did so with intent to arouse or gratify the sexual desire of any person.

c. *Explanation.*

(1) *In general.* Sexual offenses have been separated into three statutes: adults (120), children (120b), and other offenses (120c).

(2) *Definitions.* The terms are defined in Paragraph 45.a.(g).

(3) *Victim character and privilege.* See Mil. R. Evid. 412 concerning rules of evidence relating to the character of the victim of an alleged sexual offense. See Mil. R. Evid. 514 concerning rules of evidence relating to privileged communications between the victim and victim advocate.

(4) *Consent as an element.* Lack of consent is not an element of any offense under this paragraph unless expressly stated. Consent may be relevant for other purposes.

d. *Lesser included offenses.* See paragraph 3 of this part and Appendix 12A.

e. *Maximum punishments.*

(1) *Rape.* Forfeiture of all pay and allowances, and confinement for life without eligibility for parole. Mandatory minimum – Dismissal or dishonorable discharge.

(2) *Sexual assault.* Forfeiture of all pay and allowances and confinement for 30 years. Mandatory minimum – Dismissal or dishonorable discharge.

(3) *Aggravated sexual contact.* Dishonorable discharge, forfeiture of all pay and allowances, and confinement for 20 years.

(4) *Abusive sexual contact.* Dishonorable discharge, forfeiture of all pay and allowances, and confinement for 7 years.

f. *Sample specifications.*

(1) *Rape involving contact between penis and vulva or anus or mouth.*

(a) *By force.* In that (personal jurisdiction data), did (at/on board location), on or about _____, commit a sexual act upon _____ by causing penetration of _____'s (vulva) (anus) (mouth) with _____'s penis, by using unlawful force.

(b) *By force causing or likely to cause death or grievous bodily harm.* In that (personal jurisdiction data), did (at/on board location), on or about _____ 20__, commit a sexual act upon _____ by causing penetration of _____'s (vulva) (anus) (mouth) with _____'s penis, by using force likely to cause death or grievous bodily harm to _____ _, to wit: _____.

(c) *By threatening or placing that other person in fear that any person would be subjected to death, grievous bodily harm, or kidnapping.* In that (personal jurisdiction data), did (at/on board location), on or about _____ 20 ___, commit a sexual act upon _____ by causing penetration of _____'s (vulva) (anus) (mouth) with _____'s penis, by (threatening _____) (placing _____ in fear) that _____ would be subjected to (death) (grievous bodily harm) (kidnapping).

(d) *By first rendering that other person unconscious.* In that (personal jurisdiction data), did (at/on board location), on or about _____ 20__, commit a sexual act upon _____ by causing penetration of _____'s (vulva) (anus) (mouth) with _____'s penis, by first rendering _____ unconscious by _____.

(e) *By administering a drug, intoxicant, or other similar substance.* In that (personal jurisdiction data), did (at/on board location), on or about _____ 20__, commit a sexual act upon _____ by causing penetration of _____'s (vulva) (anus) (mouth) with _____'s penis, by administering to _____ (by force) (by threat of force) (without the knowledge or permission of _____ __) a (drug) (intoxicant) (list other similar substance), to wit: _____, thereby substantially impairing the ability of _____ to appraise or control his/her conduct.

(2) *Rape involving penetration of genital opening by any part of the body or any object.*

(a) *By force.* In that (personal jurisdiction data), did (at/on board location), on or about ____ 20_ _, commit a sexual act upon _____, by penetrating the (vulva) (anus) (mouth) of _____ ____ with (list body part or object) by using unlawful force, with an intent to (abuse) (humiliate) (harass) (degrade) (arouse/gratify the sexual desire of) _____ _____.

(b) *By force causing or likely to cause death or grievous bodily injury.* In that (personal jurisdiction data), did (at/on board location), on or about _____ 20__, commit a sexual act upon _____, by penetrating the (vulva) (anus) (mouth) of _____ _ with (list body part or object) by using force likely to cause death or grievous bodily harm to _____, to wit: _____, with an intent to (abuse) (humiliate) (harass) (degrade) (arouse/gratify the sexual desire of) _____.

(c) *By threatening or placing that other person in fear that any person would be subjected to death, grievous bodily harm, or kidnapping.* In that (personal jurisdiction data), did (at/on board location), on or about ____ 20__, commit a sexual act upon ____ _____, by penetrating the (vulva) (anus) (mouth) of _____ with (list body part or object) by (threatening _____) (placing _____ in fear) that _ _____ would be subjected to (death) (grievous bodily harm) (kidnapping), with an intent to (abuse) (humiliate) (harass) (degrade) (arouse/gratify the sexual desire of) _____.

(d) *By first rendering that other person unconscious.* In that (personal jurisdiction data), did (at/on board location), on or about ____ 20__, commit a sexual act upon _____, by penetrating the (vulva) (anus) (mouth) of _____ with (list body part or object) by first rendering _____ unconscious, with an intent to (abuse) (humiliate) (harass) (degrade) (arouse/gratify the sexual desire of) _____ _____.

(e) *By administering a drug, intoxicant, or other similar substance.* In that (personal jurisdiction data), did (at/on board location), on or about ____ 20__, commit a sexual act upon _____, by penetrating the (vulva) (anus) (mouth) of _____ ___ with (list body part or object) by administering to _____ (by force) (by threat of force) (without the knowledge or permission of _____ __) a (drug) (intoxicant) (list other similar substance), to wit: _____, thereby substantially impairing the ability of _____ to appraise or control his/her conduct, with an intent to (abuse) (humiliate) (harass) (degrade) (arouse/gratify the sexual desire of) _____.

(3) *Sexual assault involving contact between penis and vulva or anus or mouth.*

(a) *By threatening or placing that other person in fear.* In that (personal jurisdiction data), did (at/on

board location), on or about _____ 20__, commit a sexual act upon _____, by causing penetration of _____'s (vulva) (anus) (mouth) with _____ ___'s penis, by (threatening _____) (placing __ _____ in fear).

(b) *By causing bodily harm.* In that (personal jurisdiction data), did (at/on board location), on or about ____ 20__, commit a sexual act upon _____ , by causing penetration of _____'s (vulva) (anus) (mouth) with _____'s penis by causing bodily harm to _____, to wit: _____.

(c) *By fraudulent representation.* In that (personal jurisdiction data), did (at/on board location), on or about _____ 20__, commit a sexual act upon _ _____, by causing penetration of _____'s (vulva) (anus) (mouth) with _____'s penis by making a fraudulent representation that the sexual act served a professional purpose, to wit: _____ _.

(d) *By false pretense.* In that (personal jurisdiction data), did (at/on board location), on or about __ ___ 20__, commit a sexual act upon _____, by causing penetration of _____'s (vulva) (anus) (mouth) with _____'s penis by inducing a belief by (artifice) (pretense) (concealment) that the said accused was another person.

(e) *Of a person who is asleep, unconscious, or otherwise unaware the act is occurring.* In that (personal jurisdiction data), did (at/on board location), on or about _____ 20__, commit a sexual act upon _ _____, by causing penetration of _____'s (vulva) (anus) (mouth) with _____'s penis when he/she knew or reasonably should have known that _ _____ was (asleep) (unconscious) (unaware the sexual act was occurring due to _____).

(f) *When the other person is incapable of consenting.* In that (personal jurisdiction data), did (at/on board location), on or about _____ 20__, commit a sexual act upon _____, by causing penetration of _____'s (vulva) (anus) (mouth) with _____ __'s penis, when _____ was incapable of consenting to the sexual act because he/she [was impaired by (a drug, to wit: _____) (an intoxicant, to wit: _____) (   )] [had a (mental disease, to wit: _____) (mental defect, to wit: _____) (physical disability, to wit: _____)], a condition that was known or reasonably should have been known by the said accused.

(4) *Sexual assault involving penetration of vulva*

or anus or mouth by any part of the body or any object.

(a) *By threatening or placing that other person in fear.* In that (personal jurisdiction data), did (at/on board location), on or about _____ 20__, commit a sexual act upon _____, by penetrating the (vulva) (anus) (mouth) of _____ with (list body part or object), by (threatening _____) (placing _____ in fear), with an intent to (abuse) (humiliate) (harass) (degrade) (arouse) (gratify the sexual desire of) _____.

(b) *By causing bodily harm.* In that (personal jurisdiction data), did (at/on board location), on or about _____ 20__, commit a sexual act upon _____, by penetrating the (vulva) (anus) (mouth) of _____ with (list body part or object), by causing bodily harm to _____, to wit:_____ with an intent to (abuse) (humiliate) (harass) (degrade) (arouse) (gratify the sexual desire of) _____.

(c) *By fraudulent representation.* In that (personal jurisdiction data), did (at/on board location), on or about _____ 20__, commit a sexual act upon _____, by penetrating the (vulva) (anus) (mouth) of _____ with (list body part or object), by making a fraudulent representation that the sexual act served a professional purpose, to wit: _____, with an intent to (abuse) (humiliate) (harass) (degrade) (arouse) (gratify the sexual desire of) _____.

(d) *By false pretense.* In that (personal jurisdiction data), did (at/on board location), on or about ___ 20__, commit a sexual act upon _____, by penetrating the (vulva) (anus) (mouth) of _____ with (list body part or object), by inducing a belief by (artifice) (pretense) (concealment) that the said accused was another person, with an intent to (abuse) (humiliate) (harass) (degrade) (arouse) (gratify the sexual desire of) _____.

(e) *Of a person who is asleep, unconscious, or otherwise unaware the act is occurring.* In that (personal jurisdiction data), did (at/on board location), on or about _____ 20__, commit a sexual act upon _____, by penetrating the (vulva) (anus) (mouth) of _____ with (list body part or object), when he/she knew or reasonably should have known that _____ was (asleep) (unconscious) (unaware the sexual act was occurring due to _____), with an intent to (abuse) (humiliate)

(harass) (degrade) (arouse) (gratify the sexual desire of) _____.

(f) *When the other person is incapable of consenting.* In that (personal jurisdiction data), did (at/on board location), on or about _____ 20__, commit a sexual act upon _____, by penetrating the (vulva) (anus) (mouth) of _____ with (list body part or object), when _____ was incapable of consenting to the sexual act because he/she [was impaired by (a drug, to wit: _____) (an intoxicant, to wit: _____) (   )] [had a (mental disease, to wit: _____) (mental defect, to wit: __ _____) (physical disability, to wit: _____)], a condition that was known or reasonably should have been known by the said accused, with an intent to (abuse) (humiliate) (harass) (degrade) (arouse) (gratify the sexual desire of) _____.

(5) *Aggravated sexual contact involving the touching of the genitalia, anus, groin, breast, inner thigh, or buttocks of any person.*

(a) *By force.* In that (personal jurisdiction data), did (at/on board location), on or about _____ 20__, [(touch) (cause _____ to touch)] [(directly) (through the clothing)] the (genitalia) (anus) (groin) (breast) (inner thigh) (buttocks) of _____, by using unlawful force, with an intent to (abuse) (humiliate) (degrade) (arouse) (gratify the sexual desire of) _____.

(b) *By force causing or likely to cause death or grievous bodily harm.* In that (personal jurisdiction data), did (at/on board location), on or about _____ 20__, [(touch) (cause _____ to touch)] [(directly) (through the clothing)] the (genitalia) (anus) (groin) (breast) (inner thigh) (buttocks) of _____, by using force likely to cause death or grievous bodily harm to _____, to wit: _____, with an intent to (abuse) (humiliate) (degrade) (arouse) (gratify the sexual desire of) _____.

(c) *By threatening or placing that other person in fear that any person would be subjected to death, grievous bodily harm, or kidnapping.* In that (personal jurisdiction data), did (at/on board location), on or about _____ 20__, [(touch) (cause _____ to touch)] [(directly) (through the clothing)] the (genitalia) (anus) (groin) (breast) (inner thigh) (buttocks) of _____, by (threatening _____) (placing _____ in fear) that _____ would be subjected to (death) (grievous bodily harm) (kidnapping), with an intent to (abuse) (humiliate) (degrade) (arouse) (gratify the sexual desire of) _____.

(d) *By first rendering that other person unconscious.* In that (personal jurisdiction data), did (at/on board location), on or about _____ 20__, [(touch) (cause _____ to touch)] [(directly) (through the clothing)] the (genitalia) (anus) (groin) (breast) (inner thigh) (buttocks) of _____, by rendering _____ unconscious by _____, with an intent to (abuse) (humiliate) (degrade) (arouse) (gratify the sexual desire of) _____.

(e) *By administering a drug, intoxicant, or other similar substance.* In that (personal jurisdiction data), did (at/on board location), on or about _____ 20__, [(touch) (cause _____ to touch)] [(directly) (through the clothing)] the (genitalia) (anus) (groin) (breast) (inner thigh) (buttocks) of _____, by administering to _____ (by force) (by threat of force) (without the knowledge or permission of ____) a (drug) (intoxicant) (___) thereby substantially impairing the ability of _____ to appraise or control his/her conduct, with an intent to (abuse) (humiliate) (degrade) (arouse) (gratify the sexual desire of) _____.

(6) *Aggravated sexual contact involving the touching of any body part of any person.*

(a) *By force.* In that (personal jurisdiction data), did (at/on board location), on or about _____ 20__, [(touch) (cause _____ to touch)] [(directly) (through the clothing)] (name of body part) of _____, by using unlawful force, with an intent to (arouse) (gratify the sexual desire of) _____.

(b) *By force causing or likely to cause death or grievous bodily harm.* In that (personal jurisdiction data), did (at/on board location), on or about _____ 20__, [(touch) (cause _____ to touch)] [(directly) (through the clothing)] (name of body part) of _____, by using force likely to cause death or grievous bodily harm to _____, to wit: _____, with an intent to (arouse) (gratify the sexual desire of) _____.

(c) *By threatening or placing that other person in fear that any person would be subjected to death, grievous bodily harm, or kidnapping.* In that (personal jurisdiction data), did (at/on board location), on or about _____ 20__, [(touch) (cause _____ to touch)] [(directly) (through the clothing)] (name of body part) of _____, by (threatening _____) (placing _____ in fear) that _____ would be subjected to (death) (grievous bodily harm) (kidnapping), with an intent to (arouse) (gratify the sexual desire of) _____.

(d) *By first rendering that other person unconscious.* In that (personal jurisdiction data), did (at/on board location), on or about _____ 20__, [(touch) (cause _____ to touch)] [(directly) (through the clothing)] (name of body part) of _____, by rendering _____ unconscious by _____, with an intent to (arouse) (gratify the sexual desire of) _____.

(e) *By administering a drug, intoxicant, or other similar substance.* In that (personal jurisdiction data), did (at/on board location), on or about _____ 20__, [(touch) (cause _____ to touch)] [(directly) (through the clothing)] (name of body part) of _____, by administering to _____ (by force) (by threat of force) (without the knowledge or permission of _____) a (drug) (intoxicant) (___) and thereby substantially impairing the ability of _____ to appraise or control his/her conduct, with an intent to (arouse) (gratify the sexual desire of) _____.

(7) *Abusive sexual contact involving the touching of the genitalia, anus, groin, breast, inner thigh, or buttocks of any person.*

(a) *By threatening or placing that other person in fear.* In that (personal jurisdiction data), did (at/on board location), on or about ____ 20__, [(touch) (cause another person to touch)] [(directly) (through the clothing)] the (genitalia) (anus) (groin) (breast) (inner thigh) (buttocks) of _____ by (threatening _____) (placing _____ in fear), with an intent to (abuse) (humiliate) (degrade) (arouse) (gratify the sexual desire of) _____.

(b) *By causing bodily harm.* In that (personal jurisdiction data), did (at/on board location), on or about _____ 20__, [(touch) (cause another person to touch)] [(directly) (through the clothing)] the (genitalia) (anus) (groin) (breast) (inner thigh) (buttocks) of _____ by causing bodily harm to _____, to wit: _____, with an intent to (abuse) (humiliate) (degrade) (arouse) (gratify the sexual desire of) _____.

(c) *By fraudulent representation.* In that (personal jurisdiction data), did (at/on board location), on or about ____ 20__, [(touch) (cause another person to touch)] [(directly) (through the clothing)] the (genitalia) (anus) (groin) (breast) (inner thigh) (buttocks) of _____ by making a fraudulent representation that the sexual contact served a professional purpose, to wit: _____, with an intent to (abuse) (humiliate) (degrade) (arouse) (gratify the sexual desire of) _____.

(d) *By false pretense.* In that (personal jurisdiction data), did (at/on board location), on or about _____ 20__, [(touch) (cause another person to touch)] [(directly) (through the clothing)] the (genitalia) (anus) (groin) (breast) (inner thigh) (buttocks) of _____ by inducing a belief by (artifice) (pretense) (concealment) that the said accused was another person, with an intent to (abuse) (humiliate) (degrade) (arouse) (gratify the sexual desire of) _____.

(e) *Of a person who is asleep, unconscious, or otherwise unaware the act is occurring.* In that (personal jurisdiction data), did (at/on board location), on or about _____ 20__, [(touch) (cause another person to touch)] [(directly) (through the clothing)] the (genitalia) (anus) (groin) (breast) (inner thigh) (buttocks) of _____ when he/she knew or reasonably should have known that _____ was (asleep) (unconscious) (unaware the sexual contact was occurring due to _____), with an intent to (abuse) (humiliate) (degrade) (arouse) (gratify the sexual desire of) _____.

(f) *When that person is incapable of consenting.* In that (personal jurisdiction data), did (at/on board location), on or about _____ 20__, [(touch) (cause another person to touch)] [(directly) (through the clothing)] the (genitalia) (anus) (groin) (breast) (inner thigh) (buttocks) of _____ when _____ was incapable of consenting to the sexual contact because he/she [was impaired by (a drug, to wit: _____) (an intoxicant, to wit: _____) ( )] [had a (mental disease, to wit: _____) (mental defect, to wit: _____) (physical disability, to wit: _____)] and this condition was known or reasonably should have been known by _____, with an intent to (abuse) (humiliate) (degrade) (arouse) (gratify the sexual desire of) _____.

(8) *Abusive sexual contact involving the touching of any body part of any person.*

(a) *By threatening or placing that other person in fear.* In that (personal jurisdiction data), did (at/on board location), on or about _____ 20__, [(touch) (cause another person to touch)] [(directly) (through the clothing)] the (name of body part) of _____ by (threatening _____) (placing _____ in fear), with an intent to (arouse) (gratify the sexual desire of) _____.

(b) *By causing bodily harm.* In that (personal jurisdiction data), did (at/on board location), on or about _____ 20__, [(touch) (cause another person to touch)] [(directly) (through the clothing)] the (name of body part) of _____ by causing bodily harm to _____, to wit: _____, with an intent to (arouse) (gratify the sexual desire of) _____.

(c) *By fraudulent representation.* In that (personal jurisdiction data), did (at/on board location), on or about _____ 20__, [(touch) (cause another person to touch)] [(directly) (through the clothing)] the (name of body part) of _____ by making a fraudulent representation that the sexual contact served a professional purpose, to wit: _____, with an intent to (arouse) (gratify the sexual desire of) _____.

(d) *By false pretense.* In that (personal jurisdiction data), did (at/on board location), on or about _____ 20__, [(touch) (cause another person to touch)] [(directly) (through the clothing)] the (name of body part) of _____ by inducing a belief by (artifice) (pretense) (concealment) that the said accused was another person, with an intent to (arouse) (gratify the sexual desire of) _____.

(e) *Of a person who is asleep, unconscious, or otherwise unaware the act is occurring.* In that (personal jurisdiction data), did (at/on board location), on or about _____ 20__, [(touch) (cause another person to touch)] [(directly) (through the clothing)] the (name of body part) of _____ when he/she knew or reasonably should have known that _____ was (asleep) (unconscious) (unaware the sexual contact was occurring due to _____), with an intent to (arouse) (gratify the sexual desire of) _____.

(f) *When that person is incapable of consenting.* In that (personal jurisdiction data), did (at/on board location), on or about _____ 20__, [(touch) (cause another person to touch)] [(directly) (through the clothing)] the (name of body part) of _____ when _____ was incapable of consenting to the sexual contact because he/she [was impaired by (a drug, to wit: _____) (an intoxicant, to wit: _____) ( )] [had a (mental disease, to wit: _____) (mental defect, to wit: _____) (physical disability, to wit: _____)], a condition that was known or reasonably should have been known by __

_____, with an intent to (arouse) (gratify the sexual desire of) _____.

45a. Article 120a—Stalking

a. *Text of statute.*

(a) **Any person subject to this section:**

(1) **who wrongfully engages in a course of conduct directed at a specific person that would cause a reasonable person to fear death or bodily harm, including sexual assault, to himself or herself or a member of his or her immediate family;**

(2) **who has knowledge, or should have knowledge, that the specific person will be placed in reasonable fear of death or bodily harm, including sexual assault, to himself or herself or a member of his or her immediate family; and**

(3) **whose acts induce reasonable fear in the specific person of death or bodily harm, including sexual assault, to himself or herself or to a member of his or her immediate family; is guilty of stalking and shall be punished as a court-martial may direct.**

(b) **In this section:**

(1) **The term "course of conduct" means:**

(A) **a repeated maintenance of visual or physical proximity to a specific person; or**

(B) **a repeated conveyance of verbal threat, written threats, or threats implied by conduct, or a combination of such threats, directed at or towards a specific person.**

(2) **The term "repeated," with respect to conduct, means two or more occasions of such conduct.**

(3) **The term "immediate family," in the case of a specific person, means a spouse, parent, child, or sibling of the person, or any other family member, relative, or intimate partner of the person who regularly resides in the household of the person or who within the six months preceding the commencement of the course of conduct regularly resided in the household of the person.**

b. *Elements.*

(1) That the accused wrongfully engaged in a course of conduct directed at a specific person that would cause a reasonable person to fear death or bodily harm to himself or herself or a member of his or her immediate family;

(2) That the accused had knowledge, or should

have had knowledge, that the specific person would be placed in reasonable fear of death or bodily harm to himself or herself or a member of his or her immediate family; and

(3) That the accused's acts induced reasonable fear in the specific person of death or bodily harm to himself or herself or to a member of his or her immediate family.

c. *Explanation.* See Paragraph 54c(1)(a) for an explanation of "bodily harm".

d. *Lesser included offenses.* See paragraph 3 of this part and Appendix 12A.

e. *Maximum punishment.* Dishonorable discharge, forfeiture of all pay and allowances, and confinement for 3 years.

f. *Sample Specification.*

In that _____ (personal jurisdiction data), who (knew)(should have known) that _____ would be placed in reasonable fear of (death)(bodily harm) to (himself) (herself) (_____ , a member of his or her immediate family) did (at/on board—location), (subject-matter jurisdiction data, if required), (on or about _____ 20 __)(from about _____ to about _____ 20 __), wrongfully engage in a course of conduct directed at _____ , to wit: _____ thereby inducing in _____ , a reasonable fear of (death)(bodily harm) to (himself)(herself) (_____ , a member of his or her immediate family).

45b. Article 120b—Rape and sexual assault of a child

[Note: This statute applies to offenses committed on or after 28 June 2012. Article 120b is a new statute designed to address only child sexual offenses. Previous versions of child sexual offenses are located as follows: for offenses committed on or before 30 September 2007, *see* Appendix 27; for offenses committed during the period 1 October 2007 through 27 June 2012, *see* Appendix 28.]

a. *Text of Statute*

(a) *Rape of a Child.* **Any person subject to this chapter who—**

(1) **commits a sexual act upon a child who has not attained the age of 12 years; or**

(2) **commits a sexual act upon a child who has attained the age of 12 years by—**

(A) **using force against any person;**

(B) threatening or placing that child in fear;

(C) rendering that child unconscious; or

(D) administering to that child a drug, intoxicant, or other similar substance;

is guilty of rape of a child and shall be punished as a court-martial may direct.

(b) *Sexual Assault of a Child.* Any person subject to this chapter who commits a sexual act upon a child who has attained the age of 12 years is guilty of sexual assault of a child and shall be punished as a court-martial may direct.

(c) *Sexual Abuse of a Child.* Any person subject to this chapter who commits a lewd act upon a child is guilty of sexual abuse of a child and shall be punished as a court-martial may direct.

(d) *Age of Child.*

(1) *Under 12 years.* In a prosecution under this section, it need not be proven that the accused knew the age of the other person engaging in the sexual act or lewd act. It is not a defense that the accused reasonably believed that the child had attained the age of 12 years.

(2) *Under 16 years.* In a prosecution under this section, it need not be proven that the accused knew that the other person engaging in the sexual act or lewd act had not attained the age of 16 years, but it is a defense in a prosecution under subsection (b) (sexual assault of a child) or subsection (c) (sexual abuse of a child), which the accused must prove by a preponderance of the evidence, that the accused reasonably believed that the child had attained the age of 16 years, if the child had in fact attained at least the age of 12 years.

(e) *Proof of Threat.* In a prosecution under this section, in proving that a person made a threat, it need not be proven that the person actually intended to carry out the threat or had the ability to carry out the threat.

(f) *Marriage.* In a prosecution under subsection (b) (sexual assault of a child) or subsection (c) (sexual abuse of a child), it is a defense, which the accused must prove by a preponderance of the evidence, that the persons engaging in the sexual act or lewd act were at that time married to each other, except where the accused commits a sexual act upon the person when the accused knows or reasonably should know that the other person is

asleep, unconscious, or otherwise unaware that the sexual act is occurring or when the other person is incapable of consenting to the sexual act due to impairment by any drug, intoxicant, or other similar substance, and that condition was known or reasonably should have been known by the accused.

(g) *Consent.* Lack of consent is not an element and need not be proven in any prosecution under this section. A child not legally married to the person committing the sexual act, lewd act, or use of force cannot consent to any sexual act, lewd act, or use of force.

(h) *Definitions.* In this section:

(1) *Sexual act and sexual contact.* The terms 'sexual act' and 'sexual contact' have the meanings given those terms in section 920(g) of this title (article 120(g)).

(2) *Force.* The term 'force' means—

(A) the use of a weapon;

(B) the use of such physical strength or violence as is sufficient to overcome, restrain, or injure a child; or

(C) inflicting physical harm.

In the case of a parent-child or similar relationship, the use or abuse of parental or similar authority is sufficient to constitute the use of force.

(3) *Threatening or placing that child in fear.* The term 'threatening or placing that child in fear' means a communication or action that is of sufficient consequence to cause the child to fear that non-compliance will result in the child or another person being subjected to the action contemplated by the communication or action.

(4) *Child.* The term 'child' means any person who has not attained the age of 16 years.

(5) *Lewd act.* The term 'lewd act' means—

(A) any sexual contact with a child;

(B) intentionally exposing one's genitalia, anus, buttocks, or female areola or nipple to a child by any means, including via any communication technology, with an intent to abuse, humiliate, or degrade any person, or to arouse or gratify the sexual desire of any person;

(C) intentionally communicating indecent language to a child by any means, including via any communication technology, with an intent to abuse, humiliate, or degrade any person, or to arouse or gratify the sexual desire of any person; or

(D) **any indecent conduct, intentionally done with or in the presence of a child, including via any communication technology, that amounts to a form of immorality relating to sexual impurity which is grossly vulgar, obscene, and repugnant to common propriety, and tends to excite sexual desire or deprave morals with respect to sexual relations.**

b. *Elements.*

(1) *Rape of a child involving contact between penis and vulva or anus or mouth.*

(a) *Rape of a child who has not attained the age of 12.*

(i) That the accused committed a sexual act upon a child causing penetration, however slight, by the penis of the vulva or anus or mouth; and

(ii) That at the time of the sexual act the child had not attained the age of 12 years.

(b) *Rape by force of a child who has attained the age of 12.*

(i) That the accused committed a sexual act upon a child causing penetration, however slight, by the penis of the vulva or anus or mouth; and

(ii) That at the time of the sexual act the child had attained the age of 12 years but had not attained the age of 16 years, and

(iii) That the accused did so by using force against that child or any other person.

(c) *Rape by threatening or placing in fear a child who has attained the age of 12.*

(i) That the accused committed a sexual act upon a child causing penetration, however slight, by the penis of the vulva or anus or mouth;

(ii) That at the time of the sexual act the child had attained the age of 12 years but had not attained the age of 16 years; and

(iii) That the accused did so by threatening the child or another person or placing that child in fear.

(d) *Rape by rendering unconscious a child who has attained the age of 12.*

(i) That the accused committed a sexual act upon a child causing penetration, however slight, by the penis of the vulva or anus or mouth;

(ii) That at the time of the sexual act the

child had attained the age of 12 years but had not attained the age of 16 years; and

(iii) That the accused did so by rendering that child unconscious.

(e) *Rape by administering a drug, intoxicant, or other similar substance to a child who has attained the age of 12.*

(i) That the accused committed a sexual act upon a child causing penetration, however slight, by the penis of the vulva or anus or mouth;

(ii) That at the time of the sexual act the child had attained the age of 12 years but had not attained the age of 16 years; and

(iii) That the accused did so by administering to that child a drug, intoxicant, or other similar substance.

(2) *Rape of a child involving penetration of vulva or anus or mouth by any part of the body or any object.*

(a) *Rape of a child who has not attained the age of 12.*

(i) That the accused committed a sexual act upon a child by causing penetration, however slight, of the vulva or anus or mouth of the child by any part of the body or by any object;

(ii) That at the time of the sexual act the child had not attained the age of 12 years; and

(iii) That the accused did so with an intent to abuse, humiliate, harass, or degrade any person or to arouse or gratify the sexual desire of any person.

(b) *Rape by force of a child who has attained the age of 12.*

(i) That the accused committed a sexual act upon a child by causing penetration, however slight, of the vulva, anus, or mouth of the child by any part of the body or by any object;

(ii) That at the time of the sexual act the child had attained the age of 12 years but had not attained the age of 16 years;

(iii) That the accused did so by using force against that child or any other person; and

(iv) That the accused did so with an intent to abuse, humiliate, harass, or degrade any person or to arouse or gratify the sexual desire of any person.

(c) *Rape by threatening or placing in fear a child who has attained the age of 12.*

(i) That the accused committed a sexual act upon a child by causing penetration, however slight, of the vulva or anus or mouth of the child by any part of the body or by any object;

(ii) That at the time of the sexual act the child had attained the age of 12 years but had not attained the age of 16 years;

(iii) That the accused did so by threatening the child or another person or placing that child in fear; and

(iv) That the accused did so with an intent to abuse, humiliate, harass, or degrade any person or to arouse or gratify the sexual desire of any person.

(d) *Rape by rendering unconscious a child who has attained the age of 12.*

(i) That the accused committed a sexual act upon a child by causing penetration, however slight, of the vulva or anus or mouth of the child by any part of the body or by any object;

(ii) That at the time of the sexual act the child had attained the age of 12 years but had not attained the age of 16 years;

(iii) That the accused did so by rendering that child unconscious; and

(iv) That the accused did so with an intent to abuse, humiliate, harass, or degrade any person or to arouse or gratify the sexual desire of any person.

(e) *Rape by administering a drug, intoxicant, or other similar substance to a child who has attained the age of 12.*

(i) That the accused committed a sexual act upon a child by causing penetration, however slight, of the vulva or anus or mouth of the child by any part of the body or by any object;

(ii) That at the time of the sexual act the child had attained the age of 12 years but had not attained the age of 16 years;

(iii) That the accused did so by administering to that child a drug, intoxicant, or other similar substance; and

(iv) That the accused did so with an intent to abuse, humiliate, harass, or degrade any person or to arouse or gratify the sexual desire of any person.

(3) *Sexual assault of a child.*

(a) *Sexual assault of a child who has attained the age of 12 involving contact between penis and vulva or anus or mouth.*

(i) That the accused committed a sexual act upon a child causing contact between penis and vulva or anus or mouth; and

(ii) That at the time of the sexual act the child had attained the age of 12 years but had not attained the age of 16 years.

(b) *Sexual assault of a child who has attained the age of 12 involving penetration of vulva or anus or mouth by any part of the body or any object.*

(i) That the accused committed a sexual act upon a child by causing penetration, however slight, of the vulva or anus or mouth of the child by any part of the body or by any object;

(ii) That at the time of the sexual act the child had attained the age of 12 years but had not attained the age of 16 years; and

(iii) That the accused did so with an intent to abuse, humiliate, harass, or degrade any person or to arouse or gratify the sexual desire of any person.

(4) *Sexual abuse of a child.*

(a) *Sexual abuse of a child by sexual contact involving the touching of the genitalia, anus, groin, breast, inner thigh, or buttocks of any person.*

(i) That the accused committed sexual contact upon a child by touching, or causing another person to touch, either directly or through the clothing, the genitalia, anus, groin, breast, inner thigh, or buttocks of any person; and

(ii) that the accused did so with intent to abuse, humiliate, harass, or degrade any person or to arouse or gratify the sexual desire of any person.

(b) *Sexual abuse of a child by sexual contact involving the touching of any body part.*

(i) That the accused committed sexual contact upon a child by touching, or causing another person to touch, either directly or through the clothing, any body part of any person; and

(ii) That the accused did so with intent to arouse or gratify the sexual desire of any person.

(c) *Sexual abuse of a child by indecent exposure.*

(i) That the accused intentionally exposed his or her genitalia, anus, buttocks, or female areola or nipple to a child by any means; and

(ii) That the accused did so with an intent to abuse, humiliate or degrade any person, or to arouse or gratify the sexual desire of any person.

(d) *Sexual abuse of a child by indecent communication.*

(i) That the accused intentionally communicated indecent language to a child by any means; and

(ii) That the accused did so with an intent to abuse, humiliate or degrade any person, or to arouse or gratify the sexual desire of any person.

(e) *Sexual abuse of a child by indecent conduct.*

(i) That the accused engaged in indecent conduct, intentionally done with or in the presence of a child; and

(ii) That the indecent conduct amounted to a form of immorality relating to sexual impurity which is grossly vulgar, obscene, and repugnant to common propriety, and tends to excite sexual desire or deprave morals with respect to sexual relations.

c. *Explanation.*

(1) *In general.* Sexual offenses have been separated into three statutes: adults (120), children (120b), and other offenses (120c).

(2) *Definitions.* Terms not defined in this paragraph are defined in paragraph 45b.a.(h), *supra.*

d. *Lesser included offenses.* See paragraph 3 of this part and Appendix 12A.

e. *Maximum punishment.*

(1) *Rape of a child.* Forfeiture of all pay and allowances, and confinement for life without eligibility for parole. Mandatory minimum – Dismissal or dishonorable discharge.

(2) *Sexual assault of a child.* Forfeiture of all pay and allowances, and confinement for 30 years. Mandatory minimum – Dismissal or dishonorable discharge.

(3) *Sexual abuse of a child.*

(a) *Cases involving sexual contact.* Dishonorable discharge, forfeiture of all pay and allowances, and confinement for 20 years.

(b) *Other cases.* Dishonorable discharge, forfeiture of all pay and allowances, and confinement for 15 years.

f. *Sample specifications.*

(1) *Rape of a child involving contact between penis and vulva or anus or mouth.*

(a) *Rape of a child who has not attained the age of 12.* In that (personal jurisdiction data), did (at/on board location), on or about _____ 20__, commit a sexual act upon _____, a child who had not attained the age of 12 years, by causing penetration of _____'s (vulva) (anus) (mouth) with _____'s penis.

(b) *Rape by force of a child who has attained the age of 12 years.* In that (personal jurisdiction data), did (at/on board location), on or about _____ _ 20__, commit a sexual act upon _____, a child who had attained the age of 12 years but had not attained the age of 16 years, by causing penetration of _____'s (vulva) (anus) (mouth) with ___ _____'s penis, by using force against _____, to wit: _____.

(c) *Rape by threatening or placing in fear a child who has attained the age of 12 years.* In that (personal jurisdiction data), did (at/on board location), on or about _____ 20__, commit a sexual act upon _____, a child who had attained the age of 12 years but had not attained the age of 16 years, by causing penetration of _____'s (vulva) (anus) (mouth) with _____'s penis by (threatening _____) (placing _____ in fear).

(d) *Rape by rendering unconscious of a child who has attained the age of 12 years.* In that (personal jurisdiction data), did (at/on board location), on or about _____ 20__, commit a sexual act upon _ _____, a child who had attained the age of 12 years but had not attained the age of 16 years, by causing penetration of _____'s (vulva) (anus) (mouth) with _____'s penis by rendering _____ _____ unconscious by _____.

(e) *Rape by administering a drug, intoxicant, or other similar substance to a child who has attained the age of 12 years.* In that (personal jurisdiction data), did (at/on board location), on or about __ _____ 20__, commit a sexual act upon _____, a child who had attained the age of 12 years but had not attained the age of 16 years, by causing penetration of _____'s (vulva) (anus) (mouth) with __ _____'s penis by administering to _____ a (drug) (intoxicant) (____), to wit: _____.

(2) *Rape of a child involving penetration of the vulva or anus or mouth by any part of the body or any object.*

(a) *Rape of a child who has not attained the age of 12.* In that (personal jurisdiction data), did (at/on board location), on or about _____ 20__, commit a sexual act upon _____, a child who had not attained the age of 12 years, by penetrating the (vulva) (anus) (mouth) of _____ with (list body part or object), with an intent to (abuse) (humiliate) (harass) (degrade) (arouse) (gratify the sexual desire of) _____.

(b) *Rape by force of a child who has attained the age of 12 years.* In that (personal jurisdiction data), did (at/on board location), on or about _____ 20__, commit a sexual act upon _____, a child who had attained the age of 12 years but had not attained the age of 16 years, by penetrating the (vulva) (anus) (mouth) of _____ with (list body part or object), by using force against _____ _, with an intent to (abuse) (humiliate) (harass) (degrade) (arouse) (gratify the sexual desire of) _____ _____.

(c) *Rape by threatening or placing in fear a child who has attained the age of 12 years.* In that (personal jurisdiction data), did (at/on board location), on or about _____ 20__, commit a sexual act upon _____, a child who had attained the age of 12 years but had not attained the age of 16 years, by penetrating the (vulva) (anus) (mouth) of _____ _____ with (list body part or object), by (threatening _____) (placing _____ in fear), with an intent to (abuse) (humiliate) (harass) (degrade) (arouse) (gratify the sexual desire of) _____ .

(d) *Rape by rendering unconscious of a child who has attained the age of 12 years.* In that (personal jurisdiction data), did (at/on board location), on or about _____ 20__, commit a sexual act upon _ _____, a child who had attained the age of 12 years but had not attained the age of 16 years, by penetrating the (vulva) (anus) (mouth) of _____ ___ with (list body part or object), by rendering ___ _____ unconscious, with an intent to (abuse) (humiliate) (harass) (degrade) (arouse) (gratify the sexual desire of) _____.

(e) *Rape by administering a drug, intoxicant, or other similar substance to a child who has attained the age of 12 years.* In that (personal jurisdiction data), did (at/on board location), on or about __ _____ 20__, commit a sexual act upon _____, a child who had attained the age of 12 years but had not attained the age of 16 years, by penetrating the (vulva) (anus) (mouth) of _____ with (list body part or object), by administering to _____ ___ a (drug) (intoxicant) (____), to wit: _____ , with an intent to (abuse) (humiliate) (harass) (degrade) (arouse) (gratify the sexual desire of) _____ _____.

(3) *Sexual assault of a child.*

(a) *Sexual assault of a child who has attained the age of 12 years involving contact between penis and vulva or anus or mouth.* In that (personal jurisdiction data), did (at/on board location), on or about _____ 20__, commit a sexual act upon _____, a child who had attained the age of 12 years but had not attained the age of 16 years, by causing penetration of _____'s (vulva) (anus) (mouth) with _ _____'s penis.

(b) *Sexual assault of a child who has attained the age of 12 years involving penetration of vulva or anus or mouth by any part of the body or any object.* In that (personal jurisdiction data), did (at/on board location), on or about _____ 20__, commit a sexual act upon _____, a child who had attained the age of 12 years but had not attained the age of 16 years, by penetrating the (vulva) (anus) (mouth) of _____ with (list body part or object), with an intent to (abuse) (humiliate) (harass) (degrade) (arouse) (gratify the sexual desire of) ____ _____.

(4) *Sexual abuse of a child.*

(a) *Sexual abuse of a child involving sexual contact involving the touching of the genitalia, anus, groin, breast, inner thigh, or buttocks of any person.* In that (personal jurisdiction data), did (at/on board location), on or about _____ 20__, commit a lewd act upon _____, a child who had not attained the age of 16 years, by intentionally [(touching) (causing _____ to touch)] [(directly) (through the clothing)] the (genitalia) (anus) (groin) (breast) (inner thigh) (buttocks) of _____, with an intent to (abuse) (humiliate) (degrade) _____.

(b) *Sexual abuse of a child involving sexual contact involving the touching of any body part of any person.* In that (personal jurisdiction data), did (at/on board location), on or about _____ 20__, commit a lewd act upon _____, a child who had not attained the age of 16 years, by intentionally exposing [his (genitalia) (anus) (buttocks)] [her (genitalia) (anus) (buttocks) (areola) (nipple)] to ___ _____, with an intent to (abuse) (humiliate) (harass) (degrade) (arouse) (gratify the sexual desire of) _____.

(c) *Sexual abuse of a child involving indecent exposure.* In that (personal jurisdiction data), did (at/ on board location), on or about ____ 20__, commit a lewd act upon _____, a child who had not attained the age of 16 years, by intentionally [(touching) (causing _____ to touch)] [(directly) (through the clothing)] (name of body part) of _____, with an intent to (arouse) (gratify the sexual desire of) _____.

(d) *Sexual abuse of a child involving indecent communication.* In that (personal jurisdiction data), did (at/on board location), on or about _____ 20_ _, commit a lewd act upon _____, a child who had not attained the age of 16 years, by intentionally communicating to _____ indecent language to wit: _____, with an intent to (abuse) (humiliate) (harass) (degrade) (arouse) (gratify the sexual desire of) _____.

(e) *Sexual abuse of a child involving indecent conduct.* In that (personal jurisdiction data), did (at/on board location), on or about _____ 20__, commit a lewd act upon _____, a child who had not attained the age of 16 years, by engaging in indecent conduct, to wit: _____, intentionally done (with) (in the presence of) _____, which conduct amounted to a form of immorality relating to sexual impurity which is grossly vulgar, obscene, and repugnant to common propriety, and tends to excite sexual desire or deprave morals with respect to sexual relations.

45c. Article 120c—Other sexual misconduct

[Note: This statute applies to offenses committed on or after 28 June 2012. Article 120c is a new statute designed to address miscellaneous sexual misconduct. Previous versions of these offenses are located as follows: for offenses committed on or before 30 September 2007, *see* Appendix 27; for offenses committed during the period 1 October 2007 through 27 June 2012, *see* Appendix 28.]

a. *Text of Statute*

(a) *Indecent Viewing, Visual Recording, or Broadcasting.* **Any person subject to this chapter who, without legal justification or lawful authorization—**

(1) **knowingly and wrongfully views the private area of another person, without that other person's consent and under circumstances in which that other person has a reasonable expectation of privacy;**

(2) **knowingly photographs, videotapes, films, or records by any means the private area of another person, without that other person's consent and under circumstances in which that other person has a reasonable expectation of privacy; or**

(3) **knowingly broadcasts or distributes any such recording that the person knew or reasonably should have known was made under the circumstances proscribed in paragraphs (1) and (2); is guilty of an offense under this section and shall be punished as a court-martial may direct.**

(b) *Forcible Pandering.* **Any person subject to this chapter who compels another person to engage in an act of prostitution with any person is guilty of forcible pandering and shall be punished as a court-martial may direct.**

(c) *Indecent Exposure.* **Any person subject to this chapter who intentionally exposes, in an indecent manner, the genitalia, anus, buttocks, or female areola or nipple is guilty of indecent exposure and shall by punished as a court-martial may direct.**

(d) *Definitions.* **In this section:**

(1) *Act of prostitution.* **The term 'act of prostitution' means a sexual act or sexual contact (as defined in section 920(g) of this title (article 120(g))) on account of which anything of value is given to, or received by, any person.**

(2) *Private area.* **The term 'private area' means the naked or underwear-clad genitalia, anus, buttocks, or female areola or nipple.**

(3) *Reasonable expectation of privacy.* **The term 'under circumstances in which that other person has a reasonable expectation of privacy' means—**

(A) **circumstances in which a reasonable person would believe that he or she could disrobe in privacy, without being concerned that an image of a private area of the person was being captured; or**

(B) **circumstances in which a reasonable person would believe that a private area of the person would not be visible to the public.**

(4) *Broadcast.* **The term 'broadcast' means to electronically transmit a visual image with the intent that it be viewed by a person or persons.**

(5) *Distribute.* **The term 'distribute' means delivering to the actual or constructive possession of another, including transmission by electronic means.**

(6) *Indecent manner.* **The term 'indecent manner' means conduct that amounts to a form**

of immorality relating to sexual impurity which is grossly vulgar, obscene, and repugnant to common propriety, and tends to excite sexual desire or deprave morals with respect to sexual relations.

b. *Elements.*

(1) *Indecent viewing.*

(a) That the accused knowingly and wrongfully viewed the private area of another person;

(b) That said viewing was without the other person's consent; and

(c) That said viewing took place under circumstances in which the other person had a reasonable expectation of privacy.

(2) *Indecent recording.*

(a) That the accused knowingly recorded (photographed, videotaped, filmed, or recorded by any means) the private area of another person;

(b) That said recording was without the other person's consent; and

(c) That said recording was made under circumstances in which the other person had a reasonable expectation of privacy.

(3) *Broadcasting of an indecent recording.*

(a) That the accused knowingly broadcast a certain recording of another person's private area;

(b) That said recording was made or broadcast without the other person's consent;

(c) That the accused knew or reasonably should have known that the recording was made or broadcast without the other person's consent;

(d) That said recording was made under circumstances in which the other person had a reasonable expectation of privacy; and

(e) That the accused knew or reasonably should have known that said recording was made under circumstances in which the other person had a reasonable expectation of privacy.

(4) *Distribution of an indecent visual recording.*

(a) That the accused knowingly distributed a certain recording of another person's private area;

(b) That said recording was made or distributed without the other person's consent;

(c) That the accused knew or reasonably should have known that said recording was made or distributed without the other person's consent;

(d) That said recording was made under cir-

cumstances in which the other person had a reasonable expectation of privacy; and

(e) That the accused knew or reasonably should have known that said recording was made under circumstances in which the other person had a reasonable expectation of privacy.

(5) *Forcible pandering.* That the accused compelled another person to engage in an act of prostitution with any person.

(6) *Indecent exposure.*

(a) That the accused exposed his or her genitalia, anus, buttocks, or female areola or nipple;

(b) That the exposure was in an indecent manner; and

(c) That the exposure was intentional.

c. *Explanation.*

(1) *In general.* Sexual offenses have been separated into three statutes: adults (120), children (120b), and other offenses (120c).

(2) *Definitions.*

(a) Recording. A "recording" is a still or moving visual image captured or recorded by any means.

(b) Other terms are defined in paragraph 45c.a.(d), *supra.*

d. *Lesser included offenses.* See paragraph 3 of this part and Appendix 12A.

e. *Maximum punishment.*

(1) *Indecent viewing.* Dishonorable discharge, forfeiture of all pay and allowances, and confinement for 1 year.

(2) *Indecent visual recording.* Dishonorable discharge, forfeiture of all pay and allowances, and confinement for 5 years.

(3) *Broadcasting or distribution of an indecent visual recording.* Dishonorable discharge, forfeiture of all pay and allowances, and confinement for 7 years.

(4) *Forcible pandering.* Dishonorable discharge, forfeiture of all pay and allowances, and confinement for 12 years.

(5) *Indecent exposure.* Dishonorable discharge, forfeiture of all pay and allowances, and confinement for 1 year.

f. *Sample specifications.*

(1) *Indecent viewing, visual recording, or broadcasting.*

(a) *Indecent viewing.* In that (personal jurisdiction data), did (at/on board location), on or about __ _____ 20__, knowingly and wrongfully view the private area of _____, without (his) (her) consent and under circumstances in which (he) (she) had a reasonable expectation of privacy.

(b) *Indecent visual recording.* In that (personal jurisdiction data), did (at/on board location), on or about _____ 20__, knowingly (photograph) (videotape) (film) (make a recording of) the private area of _____, without (his) (her) consent and under circumstances in which (he) (she) had a reasonable expectation of privacy.

(c) *Broadcasting or distributing an indecent visual recording.* In that (personal jurisdiction data), did (at/on board location), on or about _____ 20_ _, knowingly (broadcast) (distribute) a recording of the private area of _____, when the said accused knew or reasonably should have known that the said recording was (made) (and/or) (distributed/ broadcast) without the consent of _____ and under circumstances in which (he) (she) had a reasonable expectation of privacy.

(2) *Forcible pandering.* In that (personal jurisdiction data), did (at/on board location), on or about __ _____ 20__, wrongfully compel _____ to engage in (a sexual act) (sexual contact) with _____ ____, to wit: _____, for the purpose of receiving (money) (other compensation) (_____).

(3) *Indecent exposure.* In that (personal jurisdiction data), did (at/on board location), on or about __ _____ 20__, intentionally expose [his (genitalia) (anus) (buttocks)] [her (genitalia) (anus) (buttocks) (areola) (nipple)] in an indecent manner, to wit: ___ _____.

46. Article 121—Larceny and wrongful appropriation

a. *Text of statute.*

(a) **Any person subject to this chapter who wrongfully takes, obtains, or withholds, by any means, from the possession of the owner or of any other person any money, personal property, or article of value of any kind—**

(1) **with intent permanently to deprive or defraud another person of the use and benefit of property or to appropriate it to his own use or the use of any person other than the owner, steals that property and is guilty of larceny; or**

(2) **with intent temporarily to deprive or**

defraud another person of the use and benefit of property or to appropriate it to his own use or the use of any person other than the owner, is guilty of wrongful appropriation.

(b) **Any person found guilty of larceny or wrongful appropriation shall be punished as a court-martial may direct.**

b. *Elements.*

(1) *Larceny.*

(a) That the accused wrongfully took, obtained, or withheld certain property from the possession of the owner or of any other person;

(b) That the property belonged to a certain person;

(c) That the property was of a certain value, or of some value; and

(d) That the taking, obtaining, or withholding by the accused was with the intent permanently to deprive or defraud another person of the use and benefit of the property or permanently to appropriate the property for the use of the accused or for any person other than the owner.

[Note: If the property is alleged to be military property, as defined in paragraph 46c(1)(h), add the following element]

(e) That the property was military property.

(2) *Wrongful appropriation.*

(a) That the accused wrongfully took, obtained, or withheld certain property from the possession of the owner or of any other person;

(b) That the property belonged to a certain person;

(c) That the property was of a certain value, or of some value; and

(d) That the taking, obtaining, or withholding by the accused was with the intent temporarily to deprive or defraud another person of the use and benefit of the property or temporarily to appropriate the property for the use of the accused or for any person other than the owner.

c. *Explanation.*

(1) *Larceny.*

(a) *In general.* A wrongful taking with intent permanently to deprive includes the common law offense of larceny; a wrongful obtaining with intent permanently to defraud includes the offense formerly known as obtaining by false pretense; and a wrongful withholding with intent permanently to appropriate includes the offense formerly known as embezzlement. Any of the various types of larceny under Article 121 may be charged and proved under a specification alleging that the accused "did steal" the property in question.

(b) *Taking, obtaining, or withholding.* There must be a taking, obtaining, or withholding of the property by the thief. For instance, there is no taking if the property is connected to a building by a chain and the property has not been disconnected from the building; property is not "obtained" by merely acquiring title thereto without exercising some possessory control over it. As a general rule, however, any movement of the property or any exercise of dominion over it is sufficient if accompanied by the requisite intent. Thus, if an accused enticed another's horse into the accused's stable without touching the animal, or procured a railroad company to deliver another's trunk by changing the check on it, or obtained the delivery of another's goods to a person or place designated by the accused, or had the funds of another transferred to the accused's bank account, the accused is guilty of larceny if the other elements of the offense have been proved. A person may "obtain" the property of another by acquiring possession without title, and one who already has possession of the property of another may "obtain" it by later acquiring title to it. A "withholding" may arise as a result of a failure to return, account for, or deliver property to its owner when a return, accounting, or delivery is due, even if the owner has made no demand for the property, or it may arise as a result of devoting property to a use not authorized by its owner. Generally, this is so whether the person withholding the property acquired it lawfully or unlawfully. *See* subparagraph c(1)(f) below. However, acts which constitute the offense of unlawfully receiving, buying, or concealing stolen property or of being an accessory after the fact are not included within the meaning of "withholds." Therefore, neither a receiver of stolen property nor an accessory after the fact can be convicted of larceny on that basis alone. The taking, obtaining, or withholding must be of specific property. A debtor does not withhold specific property from the possession of a creditor by failing or refusing to pay a debt, for the relationship of debtor and creditor does not give the creditor a possessory right in any specific money or other property of the debtor.

(c) *Ownership of the property.*

(i) *In general.* Article 121 requires that the taking, obtaining, or withholding be from the possession of the owner or of any other person. Care, custody, management, and control are among the definitions of possession.

(ii) *Owner.* "Owner" refers to the person who, at the time of the taking, obtaining, or withholding, had the superior right to possession of the property in the light of all conflicting interests therein which may be involved in the particular case. For instance, an organization is the true owner of its funds as against the custodian of the funds charged with the larceny thereof.

(iii) *Any other person.* "Any other person" means any person—even a person who has stolen the property—who has possession or a greater right to possession than the accused. In pleading a violation of this article, the ownership of the property may be alleged to have been in any person, other than the accused, who at the time of the theft was a general owner or a special owner thereof. A general owner of property is a person who has title to it, whether or not that person has possession of it; a special owner, such as a borrower or hirer, is one who does not have title but who does have possession, or the right of possession, of the property.

(iv) *Person.* "Person," as used in referring to one from whose possession property has been taken, obtained, or withheld, and to any owner of property, includes (in addition to a natural person) a government, a corporation, an association, an organization, and an estate. Such a person need not be a legal entity.

(d) *Wrongfulness of the taking, obtaining, or withholding.* The taking, obtaining, or withholding of the property must be wrongful. As a general rule, a taking or withholding of property from the possession of another is wrongful if done without the consent of the other, and an obtaining of property from the possession of another is wrongful if the obtaining is by false pretense. However, such an act is not wrongful if it is authorized by law or apparently lawful superior orders, or, generally, if done by a person who has a right to the possession of the property either equal to or greater than the right of one from whose possession the property is taken, obtained, or withheld. An owner of property who takes or withholds it from the possession of another, without the consent of the other, or who obtains it therefrom by false pretense, does so wrongfully if the other has a superior right—such as a lien—to possession of the property. A person who takes, obtains, or withholds property as the agent of another has the same rights and liabilities as does the principal, but may not be charged with a guilty knowledge or intent of the principal which that person does not share.

(e) *False pretense.* With respect to obtaining property by false pretense, the false pretense may be made by means of any act, word, symbol, or token. The pretense must be in fact false when made and when the property is obtained, and it must be knowingly false in the sense that it is made without a belief in its truth. A false pretense is a false representation of past or existing fact. In addition to other kinds of facts, the fact falsely represented by a person may be that person's or another's power, authority, or intention. Thus, a false representation by a person that person presently intends to perform a certain act in the future is a false representation of an existing fact—the intention—and thus a false pretense. Although the pretense need not be the sole cause inducing the owner to part with the property, it must be an effective and intentional cause of the obtaining. A false representation made after the property was obtained will not result in a violation of Article 121. A larceny is committed when a person obtains the property of another by false pretense and with intent to steal, even though the owner neither intended nor was requested to part with title to the property. Thus, a person who gets another's watch by pretending that it will be borrowed briefly and then returned, but who really intends to sell it, is guilty of larceny.

(f) *Intent.*

(i) *In general.* The offense of larceny requires that the taking, obtaining, or withholding by the thief be accompanied by an intent permanently to deprive or defraud another of the use and benefit of property or permanently to appropriate the property to the thief's own use or the use of any person other than the owner. These intents are collectively called an intent to steal. Although a person gets property by a taking or obtaining which was not wrongful or which was without a concurrent intent to steal, a larceny is nevertheless committed if an intent to steal is formed after the taking or obtaining and the property is wrongfully withheld with that intent. For example, if a person rents another's vehicle, later decides to keep it permanently, and then either fails to return it at the appointed time or uses

it for a purpose not authorized by the terms of the rental, larceny has been committed, even though at the time the vehicle was rented, the person intended to return it after using it according to the agreement.

(ii) *Inference of intent.* An intent to steal may be proved by circumstantial evidence. Thus, if a person secretly takes property, hides it, and denies knowing anything about it, an intent to steal may be inferred; if the property was taken openly and returned, this would tend to negate such an intent. Proof of sale of the property may show an intent to steal, and therefore, evidence of such a sale may be introduced to support a charge of larceny. An intent to steal may be inferred from a wrongful and intentional dealing with the property of another in a manner likely to cause that person to suffer a permanent loss thereof.

(iii) *Special situations.*

(A) *Motive does not negate intent.* The accused's purpose in taking an item ordinarily is irrelevant to the accused's guilt as long as the accused had the intent required under subparagraph c(1)(f)(i) above. For example, if the accused wrongfully took property as a "joke" or "to teach the owner a lesson" this would not be a defense, although if the accused intended to return the property, the accused would be guilty of wrongful appropriation, not larceny. When a person takes property intending only to return it to its lawful owner, as when stolen property is taken from a thief in order to return it to its owner, larceny or wrongful appropriation is not committed.

(B) *Intent to pay for or replace property not a defense.* An intent to pay for or replace the stolen property is not a defense, even if that intent existed at the time of the theft. If, however, the accused takes money or a negotiable instrument having no special value above its face value, with the intent to return an equivalent amount of money, the offense of larceny is not committed although wrongful appropriation may be.

(C) *Return of property not a defense.* Once a larceny is committed, a return of the property or payment for it is no defense. *See* subparagraph c(2) below when the taking, obtaining, or withholding is with the intent to return.

(g) *Value.*

(i) *In general.* Value is a question of fact to

be determined on the basis of all of the evidence admitted.

(ii) *Government property.* When the stolen property is an item issued or procured from Government sources, the price listed in an official publication for that property at the time of the theft is admissible as evidence of its value. *See* Mil. R. Evid. 803(17). However, the stolen item must be shown to have been, at the time of the theft, in the condition upon which the value indicated in the official price list is based. The price listed in the official publication is not conclusive as to the value of the item, and other evidence may be admitted on the question of its condition and value.

(iii) *Other property.* As a general rule, the value of other stolen property is its legitimate market value at the time and place of the theft. If this property, because of its character or the place where it was stolen, had no legitimate market value at the time and place of the theft or if that value cannot readily be ascertained, its value may be determined by its legitimate market value in the United States at the time of the theft, or by its replacement cost at that time, whichever is less. Market value may be established by proof of the recent purchase price paid for the article in the legitimate market involved or by testimony or other admissible evidence from any person who is familiar through training or experience with the market value in question. The owner of the property may testify as to its market value if familiar with its quality and condition. The fact that the owner is not an expert of the market value of the property goes only to the weight to be given that testimony, and not to its admissibility. *See* Mil. R. Evid. 701. When the character of the property clearly appears in evidence—for instance, when it is exhibited to the court-martial—the court-martial, from its own experience, may infer that it has some value. If as a matter of common knowledge the property is obviously of a value substantially in excess of $500.00, the court-martial may find a value of more than $500.00. Writings representing value may be considered to have the value—even though contingent—which they represented at the time of the theft.

(iv) *Limited interest in property.* If an owner of property or someone acting in the owner's behalf steals it from a person who has a superior, but limited, interest in the property, such as a lien, the value

for punishment purposes shall be that of the limited interest.

(h) *Military Property.* Military property is all property, real or personal, owned, held, or used by one of the armed forces of the United States. Military property is a term of art, and should not be confused with government property. The terms are not interchangeable. While all military property is government property, not all government property is military property. An item of government property is not military property unless the item in question meets the definition provided above. Retail merchandise of service exchange stores is not military property under this article.

(i) *Miscellaneous considerations.*

(i) *Lost property.* A taking or withholding of lost property by the finder is larceny if accompanied by an intent to steal and if a clue to the identity of the general or special owner, or through which such identity may be traced, is furnished by the character, location, or marketing of the property, or by other circumstances.

(ii) *Multiple article larceny.* When a larceny of several articles is committed at substantially the same time and place, it is a single larceny even though the articles belong to different persons. Thus, if a thief steals a suitcase containing the property of several persons or goes into a room and takes property belonging to various persons, there is but one larceny, which should be alleged in but one specification.

(iii) *Special kinds of property which may also be the subject of larceny.* Included in property which may be the subject of larceny is property which is taken, obtained, or withheld by severing it from real estate and writings which represent value such as commercial paper.

(iv) *Services.* Theft of services may not be charged under this paragraph, but *see* paragraph 78.

(vi) *Credit, Debit, and Electronic Transactions.* Wrongfully engaging in a credit, debit, or electronic transaction to obtain goods or money is an obtaining-type larceny by false pretense. Such use to obtain goods is usually a larceny of those goods from the merchant offering them. Such use to obtain money or a negotiable instrument (e.g., withdrawing cash from an automated teller or a cash advance from a bank) is usually a larceny of money from the entity presenting the money or a negotiable instrument. For the purpose of this section, the term 'credit, debit, or electronic transaction' includes the use of an instrument or device, whether known as a credit card, debit card, automated teller machine (ATM) card or by any other name, including access devices such as code, account number, electronic serial number or personal identification number, issued for the use in obtaining money, goods, or anything else of value.

(2) *Wrongful appropriation.*

(a) *In general.* Wrongful appropriation requires an intent to temporarily—as opposed to permanently—deprive the owner of the use and benefit of, or appropriate to the use of another, the property wrongfully taken, withheld, or obtained. In all other respects wrongful appropriation and larceny are identical.

(b) *Examples.* Wrongful appropriation includes: taking another's automobile without permission or lawful authority with intent to drive it a short distance and then return it or cause it to be returned to the owner; obtaining a service weapon by falsely pretending to be about to go on guard duty with intent to use it on a hunting trip and later return it; and while driving a government vehicle on a mission to deliver supplies, withholding the vehicle from government service by deviating from the assigned route without authority, to visit a friend in a nearby town and later restore the vehicle to its lawful use. An inadvertent exercise of control over the property of another will not result in wrongful appropriation. For example, a person who fails to return a borrowed boat at the time agreed upon because the boat inadvertently went aground is not guilty of this offense.

d. *Lesser included offenses.* See paragraph 3 of this part and Appendix 12A.

e. *Maximum punishment.*

(1) *Larceny.*

(a) *Military property of a value of $500 or less.* Bad-conduct discharge, forfeiture of all pay and allowances, and confinement for 1 year.

(b) *Property other than military property of a value of $500 or less.* Bad-conduct discharge, forfeiture of all pay and allowances, and confinement for 6 months.

(c) *Military property of a value of more than $500 or of any military motor vehicle, aircraft, vessel, firearm, or explosive.* Dishonorable discharge, forfeiture of all pay and allowances, and confinement for 10 years.

(d) *Property other than military property of a value of more than $500 or any motor vehicle, aircraft, vessel, firearm, or explosive not included in subparagraph e(1)(c).* Dishonorable discharge, forfeiture of all pay and allowances, and confinement for 5 years.

(2) *Wrongful appropriation.*

(a) *Of a value of $500.00 or less.* Confinement for 3 months, and forfeiture of two-thirds pay per month for 3 months.

(b) *Of a value of more than $500.00.* Bad-conduct discharge, forfeiture of all pay and allowances, and confinement for 6 months.

(c) *Of any motor vehicle, aircraft, vessel, firearm, or explosive.* Dishonorable discharge, forfeiture of all pay and allowances, and confinement for 2 years.

f. *Sample specifications.*

(1) *Larceny.*

In that _____ (personal jurisdiction data), did, (at/on board—location) (subject-matter jurisdiction data, if required), on or about _____ 20 ___ , steal _____ , (military property), of a value of (about) $ _____ , the property of _____ .

(2) *Wrongful appropriation.*

In that _____ (personal jurisdiction data), did, (at/on board—location) (subject matter jurisdiction data, if required), on or about _____ 20 ___ , wrongfully appropriate _____ , of a value of (about) $ _____ , the property of _____ .

47. Article 122—Robbery

a. *Text of statute.*

Any person subject to this chapter who with intent to steal takes anything of value from the person or in the presence of another, against his will, by means of force or violence or fear of immediate or future injury to his person or property or to the person or property of a relative or member of his family or of anyone in his company at the time of the robbery, is guilty of robbery and shall be punished as a court-martial may direct.

b. *Elements.*

(1) That the accused wrongfully took certain

property from the person or from the possession and in the presence of a person named or described;

(2) That the taking was against the will of that person;

(3) That the taking was by means of force, violence, or force and violence, or putting the person in fear of immediate or future injury to that person, a relative, a member of the person's family, anyone accompanying the person at the time of the robbery, the person's property, or the property of a relative, family member, or anyone accompanying the person at the time of the robbery;

(4) That the property belonged to a person named or described;

(5) That the property was of a certain or of some value; and

(6) That the taking of the property by the accused was with the intent permanently to deprive the person robbed of the use and benefit of the property. [Note: If the robbery was committed with a firearm, add the following element]

(7) That the means of force or violence or of putting the person in fear was a firearm.

c. *Explanation.*

(1) *Taking in the presence of the victim.* It is not necessary that the property taken be located within any certain distance of the victim. If persons enter a house and force the owner by threats to disclose the hiding place of valuables in an adjoining room, and, leaving the owner tied, go into that room and steal the valuables, they have committed robbery.

(2) *Force or violence.* For a robbery to be committed by force or violence, there must be actual force or violence to the person, preceding or accompanying the taking against the person's will, and it is immaterial that there is no fear engendered in the victim. Any amount of force is enough to constitute robbery if the force overcomes the actual resistance of the person robbed, puts the person in such a position that no resistance is made, or suffices to overcome the resistance offered by a chain or other fastening by which the article is attached to the person. The offense is not robbery if an article is merely snatched from the hand of another or a pocket is picked by stealth, no other force is used, and the owner is not put in fear. But if resistance is overcome in snatching the article, there is sufficient violence, as when an earring is torn from a person's ear. There is sufficient violence when a person's attention is diverted by being jostled by a confeder-

ate of a pickpocket, who is thus enabled to steal the person's watch, even though the person had no knowledge of the act; or when a person is knocked insensible and that person's pockets rifled; or when a guard steals property from the person of a prisoner in the guard's charge after handcuffing the prisoner on the pretext of preventing escape.

(3) *Fear.* For a robbery to be committed by putting the victim in fear, there need be no actual force or violence, but there must be a demonstration of force or menace by which the victim is placed in such fear that the victim is warranted in making no resistance. The fear must be a reasonable apprehension of present or future injury, and the taking must occur while the apprehension exists. The injury apprehended may be death or bodily injury to the person or to a relative or family member, or to anyone in the person's company at the time, or it may be the destruction of the person's habitation or other property or that of a relative or family member or anyone in the person's company at the time of sufficient gravity to warrant giving up the property demanded by the assailant.

(4) *Larceny by taking.* Robbery includes "taking with intent to steal"; hence, a larceny by taking is an integral part of a charge of robbery and must be proved at the trial. *See* paragraph 46c(1).

(5) *Multiple-victim robberies.* Robberies of different persons at the same time and place are separate offenses and each such robbery should be alleged in a separate specification.

d. *Lesser included offenses.* See paragraph 3 of this part and Appendix 12A.

e. *Maximum punishment.*

(1) *When committed with a firearm.* Dishonorable discharge, forfeiture of all pay and allowances, and confinement for 15 years.

(2) *Other cases.* Dishonorable discharge, forfeiture of all pay and allowances, and confinement for 10 years.

f. *Sample specifications.*

In that _____ (personal jurisdiction data), did, (at/on board—location) (subject-matter jurisdiction data, if required), on or about _____ 20 ___ , by means of (force) (violence) (force and violence) (and) (putting him/her in fear) (with a firearm) steal from the (person) (presence) of _____ , against his/her will, (a watch) (_____) of value of (about) $ _____ , the property of _____ .

48. Article 123—Forgery

a. *Text of statute.*

Any person subject to this chapter who, with intent to defraud—

(1) falsely makes or alters any signature to, or any part of, any writing which would, if genuine, apparently impose a legal liability on another or change his legal right or liability to his prejudice; or

(2) utters, offers, issues, or transfers such a writing, known by him to be so made or altered; is guilty of forgery and shall be punished as a court-martial may direct.

b. *Elements.*

(1) *Forgery—making or altering.*

(a) That the accused falsely made or altered a certain signature or writing;

(b) That the signature or writing was of a nature which would, if genuine, apparently impose a legal liability on another or change another's legal rights or liabilities to that person's prejudice; and

(c) That the false making or altering was with the intent to defraud.

(2) *Forgery—uttering.*

(a) That a certain signature or writing was falsely made or altered;

(b) That the signature or writing was of a nature which would, if genuine, apparently impose a legal liability on another or change another's legal rights or liabilities to that person's prejudice;

(c) That the accused uttered, offered, issued, or transferred the signature or writing;

(d) That at such time the accused knew that the signature or writing had been falsely made or altered; and

(e) That the uttering, offering, issuing or transferring was with the intent to defraud.

c. *Explanation.*

(1) *In general.* Forgery may be committed either by falsely making a writing or by knowingly uttering a falsely made writing. There are three elements common to both aspects of forgery: a writing falsely made or altered; and apparent capability of the writing as falsely made or altered to impose a legal

liability on another or to change another's legal rights or liabilities to that person's prejudice; and an intent to defraud.

(2) *False.* "False" refers not to the contents of the writing or to the facts stated therein but to the making or altering of it. Hence, forgery is not committed by the genuine making of a false instrument even when made with intent to defraud. A person who, with intent to defraud, signs that person's own signature as the maker of a check drawn on a bank in which that person does not have money or credit does not commit forgery. Although the check falsely represents the existence of the account, it is what it purports to be, a check drawn by the actual maker, and therefore it is not falsely made. *See*, however, paragraph 49. Likewise, if a person makes a false signature of another to an instrument, but adds the word "by" with that person's own signature thus indicating authority to sign, the offense is not forgery even if no such authority exists. False recitals of fact in a genuine document, as an aircraft flight report which is "padded" by the one preparing it, do not make the writing a forgery. *But see* paragraph 31 concerning false official statements.

(3) *Signatures.* Signing the name of another to an instrument having apparent legal efficacy without authority and with intent to defraud is forgery as the signature is falsely made. The distinction is that in this case the falsely made signature purports to be the act of one other than the actual signer. Likewise, a forgery may be committed by a person signing that person's own name to an instrument. For example, when a check payable to the order of a certain person comes into the hands of another of the same name, forgery is committed if, knowing the check to be another's, that person indorses it with that person's own name intending to defraud. Forgery may also be committed by signing a fictitious name, as when Roe makes a check payable to Roe and signs it with a fictitious name—Doe—as drawer.

(4) *Nature of writing.* The writing must be one which would, if genuine, apparently impose a legal liability on another, as a check or promissory note, or change that person's legal rights or liabilities to that person's prejudice, as a receipt. Some other instruments which may be the subject of forgery are orders for the delivery of money or goods, railroad tickets, and military orders directing travel. A writing falsely "made" includes an instrument that may be partially or entirely printed, engraved, written

with a pencil, or made by photography or other device. A writing may be falsely "made" by materially altering an existing writing, by filling in a paper signed in blank, or by signing an instrument already written. With respect to the apparent legal efficacy of the writing falsely made or altered, the writing must appear either on its face or from extrinsic facts to impose a legal liability on another, or to change a legal right or liability to the prejudice of another. If under all the circumstances the instrument has neither real nor apparent legal efficacy, there is no forgery. Thus, the false making with intent to defraud of an instrument affirmatively invalid on its face is not forgery nor is the false making or altering, with intent to defraud, of a writing which could not impose a legal liability, as a mere letter of introduction. However, the false making of another's signature on an instrument with intent to defraud is forgery, even if there is no resemblance to the genuine signature and the name is misspelled.

(5) *Intent to defraud.* See paragraph 49c(14). The intent to defraud need not be directed toward anyone in particular nor be for the advantage of the offender. It is immaterial that nobody was actually defrauded, or that no further step was made toward carrying out the intent to defraud other than the false making or altering of a writing.

(6) *Alteration.* The alteration must effect a material change in the legal tenor of the writing. Thus, an alteration which apparently increases, diminishes, or discharges any obligation is material. Examples of material alterations in the case of a promissory note are changing the date, amount, or place of payment. If a genuine writing has been delivered to the accused and while in the accused's possession is later found to be altered, it may be inferred that the writing was altered by the accused.

(7) *Uttering.* See paragraph 49c(4).

d. *Lesser included offenses.* See paragraph 3 of this part and Appendix 12A.

e. *Maximum punishment.* Dishonorable discharge, forfeiture of all pay and allowances, and confinement for 5 years.

f. *Sample specifications.*

(1) *Forgery—making or altering.*

In that _____ (personal jurisdiction data), did, (at/on board—location) (subject-matter jurisdiction data, if required), on or about ____ 20 __ , with intent to defraud, falsely [make (in its entirety)

(the signature of _____ as an indorsement to) (the signature of _____ to) (_____) a certain (check) (writing) (_____) in the following words and figures, to wit: _____] [alter a certain (check) (writing) (_____) in the following words and figures, to wit: _____ , by (adding thereto _____) (_____)], which said (check) (writing) (_____) would, if genuine, apparently operate to the legal harm of another [*and which _____ (could be) (was) used to the legal harm of _____ , in that _____].

[*Note: This allegation should be used when the document specified is not one which by its nature would clearly operate to the legal prejudice of another—for example, an insurance application. The manner in which the document could be or was used to prejudice the legal rights of another should be alleged in the last blank.]

(2) *Forgery—uttering.*

In that _____ (personal jurisdiction data), did, (at/on board—location) (subject-matter jurisdiction data, if required), on or about _____ 20 __ , with intent to defraud, (utter) (offer) (issue) (transfer) a certain (check) (writing) (_____) in the following words and figures, to wit: _____ , a writing which would, if genuine, apparently operate to the legal harm of another, (which said (check) (writing) (_____)) (the signature to which said (check) (writing) (_____)) (_____) was, as he/she, the said _____ , then well knew, falsely (made) (altered) (*and which _____ (could be) (was) used to the legal harm of _____ , in that _____).

[*Note: *See* the note following (1), above]

49. Article 123a—Making, drawing, or uttering check, draft, or order without sufficient funds

a. *Text of statute.*

Any person subject to this chapter who—

(1) for the procurement of any article or thing of value, with intent to defraud; or

(2) for the payment of any past due obligation, or for any other purpose, with intent to deceive; makes, draws, utters, or delivers any check, draft, or order for the payment of money upon any bank or other depository, knowing at the time that the maker or drawer has not or will not have sufficient funds in, or credit with, the bank or other depository for the payment of that check, draft, or order in full upon its presentment, shall be punished as a court-martial may direct. The making, drawing, uttering, or delivering by a

maker or drawer of a check, draft, or order, payment of which is refused by the drawee because of insufficient funds of the maker or drawer in the drawee's possession or control, is prima facie evidence of his intent to defraud or deceive and of his knowledge of insufficient funds in, or credit with, that bank or other depository, unless the maker or drawer pays the holder the amount due within five days after receiving notice, orally or in writing, that the check, draft, or order was not paid on presentment. In this section, the word "credit" means an arrangement or understanding, express or implied, with the bank or other depository for the payment of that check, draft, or order.

b. *Elements.*

(1) *For the procurement of any article or thing of value, with intent to defraud.*

(a) That the accused made, drew, uttered, or delivered a check, draft, or order for the payment of money payable to a named person or organization;

(b) That the accused did so for the purpose of procuring an article or thing of value;

(c) That the act was committed with intent to defraud; and

(d) That at the time of making, drawing, uttering, or delivery of the instrument the accused knew that the accused or the maker or drawer had not or would not have sufficient funds in, or credit with, the bank or other depository for the payment thereof upon presentment.

(2) *For the payment of any past due obligation, or for any other purpose, with intent to deceive.*

(a) That the accused made, drew, uttered, or delivered a check, draft, or order for the payment of money payable to a named person or organization;

(b) That the accused did so for the purpose or purported purpose of effecting the payment of a past due obligation or for some other purpose;

(c) That the act was committed with intent to deceive; and

(d) That at the time of making, drawing, uttering, or delivering of the instrument, the accused knew that the accused or the maker or drawer had not or would not have sufficient funds in, or credit with, the bank or other depository for the payment thereof upon presentment.

c. *Explanation.*

(1) *Written instruments.* The written instruments covered by this article include any check, draft (including share drafts), or order for the payment of money drawn upon any bank or other depository, whether or not the drawer bank or depository is actually in existence. It may be inferred that every check, draft, or order carries with it a representation that the instrument will be paid in full by the bank or other depository upon presentment by a holder when due.

(2) *Bank or other depository.* "Bank or other depository" includes any business regularly but not necessarily exclusively engaged in public banking activities.

(3) *Making or drawing.* "Making" and "drawing" are synonymous and refer to the act of writing and signing the instrument.

(4) *Uttering or delivering.* "Uttering" and "delivering" have similar meanings. Both mean transferring the instrument to another, but "uttering" has the additional meaning of offering to transfer. A person need not personally be the maker or drawer of an instrument in order to violate this article if that person utters or delivers it. For example, if a person holds a check which that person knows is worthless, and utters or delivers the check to another, that person may be guilty of an offense under this article despite the fact that the person did not personally draw the check.

(5) *For the procurement.* "For the procurement" means for the purpose of obtaining any article or thing of value. It is not necessary that an article or thing of value actually be obtained, and the purpose of the obtaining may be for the accused's own use or benefit or for the use or benefit of another.

(6) *For the payment.* "For the payment" means for the purpose or purported purpose of satisfying in whole or in part any past due obligation. Payment need not be legally effected.

(7) *For any other purpose.* "For any other purpose" includes all purposes other than the payment of a past due obligation or the procurement of any article or thing of value. For example, it includes paying or purporting to pay an obligation which is not yet past due. The check, draft, or order, whether made or negotiated for the procurement of an article or thing of value or for the payment of a past due obligation or for some other purpose, need not be intended or represented as payable immediately. For example, the making of a postdated check, delivered

at the time of entering into an installment purchase contract and intended as payment for a future installment, would, if made with the requisite intent and knowledge, be a violation of this article.

(8) *Article or thing of value.* "Article or thing of value" extends to every kind of right or interest in property, or derived from contract, including interests and rights which are intangible or contingent or which mature in the future.

(9) *Past due obligation.* A "past due obligation" is an obligation to pay money, which obligation has legally matured before making, drawing, uttering, or delivering the instrument.

(10) *Knowledge.* The accused must have knowledge, at the time the accused makes, draws, utters, or delivers the instrument, that the maker or drawer, whether the accused or another, has not or will not have sufficient funds in, or credit with, the bank or other depository for the payment of the instrument in full upon its presentment. Such knowledge may be proved by circumstantial evidence.

(11) *Sufficient funds.* "Sufficient funds" refers to a condition in which the account balance of the maker or drawer in the bank or other depository at the time of the presentment of the instrument for payment is not less than the face amount of the instrument and has not been rendered unavailable for payment by garnishment, attachment, or other legal procedures.

(12) *Credit.* "Credit" means an arrangement or understanding, express or implied, with the bank or other depository for the payment of the check, draft, or order. An absence of credit includes those situations in which an accused writes a check on a nonexistent bank or on a bank in which the accused has no account.

(13) *Upon its presentment.* "Upon its presentment" refers to the time the demand for payment is made upon presentation of the instrument to the bank or other depository on which it was drawn.

(14) *Intent to defraud.* "Intent to defraud" means an intent to obtain, through a misrepresentation, an article or thing of value and to apply it to one's own use and benefit or to the use and benefit of another, either permanently or temporarily.

(15) *Intent to deceive.* "Intent to deceive" means an intent to mislead, cheat, or trick another by means of a misrepresentation made for the purpose of gaining an advantage for oneself or for a third

person, or of bringing about a disadvantage to the interests of the person to whom the representation was made or to interests represented by that person.

(16) *The relationship of time and intent.* Under this article, two times are involved: (a) when the accused makes, draws, utters, or delivers the instrument; and (b) when the instrument is presented to the bank or other depository for payment. With respect to (a), the accused must possess the requisite intent and must know that the maker or drawer does not have or will not have sufficient funds in, or credit with, the bank or the depository for payment of the instrument in full upon its presentment when due. With respect to (b), if it can otherwise be shown that the accused possessed the requisite intent and knowledge at the time the accused made, drew, uttered, or delivered the instrument, neither proof of presentment nor refusal of payment is necessary, as when the instrument is one drawn on a nonexistent bank.

(17) *Statutory rule of evidence.* The provision of this article with respect to establishing prima facie evidence of knowledge and intent by proof of notice and nonpayment within 5 days is a statutory rule of evidence. The failure of an accused who is a maker or drawer to pay the holder the amount due within 5 days after receiving either oral or written notice from the holder of a check, draft, or order, or from any other person having knowledge that such check, draft, or order was returned unpaid because of insufficient funds, is prima facie evidence (a) that the accused had the intent to defraud or deceive as alleged; and (b) that the accused knew at the time the accused made, drew, uttered, or delivered the check, draft, or order that the accused did not have or would not have sufficient funds in, or credit with, the bank or other depository for the payment of such check, draft, or order upon its presentment for payment. Prima facie evidence is that evidence from which the accused's intent to defraud or deceive and the accused's knowledge of insufficient funds in or credit with the bank or other depository may be inferred, depending on all the circumstances. The failure to give notice referred to in the article, or payment by the accused, maker, or drawer to the holder of the amount due within 5 days after such notice has been given, precludes the prosecution from using the statutory rule of evidence but does not preclude conviction of this offense if all the elements are otherwise proved.

(18) *Affirmative defense.* Honest mistake is an affirmative defense to offenses under this article. *See* R.C.M. 916(j).

d. *Lesser included offenses.* See paragraph 3 of this part and Appendix 12A.

e. *Maximum punishment.*

(1) *For the procurement of any article or thing of value, with intent to defraud, in the face amount of:*

(a) *$500.00 or less.* Bad-conduct discharge, forfeiture of all pay and allowances, and confinement for 6 months.

(b) *More than $500.00.* Dishonorable discharge, forfeiture of all pay and allowances, and confinement for 5 years.

(2) *For the payment of any past due obligation, or for any other purpose, with intent to deceive.* Bad-conduct discharge, forfeiture of all pay and allowances, and confinement for 6 months.

f. *Sample specifications.*

(1) *For the procurement of any article or thing of value, with intent to defraud.*

In that _____ (personal jurisdiction data), did, (at/on board—location) (subject-matter jurisdiction data, if required), on or about _____ 20 ___ , with intent to defraud and for the procurement of (lawful currency) (and) (_____ (an article) (a thing) of value), wrongfully and unlawfully ((make (draw)) (utter) (deliver) to _____ ,) a certain (check) (draft) (money order) upon the (_____ Bank) (_____ depository) in words and figures as follows, to wit: _____ , then knowing that (he/she) (_____), the (maker) (drawer) thereof, did not or would not have sufficient funds in or credit with such (bank) (depository) for the payment of the said (check) (draft) (order) in full upon its presentment.

(2) *For the payment of any past due obligation, or for any other purpose, with intent to deceive.*

In that _____ (personal jurisdiction data), did, (at/on board—location) (subject-matter jurisdiction data, if required), on or about _____ 20 ___ , with intent to deceive and for the payment of a past due obligation, to wit: _____ (for the purpose of _____) wrongfully and unlawfully ((make) (draw)) (utter) (deliver) to _____ , a certain (check) (draft) (money order) for the payment of money upon (_____ Bank) (_____ depository), in words and figures as follows, to wit: _____ , then knowing that (he/she) (_____), the (maker) (drawer) thereof, did not or would not have sufficient

funds in or credit with such (bank) (depository) for the payment of the said (check) (draft) (order) in full upon its presentment.

50. Article 124—Maiming

a. *Text of statute.*

Any person subject to this chapter who, with intent to injure, disfigure, or disable, inflicts upon the person of another an injury which—

(1) seriously disfigures his person by any mutilation thereof;

(2) destroys or disables any member or organ of his body; or

(3) seriously diminishes his physical vigor by the injury of any member or organ; is guilty of maiming and shall be punished as a court-martial may direct.

b. *Elements.*

(1) That the accused inflicted a certain injury upon a certain person;

(2) That this injury seriously disfigured the person's body, destroyed or disabled an organ or member, or seriously diminished the person's physical vigor by the injury to an organ or member; and

(3) That the accused inflicted this injury with an intent to cause some injury to a person.

c. *Explanation.*

(1) *Nature of offense.* It is maiming to put out a person's eye, to cut off a hand, foot, or finger, or to knock out a tooth, as these injuries destroy or disable those members or organs. It is also maiming to injure an internal organ so as to seriously diminish the physical vigor of a person. Likewise, it is maiming to cut off an ear or to scar a face with acid, as these injuries seriously disfigure a person. A disfigurement need not mutilate any entire member to come within the article, or be of any particular type, but must be such as to impair perceptibly and materially the victim's comeliness. The disfigurement, diminishment of vigor, or destruction or disablement of any member or organ must be a serious injury of a substantially permanent nature. However, the offense is complete if such an injury is inflicted even though there is a possibility that the victim may eventually recover the use of the member or organ, or that the disfigurement may be cured by surgery.

(2) *Means of inflicting injury.* To prove the offense it is not necessary to prove the specific means by which the injury was inflicted. However, such

evidence may be considered on the question of intent.

(3) *Intent.* Maiming requires a specific intent to injure generally but not a specific intent to maim. Thus, one commits the offense who intends only a slight injury, if in fact there is infliction of an injury of the type specified in this article. Infliction of the type of injuries specified in this article upon the person of another may support an inference of the intent to injure, disfigure, or disable.

(4) *Defenses.* If the injury is done under circumstances which would justify or excuse homicide, the offense of maiming is not committed. *See* R.C.M. 916.

d. *Lesser included offenses.* See paragraph 3 of this part and Appendix 12A.

e. *Maximum punishment.* Dishonorable discharge, forfeiture of all pay and allowances, and confinement for 20 years.

f. *Sample specification.*

In that _____ (personal jurisdiction data), did, (at/on board—location) (subject-matter jurisdiction data, if required) on or about _____ 20 ___ , maim _____ by (crushing his/her foot with a sledge hammer) (_____).

51. Article 125—Forcible sodomy; bestiality

a. *Text of statute.*

(a) **Forcible Sodomy.–Any person subject to this chapter who engages in unnatural carnal copulation with another person of the same or opposite sex by unlawful force or without the consent of the other person is guilty of forcible sodomy and shall be punished as a court-martial may direct.**

(b) *Bestiality.*–**Any person subject to this chapter who engages in unnatural carnal copulation with an animal is guilty of bestiality and shall be punished as a court-martial may direct.**

(c) *Scope of Offenses.*–**Penetration, however slight, is sufficient to complete an offense under subsection (a) or (b).**

b. *Elements.*

(1) *Forcible sodomy.*

(a) That the accused engaged in unnatural carnal copulation with a certain other person.

(b) That the act was done by force or without the consent of the other person.

(2) *Bestiality.*

(a) That the accused engaged in unnatural carnal copulation with an animal.

c. *Explanation.*

(1) It is unnatural carnal copulation for a person to take into that person's mouth or anus the sexual organ of another person or of an animal; or to place that person's sexual organ in the mouth or anus of another person or of an animal; or to have carnal copulation in any opening of the body, except the sexual parts, with another person; or to have carnal copulation with an animal.

(2) For purposes of this Article, the term "unlawful force" means an act of force done without legal justification or excuse.

d. *Lesser included offenses.* See paragraph 3 of this part and Appendix 12A.

e. *Maximum punishment.*

(1) *Forcible sodomy.* Dishonorable discharge, forfeiture of all pay and allowances, and confinement for life without eligibility for parole. Mandatory minimum – Dismissal or dishonorable discharge.

(2) *Bestiality.* Dishonorable discharge, forfeiture of all pay and allowances, and confinement for 5 years.

f. *Sample specification.*

(1) *Forcible sodomy.* In that (personal jurisdiction data), did, (at/on board–location) (subject-matter jurisdiction data, if required), on or about _____ 20__, engage in unnatural carnal copulation with __ _____, by unlawful force or without the consent of the said _____.

(2) *Bestiality.* In that (personal jurisdiction data), did, (at/on board–location) (subject-matter jurisdiction data, if required), on or about _____20__, engage in unnatural carnal copulation with (type of animal).

52. Article 126—Arson

a. *Text of statute.*

(a) **Any person subject to this chapter who willfully and maliciously burns or sets on fire an inhabited dwelling, or any other structure, movable or immovable, wherein to the knowledge of the offender there is at the time a human being, is guilty of aggravated arson and shall be punished as a court-martial may direct.**

(b) **Any person subject to this chapter who**

willfully and maliciously burns or sets fire to the property of another, except as provided in subsection (a), is guilty of simple arson and shall be punished as a court-martial may direct.

b. *Elements.*

(1) *Aggravated arson.*

(a) *Inhabited dwelling.*

(i) That the accused burned or set on fire an inhabited dwelling;

(ii) That this dwelling belonged to a certain person and was of a certain value; and

(iii) That the act was willful and malicious.

(b) *Structure.*

(i) That the accused burned or set on fire a certain structure;

(ii) That the act was willful and malicious;

(iii) That there was a human being in the structure at the time;

(iv) That the accused knew that there was a human being in the structure at the time; and

(v) That this structure belonged to a certain person and was of a certain value.

(2) *Simple arson.*

(a) That the accused burned or set fire to certain property of another;

(b) That the property was of a certain value; and

(c) That the act was willful and malicious.

c. *Explanation.*

(1) *In general.* In aggravated arson, danger to human life is the essential element; in simple arson, it is injury to the property of another. In either case, it is immaterial that no one is, in fact, injured. It must be shown that the accused set the fire willfully and maliciously, that is, not merely by negligence or accident.

(2) *Aggravated arson.*

(a) *Inhabited dwelling.* An inhabited dwelling includes the outbuildings that form part of the cluster of buildings used as a residence. A shop or store is not an inhabited dwelling unless occupied as such, nor is a house that has never been occupied or which has been temporarily abandoned. A person may be guilty of aggravated arson of the person's dwelling, whether as owner or tenant.

(b) *Structure.* Aggravated arson may also be committed by burning or setting on fire any other structure, movable or immovable, such as a theater, church, boat, trailer, tent, auditorium, or any other sort of shelter or edifice, whether public or private, when the offender knows that there is a human being inside at the time. It may be that the offender had this knowledge when the nature of the structure—as a department store or theater during hours of business, or other circumstances—are shown to have been such that a reasonable person would have known that a human being was inside at the time.

(c) *Damage to property.* It is not necessary that the dwelling or structure be consumed or materially injured; it is enough if fire is actually communicated to any part thereof. Any actual burning or charring is sufficient, but a mere scorching or discoloration by heat is not.

(d) *Value and ownership of property.* For the offense of aggravated arson, the value and ownership of the dwelling or other structure are immaterial, but should ordinarily be alleged and proved to permit the finding in an appropriate case of the included offense of simple arson.

(3) *Simple arson.* "Simple arson" is the willful and malicious burning or setting fire to the property of another under circumstances not amounting to aggravated arson. The offense includes burning or setting fire to real or personal property of someone other than the offender. *See also* paragraph 67 (Burning with intent to defraud).

d. *Lesser included offenses.* See paragraph 3 of this part and Appendix 12A.

e. *Maximum punishment.*

(1) *Aggravated arson.* Dishonorable discharge, forfeiture of all pay and allowances, and confinement for 20 years.

(2) *Simple arson, where the property is—*

(a) *Of a value of $500.00 or less.* Dishonorable discharge, forfeiture of all pay and allowances, and confinement for 1 year.

(b) *Of a value of more than $500.00.* Dishonorable discharge, forfeiture of all pay and allowances, and confinement for 5 years.

f. *Sample specifications.*

(1) *Aggravated arson.*

(a) *Inhabited dwelling.*

In that _____ (personal jurisdiction data), did, (at/on board—location) (subject-matter jurisdiction data, if required), on or about _____ 20 ___ , willfully and maliciously (burn) (set on fire) an inhabited dwelling, to wit: (the residence of _____) (_____), (the property of _____) of a value of (about) $ _____ .

  (b) *Structure.*
In that _____ (personal jurisdiction data), did, (at/on board—location) (subject-matter jurisdiction data, if required), on or _____ 20 __ , willfully and maliciously (burn) (set on fire), knowing that a human being was therein at the time, (the Post Theater) (_____ , the property of _____), of a value of (about) $ _____ .

  (2) *Simple arson.*
In that _____ (personal jurisdiction data), did, (at/on board— location) (subject-matter jurisdiction data, if required), on or about _____ 20 __ , willfully and maliciously (burn) (set fire to) (an automobile) (_____), the property of _____ , of a value of (about) $ _____ .

53. Article 127—Extortion

a. *Text of statute.*

  Any person subject to this chapter who communicates threats to another person with the intention thereby to obtain anything of value or any acquittance, advantage, or immunity is guilty of extortion and shall be punished as a court-martial may direct.

b. *Elements.*

  (1) That the accused communicated a certain threat to another; and

  (2) That the accused intended to unlawfully obtain something of value, or any acquittance, advantage, or immunity.

c. *Explanation.*

  (1) *In general.* Extortion is complete upon communication of the threat with the requisite intent. The actual or probable success of the extortion need not be proved.

  (2) *Threat.* A threat may be communicated by any means but must be received by the intended victim. The threat may be: a threat to do any unlawful injury to the person or property of the person threatened or to any member of that person's family or any other person held dear to that person; a threat to accuse the person threatened, or any member of that persons's family or any other person held dear to that person, of any crime; a threat to expose or impute any deformity or disgrace to the person

threatened or to any member of that person's family or any other person held dear to that person; a threat to expose any secret affecting the person threatened or any member of that person's family or any other person held dear to that person; or a threat to do any other harm.

  (3) *Acquittance.* An "acquittance" is a release or discharge from an obligation.

  (4) *Advantage or immunity.* Unless it is clear from the circumstances, the advantage or immunity sought should be described in the specification. An intent to make a person do an act against that person's will is not, by itself, sufficient to constitute extortion.

d. *Lesser included offenses.* See paragraph 3 of this part and Appendix 12A.

e. *Maximum punishment.* Dishonorable discharge, forfeiture of all pay and allowances, and confinement for 3 years.

f. *Sample specification.*
In that _____ (personal jurisdiction data), did, (at/on board—location) (subject-matter jurisdiction data, if required), on or about _____ 20 __ , with intent unlawfully to obtain (something of value) (an acquittance) (an advantage, to wit _____) (an immunity, to wit _____), communicate to _____ a threat to (here describe the threat).

54. Article 128—Assault

a. *Text of statute.*

  (a) **Any person subject to this chapter who attempts or offers with unlawful force or violence to do bodily harm to another person, whether or not the attempt or offer is consummated, is guilty of assault and shall be punished as a court-martial may direct.**

  (b) **Any person subject to this chapter who—**

    (1) **commits an assault with a dangerous weapon or other means or force likely to produce death or grievous bodily harm; or**

    (2) **commits an assault and intentionally inflicts grievous bodily harm with or without a weapon;**

  is guilty of aggravated assault and shall be punished as a court-martial may direct.

b. *Elements.*

  (1) *Simple assault.*

(a) That the accused attempted or offered to do bodily harm to a certain person; and

(b) That the attempt or offer was done with unlawful force or violence.

(2) *Assault consummated by a battery.*

(a) That the accused did bodily harm to a certain person; and

(b) That the bodily harm was done with unlawful force or violence.

(3) *Assaults permitting increased punishment based on status of victim.*

(a) *Assault upon a commissioned, warrant, noncommissioned, or petty officer.*

(i) That the accused attempted to do, offered to do, or did bodily harm to a certain person;

(ii) That the attempt, offer, or bodily harm was done with unlawful force or violence;

(iii) That the person was a commissioned, warrant, noncommissioned, or petty officer; and

(iv) That the accused then knew that the person was a commissioned, warrant, noncommissioned, or petty officer.

(b) *Assault upon a sentinel or lookout in the execution of duty, or upon a person in the execution of law enforcement duties.*

(i) That the accused attempted to do, offered to do, or did bodily harm to a certain person;

(ii) That the attempt, offer, or bodily harm was done with unlawful force or violence;

(iii) That the person was a sentinel or lookout in the execution of duty or was a person who then had and was in the execution of security police, military police, shore patrol, master at arms, or other military or civilian law enforcement duties; and

(iv) That the accused then knew that the person was a sentinel or lookout in the execution of duty or was a person who then had and was in the execution of security police, military police, shore patrol, master at arms, or other military or civilian law enforcement duties.

(c) *Assault consummated by a battery upon a child under 16 years.*

(i) That the accused did bodily harm to a certain person;

(ii) That the bodily harm was done with unlawful force or violence; and

(iii) That the person was then a child under the age of 16 years.

(4) *Aggravated assault.*

(a) *Assault with a dangerous weapon or other means or force likely to produce death or grievous bodily harm.*

(i) That the accused attempted to do, offered to do, or did bodily harm to a certain person;

(ii) That the accused did so with a certain weapon, means, or force;

(iii) That the attempt, offer, or bodily harm was done with unlawful force or violence; and

(iv) That the weapon, means, or force was used in a manner likely to produce death or grievous bodily harm.

(Note: Add any of the following as applicable)

(v) That the weapon was a loaded firearm.

(vi) That the person was a child under the age of 16 years.

(b) *Assault in which grievous bodily harm is intentionally inflicted.*

(i) That the accused assaulted a certain person;

(ii) That grievous bodily harm was thereby inflicted upon such person;

(iii) That the grievous bodily harm was done with unlawful force or violence; and

(iv) That the accused, at the time, had the specific intent to inflict grievous bodily harm.

(Note: Add any of the following as applicable)

(v) That the injury was inflicted with a loaded firearm.

(vi) That the person was a child under the age of 16 years.

c. *Explanation.*

(1) *Simple assault.*

(a) *Definition of assault.* An "assault" is an attempt or offer with unlawful force or violence to do bodily harm to another, whether or not the attempt or offer is consummated. It must be done without legal justification or excuse and without the lawful consent of the person affected. "Bodily harm" means any offensive touching of another, however slight.

(b) *Difference between "attempt" and "offer" type assaults.*

(i) *Attempt type assault.* An "attempt" type assault requires a specific intent to inflict bodily harm, and an overt act—that is, an act that amounts to more than mere preparation and apparently tends to effect the intended bodily harm. An attempt type assault may be committed even though the victim had no knowledge of the incident at the time.

(ii) *Offer type assault.* An "offer" type assault is an unlawful demonstration of violence, either by an intentional or by a culpably negligent act or omission, which creates in the mind of another a reasonable apprehension of receiving immediate bodily harm. Specific intent to inflict bodily harm is not required.

(iii) *Examples.*

(A) If Doe swings a fist at Roe's head intending to hit Roe but misses, Doe has committed an attempt type assault, whether or not Roe is aware of the attempt.

(B) If Doe swings a fist in the direct of Roe's head either intentionally or as a result of culpable negligence, and Roe sees the blow coming and is thereby put in apprehension of being struck, Doe has committed an offer type assault whether or not Doe intended to hit Roe.

(C) If Doe swings at Roe's head, intending to hit it, and Roe sees the blow coming and is thereby put in apprehension of being struck, Doe has committed both on offer and an attempt type assault.

(D) If Doe swings at Roe's head simply to frighten Roe, not intending to hit Roe, and Roe does not see the blow and is not placed in fear, then no assault of any type has been committed.

(c) *Situations not amounting to assault.*

(i) *Mere preparation.* Preparation not amounting to an overt act, such as picking up a stone without any attempt or offer to throw it, does not constitute an assault.

(ii) *Threatening words.* The use of threatening words alone does not constitute an assault. However, if the threatening words are accompanied by a menacing act or gesture, there may be an assault, since the combination constitutes a demonstration of violence.

(iii) *Circumstances negating intent to harm.* If the circumstances known to the person menaced clearly negate an intent to do bodily harm there is no assault. Thus, if a person accompanies an apparent attempt to strike another by an unequivocal announcement in some form of an intention not to strike, there is no assault. For example, if Doe raises

a stick and shakes it at Roe within striking distance saying, "If you weren't an old man, I would knock you down," Doe has committed no assault. However, an offer to inflict bodily injury upon another instantly if that person does not comply with a demand which the assailant has no lawful right to make is an assault. Thus, if Doe points a pistol at Roe and says, "If you don't hand over your watch, I will shoot you," Doe has committed an assault upon Roe. *See also* paragraph 47 (robbery) of this part.

(d) *Situations not constituting defenses to assault.*

(i) *Assault attempt fails.* It is not a defense to a charge of assault that for some reason unknown to the assailant, an assault attempt was bound to fail. Thus, if a person loads a rifle with what is believed to be a good cartridge and, pointing it at another, pulls the trigger, that person may be guilty of assault although the cartridge was defective and did not fire. Likewise, if a person in a house shoots through the roof at a place where a policeman is believed to be, that person may be guilty of assault even though the policeman is at another place on the roof.

(ii) *Retreating victim.* An assault is complete if there is a demonstration of violence and an apparent ability to inflict bodily injury causing the person at whom it was directed to reasonably apprehend that unless the person retreats bodily harm will be inflicted. This is true even though the victim retreated and was never within actual striking distance of the assailant. There must, however, be an apparent present ability to inflict the injury. Thus, to aim a pistol at a person at such a distance that it clearly could not injure would not be an assault.

(2) *Battery.*

(a) *In general.* A "battery" is an assault in which the attempt or offer to do bodily harm is consummated by the infliction of that harm.

(b) *Application of force.* The force applied in a battery may have been directly or indirectly applied. Thus, a battery can be committed by inflicting bodily injury on a person through striking the horse on which the person is mounted causing the horse to throw the person, as well as by striking the person directly.

(c) *Examples of battery.* It may be a battery to spit on another, push a third person against another, set a dog at another which bites the person, cut another's clothes while the person is wearing them though without touching or intending to touch the person, shoot a person, cause a person to take poison, or drive an automobile into a person. A person who, although excused in using force, uses more force than is required, commits a battery. Throwing an object into a crowd may be a battery on anyone whom the object hits.

(d) *Situations not constituting battery.* If bodily harm is inflicted unintentionally and without culpable negligence, there is no battery. It is also not a battery to touch another to attract the other's attention or to prevent injury.

(3) *Assaults permitting increased punishment based on status of victims.*

(a) *Assault upon a commissioned, warrant, noncommissioned, or petty officer.* The maximum punishment is increased when assault is committed upon a commissioned officer of the armed forces of the United States, or of a friendly foreign power, or upon a warrant, noncommissioned, or petty officer of the armed forces of the United States. Knowledge of the status of the victim is an essential element of the offense and may be proved by circumstantial evidence. It is not necessary that the victim be superior in rank or command to the accused, that the victim be in the same armed force, or that the victim be in the execution of office at the time of the assault.

(b) *Assault upon a sentinel or lookout in the execution of duty, or upon a person in the execution of law enforcement duties.* The maximum punishment is increased when assault is committed upon a sentinel or lookout in the execution of duty or upon a person who was then performing security police, military police, shore patrol, master at arms, or other military or civilian law enforcement duties. Knowledge of the status of the victim is an essential element of this offense and may be proved by circumstantial evidence. *See* paragraph 38c(4) for the definition of "sentinel or lookout."

(c) *Assault consummated by a battery upon a child under 16 years of age.* The maximum punishment is increased when assault consummated by a battery is committed upon a child under 16 years of age. Knowledge that the person assaulted was under 16 years of age is not an element of this offense.

(4) *Aggravated assault.*

(a) *Assault with a dangerous weapon or other means or force likely to produce death or grievous bodily harm.*

(i) *Dangerous weapon.* A weapon is dangerous when used in a manner likely to produce death or grievous bodily harm.

(ii) *Other means or force.* The phrase "other means or force" may include any means or instrumentality not normally considered a weapon. When the natural and probable consequence of a particular use of any means or force would be death or grievous bodily harm, it may be inferred that the means or force is "likely" to produce that result. The use to which a certain kind of instrument is ordinarily put is irrelevant to the question of its method of employment in a particular case. Thus, a bottle, beer glass, a rock, a bunk adaptor, a piece of pipe, a piece of wood, boiling water, drugs, or a rifle butt may be used in a manner likely to inflict death or grievous bodily harm. On the other hand, an unloaded pistol, when presented as a firearm and not as a bludgeon, is not a dangerous weapon or a means of force likely to produce grievous bodily harm, whether or not the assailant knew it was unloaded.

(iii) *Grievous bodily harm.* "Grievous bodily harm" means serious bodily injury. It does not include minor injuries, such as a black eye or a bloody nose, but does include fractured or dislocated bones, deep cuts, torn members of the body, serious damage to internal organs, and other serious bodily injuries.

(iv) *Death or injury not required.* It is not necessary that death or grievous bodily harm be actually inflicted to prove assault with a dangerous weapon or means likely to produce grievous bodily harm.

(v) *When committed upon a child under 16 years of age.* The maximum punishment is increased when aggravated assault with a dangerous weapon or means likely to produce death or grievous bodily harm is inflicted upon a child under 16 years of age. Knowledge that the person assaulted was under the age of 16 years is not an element of the offense.

(b) *Assault in which grievous bodily harm is intentionally inflicted.*

(i) *In general.* It must be proved that the accused specifically intended to and did inflict grievous bodily harm. Culpable negligence will not suffice.

(ii) *Proving intent.* Specific intent may be

proved by circumstantial evidence. When grievous bodily harm has been inflicted by means of intentionally using force in a manner likely to achieve that result, it may be inferred that grievous bodily harm was intended. On the other hand, that inference might not be drawn if a person struck another with a fist in a sidewalk fight even if the victim fell so that the victim's head hit the curbstone and a skull fracture resulted. It is possible, however, to commit this kind of aggravated assault with the fists, as when the victim is held by one of several assailants while the others beat the victim with their fists and break a nose, jaw, or rib.

(iii) *Grievous bodily harm. See* subparagraph (4)(a)(iii).

(iv) *When committed on a child under 16 years of age.* The maximum punishment is increased when aggravated assault with intentional infliction of grievous bodily harm is inflicted upon a child under 16 years of age. Knowledge that the person assaulted was under the age of 16 years is not an element of the offense.

d. *Lesser included offenses.* See paragraph 3 of this part and Appendix 12A.

e. *Maximum punishment.*

(1) *Simple assault.*

(A) *Generally.* Confinement for 3 months and forfeiture of two-thirds pay per month for 3 months.

(B) *When committed with an unloaded firearm.* Dishonorable discharge, forfeiture of all pay and allowances, and confinement for 3 years.

(2) *Assault consummated by a battery.* Bad conduct discharge, forfeiture of all pay and allowances, and confinement for 6 months.

(3) *Assault upon a commissioned officer of the armed forces of the United States or of a friendly foreign power, not in the execution of office.* Dishonorable discharge, forfeiture of all pay and allowances, and confinement for 3 years.

(4) *Assault upon a warrant officer, not in the execution of office.* Dishonorable discharge, forfeiture of all pay and allowances, and confinement for 18 months.

(5) *Assault upon a noncommissioned or petty officer, not in the execution of office.* Bad-conduct discharge, forfeiture of all pay and allowances, and confinement for 6 months.

(6) *Assault upon a sentinel or lookout in the exe-*

cution of duty, or upon any person who, in the execution of office, is performing security police, military police, shore patrol, master at arms, or other military or civilian law enforcement duties. Dishonorable discharge, forfeiture of all pay and allowances, and confinement for 3 years.

(7) *Assault consummated by a battery upon a child under 16 years.* Dishonorable discharge, forfeiture of all pay and allowances, and confinement for 2 years.

(8) *Aggravated assault with a dangerous weapon or other means or force likely to produce death or grievous bodily harm.*

(a) *When committed with a loaded firearm.* Dishonorable discharge, forfeiture of all pay and allowances, and confinement for 8 years.

(b) *Aggravated assault with a dangerous weapon or other means or force likely to produce death or grievous bodily harm when committed upon a child under the age of 16 years.* Dishonorable discharge, total forfeitures, and confinement for 5 years.

(c) *Other cases.* Dishonorable discharge, forfeiture of all pay and allowances, and confinement for 3 years.

(9) *Aggravated assault in which grievous bodily harm is intentionally inflicted.*

(a) *When the injury is inflicted with a loaded firearm.* Dishonorable discharge, forfeiture of all pay and allowances, and confinement for 10 years.

(b) *Aggravated assault in which grievous bodily harm is intentionally inflicted when committed upon a child under the age of 16 years.* Dishonorable discharge, total forfeitures, and confinement for 8 years.

(c) *Other cases.* Dishonorable discharge, forfeiture of all pay and allowances, and confinement for 5 years.

f. *Sample specifications.*

(1) *Simple assault.*

In that _____ (personal jurisdiction data), did, (at/on board—location), (subject-matter jurisdiction data, if required), on or about _____ 20 ___ , assault _____ by (striking at him/her with a _____) (_____).

(2) *Assault consummated by a battery.*

In that _____ (personal jurisdiction data), did, (at/on board—location) (subject-matter jurisdiction data, if required), on or about _____ 20 ___ , unlawfully (strike) (_____) _____ (on) (in) the _____ with _____ .

(3) *Assault upon a commissioned officer.*

In that _____ (personal jurisdiction data), did, (at/on board—location) (subject-matter jurisdiction data, if required), on or about _____ 20 ___ , assault _____ , who then was and was then known by the accused to be a commissioned officer of (_____ , a friendly foreign power) (the United States (Army) (Navy) (Marine Corps) (Air Force) (Coast Guard)) by _____ .

(4) *Assault upon a warrant, noncommissioned, or petty officer.*

In that _____ (personal jurisdiction data), did, (at/on board—location) (subject-matter jurisdiction data, if required), on or about _____ 20 ___ , assault _____ , who then was and was then known by the accused to be a (warrant) (noncommissioned) (petty) officer of the United States (Army) (Navy) (Marine Corps) (Air Force) (Coast Guard), by _____ .

(5) *Assault upon a sentinel or lookout.*

In that _____ (personal jurisdiction data), did, (at/on board—location) (subject-matter jurisdiction data, if required), on or about _____ 20 ___ , assault _____ , who then was and was then known by the accused to be a (sentinel) (lookout) in the execution of his/her duty, ((in) (on) the _____) by _____ .

(6) *Assault upon a person in the execution of law enforcement duties.*

In that _____ (personal jurisdiction data), did, (at/on board—location) (subject-matter jurisdiction data, if required), on or about _____ 20 ___ , assault _____ , who then was and was then known by the accused to be a person then having and in the execution of (Air Force security police) (military police) (shore patrol) (master at arms) ((military) (civilian) law enforcement)) duties, by _____ .

(7) *Assault consummated by a battery upon a child under 16 years.*

In that _____ (personal jurisdiction data), did, (at/on board—location) (subject-matter jurisdiction data, if required), on or about _____ 20 ___ , unlawfully (strike) (_____) _____ a child under the age of 16 years, (in) (on) the _____ with

(8) *Assault, aggravated—with a dangerous weapon, means or force.*

In that _____ (personal jurisdiction data), did, (at/on board-location) (subject matter jurisdiction data, if required), on or about _____ 20 ___ , commit an assault upon _____ (a child under the age of 16 years) by (shooting) (pointing) (striking) (cutting) (_____) (at him/her) (him/her) (in) (on) (the _____) with (a dangerous weapon)(a (means) (force) likely to produce death or grievous bodily harm), to wit: a (loaded firearm)(pickax) (bayonet) (club) (_____).

(9) *Assault, aggravated—inflicting grievous bodily harm.*

In that _____ (personal jurisdiction data), did, (at/on board-location)(subject matter jurisdiction data, if required), on or about _____ 20 ___ , commit an assault upon _____ (a child under the age of 16 years) by (shooting) (striking) (cutting) (_____) (him/her) (on) the _____ with a (loaded firearm) (club) (rock) (brick) (_____) and did thereby intentionally inflict grievous bodily harm upon him/her, to wit: a (broken leg) (deep cut) (fractured skull) (_____).

55. Article 129—Burglary

a. *Text of statute.*

Any person subject to this chapter who, with intent to commit an offense punishable under sections 918-928 of this title (articles 118-128), breaks and enters, in the nighttime, the dwelling house of another, is guilty of burglary and shall be punished as a court-martial may direct.

b. *Elements.*

(1) That the accused unlawfully broke and entered the dwelling house of another;

(2) That both the breaking and entering were done in the nighttime; and

(3) That the breaking and entering were done with the intent to commit an offense punishable under Article 118 through 128, except Article 123a.

c. *Explanation.*

(1) *In general.* "Burglary" is the breaking and entering in the nighttime of the dwelling house of another, with intent to commit an offense punishable under Articles 118 through 128, except 123a. In addition, an intent to commit an offense which, although not covered by Article 118 through 128, necessarily includes an offense within one of these

articles, satisfies the intent element of this article. This includes, for example, assaults punishable under Article 134 which necessarily include simple assault under Article 128.

(2) *Breaking.* There must be a breaking, actual or constructive. Merely to enter through a hole left in the wall or roof or through an open window or door will not constitute a breaking; but if a person moves any obstruction to entry of the house without which movement the person could not have entered, the person has committed a "breaking." Opening a closed door or window or other similar fixture, opening wider a door or window already partly open but insufficient for the entry, or cutting out the glass of a window or the netting of a screen is a sufficient breaking. The breaking of an inner door by one who has entered the house without breaking, or by a person lawfully within the house who has no authority to enter the particular room, is a sufficient breaking, but unless such a breaking is followed by an entry into the particular room with the requisite intent, burglary is not committed. There is a constructive breaking when the entry is gained by a trick, such as concealing oneself in a box; under false pretense, such as impersonating a gas or telephone inspector; by intimidating the occupants through violence or threats into opening the door; through collusion with a confederate, an occupant of the house; or by descending a chimney, even if only a partial descent is made and no room is entered.

(3) *Entry.* An entry must be effected before the offense is complete, but the entry of any part of the body, even a finger, is sufficient. Insertion into the house of a tool or other instrument is also a sufficient entry, unless the insertion is solely to facilitate the breaking or entry.

(4) *Nighttime.* Both the breaking and entry must be in the nighttime. "Nighttime" is the period between sunset and sunrise when there is not sufficient daylight to discern a person's face.

(5) *Dwelling house of another.* To constitute burglary the house must be the dwelling house of another. "Dwelling house" includes outbuildings within the common inclosure, farmyard, or cluster of buildings used as a residence. Such an area is the "curtilage." A store is not a dwelling house unless part of, or also used as, a dwelling house, as when the occupant uses another part of the same building as a dwelling, or when the store in habitually slept in by family members or employees. The house

must be used as a dwelling at the time of the breaking and entering. It is not necessary that anyone actually be in it at the time of the breaking and entering, but if the house has never been occupied at all or has been left without any intention of returning, it is not a dwelling house. Separate dwellings within the same building, such as a barracks room, apartment, or a room in a hotel, are subjects of burglary by other residents or guests, and in general by the owner of the building. A tent is not a subject of burglary.

(6) *Intent to commit offense.* Both the breaking and entry must be done with the intent to commit in the house an offense punishable under Articles 118 through 128, except 123a. If, after the breaking and entering, the accused commits one or more of these offenses, it may be inferred that the accused intended to commit the offense or offenses at the time of the breaking and entering. If the evidence warrants, the intended offense may be separately charged. It is immaterial whether the offense intended is committed or even attempted. If the offense is intended, it is no defense that its commission was impossible.

(7) *Separate offense.* If the evidence warrants, the intended offense in the burglary specification may be separately charged.

d. *Lesser included offenses.* See paragraph 3 of this part and Appendix 12A.

e. *Maximum punishment.* Dishonorable discharge, forfeiture of all pay and allowances, and confinement for 10 years.

f. *Sample specification.*

In that _____ (personal jurisdiction data), did, at _____ , (subject-matter jurisdiction data, if required), on or about _____ 20 ___ , in the nighttime, unlawfully break and enter the (dwelling house) (_____ within the curtilage) of _____ , with intent to commit (murder) (larceny) (_____) therein.

56. Article 130—Housebreaking

a. *Text of statute.*

Any person subject to this chapter who unlawfully enters the building or structure of another with intent to commit a criminal offense therein is guilty of housebreaking and shall be punished as a court-martial may direct.

b. *Elements.*

(1) That the accused unlawfully entered a certain building or structure of a certain other person; and

(2) That the unlawful entry was made with the intent to commit a criminal offense therein.

c. *Explanation.*

(1) *Scope of offense.* The offense of housebreaking is broader than burglary in that the place entered is not required to be a dwelling house; it is not necessary that the place be occupied; it is not essential that there be a breaking; the entry may be either in the night or in the daytime; and the intent need not be to commit one of the offenses made punishable under Articles 118 through 128.

(2) *Intent.* The intent to commit some criminal offense is an essential element of housebreaking and must be alleged and proved to support a conviction of this offense. If, after the entry the accused committed a criminal offense inside the building or structure, it may be inferred that the accused intended to commit that offense at the time of the entry.

(3) *Criminal offense.* Any act or omission which is punishable by courts-martial, except an act or omission constituting a purely military offense, is a "criminal offense."

(4) *Building, structure.* "Building" includes a room, shop, store, office, or apartment in a building. "Structure" refers only to those structures which are in the nature of a building or dwelling. Examples of these structures are a stateroom, hold, or other compartment of a vessel, an inhabitable trailer, an inclosed truck or freight car, a tent, and a houseboat. It is not necessary that the building or structure be in use at the time of the entry.

(5) *Entry.* See paragraph 55c(3).

(6) *Separate offense.* If the evidence warrants, the intended offense in the housebreaking specification may be separately charged.

d. *Lesser included offenses.* See paragraph 3 of this part and Appendix 12A.

e. *Maximum punishment.* Dishonorable discharge, forfeiture of all pay and allowances, and confinement for 5 years.

f. *Sample specification.*

In that _____ , (personal jurisdiction data), did, (at/on board—location) (subject-matter jurisdiction data, if required), on or about _____ 20 ___ , unlawfully enter a (dwelling) (room) (bank) (store) (warehouse) (shop) (tent) (stateroom) (_____), the property of _____ , with intent to commit a criminal offense, to wit: _____ , therein.

57. Article 131—Perjury

a. *Text of statute.*

Any person subject to this chapter who in a judicial proceeding or in a course of justice willfully and corruptly—

(1) upon a lawful oath or in any form allowed by law to be substituted for an oath, gives any false testimony material to the issue or matter of inquiry; or

(2) in any declaration, certificate, verification, or statement under penalty of perjury as permitted under section 1746 of title 28, United States Code, subscribes any false statement material to the issue or matter of inquiry; is guilty of perjury and shall be punished as a court-martial may direct.

b. *Elements.*

(1) *Giving false testimony.*

(a) That the accused took an oath or affirmation in a certain judicial proceeding or course of justice;

(b) That the oath or affirmation was administered to the accused in a matter in which an oath or affirmation was required or authorized by law;

(c) That the oath or affirmation was administered by a person having authority to do so;

(d) That upon the oath or affirmation that accused willfully gave certain testimony;

(e) That the testimony was material;

(f) That the testimony was false; and

(g) That the accused did not then believe the testimony to be true.

(2) *Subscribing false statement.*

(a) That the accused subscribed a certain statement in a judicial proceeding or course of justice;

(b) That in the declaration, certification, verification, or statement under penalty of perjury, the accused declared, certified, verified, or stated the truth of that certain statement;

(c) That the accused willfully subscribed the statement;

(d) That the statement was material;

(e) That the statement was false; and

(f) That the accused did not then believe the statement to be true.

c. *Explanation.*

(1) *In general.* "Judicial proceeding" includes a trial by court-martial and "course of justice" includes a preliminary hearing conducted under Article 32. If the accused is charged with having committed perjury before a court-martial, it must be shown that the court-martial was duly constituted.

(2) *Giving false testimony.*

(a) *Nature.* The testimony must be false and must be willfully and corruptly given; that is, it must be proved that the accused gave the false testimony willfully and did not believe it to be true. A witness may commit perjury by testifying to the truth of a matter when in fact the witness knows nothing about it at all or is not sure about it, whether the thing is true or false in fact. A witness may also commit perjury in testifying falsely as to a belief, remembrance, or impression, or as to a judgment or opinion. It is no defense that the witness voluntarily appeared, that the witness was incompetent as a witness, or that the testimony was given in response to questions that the witness could have declined to answer.

(b) *Material matter.* The false testimony must be with respect to a material matter, but that matter need not be the main issue in the case. Thus, perjury may be committed by giving false testimony with respect to the credibility of a material witness or in an affidavit in support of a request for a continuance, as well as by giving false testimony with respect to a fact from which a legitimate inference may be drawn as to the existence or nonexistence of a fact in issue.

(c) *Proof.* The falsity of the allegedly perjured statement cannot be proved by circumstantial evidence alone, except with respect to matters which by their nature are not susceptible of direct proof. The falsity of the statement cannot be proved by the testimony of a single witness unless that testimony directly contradicts the statement and is corroborated by other evidence either direct or circumstantial, tending to prove the falsity of the statement. However, documentary evidence directly disproving the truth of the statement charged to have been perjured need not be corroborated if: the document is an official record shown to have been well known to the ac-

cused at the time the oath was taken; or the documentary evidence originated from the accused—or had in any manner been recognized by the accused as containing the truth—before the allegedly perjured statement was made.

(d) *Oath.* The oath must be one recognized or authorized by law and must be duly administered by one authorized to administer it. When a form of oath has been prescribed, a literal following of that form is not essential; it is sufficient if the oath administered conforms in substance to the prescribed form. "Oath" includes an affirmation when the latter is authorized in lieu of an oath.

(e) *Belief of accused.* The fact that the accused did not believe the statement to be true may be proved by testimony of one witness without corroboration or by circumstantial evidence.

(3) *Subscribing false statement. See* subparagraphs (1) and (2), above, as applicable. Section 1746 of title 28, United States Code, provides for subscribing to the truth of a document by signing it expressly subject to the penalty for perjury. The signing must take place in a judicial proceeding or course of justice—for example, if a witness signs under penalty of perjury summarized testimony given at an Article 32 preliminary hearing. It is not required that the document be sworn before a third party. Section 1746 does not change the requirement that a deposition be given under oath or alter the situation where an oath is required to be taken before a specific person.

d. *Lesser included offenses.* See paragraph 3 of this part and Appendix 12A.

e. *Maximum punishment.* Dishonorable discharge, forfeiture of all pay and allowances, and confinement for 5 years.

f. *Sample specifications.*

(1) *Giving false testimony.*

In that _____ (personal jurisdiction data), having taken a lawful (oath) (affirmation) in a (trial by _____ court-martial of _____) (trial by a court of competent jurisdiction, to wit: _____ of _____) (deposition for use in a trial by _____ of _____) (_____) that he/she would (testify) (depose) truly, did, (at/on board—location) (subject-matter jurisdiction data, if required), on or about _____ 20 ___ , willfully, corruptly, and contrary to such (oath) (affirmation), (testify) (depose) falsely in substance that

_____, which (testimony) (deposition) was upon a material matter and which he/she did not then believe to be true.

(2) Subscribing false statement.

In that _____ (personal jurisdiction data), did (at/on board—location) (subject-matter jurisdiction data, if required), on or about _____ 20 ___, in a (judicial proceeding) (course of justice), and in a (declaration) (certification) (verification) (statement) under penalty of perjury pursuant to section 1746 of title 28, United States Code, willfully and corruptly subscribed a false statement material to the (issue) (matter of inquiry), to wit: _____, which statement was false in that _____, and which statement he/she did not then believe to be true.

58. Article 132—Frauds against the United States

a. *Text of statute.*

Any person subject to this chapter—

(1) who, knowing it to be false or fraudulent—

(a) makes any claim against the United States or any officer thereof; or

(b) presents to any person in the civil or military service thereof, for approval or payment, any claim against the United States or any officer thereof;

(2) who, for the purpose of obtaining the approval, allowance, or payment of any claim against the United States or any officer thereof—

(a) makes or uses any writing or other paper knowing it to contain any false or fraudulent statements;

(b) makes any oath to any fact or to any writing or other paper knowing the oath to be false; or

(c) forges or counterfeits any signature upon any writing or other paper, or uses any such signature knowing it to be forged or counterfeited;

(3) who, having charge, possession, custody, or control of any money, or other property of the United States, furnished or intended for the armed forces thereof, knowingly delivers to any person having authority to receive it, any amount thereof less than that for which he receives a certificate or receipt; or

(4) who, being authorized to make or deliver any paper certifying the receipt of any property of the United States furnished or intended for the armed forces thereof, makes or delivers to any person such writing without having full knowledge of the truth of the statements therein contained and with intent to defraud the United States;

shall, upon conviction, be punished as a court-martial may direct.

b. *Elements.*

(1) Making a false or fraudulent claim.

(a) That the accused made a certain claim against the United States or an officer thereof;

(b) That the claim was false or fraudulent in certain particulars; and

(c) That the accused then knew that the claim was false or fraudulent in these particulars.

(2) Presenting for approval or payment a false or fraudulent claim.

(a) That the accused presented for approval or payment to a certain person in the civil or military service of the United States having authority to approve or pay it a certain claim against the United States or an officer thereof;

(b) That the claim was false or fraudulent in certain particulars; and

(c) That the accused then knew that the claim was false or fraudulent in these particulars.

(3) Making or using a false writing or other paper in connection with claims.

(a) That the accused made or used a certain writing or other paper;

(b) That certain material statements in the writing or other paper were false or fraudulent;

(c) That the accused then knew the statements were false or fraudulent; and

(d) That the act of the accused was for the purpose of obtaining the approval, allowance, or payment of a certain claim or claims against the United States or an officer thereof.

(4) False oath in connection with claims.

(a) That the accused made an oath to a certain fact or to a certain writing or other paper;

(b) That the oath was false in certain particulars;

(c) That the accused then knew it was false; and

(d) That the act was for the purpose of obtaining the approval, allowance, or payment of a certain claim or claims against the United States or an officer thereof.

(5) *Forgery of signature in connection with claims.*

(a) That the accused forged or counterfeited the signature of a certain person on a certain writing or other paper; and

(b) That the act was for the purpose of obtaining the approval, allowance, or payment of a certain claim against the United States or an officer thereof.

(6) *Using forged signature in connection with claims.*

(a) That the accused used the forged or counterfeited signature of a certain person;

(b) That the accused then knew that the signature was forged or counterfeited; and

(c) That the act was for the purpose of obtaining the approval, allowance, or payment of a certain claim against the United States or an officer thereof.

(7) *Delivering less than amount called for by receipt.*

(a) That the accused had charge, possession, custody, or control of certain money or property of the United States furnished or intended for the armed forces thereof;

(b) That the accused obtained a certificate or receipt for a certain amount or quantity of that money or property;

(c) That for the certificate or receipt the accused knowingly delivered to a certain person having authority to receive it an amount or quantity of money or property less than the amount or quantity thereof specified in the certificate or receipt; and

(d) That the undelivered money or property was of a certain value.

(8) *Making or delivering receipt without having full knowledge that it is true.*

(a) That the accused was authorized to make or deliver a paper certifying the receipt from a certain person of certain property of the United States furnished or intended for the armed forces thereof;

(b) That the accused made or delivered to that person a certificate or receipt;

(c) That the accused made or delivered the certificate without having full knowledge of the truth of a certain material statement or statements therein;

(d) That the act was done with intent to defraud the United States; and

(e) That the property certified as being received was of a certain value.

c. *Explanation.*

(1) *Making a false or fraudulent claim.*

(a) *Claim.* A "claim" is a demand for a transfer of ownership of money or property and does not include requisitions for the mere use of property. This article applies only to claims against the United States or any officer thereof as such, and not to claims against an officer of the United States in that officer's private capacity.

(b) *Making a claim.* Making a claim is a distinct act from presenting it. A claim may be made in one place and presented in another. The mere writing of a paper in the form of a claim, without any further act to cause the paper to become a demand against the United States or an officer thereof, does not constitute making a claim. However, any act placing the claim in official channels constitutes making a claim, even if that act does not amount to presenting a claim. It is not necessary that the claim be allowed or paid or that it be made by the person to be benefited by the allowance or payment. *See* also subparagraph (2), below.

(c) *Knowledge.* The claim must be made with knowledge of its fictitious or dishonest character. This article does not proscribe claims, however groundless they may be, that the maker believes to be valid, or claims that are merely made negligently or without ordinary prudence.

(2) *Presenting for approval or payment a false or fraudulent claim.*

(a) *False and fraudulent.* False and fraudulent claims include not only those containing some material false statement, but also claims which the claimant knows to have been paid or for some other reason the claimant knows the claimant is not authorized to present or upon which the claimant knows the claimant has no right to collect.

(b) *Presenting a claim.* The claim must be presented, directly or indirectly, to some person having authority to pay it. The person to whom the claim is presented may be identified by position or authority to approve the claim, and need not be identified by name in the specification. A false claim may be tacitly presented, as when a person who knows that there is no entitlement to certain pay accepts it nevertheless without disclosing a disqualification, even though the person may not have made any representation of entitlement to the pay. For example, a person cashing a pay check which includes an amount for a dependency allowance, knowing at the time that the entitlement no longer exists because of a change in that dependency status, has tacitly presented a false claim. *See also* subparagraph (1), above.

(3) *Making or using a false writing or other paper in connection with claims.* The false or fraudulent statement must be material, that is, it must have a tendency to mislead governmental officials in their consideration or investigation of the claim. The offense of making a writing or other paper known to contain a false or fraudulent statement for the purpose of obtaining the approval, allowance, or payment of a claim is complete when the writing or paper is made for that purpose, whether or not any use of the paper has been attempted and whether or not the claim has been presented. *See also* the explanation in subparagraph (1) and (2), above.

(4) *False oath in connection with claims. See* subparagraphs (1) and (2), above.

(5) *Forgery of signature in connection with claims.* Any fraudulent making of the signature of another is forging or counterfeiting, whether or not an attempt is made to imitate the handwriting. *See* paragraph 48(c) and subparagraph (1) and (2), above.

(6) *Delivering less than amount called for by receipt.* It is immaterial by what means—whether deceit, collusion, or otherwise—the accused effected the transaction, or what was the accused's purpose.

(7) *Making or delivering receipt without having full knowledge that it is true.* When an officer or other person subject to military law is authorized to make or deliver any paper certifying the receipt of any property of the United States furnished or intended for the armed forces thereof, and a receipt or other paper is presented for signature stating that a certain amount of supplies has been furnished by a certain contractor, it is that person's duty before signing the paper to know that the full amount of supplies therein stated to have been furnished has in fact been furnished, and that the statements contained in the paper are true. If the person signs the paper with intent to defraud the United States and without that knowledge, that person is guilty of a violation of this section of the article. If the person signs the paper with knowledge that the full amount was not received, it may be inferred that the person intended to defraud the United States.

d. *Lesser included offenses.* See paragraph 3 of this part and Appendix 12A.

e. *Maximum punishment.*

(1) Article 132(1) and (2). Dishonorable discharge, forfeiture of all pay and allowances, and confinement for 5 years.

(2) Article 132(3) and (4).

(a) *When amount is $500.00 or less.* Bad-conduct discharge, forfeiture of all pay and allowances, and confinement for 6 months.

(b) *When amount is over $500.00.* Dishonorable discharge, forfeiture of all pay and allowances, and confinement for 5 years.

f. *Sample specifications.*

(1) *Making false claim.*

In that _____ (personal jurisdiction data), did, (at/on board—location) (subject-matter jurisdiction data, if required), on or about _____ 20 ___ , (by preparing (a voucher) (_____) for presentation for approval or payment) (_____), make a claim against the (United States) (finance officer at _____) (_____) in the amount of $ _____ for (private property alleged to have been (lost) (destroyed) in the military service) (_____), which claim was (false) (fraudulent) (false and fraudulent) in the amount of $ _____ in that _____ and was then known by the said _____ to be (false) (fraudulent) (false and fraudulent).

(2) *Presenting false claim.*

In that _____ (personal jurisdiction data), did, (at/on board—location) (subject-matter jurisdiction data, if required), on or about _____ 20 ___ , by presenting (a voucher)(_____) to _____ , an officer of the United States duly authorized to (approve) (pay) (approve and pay) such claim, present for (approval) (payment) (approval and payment) a claim against the (United States) (finance officer at _____) (_____) in the amount of $ _____ for (services alleged to have been rendered to the United States by _____ during _____) (_____), which claim was (false) (fraudulent) (false and fraudulent) in the amount of $ _____ in that _____ , and was then known by the said _____ to be (false) (fraudulent) (false and fraudulent).

(3) *Making or using false writing.*

In that _____ (personal jurisdiction data), for the purpose of obtaining the (approval) (allowance) (payment) (approval, allowance, and payment), of a claim against the United States in the amount of $ _____ , did (at/on board— location) (subject-matter jurisdiction data, if required), on or about _____ 20 ___ , (make) (use) (make and use) a certain (writing) (paper), to wit: _____ , which said (writing) (paper), as he/she, the said _____ , then knew, contained a statement that _____ , which statement was (false) (fraudulent) (false and fraudulent) in that _____ , and was then known by the said _____ to be (false) (fraudulent) (false and fraudulent).

(4) *Making false oath.*

In that _____ (personal jurisdiction data), for the purpose of obtaining the (approval) (allowance) (payment) (approval, allowance, and payment) of a claim against the United States, did, (at/on board—location) (subject-matter jurisdiction data, if required), on or about _____ 20 ___ , make an oath (to the fact that _____) (to a certain (writing) (paper), to wit: _____ , to the effect that _____), which said oath was false in that _____ , and was then known by the said _____ to be false.

(5) *Forging or counterfeiting signature.*

In that _____ (personal jurisdiction data), for the purpose of obtaining the (approval) (allowance) (payment) (approval, allowance, and payment) of a claim against the United States, did (at/on board—location) (subject-matter jurisdiction data, if required), on or about _____ 20 ___ , (forge) (counterfeit) (forge and counterfeit) the signature of _____ upon a _____ in words and figures as follows: _____ .

(6) *Using forged signature.*

In that _____ , for the purpose of obtaining the (approval) (allowance) (payment) (approval, allowance, and payment) of a claim against the United States, did, (at/on board—location) (subject-matter jurisdiction data, if required), on or about _____ 20 ___ , use the signature of _____ on a certain (writing) (paper), to wit: _____ , then knowing such signature to be (forged) (counterfeited) (forged and counterfeited).

(7) *Paying amount less than called for by receipt.*

In that _____ (personal jurisdiction data), having (charge) (possession) (custody) (control) of (money) (_____) of the United States, (furnished) (intended) (furnished and intended) for the armed forces thereof, did, (at/on board—location) (subject-matter jurisdiction data, if required), on or about _____ 20 ___ , knowingly deliver to _____ , the said _____ having authority to receive the same, (an amount) (_____), which, as he/she, _____ , then knew, was ($ _____) (_____) less than the (amount) (_____) for which he/she received a (certificate) (receipt) from the said _____ .

(8) *Making receipt without knowledge of the facts.*

In that _____ (personal jurisdiction data), being authorized to (make) (deliver) (make and deliver) a paper certifying the receipt of property of the United States (furnished) (intended) (furnished and intended) for the armed forces thereof, did, (at/on board—location) (subject-matter jurisdiction data, if required), on or about _____ 20 ___ , without having full knowledge of the statement therein contained and with intent to defraud the United States, (make) (deliver) (make and deliver) to _____ , such a writing, in words and figures as follows: _____ , the property therein certified as received being of a value of about $ _____ .

59. Article 133—Conduct unbecoming an officer and gentleman

a. *Text of statute.*

Any commissioned officer, cadet, or midshipman who is convicted of conduct unbecoming an officer and a gentleman shall be punished as a court-martial may direct.

b. *Elements.*

(1) That the accused did or omitted to do certain acts; and

(2) That, under the circumstances, these acts or omissions constituted conduct unbecoming an officer and gentleman.

c. *Explanation.*

(1) *Gentleman.* As used in this article, "gentleman" includes both male and female commissioned officers, cadets, and midshipmen.

(2) *Nature of offense.* Conduct violative of this article is action or behavior in an official capacity which, in dishonoring or disgracing the person as an

officer, seriously compromises the officer's character as a gentleman, or action or behavior in an unofficial or private capacity which, in dishonoring or disgracing the officer personally, seriously compromises the person's standing as an officer. There are certain moral attributes common to the ideal officer and the perfect gentleman, a lack of which is indicated by acts of dishonesty, unfair dealing, indecency, indecorum, lawlessness, injustice, or cruelty. Not everyone is or can be expected to meet unrealistically high moral standards, but there is a limit of tolerance based on customs of the service and military necessity below which the personal standards of an officer, cadet, or midshipman cannot fall without seriously compromising the person's standing as an officer, cadet, or midshipman or the person's character as a gentleman. This article prohibits conduct by a commissioned officer, cadet, or midshipman which, taking all the circumstances into consideration, is thus compromising. This article includes acts made punishable by any other article, provided these acts amount to conduct unbecoming an officer and a gentleman. Thus, a commissioned officer who steals property violates both this article and Article 121. Whenever the offense charged is the same as a specific offense set forth in this Manual, the elements of proof are the same as those set forth in the paragraph which treats that specific offense, with the additional requirement that the act or omission constitutes conduct unbecoming an officer and gentleman.

(3) *Examples of offenses.* Instances of violation of this article include knowingly making a false official statement; dishonorable failure to pay a debt; cheating on an exam; opening and reading a letter of another without authority; using insulting or defamatory language to another officer in that officer's presence or about that officer to other military persons; being drunk and disorderly in a public place; public association with known prostitutes; committing or attempting to commit a crime involving moral turpitude; and failing without good cause to support the officer's family.

d. *Lesser included offenses.* See paragraph 3 of this part and Appendix 12A.

e. *Maximum punishment.* Dismissal, forfeiture of all pay and allowances, and confinement for a period not in excess of that authorized for the most analogous offense for which a punishment is prescribed in this Manual, or, if none is prescribed, for 1 year.

f. *Sample specifications.*

(1) *Copying or using examination paper.*
In that _____ (personal jurisdiction data), did, (at/on board—location), on or about _____ 20 __ , while undergoing a written examination on the subject of _____ , wrongfully and dishonorably (receive) (request) unauthorized aid by ((using) (copying) the examination paper of __)) (__).

(2) *Drunk or disorderly.*
In that _____ (personal jurisdiction data), was, (at/on board—location), on or about _____ 20 __ , in a public place, to wit: _____ , (drunk) (disorderly) (drunk and disorderly) while in uniform, to the disgrace of the armed forces.

60. Article 134—General article

a. *Text of statute.*

Though not specifically mentioned in this chapter, all disorders and neglects to the prejudice of good order and discipline in the armed forces, all conduct of a nature to bring discredit upon the armed forces, and crimes and offenses not capital, of which persons subject to this chapter may be guilty, shall be taken cognizance of by a general, special, or summary court-martial, according to the nature and degree of the offense, and shall be punished at the discretion of that court.

b. *Elements.* The proof required for conviction of an offense under Article 134 depends upon the nature of the misconduct charged. If the conduct is punished as a crime or offense not capital, the proof must establish every element of the crime or offense as required by the applicable law. All offenses under Article 134 require proof of a single terminal element; however, the terminal element may be proven using any of three theories of liability corresponding to clause 1, 2, or 3 offenses.

Discussion

The terminal element is merely the expression of one of the clauses under Article 134. See paragraph c below for an explanation of the clauses and rules for drafting specifications. More than one clause may be alleged and proven; however, proof of only one clause will satisfy the terminal element. For clause 3 offenses, the military judge may judicially notice whether an offense is capital. *See* Mil. R. Evid. 202.

---

(1) For clause 1 or 2 offenses under Article 134, the following proof is required:

(a) That the accused did or failed to do certain acts; and

(b) That, under the circumstances, the accused's conduct was to the prejudice of good order and discipline in the armed forces or was of a nature to bring discredit upon the armed forces.

(2) For clause 3 offenses under Article 134, the following proof is required:

(a) That the accused did or failed to do certain acts that satisfy each element of the federal statute (including, in the case of a prosecution under 18 U.S.C. § 13, each element of the assimilated State, Territory, Possession, or District law); and

(b) That the offense charged was an offense not capital.

c. *Explanation.*

(1) *In general.* Article 134 makes punishable acts in three categories of offenses not specifically covered in any other article of the code. These are referred to as "clauses 1, 2, and 3" of Article 134. Clause 1 offenses involve disorders and neglects to the prejudice of good order and discipline in the armed forces. Clause 2 offenses involve conduct of a nature to bring discredit upon the armed forces. Clause 3 offenses involve noncapital crimes or offenses which violate Federal law including law made applicable through the Federal Assimilative Crimes Act, *see* subsection (4) below. If any conduct of this nature is specifically made punishable by another article of the code, it must be charged as a violation of that article. *See* subparagraph (5)(a) below. However, *see* paragraph 59c for offenses committed by commissioned officers, cadets, and midshipmen.

(2) *Disorders and neglects to the prejudice of good order and discipline in the armed forces (clause 1).*

(a) *To the prejudice of good order and discipline.* "To the prejudice of good order and discipline" refers only to acts directly prejudicial to good order and discipline and not to acts which are prejudicial only in a remote or indirect sense. Almost any irregular or improper act on the part of a member of the military service could be regarded as prejudicial in some indirect or remote sense; however, this article does not include these distant effects. It is confined to cases in which the prejudice is reasonably direct and palpable. An act in violation of a local civil law or of a foreign law may be punished if it constitutes a disorder or neglect to the prejudice of good order and discipline in the armed forces. However, *see* R.C.M. 203 concerning subject-matter jurisdiction.

(b) *Breach of custom of the service.* A breach of a custom of the service may result in a violation of clause 1 of Article 134. In its legal sense, "custom" means more than a method of procedure or a mode of conduct or behavior which is merely of frequent or usual occurrence. Custom arises out of long established practices which by common usage have attained the force of law in the military or other community affected by them. No custom may be contrary to existing law or regulation. A custom which has not been adopted by existing statute or regulation ceases to exist when its observance has been generally abandoned. Many customs of the service are now set forth in regulations of the various armed forces. Violations of these customs should be charged under Article 92 as violations of the regulations in which they appear if the regulation is punitive. *See* paragraph 16c.

(3) *Conduct of a nature to bring discredit upon the armed forces (clause 2).* "Discredit" means to injure the reputation of. This clause of Article 134 makes punishable conduct which has a tendency to bring the service into disrepute or which tends to lower it in public esteem. Acts in violation of a local civil law or a foreign law may be punished if they are of a nature to bring discredit upon the armed forces. However, *see* R.C.M. 203 concerning subject-matter jurisdiction.

(4) *Crimes and offenses not capital (clause 3).*

(a) *In general.* State and foreign laws are not included within the crimes and offenses not capital referred to in this clause of Article 134 and violations thereof may not be prosecuted as such except when State law becomes Federal law of local application under section 13 of title 18 of the United States Code (Federal Assimilative Crimes Act— *see* subparagraph (4)(c) below. For the purpose of court-martial jurisdiction, the laws which may be applied under clause 3 of Article 134 are divided into two groups: crimes and offenses of unlimited application (crimes which are punishable regardless where they may be committed), and crimes and offenses of local application (crimes which are punishable only if committed in areas of federal jurisdiction).

(b) *Crimes and offenses of unlimited application.* Certain noncapital crimes and offenses prohibited by the United States Code are made applicable under clause 3 of Article 134 to all persons subject to the code regardless where the wrongful act or omission occurred. Examples include: counterfeiting (18 U.S.C. § 471), and various frauds against the Government not covered by Article 132.

(c) *Crimes and offenses of local application.*

(i) *In general.* A person subject to the code may not be punished under clause 3 of Article 134 for an offense that occurred in a place where the law in question did not apply. For example, a person may not be punished under clause 3 of Article 134 when the act occurred in a foreign country merely because that act would have been an offense under the United States Code had the act occurred in the United States. Regardless where committed, such an act might be punishable under clauses 1 or 2 of Article 134. There are two types of congressional enactments of local application: specific federal statutes (defining particular crimes), and a general federal statute, the Federal Assimilative Crimes Act (which adopts certain state criminal laws).

(ii) *Federal Assimilative Crimes Act (18 U.S.C. § 13).* The Federal Assimilative Crimes Act is an adoption by Congress of state criminal laws for areas of exclusive or concurrent federal jurisdiction, provided federal criminal law, including the UCMJ, has not defined an applicable offense for the misconduct committed. The Act applies to state laws validly existing at the time of the offense without regard to when these laws were enacted, whether before or after passage of the Act, and whether before or after the acquisition of the land where the offense was committed. For example, if a person committed an act on a military installation in the United States at a certain location over which the United States had either exclusive or concurrent jurisdiction, and it was not an offense specifically defined by federal law (including the UCMJ), that person could be punished for that act by a court-martial if it was a violation of a noncapital offense under the law of the State where the military installation was located. This is possible because the Act adopts the criminal law of the state wherein the military installation is located and applies it as though it were federal law. The text of the Act is as follows: Whoever within or upon any of the places now existing or hereafter reserved or acquired as provided in section 7 of this title, is guilty of any act or omission which, although not made punishable by

any enactment of Congress, would be punishable if committed or omitted within the jurisdiction of the State, Territory, Possession, or District in which such place is situated, by the laws thereof in force at the time of such act or omission, shall be guilty of a like offense and subject to a like punishment.

(5) *Limitations on Article 134.*

(a) *Preemption doctrine.* The preemption doctrine prohibits application of Article 134 to conduct covered by Articles 80 through 132. For example, larceny is covered in Article 121, and if an element of that offense is lacking—for example, intent—there can be no larceny or larceny-type offense, either under Article 121 or, because of preemption, under Article 134. Article 134 cannot be used to create a new kind of larceny offense, one without the required intent, where Congress has already set the minimum requirements for such an offense in Article 121.

(b) *Capital offense.* A capital offense may not be tried under Article 134.

(6) *Drafting specifications for Article 134 offenses.*

(a) *Specifications under clause 1 or 2.* When alleging a clause 1 or 2 violation, the specification must expressly allege that the conduct was "to the prejudice of good order and discipline" or that it was "of a nature to bring discredit upon the armed forces." The same conduct may be prejudicial to good order and discipline in the armed forces and at the same time be of a nature to bring discredit upon the armed forces. Both clauses may be alleged; however, only one must be proven to satisfy the terminal element. If conduct by an accused does not fall under any of the enumerated Article 134 offenses (paragraphs 61 through 113 of this Part), a specification not listed in this Manual may be used to allege the offense.

Discussion

Clauses 1 and 2 are theories of liability that must be expressly alleged in a specification so that the accused will be given notice as to which clause or clauses to defend against. The words "to the prejudice of good order and discipline in the armed forces" encompass both paragraph c.(2)(a), prejudice to good order and discipline, and paragraph c.(2)(b), breach of custom of the Service. A generic sample specification is provided below:

"*In that* _____ , *(personal jurisdiction data), did (at/ on board location), on or about* _____ 20__, *(commit elements of Article 134 clause 1 or 2 offense), and that said conduct (was to the prejudice of good order and discipline in the armed forces) (and) (was of a nature to bring discredit upon the armed forces)."*

If clauses 1 and 2 are alleged together in the terminal element, the word "and" should be used to separate them. Any clause not proven beyond a reasonable doubt should be excepted from the specification at findings. *See* R.C.M. 918(a)(1). *See also* Appendix 23 of this Manual, Art. 79. Although using the conjunctive "and" to connect the two theories of liability is recommended, a specification connecting the two theories with the disjunctive "or" is sufficient to provide the accused reasonable notice of the charge against him. *See* Appendix 23 of this Manual, Art. 134.

Lesser included offenses are defined and explained under Article 79; however, in 2010, the Court of Appeals for the Armed Forces examined Article 79 and clarified the legal test for lesser included offenses. *See United States v. Jones*, 68 M.J. 465 (C.A.A.F. 2010). Under *Jones*, an offense under Article 79 is "necessarily included" in the offense charged only if the elements of the lesser offense are a subset of the elements of the greater offense alleged. 68 M.J. at 472; *see also* discussion following paragraph 3b(1)(c) in this part and the related analysis in Appendix 23 of this Manual. Practitioners should carefully consider lesser included offenses using the elements test in conformity with *Jones. See* paragraph 3b(4) in Appendix 23 of this Manual. If it is uncertain whether an Article 134 offense is included within a charged offense, the government may plead in the alternative or, with the consent of the accused, the government may amend the charge sheet. *Jones*, 68 M.J. at 472-73 (referring to R.C.M. 603(d) for amending a charge sheet).

(b) *Specifications under clause 3.* When alleging a clause 3 violation, the specification must expressly allege that the conduct was "an offense not capital," and each element of the federal statute (including, in the case of a prosecution under 18 U.S.C. § 13, each element of the assimilated State, Territory, Possession, or District law) must be alleged expressly or by necessary implication. In addition, the federal statute should be identified.

Discussion

The words "an offense not capital" are sufficient to provide notice to the accused that a clause 3 offense has been charged and are meant to include all crimes and offenses not capital. A generic sample specification for clause 3 offenses is provided below:

"In that _____, (personal jurisdiction data), did (at/on board location), on or about _____ 20__, (commit: address each element), an offense not capital, in violation of (name or citation of statute)."

In addition to alleging each element of the federal statute, practitioners should consider including, when appropriate and necessary, words of criminality (*e.g.*, wrongfully, knowingly, or willfully).

---

61. Article 134—(Animal abuse)

a. *Text of statute. See* paragraph 60.

b. *Elements.*

(1) *Abuse, neglect, or abandonment of an animal.*

(a) That the accused wrongfully abused, neglected, or abandoned a certain (public*) animal (and the accused caused the serious injury or death of the animal*); and

(b) That, under the circumstances, the conduct of the accused was to the prejudice of good order and discipline in the armed forces or was of a nature to bring discredit upon the armed forces.

(*Note: Add these elements as applicable.)

(2) *Sexual act with an animal.*

(a) That the accused engaged in a sexual act with a certain animal; and

(b) That, under the circumstances, the conduct of the accused was to the prejudice of good order and discipline in the armed forces or was of a nature to bring discredit upon the armed forces.

c. *Explanation.*

(1) *In general.* This offense prohibits knowing, reckless, or negligent abuse, neglect, or abandonment of an animal. This offense does not include legal hunting, trapping, or fishing; reasonable and recognized acts of training, handling, or disciplining of an animal; normal and accepted farm or veterinary practices; research or testing conducted in accordance with approved military protocols; protection of person or property from an unconfined animal; or authorized military operations or military training.

(2) *Definitions.* As used in this paragraph:

(A) "Abuse" means intentionally and unjustifiably: overdriving, overloading, overworking, tormenting, beating, depriving of necessary sustenance, allowing to be housed in a manner that results in chronic or repeated serious physical harm, carrying or confining in or upon any vehicles in a cruel or reckless manner, or otherwise mistreating an animal. Abuse may include any sexual touching of an animal if not included in the definition of "sexual act with an animal" below.

(B) "Neglect" means allowing another to abuse an animal, or, having the charge or custody of any animal, intentionally, knowingly, recklessly, or negligently failing to provide it with proper food, drink, or protection from the weather consistent with the species, breed, and type of animal involved.

(C) "Abandon" means the intentional, knowing, reckless or negligent leaving of an animal at a location without providing minimum care while having the charge or custody of that animal.

(D) "Animal" means pets and animals of the type that are raised by individuals for resale to others, including but not limited to: cattle, horses, sheep, pigs, goats, chickens, dogs, cats, and similar animals owned or under the control of any person. Animal does not include reptiles, insects, arthropods, or any animal defined or declared to be a pest by the administrator of the United States Environmental Protection Agency.

(E) "Public animal" means any animal owned or used by the United States or any animal owned or used by a local or State government in the United States, its territories or possessions. This would include, for example, drug detector dogs used by the government.

(F) "Sexual act with an animal" means contact between the sex organ, anus, or mouth of a person and an animal or between the sex organ, mouth, or anus of an animal and a person or object manipulated by a person if done with an intent to arouse or gratify the sexual desire of any person.

(G) "Serious injury of an animal" means physical harm that involves a temporary but substantial disfigurement; causes a temporary but substantial loss or impairment of the function of any bodily part or organ; causes a fracture of any bodily part; causes permanent maiming; causes acute pain of a duration that results in suffering; or carries a substantial risk of death. Serious injury includes, but is not limited to, burning, torturing, poisoning, or maiming.

d. *Lesser included offenses.* See paragraph 3 of this part and Appendix 12A.

e. *Maximum punishment.*

(1) *Abuse, neglect, or abandonment of an animal.* Bad-conduct discharge, forfeiture of all pay and allowances, and confinement for 1 year.

(2) *Abuse, neglect, or abandonment of a public animal.* Bad-conduct discharge, forfeiture of all pay and allowances, and confinement for 2 years.

(3) *Sexual act with an animal or cases where the accused caused the serious injury or death of the animal.* Dishonorable discharge, forfeiture of all pay and allowances, and confinement for 5 years.

f. *Sample specification.*

In that _____ (personal jurisdiction data), did, (at/on board—location) (subject-matter jurisdiction data, if required), on or about (date), (wrongfully [abuse] [neglect] [abandon]) (*engage in a sexual act, to wit: _____ , with) a certain (*public) animal (*and caused [serious injury to] [the death of] the animal), and that said conduct was (to the prejudice of good order and discipline in the armed forces) (of a nature to bring discredit upon the armed forces) (to the prejudice of good order and discipline in the armed forces and was of a nature to bring discredit upon the armed forces).

62. Article 134—(Adultery)

a. *Text of statute. See* paragraph 60.

b. *Elements.*

(1) That the accused wrongfully had sexual intercourse with a certain person;

(2) That, at the time, the accused or the other person was married to someone else; and

(3) That, under the circumstances, the conduct of the accused was to the prejudice of good order and discipline in the armed forces or was of a nature to bring discredit upon the armed forces.

c. *Explanation.*

(1) *Nature of offense.* Adultery is clearly unacceptable conduct, and it reflects adversely on the service record of the military member.

(2) *Conduct prejudicial to good order and discipline or of a nature to bring discredit upon the armed forces.* To constitute an offense under the UCMJ, the adulterous conduct must either be directly prejudicial to good order and discipline or service discrediting. Adulterous conduct that is directly prejudicial includes conduct that has an obvious, and measurably divisive effect on unit or organization discipline, morale, or cohesion, or is clearly detrimental to the authority or stature of or respect toward a servicemember. Adultery may also be service discrediting, even though the conduct is only indirectly or remotely prejudicial to good order and discipline. Discredit means to injure the reputation of the armed forces and includes adulterous conduct that has a tendency, because of its open or notorious nature, to bring the service into disrepute, make it subject to public ridicule, or lower it in

public esteem. While adulterous conduct that is private and discreet in nature may not be service discrediting by this standard, under the circumstances, it may be determined to be conduct prejudicial to good order and discipline. Commanders should consider all relevant circumstances, including but not limited to the following factors, when determining whether adulterous acts are prejudicial to good order and discipline or are of a nature to bring discredit upon the armed forces:

(a) The accused's marital status, military rank, grade, or position;

(b) The co-actor's marital status, military rank, grade, and position, or relationship to the armed forces;

(c) The military status of the accused's spouse or the spouse of co-actor, or their relationship to the armed forces;

(d) The impact, if any, of the adulterous relationship on the ability of the accused, the co-actor, or the spouse of either to perform their duties in support of the armed forces;

(e) The misuse, if any, of government time and resources to facilitate the commission of the conduct;

(f) Whether the conduct persisted despite counseling or orders to desist; the flagrancy of the conduct, such as whether any notoriety ensued; and whether the adulterous act was accompanied by other violations of the UCMJ;

(g) The negative impact of the conduct on the units or organizations of the accused, the co-actor or the spouse of either of them, such as a detrimental effect on unit or organization morale, teamwork, and efficiency;

(h) Whether the accused or co-actor was legally separated; and

(i) Whether the adulterous misconduct involves an ongoing or recent relationship or is remote in time.

(3) *Marriage.* A marriage exists until it is dissolved in accordance with the laws of a competent state or foreign jurisdiction.

(4) *Mistake of fact.* A defense of mistake of fact exists if the accused had an honest and reasonable belief either that the accused and the co-actor were both unmarried, or that they were lawfully married to each other. If this defense is raised by the evidence, then the burden of proof is upon the United States to establish that the accused's belief was unreasonable or not honest.

d. *Lesser included offenses.* See paragraph 3 of this part and Appendix 12A.

e. *Maximum punishment.* Dishonorable discharge, forfeiture of all pay and allowances, and confinement for 1 year.

f. *Sample specification.*

In that _____ (personal jurisdiction data), (a married man/a married woman), did, (at/on board—location) (subject-matter jurisdiction data, if required), on or about ____ 20 __ , wrongfully have sexual intercourse with _____ , a (married) (woman/man) not (his wife) (her husband), and that said conduct was (to the prejudice of good order and discipline in the armed forces) (of a nature to bring discredit upon the armed forces) (to the prejudice of good order and discipline in the armed forces and was of a nature to bring discredit upon the armed forces).

63. Deleted—See Appendix 27

Indecent assault was deleted by Executive Order 13447, 72 Fed. Reg. 56179 (Oct. 2, 2007). *See* Appendix 25.

64. Article 134—(Assault—with intent to commit murder, voluntary manslaughter, rape, robbery, forcible sodomy, arson, burglary, or housebreaking)

a. *Text of statute. See* paragraph 60.

b. *Elements.*

(1) That the accused assaulted a certain person;

(2) That, at the time of the assault, the accused intended to kill (as required for murder or voluntary manslaughter) or intended to commit rape, robbery, forcible sodomy, arson, burglary, or housebreaking; and

(3) That, under the circumstances, the conduct of the accused was to the prejudice of good order and discipline in the armed forces or was of a nature to bring discredit upon the armed forces.

c. *Explanation.*

(1) *In general.* An assault with intent to commit any of the offenses mentioned above is not necessarily the equivalent of an attempt to commit the intended offense, for an assault can be committed with

intent to commit an offense without achieving that proximity to consummation of an intended offense which is essential to an attempt. *See* paragraph 4.

(2) *Assault with intent to murder.* Assault with intent to commit murder is assault with specific intent to kill. Actual infliction of injury is not necessary. To constitute an assault with intent to murder with a firearm, it is not necessary that the weapon be discharged. When the intent to kill exists, the fact that for some unknown reason the actual consummation of the murder by the means employed is impossible is not a defense if the means are apparently adapted to the end in view. The intent to kill need not be directed against the person assaulted if the assault is committed with intent to kill some person. For example, if a person, intending to kill Jones, shoots Smith, mistaking Smith for Jones, that person is guilty of assaulting Smith with intent to murder. If a person fires into a group with intent to kill anyone in the group, that person is guilty of and assault with intent to murder each member of the group.

(3) *Assault with intent to commit voluntary manslaughter.* Assault with intent to commit voluntary manslaughter is an assault committed with a specific intent to kill under such circumstances that, if death resulted therefrom, the offense of voluntary manslaughter would have been committed. There can be no assault with intent to commit involuntary manslaughter, for it is not a crime capable of being intentionally committed.

(4) *Assault with intent to commit rape.* In assault with intent to commit rape, the accused must have intended to complete the offense. Any lesser intent will not suffice. No actual touching is necessary, but indecent advances and importunities, however earnest, not accompanied by such an intent, do not constitute this offense, nor do mere preparations to rape not amounting to an assault. Once an assault with intent to commit rape is made, it is no defense that the accused voluntarily desisted.

(5) *Assault with intent to rob.* For assault with intent to rob, the fact that the accused intended to take money and that the person the accused intended to rob had none is not a defense.

(6) *Assault with intent to commit forcible sodomy.* Assault with intent to commit forcible sodomy is an assault against a human being and must be committed with a specific intent to commit forcible sodomy. Any lesser intent, or different intent, will not suffice.

d. *Lesser included offenses.* See paragraph 3 of this part and Appendix 12A.

e. *Maximum punishment.*

(1) *Assault with intent to commit murder or rape.* Dishonorable discharge, forfeiture of all pay and allowances, and confinement for 20 years.

(2) *Assault with intent to commit voluntary manslaughter, robbery, forcible sodomy, arson, or burglary.* Dishonorable discharge, forfeiture of all pay and allowances, and confinement for 10 years.

(3) *Assault with intent to commit housebreaking.* Dishonorable discharge, forfeiture of all pay and allowances, and confinement for 5 years.

f. *Sample specification.*

In that _____ (personal jurisdiction data), did, (at/on board—location) (subject-matter jurisdiction data, if required), on or about _____ 20 __ , with intent to commit (murder) (voluntary manslaughter) (rape) (robbery) (forcible sodomy) (arson) (burglary) (housebreaking), commit an assault upon _____ by _____ , and that said conduct was (to the prejudice of good order and discipline in the armed forces) (of a nature to bring discredit upon the armed forces) (to the prejudice of good order and discipline in the armed forces and was of a nature to bring discredit upon the armed forces).

65. Article 134—(Bigamy)

a. *Text of statute. See* paragraph 60.

b. *Elements.*

(1) That the accused had a living lawful spouse;

(2) That while having such spouse the accused wrongfully married another person; and

(3) That, under the circumstances, the conduct of the accused was to the prejudice of good order and discipline in the armed forces or was of a nature to bring discredit upon the armed forces.

c. *Explanation.* Bigamy is contracting another marriage by one who already has a living lawful spouse. If a prior marriage was void, it will have created no status of "lawful spouse." However, if it was only voidable and has not been voided by a competent court, this is no defense. A belief that a prior marriage has been terminated by divorce, death of the other spouse, or otherwise, constitutes a defense only if the belief was reasonable. *See* R.C.M. 916(j)(1).

d. *Lesser included offenses.* See paragraph 3 of this part and Appendix 12A.

e. *Maximum punishment.* Dishonorable discharge, forfeiture of all pay and allowances, and confinement for 2 years.

f. *Sample specification.*

In that _____ (personal jurisdiction data), did, at _____ , (subject-matter jurisdiction data, if required), on or about _____ 20 ___ , wrongfully marry _____ , having at the time of his/her said marriage to _____ a lawful wife/husband then living, to wit: _____ , and that said conduct was (to the prejudice of good order and discipline in the armed forces) (of a nature to bring discredit upon the armed forces) (to the prejudice of good order and discipline in the armed forces and was of a nature to bring discredit upon the armed forces).

66. Article 134—(Bribery and graft)

a. *Text of statute.* See paragraph 60.

b. *Elements.*

(1) *Asking, accepting, or receiving.*

(a) That the accused wrongfully asked, accepted, or received a thing of value from a certain person or organization;

(b) That the accused then occupied a certain official position or had certain official duties;

(c) That the accused asked, accepted, or received this thing of value (with the intent to have the accused's decision or action influenced with respect to a certain matter)* (as compensation for or in recognition of services rendered, to be rendered, or both, by the accused in relation to a certain matter)**;

(d) That this certain matter was an official matter in which the United States was and is interested; and

(e) That, under the circumstances, the conduct of the accused was to the prejudice of good order and discipline in the armed forces or was of a nature to bring discredit upon the armed forces.

(*Note: This element is required for bribery.)
(**Note: This element is required for graft.)

(2) *Promising, offering, or giving.*

(a) That the accused wrongfully promised, offered, or gave a thing of value to a certain person;

(b) That this person then occupied a certain official position or had certain official duties;

(c) That this thing of value was promised, offered, or given (with the intent to influence the decision or action of this person)* (as compensation for or in recognition of services rendered, to be rendered, or both, by this person in relation to a certain matter)**;

(d) That this matter was an official matter in which the United States was and is interested; and

(e) That, under the circumstances, the conduct of the accused was to the prejudice of good order and discipline in the armed forces or was of a nature to bring discredit upon the armed forces.

(*Note: This element is required for bribery.)
(**Note: This element is required for graft.)

c. *Explanation.* Bribery requires an intent to influence or be influenced in an official matter; graft does not. Graft involves compensation for services performed in an official matter when no compensation is due.

d. *Lesser included offenses.* See paragraph 3 of this part and Appendix 12A.

e. *Maximum punishment.*

(1) *Bribery.* Dishonorable discharge, forfeiture of all pay and allowances, and confinement for 5 years.

(2) *Graft.* Dishonorable discharge, forfeiture of all pay and allowances, and confinement for 3 years.

f. *Sample specifications.*

(1) *Asking, accepting, or receiving.*

In that _____ (personal jurisdiction data), being at the time (a contracting officer for _____) (the personnel officer of _____) (_____), did, (at/on board—location) (subject-matter jurisdiction data, if required), on or about _____ 20 ___ , wrongfully (ask) (accept) (receive) from _____ , (a contracting company) engaged in _____ (_____), (the sum of $ _____) (_____ , of a value of (about) $ _____) (_____), (*with intent to have his/her (decision) (action) influenced with respect to) ((as compensation for) (in recognition of)) service (rendered) (to be rendered) (**rendered and to be rendered) by him/her the said _____ in relation to) an official matter in which the United States was and is interested, to wit: (the purchasing of military supplies from _____) (the transfer of _____ to duty with (_____) (_____), and that said conduct was (to the prejudice of good order and discipline in the armed forces) (of a nature to bring discredit upon the armed forces) (to the prejudice of good order and discipline in the armed forces and was of a nature to bring discredit upon the armed forces).

[*Note: This language should be used to allege bribery.]
[**Note: This language should be used to allege graft.]

(2) *Promising, offering, or giving.*

In that _____ (personal jurisdiction data), did (at/on board—location) (subject-matter jurisdiction data, if required), on or about _____ 20 ___ , wrongfully (promise) (offer) (give) to _____ , (his/her commanding officer) (the claims officer of _____) (_____), (the sum of $ _____) (_____ , of a value of (about $ _____) (_____ , (*with intent to influence the (decision) (action) of the said _____ with respect to) ((as compensation for) (in recognition of)) services (rendered) (to be rendered) (**rendered and to be rendered) by the said _____ in relation to) an official matter in which the United States was and is interested, to wit: (the granting of leave to _____) (the processing of a claim against the United States in favor of _____) (_____), and that said conduct was (to the prejudice of good order and discipline in the armed forces) (of a nature to bring discredit upon the armed forces) (to the prejudice of good order and discipline in the armed forces and was of a nature to bring discredit upon the armed forces).

[*Note: This language should be used to allege bribery.]
[**Note: This language should be used to allege graft.]

67. Article 134—(Burning with intent to defraud)

a. *Text of statute. See* paragraph 60.

b. *Elements.*

(1) That the accused willfully and maliciously burned or set fire to certain property owned by a certain person or organization;

(2) That such burning or setting on fire was with the intent to defraud a certain person or organization; and

(3) That, under the circumstances, the conduct of the accused was to the prejudice of good order and discipline in the armed forces or was of a nature to bring discredit upon the armed forces.

c. *Explanation. See* paragraph 49c(14) for a discussion of "intent to defraud."

d. *Lesser included offenses.* See paragraph 3 of this part and Appendix 12A.

e. *Maximum punishment.* Dishonorable discharge, forfeiture of all pay and allowances, and confinement for 10 years.

f. *Sample specification.*

In that _____ (personal jurisdiction data), did, (at/on board—location) (subject-matter jurisdiction data, if required), on or about _____ 20 ___ , willfully and maliciously (burn) (set fire to) (a dwelling) (a barn) (an automobile), the property of _____ , with intent to defraud (the insurer thereof, to wit: _____) (_____), and that said conduct was (to the prejudice of good order and discipline in the armed forces) (of a nature to bring discredit upon the armed forces) (to the prejudice of good order and discipline in the armed forces and was of a nature to bring discredit upon the armed forces).

68. Article 134—(Check, worthless, making and uttering—by dishonorably failing to maintain funds)

a. *Text of statute. See* paragraph 60.

b. *Elements.*

(1) That the accused made and uttered a certain check;

(2) That the check was made and uttered for the purchase of a certain thing, in payment of a debt, or for a certain purpose;

(3) That the accused subsequently failed to place or maintain sufficient funds in or credit with the drawee bank for payment of the check in full upon its presentment for payment;

(4) That this failure was dishonorable; and

(5) That, under the circumstances, the conduct of the accused was to the prejudice of good order and discipline in the armed forces or was of a nature to bring discredit upon the armed forces.

c. *Explanation.* This offense differs from an Article 123a offense (paragraph 49) in that there need be no intent to defraud or deceive at the time of making, drawing, uttering, or delivery, and that the accused need not know at that time that the accused did not or would not have sufficient funds for payment. The gist of the offense lies in the conduct of the accused after uttering the instrument. Mere negligence in maintaining one's bank balance is insufficient for this offense, for the accused's conduct must reflect bad faith or gross indifference in this regard. As in the offense of dishonorable failure to pay debts (*see* paragraph 71), dishonorable conduct of the accused is necessary, and the other principles discussed in paragraph 71 also apply here.

d. *Lesser included offenses.* See paragraph 3 of this part and Appendix 12A.

e. *Maximum punishment.* Bad-conduct discharge, forfeiture of all pay and allowances, and confinement for 6 months.

f. *Sample specification.*

In that _____ (personal jurisdiction data), did, (at/on board—location) (subject-matter jurisdiction data, if required), on or about _____ 20 __ , make and utter to _____ a certain check, in words and figures as follows, to wit: _____ , (for the purchase of _____) (in payment of a debt) (for the purpose of _____), and did thereafter dishonorably fail to (place) (maintain) sufficient funds in the _____ Bank for payment of such check in full upon its presentment for payment, and that said conduct was (to the prejudice of good order and discipline in the armed forces) (of a nature to bring discredit upon the armed forces) (to the prejudice of good order and discipline in the armed forces and was of a nature to bring discredit upon the armed forces).

68a. Article 134—(Child endangerment)

a. *Text of statute.* See paragraph 60.

b. *Elements.*

(1) That the accused had a duty for the care of a certain child;

(2) That the child was under the age of 16 years;

(3) That the accused endangered the child's mental or physical health, safety, or welfare through design or culpable negligence; and

(4) That, under the circumstances, the conduct of the accused was to the prejudice of good order and discipline in the armed forces or was of a nature to bring discredit upon the armed forces.

c. *Explanation.*

(1) *In general.* This offense is intended to prohibit and therefore deter child endangerment through design or culpable negligence.

(2) *Design.* Design means on purpose, intentionally, or according to plan and requires specific intent to endanger the child.

(3) *Culpable negligence.* Culpable negligence is a degree of carelessness greater than simple negligence. It is a negligent act or omission accompanied by a culpable disregard for the foreseeable consequences to others of that act or omission. In the context of this offense, culpable negligence may include acts that, when viewed in the light of human experience, might foreseeably result in harm to a child, even though such harm would not necessarily be the natural and probable consequences of such acts. In this regard, the age and maturity of the child, the conditions surrounding the neglectful conduct, the proximity of assistance available, the nature of the environment in which the child may have been left, the provisions made for care of the child, and the location of the parent or adult responsible for the child relative to the location of the child, among others, may be considered in determining whether the conduct constituted culpable negligence.

(4) *Harm.* Actual physical or mental harm to the child is not required. The offense requires that the accused's actions reasonably could have caused physical or mental harm or suffering. However, if the accused's conduct does cause actual physical or mental harm, the potential maximum punishment increases. See Paragraph 54c(4)(a)(iii) for an explanation of "grievous bodily harm".

(5) *Endanger.* "Endanger" means to subject one to a reasonable probability of harm.

(6) *Age of victim as a factor.* While this offense may be committed against any child under 16, the age of the victim is a factor in the culpable negligence determination. Leaving a teenager alone for an evening may not be culpable (or even simple) negligence; leaving an infant or toddler for the same period might constitute culpable negligence. On the other hand, leaving a teenager without supervision for an extended period while the accused was on temporary duty outside commuting distance might constitute culpable negligence.

(7) *Duty required.* The duty of care is determined by the totality of the circumstances and may be established by statute, regulation, legal parent-child relationship, mutual agreement, or assumption of control or custody by affirmative act. When there is no duty of care of a child, there is no offense under this paragraph. Thus, there is no offense when a stranger makes no effort to feed a starving child or an individual/neighbor not charged with the care of a child does not prevent the child from running and playing in the street.

d. *Lesser included offenses.* See paragraph 3 of this part and Appendix 12A.

e. *Maximum punishment.*

(1) *Endangerment by design resulting in grievous bodily harm.* Dishonorable discharge, forfeiture of all pay and allowances, and confinement for 8 years.

(2) *Endangerment by design resulting in harm.* Dishonorable discharge, forfeiture of all pay and allowances, and confinement for 5 years.

(3) *Other cases by design.* Dishonorable discharge, forfeiture of all pay and allowances and confinement for 4 years.

(4) *Endangerment by culpable negligence resulting in grievous bodily harm.* Dishonorable discharge, forfeiture of all pay and allowances, and confinement for 3 years.

(5) *Endangerment by culpable negligence resulting in harm.* Bad-conduct discharge, forfeiture of all pay and allowances, and confinement for 2 years.

(6) *Other cases by culpable negligence.* Bad-conduct discharge, forfeiture of all pay and allowances, and confinement for 1 year.

f. *Sample specification.*

(1) *Resulting in grievous bodily harm.*

In that _____ (personal jurisdiction data), (at/on board-location) (subject matter jurisdiction data, if required) on or about _____ 20 __ , had a duty for the care of _____ , a child under the age of 16 years and did endanger the (mental health) (physical health) (safety) (welfare) of said _____ , by (leaving the said _____ unattended in his quarters for over _____ hours/days with no adult present in the home) (by failing to obtain medical care for the said _____ 's diabetic condition) (_____), and that such conduct (was by design) (constituted culpable negligence) (which resulted in grievous bodily harm, to wit:) (broken leg) (deep cut) (fractured skull) (_____), and that said conduct was (to the prejudice of good order and discipline in the armed forces) (of a nature to bring discredit upon the armed forces) (to the prejudice of good order and discipline in the armed forces and was of a nature to bring discredit upon the armed forces).

(2) *Resulting in harm.*

In that _____ (personal jurisdiction data), (at/on board-location) (subject matter jurisdiction data, if required) on or about _____ 20 __ , had a duty for the care of _____ , a child under the age of 16 years, and did endanger the (mental health) (physical health) (safety) (welfare) of said _____ , by (leaving the said _____ unattended in his quarters for over _____ hours/days with no adult present in the home) (by failing to obtain medical care for the said _____ 's diabetic condition) (_____), and that such conduct (was by design) (constituted culpable negligence) (which resulted in (harm, to wit:) (a black eye) (bloody nose) (minor cut) (_____), and that said conduct was (to the prejudice of good order and discipline in the armed forces) (of a nature to bring discredit upon the armed forces) (to the prejudice of good order and discipline in the armed forces and was of a nature to bring discredit upon the armed forces).

(3) *Other cases.*

In that _____ (personal jurisdiction data), (at/on board-location) (subject matter jurisdiction data, if required) on or about _____ 20 __ , was responsible for the care of _____ , a child under the age of 16 years, and did endanger the (mental health) (physical health) (safety) (welfare) of said _____ , by (leaving the said _____ unattended in his quarters for over _____ hours/days with no adult present in the home) (by failing to obtain medical care for the said _____ 's diabetic condition) (_____), and that such conduct (was by design) (constituted culpable negligence), and that said conduct was (to the prejudice of good order and discipline in the armed forces) (of a nature to bring discredit upon the armed forces) (to the prejudice of good order and discipline in the armed forces and was of a nature to bring discredit upon the armed forces).

68b. Article 134—(Child pornography)

a. *Text of Statute.* See paragraph 60.

b. *Elements.*

(1) *Possessing, receiving, or viewing child pornography.*

(a) That the accused knowingly and wrongfully possessed, received, or viewed child pornography; and

(b) That, under the circumstances, the conduct of the accused was to the prejudice of good order and discipline in the armed forces or was of a nature to bring discredit upon the armed forces.

(2) *Possessing child pornography with intent to distribute.*

(a) That the accused knowingly and wrongfully possessed child pornography;

(b) That the possession was with the intent to distribute; and

(c) That, under the circumstances, the conduct of the accused was to the prejudice of good order and discipline in the armed forces or was of a nature to bring discredit upon the armed forces.

(3) *Distributing child pornography.*

(a) That the accused knowingly and wrongfully distributed child pornography to another; and

(b) That, under the circumstances, the conduct of the accused was to the prejudice of good order and discipline in the armed forces or was of a nature to bring discredit upon the armed forces.

(4) *Producing child pornography.*

(a) That the accused knowingly and wrongfully produced child pornography; and

(b) That, under the circumstances, the conduct of the accused was to the prejudice of good order and discipline in the armed forces or was of a nature to bring discredit upon the armed forces.

c. *Explanation.*

(1) "Child Pornography" means material that contains either an obscene visual depiction of a minor engaging in sexually explicit conduct or a visual depiction of an actual minor engaging in sexually explicit conduct.

(2) An accused may not be convicted of possessing, receiving, viewing, distributing, or producing child pornography if he was not aware that the images were of minors, or what appeared to be minors, engaged in sexually explicit conduct. Awareness may be inferred from circumstantial evidence such as the name of a computer file or folder, the name of the host website from which a visual depiction was viewed or received, search terms used, and the number of images possessed.

(3) "Distributing" means delivering to the actual or constructive possession of another.

(4) "Minor" means any person under the age of 18 years.

(5) "Possessing" means exercising control of something. Possession may be direct physical custody like holding an item in one's hand, or it may be constructive, as in the case of a person who hides something in a locker or a car to which that person may return to retrieve it. Possession must be know-

ing and conscious. Possession inherently includes the power or authority to preclude control by others. It is possible for more than one person to possess an item simultaneously, as when several people share control over an item.

(6) "Producing" means creating or manufacturing. As used in this paragraph, it refers to making child pornography that did not previously exist. It does not include reproducing or copying.

(7) "Sexually explicit conduct" means actual or simulated:

(a) sexual intercourse or sodomy, including genital-genital, oral-genital, anal-genital, or oral-anal, whether between persons of the same or opposite sex;

(b) bestiality;

(c) masturbation;

(d) sadistic or masochistic abuse; or

(e) lascivious exhibition of the genitals or pubic area of any person.

(8) "Visual depiction" includes any developed or undeveloped photograph, picture, film or video; any digital or computer image, picture, film, or video made by any means, including those transmitted by any means including streaming media, even if not stored in a permanent format; or any digital or electronic data capable of conversion into a visual image.

(9) "Wrongfulness." Any facts or circumstances that show that a visual depiction of child pornography was unintentionally or inadvertently acquired are relevant to wrongfulness, including, but not limited to, the method by which the visual depiction was acquired, the length of time the visual depiction was maintained, and whether the visual depiction was promptly, and in good faith, destroyed or reported to law enforcement.

(10) On motion of the government, in any prosecution under this paragraph, except for good cause shown, the name, address, social security number, or other nonphysical identifying information, other than the age or approximate age, of any minor who is depicted in any child pornography or visual depiction or copy thereof shall not be admissible and may be redacted from any otherwise admissible evidence, and the panel shall be instructed, upon request of the Government, that it can draw no inference from the absence of such evidence.

d. *Lesser included offenses.* See paragraph 3 of this part and Appendix 12A.

e. *Maximum punishment.*

(1) *Possessing, receiving, or viewing child pornography.* Dishonorable discharge, forfeiture of all pay and allowances, and confinement for 10 years.

(2) *Possessing child pornography with intent to distribute.* Dishonorable discharge, forfeiture of all pay and allowances, and confinement for 15 years.

(3) *Distributing child pornography.* Dishonorable discharge, forfeiture of all pay and allowances, and confinement for 20 years.

(4) *Producing child pornography.* Dishonorable discharge, forfeiture of all pay and allowances, and confinement for 30 years.

f. *Sample specification.*
Possessing, receiving, viewing, possessing with intent to distribute, distributing, or producing child pornography.

In that _____ (personal jurisdiction data), did (at/on board-location), on or about _____ 20 __ knowingly and wrongfully (possess) (receive) (view) (distribute) (produce) child pornography, to wit: a (photograph) (picture) (film) (video) (digital image) (computer image) of a minor, or what appears to be a minor, engaging in sexually explicit conduct (, with intent to distribute the said child pornography), and that said conduct was (to the prejudice of good order and discipline in the armed forces) (of a nature to bring discredit upon the armed forces) (to the prejudice of good order and discipline in the armed forces and was of a nature to bring discredit upon the armed forces).

69. Article 134—(Cohabitation, wrongful)

a. *Text of statute.* See paragraph 60.

b. *Elements.*

(1) That, during a certain period of time, the accused and another person openly and publicly lived together as husband and wife, holding themselves out as such;

(2) That the other person was not the spouse of the accused;

(3) That, under the circumstances, the conduct of the accused was to the prejudice of good order and discipline in the armed forces or was of a nature to bring discredit upon the armed forces.

c. *Explanation.* This offense differs from adultery (*see* paragraph 62) in that it is not necessary to prove that one of the partners was married or that sexual intercourse took place. Public knowledge of the wrongfulness of the relationship is not required, but the partners must behave in a manner, as exhibited by conduct or language, that leads others to believe that a marital relationship exists.

d. *Lesser included offenses.* See paragraph 3 of this part and Appendix 12A.

e. *Maximum punishment.* Confinement for 4 months and forfeiture of two-thirds pay per month for 4 months.

f. *Sample specification.*
In that _____ (personal jurisdiction data), did, (at/on board—location) (subject-matter jurisdiction data, if required), from about _____ 20 __ , to about _____ 20 __ , wrongfully cohabit with _____ , (a woman not his wife) (a man not her husband), and that said conduct was (to the prejudice of good order and discipline in the armed forces) (of a nature to bring discredit upon the armed forces) (to the prejudice of good order and discipline in the armed forces and was of a nature to bring discredit upon the armed forces).

70. Article 134—(Correctional custody—offenses against)

a. *Text of statute. See* paragraph 60.

b. *Elements.*

(1) *Escape from correctional custody.*

(a) That the accused was placed in correctional custody by a person authorized to do so;

(b) That, while in such correctional custody, the accused was under physical restraint;

(c) That the accused freed himself or herself from the physical restraint of this correctional custody before being released therefrom by proper authority; and

(d) That, under the circumstances, the conduct of the accused was to the prejudice of good order and discipline in the armed forces or was of a nature to bring discredit upon the armed forces.

(2) *Breach of correctional custody.*

(a) That the accused was placed in correctional custody by a person authorized to do so;

(b) That, while in correctional custody, a certain restraint was imposed upon the accused;

(c) That the accused went beyond the limits of

the restraint imposed before having been released from the correctional custody or relieved of the restraint by proper authority; and

(d) That, under the circumstances, the conduct of the accused was to the prejudice of good order and discipline in the armed forces or was of a nature to bring discredit upon the armed forces.

c. *Explanation.*

(1) *Escape from correctional custody.* Escape from correctional custody is the act of a person undergoing the punishment of correctional custody pursuant to Article 15, who, before being set at liberty by proper authority, casts off any physical restraint imposed by the custodian or by the place or conditions of custody.

(2) *Breach of correctional custody.* Breach of restraint during correctional custody is the act of a person undergoing the punishment who, in the absence of physical restraint imposed by a custodian or by the place or conditions of custody, breaches any form of restraint imposed during this period.

(3) *Authority to impose correctional custody. See* Part V concerning who may impose correctional custody. Whether the status of a person authorized that person to impose correctional custody is a question of law to be decided by the military judge. Whether the person who imposed correctional custody had such a status is a question of fact to be decided by the factfinder.

d. *Lesser included offenses.* See paragraph 3 of this part and Appendix 12A.

e. *Maximum punishment.*

(1) *Escape from correctional custody.* Dishonorable discharge, forfeiture of all pay and allowances, and confinement for 1 year.

(2) *Breach of correctional custody.* Bad-conduct discharge, forfeiture of all pay and allowances, and confinement for 6 months.

f. *Sample specifications.*

(1) *Escape from correctional custody.*

In that _____ (personal jurisdiction data), while undergoing the punishment of correctional custody imposed by a person authorized to do so, did, (at/on board—location), on or about _____ 20 ___ , escape from correctional custody, and that said conduct was (to the prejudice of good order and discipline in the armed forces) (of a nature to bring discredit upon the armed forces) (to the prejudice of good order

and discipline in the armed forces and was of a nature to bring discredit upon the armed forces).

(2) *Breach of correctional custody.*

In that _____ (personal jurisdiction data), while duly undergoing the punishment of correctional custody imposed by a person authorized to do so, did, (at/on board—location), on or about _____ 20 ___ , breach the restraint imposed thereunder by _____ , and that said conduct was (to the prejudice of good order and discipline in the armed forces) (of a nature to bring discredit upon the armed forces) (to the prejudice of good order and discipline in the armed forces and was of a nature to bring discredit upon the armed forces).

71. Article 134—(Debt, dishonorably failing to pay)

a. *Text of statute. See* paragraph 60.

b. *Elements.*

(1) That the accused was indebted to a certain person or entity in a certain sum;

(2) That this debt became due and payable on or about a certain date;

(3) That while the debt was still due and payable the accused dishonorably failed to pay this debt; and

(4) That, under the circumstances, the conduct of the accused was to the prejudice of good order and discipline in the armed forces or was of a nature to bring discredit upon the armed forces.

c. *Explanation.* More than negligence in nonpayment is necessary. The failure to pay must be characterized by deceit, evasion, false promises, or other distinctly culpable circumstances indicating a deliberate nonpayment or grossly indifferent attitude toward one's just obligations. For a debt to form the basis of this offense, the accused must not have had a defense, or an equivalent offset or counterclaim, either in fact or according to the accused's belief, at the time alleged. The offense should not be charged if there was a genuine dispute between the parties as to the facts or law relating to the debt which would affect the obligation of the accused to pay. The offense is not committed if the creditor or creditors involved are satisfied with the conduct of the debtor with respect to payment. The length of the period of nonpayment and any denial of indebtedness which the accused may have made may tend to prove that the accused's conduct was dishonorable, but the court-martial may convict only if it finds from all of the evidence that the conduct was in fact dishonorable.

d. *Lesser included offenses.* See paragraph 3 of this part and Appendix 12A.

e. *Maximum punishment.* Bad-conduct discharge, forfeiture of all pay and allowances, and confinement for 6 months.

f. *Sample specification.*

In that _____ (personal jurisdiction data), being indebted to _____ in the sum of $ _____ for _____ , which amount became due and payable (on) (about) (on or about) _____ 20 ___ , did (at/on board—location) (subject-matter jurisdiction data, if required), from _____ 20 ___ , to _____ 20 ___ , dishonorably fail to pay said debt, and that said conduct was (to the prejudice of good order and discipline in the armed forces) (of a nature to bring discredit upon the armed forces) (to the prejudice of good order and discipline in the armed forces and was of a nature to bring discredit upon the armed forces).

72. Article 134—(Disloyal statements)

a. *Text of statute. See* paragraph 60.

b. *Elements.*

(1) That the accused made a certain statement;

(2) That the statement was communicated to another person;

(3) That the statement was disloyal to the United States;

(4) That the statement was made with the intent to promote disloyalty or disaffection toward the United States by any member of the armed forces or to interfere with or impair the loyalty to the United States or good order and discipline of any member of the armed forces; and

(5) That, under the circumstances, the conduct of the accused was to the prejudice of good order and discipline in the armed forces or was of a nature to bring discredit upon the armed forces.

c. *Explanation.* Certain disloyal statements by military personnel may not constitute an offense under 18 U.S.C. §§ 2385, 2387, and 2388, but may, under the circumstances, be punishable under this article. Examples include praising the enemy, attacking the war aims of the United States, or denouncing our form of government with the intent to promote disloyalty or disaffection among members of the armed

services. A declaration of personal belief can amount to a disloyal statement if it disavows allegiance owed to the United States by the declarant. The disloyalty involved for this offense must be to the United States as a political entity and not merely to a department or other agency that is a part of its administration.

d. *Lesser included offenses.* See paragraph 3 of this part and Appendix 12A.

e. *Maximum punishment.* Dishonorable discharge, forfeiture of all pay and allowances, and confinement for 3 years.

f. *Sample specification.*

In that _____ (personal jurisdiction data), did, (at/on board—location), on or about _____ 20 ___ , with intent to (promote (disloyalty) (disaffection) (disloyalty and disaffection)) ((interfere with) (impair) the (loyalty) (good order and discipline)) of any member of the armed forces of the United States communicate to _____ , the following statement, to wit: " _____ ," or words to that effect, which statement was disloyal to the United States, and that said conduct was (to the prejudice of good order and discipline in the armed forces) (of a nature to bring discredit upon the armed forces) (to the prejudice of good order and discipline in the armed forces and was of a nature to bring discredit upon the armed forces).

73. Article 134—(Disorderly conduct, drunkenness)

a. *Text of statute. See* paragraph 60.

b. *Elements.*

(1) That the accused was drunk, disorderly, or drunk and disorderly on board ship or in some other place; and

(2) That, under the circumstances, the conduct of the accused was to the prejudice of good order and discipline in the armed forces or was of a nature to bring discredit upon the armed forces.

c. *Explanation.*

(1) *Drunkenness.* See paragraph 35c(6) for a discussion of intoxication.

(2) *Disorderly.* Disorderly conduct is conduct of such a nature as to affect the peace and quiet of persons who may witness it and who may be disturbed or provoked to resentment thereby. It includes conduct that endangers public morals or

outrages public decency and any disturbance of a contentious or turbulent character.

(3) *Service discrediting.* Unlike most offenses under Article 134, "conduct of a nature to bring discredit upon the armed forces" must be included in the specification and proved in order to authorized the higher maximum punishment when the offense is service discrediting.

d. *Lesser included offenses.* See paragraph 3 of this part and Appendix 12A.

e. *Maximum punishment.*

(1) *Disorderly conduct.*

(a) *Under such circumstances as to bring discredit upon the military service.* Confinement for 4 months and forfeiture of two-thirds pay per month for 4 months.

(b) *Other cases.* Confinement for 1 month and forfeiture of two-thirds pay per month for 1 month.

(2) *Drunkenness.*

(a) *Aboard ship or under such circumstances as to bring discredit upon the military service.* Confinement for 3 months and forfeiture of two-thirds pay per month for 3 months.

(b) *Other cases.* Confinement for 1 month and forfeiture of two-thirds pay per month for 1 month.

(3) *Drunk and disorderly.*

(a) *Aboard ship.* Bad-conduct discharge, forfeiture of all pay and allowances, and confinement for 6 months.

(b) *Under such circumstances as to bring discredit upon the military service.* Confinement for 6 months and forfeiture of two-thirds pay per month for 6 months.

(c) *Other cases.* Confinement for 3 months and forfeiture of two-thirds pay per month for 3 months.

f. *Sample specification.*

In that _____ (personal jurisdiction data), was, (at/on board—location) (subject-matter jurisdiction data, if required), on or about _____ 20 __ , (drunk) (disorderly) (drunk and disorderly) (which conduct was of a nature to bring discredit upon the armed forces), and that said conduct was (to the prejudice of good order and discipline in the armed forces) (of a nature to bring discredit upon the armed forces) (to the prejudice of good order and discipline in the armed forces and was of a nature to bring discredit upon the armed forces).

74. Article 134—(Drinking liquor with prisoner)

a. *Text of statute. See* paragraph 60.

b. *Elements.*

(1) That the accused was a sentinel or in another assignment in charge of a prisoner;

(2) That, while in such capacity, the accused unlawfully drank intoxicating liquor with a prisoner;

(3) That the prisoner was under the charge of the accused;

(4) That the accused knew that the prisoner was a prisoner under the accused's charge; and

(5) That, under the circumstances, the conduct of the accused was to the prejudice of good order and discipline in the armed forces or was of a nature to bring discredit upon the armed forces.

c. *Explanation.*

(1) *Prisoner.* A "prisoner" is a person who is in confinement or custody imposed under R.C.M. 302, 304, or 305, or under sentence of a court-martial who has not been set free by proper authority.

(2) *Liquor.* For the purposes of this offense, "liquor" includes any alcoholic beverage.

d. *Lesser included offenses.* See paragraph 3 of this part and Appendix 12A.

e. *Maximum punishment.* Confinement for 3 months and forfeiture of two-thirds pay per month for 3 months.

f. *Sample specification.*

In that _____ (personal jurisdiction data), a (sentinel) (_____) in charge of prisoners, did, (at/on board—location), on or about _____ 20 __ , unlawfully drink intoxicating liquor with _____ , a prisoner under his/her charge, and that said conduct was (to the prejudice of good order and discipline in the armed forces) (of a nature to bring discredit upon the armed forces) (to the prejudice of good order and discipline in the armed forces and was of a nature to bring discredit upon the armed forces).

75. Article 134—(Drunk prisoner)

a. *Text of statute. See* paragraph 60.

b. *Elements.*

(1) That the accused was a prisoner;

(2) That while in such status the accused was found drunk; and

(3) That, under the circumstances, the conduct of

the accused was to the prejudice of good order and discipline in the armed forces or was of a nature to bring discredit upon the armed forces.

c. *Explanation.*

(1) *Prisoner. See* paragraph 74c(1).

(2) *Drunk. See* paragraph 35c(6) for a discussion of intoxication.

d. *Lesser included offenses.* See paragraph 3 of this part and Appendix 12A.

e. *Maximum punishment.* Confinement for 3 months and forfeiture of two-thirds pay per month for 3 months.

f. *Sample specification.*

In that _____ (personal jurisdiction data), a prisoner, was (at/on board— location), on or about _____ 20 ___ , found drunk, and that said conduct was (to the prejudice of good order and discipline in the armed forces) (of a nature to bring discredit upon the armed forces) (to the prejudice of good order and discipline in the armed forces and was of a nature to bring discredit upon the armed forces).

76. Article 134—(Drunkenness—incapacitation for performance of duties through prior wrongful indulgence in intoxicating liquor or any drug)

a. *Text of statute. See* paragraph 60.

b. *Elements.*

(1) That the accused had certain duties to perform;

(2) That the accused was incapacitated for the proper performance of such duties;

(3) That such incapacitation was the result of previous wrongful indulgence in intoxicating liquor or any drug; and

(4) That, under the circumstances, the conduct of the accused was to the prejudice of good order and discipline in the armed forces or was of a nature to bring discredit upon the armed forces.

c. *Explanation.*

(1) *Liquor. See* paragraph 74c(2).

(2) *Incapacitated.* Incapacitated means unfit or unable to perform properly. A person is "unfit" to perform duties if at the time the duties are to commence, the person is drunk, even though physically able to perform the duties. Illness resulting from previous overindulgence is an example of being "unable" to perform duties. For a discussion of "drunk" *see* paragraph 35c(6).

(3) *Affirmative defense.* The accused's lack of knowledge of the duties assigned is an affirmative defense to this offense.

d. *Lesser included offenses.* See paragraph 3 of this part and Appendix 12A.

e. *Maximum punishment.* Confinement for 3 months and forfeiture of two-thirds pay per month for 3 months.

f. *Sample specification.*

In that _____ (personal jurisdiction data), was, (at/on board—location), on or about _____ 20 ___ , as a result of wrongful previous over-indulgence in intoxicating liquor or drugs incapacitated for the proper performance of his/her duties, and that said conduct was (to the prejudice of good order and discipline in the armed forces) (of a nature to bring discredit upon the armed forces) (to the prejudice of good order and discipline in the armed forces and was of a nature to bring discredit upon the armed forces).

77. Article 134—(False or unauthorized pass offenses)

a. *Text of statute. See* paragraph 60.

b. *Elements.*

(1) *Wrongful making, altering, counterfeiting, or tampering with a military or official pass, permit, discharge certificate, or identification card.*

(a) That the accused wrongfully and falsely made, altered, counterfeited, or tampered with a certain military or official pass, permit, discharge certificate, or identification card; and

(b) That, under the circumstances, the conduct of the accused was to the prejudice of good order and discipline in the armed forces or was of a nature to bring discredit upon the armed forces.

(2) *Wrongful sale, gift, loan, or disposition of a military or official pass, permit, discharge certificate, or identification card.*

(a) That the accused wrongfully sold, gave, loaned, or disposed of a certain military or official pass, permit, discharge certificate, or identification card;

(b) That the pass, permit, discharge certificate, or identification card was false or unauthorized;

(c) That the accused then knew that the pass,

permit, discharge certificate, or identification card was false or unauthorized; and

(d) That, under the circumstances, the conduct of the accused was to the prejudice of good order and discipline in the armed forces or was of a nature to bring discredit upon the armed forces.

(3) *Wrongful use or possession of a false or unauthorized military or official pass, permit, discharge certificate, or identification card.*

(a) That the accused wrongfully used or possessed a certain military or official pass, permit, discharge certificate, or identification card;

(b) That the pass, permit, discharge certificate, or identification card was false or unauthorized;

(c) That the accused then knew that the pass, permit, discharge certificate, or identification card was false or unauthorized; and

(d) That, under the circumstances, the conduct of the accused was to the prejudice of good order and discipline in the armed forces or was of a nature to bring discredit upon the armed forces.

[Note: When there is intent to defraud or deceive, add the following element after (c) above: That the accused used or possessed the pass, permit, discharge certificate, or identification card with an intent to defraud or deceive.]

c. *Explanation.*

(1) *In general.* "Military or official pass, permit, discharge certificate, or identification card" includes, as well as the more usual forms of these documents, all documents issued by any governmental agency for the purpose of identification and copies thereof.

(2) *Intent to defraud or deceive. See* paragraph 49c(14) and (15).

d. *Lesser included offenses. See* paragraph 3 of this part and Appendix 12A.

e. *Maximum punishment.*

(1) *Possessing or using with intent to defraud or deceive, or making, altering, counterfeiting, tampering with, or selling.* Dishonorable discharge, forfeiture of all pay and allowances, and confinement for 3 years.

(2) *All other cases.* Bad-conduct discharge, forfeiture of all pay and allowances, and confinement for 6 months.

f. *Sample specifications.*

(1) *Wrongful making, altering, counterfeiting, or*

tampering with military or official pass, permit, discharge certificate, or identification card.

In that _____ (personal jurisdiction data), did, (at/on board—location) (subject-matter jurisdiction data, if required), on or about _____ 20 ___, wrongfully and falsely (make) (forge) (alter by _____) (counterfeit) (tamper with by _____) (a certain instrument purporting to be) (a) (an) (another's) (naval) (military) (official) (pass) (permit) (discharge certificate) (identification card) (_____) in words and figures as follows: _____ , and that said conduct was (to the prejudice of good order and discipline in the armed forces) (of a nature to bring discredit upon the armed forces) (to the prejudice of good order and discipline in the armed forces and was of a nature to bring discredit upon the armed forces).

(2) *Wrongful sale, gift, loan, or disposition of a military or official pass, permit, discharge certificate, or identification card.*

In that _____ (personal jurisdiction data), did, (at/on board—location) (subject-matter jurisdiction data, if required), on or about _____ 20 ___, wrongfully (sell to _____) (give to _____) (loan to _____) (dispose of by _____) (a certain instrument purporting to be) (a) (an) (another's) (naval) (military) (official) (pass) (permit) (discharge certificate) (identification card) (_____) in words and figures as follows: _____ , he/she, the said _____ , then well knowing the same to be (false) (unauthorized), and that said conduct was (to the prejudice of good order and discipline in the armed forces) (of a nature to bring discredit upon the armed forces) (to the prejudice of good order and discipline in the armed forces and was of a nature to bring discredit upon the armed forces).

(3) *Wrongful use or possession of a false or unauthorized military or official pass, permit, discharge certificate, or identification card.*

In that _____ (personal jurisdiction data), did (at/on board—location) (subject-matter jurisdiction data, if required), on or about _____ 20 ___, wrongfully (use) (possess) (with intent to (defraud) (deceive)) (a certain instrument purporting to be) (a) (an) (another's) (naval) (military) (official) (pass) (permit) (discharge certificate) (identification card) (_____), he/she, the said _____ , then well knowing the same to be (false) (unauthorized), and that said conduct was (to the prejudice of good order and discipline in the armed forces) (of a nature to bring discredit upon the armed forces) (to the prejudice of good order and discipline in the armed forces and was of a nature to bring discredit upon the armed forces).

78. Article 134—(False pretenses, obtaining services under)

a. *Text of statute. See* paragraph 60.

b. *Elements.*

(1) That the accused wrongfully obtained certain services;

(2) That the obtaining was done by using false pretenses;

(3) That the accused then knew of the falsity of the pretenses;

(4) That the obtaining was with intent to defraud;

(5) That the services were of a certain value; and

(6) That, under the circumstances, the conduct of the accused was to the prejudice of good order and discipline in the armed forces or was of a nature to bring discredit upon the armed forces.

c. *Explanation.* This offense is similar to the offenses of larceny and wrongful appropriation by false pretenses, except that the object of the obtaining is services (for example, telephone service) rather than money, personal property, or articles of value of any kind as under Article 121. *See* paragraph 46c. *See* paragraph 49c(14) for a definition of "intent to defraud."

d. *Lesser included offenses.* See paragraph 3 of this part and Appendix 12A.

e. *Maximum punishment.* Obtaining services under false pretenses.

(1) *Of a value of $500.00 or less.* Bad-conduct discharge, forfeiture of all pay and allowances, and confinement for 6 months.

(2) *Of a value of more than $500.00.* Dishonorable discharge, forfeiture of all pay and allowances, and confinement for 5 years.

f. *Sample specification.*

In that _____ (personal jurisdiction data), did, (at/on board—location) (subject-matter jurisdiction data, if required), on or about _____ 20 ___, with intent to defraud, falsely pretend to _____ that _____ , then knowing that the pretenses were false, and by means thereof did wrongfully obtain from _____ services, of a value of (about) $ _____ , to wit: _____ ,

and that said conduct was (to the prejudice of good order and discipline in the armed forces) (of a nature to bring discredit upon the armed forces) (to the prejudice of good order and discipline in the armed forces and was of a nature to bring discredit upon the armed forces).

79. Article 134—(False swearing)

a. *Text of statute. See* paragraph 60.

b. *Elements.*

(1) That the accused took an oath or equivalent;

(2) That the oath or equivalent was administered to the accused in a matter in which such oath or equivalent was required or authorized by law;

(3) That the oath or equivalent was administered by a person having authority to do so;

(4) That upon this oath or equivalent the accused made or subscribed a certain statement;

(5) That the statement was false;

(6) That the accused did not then believe the statement to be true; and

(7) That, under the circumstances, the conduct of the accused was to the prejudice of good order and discipline in the armed forces or was of a nature to bring discredit upon the armed forces.

c. *Explanation.*

(1) *Nature of offense.* False swearing is the making under a lawful oath or equivalent of any false statement, oral or written, not believing the statement to be true. It does not include such statements made in a judicial proceeding or course of justice, as these are under Article 131, perjury (*see* paragraph 57). Unlike a false official statement under Article 107 (*see* paragraph 31) there is no requirement that the statement be made with an intent to deceive or that the statement be official. *See* paragraphs 57c(1), c(2)(*c*) and c(2)(*e*) concerning "judicial proceeding or course of justice," proof of the falsity, and the belief of the accused, respectively.

(2) *Oath. See* Article 136 and R.C.M. 807 as to the authority to administer oaths, and *see* Section IX of Part III (Military Rules of Evidence) concerning proof of the signatures of persons authorized to administer oaths. An oath includes an affirmation when authorized in lieu of an oath.

d. *Lesser included offenses.* See paragraph 3 of this part and Appendix 12A.

e. *Maximum punishment.* Dishonorable discharge,

forfeiture of all pay and allowances, and confinement for 3 years.

f. *Sample specification.*

In that _____ (personal jurisdiction data), did, (at/on board—location) (subject-matter jurisdiction data, if required), on or about _____ 20 ___ , (in an affidavit) (in _____), wrongfully and unlawfully (make) (subscribe) under lawful (oath) (affirmation) a false statement in substance as follows: _____ , which statement he/she did not then believe to be true, and that said conduct was (to the prejudice of good order and discipline in the armed forces) (of a nature to bring discredit upon the armed forces) (to the prejudice of good order and discipline in the armed forces and was of a nature to bring discredit upon the armed forces).

80. Article 134—(Firearm, discharging—through negligence)

a. *Text of statute. See* paragraph 60.

b. *Elements.*

(1) That the accused discharged a firearm;

(2) That such discharge was caused by the negligence of the accused; and

(3) That, under the circumstances, the conduct of the accused was to the prejudice of good order and discipline in the armed forces or was of a nature to bring discredit upon the armed forces.

c. *Explanation.* For a discussion of negligence, *see* paragraph 85c(2).

d. *Lesser included offenses.* See paragraph 3 of this part and Appendix 12A.

e. *Maximum punishment.* Confinement for 3 months and forfeiture of two-thirds pay per month for 3 months.

f. *Sample specification.*

In that _____ (personal jurisdiction data), did, (at/on board—location) (subject-matter jurisdiction data, if required), on or about _____ 20 ___ , through negligence, discharge a (service rifle) (___) in the (squadron) (tent) (barracks) (_____) of _____ , and that said conduct was (to the prejudice of good order and discipline in the armed forces) (of a nature to bring discredit upon the armed forces) (to the prejudice of good order and discipline in the armed forces and was of a nature to bring discredit upon the armed forces).

81. Article 134—(Firearm, discharging—willfully, under such circumstances as to endanger human life)

a. *Text of statute. See* paragraph 60.

b. *Elements.*

(1) That the accused discharged a firearm;

(2) That the discharge was willful and wrongful;

(3) That the discharge was under circumstances such as to endanger human life; and

(4) That, under the circumstances, the conduct of the accused was to the prejudice of good order and discipline in the armed forces or was of a nature to bring discredit upon the armed forces.

c. *Explanation.* "Under circumstances such as to endanger human life" refers to a reasonable potentiality for harm to human beings in general. The test is not whether the life was in fact endangered but whether, considering the circumstances surrounding the wrongful discharge of the weapon, the act was unsafe to human life in general.

d. *Lesser included offenses.* See paragraph 3 of this part and Appendix 12A.

e. *Maximum punishment.* Dishonorable discharge, forfeiture of all pay and allowances, and confinement for 1 year.

f. *Sample specification.*

In that _____ (personal jurisdiction data), did, (at/on board—location) (subject-matter jurisdiction data, if required), on or about _____ 20 ___ , wrongfully and willfully discharge a firearm, to wit: _____ , (in the mess hall of _____) (_____), under circumstances such as to endanger human life, and that said conduct was (to the prejudice of good order and discipline in the armed forces) (of a nature to bring discredit upon the armed forces) (to the prejudice of good order and discipline in the armed forces and was of a nature to bring discredit upon the armed forces).

82. Article 134—(Fleeing scene of accident)

a. *Text of statute. See* paragraph 60.

b. *Elements.*

(1) *Driver.*

(a) That the accused was the driver of a vehicle;

(b) That while the accused was driving the vehicle was involved in an accident;

(c) That the accused knew that the vehicle had been in an accident;

(d) That the accused left the scene of the accident without (providing assistance to the victim who had been struck (and injured) by the said vehicle) or (providing identification);

(e) That such leaving was wrongful; and

(f) That, under the circumstances, the conduct of the accused was to the prejudice of good order and discipline in the armed forces or was of a nature to bring discredit upon the armed forces.

(2) *Senior passenger.*

(a) That the accused was a passenger in a vehicle which was involved in an accident;

(b) That the accused knew that said vehicle had been in an accident;

(c) That the accused was the superior commissioned or noncommissioned officer of the driver, or commander of the vehicle, and wrongfully and unlawfully ordered, caused, or permitted the driver to leave the scene of the accident without (providing assistance to the victim who had been struck (and injured) by the said vehicle) (or) (providing identification); and

(d) That, under the circumstances, the conduct of the accused was to the prejudice of good order and discipline in the armed forces or was of a nature to bring discredit upon the armed forces.

c. *Explanation.*

(1) *Nature of offense.* This offense covers "hit and run" situations where there is damage to property other than the driver's vehicle or injury to someone other than the driver or a passenger in the driver's vehicle. It also covers accidents caused by the accused, even if the accused's vehicle does not contact other people, vehicles, or property.

(2) *Knowledge.* Actual knowledge that an accident has occurred is an essential element of this offense. Actual knowledge may be proved by circumstantial evidence.

(3) *Passenger.* A passenger other than a senior passenger may also be liable under this paragraph. *See* paragraph 1 of this Part.

d. *Lesser included offenses.* See paragraph 3 of this part and Appendix 12A.

e. *Maximum punishment.* Bad-conduct discharge, forfeiture of all pay and allowances, and confinement for 6 months.

f. *Sample specification.*

In that _____ (personal jurisdiction data), (the driver of) (*a passenger in) (the senior officer/ noncommissioned officer in) (_____ in) a vehicle at the time of an accident in which said vehicle was involved, and having knowledge of said accident, did, at _____ (subject-matter jurisdiction data, if required), on or about _____ 20 __ (wrongfully leave) (*by _____ , assist the driver of the said vehicle in wrongfully leaving) (wrongfully order, cause, or permit the driver to leave) the scene of the accident without (providing assistance to _____ , who had been struck (and injured) by the said vehicle) (making his/her (the driver's) identity known), and that said conduct was (to the prejudice of good order and discipline in the armed forces) (of a nature to bring discredit upon the armed forces) (to the prejudice of good order and discipline in the armed forces and was of a nature to bring discredit upon the armed forces).

[*Note: This language should be used when the accused was a passenger and is charged as a principal. *See* paragraph 1 of this part.]

83. Article 134—(Fraternization)

a. *Text of statute. See* paragraph 60.

b. *Elements.*

(1) That the accused was a commissioned or warrant officer;

(2) That the accused fraternized on terms of military equality with one or more certain enlisted member(s) in a certain manner;

(3) That the accused then knew the person(s) to be (an) enlisted member(s);

(4) That such fraternization violated the custom of the accused's service that officers shall not fraternize with enlisted members on terms of military equality; and

(5) That, under the circumstances, the conduct of the accused was to the prejudice of good order and discipline in the armed forces or was of a nature to bring discredit upon the armed forces.

c. *Explanation.*

(1) *In general.* The gist of this offense is a violation of the custom of the armed forces against fraternization. Not all contact or association between officers and enlisted persons is an offense. Whether the contact or association in question is an offense depends on the surrounding circumstances. Factors

to be considered include whether the conduct has compromised the chain of command, resulted in the appearance of partiality, or otherwise undermined good order, discipline, authority, or morale. The acts and circumstances must be such as to lead a reasonable person experienced in the problems of military leadership to conclude that the good order and discipline of the armed forces has been prejudiced by their tendency to compromise the respect of enlisted persons for the professionalism, integrity, and obligations of an officer.

(2) *Regulations.* Regulations, directives, and orders may also govern conduct between officer and enlisted personnel on both a service-wide and a local basis. Relationships between enlisted persons of different ranks, or between officers of different ranks may be similarly covered. Violations of such regulations, directives, or orders may be punishable under Article 92. *See* paragraph 16.

d. *Lesser included offenses.* See paragraph 3 of this part and Appendix 12A.

e. *Maximum punishment.* Dismissal, forfeiture of all pay and allowances, and confinement for 2 years.

f. *Sample specification.*

In that _____ (personal jurisdiction data), did, (at/on board—location) (subject-matter jurisdiction data, if required), on or about _____ 20 __ , knowingly fraternize with _____ , an enlisted person, on terms of military equality, to wit: _____ , in violation of the custom of (the Naval Service of the United States) (the United States Army) (the United States Air Force) (the United States Coast Guard) that officers shall not fraternize with enlisted persons on terms of military equality, and that said conduct was (to the prejudice of good order and discipline in the armed forces) (of a nature to bring discredit upon the armed forces) (to the prejudice of good order and discipline in the armed forces and was of a nature to bring discredit upon the armed forces).

84. Article 134—(Gambling with subordinate)

a. *Text of statute.* See paragraph 60.

b. *Elements.*

(1) That the accused gambled with a certain servicemember;

(2) That the accused was then a noncommissioned or petty officer;

(3) That the servicemember was not then a noncommissioned or petty officer and was subordinate to the accused;

(4) That the accused knew that the servicemember was not then a noncommissioned or petty officer and was subordinate to the accused; and

(5) That, under the circumstances, the conduct of the accused was to the prejudice of good order and discipline in the armed forces or was of a nature to bring discredit upon the armed forces.

c. *Explanation.* This offense can only be committed by a noncommissioned or petty officer gambling with an enlisted person of less than noncommissioned or petty officer rank. Gambling by an officer with an enlisted person may be a violation of Article 133. *See also* paragraph 83.

d. *Lesser included offenses.* See paragraph 3 of this part and Appendix 12A.

e. *Maximum punishment.* Confinement for 3 months and forfeiture of two-thirds pay per month for 3 months.

f. *Sample specification.*

In that _____ (personal jurisdiction data), did (at/on board—location) (subject-matter jurisdiction data, if required), on or about _____ 20 __ , gamble with _____ , then knowing that the said _____ was not a noncommissioned or petty officer and was subordinate to the said _____ , and that said conduct was (to the prejudice of good order and discipline in the armed forces) (of a nature to bring discredit upon the armed forces) (to the prejudice of good order and discipline in the armed forces and was of a nature to bring discredit upon the armed forces).

85. Article 134—(Homicide, negligent)

a. *Text of statute.* See paragraph 60.

b. *Elements.*

(1) That a certain person is dead;

(2) That this death resulted from the act or failure to act of the accused;

(3) That the killing by the accused was unlawful;

(4) That the act or failure to act of the accused which caused the death amounted to simple negligence; and

(5) That, under the circumstances, the conduct of the accused was to the prejudice of good order and

discipline in the armed forces or was of a nature to bring discredit upon the armed forces.

c. *Explanation.*

(1) *Nature of offense.* Negligent homicide is any unlawful homicide which is the result of simple negligence. An intent to kill or injure is not required.

(2) *Simple negligence.* Simple negligence is the absence of due care, that is, an act or omission of a person who is under a duty to use due care which exhibits a lack of that degree of care of the safety of others which a reasonably careful person would have exercised under the same or similar circumstances. Simple negligence is a lesser degree of carelessness than culpable negligence. *See* paragraph 44c(2)(*a*).

d. *Lesser included offenses.* See paragraph 3 of this part and Appendix 12A.

e. *Maximum punishment.* Dishonorable discharge, forfeiture of all pay and allowances, and confinement for 3 years.

f. *Sample specification.*

    In that _____ (personal jurisdiction data), did, (at/on board—location) (subject-matter jurisdiction data, if required), on or about _____ 20 __ , unlawfully kill _____ , (by negligently _____ the said _____ (in) (on) the _____ with a _____) (by driving a (motor vehicle) (_____) against the said _____ in a negligent manner) (_____), and that said conduct was (to the prejudice of good order and discipline in the armed forces) (of a nature to bring discredit upon the armed forces) (to the prejudice of good order and discipline in the armed forces and was of a nature to bring discredit upon the armed forces).

86. Article 134—(Impersonating a commissioned, warrant, noncommissioned, or petty officer, or an agent or official)

a. *Text of statute. See* paragraph 60.

b. *Elements.*

(1) That the accused impersonated a commissioned, warrant, noncommissioned, or petty officer, or an agent of superior authority of one of the armed forces of the United States, or an official of a certain government, in a certain manner;

(2) That the impersonation was wrongful and willful; and

(3) That, under the circumstances, the conduct of the accused was to the prejudice of good order and

discipline in the armed forces or was of a nature to bring discredit upon the armed forces.

[Note 1: If intent to defraud is in issue, add the following additional element after (2), above: That the accused did so with the intent to defraud a certain person or organization in a certain manner;].

[Note 2: If the accused is charged with impersonating an official of a certain government without an intent to defraud, use the following additional element after (2) above: That the accused committed one or more acts which exercised or asserted the authority of the office the accused claimed to have;].

c. *Explanation.*

(1) *Nature of offense.* Impersonation does not depend upon the accused deriving a benefit from the deception or upon some third party being misled, although this is an aggravating factor.

(2) *Willfulness.* "Willful" means with the knowledge that one is falsely holding one's self out as such.

(3) *Intent to defraud. See* paragraph 49c(14).

d. *Lesser included offenses.* See paragraph 3 of this part and Appendix 12A.

e. *Maximum punishment.* Impersonating a commissioned, warrant, noncommissioned, or petty officer, or an agent or official.

(1) *With intent to defraud.* Dishonorable discharge, forfeiture of all pay and allowances, and confinement for 3 years.

(2) *All other cases.* Bad-conduct discharge, forfeiture of all pay and allowances, and confinement for 6 months.

f. *Sample specification.*

    In that _____ (personal jurisdiction data), did, (at/on board—location) (subject-matter jurisdiction data, if required), on or about _____ 20 __ , wrongfully and willfully impersonate (a (commissioned officer) (warrant officer) (noncommissioned officer) (petty officer) (agent of superior authority) of the (Army) (Navy) (Marine Corps) (Air Force) (Coast Guard)) (an official of the Government of _____) by (publicly wearing the uniform and insignia of rank of a (lieutenant of the _____) (_____)) (showing the credentials of _____) (_____) (*with intent to defraud _____ by _____) (**and (exercised) (asserted) the authority of _____ by _____), and that said conduct was (to the prejudice of good order and discipline in the armed forces) (of a nature to bring discredit upon the armed forces) (to the prejudice of good order and discipline in the armed forces and was of a nature to bring discredit upon the armed forces).

[*See subsection b note 1.]
[**See subsection b note 2.]

87. Deleted—See Appendix 27

Indecent acts or liberties with a child was deleted by Executive Order 13447, 72 Fed. Reg. 56179 (Oct. 2, 2007). See Appendix 25.

88. Deleted—See Appendix 27

Indecent exposure was deleted by Executive Order 13447, 72 Fed. Reg. 56179 (Oct. 2, 2007). See Appendix 25.

89. Article 134—(Indecent language)

a. *Text of statute.* See paragraph 60.

b. *Elements.*

(1) That the accused orally or in writing communicated to another person certain language;

(2) That such language was indecent; and

(3) That, under the circumstances, the conduct of the accused was to the prejudice of good order and discipline in the armed forces or was of a nature to bring discredit upon the armed forces.

[Note: In appropriate cases add the following element after element (1): That the person to whom the language was communicated was a child under the age of 16.]

c. *Explanation.* "Indecent" language is that which is grossly offensive to modesty, decency, or propriety, or shocks the moral sense, because of its vulgar, filthy, or disgusting nature, or its tendency to incite lustful thought. Language is indecent if it tends reasonably to corrupt morals or incite libidinous thoughts. The language must violate community standards. *See* paragraph 45 if the communication was made in the physical presence of a child.

d. *Lesser included offenses.* See paragraph 3 of this part and Appendix 12A.

e. *Maximum punishment.* Indecent or insulting language.

(1) *Communicated to any child under the age of 16 years.* Dishonorable discharge, forfeiture of all pay and allowances, and confinement for 2 years.

(2) *Other cases.* Bad-conduct discharge; forfeiture of all pay and allowances, and confinement for 6 months.

f. *Sample specification.*

In that _____ (personal jurisdiction data), did (at/on board—location) (subject-matter jurisdiction data, if required), on or about _____ 20 ___ , (orally) (in writing) communicate to _____ , (a child under the age of 16 years), certain indecent language, to wit: _____ , and that said conduct was (to the prejudice of good order and discipline in the armed forces) (of a nature to bring discredit upon the armed forces) (to the prejudice of good order and discipline in the armed forces and was of a nature to bring discredit upon the armed forces).

90. Article 134—(Indecent conduct)

a. *Text of Statute.* See paragraph 60.

b. *Elements.*

(1) That the accused engaged in certain conduct;

(2) That the conduct was indecent; and

(3) That, under the circumstances, the conduct of the accused was to the prejudice of good order and discipline in the armed forces or was of a nature to bring discredit upon the armed forces.

c. *Explanation.*

(1) "Indecent" means that form of immorality relating to sexual impurity which is grossly vulgar, obscene, and repugnant to common propriety, and tends to excite sexual desire or deprave morals with respect to sexual relations.

(2) Indecent conduct includes offenses previously proscribed by "Indecent acts with another" except that the presence of another person is no longer required. For purposes of this offense, the words "conduct" and "act" are synonymous. For child offenses, some indecent conduct may be included in the definition of lewd act and preempted by Article 120b(c). *See* paragraph 60c(5)(a).

d. *Lesser included offense.* See paragraph 3 of this part and Appendix 12A.

e. *Maximum punishment.* Dishonorable discharge, forfeiture of all pay and allowances, and confinement for 5 years.

f. *Sample specification.* In that _____ (personal jurisdiction data), did (at/on board – location) (subject-matter jurisdiction data, if required), on or about (date), (wrongfully commit indecent conduct, to wit: _____), and that said conduct was (to the prejudice of good order and discipline in the armed forces) (of a nature to bring discredit upon the armed forces) (to the prejudice of good order and discipline in the armed forces and was of a nature to bring discredit upon the armed forces).

91. Article 134—(Jumping from vessel into the water)

a. *Text of statute. See* paragraph 60.

b. *Elements.*

(1) That the accused jumped from a vessel in use by the armed forces into the water;

(2) That such act by the accused was wrongful and intentional; and

(3) That, under the circumstances, the conduct of the accused was to the prejudice of good order and discipline in the armed forces or was of a nature to bring discredit upon the armed forces.

c. *Explanation.* "In use by" means any vessel operated by or under the control of the armed forces. This offense may be committed at sea, at anchor, or in port.

d. *Lesser included offenses.* See paragraph 3 of this part and Appendix 12A.

e. *Maximum punishment.* Bad-conduct discharge, forfeiture of all pay and allowances, and confinement for 6 months.

f. *Sample specification.*

In that _____ (personal jurisdiction data), did, on board _____ , at (location), on or about _____ 20 ___ , wrongfully and intentionally jump from _____ , a vessel in use by the armed forces, into the (sea) (lake) (river), and that said conduct was (to the prejudice of good order and discipline in the armed forces) (of a nature to bring discredit upon the armed forces) (to the prejudice of good order and discipline in the armed forces and was of a nature to bring discredit upon the armed forces).

92. Article 134—(Kidnapping)

a. *Text of statute. See* paragraph 60.

b. *Elements.*

(1) That the accused seized, confined, inveigled, decoyed, or carried away a certain person;

(2) That the accused then held such person against that person's will;

(3) That the accused did so willfully and wrongfully; and

(4) That, under the circumstances, the conduct of the accused was to the prejudice of good order and discipline in the armed forces or was of a nature to bring discredit upon the armed forces.

c. *Explanation.*

(1) *Inveigle, decoy.* "Inveigle" means to lure, lead astray, or entice by false representations or other deceitful means. For example, a person who entices another to ride in a car with a false promise to take the person to a certain destination has inveigled the passenger into the car. "Decoy" means to entice or lure by means of some fraud, trick, or temptation. For example, one who lures a child into a trap with candy has decoyed the child.

(2) *Held.* "Held" means detained. The holding must be more than a momentary or incidental detention. For example, a robber who holds the victim at gunpoint while the victim hands over a wallet, or a rapist who throws his victim to the ground, does not, by such acts, commit kidnapping. On the other hand, if, before or after such robbery or rape, the victim is involuntarily transported some substantial distance, as from a housing area to a remote area of the base or post, this may be kidnapping, in addition to robbery or rape.

(3) *Against the will.* "Against that person's will" means that the victim was held involuntarily. The involuntary nature of the detention may result from force, mental or physical coercion, or from other means, including false representations. If the victim is incapable of having a recognizable will, as in the case of a very young child or a mentally incompetent person, the holding must be against the will of the victim's parents or legal guardian. Evidence of the availability or nonavailability to the victim of means of exit or escape is relevant to the voluntariness of the detention, as is evidence of threats or force, or lack thereof, by the accused to detain the victim.

(4) *Willfully.* The accused must have specifically intended to hold the victim against the victim's will to be guilty of kidnapping. An accidental detention will not suffice. The holding need not have been for financial or personal gain or for any other particular purpose. It may be an aggravating circumstance that the kidnapping was for ransom, however. *See* R.C.M. 1001(b)(4).

(5) *Wrongfully.* "Wrongfully" means without justification or excuse. For example, a law enforcement official may justifiably apprehend and detain, by force if necessary (*see* R.C.M. 302(d)(3)), a person

reasonably believed to have committed an offense. An official who unlawfully uses the official's authority to apprehend someone is not guilty of kidnapping, but may be guilty of unlawful detention. *See* paragraph 21. It is not wrongful under this paragraph and therefore not kidnapping for a parent or legal guardian to seize and hold that parent's or legal guardian's minor child.

d. *Lesser included offenses.* See paragraph 3 of this part and Appendix 12A.

e. *Maximum punishment.* Dishonorable discharge, forfeiture of all pay and allowances, and confinement for life without eligibility for parole.

f. *Sample specification.*

In that _____ , (personal jurisdiction data), did, (at/on board—location) (subject-matter jurisdiction data, if required), on or about _____ 20 _ , willfully and wrongfully (seize) (confine) (inveigle) (decoy) (carry away) and hold _____ (a minor whose parent or legal guardian the accused was not) (a person not a minor) against his/her will, and that said conduct was (to the prejudice of good order and discipline in the armed forces) (of a nature to bring discredit upon the armed forces) (to the prejudice of good order and discipline in the armed forces and was of a nature to bring discredit upon the armed forces).

93. Article 134—(Mail: taking, opening, secreting, destroying, or stealing)

a. *Text of statute. See* paragraph 60.

b. *Elements.*

(1) *Taking.*

(a) That the accused took certain mail matter;

(b) That such taking was wrongful;

(c) That the mail matter was taken by the accused before it was delivered to or received by the addressee;

(d) That such taking was with the intent to obstruct the correspondence or pry into the business or secrets of any person or organization; and

(e) That, under the circumstances, the conduct of the accused was to the prejudice of good order and discipline in the armed forces or was of a nature to bring discredit upon the armed forces.

(2) *Opening, secreting, destroying, or stealing.*

(a) That the accused opened, secreted, destroyed, or stole certain mail matter;

(b) That such opening, secreting, destroying, or stealing was wrongful;

(c) That the mail matter was opened, secreted, destroyed, or stolen by the accused before it was delivered to or received by the addressee; and

(d) That, under the circumstances, the conduct of the accused was to the prejudice of good order and discipline in the armed forces or was of a nature to bring discredit upon the armed forces.

c. *Explanation.* These offenses are intended to protect the mail and mail system. "Mail matter" means any matter deposited in a postal system of any government or any authorized depository thereof or in official mail channels of the United States or an agency thereof including the armed forces. The value of the mail matter is not an element. *See* paragraph 46c(1) concerning "steal."

d. *Lesser included offenses.* See paragraph 3 of this part and Appendix 12A.

e. *Maximum punishment.* Dishonorable discharge, forfeiture of all pay and allowances, and confinement for 5 years.

f. *Sample specifications.*

(1) *Taking.*

In that _____ (personal jurisdiction data), did, (at/on board—location) (subject-matter jurisdiction data, if required), on or about _____ 20 _ , wrongfully take certain mail matter, to wit: (a) (letter(s)) (postal card(s)) (package(s)), addressed to _____ , (out of the (_____ Post Office _____) (orderly room of _____) (unit mail box of _____) (_____)) (from _____) before (it) (they) (was) (were) (delivered) (actually received) (to) (by) the (addressee) with intent to (obstruct the correspondence) (pry into the (business) (secrets)) of _____ , and that said conduct was (to the prejudice of good order and discipline in the armed forces) (of a nature to bring discredit upon the armed forces) (to the prejudice of good order and discipline in the armed forces and was of a nature to bring discredit upon the armed forces).

(2) *Opening, secreting, destroying, or stealing.*

In that _____ (personal jurisdiction data), did, (at/on board—location) (subject-matter jurisdiction data, if required), on or about _____ , 20 _ , (wrongfully (open) (secret) (destroy)) (steal) certain mail matter, to wit: (a) (letter(s)) (postal card(s)) (package(s)) addressed to _____ , which said (letters(s)) (_____) (was) (were) then (in (the _____ Post Office _____) (orderly room of _____) (unit mail box of _____) (custody of _____) (_____)) (had previously been committed to _____ , (a representative of _____ ,) (an official agency for the transmission of communications)) before said (letter(s)) (_____) (was) (were) (delivered) (actually received) (to) (by) the (addressee), and that said conduct was (to the prejudice of good order and discipline in the armed forces) (of a nature to bring discredit upon the armed forces) (to the prejudice of good order and discipline in the armed forces and was of a nature to bring discredit upon the armed forces).

94. Article 134—(Mails: depositing or causing to be deposited obscene matters in)

a. *Text of statute. See* paragraph 60.

b. *Elements.*

(1) That the accused deposited or caused to be deposited in the mails certain matter for mailing and delivery;

(2) That the act was done wrongfully and knowingly;

(3) That the matter was obscene; and

(4) That, under the circumstances, the conduct of the accused was to the prejudice of good order and discipline in the armed forces or was of a nature to bring discredit upon the armed forces.

c. *Explanation.* Whether something is obscene is a question of fact. "Obscene" is synonymous with "indecent" as the latter is defined in paragraph 89c. The matter must violate community standards of decency or obscenity and must go beyond customary limits of expression. "Knowingly" means the accused deposited the material with knowledge of its nature.

d. *Lesser included offenses.* See paragraph 3 of this part and Appendix 12A.

e. *Maximum punishment.* Dishonorable discharge, forfeiture of all pay and allowances, and confinement for 5 years.

f. *Sample specification.*

In that _____ (personal jurisdiction data), did, (at/on board—location) (subject-matter jurisdiction data, if required), on or about ___ 20 ___ , wrongfully and knowingly (deposit) (cause to be deposited) in the (United States) (___) mails, for

mailing and delivery a (letter) (picture) (___) (containing) (portraying) (suggesting) (___) certain obscene matters, to wit: ___ , and that said conduct was (to the prejudice of good order and discipline in the armed forces) (of a nature to bring discredit upon the armed forces) (to the prejudice of good order and discipline in the armed forces and was of a nature to bring discredit upon the armed forces).

95. Article 134—(Misprision of serious offense)

a. *Text of statute. See* paragraph 60.

b. *Elements.*

(1) That a certain serious offense was committed by a certain person;

(2) That the accused knew that the said person had committed the serious offense;

(3) That, thereafter, the accused concealed the serious offense and failed to make it known to civilian or military authorities as soon as possible;

(4) That the concealing was wrongful; and

(5) That, under the circumstances, the conduct of the accused was to the prejudice of good order and discipline in the armed forces or was of a nature to bring discredit upon the armed forces.

c. *Explanation.*

(1) *In general.* Misprision of a serious offense is the offense of concealing a serious offense committed by another but without such previous concert with or subsequent assistance to the principal as would make the accused an accessory. *See* paragraph 3. An intent to benefit the principal is not necessary to this offense.

(2) *Serious offense.* For purposes of this paragraph, a "serious offense" is any offense punishable under the authority of the code by death or by confinement for a term exceeding 1 year.

(3) *Positive act of concealment.* A mere failure or refusal to disclose the serious offense without some positive act of concealment does not make one guilty of this offense. Making a false entry in an account book for the purpose of concealing a theft committed by another is an example of a positive act of concealment.

d. *Lesser included offenses.* See paragraph 3 of this part and Appendix 12A.

e. *Maximum punishment.* Dishonorable discharge,

forfeiture of all pay and allowances, and confinement for 3 years.

f. *Sample specification.*

In that _____ (personal jurisdiction data), having knowledge that _____ had actually committed a serious offense to wit: (the murder of _____) (_____), did, (at/on board—location) (subject-matter jurisdiction data, if required), from about _____ 20 ___ , to about _____ 20 ___ , wrongfully conceal such serious offense by _____ and fail to make the same known to the civil or military authorities as soon as possible, and that said conduct was (to the prejudice of good order and discipline in the armed forces) (of a nature to bring discredit upon the armed forces) (to the prejudice of good order and discipline in the armed forces and was of a nature to bring discredit upon the armed forces).

96. Article 134—(Obstructing justice)

a. *Text of statute. See* paragraph 60.

b. *Elements.*

(1) That the accused wrongfully did a certain act;

(2) That the accused did so in the case of a certain person against whom the accused had reason to believe there were or would be criminal proceedings pending;

(3) That the act was done with the intent to influence, impede, or otherwise obstruct the due administration of justice; and

(4) That, under the circumstances, the conduct of the accused was to the prejudice of good order and discipline in the armed forces or was of a nature to bring discredit upon the armed forces.

c. *Explanation.* This offense may be based on conduct that occurred before preferral of charges. Actual obstruction of justice is not an element of this offense. For purposes of this paragraph "criminal proceedings" includes nonjudicial punishment proceedings under Part V of this Manual. Examples of obstruction of justice include wrongfully influencing, intimidating, impeding, or injuring a witness, a person acting on charges under this chapter, an investigating officer under R.C.M. 406, or a party; and by means of bribery, intimidation, misrepresentation, or force or threat of force delaying or preventing communication of information relating to a violation of any criminal statute of the United States to a person authorized by a department, agency, or armed

force of the United States to conduct or engage in investigations or prosecutions of such offenses; or endeavoring to do so. *See also* paragraph 22 and Article 37.

d. *Lesser included offenses.* See paragraph 3 of this part and Appendix 12A.

e. *Maximum punishment.* Dishonorable discharge, forfeiture of all pay and allowances, and confinement for 5 years.

f. *Sample specification.*

In that _____ (personal jurisdiction data), did, (at/on board—location) (subject-matter jurisdiction data, if required), on or about _____ 20 ___ , wrongfully (endeavor to) (impede (a trial by court-martial) (an investigation) (a preliminary hearing) (_____)) [influence the actions of _____ , (a trial counsel of the court-martial) (a defense counsel of the court-martial) (an officer responsible for making a recommendation concerning disposition of charges) (_____)] [(influence) (alter) the testimony of _____ as a witness before a (court-martial) (an investigating officer) (a preliminary hearing) (_____)] in the case of by [(promising) (offering) (giving) to the said _____ , (the sum of $ _____) (_____ , of a value of about $ _____)] [communicating to the said _____ a threat to _____] [_____], (if) (unless) he/she, the said _____ , would [recommend dismissal of the charges against said _____] [(wrongfully refuse to testify) (testify falsely concerning _____) (_____)] [(at such trial)(before such investigating officer)(before such preliminary hearing officer)] [_____], and that said conduct was (to the prejudice of good order and discipline in the armed forces) (of a nature to bring discredit upon the armed forces) (to the prejudice of good order and discipline in the armed forces and was of a nature to bring discredit upon the armed forces).

96a. Art 134—(Wrongful interference with an adverse administrative proceeding)

a. *Text of statute. See* paragraph 60.

b. *Elements.*

(1) That the accused wrongfully did a certain act;

(2) That the accused did so in the case of a certain person against whom the accused had reason to believe there was or would be an adverse administrative proceeding pending;

(3) That the act was done with the intent to influence, impede, or obstruct the conduct of such ad-

ministrative proceeding, or otherwise obstruct the due administration of justice;

(4) That under the circumstances, the conduct of the accused was to the prejudice of good order and discipline in the armed forces or was of a nature to bring discredit upon the armed forces.

c. *Explanation.* For purposes of this paragraph "adverse administrative proceeding" includes any administrative proceeding or action, initiated against a servicemember, that could lead to discharge, loss of special or incentive pay, administrative reduction in grade, loss of a security clearance, bar to reenlistment, or reclassification. Examples of wrongful interference include wrongfully influencing, intimidating, impeding, or injuring a witness, an investigator, or other person acting on an adverse administrative action; by means of bribery, intimidation, misrepresentation, or force or threat of force delaying or preventing communication of information relating to such administrative proceeding; and, the wrongful destruction or concealment of information relevant to such adverse administrative proceeding.

d. *Lesser included offenses.* See paragraph 3 of this part and Appendix 12A.

e. *Maximum punishment.* Dishonorable discharge, forfeiture of all pay and allowances, and confinement for 5 years.

f. *Sample specification.*

In that _____ (personal jurisdiction data), did (at/on board-location) (subject-matter jurisdiction data, if required), on or about _____ 20 ___ , (wrongfully endeavor to) [impede (an adverse administrative proceeding) (an investigation) (_____)] [influence the actions of _____ , (an officer responsible for making a recommendation concerning the adverse administrative action) (an individual responsible for making a decision concerning an adverse administrative proceeding) (an individual responsible for processing an adverse administrative proceeding) (_____)] [(influence)(alter) the testimony of _____ a witness before (a board established to consider an administrative proceeding or elimination) (a preliminary hearing officer) (_____)] in the case of _____ , by](promising) (offering) (giving) to the said _____ , (the sum of $ _____) (_____ , of a value of about $ _____)] [communicating to the said _____ a threat to _____] [_____], (if) (unless) the said _____ , would [recommend dismissal of the

action against said _____] [(wrongfully refuse to testify) (testify falsely concerning _____) (_____)] [(at such administrative proceeding) (before such preliminary hearing officer) (before such administrative board)] [_____], and that said conduct was (to the prejudice of good order and discipline in the armed forces) (of a nature to bring discredit upon the armed forces) (to the prejudice of good order and discipline in the armed forces and was of a nature to bring discredit upon the armed forces).

97. Article 134—(Pandering and prostitution)

a. *Text of statute.* See paragraph 60.

b. *Elements.*

(1) *Prostitution.*

(a) That the accused engaged in a sexual act with another person not the accused's spouse;

(b) That the accused did so for the purpose of receiving money or other compensation;

(c) That this act was wrongful; and

(d) That, under the circumstances, the conduct of the accused was to the prejudice of good order and discipline in the armed forces or was of a nature to bring discredit upon the armed forces.

(2) *Patronizing a prostitute.*

(a) That the accused engaged in a sexual act with another person not the accused's spouse;

(b) That the accused compelled, induced, enticed, or procured such person to engage in a sexual act in exchange for money or other compensation; and

(c) That this act was wrongful; and

(d) That, under the circumstances, the conduct of the accused was to the prejudice of good order and discipline in the armed forces or was of a nature to bring discredit upon the armed forces.

(3) *Pandering by inducing, enticing, or procuring act of prostitution.*

(a) That the accused induced, enticed, or procured a certain person to engage in a sexual act for hire and reward with a person to be directed to said person by the accused;

(b) That this inducing, enticing, or procuring was wrongful;

(c) That, under the circumstances, the conduct of the accused was to the prejudice of good order and discipline in the armed forces or was of a nature to bring discredit upon the armed forces.

(4) *Pandering by arranging or receiving consideration for arranging for a sexual act.*

(a) That the accused arranged for, or received valuable consideration for arranging for, a certain person to engage in a sexual act with another person;

(b) That the arranging (and receipt of consideration) was wrongful; and

(c) That, under the circumstances, the conduct of the accused was to the prejudice of good order and discipline in the armed forces or was of a nature to bring discredit upon the armed forces.

c. *Explanation.*

(1) Prostitution may be committed by males or females.

(2) *Sexual act. See* paragraph 45.a.(g)(1).

d. *Lesser included offenses. See* paragraph 3 of this part and Appendix 12A.

e. *Maximum punishment.*

(1) *Prostitution and patronizing a prostitute.* Dishonorable discharge, forfeiture of all pay and allowances, and confinement for 1 year.

(2) *Pandering.* Dishonorable discharge, forfeiture of all pay and allowances, and confinement for 5 years.

f. *Sample specifications.*

(1) *Prostitution.*

In that _____ (personal jurisdiction data), did, (at/on board-location) (subject-matter jurisdiction data, if required), on or about _____ 20 _ , wrongfully engage in (a sexual act) (sexual acts) with _____ , a person not his/her spouse, for the purpose of receiving (money) (_____), and that said conduct was (to the prejudice of good order and discipline in the armed forces) (of a nature to bring discredit upon the armed forces) (to the prejudice of good order and discipline in the armed forces and was of a nature to bring discredit upon the armed forces).

(2) *Patronizing a prostitute.*

In that _____ (personal jurisdiction data), did, (at/on board location) (subject-matter jurisdiction data, if required), on or about _____ 20 _ , wrongfully (compel) (induce) (entice) (procure) _____ , a person not his/her spouse, to engage in (a sexual act) (sexual acts) with the accused in exchange for (money) (_____), and that said conduct was (to the prejudice of good order and

discipline in the armed forces) (of a nature to bring discredit upon the armed forces) (to the prejudice of good order and discipline in the armed forces and was of a nature to bring discredit upon the armed forces).

(3) *Inducing, enticing, or procuring act of prostitution.*

In that _____ (personal jurisdiction data), did (at/on board-location) (subject-matter jurisdiction data, if required), on or about _____ 20 _ , wrongfully (induce)(entice)(procure) _____ to engage in (a sexual act) (sexual acts for hire and reward) with persons to be directed to him/her by the said _____ , and that said conduct was (to the prejudice of good order and discipline in the armed forces) (of a nature to bring discredit upon the armed forces) (to the prejudice of good order and discipline in the armed forces and was of a nature to bring discredit upon the armed forces).

(4) *Arranging, or receiving consideration for arranging for sexual intercourse or sodomy.*

In that _____ (personal jurisdiction data), did, (at/on board-location) (subject-matter jurisdiction data, if required), on or about _____ 20 _ , wrongfully (arrange for) (receive valuable consideration, to wit: _____ on account of arranging for) _____ to engage in (an act) (acts) of (sexual intercourse) (sodomy) with _____ , and that said conduct was (to the prejudice of good order and discipline in the armed forces) (of a nature to bring discredit upon the armed forces) (to the prejudice of good order and discipline in the armed forces and was of a nature to bring discredit upon the armed forces).

97a. Article 134—(Parole, Violation of)

a. *Text of statute. See* paragraph 60.

b. *Elements.*

(1) That the accused was a prisoner as the result of a court-martial conviction or other criminal proceeding;

(2) That the accused was on parole;

(3) That there were certain conditions of parole that the parolee was bound to obey;

(4) That the accused violated the conditions of parole by doing an act or failing to do an act; and

(5) That, under the circumstances, the conduct of the accused was to the prejudice of good order and

discipline in the armed forces or was of a nature to bring discredit upon the armed forces.

c. *Explanation.*

(1) "Prisoner" refers only to those in confinement resulting from conviction at a court-martial or other criminal proceeding.

(2) "Parole" is defined as "word of honor." A prisoner on parole, or parolee, has agreed to adhere to a parole plan and conditions of parole. A "parole plan" is a written or oral agreement made by the prisoner prior to parole to do or refrain from doing certain acts or activities. A parole plan may include a residence requirement stating where and with whom a parolee will live, and a requirement that the prisoner have an offer of guaranteed employment. "Conditions of parole" include the parole plan and other reasonable and appropriate conditions of parole, such as paying restitution, beginning or continuing treatment for alcohol or drug abuse, or paying a fine ordered executed as part of the prisoner's court-martial sentence. In return for giving his or her "word of honor" to abide by a parole plan and conditions of parole, the prisoner is granted parole.

d. *Lesser included offenses.* See paragraph 3 of this part and Appendix 12A.

e. *Maximum punishment.* Bad-conduct discharge, confinement for 6 months, and forfeiture of two-thirds pay per month for 6 months.

f. *Sample specifications.*

In that _____ (personal jurisdiction data), a prisoner on parole, did, (at/on board—location), on or about _____ 20 ___ , violate the conditions of his/her parole by _____ , and that said conduct was (to the prejudice of good order and discipline in the armed forces) (of a nature to bring discredit upon the armed forces) (to the prejudice of good order and discipline in the armed forces and was of a nature to bring discredit upon the armed forces).

98. Article 134—(Perjury: subornation of)

a. *Text of statute. See* paragraph 60.

b. *Elements.*

(1) That the accused induced and procured a certain person to take an oath or its equivalent and to falsely testify, depose, or state upon such oath or its equivalent concerning a certain matter;

(2) That the oath or its equivalent was adminis-

tered to said person in a matter in which an oath or its equivalent was required or authorized by law;

(3) That the oath or its equivalent was administered by a person having authority to do so;

(4) That upon the oath or its equivalent said person willfully made or subscribed a certain statement;

(5) That the statement was material;

(6) That the statement was false;

(7) That the accused and the said person did not then believe that the statement was true; and

(8) That, under the circumstances, the conduct of the accused was to the prejudice of good order and discipline in the armed forces or was of a nature to bring discredit upon the armed forces.

c. *Explanation. See* paragraph 57c for applicable principles. "Induce and procure" means to influence, persuade, or cause.

d. *Lesser included offenses.* See paragraph 3 of this part and Appendix 12A.

e. *Maximum punishment.* Dishonorable discharge, forfeiture of all pay and allowances, and confinement for 5 years.

f. *Sample specification.*

In that _____ (personal jurisdiction data), did, (at/on board—location) (subject-matter jurisdiction data, if required), on or about _____ 20 ___ , procure _____ to commit perjury by inducing him/her, the said _____ , to take a lawful (oath) (affirmation) in a (trial by court-martial of _____) (trial by a court of competent jurisdiction, to wit: _____ of _____) (deposition for use in a trial by _____ of _____) (_____) that he/she, the said _____ , would (testify) (depose) (_____) truly, and to (testify) (depose) (_____) willfully, corruptly, and contrary to such (oath) (affirmation) in substance that _____ , which (testimony) (deposition) (_____) was upon a material matter and which the accused and the said _____ did not then believe to be true, and that said conduct was (to the prejudice of good order and discipline in the armed forces) (of a nature to bring discredit upon the armed forces) (to the prejudice of good order and discipline in the armed forces and was of a nature to bring discredit upon the armed forces).

99. Article 134—(Public record: altering, concealing, removing, mutilating, obliterating, or destroying)

a. *Text of statute. See* paragraph 60.

b. *Elements.*

(1) That the accused altered, concealed, removed, mutilated, obliterated, destroyed, or took with the intent to alter, conceal, remove, mutilate, obliterate, or destroy, a certain public record;

(2) That the act of the accused was willful and unlawful; and

(3) That, under the circumstances, the conduct of the accused was to the prejudice of good order and discipline in the armed forces or was of a nature to bring discredit upon the armed forces.

c. *Explanation.* "Public records" include records, reports, statements, or data compilations, in any form, of public offices or agencies, setting forth the activities of the office or agency, or matters observed pursuant to duty imposed by law as to which matters there was a duty to report. "Public records" includes classified matters.

d. *Lesser included offenses.* See paragraph 3 of this part and Appendix 12A.

e. *Maximum punishment.* Dishonorable discharge, forfeiture of all pay and allowances, and confinement for 3 years.

f. *Sample specification.*

In that _____ (personal jurisdiction data), did, (at/on board—location) (subject-matter jurisdiction data, if required), on or about _____ 20 __ , willfully and unlawfully ((alter) (conceal) (remove) (mutilate) (obliterate) (destroy)) (take with intent to (alter) (conceal) (remove) (mutilate) (obliterate) (destroy)) a public record, to wit: _____ , and that said conduct was (to the prejudice of good order and discipline in the armed forces) (of a nature to bring discredit upon the armed forces) (to the prejudice of good order and discipline in the armed forces and was of a nature to bring discredit upon the armed forces).

100. Article 134—(Quarantine: medical, breaking)

a. *Text of statute. See* paragraph 60.

b. *Elements.*

(1) That a certain person ordered the accused into medical quarantine;

(2) That the person was authorized to order the accused into medical quarantine;

(3) That the accused knew of this medical quarantine and the limits thereof;

(4) That the accused went beyond the limits of the medical quarantine before being released therefrom by proper authority; and

(5) That, under the circumstances, the conduct of the accused was to the prejudice of good order and discipline in the armed forces or was of a nature to bring discredit upon the armed forces.

c. *Explanation.* None.

d. *Lesser included offenses.* See paragraph 3 of this part and Appendix 12A.

e. *Maximum punishment.* Confinement for 6 months and forfeiture of two-thirds pay per month for 6 months.

f. *Sample specification.*

In that _____ (personal jurisdiction data) having been placed in medical quarantine by a person authorized to order the accused into medical quarantine, did, (at/on board—location) (subject-matter jurisdiction data, if required), on or about _____ 20 __ , break said medical quarantine, and that said conduct was (to the prejudice of good order and discipline in the armed forces) (of a nature to bring discredit upon the armed forces) (to the prejudice of good order and discipline in the armed forces and was of a nature to bring discredit upon the armed forces).

100a. Article 134—(Reckless endangerment)

a. *Text of statute. See* paragraph 60.

b. *Elements.*

(1) That the accused did engage in conduct;

(2) That the conduct was wrongful and reckless or wanton;

(3) That the conduct was likely to produce death or grievous bodily harm to another person; and

(4) That, under the circumstances, the conduct of the accused was to the prejudice of good order and discipline in the armed forces or was of a nature to bring discredit upon the armed forces.

c. *Explanation.*

(1) *In general.* This offense is intended to prohibit and therefore deter reckless or wanton conduct

that wrongfully creates a substantial risk of death or grievous bodily harm to others.

(2) *Wrongfulness.* Conduct is wrongful when it is without legal justification or excuse.

(3) *Recklessness.* "Reckless" conduct is conduct that exhibits a culpable disregard of foreseeable consequences to others from the act or omission involved. The accused need not intentionally cause a resulting harm or know that his conduct is substantially certain to cause that result. The ultimate question is whether, under all the circumstances, the accused's conduct was of that heedless nature that made it actually or imminently dangerous to the rights or safety of others.

(4) *Wantonness.* "Wanton" includes "Reckless" but may connote willfulness, or a disregard of probable consequences, and thus describe a more aggravated offense.

(5) *Likely to produce.* When the natural or probable consequence of particular conduct would be death or grievous bodily harm, it may be inferred that the conduct is "likely" to produce that result. *See* paragraph 54c(4)(a)(ii).

(6) *Grievous bodily harm.* "Grievous bodily harm" means serious bodily injury. It does not include minor injuries, such as a black eye or a bloody nose, but does include fractured or dislocated bones, deep cuts, torn members of the body, serious damage to internal organs, and other serious bodily injuries.

(7) *Death or injury not required.* It is not necessary that death or grievous bodily harm be actually inflicted to prove reckless endangerment.

d. *Lesser included offenses.* None.

e. *Maximum punishment.* Bad-conduct discharge, forfeiture of all pay and allowances, and confinement for 1 year.

f. *Sample specification.*

In that _____ (personal jurisdiction data), did, (at/on board—location) (subject-matter jurisdiction data, if required), on or about _____ 20 ___, wrongfully and (recklessly) (wantonly) engage in conduct, to wit: (describe conduct), conduct likely to cause death or grievous bodily harm to _____, and that said conduct was (to the prejudice of good order and discipline in the armed forces) (of a nature to bring discredit upon the armed forces) (to the prejudice of good order and discipline in the armed

forces and was of a nature to bring discredit upon the armed forces).

101. Deleted—See Executive Order 12708

Requesting commission of an offense was deleted pursuant to Executive Order 12708, effective 1 April 1990.

102. Article 134—(Restriction, breaking)

a. *Text of statute. See* paragraph 60.

b. *Elements.*

(1) That a certain person ordered the accused to be restricted to certain limits;

(2) That said person was authorized to order said restriction;

(3) That the accused knew of the restriction and the limits thereof;

(4) That the accused went beyond the limits of the restriction before being released therefrom by proper authority; and

(5) That, under the circumstances, the conduct of the accused was to the prejudice of good order and discipline in the armed forces or was of a nature to bring discredit upon the armed forces.

c. *Explanation.* Restriction is the moral restraint of a person imposed by an order directing a person to remain within certain specified limits. "Restriction" includes restriction under R.C.M. 304(a)(2), restriction resulting from imposition of either nonjudicial punishment (*see* Part V) or the sentence of a court-martial (*see* R.C.M. 1003(b)(6)), and administrative restriction in the interest of training, operations, security, or safety.

d. *Lesser included offenses.* See paragraph 3 of this part and Appendix 12A.

e. *Maximum punishment.* Confinement for 1 month and forfeiture of two-thirds pay per month for 1 month.

f. *Sample specification.*

In that _____ (personal jurisdiction data), having been restricted to the limits of _____, by a person authorized to do so, did, (at/on board—location), on or about _____ 20 ___, break said restriction, and that said conduct was (to the prejudice of good order and discipline in the armed forces) (of a nature to bring discredit upon the armed forces) (to the prejudice of good order and discipline in the armed forces and was of a nature to bring discredit upon the armed forces).

103. Article 134—(Seizure: destruction, removal, or disposal of property to prevent)

a. *Text of statute. See* paragraph 60.

b. *Elements.*

(1) That one or more persons authorized to make searches and seizures were seizing, about to seize, or endeavoring to seize certain property;

(2) That the accused destroyed, removed, or otherwise disposed of that property with intent to prevent the seizure thereof;

(3) That the accused then knew that person(s) authorized to make searches were seizing, about to seize, or endeavoring to seize the property; and

(4) That, under the circumstances, the conduct of the accused was to the prejudice of good order and discipline in the armed forces or was of a nature to bring discredit upon the armed forces.

c. *Explanation. See* Mil. R. Evid. 316(*e*) concerning military personnel who may make seizures. It is not a defense that a search or seizure was technically defective.

d. *Lesser included offenses.* See paragraph 3 of this part and Appendix 12A.

e. *Maximum punishment.* Dishonorable discharge, forfeiture of all pay and allowances, and confinement for 1 year.

f. *Sample specification.*

In that _____ (personal jurisdiction data), did, (at/on board—location) (subject matter jurisdiction data, if required), on or about _____ 20 ___ , with intent to prevent its seizure, (destroy) (remove) (dispose of) _____ , property which, as _____ then knew, (a) person(s) authorized to make searches and seizures were (seizing) (about to seize) (endeavoring to seize), and that said conduct was (to the prejudice of good order and discipline in the armed forces) (of a nature to bring discredit upon the armed forces) (to the prejudice of good order and discipline in the armed forces and was of a nature to bring discredit upon the armed forces).

103a. Article 134—(Self-injury without intent to avoid service)

a. *Text of statute. See* paragraph 60.

b. *Elements.*

(1) That the accused intentionally inflicted injury upon himself or herself;

(2) That, under the circumstances, the conduct of the accused was to the prejudice of good order and discipline in the armed forces or was of a nature to bring discredit upon the armed forces.

[Note: If the offense was committed in time of war or in a hostile fire pay zone, add the following element]

(3) That the offense was committed (in time of war) (in a hostile fire pay zone).

c. *Explanation.*

(1) *Nature of offense.* This offense differs from malingering (see paragraph 40) in that for this offense, the accused need not have harbored a design to avoid performance of any work, duty, or service which may properly or normally be expected of one in the military service. This offense is characterized by intentional self-injury under such circumstances as prejudice good order and discipline or discredit the armed forces. It is not required that the accused be unable to perform duties, or that the accused actually be absent from his or her place of duty as a result of the injury. For example, the accused may inflict the injury while on leave or pass. The circumstances and extent of injury, however, are relevant to a determination that the accused's conduct was prejudicial to good order and discipline, or service-discrediting.

Discussion

Bona fide suicide attempts should not be charged as criminal offenses. When making a determination whether the injury by the service member was a bona fide suicide attempt, the convening authority should consider factors including, but not limited to, health conditions, personal stressors, and DoD policy related to suicide prevention.

––––––––

(2) *How injury inflicted.* The injury may be inflicted by nonviolent as well as by violent means and may be accomplished by any act or omission that produces, prolongs, or aggravates a sickness or disability. Thus, voluntary starvation that results in a debility is a self-inflicted injury. Similarly, the injury may be inflicted by another at the accused's request.

d. *Lesser included offenses.* See paragraph 3 of this part and Appendix 12A.

e. *Maximum punishment.*

(1) *Intentional self-inflicted injury.* Dishonorable discharge, forfeiture of all pay and allowances, and confinement for 2 years.

(2) *Intentional self-inflicted injury in time of war or in a hostile fire pay zone.* Dishonorable discharge, forfeiture of all pay and allowances, and confinement for 5 years.

f. *Sample specification.*

In that _____ (personal jurisdiction data), did, (at/on board—location) (in a hostile fire pay zone) on or about _____ 20 ___ , (a time of war,) intentionally injure himself/herself by _____ (nature and circumstances of injury), and that said conduct was (to the prejudice of good order and discipline in the armed forces) (of a nature to bring discredit upon the armed forces) (to the prejudice of good order and discipline in the armed forces and was of a nature to bring discredit upon the armed forces).

104. Article 134—(Sentinel or lookout: offenses against or by)

a. *Text of statute. See* paragraph 60.

b. *Elements.*

(1) *Disrespect to a sentinel or lookout.*

(a) That a certain person was a sentinel or lookout;

(b) That the accused knew that said person was a sentinel or lookout;

(c) That the accused used certain disrespectful language or behaved in a certain disrespectful manner;

(d) That such language or behavior was wrongful;

(e) That such language or behavior was directed toward and within the sight or hearing of the sentinel or lookout;

(f) That said person was at the time in the execution of duties as a sentinel or lookout; and

(g) That, under the circumstances, the conduct of the accused was to the prejudice of good order and discipline in the armed forces or was of a nature to bring discredit upon the armed forces.

(2) *Loitering or wrongfully sitting on post by a sentinel or lookout.*

(a) That the accused was posted as a sentinel or lookout;

(b) That while so posted, the accused loitered or wrongfully sat down on post; and

(c) That, under the circumstances, the conduct of the accused was to the prejudice of good order and discipline in the armed forces or was of a nature to bring discredit upon the armed forces.
[Note: If the offense was committed in time of war or while the accused was receiving special pay under 37 U.S.C. § 310, add the following element after element (a): That the accused was so posted (in time of war) (while receiving special pay under 37 U.S.C. § 310).]

c. *Explanation.*

(1) *Disrespect.* For a discussion of "disrespect," *see* paragraph 13c(3).

(2) *Loitering or wrongfully sitting on post.*

(a) *In general.* The discussion set forth in paragraph 38c applies to loitering or sitting down while posted as a sentinel or lookout as well.

(b) *Loiter.* "Loiter" means to stand around, to move about slowly, to linger, or to lag behind when that conduct is in violation of known instructions or accompanied by a failure to give complete attention to duty.

d. *Lesser included offenses.* See paragraph 3 of this part and Appendix 12A.

e. *Maximum punishment.*

(1) *Disrespect to a sentinel or lookout.* Confinement for 3 months and forfeiture of two-thirds pay per month for 3 months.

(2) *Loitering or wrongfully sitting on post by a sentinel or lookout.*

(a) *In time of war or while receiving special pay under 37 U.S.C. § 310.* Dishonorable discharge, forfeiture of all pay and allowances, and confinement for 2 years.

(b) *Other cases.* Bad-conduct discharge, forfeiture of all pay and allowances, and confinement for 6 months.

f. *Sample specifications.*

(1) *Disrespect to a sentinel or lookout.*

In that _____ (personal jurisdiction data), did, (at/on board—location), on or about _____ 20 ___ , then knowing that _____ was a sentinel or lookout, (wrongfully use the following disrespectful language " _____ ," or words to that effect, to _____) (wrongfully behave in a disrespectful manner toward _____ , by

_____) a (sentinel) (lookout) in the execution of his/her duty, and that said conduct was (to the prejudice of good order and discipline in the armed forces) (of a nature to bring discredit upon the armed forces) (to the prejudice of good order and discipline in the armed forces and was of a nature to bring discredit upon the armed forces).

(2) *Loitering or wrongfully sitting down on post by a sentinel or lookout.*

In that _____ (personal jurisdiction data), while posted as a (sentinel) (lookout), did, (at/on board—location) (while receiving special pay under 37 U.S.C. § 310) on or about ____ 20 ___ , (a time of war) (loiter) (wrongfully sit down) on his/her post, and that said conduct was (to the prejudice of good order and discipline in the armed forces) (of a nature to bring discredit upon the armed forces) (to the prejudice of good order and discipline in the armed forces and was of a nature to bring discredit upon the armed forces).

105. Article 134—(Soliciting another to commit an offense)

a. *Text of statute. See* paragraph 60.

b. *Elements.*

(1) That the accused solicited or advised a certain person or persons to commit a certain offense under the code other than one of the four offenses named in Article 82;

(2) That the accused did so with the intent that the offense actually be committed; and

(3) That, under the circumstances, the conduct of the accused was to the prejudice of good order and discipline in the armed forces or was a nature to bring discredit upon the armed forces.

c. *Explanation. See* paragraph 6c. If the offense solicited was actually committed, *see also* paragraph 1.

d. *Lesser included offenses.* See paragraph 3 of this part and Appendix 12A.

e. *Maximum punishment.* Any person subject to the code who is found guilty of soliciting or advising another person to commit an offense which, if committed by one subject to the code, would be punishable under the code, shall be subject to the maximum punishment authorized for the offense solicited or advised, except that in no case shall the death penalty be imposed nor shall the period of confinement in any case, including offenses for which life im-

prisonment may be adjudged, exceed 5 years. However, any person subject to the code who is found guilty of soliciting or advising another person to commit the offense of espionage (Article 106a) shall be subject to any punishment, other than death, that a court-martial may direct.

f. *Sample specification.*

In that _____ (personal jurisdiction data), did, (at/on board—location) (subject-matter jurisdiction data, if required), on or about ____ 20 ___ , wrongfully (solicit) (advise) _____ (to disobey a general regulation, to wit: _____) (to steal _____ , of a value of (about) $ _____ , the property of _____) (to _____), by _____ , and that said conduct was (to the prejudice of good order and discipline in the armed forces) (of a nature to bring discredit upon the armed forces) (to the prejudice of good order and discipline in the armed forces and was of a nature to bring discredit upon the armed forces).

106. Article 134—(Stolen property: knowingly receiving, buying, concealing)

a. *Text of statute. See* paragraph 60.

b. *Elements.*

(1) That the accused wrongfully received, bought, or concealed certain property of some value;

(2) That the property belonged to another person;

(3) That the property had been stolen;

(4) That the accused then knew that the property had been stolen; and

(5) That, under the circumstances, the conduct of the accused was to the prejudice of good order and discipline in the armed forces or was of a nature to bring discredit upon the armed forces.

c. *Explanation.*

(1) *In general.* The actual thief is not criminally liable for receiving the property stolen; however a principal to the larceny (*see* paragraph 1), when not the actual thief, may be found guilty of knowingly receiving the stolen property but may not be found guilty of both the larceny and receiving the property.

(2) *Knowledge.* Actual knowledge that the property was stolen is required. Knowledge may be proved by circumstantial evidence.

(3) *Wrongfulness.* Receiving stolen property is wrongful if it is without justification or excuse. For example, it would not be wrongful for a person to

receive stolen property for the purpose of returning it to its rightful owner, or for a law enforcement officer to seize it as evidence.

d. *Lesser included offenses.* See paragraph 3 of this part and Appendix 12A.

e. *Maximum punishment.* Stolen property, knowingly receiving, buying, or concealing.

(1) *Of a value of $500.00 or less.* Bad-conduct discharge, forfeiture of all pay and allowances, and confinement for 6 months.

(2) *Of a value of more than $500.00.* Dishonorable discharge, forfeiture of all pay and allowances, and confinement for 3 years.

f. *Sample specification.*

In that _____ (personal jurisdiction data), did, (at/on board—location) (subject-matter jurisdiction data, if required), on or about ____ 20 __ , wrongfully (receive) (buy) (conceal) _____ , of a value of (about) $ _____ , the property of _____ , which property, as he/she, the said _____ , then knew, had been stolen, and that said conduct was (to the prejudice of good order and discipline in the armed forces) (of a nature to bring discredit upon the armed forces) (to the prejudice of good order and discipline in the armed forces and was of a nature to bring discredit upon the armed forces).

107. Article 134—(Straggling)

a. *Text of statute. See* paragraph 60.

b. *Elements.*

(1) That the accused, while accompanying the accuse's organization on a march, maneuvers, or similar exercise, straggled;

(2) That the straggling was wrongful; and

(3) That, under the circumstances, the conduct of the accused was to the prejudice of good order and discipline in the armed forces or was of a nature to bring discredit upon the armed forces.

c. *Explanation.* "Straggle" means to wander away, to stray, to become separated from, or to lag or linger behind.

d. *Lesser included offenses.* See paragraph 3 of this part and Appendix 12A.

e. *Maximum punishment.* Confinement for 3 months and forfeiture of two-thirds pay per month for 3 months.

f. *Sample specification.*

In that _____ (personal jurisdiction data), did, at _____ , on or about ____ 20 __ , while accompanying his/her organization on (a march) (maneuvers) (_____), wrongfully straggle, and that said conduct was (to the prejudice of good order and discipline in the armed forces) (of a nature to bring discredit upon the armed forces) (to the prejudice of good order and discipline in the armed forces and was of a nature to bring discredit upon the armed forces).

108. Article 134—(Testify: wrongful refusal)

a. *Text of statute. See* paragraph 60.

b. *Elements.*

(1) That the accused was in the presence of a court-martial, board of officer(s), military commission, court of inquiry, an officer conducting an investigation under Article 32, or an officer taking a deposition, of or for the United States, at which a certain person was presiding;

(2) That the said person presiding directed the accused to qualify as a witness or, having so qualified, to answer a certain question;

(3) That the accused refused to qualify as a witness or answer said question;

(4) That the refusal was wrongful; and

(5) That, under the circumstances, the conduct of the accused was to the prejudice of good order and discipline in the armed forces or was of a nature to bring discredit upon the armed forces.

c. *Explanation.* To "qualify as a witness" means that the witness declares that the witness will testify truthfully. *See* R.C.M. 807; Mil. R. Evid. 603. A good faith but legally mistaken belief in the right to remain silent does not constitute a defense to a charge of wrongful to testify. *See also* Mil. R. Evid. 301 and Section V.

d. *Lesser included offenses.* See paragraph 3 of this part and Appendix 12A.

e. *Maximum punishment.* Dishonorable discharge, forfeiture of all pay and allowances, and confinement for 5 years.

f. *Sample specification.*

In that _____ (personal jurisdiction data), being in the presence of (a) (an) ((general) (special) (summary) court-martial) (board of officer(s)) (military commission) (court of inquiry) (officer conducting a preliminary hearing under Article 32, Uniform Code of Military Justice) (officer taking a deposition) (_____) (of) (for) the United States, of which _____ was (military judge) (president), (_____), (and having been directed by the said _____ to qualify as a witness) (and having qualified as a witness and having been directed by the said _____ to answer the following question(s) put to him/her as a witness, " _____ "), did, (at/on board—location), on or about _____ 20 ___ , wrongfully refuse (to qualify as a witness) (to answer said question(s)), and that said conduct was (to the prejudice of good order and discipline in the armed forces) (of a nature to bring discredit upon the armed forces) (to the prejudice of good order and discipline in the armed forces and was of a nature to bring discredit upon the armed forces).

109. Article 134—(Threat or hoax designed or intended to cause panic or public fear)

a. *Text of statute.* See paragraph 60.

b. *Elements.*

(1) *Threat.*

(a) That the accused communicated certain language;

(b) That the information communicated amounted to a threat;

(c) That the harm threatened was to be done by means of an explosive; weapon of mass destruction; biological or chemical agent, substance, or weapon; or hazardous material;

(d) That the communication was wrongful; and

(e) That, under the circumstances, the conduct of the accused was to the prejudice of good order and discipline in the armed forces or was of a nature to bring discredit upon the armed forces.

(2) *Hoax.*

(a) That the accused communicated or conveyed certain information;

(b) That the information communicated or conveyed concerned an attempt being made or to be made by means of an explosive; weapon of mass destruction; biological or chemical agent, substance, or weapon; or hazardous material, to unlawfully kill, injure, or intimidate a person or to unlawfully damage or destroy certain property;

(c) That the information communicated or conveyed by the accused was false and that the accused then knew it to be false;

(d) That the communication of the information by the accused was malicious; and

(e) That, under the circumstances, the conduct of the accused was to the prejudice of good order and discipline in the armed forces or was of a nature to bring discredit upon the armed forces.

c. *Explanation.*

(1) *Threat.* A "threat" means an expressed present determination or intent to kill, injure, or intimidate a person or to damage or destroy certain property presently or in the future. Proof that the accused actually intended to kill, injure, intimidate, damage, or destroy is not required.

(2) *Explosive.* "Explosive" means gunpowder, powders used for blasting, all forms of high explosives, blasting materials, fuses (other than electrical circuit breakers), detonators, and other detonating agents, smokeless powders, any explosive bomb, grenade, missile, or similar device, and any incendiary bomb or grenade, fire bomb, or similar device, and any other explosive compound, mixture, or similar material.

(3) *Weapon of mass destruction.* A weapon of mass destruction means any device, explosive or otherwise, that is intended, or has the capability, to cause death or serious bodily injury to a significant number of people through the release, dissemination, or impact of: toxic or poisonous chemicals, or their precursors; a disease organism; or radiation or radioactivity.

(4) *Biological agent.* The term "biological agent" means any micro-organism (including bacteria, viruses, fungi, rickettsiac, or protozoa), pathogen, or infectious substance, and any naturally occurring, bioengineered, or synthesized component of any such micro-organism, pathogen, or infectious substance, whatever its origin or method of production, that is capable of causing—

(a) death, disease, or other biological malfunction in a human, an animal, a plant, or another living organism;

(b) deterioration of food, water, equipment, supplies, or materials of any kind; or

(c) deleterious alteration of the environment.

(5) *Chemical agent, substance, or weapon.* A chemical agent, substance, or weapon refers to a toxic chemical and its precursors or a munition or device, specifically designed to cause death or other harm through toxic properties of those chemicals

that would be released as a result of the employment of such munition or device, and any equipment specifically designed for use directly in connection with the employment of such munitions or devices.

(6) *Hazardous material.* A substance or material (including explosive, radioactive material, etiologic agent, flammable or combustible liquid or solid, poison, oxidizing or corrosive material, and compressed gas, or mixture thereof) or a group or class of material designated as hazardous by the Secretary of Transportation.

(7) *Malicious.* A communication is "malicious" if the accused believed that the information would probably interfere with the peaceful use of the building, vehicle, aircraft, or other property concerned, or would cause fear or concern to one or more persons.

d. *Lesser included offenses.* See paragraph 3 of this part and Appendix 12A.

e. *Maximum punishment.* Dishonorable discharge, forfeitures of all pay and allowances, and confinement for 10 years.

f. *Sample specifications.*

(1) *Threat.*

In that _____ (personal jurisdiction data) did, (at/on board—location) on or about _____ 20 __ , wrongfully communicate certain information, to wit: _____ , which language constituted a threat to harm a person or property by means of a(n) [explosive; weapon of mass destruction; biological agent, substance, or weapon; chemical agent, substance, or weapon; and/or (a) hazardous material(s)], and that said conduct was (to the prejudice of good order and discipline in the armed forces) (of a nature to bring discredit upon the armed forces) (to the prejudice of good order and discipline in the armed forces and was of a nature to bring discredit upon the armed forces).

(2) *Hoax.*

In that _____ (personal jurisdiction data) did, (at/on board—location), on or about _____ 20 __ , maliciously (communicate) (convey) certain information concerning an attempt being made or to be made to unlawfully [(kill) (injure) (intimidate) _____] [(damage) (destroy) _____] by means of a(n) [explosive; weapon of mass destruction; biological agent, substance, or weapon; chemical agent, substance, or weapon; and/or (a) hazardous material(s)], to wit: _____ , which information was false and which the accused

then knew to be false, and that said conduct was (to the prejudice of good order and discipline in the armed forces) (of a nature to bring discredit upon the armed forces) (to the prejudice of good order and discipline in the armed forces and was of a nature to bring discredit upon the armed forces).

110. Article 134—(Threat, communicating)

a. *Text of statute. See* paragraph 60.

b. *Elements.*

(1) That the accused communicated certain language expressing a present determination or intent to wrongfully injure the person, property, or reputation of another person, presently or in the future;

(2) That the communication was made known to that person or to a third person;

(3) That the communication was wrongful; and

(4) That, under the circumstances, the conduct of the accused was to the prejudice of good order and discipline in the armed forces or was of a nature to bring discredit upon the armed forces.

c. *Explanation.* For purposes of this paragraph, to establish that the communication was wrongful it is necessary that the accused transmitted the communication for the purpose of issuing a threat, with the knowledge that the communication would be viewed as a threat, or acted recklessly with regard to whether the communication would be viewed as a threat. However, it is not necessary to establish that the accused actually intended to do the injury threatened. Nor is the offense committed by the mere statement of intent to commit an unlawful act not involving injury to another. *See also* paragraph 109, Threat or hoax designed or intended to cause panic or public fear.

d. *Lesser included offenses.* See paragraph 3 of this part and Appendix 12A.

e. *Maximum punishment.* Dishonorable discharge, forfeiture of all pay and allowances, and confinement for 3 years.

f. *Sample specification.*

In that _____ (personal jurisdiction data), did, (at/on board—location) (subject-matter jurisdiction data, if required), on or about _____ 20 __ , wrongfully communicate to _____ a threat (injure _____ by _____) (accuse _____ of having committed the offense of _____) (_____), and that said conduct was (to the prejudice of good order and discipline in the armed forces) (of a nature to bring discredit upon the armed forces) (to the prejudice of good order and discipline in the armed forces and was of a nature to bring discredit upon the armed forces).

111. Article 134—(Unlawful entry)

a. *Text of statute. See* paragraph 60.

b. *Elements.*

(1) That the accused entered the real property of another or certain personal property of another which amounts to a structure usually used for habitation or storage;

(2) That such entry was unlawful; and

(3) That, under the circumstances, the conduct of the accused was to the prejudice of good order and discipline in the armed forces or was of a nature to bring discredit upon the armed forces.

c. *Explanation. See* paragraph 55 for a discussion of "entry." An entry is "unlawful" if made without the consent of any person authorized to consent to entry or without other lawful authority. No specific intent or breaking is required for this offense. *See* paragraph 56 for a discussion of housebreaking. The property protected against unlawful entry includes real property and the sort of personal property which amounts to a structure usually used for habitation or storage. It would usually not include an aircraft, automobile, tracked vehicle, or a person's locker, even though used for storage purposes. However, depending on the circumstances, an intrusion into such property may be prejudicial to good order and discipline.

d. *Lesser included offenses.* See paragraph 3 of this part and Appendix 12A.

e. *Maximum punishment.* Bad-conduct discharge, forfeiture of all pay and allowances, and confinement for 6 months.

f. *Sample specification.*

In that _____ (personal jurisdiction data), did, (at/on board—location) (subject-matter jurisdiction data, if required), on or about _____ 20 __ , unlawfully enter the (dwelling house) (garage) (warehouse) (tent) (vegetable garden) (orchard) (stateroom) (_____) of _____ , and that said conduct was (to the prejudice of good order and discipline in the armed forces) (of a nature to bring discredit upon the armed forces) (to the prejudice of good order and discipline in the armed forces and

112. Article 134—(Weapon: concealed, carrying)

a. *Text of statute. See* paragraph 60.

b. *Elements.*

(1) That the accused carried a certain weapon concealed on or about the accused's person;

(2) That the carrying was unlawful;

(3) That the weapon was a dangerous weapon; and

(4) That, under the circumstances, the conduct of the accused was to the prejudice of good order and discipline in the armed forces or was of a nature to bring discredit upon the armed forces.

c. *Explanation.*

(1) *Concealed weapon.* A weapon is concealed when it is carried by a person and intentionally covered or kept from sight.

(2) *Dangerous weapon.* For purposes of this paragraph, a weapon is dangerous if it was specifically designed for the purpose of doing grievous bodily harm, or it was used or intended to be used by the accused to do grievous bodily harm.

(3) *On or about.* "On or about" means the weapon was carried on the accused's person or was within the immediate reach of the accused.

d. *Lesser included offenses.* See paragraph 3 of this part and Appendix 12A.

e. *Maximum punishment.* Bad-conduct discharge, forfeiture of all pay and allowances, and confinement for 1 year.

f. *Sample specification.*

In that _____ (personal jurisdiction data), did, (at/on board—location) (subject-matter jurisdiction data, if required), on or about _____ 20 __ , unlawfully carry on or about his/her person a concealed weapon, to wit: a _____ , and that said conduct was (to the prejudice of good order and discipline in the armed forces) (of a nature to bring discredit upon the armed forces) (to the prejudice of good order and discipline in the armed forces and was of a nature to bring discredit upon the armed forces).

113. Article 134—(Wearing unauthorized insignia, decoration, badge, ribbon, device, or lapel button)

a. *Text of statute. See* paragraph 60.

b. *Elements.*

(1) That the accused wore a certain insignia, decoration, badge, ribbon, device, or lapel button upon the accused's uniform or civilian clothing;

(2) That the accused was not authorized to wear the item;

(3) That the wearing was wrongful; and

(4) That, under the circumstances, the conduct of the accused was to the prejudice of good order and discipline in the armed forces or was of a nature to bring discredit upon the armed forces.

c. *Explanation.* None.

d. *Lesser included offenses.* See paragraph 3 of this part and Appendix 12A.

e. *Maximum punishment.* Bad-conduct discharge, forfeiture of all pay and allowances, and confinement for 6 months.

f. *Sample specification.*

In that _____ (personal jurisdiction data), did, (at/on board—location), on or about _____ 20 ___ , wrongfully and without authority wear upon his/her (uniform) (civilian clothing) (the insignia or grade of a (master sergeant of _____) (chief gunner's mate of _____)) (Combat Infantryman Badge) (the Distinguished Service Cross) (the ribbon representing the Silver Star) (the lapel button representing the Legion of Merit) (_____), and that said conduct was (to the prejudice of good order and discipline in the armed forces) (of a nature to bring discredit upon the armed forces) (to the prejudice of good order and discipline in the armed forces and was of a nature to bring discredit upon the armed forces).

PART V
NONJUDICIAL PUNISHMENT PROCEDURE

1. General

a. *Authority.* Nonjudicial punishment in the United States Armed Forces is authorized by Article 15.

b. *Nature.* Nonjudicial punishment is a disciplinary measure more serious than the administrative corrective measures discussed in paragraph 1g, but less serious than trial by court-martial.

c. *Purpose.* Nonjudicial punishment provides commanders with an essential and prompt means of maintaining good order and discipline and also promotes positive behavior changes in servicemembers without the stigma of a court-martial conviction.

d. *Policy.*

(1) *Commander's responsibility.* Commanders are responsible for good order and discipline in their commands. Generally, discipline can be maintained through effective leadership including, when necessary, administrative corrective measures. Nonjudicial punishment is ordinarily appropriate when administrative corrective measures are inadequate due to the nature of the minor offense or the record of the servicemember, unless it is clear that only trial by court-martial will meet the needs of justice and discipline. Nonjudicial punishment shall be considered on an individual basis. Commanders considering nonjudicial punishment should consider the nature of the offense, the record of the servicemember, the needs for good order and discipline, and the effect of nonjudicial punishment on the servicemember and the servicemember's record.

(2) *Commander's discretion.* A commander who is considering a case for disposition under Article 15 will exercise personal discretion in evaluating each case, both as to whether nonjudicial punishment is appropriate, and, if so, as to the nature and amount of punishment appropriate. No superior may direct that a subordinate authority impose nonjudicial punishment in a particular case, issue regulations, orders, or "guides" which suggest to subordinate authorities that certain categories of minor offenses be disposed of by nonjudicial punishment instead of by court-martial or administrative corrective measures, or that predetermined kinds or amounts of punishments be imposed for certain classifications of offenses that the subordinate considers appropriate for disposition by nonjudicial punishment.

(3) *Commander's suspension authority.* Commanders should consider suspending all or part of any punishment selected under Article 15, particularly in the case of first offenders or when significant extenuating or mitigating matters are present. Suspension provides an incentive to the offender and gives an opportunity to the commander to evaluate the offender during the period of suspension.

e. *Minor offenses.* Nonjudicial punishment may be imposed for acts or omissions that are minor offenses under the punitive articles (*see* Part IV). Whether an offense is minor depends on several factors: the nature of the offense and the circumstances surrounding its commission; the offender's age, rank, duty assignment, record and experience; and the maximum sentence imposable for the offense if tried by general court-martial. Ordinarily, a minor offense is an offense which the maximum sentence imposable would not include a dishonorable discharge or confinement for longer than 1 year if tried by general court-martial. The decision whether an offense is "minor" is a matter of discretion for the commander imposing nonjudicial punishment, but nonjudicial punishment for an offense other than a minor offense (even though thought by the commander to be minor) is not a bar to trial by court-martial for the same offense. *See* R.C.M. 907(b)(2)(D)(iv). However, the accused may show at trial that nonjudicial punishment was imposed, and if the accused does so, this fact must be considered in determining an appropriate sentence. *See* Article 15(f); R.C.M. 1001(c)(1)(B).

f. *Limitations on nonjudicial punishment.*

(1) *Double punishment prohibited.* When nonjudicial punishment has been imposed for an offense, punishment may not again be imposed for the same offense under Article 15. *But see* paragraph 1e concerning trial by court-martial.

(2) *Increase in punishment prohibited.* Once nonjudicial punishment has been imposed, it may not be increased, upon appeal or otherwise.

(3) *Multiple punishment prohibited.* When a commander determines that nonjudicial punishment is appropriate for a particular servicemember, all known offenses determined to be appropriate for disposition by nonjudicial punishment and ready to be considered at that time, including all such offenses arising from a single incident or course of conduct,

shall ordinarily be considered together, and not made the basis for multiple punishments.

(4) *Statute of limitations.* Except as provided in Article 43(d), nonjudicial punishment may not be imposed for offenses which were committed more than 2 years before the date of imposition. *See* Article 43(c).

(5) *Civilian courts.* Nonjudicial punishment may not be imposed for an offense tried by a court which derives its authority from the United States. Nonjudicial punishment may not be imposed for an offense tried by a State or foreign court unless authorized by regulations of the Secretary concerned.

g. *Relationship of nonjudicial punishment to administrative corrective measures.* Article 15 and Part V of this Manual do not apply to include, or limit use of administrative corrective measures that promote efficiency and good order and discipline such as counseling, admonitions, reprimands, exhortations, disapprovals, criticisms, censures, reproofs, rebukes, extra military instruction, and administrative withholding of privileges. *See also* R.C.M. 306. Administrative corrective measures are not punishment, and they may be used for acts or omissions which are not offenses under the code and for acts or omissions which are offenses under the code.

h. *Applicable standards.* Unless otherwise provided, the service regulations and procedures of the service member shall apply.

i. *Effect of errors.* Failure to comply with any of the procedural provisions of Part V of this Manual shall not invalidate a punishment imposed under Article 15, unless the error materially prejudiced a substantial right of the servicemember on whom the punishment was imposed.

2. Who may impose nonjudicial punishment

The following persons may serve as a nonjudicial punishment authority for the purposes of administering nonjudicial punishment proceedings under this Part:

a. *Commander.* As provided by regulations of the Secretary concerned, a commander may impose nonjudicial punishment upon any military personnel of that command. "Commander" means a commissioned or warrant officer who, by virtue of rank and assignment, exercises primary command authority over a military organization or prescribed territorial area, which under pertinent official directives is recognized as a "command." "Commander" includes a commander of a joint command. Subject to subparagraph 1d(2) and any regulations of the Secretary concerned, the authority of a commander to impose nonjudicial punishment as to certain types of offenses, certain categories of persons, or in specific cases, or to impose certain types of punishment, may be limited or withheld by a superior commander or by the Secretary concerned.

b. *Officer in charge.* If authorized by regulations of the Secretary concerned, an officer in charge may impose nonjudicial punishment upon enlisted persons assigned to that unit.

c. *Principal assistant.* If authorized by regulations of the Secretary concerned, a commander exercising general court-martial jurisdiction or an officer of general or flag rank in command may delegate that commander's powers under Article 15 to a principal assistant. The Secretary concerned may define "principal assistant."

3. Right to demand trial

Except in the case of a person attached to or embarked in a vessel, punishment may not be imposed under Article 15 upon any member of the armed forces who has, before the imposition of nonjudicial punishment, demanded trial by court-martial in lieu of nonjudicial punishment. This right may also be granted to a person attached to or embarked in a vessel if so authorized by regulations of the Secretary concerned. A person is "attached to" or "embarked in" a vessel if, at the time nonjudicial punishment is imposed, that person is assigned or attached to the vessel, is on board for passage, or is assigned or attached to an embarked staff, unit, detachment, squadron, team, air group, or other regularly organized body.

4. Procedure

a. *Notice.* If, after a preliminary inquiry (*see* R.C.M. 303), the nonjudicial punishment authority determines that disposition by nonjudicial punishment proceedings is appropriate (*see* R.C.M. 306: paragraph 1 of this Part), the nonjudicial punishment authority shall cause the servicemember to be notified. The notice shall include:

(1) a statement that the nonjudicial punishment

authority is considering the imposition of nonjudicial punishment;

(2) a statement describing the alleged offenses—including the article of the code—which the member is alleged to have committed;

(3) a brief summary of the information upon which the allegations are based or a statement that the member may, upon request, examine available statements and evidence;

(4) a statement of the rights that will be accorded to the servicemember under paragraphs 4c(1) and (2) of this Part;

(5) unless the right to demand trial is not applicable (*see* paragraph 3 of this Part), a statement that the member may demand trial by court-martial in lieu of nonjudicial punishment, a statement of the maximum punishment which the nonjudicial punishment authority may impose by nonjudicial punishment; a statement that, if trial by court-martial is demanded, charges could be referred for trial by summary, special, or general court-martial; that the member may not be tried by summary court-martial over the member's objection; and that at a special or general court-martial the member has the right to be represented by counsel.

b. *Decision by servicemember.*

(1) *Demand for trial by court-martial.* If the servicemember demands trial by court-martial (when this right is applicable), the nonjudicial proceedings shall be terminated. It is within the discretion of the commander whether to forward or refer charges for trial by court-martial (*see* R.C.M. 306; 307; 401–407) in such a case, but in no event may nonjudicial punishment be imposed for the offenses affected unless the demand is voluntarily withdrawn.

(2) *No demand for trial by court-martial.* If the servicemember does not demand trial by court-martial within a reasonable time after notice under paragraph 4a of this Part, or if the right to demand trial by court-martial is not applicable, the nonjudicial punishment authority may proceed under paragraph 4c of this Part.

c. *Nonjudicial punishment accepted.*

(1) *Personal appearance requested; procedure.* Before nonjudicial punishment may be imposed, the servicemember shall be entitled to appear personally before the nonjudicial punishment authority who offered nonjudicial punishment, except when appearance is prevented by the unavailability of the nonjudicial punishment authority or by extraordinary circumstances, in which case the servicemember shall be entitled to appear before a person designated by the nonjudicial punishment authority who shall prepare a written summary of any proceedings before that person and forward it and any written matter submitted by the servicemember to the nonjudicial punishment authority. If the servicemember requests personal appearance, the servicemember shall be entitled to:

(A) Be informed in accordance with Article 31(b);

(B) Be accompanied by a spokesperson provided or arranged for by the member unless the punishment to be imposed will not exceed extra duty for 14 days, restriction for 14 days, and an oral reprimand. Such a spokesperson need not be qualified under R.C.M. 502(d); such spokesperson is not entitled to travel or similar expenses, and the proceedings need not be delayed to permit the presence of a spokesperson; the spokesperson may speak for the servicemember, but may not question witnesses except as the nonjudicial punishment authority may allow as a matter of discretion;

(C) Be informed orally or in writing of the information against the servicemember and relating to the offenses alleged;

(D) Be allowed to examine documents or physical objects against the member which the nonjudicial punishment authority has examined in connection with the case and on which the nonjudicial punishment authority intends to rely in deciding whether and how much nonjudicial punishment to impose;

(E) Present matters in defense, extenuation, and mitigation orally, or in writing, or both;

(F) Have present witnesses, including those adverse to the servicemember, upon request if their statements will be relevant and they are reasonably available. For purposes of this subparagraph, a witness is not reasonably available if the witness requires reimbursement by the United States for any cost incurred in appearing, cannot appear without unduly delaying the proceedings, or, if a military witness, cannot be excused from other important duties;

(G) Have the proceeding open to the public unless the nonjudicial punishment authority determines that the proceeding should be closed for good cause, such as military exigencies or security interests, or unless the punishment to be imposed will not exceed extra duty for 14 days, restriction for 14 days, and an oral reprimand; however, nothing in this subparagraph requires special arrangements to be made to facilitate access to the proceeding.

(2) *Personal appearance waived; procedure.* Subject to the approval of the nonjudicial punishment authority, the servicemember may request not to appear personally under paragraph 4c(1) of this Part. If such request is granted, the servicemember may submit written matters for consideration by the nonjudicial punishment authority before such authority's decision under paragraph 4c(4) of this Part. The servicemember shall be informed of the right to remain silent and that matters submitted may be used against the member in a trial by court-martial.

(3) *Evidence.* The Military Rules of Evidence (Part III), other than with respect to privileges, do not apply at nonjudicial punishment proceedings. Any relevant matter may be considered, after compliance with paragraphs 4c(1)(C) and (D) of this Part.

(4) *Decision.* After considering all relevant matters presented, if the nonjudicial punishment authority—

(A) Does not conclude that the servicemember committed the offenses alleged, the nonjudicial punishment authority shall so inform the member and terminate the proceedings;

(B) Concludes that the servicemember committed one or more of the offenses alleged, the nonjudicial punishment authority shall:

(i) so inform the servicemember;

(ii) inform the servicemember of the punishment imposed; and

(iii) inform the servicemember of the right to appeal (*see* paragraph 7 of this Part).

d. *Nonjudicial punishment based on record of court of inquiry or other investigative body.* Nonjudicial punishment may be based on the record of a court of inquiry or other investigative body, in which proceeding the member was accorded the rights of a party. No additional proceeding under paragraph 4c(1) of this Part is required. The servicemember shall be informed in writing that nonjudicial punishment is being considered based on the record of the proceedings in question, and given the opportunity, if applicable, to refuse nonjudicial punishment. If the servicemember does not demand trial by court-martial or has no option, the servicemember may submit, in writing, any matter in defense, extenuation, or mitigation, to the officer considering imposing nonjudicial punishment, for consideration by that officer to determine whether the member committed the offenses in question, and, if so, to determine an appropriate punishment.

5. Punishments

a. *General limitations.* The Secretary concerned may limit the power granted by Article 15 with respect to the kind and amount of the punishment authorized. Subject to paragraphs 1 and 4 of this Part and to regulations of the Secretary concerned, the kinds and amounts of punishment authorized by Article 15(b) may be imposed upon servicemembers as provided in this paragraph.

b. *Authorized maximum punishments.* In addition to or in lieu of admonition or reprimand, the following disciplinary punishments subject to the limitation of paragraph 5d of this Part, may be imposed upon servicemembers:

(1) *Upon commissioned officers and warrant officers—*

(A) By any commanding officer—restriction to specified limits, with or without suspension from duty for not more than 30 consecutive days;

(B) If imposed by an officer exercising general court-martial jurisdiction, an officer of general or flag rank in command, or a principal assistant as defined in paragraph 2c of this Part—

(i) arrest in quarters for not more than 30 consecutive days;

(ii) forfeiture of not more than one-half of one month's pay per month for 2 months;

(iii) restriction to specified limits, with or without suspension from duty, for not more than 60 consecutive days;

(2) *Upon other military personnel of the command—*

(A) By any nonjudicial punishment authority—

(i) if imposed upon a person attached to or embarked in a vessel, confinement on bread and water or diminished rations for not more than 3 consecutive days;

(ii) correctional custody for not more than 7 consecutive days;

(iii) forfeiture of not more than 7 days' pay;

(iv) reduction to the next inferior grade, if the grade from which demoted is within the promotion authority of the officer imposing the reduction or any officer subordinate to the one who imposes the reduction;

(v) extra duties, including fatigue or other duties, for not more than 14 consecutive days;

(vi) restriction to specified limits, with or without suspension from duty, for not more than 14 consecutive days;

(B) If imposed by a commanding officer of the grade of major or lieutenant commander or above or a principal assistant as defined in paragraph 2c of this Part—

(i) if imposed upon a person attached to or embarked in a vessel, confinement on bread and water or diminished rations for not more than 3 consecutive days;

(ii) correctional custody for not more than 30 consecutive days;

(iii) forfeiture of not more than one-half of 1 month's pay per month for 2 months;

(iv) reduction to the lowest or any intermediate pay grade, if the grade from which demoted is within the promotion authority of the officer imposing the reduction or any officer subordinate to the one who imposes the reduction, but enlisted members in pay grades above E-4 may not be reduced more than one pay grade, except that during time of war or national emergency this category of persons may be reduced two grades if the Secretary concerned determines that circumstances require the removal of this limitation;

(v) extra duties, including fatigue or other duties, for not more than 45 consecutive days;

(vi) restriction to specified limits, with or without suspension from duty, for not more than 60 consecutive days.

c. *Nature of punishment.*

(1) *Admonition and reprimand.* Admonition and reprimand are two forms of censure intended to express adverse reflection upon or criticism of a person's conduct. A reprimand is a more severe form of censure than an admonition. When imposed as nonjudicial punishment, the admonition or reprimand is considered to be punitive, unlike the nonpunitive admonition and reprimand provided for in paragraph 1g of this Part. In the case of commissioned officers and warrant officers, admonitions and reprimands given as nonjudicial punishment must be administered in writing. In other cases, unless otherwise prescribed by the Secretary concerned, they may be administered either orally or in writing.

(2) *Restriction.* Restriction is the least severe form of deprivation of liberty. Restriction involves moral rather than physical restraint. The severity of this type of restraint depends on its duration and the geographical limits specified when the punishment is imposed. A person undergoing restriction may be required to report to a designated place at specified times if reasonably necessary to ensure that the punishment is being properly executed. Unless otherwise specified by the nonjudicial punishment authority, a person in restriction may be required to perform any military duty.

(3) *Arrest in quarters.* As in the case of restriction, the restraint involved in arrest in quarters is enforced by a moral obligation rather than by physical means. This punishment may be imposed only on officers. An officer undergoing this punishment may be required to perform those duties prescribed by the Secretary concerned. However, an officer so punished is required to remain within that officer's quarters during the period of punishment unless the limits of arrest are otherwise extended by appropriate authority. The quarters of an officer may consist of a military residence, whether a tent, stateroom, or other quarters assigned, or a private residence when government quarters have not been provided.

(4) *Correctional custody.* Correctional custody is the physical restraint of a person during duty or nonduty hours, or both, imposed as a punishment under Article 15, and may include extra duties, fatigue duties, or hard labor as an incident of correctional custody. A person may be required to serve correctional custody in a confinement facility, but if practicable, not in immediate association with persons awaiting trial or held in confinement pursuant to trial by court-martial. A person undergoing correctional custody may be required to perform those regular military duties, extra duties, fatigue duties, and hard labor which may be assigned by the authority charged with the administration of the punishment. The conditions under which correctional custody is served shall be prescribed by the Secretary concerned. In addition, the Secretary concerned may limit the categories of enlisted members upon

whom correctional custody may be imposed. The authority competent to order the release of a person from orrectional custody shall be as designated by the Secretary concerned.

(5) *Confinement on bread and water or diminished rations.* Confinement on bread and water or diminished rations involves confinement in places where the person so confined may communicate only with authorized personnel. The ration to be furnished a person undergoing a punishment of confinement on bread and water or diminished rations is that specified by the authority charged with the administration of the punishment, but the ration may not consist solely of bread and water unless this punishment has been specifically imposed. When punishment of confinement on bread and water or diminished rations is imposed, a signed certificate of a medical officer containing an opinion that no serious injury to the health of the person to be confined will be caused by that punishment, must be obtained before the punishment is executed. The categories of enlisted personnel upon whom this type of punishment may be imposed may be limited by the Secretary concerned.

(6) *Extra duties.* Extra duties involve the performance of duties in addition to those normally assigned to the person undergoing the punishment. Extra duties may include fatigue duties. Military duties of any kind may be assigned as extra duty. However, no extra duty may be imposed which constitutes a known safety or health hazard to the member or which constitutes cruel or unusual punishment or which is not sanctioned by customs of the service concerned. Extra duties assigned as punishment of noncommissioned officers, petty officers, or any other enlisted persons of equivalent grades or positions designated by the Secretary concerned, should not be of a kind which demeans their grades or positions.

(7) *Reduction in grade.* Reduction in grade is one of the most severe forms of nonjudicial punishment and it should be used with discretion. As used in Article 15, the phrase "if the grade from which demoted is within the promotion authority of the officer imposing the reduction or any officer subordinate to the one who imposes the reduction" does not refer to the authority to promote the person concerned but to the general authority to promote to the grade held by the person to be punished.

(8) *Forfeiture of pay.* Forfeiture means a permanent loss of entitlement to the pay forfeited. "Pay," as used with respect to forfeiture of pay under Article 15, refers to the basic pay of the person or, in the case of reserve component personnel on inactive-duty, compensation for periods of inactive-duty training, plus any sea or hardship duty pay. "Basic pay" includes no element of pay other than the basic pay fixed by statute for the grade and length of service of the person concerned and does not include special pay for a special qualification, incentive pay for the performance of hazardous duties, proficiency pay, subsistence and quarters allowances, and similar types of compensation. If the punishment includes both reduction, whether or not suspended, and forfeiture of pay, the forfeiture must be based on the grade to which reduced. The amount to be forfeited will be expressed in whole dollar amounts only and not in a number of day's pay or fractions of monthly pay. If the forfeiture is to be applied for more than 1 month, the amount to be forfeited per month and the number of months should be stated. Forfeiture of pay may not extend to any pay accrued before the date of its imposition.

d. *Limitations on combination of punishments.*

(1) Arrest in quarters may not be imposed in combination with restriction;

(2) Confinement on bread and water or diminished rations may not be imposed in combination with correctional custody, extra duties, or restriction;

(3) Correctional custody may not be imposed in combination with restriction or extra duties;

(4) Restriction and extra duties may be combined to run concurrently, but the combination may not exceed the maximum imposable for extra duties;

(5) Subject to the limits in subparagraphs d(1) through (4) all authorized punishments may be imposed in a single case in the maximum amounts.

e. *Punishments imposed on reserve component personnel while on inactive-duty training.* When a punishment under Article 15 amounting to a deprivation of liberty (for example, restriction, correctional custody, extra duties, or arrest in quarters) is imposed on a member of a reserve component during a period of inactive-duty training, the punishment may be served during one or both of the following:

(1) a normal period of inactive-duty training; or

(2) a subsequent period of active duty (not including a period of active duty under Article 2(d)(1),

unless such active duty was approved by the Secretary concerned).

Unserved punishments may be carried over to subsequent periods of inactive-duty training or active duty. A sentence to forfeiture of pay may be collected from active duty and inactive-duty training pay during subsequent periods of duty.

f. *Punishments imposed on reserve component personnel when ordered to active duty for disciplinary purposes.* When a punishment under Article 15 is imposed on a member of a reserve component during a period of active duty to which the reservist was ordered pursuant to R.C.M. 204 and which constitutes a deprivation of liberty (for example, restriction, correctional custody, extra duties, or arrest in quarters), the punishment may be served during any or all of the following:

(1) that period of active duty to which the reservist was ordered pursuant to Article 2(d), but only where the order to active duty was approved by the Secretary concerned;

(2) a subsequent normal period of inactive-duty training; or

(3) a subsequent period of active duty (not including a period of active duty pursuant to R.C.M. 204 which was not approved by the Secretary concerned).

Unserved punishments may be carried over to subsequent periods of inactive-duty training or active duty. A sentence to forfeiture of pay may be collected from active duty and inactive-duty training pay during subsequent periods of duty.

g. *Effective date and execution of punishments.* Reduction and forfeiture of pay, if unsuspended, take effect on the date the commander imposes the punishments. Other punishments, if unsuspended, will take effect and be carried into execution as prescribed by the Secretary concerned.

6. Suspension, mitigation, remission, and setting aside

a. *Suspension.* The nonjudicial punishment authority who imposes nonjudicial punishment, the commander who imposes nonjudicial punishment, or a successor in command over the person punished, may, at any time, suspend any part or amount of the unexecuted punishment imposed and may suspend a reduction in grade or a forfeiture, whether or not executed, subject to the following rules:

(1) An executed punishment of reduction or forfeiture of pay may be suspended only within a period of 4 months after the date of execution.

(2) Suspension of a punishment may not be for a period longer than 6 months from the date of the suspension, and the expiration of the current enlistment or term of service of the servicemember involved automatically terminates the period of suspension.

(3) Unless the suspension is sooner vacated, suspended portions of the punishment are remitted, without further action, upon the termination of the period of suspension.

(4) Unless otherwise stated, an action suspending a punishment includes a condition that the servicemember not violate any punitive article of the code. The nonjudicial punishment authority may specify in writing additional conditions of the suspension.

(5) A suspension may be vacated by any nonjudicial punishment authority or commander competent to impose upon the servicemember concerned punishment of the kind and amount involved in the vacation of suspension. Vacation of suspension may be based only on a violation of the conditions of suspension which occurs within the period of suspension. Before a suspension may be vacated, the servicemember ordinarily shall be notified and given an opportunity to respond. Although a hearing is not required to vacate a suspension, if the punishment is of the kind set forth in Article 15(e)(1)-(7), the servicemember should, unless impracticable, be given an opportunity to appear before the officer authorized to vacate suspension of the punishment to present any matters in defense, extenuation, or mitigation of the violation on which the vacation action is to be based. Vacation of a suspended nonjudicial punishment is not itself nonjudicial punishment, and additional action to impose nonjudicial punishment for a violation of a punitive article of the code upon which the vacation action is based is not precluded thereby.

b. *Mitigation.* Mitigation is a reduction in either the quantity or quality of a punishment, its general nature remaining the same. Mitigation is appropriate when the offender's later good conduct merits a reduction in the punishment, or when it is determined that the punishment imposed was disproportionate. The nonjudicial punishment authority who imposes nonjudicial punishment, the commander who imposes nonjudicial punishment, or a successor in command may, at any time, mitigate any part or amount of the unexecuted portion of the punishment imposed. The nonjudicial punishment authority who imposes nonjudicial punishment, the commander who imposes nonjudicial punishment, or a successor in command may also mitigate reduction in grade, whether executed or unexecuted, to forfeiture of pay, but the amount of the forfeiture may not be greater than the amount that could have been imposed by the officer who initially imposed the nonjudicial punishment. Reduction in grade may be mitigated to forfeiture of pay only within 4 months after the date of execution.

When mitigating—

(1) Arrest in quarters to restriction;

(2) Confinement on bread and water or diminished rations to correctional custody;

(3) Correctional custody or confinement on bread and water or diminished rations to extra duties or restriction, or both; or

(4) Extra duties to restriction, the mitigated punishment may not be for a greater period than the punishment mitigated. As restriction is the least severe form of deprivation of liberty, it may not be mitigated to a lesser period of another form of deprivation of liberty, as that would mean an increase in the quality of the punishment.

c. *Remission.* Remission is an action whereby any portion of the unexecuted punishment is cancelled. Remission is appropriate under the same circumstances as mitigation. The nonjudicial punishment authority who imposes punishment, the commander who imposes nonjudicial punishment, or a successor in command may, at any time, remit any part or amount of the unexecuted portion of the punishment imposed. The expiration of the current enlistment or term of service of the servicemember automatically remits any unexecuted punishment imposed under Article 15.

d. *Setting aside.* Setting aside is an action whereby the punishment or any part or amount thereof, whether executed or unexecuted, is set aside and any property, privileges, or rights affected by the portion of the punishment set aside are restored. The nonjudicial punishment authority who imposed punishment, the commander who imposes nonjudicial punishment, or a successor in command may set aside punishment. The power to set aside punish-

ments and restore rights, privileges, and property affected by the executed portion of a punishment should ordinarily be exercised only when the authority considering the case believes that, under all circumstances of the case, the punishment has resulted in clear injustice. Also, the power to set aside an executed punishment should ordinarily be exercised only within a reasonable time after the punishment has been executed. In this connection, 4 months is a reasonable time in the absence of unusual circumstances.

7. Appeals

a. *In general.* Any servicemember punished under Article 15 who considers the punishment to be unjust or disproportionate to the offense may appeal through the proper channels to the next superior authority.

b. *Who may act on appeal.* A "superior authority," as prescribed by the Secretary concerned, may act on an appeal. When punishment has been imposed under delegation of a commander's authority to administer nonjudicial punishment (*see* paragraph 2c of this Part), the appeal may not be directed to the commander who delegated the authority.

c. *Format of appeal.* Appeals shall be in writing and may include the appellant's reasons for regarding the punishment as unjust or disproportionate.

d. *Time limit.* An appeal shall be submitted within 5 days of imposition of punishment, or the right to appeal shall be waived in the absence of good cause shown. A servicemember who has appealed may be required to undergo any punishment imposed while the appeal is pending, except that if action is not taken on the appeal within 5 days after the appeal was submitted, and if the servicemember so requests, any unexecuted punishment involving restraint or extra duty shall be stayed until action on the appeal is taken.

e. *Legal review.* Before acting on an appeal from any punishment of the kind set forth in Article 15(e)(1)-(7), the authority who is to act on the appeal shall refer the case to a judge advocate or to a lawyer of the Department of Homeland Security for consideration and advice, and may so refer the case upon appeal from any punishment imposed under Article 15. When the case is referred, the judge advocate or lawyer is not limited to an examination of any written matter comprising the record of proceedings and may make any inquiries and examine any additional matter deemed necessary.

f. *Action by superior authority.*

(1) *In general.* In acting on an appeal, the superior authority may exercise the same power with respect to the punishment imposed as may be exercised under Article 15(d) and paragraph 6 of this Part by the officer who imposed the punishment. The superior authority may take such action even if no appeal has been filed.

(2) *Matters considered.* When reviewing the action of an officer who imposed nonjudicial punishment, the superior authority may consider the record of the proceedings, any matters submitted by the servicemember, any matters considered during the legal review, if any, and any other appropriate matters.

(3) *Additional proceedings.* If the superior authority sets aside a nonjudicial punishment due to a procedural error, that authority may authorize additional proceedings under Article 15, to be conducted by the officer who imposed the nonjudicial punishment, the commander, or a successor in command, for the same offenses involved in the original proceedings. Any punishment imposed as a result of these additional proceedings may be no more severe than that originally imposed.

(4) *Notification.* Upon completion of action by the superior authority, the servicemember upon whom punishment was imposed shall be promptly notified of the result.

(5) *Delegation to principal assistant.* If authorized by regulation of the Secretary concerned a superior authority who is a commander exercising general court-martial jurisdiction, or is an officer of general or flag rank in command, may delegate the power under Article 15(e) and this paragraph to a principal assistant.

8. Records of nonjudicial punishment

The content, format, use, and disposition of records of nonjudicial punishment may be prescribed by regulations of the Secretary concerned.

MCM INDEX

Made in the USA
Columbia, SC
19 August 2018